"By the policy to which we have adhered since the days of Washington, we have prospered beyond precedent—we have done more for the cause of liberty in the world than arms could effect. . . . Far better is it for ourselves . . . and for the cause of liberty, that, adhering to our wise, pacific system, and avoiding the distant wars of Europe, we should keep our lamp burning brightly on this Western shore as a light to all nations, than to hazard its utter extinction amid the ruins of fallen or falling republics . . ."

—HENRY CLAY, remarks to the Hungarian
patriot Louis Kossuth, January 9, 1852[1]

"It is a fearful thing to lead this great peaceful nation into war. . . . But the right is more precious than peace, and we shall fight for the things to which we have always carried nearest our hearts—for democracy, for the right of those who submit to authority to have a voice in their own governments, for the rights and liberties of small nations, for a universal dominion of right by such a concert of free peoples as shall bring peace and safety to all nations and make the world itself at last free."

—WOODROW WILSON, address to Congress
requesting a declaration of war with
Germany, April 2, 1917

MORE PRECIOUS THAN PEACE

THE COLD WAR AND THE STRUGGLE FOR THE THIRD WORLD

PETER W. RODMAN

CHARLES SCRIBNER'S SONS

NEW YORK · LONDON · TORONTO · SYDNEY · TOKYO · SINGAPORE

CHARLES SCRIBNER'S SONS
Rockefeller Center
1230 Avenue of the Americas
New York, NY 10020

Designed by Diane Stevenson/Snap-Haus Graphics

1 3 5 7 9 10 8 6 4 2

Library of Congress Cataloging-in-Publication Data

Rodman, Peter W.
More precious than peace / Peter W. Rodman.
p.   cm.
Includes bibliographical references and index.
1. Developing countries—Politics and government.   2. Cold war.
I. Title.
D883.R64   1994
909'.09724—dc20   94-30733   CIP

ISBN 0-684-19427-9

FOR MY WIFE VERONIQUE
AND
FOR MY PARENTS

CONTENTS

PREFACE

This book originated from my own experience in the U.S. government, which included a long involvement in the issues dealt with here. As a White House assistant to Henry Kissinger in the Nixon and Ford administrations from August 1969 to January 1977, I accompanied Dr. Kissinger on most of his important diplomatic missions—China, the Soviet Union, the Vietnam negotiations, the Middle East shuttles, southern Africa, and others. In the Reagan administration, I was a senior member and then director of the policy planning staff of the State Department under George Shultz from March 1983 to March 1986. In that capacity, I was a general adviser on foreign policy issues, particularly U.S.-Soviet relations and the Middle East. In March 1986, I rejoined the White House/National Security Council staff as a deputy assistant to the president (subsequently special assistant to the president), with a broad portfolio. As a generalist, I continued to take a special interest in all the so-called regional issues in the U.S.-Soviet relationship, a topic that cut across the regional and functional compartments into which our bureaucracy is organized. I took part in several senior-level talks with the Soviets on regional conflicts, including leading a working-group discussion at the Reykjavik summit in October 1986 and taking part in similar talks during the December 1987 Washington summit. I was involved in the review of U.S. policies and intelligence programs in these areas. I was reappointed a special assistant by President Bush and served until September 1990, when I left with the intention of writing this book.

I owe a debt to the Johns Hopkins Foreign Policy Institute, part of the Paul H. Nitze School of Advanced International Studies (SAIS) of the Johns Hopkins University, for providing a congenial and stimulating environment in which to think, write, and teach. Particular thanks go to those who were then my colleagues at SAIS—Dr. George Packard, dean of SAIS, Dr. Harold Brown, chairman of the Foreign Policy Institute, and Dr. Simon Serfaty, executive director of the institute. The book project was aided at its inception by a grant from the United States Institute of Peace, an independent federal institution created and funded by Congress for the support of research into conflict resolution. (The opinions, findings, and conclusions or recommendations in this book are of course mine and do not necessarily reflect the views of the United States Institute of Peace.) I must also thank the Lynde and Harry Bradley Foundation, which generously supported my activities at the Johns Hopkins Foreign Policy Institute. Additional support was provided by the Historical Research Foundation, for which I am grateful.

In the preparation of this book, I have had the benefit of information, advice, or other assistance from many individuals, including: Morton Abramowitz, Elliott Abrams, Frederick Z. Brown, Vincent Cannistraro, John Carbaugh, Mark Falcoff, Margaret Calhoun Hemenway, Fred C. Iklé, Robert W. Kagan, Zalmay Khalilzad, Christopher Lehman, Robert C. McFarlane, Robert B. Oakley, Don Oberdorfer, and Stephen Sestanovich. Nancy Menan, senior director for information policy at the National Security Council, patiently helped shepherd the manuscript through the process of declassification review.

My editors at Scribners, Robert Stewart, Ned Chase, and Hamilton Cain, helped make this a coherent work. My agent, Ronald L. Goldfarb, proved himself a master negotiator in the best tradition of this book. My assistants—Daliah Korsun, Tanya James, Laura Howenstein, and Natalie Reeves—produced portions of the typescript through infinite drafts, with dedication and skill.

I cannot omit here an expression of particular gratitude to and admiration for two distinguished American statesmen with whom I had the privilege to work closely. Secretary of State George P. Shultz was a wise and strong public servant who gave me an opportunity to play a role in exciting times, supporting him in a period of great accomplishment. He was a pleasure to work with and learn from.

But most of all, I must acknowledge my debt to Henry Kissinger. He was my teacher at Harvard College when I was an innocent nineteen-year-old senior. Little did I know then how far my tutoring at his hands would take me. The excitement of taking part in historic events in his company, the depth of understanding of the world that he embodied and (to the extent of the recipient's capacity) imparted, and the example of conviction and moral courage he displayed in a period of prolonged national crisis—these are his gifts to me.

Lastly, I want to thank my wife, Veronique, for encouraging me to undertake the project, for her wise advice, and for her very special support throughout. My children, Theodora and Nicholas, were also a very special source of inspiration.

The usual disclaimer must be repeated here. The opinions and conclusions in this book are not the responsibility of any of the aforementioned individuals or institutions but are solely mine.

Peter W. Rodman
Washington, D.C.
May 1994

MORE

PRECIOUS

THAN

PEACE

INTRODUCTION

Just before noon on Wednesday, February 15, 1989, Lt. Gen. Boris V. Gromov, commander of the Soviet Fortieth Army, walked alone across the bridge over the Amu Darya river that marked the border between Afghanistan and the Soviet Union. Gromov was young (forty-five), charismatic, a war hero with expectations of a political future ahead of him. He had lost his wife tragically in an airplane crash four years earlier. His father had been killed in World War II in the great tank battle at Kursk before he was born.

As the world's cameras rolled, Gromov strode confidently from the Afghan to the Soviet end of the bridge and was embraced emotionally by his fourteen-year-old son Maksim, who handed him a bouquet of carnations. In this fashion, in a theatrical flourish, the commander of all Soviet forces in Afghanistan became the last Soviet soldier to leave Afghan soil, completing the troop withdrawal that his government had pledged the year before.[1] It was one of those rare media-staged events that lives up to its billing, for it marked one of the turning points of contemporary history.

MORALITY AND POWER

The Cold War rivalry between the United States and the Soviet Union, as it unfolded after 1945, was fought on many fronts. It was first a contest for domination of Europe—triggered by the Soviet absorption of Central and Eastern Europe, punctuated by dangerous crises over Berlin, and hardened into a military confrontation in the center of the Continent. Second, it was a competition in strategic weapons, impelled by the deadly technology of the nuclear and missile age.

This is a book about a third front of the Cold War—the struggle for influence and dominance in the developing world, those vast and populous regions of Latin America, Asia, the Middle East, and Africa that emerged as a new arena of international politics as the European colonial empires disintegrated.

Historians can debate forever which front of the Cold War was the most important, but in many ways the contest in the developing world is intellectually the most interesting. The process of decolonization was one of the great human dramas of the twentieth century. Many of the Cold War's sharpest confrontations took place in these regions—in Korea, the Congo, Cuba, Indochina, the Middle East, as well as Afghanistan. As the Cold War ended at the end of the 1980s, the first signs of its easing came in this arena. And this dimension of the U.S.-Soviet rivalry, more than any other, illuminated deep-seated American attitudes toward international involvement.

The Cold War was a conflict of philosophies as well as of interests. Thus, its origins go back well before 1945. We will begin our story with Woodrow Wilson and Vladimir Ilyich Lenin, thinkers as well as men of action, who put their indelible stamp on their countries' international agendas and gave the ensuing conflict much of its intellectual content. It was at their moment on the world stage, at the end of the First World War, that the European colonial empires began to crack. Both Wilson's America and Lenin's Russia—believing themselves to be free of the taint of European colonialism and espousing contrary doctrines claiming universal validity—saw a historic opportunity, if not a historic duty. Each thrust itself forward as a model and patron for the political movements that sought, and later won, national independence.

The Second World War completed the unraveling of the old empires. That war and its aftermath propelled the United States and Soviet Union into superpower status and simultaneously launched Latin America and the ex-colonial lands of Asia and Africa into an uncertain future as significant players in their own right. For Wilson's and Lenin's successors, the developing regions then became a furious testing ground of competing political and economic ideas: Marxist and capitalist theories of economic progress, totalitarian and democratic models of political organization, and class struggle and collective security as principles of the international order. What path would the new nations choose? This was the critical question that drove the Cold War in what came accordingly to be known as the Third World—the regions seemingly poised between East and West.

Each superpower's response to the stirrings of independence in the colonial domains went to the heart of its sense of mission, its image of itself. There were times, especially in the 1950s and 1960s, when one side or the other, or both, believed that the future of the global balance of power was being decided in such places as the Congo, Cuba, and Indochina. There were times, especially in the 1960s, when American and Soviet leaders' confidence in the destiny of their own political and economic systems was deeply affected by their perception of which system was gaining adherents in these regions.

It would be absurd, however, to carry the moral equivalence too far. As the reader will soon see, that is hardly my thesis. The differences between the two superpowers, from the beginning, are more illuminating than the parallels.

For the Soviet leaders throughout the century, the foreign policy questions seem to have been clear and straightforward: Lenin saw the immense value of anticolonialism as a weapon against the Western powers. World War I had not only destroyed the Tsarist, Ottoman, and German colonial empires but had shaken the stability of the other European holdings as well. Thus, Britain and France were vulnerable; their colonial possessions in Africa, the Near East, India, and Southeast Asia might prove to be their Achilles' heel. Marxists who believed that imperialism depended on colonial exploitation had to believe that revolution in the Third World would seriously undermine the remaining imperialist powers.

The Soviets, through the years, faced choices that in retrospect seem mainly tactical: Should they back only Communist or radical parties in these colonial domains or ally themselves with "bourgeois" nationalist forces (sometimes enemies of the local Communists) that might be more significant factors in the fight against the West? How hard should Moscow press to exploit its political openings when faced with Western resistance? Whatever the Soviets' tactical dilemmas, however, the golden strategic opportunity of capitalizing on anti-Western resentments was always obvious.

But for Americans the issues went far deeper. Our very willingness to engage in world politics was never entirely a settled question. For a century and a half, we had considered ourselves above the fray. Not surprisingly, the same moral sensibility that had fostered our isolation was now appealed to as the argument for engagement: Our championing of independence for colonial peoples in the twentieth century was an echo of America's own origins, the mandate of our ideals. To Woodrow Wilson's mind, "The United States was not founded upon any principle of expediency. It was founded upon a profound principle of human liberty and of humanity, and, whenever it bases its policy upon any other foundations than those, it builds on the sand and not upon solid rock."[2] Wilson's philosophy was really the legacy of Lincoln: Could America remain safe in a world "half slave, half free"? And of Jefferson, who wrote to Lafayette in 1822 of his firm conviction that the "general insurrection of the world against all tyrants will ultimately prevail."[3]

However, as America emerged as a great power, especially after World War II, a tension developed between our idealism and our growing sense of responsibility for international order. As the Soviet state launched itself on the mission of capturing the anticolonial revolution for its own purposes, Americans wrestled with the moral dilemmas of whether certain ends (like resisting communism) justified certain means (like military force or covert action or backing rightist dictatorships); sometimes we found ourselves on the unsteady ground of defending morally flawed but friendly governments against Soviet or radical assaults when more palatable alternatives were not available. The example of the American Revolution had inspired the anticolonial cause in the first place. But how were we to reconcile our ties to our allies the European colonial powers, or to our strategic interest in stability, with this revolutionary tradition? Could we do what seemed necessary to combat Soviet machinations while remaining faithful to our own moral standards? Americans agonized over such questions. From the 1940s to the 1980s, from China to Cuba to Vietnam to Central America, we tore ourselves apart in controversies of this kind, in the distant wars of the Third World.

It is easy to be skeptical about the American propensity to moralize. Dean Acheson wrote teasingly: "We are all—as the Book of Common Prayer says—'miserable offenders,' and our professions are beyond our practice; both we and our critics have erred and strayed from true ways 'like lost sheep,' the remembrance of our misdoings should be 'grievous unto us,' though it seldom is."[4] But this does scant justice to the degree to which our foreign policy debates have been infused, indeed often driven, by moral and ideological arguments.

I remember when Richard Nixon, newly in office as president in 1969, hung Woodrow Wilson's portrait in a place of honor in the Cabinet Room. I was cynical. Nixon was a hard-nosed believer in realpolitik, the antithesis of Wilsonianism; Nixon's administration aspired to educate Americans in a more mature understanding of the world, free of what he saw as the excesses of moralism and naïveté that had bedeviled our foreign policy. Yet Nixon was also a man formed by the Second World War; he, along with John F. Kennedy, was part of the class of young returning veterans elected to Congress in 1946 who voted for the Marshall Plan and the formative policies of the Truman era. Of course, Truman's policies later became the subject of acrimonious partisan debate in which the young Nixon took a vigorous part. But to that postwar generation of young internationalists, Woodrow Wilson was nonetheless a noble figure. Even for a Republican, Wilson was the father of modern American internationalism and world leadership, the pioneer vindicated by the disaster of isolationism in the 1930s, all the more heroic for the tragic failure he had suffered in his own time.

As Nixon would ironically rediscover from his own experience in the presidency—such as the vehement protests over his policy toward Vietnam and the Soviet Union and his alleged neglect of human rights—it was impossible in practice to separate American international engagement from the moral impulse that Woodrow Wilson so quintessentially expressed. This was precisely the critique of Nixon in the mid-1970s. "Because we are free we can never be indifferent to the fate of freedom elsewhere," Jimmy Carter pointedly proclaimed in his inaugural address on January 20, 1977. To Daniel Patrick Moynihan, writing later in the same year, "concepts of human rights should be as integral to American foreign policy as is Marxism-Leninism to Soviet or Chinese or Yugoslav operations and planning. . . . Human rights is the single greatest weapon we have left for the defense of liberty."[5]

America's most profound task in foreign policy in the twentieth century has been to find the way to reconcile its moral convictions and its strategic responsibilities. Whenever America succeeded in foreign policy, it did exactly this—most notably after World War II in the grand alliance of the industrial democracies of the Atlantic community and Japan, which was sustained by bipartisan support for over four decades. What was this grand alliance if not a defense of *both* our democratic values and our strategic interests? That was the winning formula. In the end, having remained steadfast, we outlasted our totalitarian adversary and saw its system collapse—the result of its internal rot and the renewed pressures it faced from the outside.

In the developing world, essentially the same result occurred: When the West put up firm resistance, as in the Cuban Missile Crisis or Afghanistan, the Soviets gave way. But for the United States, the contest in these outlying regions was a more complex and agonizing process; domestic controversy dogged our involvement. Some saw us as guilty of colonial or neocolonial sins; some thought there would be a "middle way" for the developing countries between capitalism and communism (i.e., that both systems were equally inappropriate). Vietnam, especially, taught us our limits; our ways of thinking about foreign policy were irrevocably altered by that experience. Our Third World engagement seemed to be squarely situated on a basic fault line in American attitudes toward foreign policy, about the use of our power and its relationship to our moral and political purposes. The debate was often in Wilsonian terms—our own misdeeds and failings chastised (sometimes excessively) by Americans, always self-critical, self-questioning.

RESTORING THE BALANCE

This book will tell the story of American and Soviet policies in the Third World—their origins and their interactions—from these two powers' emergence on the world scene early in the twentieth century to the Cold War and to the present period of the aftermath of the Soviet Union's collapse. Of necessity I have been selective, focusing on what strikes me as the pivotal episodes and dominant themes. It is not an exhaustive history.

Throughout the ex-colonial world, from Africa to Southeast Asia, the local folklore seems invariably to include a version of a familiar fatalistic maxim: "When the elephants (or the buffalo) fight, the grass suffers." Accordingly, if I am accused of viewing the rich variety of the developing world through the prism of the U.S.-Soviet rivalry, I plead guilty to that as well. Others are more expert than I in the details of regional history— political, economic, social, cultural. I am interested here in the overlay of the Cold War competition. What was at stake was precisely the freedom of these nations to develop in their own right. The end of the superpower conflict may now permit these countries to recover control over their own destinies.

The story as it unfolds is filled with miscalculations and blunders, controversies (some not yet over), clashes of powerful personalities, and many surprising turns of history's wheel:

- Wilson and Lenin bequeathed to their successors the task of applying their new ideology to a changing reality. In the 1920s and 1930s, Josef Stalin retreated from the fray to consolidate Soviet power at home. America turned isolationist. During the Second World War, Franklin Roosevelt seized on the opportunity to press Wilson's anticolonialist cause even more passionately than Wilson had done.

- The 1950s and 1960s were the heyday of decolonization; it was also the time of an ambitious Soviet policy under Nikita Khrushchev to mobilize the Third World against the West, exactly as Lenin had envisioned. American policy reflected a strategic panic—that the Cold War was about to be won or lost in the Third World. When Khrushchev affirmed Moscow's backing of "wars of national liberation," the Kennedy administration treated it as a mortal challenge and chose Indochina as the place to draw the line.

- Indochina in the 1970s was a debacle, after which America withdrew into itself, once again disillusioned with engagement, morally uncertain of its role in the world. Meanwhile, the Soviet Union under Leonid Brezhnev grew to the full status of a military superpower. The American retreat led the Soviets to conclude that what they called the historical "correlation of forces" had shifted decisively in their favor. The late 1970s became a period of new Soviet boldness in the Third World—in fact, a serious overreaching by the Soviets and their allies—in such places as Angola, Nicaragua, Cambodia, and Afghanistan. A decade of global instability and deteriorating East-West relations was in considerable part triggered by these regional conflicts.

• In the 1980s, the drama played itself out to a climax. America recovered from its post-Vietnam disillusionment; it reengaged in the world with renewed energy, even giving aid to guerrilla insurgents fighting against Marxist dictatorships on four continents. The Soviet system and its foreign policy came under pressure internally and externally. The tables were turned.

Under Mikhail Gorbachev, there was a revolution in Soviet foreign policy. Gorbachev saw the exuberant expansionism of the Brezhnev era run aground; he retreated from foreign overcommitments near and far and supported negotiations in Afghanistan, Angola, Nicaragua, and Cambodia. Soviet reformers saw the costly failures of Brezhnev's foreign policy—including the Third World adventures that had now turned into quagmires, especially in Afghanistan—as the other side of the coin of the system's domestic failures. The regime's foreign disasters, especially in Afghanistan, helped to discredit it.

In the end, the American recovery in the 1980s had succeeded in restoring the balance of the international system. Troops of the Soviet Union or of Soviet allies retreated from Afghanistan, Angola, and Cambodia; diplomacy suddenly made progress in resolving the big-power conflict in these countries and in Central America. It was in these regional confrontations, as I have said, that the global truce of the superpowers began. And the Soviet retrenchment turned out to have ramifications *inside* the Soviet Union far beyond most participants' expectations.

Yet of all the battlefronts of the Cold War, the American reengagement in the regional conflicts continued to be the most traumatic. Americans wrestled with the host of divisive issues that this involvement raised: the instinctive American discomfort with military intervention overseas; ideological divisions between the Left and Right, especially over Central America; debates over the morality of clandestine operations and the keeping of secrets; the perennial struggle between Congress and the president over control of foreign policy; disagreements over how to negotiate with the Soviets; attacks on the State Department's conduct of diplomacy; and bureaucratic battles within the U.S. government over turf and control of policy. Liberals disliked the assertion of military power or covert action or the support of rightist allies; conservatives mistrusted negotiations and the American diplomats who conducted them. Woodrow Wilson would have recognized in this debate some of the moral issues with which he had wrestled over how a democracy should conduct foreign policy—issues of openness, international law, and democratic purpose. Wracked by bureaucratic and intellectual confusion, the Reagan administration struggled for a policy that would reconcile America's idealism and its strategic necessity of restoring the global balance after a decade of Soviet advances.

The paradox that the successful outcome on this front of the Cold War was the product of such a contentious process at home is deeply revealing of the ambivalence in America about its role and conduct in the world. For all our achievements and even with the historic success in our contest with the Soviet Union, we are still a nation not yet comfortable with the relationship between our interests and our morality, between our power and our diplomacy.

These are enduring issues for our present and future. The turbulence of the developing world continues in the 1990s, in some places even intensified without the restraints that the Cold War imposed. New dangers await us. Post-Communist Russia gropes for a new foreign policy, without the hostile Leninist ideological impulse but also with an increasing willingness to assert national interests not identical to ours. The United States is once again challenged to define its purpose and its commitment.

PART
ONE
EVOLUTION

1

WILSON, LENIN, AND THE
COLONIAL QUESTION

For Woodrow Wilson, as he watched the European war clouds approach American shores, the beginning of 1917 was a time of "spiritual agony."[1] He had won reelection the year before on a platform not only promising American abstention from the war but championing an ambitious program of domestic reform. Wilson feared war not only because of its intrinsic horror but for what it would mean to his agenda for the country. On January 4, he told his close adviser Col. Edward House, "There will be no war . . . and it would be a crime against civilization for us to go in."[2]

At that very moment the imperial German leadership was deciding on the policies that were to drag us into the conflict—the unrestricted submarine warfare and the plotting with Mexico that was soon to be uncovered in the Zimmerman telegram.

In his 1916 presidential campaign, Wilson had desperately needed to win over large numbers of progressives and socialists in order to eke out victory in an extremely close contest. In 1916 alone, landmark legislation was passed on worker's compensation, child labor, rural credit, and the eight-hour workday; the controversial liberal jurist Louis D. Brandeis was appointed to the Supreme Court. By seizing this reformist agenda, Wilson had forged the grand coalition of labor, farmers, and intellectuals that was to be the foundation of the Democratic party for decades.[3]

Wilson's antiwar position went hand in hand with this domestic thrust. To his secretary of the navy, Josephus Daniels, he said: "If war comes, we shall have to get the cooperation of the big businessmen and, as a result, they will dominate the nation for 20 years after the war. . . ."[4] As he agonized over his decision in March 1917, Wilson summoned Frank Cobb, editor of the *New York World*, and poured out his forebodings: " 'Once lead this people into war,' " he said, " 'and they'll forget there ever was such a thing as tolerance. To fight you must be brutal and ruthless, and the spirit of ruthless brutality will enter into the very fibre of our national life, infecting Congress, the courts, the policeman on the beat, the man in the street.' "[5]

Woodrow Wilson's America was an economic powerhouse, on the threshold of becoming a major force in the world whether it wished it or not. The phenomenal economic expansion in the nineteenth century had produced a dynamo of 100 million people that by 1913 accounted for 36 percent of the world's industrial production—equal to that of Britain, Germany, and France combined. Though a vast continental market in its own right, it had amassed a share of world trade comparable to that of Britain or Germany. As the Great War devastated the European economies, America's industrial and financial preeminence loomed as a certainty of the postwar period.[6]

The United States was destined for greatness on the international stage. Its Pacific acquisitions at the end of the nineteenth century, after the Spanish-American War, and Theodore Roosevelt's muscular nationalism foreshadowed America's becoming a great power, especially in the Pacific. Similarly, Roosevelt's acquisition of the Panama Canal. It was a nation gradually acquiring a self-confidence commensurate with its strength. What it lacked was a definition of its new role in the world at large.

The country was fortunate to have at that moment a leader distinguished by both his awareness of international affairs and his intellectual depth. Such presidents are rare in our history. Wilson the scholar had seen clearly, after the war with Spain, that our isolation was a thing of the past.[7] He had even had the prescience to see in 1900 how America's new power and role would transform our political system: "Much the most important change to be noticed is the result of the war with Spain upon the lodgment and exercise of power within our federal system: the greatly increased power and opportunity for constructive statesmanship given the President, by the plunge into international politics and into the administration of distant dependencies, which has been that war's most striking and momentous consequence."[8] As we shall see in this book, this change in the balance of power between Congress and the president was to be a source of permanent controversy in the twentieth century as the United States responded to the pull of international engagement.

But the European war forced on President Wilson and his intellectual supporters a particular problem. It was one thing to pluck off Pacific islands or a Panama isthmus at one's leisure, like ripe fruit from a tree, but Europe was the main theater of international politics. The classical balance of power had broken down utterly. It was precisely this European cockpit that our Founding Fathers had warned against involvement in. Now that isolation was no longer an option, what was our policy?

Wilson's answer was, at first, neutrality, but it went far beyond that. The Wilsonian vision of America was of a nation born with a commitment to justice, a people that were exceptional among the nations for their decency and their disinterestedness. Soon after the war in Europe broke out, therefore, Wilson told Congress in his December 8, 1914, State of the Union address that America's unique moral position gave it a special responsibility to help end that war: "We are, indeed, a true friend to all the nations of the world, because we threaten none, covet the possessions of none, desire the overthrow of none. Our friendship can be accepted and is accepted without reservation, because it is offered in a spirit and for a purpose which no one need ever question or suspect. Therein lies our greatness." As the war raged, Wilson actively sought to mediate. He sent Colonel House to Europe in early 1915 and again in early 1916. At the end of 1916, as a prelude to another mediation effort, Wilson sent all the European belligerents a diplomatic note inviting them to state their war aims.

These efforts failed, to Wilson's great pain, but gradually there was evolving in his mind an even more ambitious idea—not only a concept of a fair, negotiated end to the war but a theory of a more benign international system that should follow. In an address to the Senate on January 22, 1917, he spoke of a durable future peace that would banish the balance of power and rest instead on the democratic legitimacy of governments, on forswearing the practice of "hand[ing] peoples about from sovereignty to sovereignty, as if they were property." It was a ringing declaration of the principle that later came to be called "self-determination":

> No peace can last, or ought to last, which does not recognize the principle that governments derive all their just powers from the consent of the governed, and that no right anywhere exists to hand peoples about from sovereignty to sovereignty as if they were property. . . . Any peace which does not recognize and accept this principle will inevitably be upset. It will not rest upon the affections or the convictions of mankind. The ferment of spirit of whole populations will fight subtly and constantly against it, and all the world will sympathize. The world can be at peace only if its life is stable, and there can be no stability where the will is in rebellion, where there is not tranquillity of spirit and a sense of justice, of freedom, and of right.

Entry into the war in April 1917, wrenching as it was, did not alter this idealistic conception of America's purposes. On the contrary, it intensified the fervor with which the concept was advanced. The progressive coalition that Wilson had brought together at home could not have been held together otherwise. The Republican opposition clamored for all-out war to smash the German threat; even the American labor movement was caught up in the patriotic emotion. If there was to be any possibility of maintaining a liberal program at home or pursuing a decent outcome abroad, Wilson was convinced he needed to keep before the country the clearest definition of the moral aims for which America was fighting.[9] Wrote Eric Goldman: "The Wilson formula, conceived out of his own doubts and stated with rousing artistry, became the ideological bridge by which most progressives moved with their leader from neutrality to intervention."[10]

The political necessity of a liberal peace program was not confined to the American scene. In Europe, especially as the war dragged on, social and political unrest buffeted all the belligerent countries. In Britain and France, labor movements and intellectuals grew restless and agitated against their governments, threatening to weaken the allied cause. In Russia, in March 1917, the storm blew away the monarchy and threatened to drive Russia out of the war. In imperial Germany, social unrest gave hope to the West that the resolve of the Central Powers might weaken. There was revolution in the air.

As 1917 proceeded, Wilson felt the growing need to state again, this time in more detail, the progressive war aims that would rally the peoples of the allied side (including the beleaguered Russians) and challenge the governments of the Central Powers. In October, he dispatched Colonel House to London and Paris again for military consultations, but also to press for agreement on war aims.[11] It seemed an opportunity to begin the task of reforming the way the world did business, to prevent future wars.

Then came a shock that gave dramatic urgency to the issue and threw the Western powers onto the defensive: the Bolshevik Revolution in Petrograd in November 1917. The appearance of the Soviets transformed the world diplomatic scene. The Bolsheviks called for an immediate peace and moved into a negotiation for a separate armistice with Germany. Social unrest on the Continent suddenly became a tempting target not just for weakening the martial resolve of governments but for revolution. And the Bolsheviks had their own peace program, aimed at advancing their own revolutionary cause not only in Europe but in the colonial realms outside of Europe. It was a sweeping, wholesale, global challenge to the international system as the West had known it. It was a radically different vision of the world.

Lenin's Decree on Peace in November 1917 laid down new rules of international relations: the abolition of secret diplomacy; the equality of all nations; an end to annexation of foreign lands. The Bolsheviks proclaimed a policy of self-determination for all the peoples of the Russian Empire and all other empires (though within five years the Red Army would reconquer most of the Russian imperial territory). At Brest-Litovsk, where Russo-German negotiations on peace began in December 1917, the Bolsheviks launched an all-out propaganda war on "imperialism," putting forward Lenin's new rules of international relations as weapons against all the other belligerents. Backing up their advocacy of open diplomacy, for example, they published all the secret treaties that tsarist Russia had concluded with its allies.

At Brest-Litovsk, the Bolshevik diplomats made dramatically clear that a new diplomacy was replacing the old. They dispensed with the usual diplomatic amenities of cordiality, harangued their counterparts, and appealed to the peoples of the world over the heads of governments through the media (CNN's ancestor the radiotelegraph). Trotsky proclaimed on December 12: "We are conducting these negotiations . . . so as to accelerate the rising of the working masses against the imperialist cliques."[12] It was a style that would be imitated by many of their spiritual descendants in decades thereafter, from North Vietnam to Nicaragua. Negotiation was sometimes secondary to political warfare.

It was this Bolshevik challenge that prompted Wilson's famous Fourteen Points. Colonel House, in Europe at the moment of the Bolshevik Revolution, pleaded once again with conservative British and French leaders to agree on a statement of progressive war aims—to hold the American and European peoples' loyalty to the cause. Wilson even cabled House on December 1 to warn the Europeans that "our people and Congress will not fight for any selfish aim on the part of any belligerent."[13] Wilson went ahead with his own statement, which he prepared in great secrecy and then unveiled before a joint session of Congress on January 8, 1918.

The Russian debacle was in the forefront of Wilson's mind. In his address to Congress he expressed sympathy for the agony of the Russian people; he took note of the Bolsheviks' program for a new international order; he warned Germany and other states of Europe not to prey on the Russian Empire. As he outlined his own peace program, Wilson left it ambiguous whether the United States was prepared to work with the new

Russian leadership. Some of Wilson's advisers, such as Secretary of State Robert Lansing, were adamantly anti-Bolshevik. Others, like House, had not quite given up on it.

Wilson then announced the details of his own program, long in preparation. Many of its fourteen points are familiar: "open covenants openly arrived at"; freedom of navigation and free trade; arms reduction; a League of Nations; and various strictures against annexation of territory or settlement of colonial claims against the wishes of indigenous populations.

Wilson's uplifting vision of a more just and decent world order guaranteed his ascendancy as the leader of the West. It was, no less than the Bolsheviks' program, a vision of a transformed international system. While it did not succeed in keeping Russia in the war, it helped, as intended, to neutralize the Bolshevik appeal to the European Left. Whatever misgivings the conservative governments of our European "associates" may have felt (Wilson shunned the term "allies"), American economic power and the prospect of American postwar preponderance— in addition to its mass appeal—made Wilson's blueprint the dominant one among the Western powers.

For Wilson, there was no alternative, and not simply because of the Bolsheviks. After such a conflagration as the Great War, he was convinced the world's peoples would not stand for a return to the reactionary politics that had governed the world before. In Paris, during the peace conference, in a Memorial Day address on May 31, 1919, he warned: "The peoples of the world are awake and the peoples of the world are in the saddle."

THE COLONIAL QUESTION

It was the Bolsheviks who first thrust the colonial question to the fore, if only because the Russian Empire was the first to crumble. But the formal diplomacy for a peace settlement would inevitably come to the question of the disposition of German colonies in Africa and East Asia and of the various states and peoples of the Ottoman Empire. Whether or not the victorious statesmen of Britain and France realized it, the viability of their own empires was now under a cloud as well. The British, for example, had ambitions to fill the vacuum in much of the Middle East, shoving aside the French and blocking the Russians, but very shortly they would run into financial constraints that forced them to scale back their aspirations.[14] It would take the Second World War to exhaust the colonial powers utterly and usher in the great flood tide of decolonization.

While the principle of self-determination was a feature of both Wilson's and Lenin's doctrines, it was the Soviets who extended it most categorically to the colonial empires. Most of Wilson's attention was devoted to Eastern and Central Europe. After Lenin's Decree on Peace, with its general call for colonial independence, came the Bolshevik "Appeal to the Moslems of Russia and the East" on December 3, urging all the peoples of the Middle East and South Asia to rise up: "Moslems of the East! Persians, Turks, Arabs, and Hindus . . . It is not from Russia and its revolutionary government that you have to fear enslavement, but from the European imperialist robbers, from those who laid waste your native lands and converted them into their colonies."[15] At Brest-Litovsk, as noted, the Soviet diplomats raised the banner of universal self-determination.

Wilson's anti-imperialism, in contrast, came from different intellectual sources—not class struggle, but from a nineteenth-century liberal belief in a cooperative world community in which the colonial peoples should be enabled to take part. His economic analysis—as with other nonsocialist anti-imperialists like J. A. Hobson—was that the world economy, including the industrial powers, would only benefit from the expansion of global trade deriving from development in the colonial lands. His political vision—of a world organization enforcing collective security, guiding a system of international law and arbitration of disputes, and protecting freedom of the seas—was a classical liberal belief in an ordered world of independent states and peoples acting on their common interests and interdependence.

Revisionist historians have mocked the Wilsonian economic policy as a self-serving agenda for the interests of American capitalism.[16] But Wilson was for equal access to the markets of developing regions—the "Open Door"—as a way to weaken colonialist dominance.[17] He favored low tariffs globally and the dismantling of systems of special privilege and monopoly that he considered that high tariffs sustained. Predatory, exploitative imperialism was anathema to him. In a Fourth of July speech in 1914, Wilson had declared:

> There is no man who is more interested than I am in carrying the enterprise of American businessmen to every quarter of the globe. . . . But observe the limit to all that which is laid upon us, perhaps more than upon any other nation in the world. We set this nation up, at any rate we professed to set it up, to vindicate the rights of man. We did not name any differences between one race and another. . . . If American enterprise in foreign countries, particularly in those foreign countries which are not strong enough to resist us, takes the shape of imposing upon and exploiting the mass of the people of that country, it ought to be checked and not

encouraged. I am willing to get anything for an American that money and enterprise can obtain, except the suppression of the rights of other men. I will not help any man buy a power which he ought not to exercise over his fellow beings.

On December 2, 1913, in a message to Congress, Wilson had spoken of America's support for constitutional government in Mexico as indispensable to our neighbors' chance to "work out their own development in peace and liberty." The British ambassador, Sir Cecil Spring Rice, met with Wilson in early February 1914 and came away with the realization (which shocked him) that Wilson's use of the word "development" reflected an aspiration to transform not only Mexico's political system but its social and economic organization: To Wilson "the real cause of the trouble in Mexico was not political but economic. The real cause in fact was the land question." Only a fair distribution of land could ensure political stability.[18] Thus did Wilson foreshadow the stress on economic development and land reform that characterized U.S. policy in the Third World in the second half of the twentieth century, yet another area of his prescience—and influence.

On a visit to London in the summer of 1914, House outlined to British leaders a proposal for the advanced countries to cease their competitive exploitation of the underdeveloped world in favor of a general agreement on an Open Door for expansion of investment. The result would be cooperative relations, political stability, and economic progress for all concerned.[19]

Wilson, as president, protected prostrate China against the depredations of the bankers and of the Japanese army. He defended the Mexican Revolution against both European and American reaction. He moved the Philippines closer to autonomy and gained territorial status and American citizenship for Puerto Rico. He pressed the British during the Paris Peace Conference to grant self-government to Ireland. Wilson was also the godfather of the League of Nations Mandate system, which he intended to begin the transition to independence of the former German colonies and Ottoman provinces.[20]

The theory of the Mandate system was to ensure more enlightened administration of underdeveloped areas by making it subject to the moral and political supervision of the international community as well as by removing these regions of the world from the traditional rivalries of the Great Powers. The notion was fiercely resisted by several governments when the Americans advanced it in Paris in 1919. Britain's self-governing

dominions, especially Australia, wanted possession of German-held islands in the Pacific as recompense for their sacrifices at Gallipoli and
elsewhere; Japan had its eye on these islands as well. France and Italy
wanted unfettered control of their new African holdings.

The colonial issues outside of Europe were not a high priority at Paris.
As the competing claims for individual territories were debated endlessly,
according to one scholar, "The delegates sat in stodgy boredom. Three
appeared to be sleeping soundly."[21] Wilson decided not to get into the
business of allocating all the defeated powers' territories, partly because
it would look too much like dividing up the spoils of war in the discredited
traditional way; he opted to establish just the basic principles at Paris,
leaving it to the soon-to-be-formed League of Nations to make the assignments. In the end, a British proposal was adopted that divided the
losers' colonies into three classes:

• Class A Mandates, covering the more advanced portions of the Ottoman
Empire that could be "provisionally recognized" as independent states and
in which the wishes of the inhabitants must be a prime consideration in
selecting the Mandatory powers;

• Class B Mandates, especially in Central Africa, where the main concern
was to prevent abuses in administration and to ensure equal trade access
for the major powers; and

• Class C Mandates, such as South-West Africa (now Namibia) and some
strategic South Pacific islands, to which the Mandatory states would be
given more or less exclusive rights, subject to certain safeguards for the
populations.[22]

The Mandate system was a compromise, necessarily, between Wilson's
lofty principle of self-determination and his partners' eagerness to gobble
up new spoils and their refusal to put their own possessions at risk. But
for all its caution it was a crucial innovation that delegitimized colonialism. Never again could subject peoples be simply seized as booty;
henceforward the fate of subject peoples would be treated as a matter for
the international community according to some inexorably evolving standard of justice. For that very reason it was resisted in Paris.

The dilemmas were obvious. As noted, the British, French, Dutch,
and Italians were not eager to relinquish their own empires, which they
had fought and sacrificed so much to preserve. Many of the colonial

lands were only at the earliest stages of the political development that would take them, in the course of a few more decades, to independence. Extremism and violence, moreover, were beginning to rear their ugly heads as fledgling nationalist movements from Turkey to India to China to the Dutch East Indies flirted with radicalism—with the Bolsheviks beginning to mobilize those radical forces. Like predatory capitalism, revolutionary violence, too, was anathema to Wilson.

Secretary of State Lansing, less enlightened on the issue than either Wilson or House, confided to his notebook at the end of 1918 that Wilson's championing of self-determination was "loaded with dynamite":

> The more I think about the President's declaration as to the right of "self-determination," the more convinced I am of the danger of putting such ideas into the minds of certain races. It is bound to be the basis of impossible demands on the Peace Congress, and create trouble in many lands. What effect will it have on the Irish, the Indians, the Egyptians, and the nationalities among the Boers? Will it not breed discontent, disorder and rebellion? Will not the Mohammedans of Syria and Palestine and possibly of Morocco and Tripoli rely on it? How can it be harmonized with Zionism, to which the president is practically committed? The phrase is simply loaded with dynamite. It will raise hopes which can never be realized. It will, I fear, cost thousands of lives. In the end it is bound to be discredited, to be called the dream of an idealist who failed to realize the danger until too late to check those who attempted to put the principle into force.[23]

Lansing's expectation that the notion would be discredited was, of course, a wrongheaded perception of the new age that had begun. His assessment of the turbulence that would accompany it, alas, was not.

LENIN

"Indian society has no history at all, at least no known history," Karl Marx wrote contemptuously in 1853.[24] This was the patronizing Victorian attitude toward colonial peoples that Marx and Engels often displayed in their writings on colonialism—an attitude "painfully embarrassing to the orthodox communist," a scholar observed wryly a century later.[25] The fathers of Communist doctrine tended quite frankly to treat colonialism as a positive and necessary historical force pulling the subject peoples out of their backward way of life toward the ultimate fulfillment of socialism.

"Asiatic society" was too primitive in its modes of production to create the basis for its own evolution without an outside agent, Marx argued: "England has to fulfill a double mission in India: one destructive, the other regenerating—the annihilation of old Asiatic society, and the laying of the material foundation of Western society in Asia."[26] "The jealousy, the intrigues, the ignorance, the cupidity and corruption of the Orientals" was a typical outburst of Engels, in a discussion on China.[27]

Nor did Lenin romanticize the colonial peoples. In February 1920, he cautioned that "our policy in the East must be even more cautious and patient, for here we are dealing with countries that are much more backward, are under the oppressive influence of religious fanaticism, [and] are imbued with greater distrust of the Russian people. . . ."[28]

Lenin's major work, *Imperialism: The Highest Stage of Capitalism*, written in the spring of 1916 during his exile in Zurich, is a theoretical analysis, in the Marxian mode, of the evolution of capitalism. The increasingly monopolistic concentration of production, the growth of a banking oligopoly, the need for new markets in which to invest capital— all these forces drove the system to increase its dependence on colonies. The great powers competed with increasing ferocity for control of underdeveloped areas. While the colonies benefited in terms of their own economic development, imperialism, to Lenin, was essentially parasitic and a form of rapacity; its survival required suppression of the gradually awakening colonial aspirations for independence. The inexorable laws of history would produce a profound crisis.[29]

In the spring of 1916, Lenin also produced his *Theses on the Socialist Revolution and the Right of Nations to Self-Determination*, which has been described by Arno Mayer as "the political extension of Lenin's primarily economic analysis of imperialism."[30] In the *Theses*, Lenin straightforwardly embraced national self-determination as a universal principle and as a principle consistent with Marxist class analysis and political theory.

This required a certain amount of fancy analytic footwork. Nationalism, strictly speaking, was inconsistent with Marxism. If the world's turbulence was in essence a struggle between classes, with the oppressed of the world finding salvation in their class solidarity across borders, then nationalism was its negation, indeed its dangerous enemy. Lenin's answer, at one level, was that the ultimate purpose of self-determination was not national liberation for its own sake but the promotion of revolution globally. In other writings on the subject in the prolific year 1916, he made even clearer that the revolution in *Europe* was his main focus and that his interest in revolution in the outlying regions derived from the reinforcement it could bring to the main battlefield: "[T]he interests of the liberation of a number of big and very big nations in Europe stand higher than the interests of the movement for liberation of small nations. . . . [A] democratic demand must not be considered in isolation, but on a European—today we should say a world—scale."[31]

Yet for all the contradictory veins in Marx's, Engels's, and Lenin's writings, which Soviet theorists long mined for their own shifting purposes in order to prove the Moscow line of the moment, what comes through in Lenin's colonial policy was its single-mindedness and clarity of objective: the possibility of revolution in the colonial realms could be of enormous help as a weapon of Soviet policy against the major powers. For a time, hope persisted that colonial revolutions could help spur the cause of revolution in Europe; this hope, of course, was not borne out. But in one form or another, there was a consistent underlying confidence that the anti-Western impulse at work in the independence movements could be a powerful political force weakening Western rivals and therefore a natural ally of the young Soviet state.

The Americans were wrestling with the dilemmas of fostering change while trying to prevent its more malign variants; the Soviets suffered no hesitations. Nikolai Bukharin told the Eighth Congress of the Soviet Communist party in early 1919: "If we propound the solution of self-determination for the colonies . . . we lose nothing by it. On the contrary, we gain. . . . The most outright nationalist movement . . . is only water for our mill, since it contributes to the destruction of English imperialism."[32] As Lenin before him, Bukharin was referring to what might have been a fatal intellectual contradiction in the Soviet policy. Despite Lenin's theoretical analyses seeking, as we have seen, to establish the consistency between national self-determination and proletarian internationalism, a practical problem remained. It was not an accident that the independence movements in many colonial lands were headed by bourgeois or upper-class figures, often educated at the best schools of the metropolitan country, whose social position made them an unlikely partner of the oppressed peasantry or proletariat upon whom Communists ostensibly rested their hopes for revolution. The issue may seem quaintly doctrinaire today; yet there was an earnest debate on the question in the early years of the Communist movement. Lenin cut through the confusion with characteristic acumen.

It came to a head in the summer of 1920, at the Second Congress of the Communist International (the Comintern). The Comintern had been founded the year before as the Leninist rival to the Socialist International, which had clung to its democratic socialist tradition despite Lenin's vicious attacks.

The Second Comintern Congress took place in conditions of exuberant optimism over what was called the "national-colonial question" in light of the Red Army's successes in driving the British away from Central Asia and regaining some of the ground on the Western front, in Ukraine and Poland, that had been sacrificed at Brest-Litovsk. The First Comintern Congress the year before had been primarily organizational and sparsely attended. By 1920, the movement had grown, and the Second Congress was in a sense its real debut.

Of the delegates, only 25 out of the total of 218 came from what we could call colonial regions, and many of these were from nationalities of the former Russian Empire. There were delegates representing Azerbaijan, Armenia, Bukhara, Georgia, Turkey, Persia, India, Korea, the Dutch East Indies, China, and Mexico.[33] Most of the congress's reports and deliberations were devoted to European issues, but Lenin had decided also to prepare an important policy pronouncement on the national and colonial questions.

Lenin argued, in his opening report on July 19, that 70 percent of the world's peoples (about 1.25 billion persons) were living under colonial subjugation, with a minority of 250 million benefiting from that situation. He was pleased that this congress was truly a "world" congress, because it included participation from the colonial regions. The Communists were "more and more becoming representatives and genuine defenders" of this oppressed 70 percent of the world's population.[34]

Lenin circulated, first to a selected few of the delegates, his own draft of *Theses on the National and Colonial Questions*, which were to be put before the congress. The *Theses* were a scathing attack on the "lies and deceptions" perpetuated by the "bourgeois democracies" on the colonial question, which went under the "false motto of the freedom of nations and national self-determination. . . . The so-called 'League of Nations' is nothing but an insurance policy in which the victors mutually guarantee each other their prey," he wrote. Thus, the independence movements had to know that "there can be no salvation for them outside a union with the revolutionary proletariat, and the triumph of the Soviet power over Imperialism."[35] One of Lenin's final points was that the Comintern "must conclude a temporary alliance with the bourgeois democrats in the colonies and backward countries, without, however, amalgamating with them, but preserving the independent character of the proletarian movement, even though it be still in its embryonic state."[36]

Just as Wilson had responded somewhat defensively to the challenge thrown down by the Bolsheviks at Brest-Litovsk, now Lenin was reacting defensively to Wilson's program as embodied in the Versailles peace. Wilson had captured the cause of self-determination as his own, and Lenin was determined to take it back.

One of the selected few delegates to receive an advance copy of Lenin's draft was a twenty-seven-year-old Indian Marxist, M. N. Roy, whom he had never met. When Roy was ushered into Lenin's Kremlin office for their first private meeting, the young man was thrilled and flattered that the great leader so valued his opinion. Roy was an "awe-struck worshipper," he later admitted, but was put at ease by Lenin's modest manner and human scale. (Roy estimated him to be five feet four inches tall.)[37] But Roy, once he had studied Lenin's draft, strongly objected to the recommendation for alliances with the bourgeois nationalists. Roy considered the nationalist bourgeoisie a reactionary force that suppressed native Communists and stood in the way of true socialist revolution in colonial countries.

Roy gave Lenin his comments, and the two met privately a number of times during the congress with the hope of resolving the dispute in private rather than in public. Lenin seemed open-minded. "In our first discussion, he frankly admitted his ignorance of facts [in the colonial countries], but took his stand on theoretical grounds."[38] The role of Mohandas Gandhi was, for Roy, the crucial and symbolic point of difference between him and Lenin: "Lenin believed that, as the inspirer and leader of a mass movement, he [Gandhi] was a revolutionary. I maintained that, a religious and cultural revivalist, he was bound to be a reactionary socially, however revolutionary he might appear politically."[39] Lenin remained skeptical of the effectiveness of native Communists. In a subcommittee meeting, their debate broke briefly into the open. Lenin pointed out sarcastically that although India had 5 million proletarians and 37 million landless peasants, the Hindu Communists had not even succeeded in forming a Communist party in the country.[40]

Lenin then came up with a clever compromise. First, he invited Roy to draw up his own alternative *Theses*. Roy did so, offering up several points that cautioned against too close an alignment with bourgeois nationalists who only sought to smother the proletariat. Roy also stressed the importance of Communist revolution in the colonial countries as crucial to the hopes for the revolutionary cause in Europe. Then Lenin suggested that *both* drafts be published, with Roy's points appended as "Supplementary Theses." Lenin suggested some editorial changes on

Roy's and accepted a few of Roy's edits on his. (For example, Lenin's final text called for temporary alliance with "revolutionary forces" in the colonial countries rather than "bourgeois democrats.") The congress then adopted both texts. Roy was even more thrilled.

In the end, however, there is no doubt who won the debate. Later scholars agree that Roy's draft underwent more substantial editorial change than Lenin's.[41] And with the passage of time, Lenin's policy, which perfectly suited the interests of the new Soviet state, dominated the policy of the Comintern. The Soviets nurtured the more extreme radical movements wherever such a policy made sense; they formed alliances with "bourgeois nationalists," however, wherever doing so served better as a weapon against the colonial powers. It was a policy to be followed over most of the next seven decades. The variations were mostly tactical; the strategic goal was consistent.

The outcome of the debate with Roy confirmed not only that the supposedly independent Comintern was becoming an instrument of Soviet state policy; it confirmed also the clarity of Lenin's strategic perception. Long-term dreams of social revolution were to be subordinated to the near-term value of weakening the Western grip over the colonial domains—which was a way of weakening imperialism on the larger world stage.

In the meantime, the Comintern trumpeted the revolutionary cause. In September 1920, it convened in Baku a "Congress of the Peoples of the East," making a further appeal to the "enslaved masses" of, especially, the Middle East. At Baku, Grigorii Zinoviev called for a "genuine holy war against English and French capitalists."[42] Karl Radek cited the interdependence of the cause of revolution in Europe and in the East: "We are linked with you by fate: either we will unite with the peoples of the East and will promote the victory of the Western European proletariat, or we will perish and you will stay in slavery." Radek, like Zinoviev, invoked bloody historical memories of "holy war" to flatter and stir his audience into a new campaign against the West: "We appeal, comrades, to the feeling of struggle which used to inspire the peoples of the East at the time when these peoples, led by their great conquerors, went against Europe."[43]

Probably it is unwise to take all this rhetoric too seriously, especially in retrospect. M. N. Roy chose to skip the Baku congress entirely, deriding it as "Zinoviev's Circus." He thought it "a wanton waste of time, energy and material resources in frivolous agitation."[44] The exuberance of Baku may seem comical today, but Lenin's more hard-nosed strategic instinct was to have important consequences.

THE LEGACY

Thus were shaped some of the basic themes of the U.S.-Soviet rivalry of the next seventy years. "[T]he encounter had a certain absolute quality right from the beginning," Henry L. Roberts wrote.[45] Both Wilson and Lenin rejected the traditional state system of European politics; indeed, they rejected history itself. Neither man had much international experience; in each case it could be said that his view of world politics was "a projection of domestic considerations outward upon the international scene"—Wilson's democratic progressivism and Lenin's analysis of the internal mechanism of class struggle. "The very universality of their prescriptions for a world order," Roberts observed shrewdly, "betrayed a parochial origin."[46]

Neither man knew much about the other's country. As George Kennan noted of the American president:

> . . . Wilson was a man who had never had any particular interest in, or knowledge of, Russian affairs. He had never been in Russia. There is no indication that the dark and violent history of that country had ever occupied his attention. Like many other Americans, he felt a distaste and antipathy for Tsarist autocracy as he knew it, and a sympathy for the revolutionary movement in Russia. Precisely for this reason, the rapid degeneration of the Russian Revolution into a new form of authoritarianism, animated by a violent preconceived hostility toward western liberalism, was a phenomenon for which he was as little prepared, intellectually, as a great many of his compatriots.[47]

At the end of the nineteenth and beginning of the twentieth century, Americans were coming around to the general view that only democracies could conduct moral and peaceful foreign policies, that autocracies had an inherent tendency toward aggressiveness. Wilson was a prominent adherent of this view—a suspicion heightened in this case by the militantly subversive rhetoric of the Communist revolution.[48]

As for Lenin, he casually lumped England and America together as equally imperialist powers, dismissing all differences. He attributed America's entry into World War I, rather bizarrely, to the need of this country's capitalists to have "a pretext, while hiding behind the high ideals of a struggle for the rights of little nationalities, for creating a strong permanent army." Wilson's peace aims he dismissed as "a downright lie and hypocrisy."[49]

Thus, their visions of the future of the Third World were bound to clash violently. For American policy it was a twofold challenge: to guide the underdeveloped regions of the world through a transition to full-fledged participation in the international system and to do so in the face of a Soviet attempt to suborn them as allies in a radical assault on that international system. American idealism called for emancipation; but our hopes for a progressive international order presupposed a moderate evolution consistent with our humane principles. Those hopes also presupposed an international order based on interdependence and the possibility of harmony among nations. The Soviet vision of the colonial world—and of the international system that the colonial world was to join—was a wholesale rejection of that Wilsonian concept. It was a doctrine of mortal struggle, of irreconcilable class conflict. While there were Western hesitations about emancipation (such as Lansing's), which read embarrassingly today, Lenin challenged not merely the hesitations but the positive Wilsonian vision in its entirety. Ironically, the Wilsonianism that Lenin derided as a cover for sinister aims was faulted in Western Europe for its naive idealism. Witness Harold Nicolson's bitter disillusionment after Versailles.[50]

The two goals, the moral and the strategic, would often enmesh U.S. policy in tactical contradictions. Yet American statesmen would also find on many a later occasion that the two components of the challenge could not easily be separated, either. The great enterprise of integrating the developing countries into a peaceful world community could not be safely accomplished without at the same time checking the Soviet thrust (even though there were those who thought the Cold War too much colored American policy). Nor could Soviet exploitation of colonial turbulence be successfully checked without a positive American policy that responded to the aspirations of the emerging nations (though there were those who focused on the Soviet problem as the dominant issue).

Other presidents after Wilson would be challenged by the Soviets and would respond, as he attempted to do, with a positive political message that proclaimed what America was for, not only what it was against. They would find, as he did, that such a posture suited not only the international requirement but also the domestic requirement of mobilizing support in our democracy for a committed policy abroad. American foreign policy could never escape its domestic roots.

In that brief, tumultuous moment at the end of the Great War, the gauntlet was thrown down. A Swiss intellectual, Hermann Kesser, wrote in October 1918 that an exhausted Europe had been without hope until Wilson—and then Lenin—appeared. Now the world had a fateful choice to make:

[I]n one deed, the only truly great statesman-like deed, the first signal of world improvement rang out: Wilson announced the League of Nations; he foresaw that without it the peoples could no longer carry on their existence. The second attempt at world improvement . . . has been undertaken in Russia, and it is yet too soon to pronounce upon it. . . . It is certain that mankind must make up its mind either for Wilson or for Lenin.[51]

2

EMERGING POWERS

The conflict of basic principles that Wilson and Lenin embodied was not to become a direct confrontation for another generation. Both countries withdrew into their own spheres after the First World War, for different reasons, still groping their way toward a coherent response to the stirrings in the world outside Europe.

For Lenin's successor, Josef Stalin, the interwar years proved to be a time of frustration. Lenin's strategic decision to deal with bourgeois nationalists in the colonial world led to a series of failures of Soviet policy. The moment when the strategy would bear fruit was not yet at hand. The frustrations did not necessarily prove M. N. Roy to be correct; rather, they reflected the weakness of the new Soviet state and its inability to impose its will or project its doctrine. Roy's strategy of all-out support for local Communist parties would not have achieved much, either. Stalin's failures, however, would induce a caution in his approach that two decades later probably delayed the Soviets' emergence as a factor in the Third World.

For the Americans, of course, the interwar years saw a retreat into isolation. The Senate's failure in 1920 to support the League of Nations doomed the international system that Wilson had labored at Versailles to create and paved the way for renewed European conflict. The United States retreated to its own neighborhood—the Western Hemisphere—where its interventionism made a notable contrast with its abdication everywhere else and where it entangled itself in moral dilemmas that would bedevil American policy and American politics in a variety of ways for the next several generations.

BOLSHEVIK FRUSTRATIONS

Stalin held no major position in the Comintern in the early 1920s; that arena was dominated by his rivals Trotsky and Zinoviev. Yet, as a Georgian, Stalin had had a keen interest in the "national and colonial question" since the earliest days of Bolshevik power. The colonial revolution against imperialism, he had written, could be the great reliable "rear" supporting the "vanguard" of the socialist revolution in the developed world; however, the proletariat's success in the West could be assured only if its comrades in the colonial world succeeded as well. In the famous debate between Lenin and M. N. Roy, Stalin had sided with Lenin, viewing nationalism as a valuable potential ally of Bolshevik foreign policy.[1]

Soviet Russia emerged from civil war in the early 1920s, moreover, into the recognition that its dreams of igniting revolutions in Europe were not to be realized. It was more successful, once it recovered its breath, in reconquering the various non-Russian provinces of the old empire, the regions whose independence Lenin had conceded either at Brest-Litovsk or out of weakness in the early years. Ukraine, Belorussia, Azerbaijan, Armenia, and Georgia were occupied by the Red Army; the Moslem borderlands and Far Eastern provinces were retaken; satellite regimes were established in Outer Mongolia and northern Iran. In this context, it was not wrong for the Baku conference of 1920 to exude optimism about the prospect of new advances in "the East."

The Near East, in particular, seemed a tempting vacuum. With the collapse of the Ottoman Empire, the traditional "Great Game" of Russian-British competition seemed on again.

The British first thought they had a clear field ahead of them, deftly outmaneuvering the French in Palestine, for example, to claim the lion's share of the spoils. The League of Nations Mandate system proved (as Lloyd George had anticipated) a convenient cover for this effort.[2] But the British statesmen plotting these maneuvers were oblivious to the degree to which Britain's stamina had been gravely weakened by the Great War. Winston Churchill, war minister and later colonial secretary in Lloyd George's postwar government, warned that Britain simply no longer had the resources to build a new empire in the East.[3] The British had persisted, however; their armies were occupying much of the Middle East when the war ended. But then reality caught up with them.

Uprisings began to occur all over the region, responding to the stirrings of nationalism. The eager Bolsheviks were there to exploit it—and they made an impressive showing. In Turkey, Persia, and Afghanistan, they made alliances with bourgeois nationalists as Lenin had envisioned. In Turkey, they signed a treaty of friendship in March 1921 with Mustapha Kemal Pasha (later Ataturk). They furnished Kemal enough military equipment to outfit perhaps three divisions and to support him in his efforts to resist the Greek occupation of Anatolia (to which the Greeks were given rights under the 1920 Treaty of Sevres, imposed on the Ottomans by the British and French). Kemal's success, the Soviets expected, would weaken the influence of Britain and the other great powers in the area. It was, in effect, the first example of Soviet military assistance to a foreign regime at war against the Western powers.[4]

In Afghanistan in early 1919, the emir was murdered, and the British looked on with dismay as this vital buffer protecting their lifeline to India seemed to dissolve into anarchy. The Tsar had conceded in 1907 that the kingdom should be a British protectorate, but Amanullah Khan, the slain ruler's son, brashly declared the kingdom's independence and even launched a military excursion into British India in hopes of igniting an Indian uprising. The British succeeded in expelling the Afghans from India, only to see Amanullah afterward sign a friendship treaty with the Bolsheviks.[5] The Soviets embraced Amanullah and showered Afghanistan with assistance, including a radiotelegraphic station, a gunpowder plant, aviation school, several aircraft, five thousand rifles with ammunition, and a million gold rubles.[6]

The independence and integrity of Persia, or Iran, had been considered by the British throughout the nineteenth century as, in Lord Curzon's words, "a cardinal precept of our Imperial creed."[7] Persia's independence from Russian dominance, like that of Afghanistan, was a vital interest in ensuring the lifeline to India. In August 1919, the British imposed an agreement on the Persians admitting British civilian advisers, aid projects, naval facilities, and other forms of "cooperation." It was, in effect, another protectorate. The Bolsheviks found it easy to stir up Persian nationalism against this, which they did with great bravado. In May 1920, thirteen Soviet warships attacked and captured Enzeli, a Royal Navy–controlled port on the Persian Caspian coast. The Soviet goal was to weaken the British position not only in Persia but also in Iraq, where yet another nationalist uprising against the British had begun.

The humiliation on the Caspian hastened the British withdrawal from Persia in 1921. Reza Khan, the strongman whom the British sought to install as the new ruler, repudiated the Anglo-Persian agreement and signed a treaty with the Bolsheviks—directed, as were the similar Turkish and Afghan treaties, against "imperialism."[8]

From the perspective of later history, however, the political payoff for the Soviets from this youthful boldness proved limited. Kemal Pasha succeeded, with his Soviet military supplies, in pushing back the Greeks; Turkey remained outside the British sphere of influence. But Kemal's focus as ruler of Turkey was on internal modernization, not on stimulating further regional upheavals, nor had he any interest in being an instrument of any of the Soviets' broader ideological or political schemes. Similarly in Afghanistan and Persia, the Soviet gains were not of a long-term nature—more of a nuisance, as Adam Ulam puts it, than a mortal threat to the British position.[9] Nationalism displayed its resilence.

Much to the frustration of the Comintern, moreover, these Near Eastern leaders turned out to be staunchly anti-Communist at home (a pattern that would be repeated in the Middle East a generation later). While progressive in the sense that they were secular modernizers, they had no particular sympathy for socialism or proletarian revolution (or democracy). The weak young Turkish Communist party, for example, was suppressed under Kemal. The Turkish Communist delegates who had attended the Second Comintern Congress and Baku conference in 1920 returned home early in 1921 to be stoned by the local population, arrested, tortured, and literally thrown into the Black Sea. The Soviets, then in the process of negotiating the Russo-Turkish treaty, had to choose between Kemal and the Turkish Communists; they stuck with Kemal—and ended up with little to show for it.[10] Analogously in the case of Afghanistan (which had no significant Communist party), Amanullah later furnished aid to the *basmachi*, the fierce Muslim partisans who resisted Soviet rule in Central Asia in the 1920s.[11]

The most notorious setback to the Leninist policy of collaboration with bourgeois nationalists, however, was the disaster in China. China had seemed especially promising. The collapse of the ancient dynasty was a harbinger of the collapse of empires; it was expected not only to frustrate the predations of the Western powers in China but also to inspire all other victimized peoples to rise up against them. Assessing the Chinese Communist party as weak, the Comintern pressed it to ally with Sun Yat-sen's popular Kuomintang (KMT), which it did in 1923. Stalin blessed Sun Yat-sen's nationalist revolution, in Leninist terms, as a "bourgeois revolution of an anti-imperialist type."[12] Soviet political advisers like Mikhail Borodin helped build the KMT into an effective mass party. Soviet military advisers helped build, train, and equip the KMT's National Revolutionary Army; the Soviets sent $2 million worth of arms and ammunition and established the famous Whampoa military academy near Canton. Soviet military personnel took part in combat alongside Gen. Chiang Kai-shek's Nationalist forces in campaigns against resistant warlords.[13]

From 1924 to 1927, Stalin pursued this policy of active support for the KMT, at the same time nurturing the small Chinese Communist party and reconciling the two conflicting policies by the hope that Communist influence would gradually grow within the KMT. It turned into a disaster when Chiang treacherously turned on the Communists in March and April 1927, arresting and massacring their forces and cadre in Shanghai.

As scholar Franz Borkenau later noted, there was a flaw at the heart of such a policy if the Bolsheviks ever seriously intended to foment Communist revolution against the nationalist regimes with which they were simultaneously allied: "The root of the . . . catastrophe in China lies in this duplicity, in this childlike conviction that your adversary will not understand your intentions, though you express them quite openly, that he will continue to cooperate with you as long as *you* want it, and allow himself to be overthrown when it suits *you*."[14] The Soviets would have to make hard choices.

After this debacle in China, Stalin made the choice of turning Soviet foreign policy inward. At the Sixth Comintern Congress in September 1928, the new line repudiated Lenin's confident appeal to the nationalist bourgeoisie in the colonial countries. Building up and developing the indigenous Communist parties was, rhetorically at least, the preeminent task. The Comintern denounced Sun Yat-sen's nationalist philosophy in China; it denounced Gandhi in India. (If M. N. Roy felt vindicated, his triumph was short-lived: Stalin had him expelled in 1929.) In reality, Stalin's policy of "socialism in one country"—the forced-draft industrialization of Russia's primitive economy—now took priority.

As the 1930s dawned and new dangers emerged from Japan in the East and Germany in the West, adventurism in the colonial world (by whatever strategy) sank to even lower priority; it conflicted with the imperative of national survival. The Japanese occupied Manchuria in September 1931; Hitler came to power in January 1933. The thrust of Soviet policy in the 1930s was to mend fences internationally in order to contribute to a united front against the growing Fascist threat.

The Soviets provided substantial military aid to two provincial warlords in Sinjiang during the 1930s in order to establish a strategic presence in an area that might prove crucial in blocking the Japanese.[15] But in what must have involved a painful dose of swallowed pride, Stalin resumed relations with the Kuomintang regime in 1932. Five years later, as the Sino-Japanese War heated up, the Soviet Union and Nationalist China signed a treaty by which the Soviets supplied arms to China for defense against Japan. Again, the Soviets sent massive supplies of weapons— equipping between ten and twenty divisions—and a squadron of Soviet bombers and fighter planes flew combat missions in December 1937 in support of Nationalist forces.[16]

Thus, Stalin renewed the policy of relations with bourgeois nationalists, but out of necessity, not conviction. He would reconfirm after World War II his profound suspicion of these political and social forces that was burned into him by his failures in the 1920s. Yet, at the same time, the still-young Soviet state was learning its way. It was developing and testing the instruments of policy—arms aid and economic assistance—that would serve it in good stead in later decades when the decolonization process accelerated and offered opportunities that vindicated Lenin's original strategy.

AMERICAN ISOLATION

The United States, after the defeat of the League, abandoned the European field. It had a foreign policy to speak of—humanitarian relief efforts (such as Herbert Hoover's programs in Europe after the war) and participation in multilateral forums to promote disarmament and international law. The 1928 Kellogg-Briand Pact, which attempted to outlaw war, expressed the American idea of benign international involvement. Yet the characteristic of America's global policy, especially in Europe, was an aversion to the factor of power—which, indeed, is the best definition of isolationism. The United States sought no role in Europe's security and felt no stake in Europe's political destiny.

One place where the United States could not be called isolationist was Latin America. The United States's turbulent relationship with its poorer neighbors to the south has fluctuated over the centuries between the sublime and the sordid and is, to this day, marked by deep-seated emotions on both sides.

In the eighteenth and nineteenth centuries, as Latin American nations sought and won their independence from Spain and France, the United States was their exemplar and champion. The moral example of British America's successful rebellion and proclamation of basic democratic rights inspired the great liberator Simón Bolívar and his followers. The Monroe Doctrine, proclaimed in 1823, was an assertion of the new North American democracy's brave pledge to interpose itself before the European colonial powers lest the Holy Alliance crush liberalism in the Western Hemisphere as it was seeking to do in Europe.

As the Western Hemisphere developed, however, the relationship between north and south changed. By the twentieth century, the United States was claiming its own right of intervention in the name of liberal principles. Whatever the motives of U.S. policy, objective circumstances were conspiring against a continuation of natural harmony. From fraternal provider of moral support, the United States had become the paternalistic protector, the political and economic evolution over the nineteenth century having changed the relationship into one of enormous inequality, with all the complexes that that brought in train.

In 1850, the economic and social condition and status of North America and Latin America were not that different. The two regions were about the same in population (Latin America about 33 million in 1850; North America, 26 million); both were predominantly agricultural societies dependent on Europe for manufactures. Some areas in both North and South America were developing relatively rapidly though, and attracted immigrants from the poorer parts of Europe.[17] After 1850, however, the paths of North and South America diverged so sharply that today the economy of the United States is six times larger than that of Latin America. In chapter 10 we will examine why. Whatever the explanation, the disproportion of power was bound to exact a psychological price, generating resentment on the Latin American side and callousness, guilt, or moral confusion on the North American side.

In the early decades of the twentieth century, the United States found itself actively intervening, politically and militarily, in its neighbors' affairs. Theodore Roosevelt's bold intrigues over Panama were only the beginning. In 1912, President William Howard Taft sent U.S. Marines into Nicaragua to stabilize the country when it was wracked by civil war. Woodrow Wilson sent U.S. forces to take and occupy Vera Cruz for six months in 1914 to protect American lives and property against a hostile and undemocratic Mexican regime. Haiti degenerated into anarchy in 1915, and the violence resulted in the murder of successive presidents until Wilson sent U.S. Marines and naval forces. They remained in Haiti for nineteen years. The violence also erupted in Santo Domingo (now the Dominican Republic), until Wilson sent the marines in May 1916 to restore order after a revolution that had degenerated into chaos. They remained for twelve years. President Calvin Coolidge sent U.S. forces to Nicaragua again in 1927. The motives ranged from high-minded concern for democracy, civil peace, and international law to more mundane defense of U.S. business interests and of the Latin American plutocracy that served them.

FRANKLIN ROOSEVELT

It was under President Herbert Hoover that the United States was converted to the view that intervention was no longer respectable: "True democracy is not and cannot be imperialistic," Hoover remarked while on a South American tour as president-elect in 1928.[18] But the most decisive shift not only in U.S. policy in the hemisphere but in our colonial policy as a whole came with Franklin D. Roosevelt. Roosevelt inherited the idealism that Woodrow Wilson represented, but he sought to perfect it. Wilson had been an unapologetic interventionist in Central America; the upright Presbyterian, bred in Victorian certitudes, had the moral self-assurance to use American power without guilt to oppose tinhorn dictators and promote democracy. "I am going to teach the South American republics to elect good men!" Wilson had reportedy expostulated to a British diplomat in the fall of 1913.[19] But a new century—shaped, iron-ically, by the shattering horrors of Wilson's Great War for Democracy—would leave few certitudes. In a relativist age, the American idealism that Wilson expressed was probably bound to turn into self-doubt. It is this self-doubt, so uncharacteristic of Woodrow Wilson himself, that infused liberal attitudes toward Third World involvement for most of the rest of the century.

Franklin Roosevelt had been assistant secretary of the navy in Woodrow Wilson's first term when the latter ordered the fleet to take Vera Cruz. Roosevelt was shaken by the event and later cited it as seminal in his thinking about Latin America.[20] In a 1928 article in *Foreign Affairs*, he broadly deplored our interventionism in Latin America, whether by Re-publican or Democratic administrations: "[N]ever before in our history have we had fewer friends in the Western Hemisphere than we have today. . . . The time has come when we must accept not only certain facts but many new principles of a higher law, a newer and better standard in international relations."[21] He thought that the ill will engendered by our interventionism was bound ultimately to harm our trading relations, so that "[n]either from the argument of financial gain, nor from the sounder reasoning of the Golden Rule, can our policy, or lack of policy, be approved."[22]

Therefore, in his own first inaugural address on March 4, 1933, Roo-sevelt announced the Good Neighbor Policy: "In the field of world policy I would dedicate this Nation to the policy of the good neighbor—the neighbor who resolutely respects himself and, because he does so, respects the rights of others—the neighbor who respects his obligations and re-spects the sanctity of his agreements in and with a world of neighbors." In 1933 and 1934, Roosevelt refused to get involved in a civil war in Cuba; he completed the withdrawal of the marines from Haiti. Outside of Latin America he promoted and signed legislation setting a date for Philippine independence, and he authorized the State Department to negotiate with China on terminating American extraterritorial rights. Before America's entry into World War II, he surprised the British by his lack of interest in acquiring British islands in the Western Hemisphere as part of the destroyer trade in 1940.[23]

The Atlantic Charter, the declaration of principled aims that Roosevelt and Winston Churchill issued after their meeting on the presidential cruiser *Augusta* in Argentia Bay, Newfoundland, on August 14, 1941, included a joint renunciation of ambitions for acquiring territory as well as language that recalled Woodrow Wilson's theme of self-determination:

> First, their countries seek no aggrandizement, territorial or other;
>
> Second, they desire to see no territorial changes that do not accord with the freely expressed wishes of the peoples concerned;
>
> Third, they respect the right of all peoples to choose the form of government under which they will live; and they wish to see sovereign rights and self-government restored to those who have been forcibly deprived of them. . . .

Roosevelt, like Wilson before him, viewed it as essential for both domestic and international public opinion that unselfish goals be seen as motivating the coalition that he was striving to build (and join) against the Axis. But at some point during the war, Roosevelt's anticolonial instinct hardened into a determined assault on the imperial possessions even of his wartime allies. The protectiveness that Wilson had shown toward our European partners amid the first great world struggle was not to be repeated. On the contrary.

A dispute soon developed with the British over the very meaning of the Atlantic Charter. Roosevelt and Churchill had a testy exchange at Argentia over "imperial preference," the British Empire's exclusive trading arrangements, but Churchill firmly believed that the language on self-determination in the press statement applied only to Axis-occupied Europe. Churchill, indeed, had personally inserted the words "sovereign rights" before the phrase "self-government" in order to preserve existing British relationships. But no sooner was the document published than others began to read into its ambiguous phraseology a broader meaning. Labour leader Clement Atlee, deputy prime minister in the wartime coalition, assured a group of West African students the next day that the Atlantic Charter articulated principles of freedom that applied to all peoples. Colonial officials cabled London with their concern that subject peoples might indeed interpret the charter that way, and the colonial office began anxious speculations on Britain's postwar policy.[24] But Churchill was adamant, and told both his cabinet and Parliament in

September 1941 that the Atlantic declaration applied only to liberated Europe. [25]

For Roosevelt, however, there was no such limitation of basic principle, and American policy became more insistent on this point after we entered the war. When Singapore fell in February 1942, Americans drew a sharp contrast between the courageous performance of the Filipinos under Gen. Douglas MacArthur and the allegedly weak performance of the Malays. Suddenly, it seemed clear: The Filipinos fought well because the United States had already promised them independence; the Malays—and, by extension, all British colonial subjects in jeopardy to the Japanese—could not be expected to fight unless they, too, had the prospect of national independence. Walter Lippmann wrote in the *Washington Post*: "[The] western nations must . . . identify their cause with the freedom and the security of the peoples of the East, putting away the 'White man's burden' and purging themselves of the taint of an obsolete and obviously unworkable white man's imperialism."[26]

Sumner Welles, under secretary of state and presidential confidant, was particularly passionate on this score. In a Memorial Day address in 1942, he made it official: "If this war is in fact a war for the liberation of peoples, it must assure the sovereign equality of peoples throughout the world. . . . Discrimination between peoples because of their race, creed, or color must be abolished. The age of imperialism is ended. . . . The principles of the Atlantic Charter must be guaranteed to the world as a whole—in all oceans and in all continents." Roosevelt made clear on many occasions to his secretary of state, Cordell Hull, that this interpretation was authoritative.[27]

Most wounding of all, Roosevelt made a special point of repeatedly urging Churchill to speed independence for India, the "jewel in the imperial crown." On March 11, 1942, Roosevelt sent Churchill a telegram suggesting a "temporary Government" in India based loosely on the experience of the American colonies in setting up first the Continental Congress, then the Articles of Confederation, and finally the federal Constitution—the voting procedures of each of which the president explained in detail.[28] Churchill printed FDR's telegram in his memoirs, adding a curt commentary: "This document is of high interest because it illustrates the difficulties of comparing situations in various centuries and scenes where almost every material fact is totally different, and the dangers of trying to apply any superficial resemblances which may be noticed to the conduct of war."[29] "The look that Churchill gets on his face when you mention India!" Elliott Roosevelt exclaimed gleefully to his father. [30]

The mounting pressure led Churchill in a November 1942 radio address to utter his famous words of defiance: "I have not become the King's First Minister in order to preside over the liquidation of the British Empire."[31] As late as 1945, Churchill persisted in publicly minimizing the scope of the Atlantic Charter. FDR was asked about it at a shipboard press conference on February 23, 1945, on the journey back from the Yalta Conference, and teased: "Dear old Winston will never learn on that point."

The British regarded all this as historical ignorance and arrant hypocrisy. Churchill thought the Americans' imaginations were stuck in 1776 and they had George III too much on the brain.[32] His colleagues noted that America's historical territorial expansion overland, or that of the Russians and Chinese, was not subject to the same strictures; it seemed to be only the powers that had accumulated *overseas* possessions that were under such moral assault, they noted bitterly. The "salt-water fallacy," they jibed.[33]

American militancy on the subject of colonialism had many sources. One argument was economic. Roosevelt, Hull, and Welles were all convinced free-traders and objected to colonialism as a form of protectionism. Imperial preference was anathema in a postwar world that was to be governed by the Open Door. "It's something that's not generally known," Elliott Roosevelt records his father as saying to him the afternoon before the Argentia meeting, "but British bankers and German bankers have had world trade pretty well sewn up in their pockets for a long time. Despite the fact that Germany lost in the last war. Well, that's not so good for American trade, is it?"[34] The topic came up at Argentia, as noted earlier, and the Americans frequently denounced the imperial preference system as exclusionary.

Roosevelt believed, beyond this, that the competition among colonial powers for raw materials and markets, impoverishing subject peoples, was dangerous because it was a source of war. This notion of the struggle for markets sounds Leninist in its thrust, but in FDR it was turned into another argument for the more positive postwar order he envisioned. Again, he confided in his son Elliott:

"The thing is," he remarked thoughtfully, replacing a smoked cigarette in his holder with a fresh one, "the colonial system means war. Exploit the resources of an India, a Burma, a Java; take all the wealth out of those countries, but never put anything back into them, things like education, decent standards of living, minimum health requirements—all you're doing is storing up the kind of trouble that leads to war. All you're doing is negating the value of any kind of organizational structure for peace before it begins."[35]

This reflected, thirdly, the conviction of American leaders that the colonial peoples' liberation was inevitable and that it was essential for the West not to be the target of their antagonism. Roosevelt explained to Charles Taussig, one of his many confidential advisers, shortly before his death: "The President said he was concerned about the brown people in the East. He said that there are 1,100,000,000 brown people. In many Eastern countries, they are ruled by a handful of whites and they resent it. Our goal must be to help them achieve independence—1,100,000,000 potential enemies are dangerous. He said he included the 450,000,000 Chinese in that. He then added, Churchill doesn't understand this."[36]

A fourth source of anticolonialist passion in American policy was the American vision of postwar world alignments. It was the vision of a world in which Britain's and France's struggle to recover their empires would be a bigger problem for U.S. foreign policy than Stalin's Soviet Union. Roosevelt proclaimed to his son at the time of the Casablanca Conference: " 'When we've won the war, I will work with all my might and main to see to it that the United States is not wheedled into the position of accepting any plan that will further France's imperialistic ambitions, or that will aid or abet the British Empire in *its* imperial ambitions.' "[37] In the Far East, for example, FDR saw China as a crucial player and major power; it was with Chiang Kai-shek that he shared much of his thinking on postwar Asia, with minimal consultation with Churchill, and it was because of Chiang that he concluded that the British had to relinquish not only their Shanghai and Canton privileges but also Hong Kong.[38]

This was of a piece with Roosevelt's well-known suspicion of Churchill's anti-Sovietism. Britain's primary aim after the war would be to recover its dominance of world trade, Roosevelt thought, and it was seeking to accomplish this by playing off the Soviets and Americans against each other. Roosevelt was determined not to fall into the British trap. He told Elliott: " 'The one thing that could upset the apple cart after the war is if the world is divided again, Russia against England and us. That's our big job now, and it'll be our big job tomorrow, too: making sure that we continue to act as referee, as intermediary between Russia and England.' "[39]

Fifth, and perhaps most important, was the powerfully anticolonialist feeling of the American public. Roosevelt was only reflecting a nearly universal, bipartisan sentiment. Henry Luce's *Life* magazine published an "Open Letter . . . to the People of England" in the edition of October 12, 1942: "[O]ne thing we are sure we are *not* fighting for is to hold the British Empire together. We don't like to put the matter so bluntly, but we don't want you to have any illusions. If your strategists are planning a war to hold the British Empire together they will sooner or later find themselves strategizing all alone."[40] Wendell Willkie, who had been the Republican challenger to Roosevelt in 1940, came home from a round-the-world tour in October 1942 to declare that "there is no more place for imperialism."[41] President Roosevelt responded positively to Willkie with a reference to his own Atlantic Charter. It was this that triggered Churchill's defiant public "First Minister" declaration two weeks later.

For Roosevelt, what he knew and saw of colonialism deeply offended his sense of justice. The same moral feeling that infused his 1928 *Foreign Affairs* article led him to the conviction that colonialism was exploitation pure and simple and that the sooner it ended, the better. Roosevelt's journey to the Casablanca Conference in January–February 1943 was a reinforcing moment, if not a turning point. On his way to Casablanca, his aircraft stopped in British Gambia and French Morocco, and what he saw appalled him.

The Gambia was the most horrid place he had ever seen, he repeated many times. Wages were fifty cents a day, he told his son in a tone of shock: " 'Dirt. Disease. Very high mortality rate. I asked. Life expectancy—you'd never guess what it is. Twenty-six years. Those people are treated worse than the livestock. Their cattle live longer!' "[42] In a later message to Churchill he called the country a "hellhole."[43] A few months after Casablanca, Roosevelt declared in a speech in Mexico that "the day of the exploitation of the resources and the people of one country for the benefit of any group in another country is definitely over."[44]

The French did not get off any more easily. In the effort to persuade Vichy not to cooperate with the Nazis, Roosevelt assured the French of American support for their overseas empire.[45] But in private conversations with others, he made clear his intention that French colonies, Indochina in particular, should be placed under international trusteeship, not returned to French control. France had "milked" Indochina for 100 years, and the people were worse off than before, the president declared variously to British ambassador Lord Halifax, to Churchill, to Cordell Hull and others.[46] He said the same thing to Stalin at the Tehran Conference in 1943; Stalin, of course, readily agreed, observing in avuncular fashion that the French ruling class was "rotten to the core."[47] Even the British thought all this unfair to the French.

The war ended with a big-power agreement—largely the product of

American planning and under American pressure—on a United Nations trusteeship system for former colonies. The Americans saw it as successfully negating the economic exclusivity of colonialism. Unlike the League of Nations Mandate system, with its "Class A," "B," and "C" categories of colonies to which different criteria applied, the UN trusteeship system had the explicit goal of eventual independence for *all*, according to appropriate timetables. The UN Trusteeship Council not only would receive reports on how humanely trustees were administering their wards, it would have authority to inspect (putting the British Empire "in the dock," as Churchill complained).[48]

Thus, an American president had reached back into the American tradition and put this country categorically on the side of colonial independence, with as much forthrightness as the Bolsheviks had ever done and with more practical effect. It was classically American, translating our most fundamental ideals into policy. Without Wilson's compromises, it shared with Wilson's broader program of world order the commitment that new rules of the game were now in play, to be enforced by American power. The strategic dilemma—the unpredictable consequences for international order at a time of looming East-West differences—was finessed by the confident hope that a new universal organization, the United Nations, would prevent any regression to old-style rivalries. In his March 1, 1945, address to Congress upon returning home from Yalta, Roosevelt said he thought the conference he had just attended with Stalin and Churchill "ought to spell the end of the system of unilateral action, the exclusive alliances, the spheres of influence, the balances of power, and all the other expedients that have been tried for centuries—and have always failed."

Whereas Wilson's commitment was nullified by a recalcitrant Senate, Roosevelt's was undercut by a successor president who did not share the anticolonialist passion to quite the same degree—and, even more, by a Cold War that shattered the easy illusions of postwar international harmony. Suddenly, to Harry Truman, the strategic dilemma reappeared like Banquo's ghost. While a Labour government in Britain voluntarily began the liquidation of empire that Churchill had shunned, the British and French empires won a respite from American pressure. The Soviet challenge began to dominate.

CONTAINMENT AND KOREA

Suddenly, Tocqueville's vision had come true: The two sleeping giants, America and Russia, occupied center stage in world affairs. Both of them had declared war on the colonial system, even at the expense of their own allies in the recent conflict. The first two decades of the postwar era thus saw the dismantling of most of what was left of the European overseas empires. But history played its tricks, especially on the Americans. Instead of an easy harmony among the great powers and a liberal world order in which the newly independent peoples would eagerly join, the Third World was caught up in a new global ideological struggle.

Indeed, the Third World would be torn apart by its own ideological civil wars that mirrored the contest of the superpowers. Third World societies would often find themselves split between moderates and radicals, between the middle- or upper-class elites whose dream was to be part of the civilized world (the Habib Bourguibas and Léopold Senghors) and the revolutionaries who saw the Western-dominated "civilized world" as still the main enemy (the Ho Chi Minhs and Fidel Castros). Each superpower looked for clients and proxies among the developing nations, and within them. The outcome between these two visions of the Third World's future would be decided only after four decades of bloody conflict.

Roosevelt's desire to free the Indochinese from French rule was one of the early casualties of the Cold War. Even before World War II ended, Truman decided that while he would press France to implement reforms in Indochina, he would not impose any UN trusteeship without French consent. Southeast Asia remained a low-priority concern, and the United States settled into a posture of neutrality as the French battled the Communist Vietminh (at least until the Communist victory in nearby China).[49] There was also a spate of Communist uprisings in Burma, Indonesia, the Philippines, Malaya, and part of India in the late 1940s.

A Central Intelligence Agency (CIA) assessment in September 1948 expressed great concern: "In contrast to the ever closer integration of the [East European] Satellites into the Soviet system, there is an increasing fragmentation of the non-Soviet world. . . . The USSR is effectively exploiting the colonial issue and the economic nationalism of the underdeveloped areas as a means of dividing the non-Soviet world, weakening the Western Powers, and gaining the good will of colonial and former colonial areas."[50]

As the CIA document suggested, Stalin's behavior in Europe only reinforced the fears. A speech by Stalin on February 9, 1946, reasserted the fundamental nature of the conflict between capitalism and communism and seemed to imply the inevitability of war.[51] Then Stalin gradually absorbed Eastern Europe, violating wartime accords. In Western Europe, the weakness of postwar democracies heightened anxiety that the Communist parties, backed by Moscow and skilled in infighting in the labor movement, would dominate the Western half of the continent as well. These dangers were beaten back by a historic series of initiatives by the United States that represented a decisive break with its isolationist past.

It all began on a gray Friday afternoon, February 21, 1947, when a British diplomat dropped off at the State Department copies of two notes about which the British ambassador wished to speak urgently to the secretary of state. The notes referred to the situations in Greece, where Communist insurgents, aided by Moscow, were waging a brutal civil war, and in Turkey, which was in dire need of economic and military assistance in the face of Soviet pressures. His Majesty's government, which had carried the burden of support for these two countries, was on the brink of economic crisis at home and could simply no longer play this role beyond the end of March.[52] Franklin Roosevelt's campaign against our European allies' "spheres of influence" was being fulfilled with a vengeance.

Within three weeks, on March 12, 1947, President Truman stepped before a joint session of Congress and declared that America had no choice but to step in with an extensive program of economic and military assistance: "I believe that it must be the policy of the United States to support free peoples who are resisting attempted subjugation by armed minorities or by outside pressures."

This became known as the Truman Doctrine—stated in terms that, on their face, appeared to apply globally, not only to southeastern Europe. Congress, in an unprecedented show of bipartisan responsibility, voted an aid program for Greece and Turkey in May. This confirmed the demise of Britain's role as the dominant world power (India was already headed for independence later in the year) and the beginning of America's role as principal guardian of the postwar peace.

Then, in June 1947, came the Marshall Plan, announced in Secretary of State George Marshall's commencement speech at Harvard. This was in considerable part a response to the advances of Communist parties and Communist-led labor organizations in Western Europe. The American commitment of aid bolstered the confidence of democratic forces and also promoted Western European economic cooperation and integration. Congress passed an initial appropriation in December 1947. Economic hardship was inhospitable ground for rebuilding political and economic institutions. The Marshall program of economic aid is justly famous; inadequately appreciated is the American labor movement's vigorous contribution to the struggle against Communist dominance of Western European labor unions. There is direct continuity between it and the AFL-CIO's hostility to Central American communism in the 1980s.

Two years later, the North Atlantic Treaty, signed in Washington in April 1949, was the response to the culminating event in Stalin's brutal suppression of Eastern Europe, the Czechoslovakia coup of 1948 in which the Communists, having come to power as part of a broad anti-Fascist coalition, squeezed out all their non-Communist rivals. (This, too, would have its later analogue in Nicaragua.) The Berlin blockade also played a major part in galvanizing the Western coalition. The stability and recovery of Western Europe were now seen to require not only American financial aid but a tangible American participation in European defense.

Stalin's pressures in Europe had provoked a direct American response. The Red Army's physical capacity to overrun Western Europe was probably exaggerated, but the danger of *political* collapse in Western Europe was real, and the increasing brutality of Stalin's absorption of Eastern and Central Europe heightened the sense of a growing preponderance of Soviet power on the Continent. The economic devastation and political demoralization of allies—compounded, to some degree at least, by our own prior efforts to diminish their global role—left a vacuum. Either we would fill it ourselves, or we would face geopolitical disaster.

Outside of Europe, the picture was not yet clear. Truman had proclaimed a doctrine that (critics charged) could draw us into engagements all over the world. Walter Lippmann's critique was, as usual, the most perceptive. Lippmann considered Western Europe the main battleground and feared that the Truman Doctrine, in its literal terms, committed us to a strategy of holding the line in a chain of weak states in peripheral areas. The sweeping terms of containment obliged us to rely on the likes of "Chinese, Afghans, Iranians, Turks, Kurds, Arabs, Greeks, Italians, Austrians, . . . anti-Soviet Poles, Czechoslovaks, Bulgars, Yugoslavs, Albanians, Hungarians, Finns and Germans." This was to Lippmann a distraction from the main strategic prize—our Western European allies— as well as a probable source of messy problems as we got into the business of "recruiting, subsidizing and supporting a heterogeneous army of satellites, clients, dependents and puppets." Given the vulnerability of such a defense line, the Communists, not we, "would define the issues, would make the challenges, would select the ground where the conflict was to be waged, and would choose the weapons." They could "defeat us," he feared, "by disorganizing states that are already disorganized, by disuniting peoples that are torn with civil strife, and by inciting their discontent which is already very great."[53]

It was, of course, a brilliant prediction of the agonizing challenges we would confront in China, Korea, Indochina, Central America, and elsewhere in the decades following. While Truman and his senior officials would strive in their exegesis to deny that America's commitments were indiscriminate—democracy was a key criterion for our support, Truman often stressed[54]—the challenges would not come where the American responses would be easiest.

But in 1947 no crisis of this kind had yet occurred. Stalin, for his part, was still groping hesitantly toward a policy. The uprisings in the Far East received little Soviet material help. At first, Stalin continued to think the Chinese Communists' prospects were not great; he urged Mao Zedong again to seek a modus vivendi with Chiang Kai-shek.[55] Stalin's attempt to maintain a Soviet occupation of northern Iran in 1946, in violation of wartime agreements, had been checked by a vigorous American and British campaign of protest.[56] Having disbanded the Comintern in 1943 as a gesture to his wartime allies, Stalin found it expedient in 1947 to reincarnate it as the Communist Information Bureau (the Cominform) to coordinate the policies of the world's Communist parties, though it was a shadow of its former self.

At the first Cominform conference in September 1947, Stalin's Politburo colleague Andrei Zhdanov, in a famous speech, surveyed the global situation as it had emerged from World War II. The tone was a combination of both militancy and unease. The world was now divided into two camps, Zhdanov declared—the "imperialist and anti-democratic camp" and the "anti-imperialist and democratic camp." The "principal driving force of the imperialist camp" was the United States, emboldened by its newfound power and "temporary" atomic monopoly to "extort" from Britain and France the dominant role among capitalist powers around the globe.[57] America's "predatory and expansionist" policies led it to absorb the colonies of its allies into its own sphere of influence. While some individual countries were thought to be sympathetic to the anti-imperialist cause (Egypt, India, Indonesia, Vietnam), most nations in the Near East and Latin America were relegated to the imperialist camp, treated as incorrigible bourgeois nationalists, inevitable supporters of the colonial powers on whom they were politically and economically dependent. The memory of the 1920s still burned.

As decolonization unfolded, Stalin continued to distrust such figures as Gandhi, Jawaharlal Nehru, and Sukarno. In 1949, a Soviet commentator denounced the "nationalist bourgeoisie and its national-reformist lackeys," among whom was Nehru, "a bloody strangler of the progressive forces in India." Only the Communist parties were reliable champions of national liberation. Neutralism, or the idea that these new states could be a "third force" between the two sides, was a "rotten idea"

that only served the interests of imperialism.[58] (The principal exception
to this shunning of national movements, ironically enough, was the
Zionists in Palestine: Stalin permitted Czechoslovakia to ship weapons
to the Haganah in 1947–49 [including Spitfire and Messerschmitt fighter
planes], apparently viewing Israel as a spearhead against British influence
in the Middle East.)[59]

In 1949, however, came two breakthroughs—the explosion of the first
Soviet atomic bomb in August and the Communist victory in China in
October. Then came Korea—Communist North Korea's surprise inva-
sion of the South in June 1950 to unify the peninsula by force.

Before the attack, the entire U.S. national security establishment had
treated South Korea as not important enough to be inside the Western
defense perimeter. While Secretary of State Dean Acheson was vilified
later for saying this publicly in January 1950, Far East commander Gen.
Douglas MacArthur and others had said the same.[60] Nor was the South
Korean regime of strongman Syngman Rhee a democracy. By any seemingly objective standard, therefore, the impulse to rush to South Korea's
defense was a perfect illustration of what Walter Lippmann had warned
against—letting the containment doctrine drag us into miserable conflicts
in behalf of unworthy clients in the most peripheral areas. Lippmann,
not surprisingly, thought the dispatch of U.S. ground troops to Korea a
mistake.[61]

And yet the provocation in Korea was also a perfect illustration of why
Lippmann's critique of containment, wise as it was, only illuminated one
horn of America's dilemma: Lippmann's static model of a U.S. strategy
centered on Europe did not do justice to the fluidity, dynamism, and
cumulative quality of the conflict that was about to unfold in the world
outside of Europe. The Truman administration concluded, in effect, that
it would be as dangerous to let its opponent commit aggression in the
Third World without limit as it would be to risk exhaustion by counter-
interventions without limit. The bell had rung, and it was not up to the
sole discretion of the United States what punches would be thrown, and
where, and what blows could be taken without consequence.

It is in the nature of politics that one judges the meaning of events by
their context as well as their intrinsic reality. Indeed, there is no "intrinsic
reality" aside from the most mechanistic analysis of physical resources
and real estate. In the Gulf in 1990, the Iraqi invasion of Kuwait transformed what had been an inter-Arab dispute over borders and oil prices
into a despot's bid for hegemonic control over a strategic region; even
without any prior formal U.S. defense commitment to Kuwait itself,
American interests in the Arab world as a whole were correctly seen as

threatened, not to mention the broader interests of the international community in the principle that such aggression must not succeed.

In Korea forty years earlier, the North's attempt to swallow up the South seemed to fit into a global pattern of Stalinist boldness. It came against the background of Stalin's consolidation in Eastern Europe, the vulnerability of Western Europe, and the breakthroughs of 1949 in atomic power and in China. So it was inevitably seen as part of a trend—indeed, of a tide—that had to be stopped somewhere. Our "intrinsic" stake in Korea might have been marginal before June 25; our stake in Japan's security, in the security of the broader Pacific region, and in the global balance of power, all of which were inevitably seen as affected, could not be considered marginal then or now.

We will probably never know what larger ambition, if any, the invasion of South Korea truly reflected in Stalin's mind subjectively. Recent archival discoveries in Moscow confirm that he was deeply involved in the military planning for the attack, as was widely assumed at the time.[62] But the idea seems to have been Kim Il-sung's initiative, and Stalin had to be persuaded. Stalin's motivation for going along in the end was probably simple opportunism, reflecting, as Khrushchev later recounted, his conclusion that Kim's aggressive plan would succeed and that the United States would not react.[63] (Stalin had a low opinion of Truman, dismissing him to his Kremlin colleagues as "worthless.")[64] For the West, therefore, the strategic issue was unmistakable—objectively. The aggression was so brazen that its broadly threatening message about the ambitions of the aggressors became a new geopolitical reality. The absence of a response would probably have created new temptations elsewhere even if none existed beforehand.

The military buildup that the United States undertook after the North Korean attack was the most decisive step in its emergence as a permanent global military power. The U.S. troop commitment to Western Europe under the North Atlantic Treaty had been conceived as temporary; no grandiose long-term rearmament was yet planned. In April 1950, President Truman and his National Security Council had approved the famous staff report NSC 68, which expressed alarm at the recent Soviet advances—Europe, the bomb, China—and called for "substantially increased" military forces in every category.[65] But this call for a military buildup remained on paper—until Korea. A follow-up report, NSC 73/4 in August 1950, warned that the invasion of South Korea "should be regarded not as an isolated phenomenon but possibly as part of a general plan which might involve correlated action in other parts of the world."[66] Total U.S. defense spending more than tripled in the first year of the Korean War and did not quickly fall after the war was over.[67] The U.S. Army grew; the North Atlantic Treaty signatories formed an integrated military command; the U.S. Seventh Fleet interposed itself between mainland China and Chiang Kai-shek's remnant of the Republic of China on Taiwan.

Thus, Stalin's and Kim Il-sung's throw of the dice in June 1950 goes down in history as a great blunder—a monumental overreaching. Stalin had been growing bolder in the Third World as the postwar period evolved, after the lines stabilized in Europe. He was slowly recovering the confidence he had lost from his early failures. The very gains that had so alarmed the drafters of NSC 68 must have boosted his confidence in the Soviet Union's ability to play a global role. But Korea provoked a response—*America's* definitive undertaking of a global role, including outside Europe—that he cannot have intended or welcomed.

The Cold War in the Third World was on.

3
KHRUSHCHEV AND EISENHOWER

Over the grave of Nikita Khrushchev, in Novodevichii Cemetery along the Moscow River, is a modernistic memorial crafted by the dissident (and later émigré) sculptor Ernst Neizvestnii. It is a disjointed and jarring marble structure, with odd angles and boxes of black and white, reflecting the contradictions in Khrushchev's character and in what he represented. That he is buried in such a place, with such a monument, is itself an anomaly. Novodevichii is an exclusive cemetery, on the grounds of an old and beautiful convent, where, as in Paris's Père Lachaise, rest historical figures—writers, artists, and statesmen from both the pre- and postrevolutionary eras. The grounds are small, the paths narrow, the graves packed closely together. Khrushchev's grave usually draws a knot of onlookers who crane for a look at the resting place of the only supreme Communist leader denied interment in the usual honorific place at the Kremlin wall.

Khrushchev was, indeed, the first top Soviet leader not to die in office; he lived seven years in retirement after losing power in 1964—at the time a remarkable sign of the mellowing in the Soviet system that owed much to his own stunning campaign to exorcise the ghost of Stalin. He was brought down by an entrenched party apparat that was fed up with his chaotic economic reorganizations and frightened by the loss of control that his cultural liberalization seemed to threaten. He is remembered today in his homeland with some sympathy, as a man of some decent instincts who foreshadowed the farther-reaching change that came under Mikhail Gorbachev (thus, Neizvestnii's tribute). Abroad, Khrushchev is remembered for his moves toward détente with the West following the Cuban Missile Crisis, including the 1963 Limited Test Ban Treaty, the first significant achievement curbing the nuclear arms race.

For our purposes, however, there is yet another paradox. This pioneer of internal thaw and East-West détente was also the Soviet leader who launched a bold political offensive against the West in the Third World, letting loose three decades of often violent conflict.

When Stalin died in March 1953, Soviet foreign policy had run out of steam. Stalin and his North Korean comrades had alarmed the West into a rearmament and reawakening. The United States and Japan, in response, had signed a peace treaty. In Europe, the allies were consolidating the Western position in the new Federal Republic of Germany; Stalin was deterred from smashing the rebellious Yugoslavia partly because, after Korea, Secretary of State Acheson had warned pointedly that another aggression would strain the overall fabric of peace.[1] While Stalin and some of his experts had begun a tentative reevaluation of their Third World policy,[2] his successors were acutely aware of the need for more significant moves to break out of their isolation. In Khrushchev's account, he and his colleagues saw some of the American success in building alliances and bases around the Soviet periphery as the direct result of Stalin's misguided policy.[3]

The post-Stalin leaders feared for their own personal survival in a deadly domestic environment, and for the very survival of the regime and its international position at a moment of such internal vulnerability. Instead of applying pressure, the Eisenhower administration (itself new in office) extended an olive branch. The president, in a major speech on April 16, 1953, signaled the West's interest in solving lingering problems, the Korean conflict prominent among them.[4] The new team in the Kremlin seized the opening eagerly to win a breathing space, and an armistice was reached in Korea in June 1953.

In an August speech, Premier Georgii Malenkov stressed the desire of the new Soviet leadership to lessen tension in Europe and elsewhere. He had some kind words about India, as well as Pakistan, Afghanistan, Burma, Turkey, and Iran.[5] Within a few years' time, the new Soviet leaders would sign the Austrian State Treaty (withdrawing their troops from Austria), heal the breach with Marshal Tito of Yugoslavia, establish relations with the Federal Republic of Germany, and restore relations with Japan.

The new conciliatory line toward the ex–colonial countries in particular amounted to a substantial change of policy. In July 1953, in the United Nations Economic and Social Council, the Soviets announced a 4-million-ruble contribution to the UN program of technical assistance to the underdeveloped nations. Until then, they had contributed only lip service to the program.[6] In September 1953, the Soviet government signed a five-year trade agreement with India. In 1954, Afghanistan became the first Third World nation to receive Soviet credits since World War II. In a major initiative toward the Arab world, which Stalin had shunned, the Soviet Union on two occasions in 1954 cast vetoes in the

UN Security Council that protected the Arabs' position—one blocking a Western resolution on the division of Jordan River waters, the other blocking a New Zealand resolution that would have reaffirmed the 1951 condemnation of Egypt's denial to Israel of access to the Suez Canal.[7]

In February 1955, the Soviets and Indians announced a million-ton steel-mill project at Bhilai, for which the Soviets gave a $100 million credit. In April 1955, a conference of nonaligned states was held in Bandung, Indonesia; the Soviets gave it their blessing and managed to wangle an invitation for their Chinese allies. The nonaligned were courted; no longer was the world divided rigidly into "two camps." In June 1955, India's prime minister Nehru—once denounced by Stalin's men as an imperialist lackey—visited the Soviet Union as an honored guest.

In February 1955, Malenkov was ousted, replaced as premier by Nikolai Bulganin. Later in the year, he and Party First Secretary Khrushchev felt secure enough at home to venture abroad (although presumably keeping an eye on each other). In November and December they made a highly publicized monthlong tour of India, Burma, and Afghanistan. The visit to India was the highlight. The Soviet guests went out of their way to flatter their hosts, dispensing not only economic goodies but political ones as well: Nehru was bowled over by unexpected Soviet support for the Indian position on the Kashmir dispute with Pakistan and the Goa dispute with Portugal.[8] As Adam Ulam later observed, the high-level visit itself was a tribute to neutralist India, which was then "at the height of her self-congratulatory phase," and enabled the Soviets to score points at the expense of not only the British and Americans but also the Chinese, the other major power wooing the Indians. Ulam wryly added:

> Khrushchev's inherent boorishness was still being kept under restraint. He submitted to being garlanded with flowers by young girls, suffered through official receptions, where in deference to the Congress Party's ban on alcohol orange juice was substituted, and only occasionally uttered tactless remarks about wicked British and American imperialism, which had not as yet abandoned its evil designs on the Indian people. While his hosts could not but contrast his manners with the mandarin graces of Chou [Zhou Enlai], the ebullient Soviet leader could dispense economic help and his Chinese counterpart only Asian solidarity.[9]

The India trip was the first of Khrushchev's many successful Third World encounters. (In 1960 he would visit India and Burma again and spend twelve days in Indonesia; in 1964 he would visit Egypt.) The Soviet leader was fascinated by the colorful personalities he met on trips or received in Moscow, from Indonesia's Sukarno and Egypt's Gamal Abdel Nasser to Algeria's Ahmed Ben Bella and Ghana's Kwame Nkrumah. Khrushchev's memoirs are filled with vivid descriptions of his meetings and conversations with them—his identification with their successful defiance of colonialism, his sadness at their setbacks. [10]

The most dramatic and significant event of the period, however, came on September 27, 1955, with Nasser's announcement that Egypt was purchasing advanced weapons from Czechoslovakia. Frustrated by a cycle of clashes with Israel (and by the West's unwillingness to sell him weapons), Nasser defied the West and turned to the Soviets. Although Czechoslovakia was the supplier of record, Nasser admitted soon enough that the deal had been negotiated with the Soviets. The package included Soviet MiG-15 and MiG-17 jet fighters, Ilyushin-28 jet bombers, medium and heavy tanks, artillery, submarines, torpedo boats, two destroyers, and ammunition, plus training of Egyptian personnel at Warsaw Pact facilities. Egyptian cotton and rice were the barter price; the best estimates of the value of the weapons range from $200–$250 million (while some go as high as $400 million). [11] The post-Stalin Soviet leadership had quickly graduated from ceremonial visits, trade deals, and steel mills, on the edges of the Cold War competition, to massive arms supply in a region of vital strategic importance to the West.

As the former colonial countries emerged on the world scene, the advantage to the Soviets of wooing them was obvious; in that sense, to do so was perfectly natural. Yet for Communist leaders some ideological readjustment was required, especially after the rigid "two camps" doctrine of Stalin and Zhdanov. This theoretical grounding for a new policy was provided by Khrushchev, after the fact, in his report to the Twentieth Party Congress on February 14, 1956. (It was at the same party congress that Khrushchev, in a secret session, revealed and denounced the mass murder and terror of the Stalin era.) Soviet leaders routinely quoted Lenin to support every twist and turn in foreign policy, but in this case the return to an original Leninist insight was genuine.

The new nations born of the breakup of the colonial empires, while they "proclaimed nonparticipation in blocs as a principle of their foreign policy," were nevertheless natural partners of the socialist countries in a "vast zone of peace," Khrushchev declared. The Soviet Union would help them to develop and to end their dependency on their former colonial masters: "The very fact that the Soviet Union and other countries of the socialist camp exist, that they are ready to help the underdeveloped countries with their industrial development on terms of equality and mutual benefit, is a major stumbling block to colonial policy."[12]

Soviet commentators reassessed other issues in Marxist theory, such as whether these Third World nations had legitimate "socialist" credentials. Certainly, state ownership of key industries and elaborate planning bureaucracies were features of many of the new states (as much the inheritance of the postwar European socialists, London School of Economics–style, as of orthodox Marxism). Nevertheless, new theories had to be elaborated as to how these societies could advance all the way to true socialism without an intermediate state of developed capitalism. There was no precedent in Marxist analysis for a noncapitalist path of development or for a proletarian revolution without a proletariat. It had been enough of a challenge to Soviet theoreticians to explain Russia's twentieth-century experience, which contradicted Marx's expectation that revolution would occur first in the most advanced industrial countries of Europe. The developing world was even further from the Marxist norm.

To sum up a tortuous evolution in Soviet commentaries that proceeded over decades, the experts in the Khrushchev period began to make much of the small industrial working classes that seemed to exist in these countries and to hail their potential as a vanguard. The large peasantry, said to be much exploited under colonialism, was seen as an even more potent revolutionary force. And with the material help of the newly strong Soviet Union and other advanced socialist countries, these former colonies could be given the needed extra push down the path of socialist development. While in later years more honest commentary would grow skeptical of these confident assertions, in the 1950s they were enough to give philosophical grounding to the leadership's geopolitically shrewd campaign to woo the newly independent "bourgeois" nationalist regimes. In the same post-1956 period, the prestigious Institute of World Economy and International Relations was reopened (having been closed down under Stalin), new academic institutes were established, and the Soviets began developing a new generation of experts capable of advising the leadership on Third World affairs.[13]

Whether the emerging nations would accept Khrushchev's claim that the Soviets were their natural allies was, of course, another matter altogether. Most of them were to prove jealous of their independence; only a handful (North Korea, Cuba, North Vietnam) declared themselves fully "Marxist-Leninist" in the 1940s and 1950s. The ideological grounding of Soviet policy was, at bottom, shoddy. Khrushchev personalized his foreign relations to a remarkable degree. He exaggerated the depth of the personal relationships he formed and he most certainly exaggerated the "socialist" character of his new friends. In the Arab world, for example, by and large, Nasser and his brethren were petty military dictators of a less exalted sort, adopting statist economic methods as a means of political control and anti-Western ideological slogans for the same reason. It was not only that these leaders turned as brutally against local Communists as against other internal rivals; the political structures and institutions bore little significant relationship to Khrushchev's (and the commentators') crude, wishful, and un-Marxist thinking.[14]

Whatever the ideological weakness of the new bond between the Soviet Union and its clients, however, it would take the West thirty years to break it. Khrushchev's policy made enormous headway. The parallelism of interest in the 1950s between the Soviets and some of the most important developing nations was evident enough, made concrete in the burgeoning of their relations—most dramatically in the security sphere. As Nasser's extreme anti-Western policies exemplified, the parallelism of interest consisted in a common desire to weaken the position of the traditional Western powers. And whatever the physical limits of Soviet military reach in the Khrushchev period, his successors would take steps to remedy them.

THE AMERICAN RESPONSE TO KHRUSHCHEV

In March 1956, Secretary of State John Foster Dulles visited New Delhi, a few months after Bulganin and Khrushchev's triumphal tour. India was the country on behalf of whose independence Franklin Roosevelt had spent most of World War II badgering Churchill; its leaders had been regularly insulted for a generation by Stalin and his toadies. The United States had shipped huge quantities of emergency wheat and rice in 1951 and subsequent years to relieve famine. From 1945 to 1956, U.S. economic aid delivered to India, including both loans and grants, totaled nearly $435 million. (Soviet aid delivered through 1956 totaled some $40 million, though over $360 million was pledged.) U.S. aid was predominantly in the form of grants; Soviet aid was then entirely credits.[15] Yet when Dulles arrived at Palam Airport, Nehru was not there to greet him, on the grounds that he (Nehru) was not only foreign minister but also head of government and therefore their ranks were not equal. Dulles drove into New Delhi under tight security, without crowds and without fanfare. While Nehru graciously received him for a four-hour meeting shortly after his arrival, complete with photo opportunity, and he was put up in the same suite at the presidential palace that Premiers Bulganin and Zhou Enlai had slept in, there was sensitivity on the American side about the treatment.[16]

To many Americans, there seemed to be a double standard at work. This double standard itself represented a more sophisticated—and effective—challenge from the Soviet Union, and it raised a host of questions about America's role and prospects in the growing Third World of new nations.

President Eisenhower and his secretary of state were not shy about taking up the strategic challenges that the Soviets presented. In what some derided as "pactomania," they devoted considerable diplomatic effort to constructing a worldwide network of alliances to block Soviet expansion—in Latin America, by reinforcing the Rio Pact; in Southeast Asia, with the Manila Pact of 1954; in the western Pacific, with mutual defense treaties in 1954 with the Republic of Korea and the Republic of China; in the Near East, with the 1955 Baghdad Pact; and, in 1960, with the security treaty with Japan. In the less elevated dimension of covert action, the Eisenhower administration reversed a leftist takeover of power in Iran in 1953 and in Guatemala in 1954. Its reconnaissance overflights of the Soviet Union, embarrassingly brought to a halt by the U-2 shootdown of May 1960; the Dulles doctrine of "massive retaliation," threatening a nuclear response to any kind of Communist challenge, even in the Third World—these reflected the ideological energy of a Republican administration seriously concerned about, if not alarmed by, the apparent ambitions of the post-Stalin Soviet leadership in the world at large.

The new face of Soviet policy seemed a "strategy of ambiguity"[17]—moves toward liberalization at home, proclamation of a general line of "peaceful coexistence" with the West, and a new activism in the Third World. After the Twentieth Party Congress, the administration took pains to stress that the West had to keep up its guard. There were constructive changes, Dulles acknowledged in an important speech in Philadelphia on February 26, 1956. But he was loath to attribute them to any more than a change of tactics prompted by the firmness of Western policies: "The Soviet rulers trumpeted this throughout the world as proof that Soviet Communist policy was no longer predatory.

"We hoped that this was so. But we were highly skeptical. We well knew that under Leninism any tactic is admissible and that the change had come about, not through change of heart, but because old methods had failed." Deputy Under Secretary of State Robert D. Murphy gave an authoritative assessment of the post-Stalin Soviet policy in a speech on April 19, 1956. The new external face of the system, Murphy said, was only a more subtle and complex challenge: "In terms of the ultimate fate of free civilization, this new strategy is no less dangerous than the old. We assume it to be equally hostile but more deceptive to combat. It is more subtle, more complex, and geared to a longer time period."

After the shocking suppression of the Hungarian Revolution at the end of 1956, the rhetoric grew harsher. Thus, President Eisenhower stated in his second inaugural address, on January 21, 1957: "The designs of that power, dark in purpose, are clear in practice. It strives to seal forever the fate of those it has enslaved. It strives to break the ties that unite the free. And it strives to capture—to exploit for its own greater power—all forces of change in the world, especially the needs of the hungry and the hopes of the oppressed."

Behind the rhetoric was, in reality, a rather more accommodating policy toward the Soviets. The president's olive branch of April 1953 led to the Geneva summit with Bulganin and Khrushchev in July 1955, and Budapest did not prevent the visit of Vice President Richard Nixon to Moscow in 1958 and Khrushchev's visit to the United States in 1959. The military doctrine of "massive retaliation" turned out to be not a prelude to nuclear war but rather a cover for an American reluctance to challenge the Soviets and their allies on the ground in, for example, Indochina at the time of the French debacle at Dien Bien Phu in 1954. (Korea had taught a lesson about the folly of fighting faraway ground wars.) American conventional military power began to be cut back after the Korean War ended; the Republican administration promoted a "new look" in defense policy that trimmed the budget and promised "more bang for the buck"—leaving us little option, perhaps, but to bluff with nuclear weapons against conventional challenges we might no longer have the capability to respond to on the ground.

In its internal strategy papers, the administration fretted that the economic costs of opposing Soviet expansionism over a long period might be a threat to our way of life almost as deadly as Soviet communism itself. A TOP SECRET National Security Council (NSC) document of June 1953 stated it bluntly:

1. There are two principal threats to the survival of fundamental values and institutions of the United States:

a. The formidable power and aggressive policy of the communist world led by the USSR.
b. The serious weakening of the economy of the United States that may result from the cost of opposing the Soviet threat over a sustained period.

The basic problem facing the United States is to strike a proper balance between the risks arising from these two threats.[18]

It followed—as another NSC document four months later, in October 1953, concluded—that the United States needed to "keep open the possibility of negotiating with the USSR and Communist China acceptable and enforceable agreements, whether limited to individual issues now outstanding or involving a general settlement of major issues, including control of armaments."[19]

Aside from this economic ground of hesitancy, there was a deeper uncertainty in American policy, if not a profound insecurity, about our role and our prospects in the developing world. American leaders, especially in the Eisenhower administration, did not doubt that the Soviet activism in the Third World was a strategic menace to the West, designed to exploit residual colonial resentments and harness them to Soviet strategic designs. Yet American statesmen also understood that the United States had to have a *positive* program to respond to it. That is, opposing the Soviets' designs was not enough; the United States also had to distance itself from the colonial legacy and respond to the aspirations of peoples for economic advance, social progress, and political independence.

To a poor country desperate for help, the evils of communism or ulterior motives of the Soviet Union were an abstraction, while the aid proffered by Moscow seemed a benefit and the West's warnings hypocritical, if not incomprehensible. The West therefore had to offer a convincing alternative model for peaceful change or else its influence would shrink among the great millions in the developing world, who came to be referred to, with some trepidation, as the "uncommitted." Even more, there was sometimes apparent in American policy a fear that the moral validity of our own democratic system would be diminished if we did not prove our relevance, and the relevance of our system, to the great challenge of nation building that Third World countries had undertaken. This was a bipartisan concern, as evident in the Eisenhower administration as in the Democratic administrations that preceded and followed it.

The uncertainties reflected the uneasy relationship between our moral mission in the world, which we had inherited from Jefferson and Woodrow Wilson, and our strategic mission, which had befallen us with the onset of the Cold War. We were more or less convinced of the morality of our essential position, yet unsure whether it would appeal to the new nations and anguished when it seemed not to. On one level our uncertainties were displayed, for example, in a prolonged national debate over the purposes of foreign aid. On a deeper level it was a debate about our image of ourselves and our confidence in the future.

THE FOREIGN AID DEBATE

The seminal period was that of the Truman administration, as we saw in the last chapter. The Truman Doctrine of 1947 put us on the front line, supporting two small, weak European countries, Greece and Turkey, with military and economic assistance to strengthen them against both internal and external pressures; the policy was stated in universal terms, however, as an obligation "to support free peoples who are resisting attempted subjugation by armed minorities or by outside pressures." On January 20, 1949, in his inaugural address, Truman's "Point Four" announced in less Cold War–oriented terms a policy of assisting the less developed countries—a famous early pronouncement of U.S. policy on economic assistance to the developing world:

> Fourth, we must embark on a bold new program for making the benefits of our scientific advances and industrial progress available for the improvement and growth of underdeveloped areas. . . .
> I believe that we should make available to peace-loving peoples the benefits of our store of technical knowledge in order to help them realize their aspirations for a better life. And, in cooperation with other nations, we should foster capital investment in areas needing development.

Truman's Point Four, on closer reading, was quite limited in practical scope. Unlike the Marshall Plan, it envisioned no massive transfer of official capital; rather, it was confined to technical assistance and the promotion of private external investment. But Point Four nevertheless represented the beginning of a response to the emergence of the new nations. A very modest UN technical assistance program had already begun in late 1948. In 1950 came the Colombo Plan, which emerged from a meeting in Ceylon of what was evolving into the British Commonwealth; the United States and other countries joined it.

The idea of assistance for economic development caught on, though neither its economic nor its political premises were entirely thought through at the beginning. The model was Europe, with the success of the Marshall Plan and the institutions of multilateral cooperation, yet clearly the problem had been different in Europe. The Europeans (and

Japanese) had the heritage of capitalism and industrialization and the requisite institutions that could all be brought back to life by an infusion of capital. On its face, the European "model" had nothing to do with the enormous task of *creating* modern economies and societies, which is what the ex–colonial countries faced.

In the United States, the idea of development assistance was pushed strongly by liberal political figures and academic experts who shaped its theoretical basis. There was a school of thought, personified by Truman's liberal opponent Henry A. Wallace, that insisted on a purely altruistic, humanitarian aim for our aid and decried its corruption by Cold War motives. Wallace believed that even Marshall Plan aid should have been distributed by the United Nations and that the United States was only resented for using it to block communism.[20] In the developing world, Wallace thought we would be blessed many times over if we simply sought to advance the well-being of others: "The time has come for a modern Johnny Appleseed animated by the missionary spirit to go into all the world and preach the gospel to every creature. Broadcast the seeds of investment, science, technology, and productivity to all peoples. Bread cast upon the waters will come back many-fold after not too many days."[21]

Another, seemingly more hardheaded analysis was put forward in a 1948 CIA assessment of the strategic implications of the breakup of colonialism: "[T]he good will of the recently liberated and emergent independent nations becomes a vital factor in the future strategic position of the US in the Near and Far East. . . . [U]nless the US . . . adopts a more positive and sympathetic attitude toward the national aspirations of these areas and at least partially meets their demands for economic assistance, it will risk their becoming actively antagonistic toward the US."[22]

But as academic specialists studied the problems of economic underdevelopment, a more sophisticated theory was elaborated based on an American political interest in promoting evolutionary change. The major intellectual contribution came from Harvard and the Massachusetts Institute of Technology (MIT), where economists in the early 1950s conducted intensive investigations of countries like India, Pakistan, and Indonesia. At MIT, Max Millikan, Walt W. Rostow, and others analyzed the different stages of development and concluded that the conceptual tools now existed to determine what forms of capital and technical assistance were suited to promoting modernization at each stage.[23] "In many situations a favorable environment for private investment can be established only after a period of rather heavy capital formation under government auspices," Millikan and Rostow had written.[24]

The political aim for the United States, in these authors' view, should not be "to insure friendship and gratitude" or "to enable the recipient countries to carry a much larger share of the burden of military buildup against Communist armed forces" or even "to stop Communism by eliminating hunger." Rather, the appropriate policy goal should be to "use our influence to promote the evolution of societies that are stable in the sense that they are capable of rapid change without violence, effective in the sense that they can make progress in meeting the aspirations of all their citizens, and democratic in the sense that ultimate power is widely shared through the society. Such societies are not likely to constitute a military threat to us or to attach themselves to others who pose such a threat."[25] Thus, at bottom, the theory was a positive alternative to Marxist theories of development, combining humanitarian aims, sophisticated analysis, and enlightened American political self-interest.

The Cambridge concept was influential, and it was propagated by the Harvard-educated Democratic senator from Massachusetts John F. Kennedy, who pushed hard in the 1950s for legislation to promote more generous foreign assistance. The concept also attracted bipartisan support, as exemplified by a concurrent resolution that Kennedy cosponsored in 1958 with Republican senator John Sherman Cooper of Kentucky. The Kennedy-Cooper Resolution declared it "the sense of Congress" that the United States should organize an international mission to study the development needs of India. This was hardly earthshaking legislation, but the symbolism was important. The resolution was at first resisted by the Eisenhower administration, which held that individual countries should not be singled out and that new efforts were unnecessary in view of the credits and commodities already being furnished to India. The administration was mollified when the resolution was broadened to include all South Asian countries; the Senate passed it in September 1959, and a group of distinguished financial experts visited the region in 1960 under the general auspices of the World Bank.[26]

Inside the administration there were those in the mid-1950s who wanted the United States to expand its programs beyond the modest credits, commodity grants, and technical assistance that in those days constituted the U.S. effort. Eisenhower was wary, however, on the basis of Republican economic principles that taught him that private investment, trade, and technical assistance were more important and more reliable spurs to growth than large-scale handouts of official capital. In a message to Congress on March 30, 1954, he summarized the principles of his foreign economic policy as follows:

Aid—which we wish to curtail;
Investment—which we wish to encourage;
Convertibility—which we wish to facilitate;
Trade—which we wish to expand.

This conservative philosophy was reinforced by a body of scholarly work by economists such as P. T. Bauer of the London School of Economics, who questioned the theoretical and practical grounding of development assistance. Especially critical of India's development plans, Bauer and others challenged the preoccupation with rapid industrialization and, most fundamentally, the statism and slighting of the private sector that the prevailing development theory seemed to foster.[27] But Bauer's dissent was a lonely minority then.

Development aid was challenged on political grounds as well, and there was a full-fledged academic debate on this subject through the late 1950s and early 1960s. *Why Foreign Aid?* was the title of a set of essays published in 1963.[28] Aside from the debate about economic theory, there was disagreement over the foreign policy purpose of our economic aid. Did we expect to ensure a democratic political evolution? Did we seek political influence over foreign governments? Millikan and Rostow answered the question with the formula already cited—the hope of giving impetus to social progress that would reinforce a moderate political evolution in these societies. Their formulation, while the most intelligent and serious, was not without its challengers who questioned its political premises. If our goal was long-term stability in the interest of avoiding radicalism and encouraging democracy, critics argued, significant economic and social change was equally likely to be highly destabilizing. Professor Hans Morgenthau, doyen of the "realist" school of postwar American foreign policy, argued in 1963:

Economic development, especially by way of industrialization, is likely to disrupt the social fabric of the underdeveloped nation. By creating an urban industrial proletariat, it loosens and destroys the social nexus of family, village, and tribe in which the individual had found himself secure. And it will not be able, at least not right away, to provide a substitute for this lost social world. The vacuum thus created will be filled by social unrest and political agitation. Furthermore, it is not the downtrodden masses living in a static world of unrelieved misery which are the likely protagonists of revolution, but rather those groups that have begun to rise in the social and economic scale but not enough to satisfy their aroused expectations. Thus, economic development is bound to disturb not only the economic *status quo* but, through it, the political *status quo* as well. If the change is drastic enough, the social and political effects of economic development may well amount to a prerevolutionary or revolutionary situation. And while the United States may have started the revolutionary process, it will again be uncertain under whose auspices it will be ended.[29]

This was a prescient passage, foreshadowing, for example, the upheaval in the shah's Iran fifteen years later. Responsibility for the Iran debacle may be a heavy moral burden to lay at the door of our foreign aid program, whose impact may not have been all that great. But to Morgenthau the ineffectuality of our aid program was a "blessing in disguise."[30]

Harvard professor Henry Kissinger, writing at the end of the Eisenhower administration, suggested also that the political analysis of his Cambridge neighbors was grounded in a faulty reading of history:

Indeed, there is no country in which democratic institutions developed *after* industrialization and *as a result of* economic development. Where the rudiments of democratic institutions did not exist at the beginning of the industrial revolution, they did not receive impetus from industrial growth. . . . In all the traditional democratic societies, the essentials of the governmental system antedated the industrial revolution. The American Constitution was developed in a largely agricultural society and so were the fundamental institutions of the British system. These institutions were broadened and elaborated as the countries prospered—but their significant features preceded economic development and are not attributable to it.[31]

Decades later, other scholars would develop yet another critique of the traditional approach to economic modernization, investigating the role of culture—values and attitudes—in determining which societies advance and which do not. Attitudes toward work, sacrifice, excellence, family, and community, often shaped by religious traditions, turn out to be a pivotal variable. Comparisons of East Asia and Latin America, of differences within regions and among ethnic groups within societies, have produced a much more complex picture of the development process than the economic models of the 1950s.[32]

By Eisenhower's second term, nonetheless, the political pressures on the United States to engage in the aid business had become inexorable.

C. D. Jackson, an influential business executive and former White House national security aide, insistently and successfully urged on Dulles and the president the need for a more ambitious program, in large part as a way to meet the Soviet challenge. Eisenhower's second inaugural address, on January 20, 1957, included more forthcoming language: "We must use our skills and knowledge and, at times, our substance, to help others rise from misery, however far the scene of suffering may be from our shores. For wherever in the world a people knows desperate want, there must appear at least the spark of hope, the hope of progress—or there will surely rise at last the flames of conflict. . . ." The upshot was the Development Loan Fund, which Dulles unveiled in Senate testimony in April 1957. He foresaw a fund eventually dispensing as much as $750 million a year (in parallel with the $150 million spent annually for technical assistance). Eisenhower vigorously supported the new concept in a nationally televised address on May 21, 1957, devoted entirely to the subject of foreign aid. To the Democrats' arguments from compassion and development theory, the president added the strategic case for foreign aid as a positive way to combat communism: "The whole design of this defense against Communist conspiracy and encirclement cannot be with guns alone. For the freedom of nations can be menaced not only by guns but by the poverty that communism can exploit." Eisenhower pointed out that there were 1 billion people in the world, across three continents, living in countries whose average annual income per capita was $100 or less. Among these were the nineteen nations that had won their independence since World War II:

> Most of them are on the frontier of the Communist world, close to the pressure of Communist power. For centuries the peoples of these countries have borne a burden of poverty. Now they are resolved to hold on to political independence, and to support rising standards of living.
>
> In these lands no government can justly rule, or even survive, which does not reflect this resolve, which does not offer its people hope of progress. And wherever moderate government disappears, Communist extremists will extend their brand of despotic imperialism.

And so the United States got into the business of foreign aid—as it often tends to—by a brokered political compromise that masked an unresolved confusion about both the program's aims and its effectiveness. Democrats supported foreign aid for its humanitarianism or on the basis of development theory; Republicans were motivated by fears of Soviet political inroads in the Third World. They came together on the common ground of the vague hope that aid actually promoted development and that development actually ensured a democratic, or at least moderate, alternative to anti-Western radicalism. But the conflicting motives that lay just beneath the surface consensus were the seeds of the later controversies that burst forth when the optimistic hopes were not fulfilled.

By the time the Cold War ended decades later, the net financial flow to aid-receiving countries since the mid-1950s, both commercial and concessional, had reached the phenomenal total of some $2 trillion in 1980s prices.[33] The results of all this largess can only be said to be mixed. Disillusionment was inevitable, and it came early on. While the economic suppositions could not be tested until decades had passed, the political assumptions would encounter immediate problems. Development did not show signs of ensuring either democracy or stability. While the United States hoped to bring the developing countries into a liberal democratic world order, many of the recipients were statist regimes, if not dictatorships, whose domestic imperative was to consolidate power; they were happy to have our aid and use it for their own ends. "[P]rosperity," Nicholas Eberstadt has written, "is neither a necessary nor a sufficient condition for liberal democratic rule."[34]

Nor did foreign assistance offer any assurance of political influence for the United States. Experience with India (as we have seen) proved especially painful in this regard. In the 1950s, the hope was that democratic India could be made a showcase model to compete with Communist China. Disturbingly, China's economic performance far outpaced India's in the 1950s (though India was to outperform China in the early 1960s.)[35] It was the fond hope of American liberals—figures such as Chester Bowles, Walter Lippmann, and Hubert Humphrey, as well as John Kennedy—that Western foreign assistance could make the difference for India (which was the motive of the original Kennedy-Cooper Resolution). But India lost much American goodwill when it recognized the People's Republic of China in 1949 and meddled unhelpfully in Korean War diplomacy (and later at Suez). The political glow of the generous U.S. aid programs of the early 1950s was tarnished for Indians, in turn, by bitter congressional debates attacking India's neutralist foreign policies. Nehru was disdainful of the Americans. In May 1953 he wrote to his sister, Madame Pandit, who was ambassador in Washington: "It surprises me how immature in their political thinking Americans are!"[36]

In 1954, the United States began supplying military equipment to Pakistan, including F-84 jet fighters, and included Pakistan in the anti-

Communist alliance network (in both the Manila and Baghdad pacts). India turned increasingly to Moscow for arms supply. Thus, we should not have been totally surprised by the warm Indian reception of Bulganin and Khrushchev and the less than overwhelming warmth for Dulles on his 1956 visit.

The very concept of neutralism was a problem for Dulles, as is well known. Without citing India by name, Dulles, in a speech at Iowa State College on June 9, 1956, uttered his famous critique of neutralism as "immoral." It was a policy "which [he said] pretends that a nation can best gain safety for itself by being indifferent to the fate of others. This has increasingly become an obsolete conception, and, except under very exceptional circumstances, it is an immoral and short-sighted conception." Yet Dulles, in a *Foreign Affairs* article in October 1957, also acknowledged the vitality of nationalism in the Third World and the moral as well as strategic arguments for assisting the new nations whether they were members of our anti-Communist alliance system or not:

Another vast force for change is political nationalism. This is operating strongly in Asia and Africa. . . . It is going to be necessary to find policies to cope with new demands of colonial peoples, with strident and embittered nationalisms, and with social unrest among those who tend to feel that political liberty automatically should provide them with new economic opportunity.

The United States, once itself a colony, shares and sympathizes with the aspirations of peoples for political independence. . . . We can and should play an important part in finding the policies to cope with the political and social ferment of much of the human race.[37]

In his Philadelphia speech of February 26, 1956, Dulles had shown the same understanding of Third World independence: "Our interests will be fully served if other nations maintain their independence and strengthen their free institutions. We have no further aims than these."

But in the real world of day-to-day foreign policy, American frustration began to show. In his Philadelphia speech, Dulles went on to note with evident unease (undoubtedly thinking of India) that the leaders of the new nations, while capable of defending their national independence, were regrettably prey to Soviet blandishments. The Soviet Communist experiment seemed to have prestige, and the human costs of communism were less visible or tangible to the new nations than the outward evidence of Soviet accomplishments:

> The neighboring Asian peoples have seen the Soviet Union within a generation develop itself into a major industrial power. These observers are but only dimly aware of the fact that the Soviet rate of progress was possible only because natural conditions favored, and that even so, its cost in human servitude has been tragically high. They are like those of us who admire the pyramids, the palaces, the temples and the coliseums which despotic rulers once produced out of slave labor. We are only dimly conscious of the cost in terms of human misery. . . .

> The political leaders of these countries, however wise they may be and however patriotic they may be, will find it difficult to resist the public pressures which Soviet propaganda arouses, unless there is some alternative.

> The industrial nations of the West . . . can and must provide such an alternative.

Dulles poured out his heart to C. D. Jackson in a private conversation on April 14, 1957. The moderate new face of Soviet policy made it much harder to maintain Western vigilance:

> Now all of a sudden the outward Soviet appearance, mood, behavior, has materially changed. . . . Frowns have given way to smiles. Guns have given way to offers of economic aid. . . .

> Now I don't know if they are sincere or not, if this is a trick or not—but I do know two things. The first is that this "change" is not superficial, is not limited to a few speeches and Pravda editorials. It goes quite deep. . . . The other thing that I know is that with all of these outward improvements—with the repudiation of Stalin, with the rehabilitation of scores of officials, scientists, soldiers, dead and alive, with the apparent acceptance of Tito, and therefore of Titoism—with all these things going on, it is very difficult for the United States to say to its allies that all of this means nothing, that it is a trick, that the ostracism must be maintained. [38]

In the Third World, Dulles lamented to Jackson, the Soviets also enjoyed a unique advantage in that in their foreign assistance they did not have to conform to Western commercial practices:

This new competitor, because of his economic setup, which includes slave labor, does not play according to any of the rules. If an interest rate is 5 percent, he can offer 2 percent. If he takes some Egyptian cotton in payment of some arms from Czechoslovakia, he doesn't have to worry about the Liverpool Cotton Exchange when he wants to unload his cotton. And so on.

We could be witnessing the beginning of economic piracy on a scale never before practiced, and we frankly do not yet know what to do about it. But we do know that this economic piracy will be far too welcome in far too many parts of the world.[39]

The United States continued to try hard to distance itself from the colonial legacy that the European powers had left—the resentments and mistrust. President Truman, in a Rooseveltian touch, had taken pains to stress in his Point Four address that our promotion of capital investment bore no resemblance to the old-style "exploitation." The key here was democracy—our "fair-dealing" with these countries on the basis of our own democratic principles: "The old imperialism—exploitation for foreign profits—has no place in our plans. What we envisage is a program of development based on the concepts of democratic fair-dealing. . . . Democracy alone can supply the vitalizing force to stir the peoples of the world into triumphant action, not only against their human oppressors, but also against their ancient enemies—hunger, misery, despair."

Sen. John Kennedy, who made a famous speech in July 1957 endorsing Algerian independence from the French, had made an earlier speech in June 1956 calling upon the United States to dissociate itself once and for all from its allies' efforts to hang on to their colonial empires. It was time to recognize that "the day of the colonial is through," Kennedy proclaimed (echoing Roosevelt and Sumner Welles fourteen years earlier). If we had to choose between our allies and our commitment to human freedom, we must choose the latter, because it was the source of our political strength in the developing world in our competition with the Communists:

Of course such a stand will displease our allies—but it will displease the Soviets even more. For whether our allies like it or not, and whether they act to impede it or not, sooner or later, one by one, the traditional colonies of the western powers are breaking free. The primary question is whether they will then turn for association and support to the West—which has thus far too often hampered and discouraged their efforts for self-determination—or turn to the Communist East—which has (however hypocritically, in view of its own colonial exploitation) inflamed their nationalistic spirits and assumed the role of freedom's defender. . . . If we are to secure the friendship of the Arab, the African and the Asian, we cannot hope to accomplish it solely by means of military pacts and assistance. . . . No: the strength of our appeal to these key populations—and it is rightfully our appeal, and not that of the Communists—lies in our traditional and deeply felt philosophy of freedom and independence for all peoples everywhere.[40]

During World War II this American anticolonialist impulse had been thoroughly bipartisan. Although as the Cold War progressed it was occasionally more passionate among the Democrats, Eisenhower as president demonstrated how powerfully American policy under both parties continued to reflect that Rooseveltian idealism. Eisenhower, too, had no sympathy for the French enterprise in Algeria, telling Christian Herter, Dulles's successor as secretary of state: "We cannot abandon our old principles of support for national freedom and self-determination, and we cannot join the colonialists."[41] The "strongest reason of all" for his unwillingness to back the French at Dien Bien Phu, Eisenhower later wrote, was his unwillingness to tarnish America's "tradition of anticolonialism" by association with the French.[42] The same impulse was to reappear in Eisenhower's handling of the Suez crisis.

Nothing seemed to work, however. The genuine generosity and anticolonialist intentions that lay behind much of the American contribution to Third World development seemed to be of no avail. The more hardheaded strategic approach succeeded in bolstering those nations that were willing to join us in alliances, but this policy had its obvious hazards, too—witness the collapse of the Baghdad Pact after the leftist military coup in Iraq in 1958—and (as John Kennedy pointed out) it did nothing to win over the uncommitted, even if it helped guarantee their independence by assuring the overall and regional balance of power.

These seeming failures led to a variety of responses. There was an outpouring of self-doubt and self-criticism—the soul-searching book *The*

Ugly American by William J. Lederer and Eugene Burdick in 1958 told of an introspective American ambassador in Southeast Asia anguished by the insensitivity and clumsiness of much of our official presence abroad. (It was made into a movie in 1962 with Marlon Brando as the hero.)[43] More lasting, perhaps, was the popular reaction of neo-isolationism—a grass-roots assessment that it was the foreigners who were ungrateful and undeserving, not the Americans who were guilty of in-sensitivity. The absence of a large popular constituency in support of foreign aid has plagued the program in Congress since its inception and until this day in spite of valiant efforts by presidents of both parties who continued to push for it. For the duration of the Cold War, the idealistic and the strategic arguments for foreign assistance coexisted in an uneasy partnership and managed to sustain U.S. programs of a modest scale, though less than many other countries in terms of the proportion of our GNP. (With the end of the Cold War, these programs today face a renewed search for a sustainable rationale.)

In the spring of 1956, a skeptical French journalist, Raymond Cartier, editor of *Paris-Match*, wrote a thoughtful essay chiding Americans for their yearning to be loved. Certainly he wrote out of French self-interest, complaining of the American impulse to identify with every colonial rebellion. But he put his finger on a useful point: Our self-abasement only bred contempt, and this, in his view, accounted for much of the anti-Americanism that seemed to be spreading even in (and perhaps especially in) regions blessed by our assertive generosity. We should think harder about defining and defending our national interest:

> It is terribly difficult to be the dominant power of an epoch. The Wash-ington officials are not wrong in saying that anti-Americanism will exist, no matter what America does, so long as the U.S. holds its present rank. But anti-Americanism is also maintained by faults in judgment and by grave and avoidable errors. . . . There would be less anti-Americanism in the world if America abandoned its philanthropic aspirations, its vocation of Santa Claus, its transcendental morality, all its missionary trappings, all its boy-scout gear, and if, at last, it followed openly and intelligently the policy of its own interest.[44]

A clear and realistic concept of foreign aid as a *political* tool was precisely what was lacking. As we have seen, its economic rationale was fuzzy and its foreign policy rationale fuzzier.

There was another factor at work, not yet as obvious to the beleaguered policymakers in Washington as it is today. The quest for political influence through economic aid ran up against an insoluble *structural* problem: The Third World leaders were masters at playing the two sides off against each other. They were operating according to cold-blooded calculations of how to maximize their own national interest, not judging a popularity contest or making any kind of moral judgment as to the virtue of the two superpowers.

The Soviets understood this game better than we. Soviet foreign aid to India, though modest in total comparison with ours, worked wonders when it came to panicking us into giving more. Khrushchev even boasted to Indian foreign minister Morarji Desai in Moscow in June 1960: "We help you in order that the Americans might give you more aid. They will give you more aid as soon as we give you aid."[45] He was right: American annual aid commitments to India, which were $4.5 million in 1951, jumped to $87 million in 1954 and to over $100 million in 1959 despite Dulles's torment about India's neutralism.[46]

The Soviets would suffer their own setbacks in the 1960s and 1970s, as in earlier periods. Their doctrines, as noted earlier, may have been even less suited to the realities of underdevelopment than ours; if Soviet leaders really believed their class analysis of the "socialist" character of their Third World friends, then they must have been caught by surprise many times by the latter's behavior. Many of Khrushchev's favorite Third World leaders ended up overthrown. But the Soviets, unlike the Americans, never externalized their frustrations. They never seemed to feel (or express) the enormous self-doubt that America gave vent to; they did not have our habit of psychoanalyzing ourselves in public. Whatever Marxist rationales the Soviet theorists may have devised, it is hard to imagine that the Politburo leaders saw aid in the first place as anything other than an instrument of policy. Not placing such a moral importance on it, they could assess its political successes and failures with more equanimity.

And the Soviets went about their business with a certain bravado, which Khrushchev embodied brilliantly. A British writer, Barbara Ward (later Lady Jackson), observed in 1956:

> Soviet propaganda does not make its offers negatively—as a means of *defending* either itself or Asia against the West. The underlying theme is the collapse and decadence of capitalist imperialism. Not out of fear but out of success, generosity and confidence the new economic offers are made.

All this may make Mr. Khrushchev sound unbearably brash in Western ears. But to the new nations of Asia, it may seem more like the voice of achievement and self-respect.[47]

Ms. Ward was an idealist, one of those who believed foreign assistance was a humanitarian obligation of the West. She decried its Cold War distortions, pointing out quite logically that if our motive for giving aid was self-defense against communism, how could we be surprised when recipient countries showed no great gratitude for our generosity?

Nearly every program of assistance is finally rammed through the Legislature with the techniques of Dickens' Fat Boy—"I wants to make yer flesh creep." Refuse this appropriation and Bongaland will slip forever under the Communist yoke.

But then, by a remarkable psychological somersault, the same legislators who have grimly consented in pure self-interest to provide perhaps half the necessary funds, denounce the recipient people as ungrateful scoundrels who show no due appreciation of the magnificent generosity shown them (in strict preservation of Western skins). Yet is it logical to expect gratitude for steps taken openly and crudely in self-defense?[48]

We would never learn how to square this circle. More recently, in the 1980s and 1990s, U.S. foreign assistance has tended to be guided by more mundane instrumental purposes, such as to signify political support to countries we felt we had a stake in, to bolster regional security, or to promote particular social goals (combating narcotics, protecting the environment, etc.). But the desire to use foreign aid to promote democracy remains a hallowed if unfocused goal, especially in the Clinton administration.[49] In the economic realm, U.S. assistance, along with the increasingly important multilateral aid furnished through the World Bank and other international financial institutions, has come to be used as leverage to force market-oriented structural reforms—in other words, to dismantle the very same statist structures that foreign aid in the 1950s and 1960s had been promoting.

The confusion of moral and strategic elements in American thinking in the 1950s, evident in the foreign aid debate, would soon reappear with a vengeance in the Suez affair. Not coincidentally, the crisis began with American indecision over a foreign aid project—the Aswan High Dam.

THE SUEZ CRISIS

The Suez crisis of 1956 marked a transition for the Middle East, signaling the end of the colonial era and the beginning of a generation in which the region was to be buffeted by Cold War geopolitics and leftist radicalism.

Within two years of the Egyptian revolution that deposed King Farouk in July 1952, Britain and Egypt negotiated a treaty that called for the final departure of British troops from Egypt. They duly left in June 1956, after a seven-decade run that had represented one of the great triumphs of the British Empire. While the British military presence had ended, however, London retained its dominant role in the autonomous Suez Canal Company, which ran the canal, and also considered that its interests were embodied in the 1888 Convention of Constantinople, which had established the canal's status as an international waterway.

The Egyptian revolution had been unnerving, an expression of defiant nationalism. But the United States, and to some degree Britain (at least at first), came to see in the Egyptian revolution the harbinger of a trend in the Middle East that might not be entirely negative. The traditional monarchies (of which Farouk had been an extreme case) all seemed inept, ineffectual, and vulnerable; the new military caste seemed to represent a secular, meritocratic, modernizing class that, precisely because of its strong nationalism, might be the most reliable bulwark against Communist radicalism. The new military leadership might also prove a viable negotiating partner for the Israelis—certainly more so than the weak, discredited monarchies.

On the American side, the Central Intelligence Agency, in particular, was assiduous in establishing its own personal contacts and channels with the military in Egypt as well as elsewhere. The CIA station chief in Cairo had better access to Nasser than did the American ambassador. If Miles Copeland's exuberant account is to be believed, the CIA went so far as to encourage one of the first military coups in Syria and it is even suspected of having a hand in bringing the Ba'ath party to power in Iraq in 1963.[50] Efforts were made to promote indirect and even direct exchanges between Nasser and senior Israeli leaders, but they failed.[51] Even after Nasser stunned the West in September 1955 with his acceptance of Soviet weapons, CIA operative Kermit Roosevelt cabled from Cairo to CIA director Allen Dulles that "Nasser remains our best, if not our only, hope here."[52]

In any event, Nasser's arms deal with the Soviets threw the United States and Britain into a quandary. The British achieved an intelligence coup toward the end of 1955 in the form of a source within Nasser's entourage, who was given the appropriate code name "Lucky Break." Information from this source (which the British were not slow to feed to their American counterparts) indicated that Nasser was moving closer and closer to the Soviets; the fear grew that in return for Soviet support for his regional ambitions Nasser would allow the Soviets greater freedom of action in Egypt and throughout the region.[53] By March 1956 both Britain and the United States were actively exploring the possibilities of covert action to overthrow him or influence him as well as coordinating plans for economic and political pressures.[54] Yet this "hard-line" approach was hobbled by the fear of pushing him too far. John Foster Dulles advised in a memorandum to the president at the end of March: "We would want for the time being to avoid any open break which would throw Nasser irrevocably into a Soviet satellite status and we would want to leave Nasser a bridge back to good relations with the West if he so desires."[55]

As a practical matter, the original Western schizophrenia over whether Nasser was a potential enemy or friend only reappeared in another guise when a specific issue of policy toward Egypt presented itself. This was the dramatic idea, put forward by the new Egyptian leaders, of a High Dam to be built on the Nile at Aswan, in Upper Egypt. It would be the most ambitious civil engineering project in the world, harnessing the Nile waters for hydroelectric power and regulating its flood to improve irrigation in the fertile delta on which Egypt's livelihood depended. The World Bank vouched for the idea, and both the American and British governments were tempted into an offer of grant aid to supplement World Bank credits as a way to counter the growing Soviet influence. The offer was thought to demonstrate, moreover, that while the Soviets furnished weapons of destruction, the West was more concerned with aiding the welfare and development of Third World peoples. In December 1955, a joint Anglo-American offer was formally presented to the Egyptians. Egypt was simultaneously discussing the project with the Soviets, who made their own offer.

Whether to freeze out Nasser to teach him a lesson or woo him away from the Soviets—the dilemma of how to deal with a radical neutralist regime was to recur countless times in American policy in the Third World. Whenever the United States resorted to the extraordinary measure of an economic embargo, whether against Cuba or Nicaragua, the criticism would be made that we were only pushing them further into the arms of the Soviets. Yet whenever we maintained or even expanded economic ties to troublesome Third World nations, as with Egypt or

India, the question could always be asked whether we were not merely encouraging them in their course. It was, at bottom, insoluble.

In the case of the Aswan High Dam, the Americans and British both lost their enthusiasm for the project as they grew increasingly nervous about the encroaching Soviet influence in Egypt and Nasser's growing (and unhealthy) influence in the region. In Jordan in March 1956, the young king Hussein abruptly dismissed Sir John Bagot Glubb ("Glubb Pasha"), the British officer who had built Jordan's Arab Legion; this stunned the British, who blamed Nasser. In May, Nasser recognized Communist China and arranged a barter trade of Egyptian cotton for Chinese steel. China was a neuralgic point for Dulles, and it was in early June that he publicly vented his famous irritation at "short-sighted" and "immoral" policies of neutralism.

The more that American and British officials examined the dam project, the less appealing it was. There were considerable concerns about its high cost; Nasser's flirtation with the Communists as well as his confrontation with Israel were more than enough to solidify what may well have been an insuperable obstacle in Congress. Thus, retraction of the American offer may have been inevitable. But Foster Dulles ruminated to the Senate Foreign Relations Committee in executive session on June 26, 1956, that dumping the project in the Russians' lap might not be such a bad thing: Let the Russians take the blame for the austerity and distortion of the Egyptian economy that the dam's financing would entail; let the Soviets take the risk of building a white elephant that might earn no gratitude at all from the Egyptian people or government.[56] Over lunch with Henry Luce and C. D. Jackson, Dulles claimed that the West could even reap propaganda benefits behind the Iron Curtain from such an extravagant Soviet foreign aid project lavished on a developing country.[57]

The result was that on July 19, Dulles informed the Egyptian ambassador that the U.S. offer to finance the dam was withdrawn. A Department of State press statement hinged the decision, for public consumption, on the supposed inability of the Egyptian economy to sustain such a project; this was intended to soften the blow.[58] The statement did the opposite. The Egyptians were insulted as well as disappointed.

The timing, too, was terrible. Nasser had two big public speeches coming up—one on July 23, the anniversary of the 1952 revolution, and one on July 26, the anniversary of Farouk's abdication. He was not totally surprised, and he had already begun preparing his countermove. While Nasser worked out his plans, he confined himself on July 23 to a ferocious denunciation of the Americans and British: "Let them choke in their

fury, for they will not be able to dominate us or control our existence."
On July 26, Nasser announced the seizure of all the assets and facilities
of the Suez Canal Company, and even as he spoke, Egyptian troops
carried out the seizure of the company's headquarters at Ismailia.[59]

To the British, it was not only an affront but a threat to their strategic
interest. They were convinced that Nasser's unilateral action violated the
canal's international status under the 1888 Constantinople Convention.
No longer was the canal the lifeline to imperial India; it was the lifeline
to the Persian Gulf, where Britain continued as protecting power over a
number of small sheikhdoms in an oil-rich region that duly qualified as
a vital interest of the entire West.

To British prime minister Sir Anthony Eden, the seizure of the canal
was a replay of the 1930s: Nasser, if not a Hitler, was at least a Mussolini,
playing cat's paw to the Soviets' aggressive designs. As in the 1930s,
appeasement of Nasser would prove to be a grave mistake. Eden informed
President Eisenhower on July 29 that "I have this morning instructed
our Chiefs of Staff to prepare a military plan accordingly."[60] On October
1, Eden sent a telegram to Eisenhower warning of the danger of Soviet
penetration into the Middle East and raising again the parallel with the
1930s:

> You can be sure we are fully alive to the wider dangers of the Middle East
> situation. They can be summed up in one word—Russia. . . .
>
> There is no doubt in our minds that Nasser, whether he likes it or not, is
> now effectively in Russian hands, just as Mussolini was in Hitler's. It would
> be as ineffective to show weakness to Nasser now in order to placate him
> as it was to show weakness to Mussolini. The only result was and would
> be to bring the two together.[61]

Over the ensuing months, the British linked up with the French, who
viewed Nasser's radicalism as the main instigator of the festering Algerian
rebellion against French rule. The two then linked up with the Israelis,
who welcomed the offer of Western support for a decisive blow against
Nasser's belligerence and sponsorship of terrorist raids.

The Americans, too, were shocked by the seizure of the canal and
came forward in the coming months with proposals to organize the canal's
user countries to ensure against a temperamental dictator's unilateral
control of an international waterway. But the Americans did not share

the urgency felt by the British or French. Washington set great store by what it saw as Egypt's valid legal position: it saw Nasser's nationalization as within Egypt's rights under international law (since Egypt had sovereignty and Nasser had promised compensation to the Suez Canal Company's shareholders).

Through the summer of 1956, the United States tried to straddle the fence. Just as it had been uncertain from the beginning about whether Nasser was a positive or a negative factor and whether wooing him or punishing him was the best tactic, now the United States was torn between its fear of the threat to Western interests that Nasser's move represented and its fear of siding openly against him and thereby alienating him and other Third World nationalists forever. The United States decided to stress formally the importance of international legality and compromise; politically, its priority was not to be tainted by the colonialist implications of what Britain and France were impulsively threatening to do.

This American straddle had its odd manifestations. The administration looked the other way when the British and French moved military equipment earmarked for NATO out of Europe toward the Middle East.[62] But if the British and French saw this as implying American acquiescence in their military plans (about which they were essentially keeping Washington in the dark, in any case), they were wrong.

President Eisenhower, especially, was strongly opposed to the use of force on moral, legal, and political grounds. The United States was tempted, therefore, into playing the Wilsonian role of mediator, proposing, for example, an international organization of user countries to involve itself in canal management. The Americans even seemed eager to have the Soviets as participants in the hope that the Soviets would deliver the Egyptians to a compromise. Dulles sent a message to Moscow for the Soviets in August stressing the difficulties we were having in restraining the British and French. Our ambassador in Moscow, the estimable Charles Bohlen, thought the message demeaning to our allies as well as tactically unwise; Bohlen's *reclama* was overruled, and he dutifully made the presentation to Marshal Bulganin.[63] The Soviets, meanwhile, publicly championed the Egyptian case and vetoed a UN Security Council resolution in October that would have pressed Egypt to accept some version of a users' organization.

Dulles had a strategy session with the president on August 30. As Dulles later recorded, his analysis was different than Eden's. He thought the Soviets would benefit more from a British-French military action than from letting Nasser get away with what he had done:

I could not see any end to the situation that might be created if the British and the French occupied the Canal and parts of Egypt. They would make bitter enemies of the entire population of the Middle East and much of Africa. . . . The Soviet Union would reap the benefit of a greatly weakened Western Europe and would move into a position of predominant influence in the Middle East and Africa. No doubt it was for this reason that the Soviets were seeking to prevent a peaceful adjustment of the Suez problem.

Eisenhower agreed completely, adding that this was the wrong issue on which to confront Nasser.[64] A few days later, on September 2, Eisenhower wrote Eden that the whole developing world would turn against the West if force were used: "[T]he peoples of the Near East and of North Africa and, to some extent, of all of Asia and all of Africa, would be consolidated against the West to a degree which, I fear, could not be overcome in a generation and, perhaps, not even in a century particularly having in mind the capacity of the Russians to make mischief."[65]

Dulles, in a public remark that infuriated the British, made clear in a news conference on October 2 that the United States was determined to keep its distance from anything that smacked of "colonialism." The Atlantic Alliance, he pointed out, did not obligate us to support allied actions out of the Alliance area, and the United States had to preserve its independence on an issue that raised the question of colonialism:

There is some difference in the approaches to the Suez Canal problem. That difference relates perhaps to some rather fundamental things. In some areas the three nations are bound together by treaties, such as the Atlantic pact area, the three nations are bound together by treaty to protect. In those the three areas stand together.

Other problems relate to other areas and touch the so-called problem of colonialism in some way or other. On these problems the United States plays a somewhat independent role.[66]

In the end, the British, French, and Israelis went ahead with their military plan. On October 29, the Israelis invaded the Sinai, seizing strategic positions and posing an ostensible threat to the Suez Canal. On October 31, Britain and France, by prearrangement, announced their intervention to seize the canal and protect it from hostilities (which they themselves had instigated). Not until November 5, however, did their

forces arrive at the canal, and instead of a *fait accompli*, they had per-
petrated a fiasco. In the interval, as financial markets put pressure on
the pound sterling, the British faced the humiliation of a devaluation
and the possible collapse of the pound's international role as a reserve
currency. The only hope was an American loan—which the United States
refused until the military operation was halted and arrangements were
in place for a UN Expeditionary Force (UNEF) to police the Sinai. The
Anglo-French intervention collapsed, and the Israelis, too, were pressured
into withdrawing.

As with Roosevelt's pressure on Churchill, American power had
again—this time even more humiliatingly—been brought to bear against
an attempt by Britain and France to continue to play a role in their former
colonial domains. The Americans were quite proud that a blow had been
struck against colonialism and that they could take the credit. What Dulles
had said in his October 2 news conference was stated even more exu-
berantly by Vice President Richard Nixon in a campaign speech on
November 2 in Hershey, Pennsylvania. A few days earlier, an American-
sponsored resolution had passed by an overwhelming vote in the UN
General Assembly calling for an immediate cease-fire and withdrawal of
all intervening forces. The American position, Nixon said, was like a
second American "declaration of independence" from the European powers: "For the first time in history we have shown independence of Anglo-
French policies toward Asia and Africa which seemed to us to reflect the
colonial tradition. That declaration of independence has had an electri-
fying effect throughout the world."[67]

The Americans were particularly upset that the British-French action
had taken the spotlight away from the Soviets' brutal suppression of the
Hungarian uprising. Dulles complained bitterly to a group of reporters
on October 30 that just when the West was in a position to tar the Soviets
with the colonialist brush, our British and French allies were making us
declare ourselves for or against old-style Western colonialism. Since the
Second World War, he said at the off-the-record dinner, the United States
had walked a tightrope between maintaining our old and valued alliance
ties and securing the friendship and understanding of the new nations
that had emerged from colonialism. Suez complicated all this.[68]

By dissociating from the Suez affair—indeed, by having the decisive
role in ending it—the United States hoped to preserve or enhance its
moral standing in the Third World. Thereby, among other things, it
hoped to minimize the Soviets' presumed propaganda and political windfall. The United States now flaunted its independent stance in the Middle
East, putting forward in a presidential message to Congress in January

1957 (the "Eisenhower Doctrine") a policy of American support for Middle Eastern states threatened by aggression from "International Communism." Having seized the moral high ground at Suez, we felt we were in a better position to oppose the Soviets. While some critics, even in the administration, deplored the Cold War focus of the new doctrine, the policy reflected overall that the United States was stepping into the shoes of the British and French in yet another region of the world, but hopefully free of their colonialist baggage.

The longer-term results of Suez, however, were more complicated. Deeper political forces were at work than assessments of our goodwill.

The humiliation of our allies, for one thing, was bound to have consequences. For the French (and Israelis), the event gave rise to their independent nuclear weapons programs, as they both vowed never again to be in such a position of dependence on the United States. For the British, the humiliation heightened the determination of key figures in the Conservative party, such as Chancellor of the Exchequer Harold Macmillan (soon to succeed Eden as prime minister) and the young chief whip, Edward Heath, to bring Britain into the European Community— for the same reason; namely, to gain independence of us. As for our allies' willingness and ability to take some responsibility for security in the domain of their former colonies, we succeeded in dealing it a severe blow.

Soon enough, as we found ourselves more and more engaged in ensuring regional security ourselves, we were to lament how little help we received from them. When we were enmeshed in Indochina, it was the British and French who insisted that Alliance obligations did not apply out of the Atlantic area. When a later British government (Harold Wilson's in 1968) decided that on economic grounds it could no longer afford to maintain its protectorate arrangements "East of Suez" in the Persian Gulf, the United States begged it to stay. Our pleas went unheeded, and the withdrawal decision was carried out in 1971 under Wilson's successor—Edward Heath. On various occasions we would turn to our allies for help in the Middle East—Lebanon in 1958, Lebanon again in 1983–84, the Gulf in 1987–88 and 1990–91—and sometimes (not always) grouse that they were not doing enough to share the responsibility that at an earlier moment of history we had abruptly wrenched from their hands.

Our policy in Suez also had its powerful effect on the politics of the Arab world. Our hope was to win goodwill in the Arab world and thereby strengthen the forces of moderation (including particularly our expanding relations with Saudi Arabia). In Arab eyes, however, Suez was seen as

a victory not for the United States but for *Nasser* and what he represented—a defiant anti-Western policy that had made common cause with
the Soviets and profited by it. For a period after Suez there was a wave
of radical upheavals in the Middle East. In 1958, the pro-Western regime
of Nuri es-Said in Iraq was overthrown in a bloody coup that, among
other things, took Iraq out of the Baghdad Pact (requiring that we drop
the name, too); in the same year, pro-Nasser Syrians announced they
were joining their country in a political union with Egypt. In 1962, a
pro-Nasser coup in Yemen overthrew the pro-Western emir, and Nasser's
army became involved in a prolonged intervention that prompted emergency military support from the United States to the terrified Saudis.
Nasser became a major world figure and leader of the nonaligned, setting
himself up, for example, as a champion of "enlightenment and civilization" even in Africa.[69] The radical wave ebbed eventually, but not
without significant and lasting damage.

Thus, in a perverse outcome, it was the Soviets, who had played only
a minor role in the Suez affair, who found events moving in their direction
in its aftermath. On November 5—when the crisis had already passed
its climax—the Soviets sent warnings to Britain, France, and Israel threatening to intervene and a note to the United States proposing joint intervention (an idea they would try out again during the October 1973
war). The Eisenhower administration, correctly, reacted sharply to this,
rejecting the suggestion of joint intervention as "unthinkable" and declaring the Soviets an unfit partner in any enterprise so long as they
committed atrocities as in Hungary. Dulles later denounced the Soviets'
Middle East policy as "a cynical performance" and "inexcusably mischievous," based as it was on the selling of arms and the stimulation of
tensions.[70]

Nasser, on the other hand, was decidedly unimpressed by the Soviet
contribution to his success. In a speech in Damascus on March 22, 1959,
he pointed out that the Soviets had waited nine days before their famous
diplomatic "ultimatum." In that interval, Nasser said, "we had not the
slightest intimation of support from any foreign state, even the Soviet
Union. We relied on God and ourselves. . . ." Khrushchev complained
about this rebuke, writing Nasser a letter claiming credit for turning the
tide. Nasser's reply reiterated that the Soviet ultimatum had been issued
without his knowledge after nine days had passed, during which Egypt
was alone in the battle. "Of what use would the ultimatum have been
that day, Mr. Chairman, if we had come to an end and fallen?"[71] Yet
neither was the United States given any credit for what was, after all,
indisputably the decisive intervention that saved him. In Nasser's mind,

and in the minds of other Arabs who saw him vindicated, the victory was his own achievement (and Allah's).

Nasser, made a hero by the outcome, thereupon gained imitators who followed not only his anti-Western radicalism but also his clever use of Soviet backing. Up to 1955, Soviet arms transfers had been small, scattered, and directed only to Communist allies like North Korea. After 1955, the floodgates opened to a series of nonaligned countries. Syria and Yemen had received Soviet arms supplies during 1956, before Suez. Czech and Soviet military advisers went to Egypt, Syria, and Yemen to assist in training and maintenance. In 1956, Soviet weapons were sent for the first time to Afghanistan; in 1958, to Iraq and Indonesia; in 1959, to Guinea. Between 1960 and 1964, the Soviet customer list expanded to include Laos, India, Algeria, Sudan, Ghana, Mali, Cambodia, Somalia, Tanzania (via Zanzibar), and Zaire. From 1954 to 1964, Soviet weapons transfers to nonaligned countries exceeded $2.7 billion, according to the Stockholm International Peace Research Institute. In that period, 80 percent of Soviet arms exports went to nonaligned nations.[72]

In Arab folklore, to be sure, Eisenhower's pressure on the Israelis to withdraw from Sinai is fondly remembered. In the peace process that began under American auspices after 1973, American diplomats often heard this example invoked as a model. Recollection of Suez has been a staple of Jordanian king Hussein's dialogue with us: Why don't we just pressure Israel to withdraw the way Eisenhower did? By 1973 the wave of radicalism had already been halted—largely by the fiasco that Nasser's hubris led him into in 1967, by his own death from a heart attack in 1970, and by a U.S. policy under Nixon that deliberately penalized Arab connections with the Soviets (see chapter 17). The balance of forces in the Arab world between the radicals and the moderates had thus been restored by the early 1970s, and the American role had been bolstered by objective conditions. But it was not gratitude for 1956 that brought this about.

In the fifteen years following Suez, on the contrary, the Nasserite model—a military thug with a leftist program—was in the ascendant in the Middle East, Africa, even Latin America. Perversely, therefore, the Soviets were the objective beneficiary of an outcome that the United States had engineered and in which even Nasser belittled the Soviet role. Instead of helping Arab moderates, we had undermined or weakened them; instead of restoring stability in the Middle East, we had unbalanced it against us.

Amazingly enough, there is reason to believe that the Dulles brothers understood all this full well and had been privately rooting for the British and French to succeed. At dawn on November 3, while British and French forces were still stalled off the Egyptian coast, the CIA station chief in London, Chester Cooper, received an exasperated telephone call over a secure line from Robert Amory, Allen Dulles's deputy director: " 'Tell your friends,' he [Amory] shouted so loudly that I could have heard him across the Atlantic without a telephone, 'to comply with the goddamn cease-fire or go ahead with the goddamn invasion. Either way, we'll back 'em up if they do it fast. What we can't stand is their goddamn hesitation waltz while Hungary is burning.' "[73] In mid-November, after the crisis was over, British foreign secretary Selwyn Lloyd visited John Foster Dulles in Walter Reed Army Hospital, where the U.S. secretary of state was recuperating from the cancer operation that had taken him out of action from November 3 onward. Lloyd recounted the surprising question with which he was greeted: "Dulles said at once with a kind of twinkle in his eye, 'Selwyn, why did you stop? Why didn't you go through with it and get Nasser down?' If ever there was an occasion when one could have been knocked down by the proverbial feather, this was it."[74] Sometime later, in a private talk with Christian Pineau, the French foreign minister, Dulles startled the Frenchman, too, with a confession. "A Suez," Dulles said, "nous nous sommes trompés. C'est vous qui aviez raison."[75] Selwyn Lloyd reports that Dulles confessed the same thing to Dean Rusk, to Lloyd himself again on other occasions, and even to the general commanding Walter Reed Hospital, citing his illness as an excuse for a policy gone wrong.[76]

As years passed and Nasser stumbled into the 1967 war—abruptly expelling the UNEF and blockading the Straits of Tiran—Dulles's boss, President Eisenhower himself, came to the conclusion that he had seriously misjudged the issue he faced at Suez. Our sincere anticolonialist motives were not enough as a basis for policy. Instead of a last roar of colonialism, the issue posed by Suez was the first roar of a new era— the first case of a Third World radical taking Soviet arms and playing the anti-Western card. As the 1967 crisis came to a head in late May of that year, Israeli ambassador Avraham Harman visited Eisenhower in retirement at Gettysburg and heard him express his regret at how he had handled the 1956 crisis.[77] In another conversation at Gettysburg, in the fall of 1967, Eisenhower said something similar to Nixon:

He told me it was his major foreign policy mistake [Nixon wrote]. He gritted his teeth as he remarked "Why couldn't the British and the French have done it more quickly?" He went on to observe that the U.S. action in saving Nasser at Suez didn't help as far as the Middle East was con-

4

KHRUSHCHEV AND KENNEDY

If the Western alliance was rudely shaken by the Suez crisis, so, too, was the Sino-Soviet alliance torn apart—but far more decisively—in the same period. China played a pivotal role in the U.S.-Soviet rivalry in the Third World through most of the Cold War.

THE CHINA FACTOR

I met Mao Zedong in October 1975, on a visit to Beijing with Henry Kissinger. The legendary chairman of the Chinese Communist party was at the end of his days, capable of receiving visitors only at carefully selected intervals, and had enormous difficulty articulating because of muscle failure in his jaw. He would spew out a string of sounds with great force; his interpreters and aides would repeat back to him what they thought he had said. If they got it right, he would nod and they would translate. If they got it wrong, the chairman would shout it out again; if they could not get it right after several tries, he would heave a great sigh, plump himself down, and scribble the characters on a pad of paper. The intellectual energy and a hint of his prodigious physical energy were still there, in a sense all the more impressive as he railed against his infirmities and bombarded Kissinger with his usual pungent observations about world events and personalities.[1] The man had led a successful revolutionary war in a nation of hundreds of millions and was probably responsible for the deaths of tens of millions. Monster or revolutionary hero, he was a figure out of human scale. Through almost pure force of will, he had taken a prostrate China and made it a major power in the postwar period, tormenting the United States and the Soviet Union in turn and sometimes simultaneously.

It is hard to recapture today how traumatic an event the Chinese Revolution of 1949 had been in American and international politics. The upheaval in China posed for the first time in the postwar period many of the agonizing problems that would later recur in U.S. policy toward Third World conflicts. Both Franklin Roosevelt and Harry Truman had strived to hold Chiang Kai-shek's Nationalist China together so as to realize FDR's dream of a democratic China that could be the main pillar of postwar peace in the Far East. As has been noted in chapter 2, Stalin had made his own peace with Chiang Kai-shek and thought the Chinese Communists' prospects for coming to power were dim in any case. In the years after 1945, both the Soviets and the Americans were thus paradoxically seeking preservation of the wartime coalition of the two Chinese factions.

The Americans, typically, tried to mediate, sending emissaries of invariable goodwill and varying competence to promote reconciliation between Mao Zedong's Communists and Chiang's Nationalists. These efforts failed. The United States then stepped up its economic and military aid to the Nationalist government, its wartime ally, only to find itself embroiled in a policy debate at home about whether the Nationalist government was too authoritarian (or corrupt or incompetent) to hold the loyalty of the people and whether our aid should not be conditioned on wholesale reforms in the Chinese government. American military advisers, notably Gen. Joseph Stilwell, came to the conclusion that Chiang's regime was so rotten as to be unsalvageable.[2]

Meanwhile, Mao's Communists were bringing to fruition one of the most brilliant military campaigns in history. Guerrilla warfare had a variety of historical precedents, but Mao was both theoretician and practitioner of a new, modern style of "revolutionary war"—"people's war," he called it—that combined a Marxist-Leninist political and economic analysis with classical tactics of insurgent warfare. The Communists' base of power was the countryside—the long-suffering Chinese peasantry—and the strategy was to strangle the urban areas by gradually isolating them. Guerrilla forces usually had an enormous tactical advantage; they could harass government forces at times and places of their own choosing, concentrating their forces to achieve local tactical superiority, then melting away into the countryside. Over time, the exhaustion and demoralization of the central government were almost inevitable. Mao's writings on his military strategy in both the anti-Japanese war and the Chinese civil war were an ominous signal to the West of the menace that lay in the turbulence of the Third World.

Chiang's regime fell ignominiously, and the People's Republic of China was proclaimed on the mainland on October 1, 1949. There were bitter recriminations in the United States as conservative Republicans accused President Truman and Secretary of State Dean Acheson of betrayal, cowardice, and appeasement of communism. The administration was almost certainly correct that the main causes of Chiang Kai-shek's fall lay in the internal weaknesses of the regime and that he could not have been saved without a massive American military intervention of unthinkable proportions. As Acheson put it in the famous State Department "White Paper" of July 1949: "The unfortunate but inescapable fact is that the ominous result of the civil war in China was beyond the control of the government of the United States. Nothing that this country did or could have done within the reasonable limits of its capabilities could have changed that result; nothing that was left undone by this country has contributed to it. It was the product of internal Chinese forces, forces which this country tried to influence but could not."[3]

The debate among Americans continued for decades, with liberals making the case for democratic reforms as essential to the survival of Third World allies and conservatives seeing the U.S. pressure on allies as only weakening them in a mortal struggle with their totalitarian enemies. The China debacle had led, as part of its legacy, to the rise of Sen. Joseph McCarthy and a shameful period of witch-hunts that attempted to root out domestic traitors who were presumed responsible for a multitude of foreign policy setbacks; this would play no small role in the motivations of two future Democratic presidents, Kennedy and Johnson, who feared being accused of "losing" Indochina. Similarly, the liberal analysis would also leave its legacy, as later clients would be subjected to stringent pressures for democratization and internal reform as the price for American support, even against ruthless totalitarian foes.

There were American analysts of China who were perceptive enough to see beneath the surface the tensions between the Communist Chinese and their Soviet allies. Some of them were targets of McCarthyism. Our sympathy for what they went through, however, does not mean that their analysis was 100 percent correct. Someday, indeed, there would be a clash of Chinese and Russian nationalisms, as they predicted. But for a whole two decades after the Chinese Revolution, there was no good news in this for the West. The accretion of power represented by the alliance of 600 million Chinese with the growing Soviet superpower was a geopolitical disaster of the first order. In the Third World, the Chinese only seemed to add to the Soviets' capacity to promote radicalism, being, if anything, more ferociously anti-imperialist than the Soviets. Giventhe depths of Mao's ideological commitment, it is implausible that he and his colleagues could have been wooed by the West into a more conciliatory posture that would have contradicted the essence of his philosophy.

Some had even seen Mao's Communists as an impressive group of agrarian reformers, with whose aspirations we should want to identify.

This mystique was later to be shattered by the regime's extraordinary brutality after it took power—a record of arbitrariness and bloodletting condemned even by the party leadership under Deng Xiaoping after Mao died.[4]

That American liberals and conservatives came away from the 1949 revolution with totally opposite analyses of what went wrong was an ominous precedent for the bitter divisions in the United States that later occurred over Vietnam and Central America.

Gradually, China did begin to play a more independent role on the world stage, complicating its relations with Moscow. But the implications of this for the West were no blessing. The Sino-Soviet alliance that so frightened the West had never, of course, been a monolith of any kind. While Moscow and Beijing signed a treaty of alliance in 1950, their antagonism had a depth and bitterness whose full dimensions were probably not grasped by any outsiders at the time. Harrison Salisbury has enumerated an extraordinary series of slights and humiliations suffered by Mao at Stalin's hand going back to the 1920s. Not only did Stalin constantly press Mao into compromises with Chiang Kai-shek during the civil war, but when Chiang smashed the Communists in Shanghai in 1927, Stalin had reacted by rounding up all the Chinese in Moscow and other major cities, including loyal Chinese members of the Comintern; hundreds of thousands were sent to the gulags or shot. When Mao captured Chiang Kai-shek in 1936 and was about to execute him, Stalin sent Mao a peremptory telegram ordering Chiang's immediate release and threatening to break all relations with the Chinese Communists if it was not done. In early 1949, when Mao's army was on the verge of crossing the Yangtze to finish off Chiang, Stalin tried to prevent the attack. When Chiang fled his capital, Nanjing, most foreign ambassadors stayed behind to prepare for the Communist takeover—but not the Soviet ambassador, who fled with Chiang. Mao "had a keen ear for insults," Salisbury wrote, "and a long memory."[5]

The U.S. government—contrary to the conventional wisdom today— did perceive the cracks in the Sino-Soviet alliance at the time.[6] In March 1949, President Truman approved a formal strategy of seeking "to exploit through political and economic means any rifts between the Chinese Communists and the USSR . . ."[7] And even John Foster Dulles expressed the view in November 1950 that, in the long run, "our best defense lies in exploiting potential jealousies, rivalries, and disaffections within the present area of Soviet Communist control . . ."[8]

Nonetheless, the problem of how to deal with Communist China remained traumatic for the United States. An important milestone in the complex evolution of the Chinese-Soviet-American triangular relationship was the Korean War. China's intervention in that war in late 1950 may well have been motivated only by self-preservation. As Gen. Douglas MacArthur's UN forces, having blunted the North Korean invasion, pushed northward to liberate all of North Korea, China feared the consequences for itself—and for the Communist position in all of Asia—if the Americans were to succeed. Mao cabled to Stalin on October 2, 1950: "If we allow the United States to occupy all of Korea, the revolutionary strength of Korea will suffer a fundamental defeat, and the American invaders will run more rampant, with negative effects for the entire Far East."[9] (This was Mao's domino theory.) But, by their intervention, the Chinese also won their spurs as a major power. Their forces performed creditably against the Americans and carried the brunt of the Korean fighting on behalf of their North Korean and Soviet allies.

In 1954, at the Geneva Conference on Indochina, the Chinese played an important diplomatic role; they are generally given credit for persuading North Vietnam to accept the compromise with the French that divided Vietnam at the 17th parallel. In April 1955, as noted in the preceding chapter, Premier Zhou Enlai was a star at the gathering of nonaligned nations at Bandung, Indonesia. Zhou charmed the delegates as he would two generations of foreigners; he made a conciliatory speech commending the new nations in their just struggle for national sovereignty and independence from colonialism.

There is reason to believe the Soviets were growing jealous of their Chinese ally's appeal. As a developing country itself, China could claim a special solidarity with the new nations struggling not only for their national identity but for rapid modernization. China's economic performance in the 1950s outstripped India's and seemingly offered a far more relevant economic model than the Soviet Union, which was then regarded as a formidable, developed industrial power. In the vocabulary that soon became standard, the USSR and its East European satellites were the Second World; China was free to claim—at Moscow's expense—that it was part of the Third. This has been a cardinal principle of China's foreign policy to this day.

As early as 1956, Nikita Khrushchev confided to Indian vice president S. Radhakrishnan his premonition that in ten years' time, the Soviets' chief enemy in the world would be China.[10]

In November 1957, Khrushchev convened a world conference of sixty-four Communist parties in Moscow. Stalin's and Zhdanov's Cominform had been disbanded the year before, and the conference was a new way to try to ensure some unity in the international Communist movement.

It came at a triumphant moment for the Soviet hosts. After Suez, the Western alliance still seemed in disarray, while the turmoil in Eastern Europe following Khrushchev's de-Stalinization campaign seemed behind him. (In June 1957, Khrushchev had ousted the "anti-Party group" of his Kremlin opponents.) Soviet foreign policy, especially in the Third World, was impressing the West with its boldness as Khrushchev broke out of Stalin's self-imposed shell.

A month before the conference, on October 4, 1957, the Soviets had launched Sputnik, the world's first artificial earth satellite, stunning the world with its vivid demonstration of their technological prowess. Sputnik's true significance was not the scientific curiosity of this beeping metal basketball in orbit but the military implications of the powerful ballistic missile with which the Soviets had put it there. For the rest of the Cold War, intercontinental ballistic missiles capable of delivering thermonuclear warheads would be the mainstay of the two sides' arsenals in the strategic military competition.

Paradoxically, this success was to contribute to the unraveling of Communist unity. The 1957 Moscow conference was Mao's star turn on the international stage. Instead of the smooth, urbane Zhou Enlai, the Chinese representative was now the crude, ebullient Communist party chairman, about whom it needs only be said that he made Nikita Khrushchev seem shy and urbane.

Mao had a message, namely that the new strength of the Communist bloc argued for an unrelenting, militant campaign against imperialism. He insisted that Moscow remained the true leader of the Communist world, but even this flattery of Moscow had a tendentious thrust: The Soviets, Mao was saying, had the obligation to lead the renewed charge against the West.[11] There was no longer any excuse for appeasement, Mao told the delegates: "It is my opinion that the international situation has now reached a new turning point. . . . There is a Chinese saying, 'Either the East wind prevails over the West wind or the West wind prevails over the East wind.' It is characteristic of the situation today, I believe, that the East wind is prevailing over the West wind. That is to say, the forces of socialism are overwhelmingly superior to the forces of imperialism."[12]

Mao went beyond this, however, to shock his audience with his famous (or infamous) pronouncement that there was no reason even to be afraid of a nuclear war. In an earlier day, during the West's atomic monopoly, Mao had once bravely claimed that the atomic bomb, like imperialism itself, was a "paper tiger."[13] Now that the Soviets had apparently matched and surpassed Western nuclear strength, why fear a war? And what if a nuclear war destroyed half of mankind? Mao asked. The other half would survive—and so would socialism. Khrushchev, trying years later in his exile to recall Mao's exact words, summed up the gist as follows:

> No matter what kind of war breaks out—conventional or thermonuclear— we'll win. As for China, if the imperialists unleash war on us, we may lose more than three hundred million people. So what? War is war. The years will pass, and we'll get to work producing more babies than ever before.

> This last statement [Khrushchev recalled] he put more crudely than I've related here. He allowed himself to use an indecent expression, though I don't remember exactly what it was.[14]

Khrushchev was appalled. For all his own bravado and bluster, he knew full well both the actual weaknesses of the Soviet strategic arsenal and, from the experience of World War II, the horror of general war. He had no stomach for such recklessness. The shock of Mao's performance was to have its consequence for Sino-Soviet relations: The Soviets, who had earlier promised to help China develop its own nuclear capability, were to renege on their promise. The Chinese responded by, among other things, harassing the Soviet specialists in China who were providing technical assistance in other fields. The Soviets pulled all their twelve thousand advisers out of China in the summer of 1960. The Sino-Soviet dispute then broke out in open polemics over ideology and policy.

All this had its impact on Moscow's relations with the West. The dispute with China was to kindle in the Soviets, over time, a sense that they might have more in common with the West than with the militant Chinese, especially where the central issue of nuclear war was concerned. In the Third World, however, it was to impel the Soviets into a more vigorous competitive effort, in some places to head off Chinese inroads as well as to supplant Western influence. At the November 1960 Moscow Conference of Communist parties, the largest such gathering ever (eighty-one countries represented), the final declaration summoned all the participants to their "internationalist duty": "Communists have always recognized the progressive, revolutionary importance of national-liberation wars." While the fight for national liberation could be carried on by military or by nonmilitary means, as conditions warranted, the Moscow Declaration called for a "resolute struggle against imperialism and the vestiges of feudalism." As Lenin had argued in 1920, Communist parties, representing the alliance of the workers and the peasantry, were to ally with bourgeois nationalist forces in a "single national democratic front." The declaration rejected the "export of revolution" but also announced a determination to resist the imperialists' "export of counter-revolution."[15]

The Soviets' eagerness to cultivate Asian countries like Indonesia, India, and Burma, for example, can thus be explained by as great a desire to contain Chinese influence as American. We were not the only ones hoping that India would be a counterweight to China. Likewise, the growing Soviet aid programs in African countries such as Tanzania and Ghana, where the Chinese were active.[16] But the West could take little comfort from this. In the Third World, both Moscow and Beijing were seeking to supplant Western influence, and the Chinese goad only spurred the Soviets. The new theme of "wars of national liberation" was particularly ominous. In Indochina, war was continuing; a crisis loomed in the former Belgian Congo. The issue now was not simply economic aid for steel mills or even arms aid for Nasserite posturing; it was a doctrine— which the Soviets, too, espoused—that legitimated global revolutionary violence.

Revolution in the Third World caused no qualms in Khrushchev, repelled though he was by Mao's recklessness on nuclear matters. In 1958 he discussed it with visiting columnist Walter Lippmann, who came away convinced that "the Russian and Chinese challenge for the leadership of Asia and Africa" was "the most pressing issue" for the United States.[17] To Khrushchev, Soviet support for revolution was not intervention at all. Revolution was part of the contemporary historical reality. It was the *Western* attempt to block the process of history that constituted intervention. "In his mind," Lippmann explained, "opposition to this revolution is an attempt to change the status quo."[18]

To bourgeois Americans, desperate to preserve global stability and the possibilities for *peaceful* political change and economic development, this was a source of dismay.

WARS OF NATIONAL LIBERATION

In early January 1961, Khrushchev delivered a speech to a gathering of the party's ideological elite.[19] He was brimming with historical confidence: over vast expanses of Europe and Asia, there was "a mighty upsurge of anti-imperialist, national-liberation revolutions." The crisis of capitalism was acute, what with the rapid disintegration of the colonial system and the economic slump in the United States. In an important formulation that Brezhnev, too, would use, Khrushchev saw "a growing change in the correlation of forces in favor of socialism."

Khrushchev went on to discuss the different dimensions of the struggle against imperialism. There were different kinds of wars: world wars, local wars, and wars of national liberation. In a clear rebuke to the Chinese, Khrushchev warned that nuclear war would be an "incalculable disaster" for the working class and for the world. Therefore, at this level, the Soviet policy was to prevent war; it stood for "peaceful co-existence among states with different social systems," which was, he said, a form of intensive struggle against the aggressive forces of imperialism in the international arena. So-called local wars, like the Suez adventure, were dangerous because they could escalate into nuclear war.

"Wars of national liberation," however, were something else entirely: "There will be wars of national liberation as long as imperialism exists, as long as colonialism exists. These are revolutionary wars. Such wars are not only possible but inevitable. . . . Communists fully and unreservedly support such just wars and march in the van of the peoples fighting wars of liberation." Having just hosted the 1960 Moscow Conference of Communist parties in November, Khrushchev repeated that conference's declaration that denied any interest in the "export of revolution" but called for Communists "resolutely [to] struggle against imperialist export of counter-revolution."

This speech, delivered behind closed doors on January 6, 1961, was published in the Soviet press on January 18, two days before John F. Kennedy's inauguration as president. It had a stunning effect. Kennedy ploughed through the twenty-thousand-word text himself. On the advice of the American ambassador in Moscow, Llewellyn Thompson, Kennedy gave copies of it to all his top people and told them to "read, mark, learn, and inwardly digest" it.[20] He read portions of it aloud to the first session of his National Security Council. His new secretary of defense, Robert McNamara, recalled years later, "It was a significant event in our lives."[21] The new administration treated the speech as a shot across its bow, a grave challenge to the West.

Kennedy appeared before a joint session of Congress on January 30 for a brief State of the Union address and declared that all the nation's domestic problems "pale when placed beside those which confront us around the world. . . . Each day the crises multiply. Each day their solution grows more difficult. Each day we draw nearer the hour of maximum danger, as weapons spread and hostile forces grow stronger. I feel I must inform the Congress that our analyses over the last ten days make it clear that—in each of the principal areas of crisis—the tide of events has been running out, and time has not been our friend." He cited Chinese pressures against India, the insurgencies in South Vietnam and Laos, and the crisis in the Congo. In Latin America, "Communist agents seeking to exploit that region's peaceful revolution of hope have established a base in Cuba, only 90 miles from our shores." The Atlantic Alliance was in "some disarray." Our difficult relations with the Soviet Union and Communist China were the obstacle to a better world: "We must never be lulled into believing that either power has yielded its ambitions for world domination—ambitions which they forcefully re-stated only a short time ago" (meaning the Moscow Declaration and the Khrushchev speech).

On May 25, Kennedy appeared again before a joint session of Congress to deliver an urgent and more detailed legislative program. This "special message" covered the full range of domestic and foreign topics that a State of the Union program might be expected to cover—fiscal and monetary policy, manpower training, the space program, NATO, foreign assistance, arms control, and so forth. What is remarkable in retrospect is that such a broad-gauged message on his legislative program should be so dominated by strategic fear about the competition in the Third World:

> The great battleground for the defense and expansion of freedom today is the whole southern half of the globe—Asia, Latin America, Africa and the Middle East—the lands of the rising peoples. Their revolution is the greatest in human history. . . .

> [T]he adversaries of freedom did not create the revolution; nor did they create the conditions which compel it. But they are seeking to ride the crest of its wave—to capture it for themselves.

> Yet their aggression is more often concealed than open. They have fired no missiles; and their troops are seldom seen. They send arms, agitators, aid, technicians and propaganda to every troubled area. But where fighting is required, it is usually done by others—by guerrillas striking at night, by assassins striking alone—assassins who have taken the lives of four thousand civil officers in the last twelve months in Vietnam alone—by subversives and saboteurs and insurrectionists, who in some cases control whole areas inside of independent nations. . . .

> It is a contest of will and purpose as well as force and violence—a battle for minds and souls as well as lives and territory. And in that contest, we cannot stand aside.

Other interpretations of the Khrushchev speech are possible, and some were given at the time. Outgoing President Eisenhower read the text and dismissed it as the usual Khrushchev bluster. Ambassador Thompson's analysis, to which Kennedy reacted so passionately, included the qualifying observation that much of it was Khrushchev the propagandist.[22] Walter Lippmann, on yet another visit with Khrushchev (in April 1961), came to the conclusion that Khrushchev was now really more concerned with Great Power relations (including the German and the Chinese problem) than with the underdeveloped world.[23]

Later scholars, too, have argued that the Kennedy administration's response was a tremendous overreaction. For one thing, much of the Kremlin rhetoric about Third World revolution was not even new; it harked back to Khrushchev's own 1956 speech to the Twentieth Party Congress. Much of Khrushchev's 1961 speech was clearly directed at the Chinese more than at the Americans, indeed to reject Beijing's brand of militancy, especially on nuclear issues, and also to reassert Moscow's discipline over the world Communist movement. In an important sense, therefore, the speech did include a conciliatory signal to the West.[24]

Beneath all the historical bravado about the "correlation of forces," moreover, were hints of Moscow's worries about its prospects in the Third World. There was a worried reference to the Third World's continuing economic dependence on the West, which Khrushchev (correctly) saw as a powerful and enduring source of Western influence. There was an agitated reference, also, to the idea that the developing countries could be a "third force" in the world, between capitalists and Communists; Khrushchev slapped this idea down ("utter chicanery," he called it), insisting that socialism had played a key role in the death of colonialism and was the new nations' natural ally. Obviously, there was some insecurity on that point. While advocating a united front between local Communists and bourgeois nationalists, Khrushchev advised Communists to keep explaining to the masses that the policies of nationalist governments, even if "democratic," were not the same as authentic socialism—betraying nervousness, in other words, about the local Communists' ability to survive while subordinated to the bourgeois nationalists.

Khrushchev hailed the Algerian Revolution as a "sacred war," but this praise was hollow. The Soviets were already cultivating French president Charles de Gaulle to encourage his disruptive influence in NATO and were soft-pedaling significant support for the Algerian rebels. The Chinese were making the telling point that in Algeria and elsewhere, the

Soviets were subordinating the interests of Third World revolution to their Great Power interests.[25]

If our Vietnam debacle was the product of the Kennedy reaction to this speech, then "overreaction" is an understatement. But to dismiss the Khrushchev performance as innocuous, or even as an attempt at "reassuring the West," is too simple. The Soviets' effort to contrast themselves with the Chinese was welcome enough when it came to avoiding nuclear war or local conflicts that could lead to it. But there was no mistaking the Soviets' own decision, in most of the Third World, to compete with the Chinese over who could be the more effective challenger to the West.

It was easy for the Chinese to score a point off the Soviets over Algeria, and there would be many other occasions (Cuba in 1962, Indochina in 1972, to take two dramatic examples) when the Soviets would subordinate their Third World clients to their Great Power relationships. The Chinese, however, were to do exactly the same when they considered vital interests at stake (as when their fear of the Soviets in the Brezhnev era led them to a rapprochement with the United States). In the 1960s, however, the Soviet and Chinese attempt to destabilize the Third World and capture its revolution was real enough. The challenge manifested itself in a burgeoning of military, economic, and political relations designed to undercut Western influence.

Both the Soviets and the Chinese without doubt viewed the Third World as intrinsically less important than relations among the Great Powers, but that was not the issue. Certainly Moscow and Beijing viewed their Third World policies in instrumental terms—as a means of outflanking the West or weakening it—just as Lenin had done. That they were both willing to subordinate Third World clients when more important interests were at stake, however, is not proof that they were not seriously devoted to creating problems for us; on the contrary, it is a tribute to the West's occasional success in forcing them to choose. When *we* imposed some penalty for their Third World conduct, exacting a price in the coin of relations with us, they usually did back off (as in Cuba or the Middle East). But this was an argument *for* a determined Western response in the Third World, not against it. Later, this counterstrategy went by the name of "linkage."

THE KENNEDY RESPONSE

If the Kennedy team was right to take the Khrushchev challenge seriously, the way it responded was nonetheless a triumph of emotion over analysis. Khrushchev's exuberance about the shifting "correlation of forces" struck a raw nerve because (not to put too fine a point on it) the new American administration agreed with him. John Kennedy had campaigned in 1960 against the inadequacy of Eisenhower's foreign and defense policies: We were losing the Third World; we were losing the Cold War; we had lost the strategic initiative. When Khrushchev needled the Americans over the U.S. economic recession, he was only borrowing from the Democratic challenger's campaign material. Until the Cuban Missile Crisis in October 1962, the Kennedy administration's Third World posture can only be described as one of insecurity, if not strategic panic. The global balance of power, it believed, was being decided in the Third World—and we were losing.

The administration's response to this challenge was manifold, as reflected in the president's multifaceted May 25, 1961, address on urgent national needs.

The preoccupation with guerrilla warfare was high on the list. This is the administration that came into office calling for a military buildup, particularly in conventional forces (rejecting the Dulles doctrine of relying on "massive [nuclear] retaliation" to deter conventional challenges). Now counterinsurgency in the developing world became a national priority. Whereas Khrushchev's nightmare was the Third World's continuing economic dependence on the West, Kennedy's was a vision of guerrillas and assassins tipping the balance in shadowy faraway conflicts.

One of the first questions the new president asked his aides when he came into office was: "What are we doing about guerrilla warfare?"[26] In January 1962 the Marine Corps *Gazette* published a special issue devoted to guerrilla warfare and counterinsurgency; Kennedy read it "from cover to cover" (in his own words) and wrote the *Gazette* a laudatory letter, which was reproduced as the frontispiece when the special issue was subsequently published as a book.[27] A U.S. Army directorate for special warfare, established at the end of the Eisenhower administration, was expanded. Army Special Forces were upgraded to elite status—the "Green Berets." Kennedy established an NSC subcommittee called the Special Group, Counter-insurgency; it was chaired by Gen. Maxwell Taylor, then military representative of the president, and included some of the most senior officials in the U.S. government, such as the deputy secretary of defense, deputy under secretary of state for political affairs, the chairman of the Joint Chiefs of Staff, director of central intelligence, administrator of the Agency for International Development, director of the U.S. Information Agency, and Atty. Gen. Robert Kennedy, the president's closest confidant. In March 1962, the U.S. Army convened a three-day Washington symposium of 350 social and behavioral scientists and military leaders to investigate all the ramifications of this complex new variety of warfare.[28]

The president told the graduating class at West Point on June 6, 1962: "This is another type of War, new in its intensity, ancient in its origins— war by guerrillas, subversives, insurgents, assassins. War by ambush instead of by combat; by infiltration instead of aggression; seeking victory by eroding and exhausting the enemy instead of engaging him. . . . It requires in those situations where we must counter it . . . a wholly new kind of strategy; a wholly different kind of force and therefore a new and different kind of military training."

Most disturbing to American analysts of the problem was that the Soviets had a doctrine for such a form of conflict and the West did not. Marxist class analysis and Leninist prescriptions for disciplined political violence together provided a sophisticated doctrine for revolutionary wars. For Lenin, an avid reader of Karl von Clausewitz, revolutionary war was part and parcel of a political strategy to outflank the West, and warfare on the ground was viewed similarly as a component of a political struggle.[29] Sapping the will of the central government, winning over (or intimidating) the local population, and, just as important, wearing down the psychological stamina of the imperialist powers supporting the local regime—these were the political auxiliary to the military tactics. For Americans and most other Westerners, in contrast, politics and warfare were usually distinct categories. The conduct of war was traditionally left to the military experts; political theory was predicated on the legitimacy of the state system (not class struggle), on the hopes for international order and international law (not mortal ideological combat), and on a belief in peaceful progress.

The American "doctrine" that was devised by a liberal administration to counter this new threat included a strong reaffirmation of the need to offer a peaceful, progressive alternative. This was the cautionary lesson absorbed from Chiang Kai-shek's unhappy experience in China. In his Special Message of May 25, 1961, President Kennedy spoke of Third World nations under stress:

> We would be badly mistaken to consider their problems in military terms alone. For no amount of arms and armies can help stabilize those governments which are unable or unwilling to achieve social and economic reform and development. Military pacts cannot help nations whose social injustice and economic chaos invite insurgency and penetration and subversion. The most skillful counter-guerilla efforts cannot succeed where

the local population is too caught up in its own misery to be concerned about the advance of communism.

But for those who share this view, we stand ready now, as we have in the past, to provide generously of our skills, and our capital, and our food to assist the peoples of the less developed nations to reach their goals in freedom—to help them before they are engulfed in crisis.

The Kennedy administration wholeheartedly embraced the theory and philosophy of economic development, hiring many of its academic and political originators (Walt Rostow, John Kenneth Galbraith, Chester Bowles). On March 1, 1961, Kennedy established the Peace Corps by Executive Order. On March 13, he launched the Alliance for Progress (foreshadowed in his inaugural address), representing a special commitment to promote economic advance in our own hemisphere. On March 22, he sent Congress a message endorsing the UN concept of a "Development Decade." It was this message that created the Agency for International Development to unify the hitherto separate activities of technical assistance, development lending, and food aid and to institutionalize the national commitment to a more substantial program of grants and credits. More emphasis was to be placed on development planning, promoted by longer-term (multiyear) authorizations; multilateral consortia were organized in the World Bank for India and Pakistan, as Kennedy had long urged as a senator. In the early 1960s, U.S. official assistance to international development rose by one-third.[30]

Thus did the United States hope to respond to the revolution of rising expectations among the former colonial nations. Narrowing the gap between rich and poor was seen as a crucial strategic interest. Conservatives may not have needed such a doctrinal justification for resisting Soviet communism, whose moral and strategic evil seemed self-evident. For liberals in the Cold War, however (as for Woodrow Wilson and Franklin Roosevelt in two world wars), the struggle could be supported morally or analytically only on a platform of progressive objectives. As we saw in the last chapter, there was a certain diffidence about private enterprise, and there was also a noticeable relativism about whether our own political model was really suitable for export. "We cannot expect that all nations will adopt like systems . . ." Kennedy conceded to the UN General Assembly on September 25, 1961.

The liberal analysis of Communist advances in Latin America, indeed, was that social and political revolution was essentially justified. We held no brief for rightist tyrants. The Communists were betraying this legitimate revolution, however, by turning it in violent directions and rendering it subservient to a foreign power. This was the case argued in the famous "White Paper" of April 1961, just before the Bay of Pigs invasion by U.S.-backed Cuban exiles. The sympathy for radical change reflected the moral conviction of a president who, as a senator, had stressed the need to keep America free of the taint of colonialism and who had championed the Algerian Revolution against the French. This approach also reflected the scruple of an administration that when it launched the Bay of Pigs operation, let it fail rather than involve American military power more openly.

FROM THE BAY OF PIGS TO THE MISSILE CRISIS

Kennedy and Khrushchev had a turbulent relationship over the three years of Kennedy's tragically foreshortened term of office. The small island of Cuba, "only 90 miles from our shores," as Kennedy had said, was to play a central role.

The American reaction to the Cuban Revolution demonstrated again the ambivalences and hesitations of the American posture in the developing world. The conservative Eisenhower administration was profoundly suspicious of Fidel Castro and his band of guerrillas who swept down from the Sierra Maestra at the end of 1958 to seize power from the dictator Fulgencio Batista. The Republicans had economic concerns, knowing of the revolutionaries' antipathy to the extensive U.S. business and land holdings in Cuba, and strategic concerns, fearing Castro as a kind of Latin Nasser with aspirations of radicalizing the Western Hemisphere. The rebels seemed heavily influenced by Communist ideology; their anti-Yankee rhetoric and expropriation of U.S. property ($1 billion in the first two years) confirmed the Eisenhower administration's worst fears.[31] After some initial conciliatory gestures, Eisenhower was prompted to impose economic sanctions, most importantly an end to Cuba's quota for sugar exports to the United States.

Castro, meanwhile, sought shrewdly to appeal to Americans by portraying himself as a social and agrarian reformer whose revolution had indigenous roots and no inherent hostility toward the United States. As with the Chinese before him and the Vietnamese after him, this argument had its takers. Castro's roguish charm and eloquence were evident on the U.S. tour he made in April 1959, speaking in Washington, in New York, and at Harvard. A debate raged in the United States over whether we were missing an opportunity for better relations. But as time passed, the regime's policies—its blatant anti-Americanism, its ruthless suppression of opposition at home, and its enthusiastic championing of hemispheric upheaval (all personified in Castro's Argentine-born comrade Ernesto "Che" Guevara) undercut Castro's U.S. sympathizers (at least in the mainstream of our politics) and earned him bipartisan hostility here. The suspicion persisted that the Cuban regime's policies had been Communist dominated from the day it came into power (which was eventually proved to be totally correct). [32]

For President-elect Kennedy, the dilemma was not simply an analytic one. He was inheriting from Eisenhower a full-fledged plan for a CIA-trained exile army to invade the island—a plan that would be ready soon after his inauguration. For all his sympathy for the Algerian revolutionaries and his distaste for European colonialism, Kennedy in his campaign had not shrunk from challenging Eisenhower and Nixon for not doing enough to stop Castro. Yet an outright invasion ran up against the scruples of an American political class, especially the Democratic heirs of FDR, to whom the swaggering interventionism of the early decades of the century was no longer respectable.

The solution adopted by the new administration was to reduce the scale of the operation and the overt quality of the official U.S. involvement in it and also to try to improve the political coloration of the exile organization. The CIA had favored the ex-Batista types, who had fled Cuba first, formed their U.S. contacts first, and seemed to have the clearest motivation. The Communist influence that was daily becoming more evident in Havana, however, was spawning a second wave of exiles—moderates, liberals, and other non-Communists who had been a part of the revolution against Batista but found themselves either deeply disillusioned or squeezed out by the Leninist vanguard that dominated. These included men like Manuel Ray, a young liberal engineer who had directed sabotage operations for the guerrillas and then been minister of public works in Castro's first government. Ray quit and formed his own movement, opposing communism but committed to continuing Castro's social reforms. He, too, visited Harvard and garnered much support among academics who had influence with the new administration. Kennedy ordered that the exile organization, in its political and military operations, be broadened to include these more democratic groups. It stood to reason that such a broad-based, progressive democratic force would have a far better chance of gaining popular support in Cuba against the new dictatorship. [33]

The Kennedy administration made clear (in a way the Eisenhower administration might not have done) its categorical rejection of Batista and its endorsement of many of the social reforms in Castro's original program. Ex-Harvard professor Arthur Schlesinger, Jr., an intellectual with a long and honorable record as an anti-Communist liberal, helped as a White House adviser to draft the "White Paper" issued by the State Department in April, shortly before the Bay of Pigs. The Cuban people's rallying to Castro, the document declared, was a response to his promise of "a free and democratic Cuba dedicated to social and economic justice."[34] For a while after taking power, Castro had seemed to be making good on his promise:

> The positive programs initiated in the first months of the Castro regime— the schools built, the medical clinics established, the new housing, the early projects of land reform, the opening up of beaches and resorts to the people, the elimination of graft in government—were impressive in their conception; no future Cuban government can expect to turn its back on such objectives. But so far as the expressed political aims of the revolution were concerned, the record of the Castro regime has been a record of the steady and consistent betrayal of Dr. Castro's prerevolutionary promises; and the result has been to corrupt the social achievements and make them the means, not of liberation, but of bondage.

The betrayal consisted of two things: the supplanting of the originally broad-based "26th of July" Movement by the Communist party and the "delivery of the revolution to the Sino-Soviet bloc." In sum: "[T]he Castro regime in Cuba offers a clear and present danger to the authentic and autonomous revolution of the Americas—to the whole hope of spreading political liberty, economic development, and social progress through all the republics of the hemisphere."

This was the liberal case against Castro. Unfortunately, it proved bureaucratically impossible to translate this enlightened commitment to the "authentic and autonomous revolution of the Americas" into a broadening of the Cuban exile movement gathering in southern Florida for the liberation of their country. The CIA, and the early exiles it was working with, resisted collaboration with a left-of-center movement like Manuel Ray's. The White House insisted on a shotgun marriage, but the union never held together, and the disarray contributed significantly to the failed outcome.[35] The desperate efforts to make the anti-Castro legion a broader-based force foreshadowed the similar struggle of U.S. policymakers three decades later to enhance the democratic credentials of the Nicaraguan resistance (the "Contras"). But whereas Reagan was pushed to confront the same contradictions by considerable political pressures at home from the Left, Kennedy faced mainly pressures from the Right, and his scruples about the counterrevolutionaries were mostly his own.

After the Bay of Pigs fiasco of April 1961, Khrushchev warned Kennedy of the dangers of escalation if such escapades were repeated. In a rather humiliating public message to the president on April 18, Khrushchev warned—applying the doctrine of his January speech—that "[a]ny so-called 'small war' can produce a chain reaction in all parts of the world." In effect, he was rubbing Kennedy's nose in it and hoping to reinforce Kennedy's caution.[36]

For after the Bay of Pigs and a weak presidential performance at a Vienna summit in June, Khrushchev formed a low opinion of Kennedy's personal courage. "Too liberal to fight" was Khrushchev's later blunt description to the visiting New England poet Robert Frost.[37] There was a Berlin crisis in the summer of 1961, and Kennedy was forced to call up reserves and prepare to send six divisions to Europe to reinforce West Berlin and face down Soviet threats to the city. Then the Berlin Wall went up in August, to stanch the flow of fleeing East Berliners and reinforce the Communist East German regime. The new Program of the Communist Party of the Soviet Union trumpeted: "A mighty wave of national-liberation revolutions is sweeping away the colonial system and undermining the foundations of imperialism."[38] Khrushchev's dramatic announcements of multimegaton nuclear tests, following up on the triumph of the first launches of cosmonauts into earth orbit, heightened the administration's sense of beleaguerment and strategic fear.

In the Third World, in addition to Latin America, the immediate challenges seemed to come in Indochina and Africa.

Kennedy confronted a minicrisis in Laos in the first two months of his term as Communist guerrilla forces, armed with new shipments of Soviet weapons, undermined that country's delicate internal political balance. Eisenhower had dumped this in Kennedy's lap, warning him before inauguration of Laos's importance.[39] A multilateral negotiation in Geneva produced a new treaty in 1962 reaffirming Laotian neutrality (which was supposedly already guaranteed by the 1954 Geneva Accords). It was a precarious arrangement, but Kennedy was too shaken by the Bay of Pigs to press for a military solution. "If it hadn't been for Cuba," he reportedly told an aide in the summer of 1961, "we would be fighting in Laos today."[40] Kennedy compensated by stepping up the U.S. military advisory role in South Vietnam. It rose to a level of sixteen thousand men, in response to the building guerrilla insurgency there. After the difficult summit with Khrushchev in Vienna in June, Kennedy told James Reston: "Now we have a problem in trying to make our power credible, and Vietnam looks like the place."[41]

Africa was a drama in itself. In 1960 alone, seventeen of its countries won independence from colonial rule as the principal European colonial powers (with a few exceptions) bowed out of their historical role.

John Kennedy had a strong reputation in Africa. His Algerian stance had made him a hero; he had briefly chaired the Senate African Affairs Subcommittee, and he had strived to bring Africa's cause to the forefront of national attention. (There are 479 references to Africa in the index to his 1960 campaign speeches.)[42] Whatever its domestic political utility for a Democratic politician, it was also another testimony to the deep-seated American desire to identify with the aspirations of the new nations.

The new nations, for their part, insisted on their lack of interest in the Cold War U.S.-Soviet rivalry. As Julius Nyerere, leader of Tanzania (then Tanganyika), put it, "Our desire is to be friendly to every country in the world, but we have no desire to have a friendly country choosing our enemies for us."[43]

This is the kind of neutralism that had led John Foster Dulles to protest, and that led Vice President Nixon to worry that the United States should be "winning the battle for men's minds" in Africa. Kennedy mocked this notion in a June 1959 speech: "[T]he people of Africa are more interested in development than they are in doctrine. They are more interested in achieving a decent standard of living than following the standards of either East or West."[44] Kennedy more than doubled U.S. economic aid to Africa (to $459.6 million) in his first year in office, expanded the U.S. diplomatic presence in Africa, hosted twenty-six African heads of government at the White House, and preceded the United Nations in declaring an arms embargo against South Africa[45]—all of which can only be seen as a determined attempt to "win the battle for men's minds" in Africa, as he had chided Nixon for recommending.

There can be no doubt that Kennedy, for all his disavowals, was powerfully motivated by the competition with the Soviets. It was impossible to separate the generous program for Africa from the hope that it would appeal to the continent's peoples as a more attractive alternative to the Soviet and Chinese challenge to which Kennedy himself had so passionately called attention in the early months of 1961. The confidential report of an advisory committee warned the new president: "We see Africa as probably the greatest open field of maneuver in the worldwide competition" between the Communist bloc and the West.[46] Kennedy and many of his advisers may have believed, as Sanford Ungar comments, that the United States could court the emerging nations with "kindness, decency, and demonstrations of the success of the American free-market economy and open society."[47] But in the Belgian Congo, Kennedy was to discover that the game was played by rougher rules and that it was impossible to deal with Africa without attention to the Cold War overlay that inevitably imposed itself.

The Belgians deserve some sort of prize for one of the most disorderly exercises of decolonization. In 1960 they turned over power in the Congo to a left-wing radical government headed by Prime Minister Patrice Lumumba, which prompted mineral-rich Katanga Province, under the influence of Belgian mining interests, to secede. A civil war began that took on a Cold War dimension for a variety of reasons. As the largest and richest of the African colonies newly independent in 1960, the Congo was seen by both East and West as a potential leader or bellwether or trendsetter for the rest of Africa. The confrontation of leftist radicals versus monopoly capitalists could hardly avoid forcing outsiders to choose sides on ideological grounds. While the Soviets were not responsible for putting Lumumba into power, Khrushchev decided they had a stake in him: At a key moment in 1960, Khrushchev shipped aircraft, weapons, and military advisers to aid him. To the Eisenhower administration, this was another ominous development—an unprecedented projection of Soviet influence by military means in a place of strategic importance to the West, thousands of miles from Soviet borders.[48]

Lumumba was murdered by his opponents just at the time Kennedy came into office. (While the CIA seems to have wanted Lumumba's elimination, evidence of its direct involvement is elusive.)[49] The crisis continued, but the Congo turned out to be one place where the United States outmaneuvered the Soviets. Soviet help for Lumumba (and his leftist successor Antoine Gizenga) was woefully inadequate; likewise, help from surrogates like the egregious Nasser. The United Nations, embodied in its mystical secretary-general, Dag Hammarskjöld, and UN peacekeeping forces, tended to press for cease-fires, which objectively helped the Katangans survive the offensives of the Congolese army. Khrushchev embarrassed all his potential Third World allies by announcing his 100-megaton-bomb test on the eve of the first nonaligned summit, held in Belgrade in September 1961. The Kennedy administration pushed for a compromise between Katanga and the central government, which was not so difficult for us to contemplate, given that the central government had by then fallen under the sway of the pro-Western strongman Joseph Mobutu.

Hammarskjöld died in a plane crash in the Congo in September 1961.

Arkady Shevchenko, a high-ranking Soviet diplomat who was then handling UN affairs and later defected, takes seriously the speculation that
the Soviet Union may have had something to do with it; Soviet colleagues
told him of a report that KGB operatives had guided a group of Congolese
to shoot down the plane.[50] Other theories blame mercenaries hired by
American, British, and Belgian mining interests (though in this case the
motive is less clear).[51] In the end, the Congo crisis should have taught
the lesson that neither side in the Third World competition was likely to
prevail only by the purity of its motives.

As the Congo crisis subsided, the Kennedy administration tried by
various means to restore some sense of balance and perspective to the
overall U.S.-Soviet relationship. To counter the growing perception of
Soviet military superiority, Deputy Secretary of Defense Roswell Gilpatric
delivered a major speech to the Business Council on October 21, 1961,
enumerating the specifics of the strategic nuclear balance and demonstrating that for all Khrushchev's bluster and weapons testing, the United
States possessed overwhelming superiority in long-range missiles and
bombers and missile-carrying submarines.[52] Historian Michael Beschloss
is of the view that the Gilpatric speech humiliated Khrushchev and forced
him to contemplate some reckless action to restore the perception of the
strategic balance.[53] It is equally possible, however, that the speech was a
justifiable answer to the major strategic problem Kennedy faced, which
was the doubt about American resolve.

Kennedy's domestic problem was a reflection of this. He was the target
of a barrage of criticism from Republicans who essentially shared Khrushchev's assessment that he was weak. The administration responded by
confident pronouncements like the Gilpatric speech as well as by somewhat defensive rebuttals answering back the critics of the Right. A speech
in Minnesota on May 4, 1962, by Thomas L. Hughes, deputy director
of the State Department Bureau of Intelligence and Research, is an
example. Hughes criticized the "amateur anti-Communists" and "great
simplifiers"—the dogmatic, strident, bellicose critics who suffered from
a kind of "Cold War battle fatigue" and failed to comprehend the complex
new challenge that Khrushchev represented:

The Great Simplifiers—the amateur anti-Communists—in fact leave all
the really challenging questions unanswered.

How do we evaluate the changes now going on in the Soviet Union? The
amateur anti-Communists can't help us.

Will Khrushchev's successors be better or worse? The amateur anti-Communists aren't interested.

What is the spectrum of pressures, incentives, rejections, inducements, and initiatives which we can bring to bear on Soviet foreign policy?

What are the fundamental and what are the peripheral areas in our own policy vis-à-vis the Soviet Union? . . .

To none of these questions do the amateur anti-Communists have any constructive comments or suggestions.

They cannot contemplate the gradual possibility of a fractionalized Communist world without going to pieces themselves.

They are uncomfortable over any notions of complexity or movement inside the Sino-Soviet bloc. . . .

When it comes to the tactical uses of American power—a sophisticated application of pressures, toughness here, relative accommodation here, negotiations there, initiatives somewhere else—once more the amateur anti-Communists have few if any recommendations.

The Soviet challenge was indeed complex. Khrushchev was certainly more pragmatic as he wrestled with the Chinese and suffered setbacks like the Congo. But the near catastrophe into which he (and we) soon stumbled—namely, the Cuban Missile Crisis of October 1962—cannot be blamed on boisterous speeches either by Roswell Gilpatric inside the administration or by Republicans outside it. Nor is it entirely fair to lay the main blame on the administration for a hesitant foreign policy that may have misled Khrushchev into thinking he would win a high-stakes gamble. Nikita Khrushchev has to bear the responsibility himself for a reckless move. For just as he provoked a confrontation over Berlin in 1961, he provoked an even greater crisis in 1962 by secretly emplacing missiles in Cuba. The missile crisis turned out, of course, to be a major milestone in U.S.-Soviet relations, not only in the strategic relationship but also in the Third World.

The decision to install medium- and intermediate-range nuclear ballistic missiles in Cuba was, by all accounts, Khrushchev's, not Castro's. The Soviet leader's motivation, according to much of his own testimony, was to prevent another U.S.-sponsored invasion of Cuba.[54] Yet the context of the time suggests the incompleteness, if not disingenuousness, of such an explanation. American opposition to Castro after the Bay of Pigs, while indulging in incompetent and half-baked assassination plots, was decidedly nonmilitary. Khrushchev himself later admitted in his memoirs that an important part of his motivation was to equalize "what the West likes to call the balance of power" by giving his own shorter-range ballistic missiles a strategic capability against the United States.[55] And Berlin—perhaps the main prize—could not possibly have been far from his calculation. The Soviets let it be known through deliberate press leaks in early October that they were preparing a new diplomatic initiative on Berlin for November to coincide with a dramatic visit by Khrushchev to the UN General Assembly.[56] Thus, it is difficult to avoid the conclusion that Khrushchev had in mind the masterstroke of simultaneously redressing the strategic nuclear imbalance and reopening the Berlin issue on more advantageous terms.

Kennedy's great success in the Cuban Missile Crisis was to force the withdrawal of the threatening Soviet rockets, head off the Berlin crisis, and then engage Khrushchev in a more constructive dialogue on issues ranging from nuclear testing to economic relations. He accomplished this by imposing a limited naval blockade on Cuba and by gradually stepping up pressures on Cuba until the Soviets were induced to withdraw their missiles.

There were limits to the American victory, however. Castro's regime was left intact, still championing revolution throughout Latin America; not until Che Guevara was captured and killed by CIA-trained Bolivians in 1967 was the specter of endless warfare in Latin America to be laid to rest. An opportunity was missed in the missile crisis to force a change in Cuba's status: Brazilian president Joao Goulart—no stooge of the United States—had proposed that Cuba declare itself neutral and denuclearized in exchange for an American pledge not to invade it. The result, as a Latin diplomat put it, could have been the "Finlandization" of Cuba, disconnecting it decisively from its Soviet military patron. The administration, persuaded that the limitation of its objectives was the key to its success,[57] ignored the Brazilian initiative. "Select your objective carefully, for *if it is limited enough* you are quite likely to achieve it," wrote State Department official Harlan Cleveland, citing this as "Lesson No. 1" of the affair.[58] The Soviets, after initially distancing themselves from Cuba in the wake of the crisis, then found it safe to gradually resume and expand their role as Cuba's economic and military supplier.

Perhaps of even more significance was that the outcome of the missile crisis lulled the United States into an extraordinary complacency about the durability of its strategic nuclear superiority. Secretary of Defense McNamara told an interviewer in April 1965 that the Soviet leaders "have decided that they have lost the quantitative race, and they are not seeking to engage us in that contest. . . . [T]here is no indication that the Soviets are seeking to develop a strategic nuclear force as large as ours."[59] This, of course, was a major misjudgment.

The administration, just as it believed that the limitation of its objectives had been a key to its success, also talked itself into the assessment that our conventional superiority, especially our naval superiority in the Caribbean, had played *the* crucial role in the outcome. "[P]erhaps most significantly," Secretary McNamara told a group of NATO ministers in early 1963, "the forces that were the cutting edge of the action were the non-nuclear ones. Nuclear force was not irrelevant, but it was in the background. Non-nuclear forces were our sword, our nuclear forces were our shield."[60]

To Khrushchev and his successors, however, all this was nonsense. The Soviet assessment of the significance of *nuclear* weapons was made clear in Khrushchev's postcrisis speech to the Supreme Soviet on December 12, 1962, in answer to the Chinese, who were lambasting him for backing down: "If [imperialism] is a "paper tiger" now, those who say this know that this "paper tiger" has atomic teeth. It can put them to work; and it cannot be regarded frivolously."[61] And in his memoirs Khrushchev reaffirmed the point: "The experience of the Cuban crisis also convinced us that we were right to concentrate on the manufacture of nuclear missiles rather than on the expansion of our surface navy. . . ."[62]

Khrushchev and his successors, in any event, did not trouble themselves much over the intellectual problem of which category of weaponry had been the more important in Cuba. They began a massive program of rearmament in *all* categories of military power—nuclear and conventional, strategic and tactical naval, air, and ground. This was to affect the American reaction in another crisis—the 1973 war in the Middle East—when the strategic balance was no longer favorable to us, as it had been in Cuba. Contrary to the Kennedy administration's assumption, the ability to escalate to a higher level of violence *is* relevant to the outcome of a crisis; the overall balance is a central part of the context that determines a side's willingness to take risks. This was very much in Henry Kissinger's mind in the 1973 crisis, when the Soviets threatened to intervene in the Sinai and U.S. forces went on alert to face them down. ("This is the last time we'll ever be able to get away with this,"

Kissinger lamented to his aides.)[63] Nikita Khrushchev understood all this perfectly well in 1962.

That being said, in retrospect it is also clear that the Cuban Missile Crisis set a limit to U.S.-Soviet confrontation in the Third World. Aside from that momentary face-off at the end of the 1973 Middle East war, the two superpowers never again allowed a Third World conflict to drag them to such a point of direct confrontation. Perhaps this was the result of circumstance; most of the succeeding conflicts were more in the nature of conflicts by proxy, even in Vietnam and Afghanistan. But Cuba had also probably brought home the realization that no Third World issue was important enough to risk nuclear war. Khrushchev said as much in his riposte to the Chinese, quoted above. As we shall see, however, the violence in the Third World, fueled by the doctrine of "wars of national liberation," had by no means run its course.

5

VIETNAM AND ITS STRATEGIC
CONSEQUENCES

Ho Chi Minh, father of the Indochinese Revolution, was a young expatriate scraping for a living in Europe when he was caught up in the political cause of anticolonialism and Vietnamese independence. In a rented tuxedo he appeared at the Versailles Peace Conference in 1919, where he presented an eight-point program of grievances and pleas for Vietnamese autonomy. The assembled peacemakers, as we have seen in chapter 1, applied the Wilsonian principle of self-determination rather selectively, and the appeal of the young Vietnamese nationalist went unheeded. In 1920, a friend showed him a copy of Lenin's *Theses on the National and Colonial Questions*, which had been published in the French Socialist party newspaper *L'Humanité*. Like M. N. Roy, he was enormously impressed. Ho later wrote:

These theses contained political terms that were difficult to understand. However, by reading them several times over I managed to get the gist of them. Lenin's theses roused me to great emotion, great enthusiasm, great faith, and helped me see the problems clearly. My joy was so great that at times I was reduced to tears. Alone in my room, I would cry out as though standing before a great crowd: 'My beloved, downtrodden, luckless compatriots! This is what we need, this our road to freedom!'
After that, I put all my trust in Lenin and the Third International.[1]

In September 1920, Ho attended the notorious Comintern gathering in Baku (the "Congress of the Peoples of the East") and unlike M. N. Roy, he was impressed with this, too. In December, back in Paris, he took part in the founding of the French Communist party. Ho remained an active worker for the Comintern in the 1920s, organizing Vietnamese Communists while based in China. When the Second World War began, he organized Vietnamese resistance to the Japanese occupation and, of course, simultaneously prepared for a war of independence against the French.[2]

During and after the war, Ho Chi Minh made contact with U.S. officials, lying to them flatly in 1946 that he was not a Communist.[3] The United States remained wary of Ho throughout the Truman administration, knowing full well of his Communist loyalties, even while adopting a hands-off posture toward French colonialism. The United States linked itself more closely with the French only after the Communist victory in China in 1949 (one of many grievances the Vietnamese must nurse against their Chinese "comrades").

A debate has raged ever since then over whether Ho Chi Minh was more a nationalist or a Communist. Was his radicalism only triggered by the rejection of his plea at Versailles? Did the United States miss an opportunity during and after World War II to establish a relationship with his independence movement and turn him into an "Asian Tito," a nominally Communist ruler maintaining his independence from any Soviet or Chinese imperial designs? Most of those who advance the thesis do not dispute that Ho was a convinced Communist; rather, they argue that he subordinated his ideology to his aims as a nationalist and that our geopolitical interest should have been to separate him from Soviet or Chinese influence, not to push him into the arms of those two Communist powers.[4]

The answers are probably unknowable. A similar debate recurs again and again in the history of America's relations with Third World radicals, whether Gamal Abdel Nasser or Mao Zedong or Fidel Castro or Daniel Ortega: One school of thought sees this radicalism as implacably hostile to us, driven by its core ideology, only to be combated. Others see the hostility as rooted in circumstances, to be eased by more conciliatory policies on our part.

In the Vietnamese case, certain things do seem clear. There can be no doubt of Hanoi's determination to dominate all of Vietnam plus Laos and Cambodia, its immediate neighbors: "Indochina is a strategic unit, a single theater of operations," avowed Gen. Vo Nguyen Giap in 1950. "Therefore, we have the task of helping to liberate all of Indochina. . . ."[5] Likewise, there is no doubt of the brutality and ideological rigidity of Hanoi's practice of governance, which was thoroughly Stalinist. Yet Ho Chi Minh was not the stooge of either Moscow or Beijing, and it is not impossible that the *global* strategic consequences for the United States of a nationalist Communist Indochina in the 1940s might have been manageable—and certainly would not have been as damaging as the involvement that the United States later undertook, with all its disastrous impact on our body politic. Even more than Korea, Indochina was the kind of peripheral engagement that Walter Lippmann had warned against when containment was born in 1947.

Whatever the strategic implications of Ho's nationalism, the implications *within* Vietnam were, in the end, fatal to the French and, later, the American effort. By his leadership of the independence struggle against the French, Ho Chi Minh won for his movement a credential of Vietnamese patriotism that proved impossible for any others to match. In 1950, the French (with U.S. diplomatic support) installed the emperor Bao Dai as head of a quasi-independent Vietnam. Later, the United States would back Ngo Dinh Diem and then a succession of military figures, most notably Nguyen Van Thieu, as leaders of South Vietnam. All would strive mightily to establish their own nationalist legitimacy, to shape a society with the moral cohesion to fight for *its* independence against the military and political onslaught of the North. They failed.

Acutely aware of the problem, the Americans would strive to enhance the legitimacy of their South Vietnamese clients by insisting on democratic reforms. While internal democracy seemed no part of North Vietnam's strength (on the contrary), this effort was believed to hold the key to the South's cohesion and will to fight. The lesson of the failure of Chiang Kai-shek's Chinese Nationalist regime, as spelled out in the State Department's 1949 "White Paper," was seen as bolstering the argument. Defined this way, however, the problem was insoluble, since the time frame for a Third World country's evolution into a democracy is far longer, even in the best of circumstances, than the time frame for winning a war. The task of creating a civil society is difficult enough in Third World countries with non-Western traditions; to achieve this while fighting off an invading army and armed insurgents is probably impossible. The South Vietnamese were whipsawed between their implacable enemy in Hanoi and their importunate ally in Washington.[6]

Pressure on the authoritarian Diem to reform was nonetheless a constant feature of the Eisenhower administration's policy. Likewise, the Kennedy administration. "Looking under bushes for the Vietnamese George Washington," Gen. Maxwell Taylor called it.[7] The heavy-handedness of the Kennedy policy (which resulted in Diem's murder during a U.S.-encouraged coup) needs no elaboration here.[8] Lyndon Johnson came into office intending to downplay the push for reform,[9] but the impulse had a life of its own. Even during the supposedly hard-nosed Nixon administration, under mounting pressure from Congress and public opinion, the United States exerted its leverage vigorously on the South Vietnamese to create a structure of pluralistic politics and free elections.

Such a policy was, at bottom, a mass of contradictions. "Colonialism by ventriloquy" is William Odom's sarcastic description of the American approach.[10] Like the British in the nineteenth century, we wanted to uplift the quality of our client's internal administration, but unlike the British in the nineteenth century, we had anticolonialist scruples that ruled out taking direct control. The result was clumsy, unremitting—and demeaning—pressure from far away, which, despite its supposed indirection, undercut the prestige of the very client we were trying to build up. By the time of the Nixon administration, of course, the United States was also disengaging from Vietnam, so the humiliating image of colonial dictation to a client was compounded by the image of the colonial patron simultaneously abandoning its client.

By the end, South Vietnam was a democratic paragon by regional standards, with a multiparty system and an obstreperous press. The moral importance of this should not be slighted. In its practical effect, however, it cannot be demonstrated to have won South Vietnam the legitimacy that its advocates implicitly assured would follow. In part, this was because the loudest American advocates of democratic reform gave the reforming leadership in Saigon no credit or respite from continuing pressures.[11] In perhaps greater part, it was because North Vietnam's advantage lay not only in its nationalist credential but in its totalitarian discipline and the utter ruthlessness of the war it waged against the hapless South.

Did the advocacy of democratic reform miss the point of what was at issue? Or did it not go far enough? Was there a fatal flaw inherent all along in the historical weakness of South Vietnam's claim to a national identity? All this, too, is probably unknowable. But the democratic merits or demerits of our Third World allies have been a recurring preoccupation of our foreign policy, and the dilemmas persist.

KENNEDY AND JOHNSON

When French forces were overwhelmed at Dien Bien Phu in 1954, President Eisenhower rejected the recommendation of some in his administration to intervene militarily to save them.[12] A war hero, Eisenhower was not afraid of political attack on his right flank on such an issue. Nor did John Foster Dulles, the scourge of neutralism, object to the 1954 Geneva Accords that (at least in theory) established the neutrality of the Indochinese states. The area seemed remote from America's most important strategic concerns.

It was in the Kennedy administration that this changed. As we have seen, Kennedy was confronted in early 1961 by a challenge in Laos that was attributable to a Soviet airlift of arms to the Communist Pathet Lao and that seemed to embody the menacing Khrushchevian doctrine of "wars of national liberation." A Communist takeover in Laos would put South Vietnam inevitably at greater risk. The Soviet intervention involved only a few million dollars in small arms, but it has been termed "probably the most politically successful military effort made under Khrushchev."[13] The Soviet airlift enabled the Pathet Lao to rout the U.S.-backed forces and to control four-fifths of the country by May 1961, shortly after the airlift began. The United States sued for peace.

Ironically, after the Cuban Missile Crisis the American attitude toward Soviet foreign policy became much less alarmist, yet American policy in Indochina was impelled by a strange momentum. There is evidence that Khrushchev was even reducing the Soviet investment in Indochina, which he considered of minor importance.[14] As Khrushchev's quarrel with Mao burst into the open, moreover, there seemed no doubt in the West that the Soviet leader wore the white hat. On most issues of relations with the West, the Soviets—especially after the missile crisis—seemed the more conciliatory, with the Chinese position degenerating into a rabid anti-Americanism. In a televised interview on December 17, 1962, Kennedy observed that Khrushchev "realizes how dangerous a world we live in" and therefore that we were "better off with the Khrushchev view" than with the Chinese. The tone and substance of U.S.-Soviet relations improved enormously. The pressure on Berlin ceased. Kennedy made a conciliatory speech at American University in Washington on June 10, 1963, proposing to complete a ban on nuclear tests in the atmosphere (putting an end to all the multimegaton fireworks); it was soon accomplished.

The mood of the time was captured in our culture. The 1966 film *The Russians Are Coming! The Russians Are Coming!* told of a Soviet submarine stranded off the coast of a Connecticut holiday island, its sailors rescued by Americans in a celebration of a new spirit of cooperation.[15] As an indicator of how far this new trend reached, even Ian Fleming's James Bond oeuvre, and the films it spawned, began to portray MI6, the CIA, and the KGB battling on the same side against more radical and destructive forces, which were sometimes freelance but other times aligned with the Chinese.

None of this seemed to affect U.S. concern over Vietnam. In part, the deepening U.S. commitment was driven by Kennedy and Johnson's political fear of "losing Vietnam," as Truman and Acheson had been vilified for "losing China." But also, as the administration's argumentation made clear, the problem of guerrilla war was still viewed in strategic terms. The vulnerability of Western positions in the Third World seemed still a serious problem; the moral unacceptability of letting the Communists capture by force of arms the legitimate aspirations of ex–colonial peoples seemed still a global imperative; the West still needed to show that it could defeat guerrilla insurgencies as a practical matter. The ideological inspiration for the threat, however, was now no longer the Soviet Union but China.

As the American involvement in Indochina deepened in the mid-1960s, the Chinese threat became paramount. After all, it was Mao who had brilliantly created and elaborated the modern doctrine of guerrilla warfare. Nor could anyone doubt the virulence of Chinese ideological hostility to the West and to Western influence in the Third World. "The rulers of Hanoi are urged on by Peiping,"* President Lyndon Johnson declared in a speech at Johns Hopkins University on April 7, 1965; the struggle in Vietnam was "part of a wider pattern of aggressive purposes." The anti-Chinese rationale of the American involvement reached its apogee in September 1965 (after Johnson's buildup of combat troops and bombing had begun), when Chinese minister of defense Marshal Lin Biao published "Long Live the Victory of People's War!," a long article that discussed Vietnam in the context of a long diatribe on the need for revolutionary upheaval in the Third World.[16] Lin Biao's seventeen-thousand-word manifesto immediately took the place in American demonology that Khrushchev's January 1961 speech on "wars of national liberation" had occupied four and a half years earlier.

What was menacing in Lin Biao's thesis was the vivid way he described how the lessons learned by the Chinese Communists in their successful guerrilla wars against both the Nationalists and the Japanese could now be applied by the Third World as a whole against Western imperialism. Just as the Chinese Communists developed their power in the vast countryside of China and then encircled and strangled their enemies in the cities, similarly the contemporary world revolution in Asia, Africa, and Latin America occupied the "rural base areas" from which it could ultimately surround and defeat "the cities of the world," namely, the imperialist strongholds of North America and Western Europe. The Third World thus represented the main battlefront against imperialism and now had an unstoppable strategy for winning the war for world revolution.

It was not entirely a new formulation. The Chinese had long believed that the methods that had worked for them could well apply elsewhere.

---

*"Peiping" was the name the Nationalist Chinese still gave to Beijing, which the Communists had renamed when they made it their capital.

Lin and Mao's revolutionary colleague Liu Shaoqi had made such an observation as far back as 1949.[17] It reflected some of Mao's original contribution to the Leninist doctrine of revolutionary war, such as the mobilization of the peasantry. Likewise, Mao (like M. N. Roy in 1920), from the perspective of an authentic Third Worlder, had always laid stress on the historical importance of the anticolonial struggle in the Third World in its own right, as the main front of the struggle against Western imperialism and not simply a flanking maneuver.

While not new, however, the theory of "people's war" was elaborated more fully by the Chinese under the stimulus of the rivalry with the Soviets in the 1960s. It was another rebuke to the Soviets for their seeming reluctance to press the fight against the imperialists. Unlike Soviet "revisionism," Chinese ideology did not shrink from encouraging the world's peoples to make the transition to socialism through armed revolution.[18]

Lin Biao's article touched explicitly on Vietnam: "Viet Nam is the most convincing current example of a victim of aggression defeating U.S. imperialism by a people's war. . . . The U.S. aggressors are in danger of being swamped in the people's war in Viet Nam. They are deeply worried that their defeat in Viet Nam will lead to a chain reaction. They are expanding the war in an attempt to save themselves from defeat. But the more they expand the war, the greater will be the chain reaction."[19] To American policymakers already steeped in the Maoist lore, this was a defiant thrust, and it impressed the Johnson administration as a confirmation of the broader strategic significance of what they faced in Vietnam. Vietnam was—for both the Americans and the Chinese—the test case of a global strategy of revolution.

Other analysts, reading Lin Biao's text more closely, found different signals. According to a RAND Corporation study in November 1965, the more significant passages in Lin's manifesto were the operational paragraphs in which he stressed the need for "self-reliance." The Vietnamese Communists could win, Lin seemed to be saying, only if they relied primarily on their own resources and their own revolutionary spirit. Similarly, Lin seemed to be offering comradely criticism of Hanoi's political and military strategy. While the Chinese pledged more assistance, the thrust of the message (in this interpretation) was that the Vietnamese were basically on their own.[20] Mao, after all, had told writer Edgar Snow earlier in the year that China had no troops outside her own frontiers and had no intention of fighting anybody unless her own territory was attacked.[21]

The Johnson administration found no consolation in any of this. To them, the problem was China's growing influence as the fount of militancy, coupled with the frustrating effectiveness of guerrilla strategy. Secretary of State Dean Rusk told the Far East and Pacific Subcommittee of the House Foreign Affairs Committee on March 16, 1966, that the Chinese continued to seek dominance in Asia as well as leadership of the international Communist movement: "Peiping is striving to restore traditional Chinese influence or dominance in South, Southeast, and East Asia." Nor was Rusk impressed by RAND-style analysis that Beijing's active, material support for revolutions was limited:

> It is true that this doctrine calls for revolution by the natives of each country. In that sense it may be considered a "do-it-yourself kit." But Peiping is prepared to train and indoctrinate the leaders of these revolutions and to support them with funds, arms, and propaganda, as well as politically. . . .

> Peiping has sought to promote Communist coups and "wars of liberation" against independent governments in Africa and Latin America as well as in Asia.

VIETNAM AND CUBA

Another feature of the Kennedy-Johnson team's approach to Vietnam deserves to be noted. Fidel Castro's comrade Che Guevara used to boast that the Third World would inflict "one, two, three, many Vietnams" on the West. In an ironic twist, after the triumph of the Cuban Missile Crisis, American officials decided optimistically that Vietnam could be another Cuba.

From their success in crisis management and the skillful use of power in the Cuban affair of October 1962, they drew specific lessons. The gradual escalation of American military pressures during the week of that crisis—verbal warnings backed by menacing and well-publicized troop deployments around the Caribbean—seemed an attractive example of how, in the nuclear age, one could apply power without actually having to use it. The crisis had "extraordinary pedagogical importance," White House national security adviser McGeorge Bundy insisted afterward.[22] It vindicated the sophisticated reasoning of academic strategists and bargaining theorists like Thomas C. Schelling of Harvard, who had written in his classic *The Strategy of Conflict* that strategy, properly conceived, was "not concerned with the efficient *application* of force but with the *exploitation of potential force*." Thus, in the nuclear age a strategy of deterrence was "a theory of the skillful *nonuse* of military forces."[23]

Under Secretary of State George Ball saw as one lesson of Cuba "the wisdom—indeed the necessity—of the measured response." Instead of launching an immediate air strike, the president had escalated pressures gradually, which gave flexibility to American policy. The president chose, as Ball put it in an address to NATO parliamentarians on November 16, 1962, to "avoid resort to an immediate use of force that might have led the United States and the Soviet Union, and with them their allies, up an ascending scale of violence. That choice enabled the President to gain time. . . . Lastly, it enabled him to keep—and he still keeps—an option for further pressure if the situation should require it."

Others repeated the theme. Defense Secretary McNamara told the Senate Armed Services Committee on February 20, 1963, that the "power of escalation" had been an important component of the "controlled response" that had signaled to the Soviet Union our determination to achieve our objective in the Cuban crisis.[24] Assistant Secretary of State Harlan Cleveland, in a *Foreign Affairs* article on crisis diplomacy in July 1963, cited Cuba as an example of the maxim "Creep Up Carefully on the Use of Force." Echoing Schelling's bargaining theory, Cleveland explained:

> The use of force in a dangerous world demands adherence to a doctrine of restraint—the cool, calm, and collected manipulation of power for collective security—and the sophisticated mixture of diplomacy with that power. . . . [F]orce is just another manner of speaking—with a rather expensive vocabulary. But if force is to be a persuasive form of discourse, its modulations must carry not only the latent threat of more force but equally the assurance that it is under the personal control of responsible men.[25]

Arthur M. Schlesinger, Jr., in his memoir A *Thousand Days*, praised the president's "combination of toughness and restraint . . . so brilliantly controlled, so matchlessly calibrated, that dazzled the world."[26]

One of the most important consequences of this line of analysis—the faith in the fine-tuning of force—was the effect it had on our unfolding involvement in Vietnam within a few years of the events in the Caribbean. The analogy of the Cuban Missile Crisis—the "slow, judicious" use of power "signaling clearly and cautiously their intentions"—was vivid in the minds of McNamara and others in early 1965 as they developed the plan of gradually escalated bombing that marked our first direct military involvement in Indochina, David Halberstam later recorded.[27] Johnson aide Bill Moyers was a witness:

> [T]here was an unspoken assumption in Washington that a major war was something that could be avoided if we injected just a little power at a time.

There was an assumption that the people in Hanoi would interpret the beginning of the bombing and the announcement of a major buildup as signals of resolve on our part which implied greater resistance to come if they did not change their plans. . . . There was a confidence—it was never bragged about, it was just there—a residue, perhaps, of the confrontation over the missiles in Cuba—that when the chips were really down, the other people would fold.[28]

The "Pentagon Papers" and other documents bear this out. A memorandum from Walt Rostow, then head of the State Department Planning Staff, to Secretary Rusk on November 23, 1964, spoke of the need to convey some "decisive signal" to the North Vietnamese that we were prepared to prevent their conquest of Indochina. Rostow recommended an initial introduction of U.S. ground forces and retaliation against North Vietnam coupled with the same kind of "determination and staying power" that we had shown in Cuba as well as Berlin.[29]

Even where Cuba is not mentioned, the same conceptual apparatus recurs with unmistakable frequency. Thus, McGeorge Bundy, en route home after a visit to Saigon, wrote a lengthy memorandum to President Johnson on February 7, 1965, recommending a bombing strategy of "graduated and continuing reprisal" in which the "level of force and pressure" would "begin at a low level" and "be increased only gradually." Its aim was not to "win" an air war in the North but to "influence the course of the struggle in the South."[30] Maxwell Taylor, by then our ambassador in South Vietnam, similarly favored "a measured, controlled sequence of actions" against North Vietnam, but in his mind the focus should be on influencing Hanoi's behavior—to give its leaders "serious doubts as to their chances for ultimate success."[31] Adm. U. S. G. Sharp, our Pacific commander, also endorsed a " 'graduated pressures' philosophy" that would convey "steady, relentless movement toward our objective of convincing Hanoi and Peiping of the prohibitive cost to them of their program of subversion, insurgency and aggression" in Southeast Asia.[32] President Johnson cabled to Ambassador Taylor on February 8, 1965, that he had approved a plan for "continuing action" against North Vietnam "with modifications up and down in tempo and scale in the light of your recommendations . . . and our own continuing review of the situation."[33]

Thus began Lyndon Johnson's initial bombing campaign over North Vietnam known as Rolling Thunder. One of its purposes, Admiral Sharp wrote in a summary report in 1968, was "to drive home to the North

Vietnamese leaders that our staying power was superior to their own."[34] This of course is precisely what it did *not* do. The fine-tuned, constrained, and demonstrative uses of force, which according to the administration's rationales were to convey our willingness to commit overwhelming power, implied, in fact, the opposite: that we were not really eager or willing to engage ourselves more fully. If the hope was to *avoid* a major commitment of American troops and American power, as indeed it was, then the North Vietnamese were as capable of discerning this strategy as we were of devising it.

Twenty months later, at the end of December 1966, North Vietnamese premier Pham Van Dong gave *New York Times* correspondent Harrison Salisbury his own assessment of the relative staying power of the two sides. The escalation of our bombing had made no decisive military difference, said the premier. North Vietnam had adjusted to the early difficulties and was now prepared to outlast us—to fight on for ten years, twenty years, as long as needed.[35] Pham Van Dong turned out to be right.

It was not the Cuban Missile Crisis that enmeshed us in Vietnam, of course. But one can easily trace how certain intellectual preconceptions that administration figures had seen as vindicated in Cuba turned up again in the same vocabulary when basic decisions were being made in Vietnam. The phenomenon was a tribute to the power of academic theories in the minds of sophisticated men. Thus did the Kennedy and Johnson administrations combine panic at the strategic level with hubris at the tactical level—a sure formula for a fiasco.

NIXON AND THE SOVIETS: "LINKAGE"

The strategic rationale for our Vietnam intervention, as articulated by the Kennedy and Johnson administrations, seems, with the benefit of hindsight, to have been seriously wrong. Vietnam was considered a test case of Communist, particularly Chinese Communist, theories of revolutionary guerrilla warfare that had global implications and had to be blocked if upheaval was not to engulf the Third World. However, soon after Lyndon Johnson's major escalation of U.S. combat involvement in 1965, China found itself convulsed for a decade in the internal madness of the "Great Proletarian Socialist Cultural Revolution." Even Lin Biao's manifesto of September 1965 on "people's war," as we have seen, mitigated its sweeping global visions with subtle indications that China's contribution to other countries' revolutions would be verbal and little else. Within a few years, moreover, heavy-handed Soviet military pressures against China would force China to call off its revolutionary militancy and turn, in some desperation, to the West.

North Vietnam's assault on the South turns out in retrospect to have been mainly the reflection of Hanoi's own thirty-year drive for regional hegemony, not a Soviet or Chinese global campaign. It is possible to regard Hanoi's relentless drive for regional domination as evil and morally worthy of resistance (as I do) and yet to conclude with Lippmann that it was the wrong place strategically for such a huge, and ultimately exhausting, American effort. Whether North Vietnam was a geopolitical menace posing a wider global threat can be legitimately questioned. (The point has been made, however, that U.S. combat intervention in Vietnam was a necessary psychological precondition for Indonesia's successful resistance to the Communist takeover attempt in the fall of 1965.[36] That argument deserves to be taken seriously, given Indonesia's strategic importance and the degree to which the United States had already committed its prestige in South Vietnam in the early 1960s.)

When Richard Nixon entered the White House on January 20, 1969, in any case, the American commitment in Vietnam was an inherited fact. The task he faced was how to get out. Nixon spent little time in his public rhetoric or private rumination regurgitating the rationale for getting in. For one thing, the preoccupation with guerrilla warfare was gone. The Vietcong had been shattered in the Tet offensive; according to our military's assessment, two-thirds of the fighting was now being done by North Vietnamese army (NVA) regular units.[37] For another thing, Nixon and his White House adviser Henry Kissinger made sure that the antiChinese rationale for our involvement was abruptly dropped. From the very first weeks of the administration, Nixon and Kissinger were exploring paths to rapprochement with Beijing.[38]

The Soviets, however, were reserved a special role. During his 1968 presidential campaign, Nixon had promised to end the war but kept silent about how he planned to go about it. This was transmogrified into a journalistic cliché that he had claimed he had a "secret plan." He never actually said this.[39] On the other hand, he did have in mind an approach that he felt the Johnson administration had not tried hard enough—namely, using our leverage with the Soviets to get them to use their influence with Hanoi. When Nixon and Kissinger came into office, they devised the theory of "linkage," with Vietnam uppermost in mind.

Linkage was the theory that the various issues on which the United States and Soviet Union interacted should be viewed as interconnected. Nixon and Kissinger did not believe that arms control negotiations, for example, could or should be able to proceed in isolation from other issues reflecting the political sources of tension, such as Berlin or Third World conflicts in Vietnam or the Middle East. More positively, it was believed that an improvement in U.S.-Soviet relations would be more durable if it proceeded on a broad front, embracing progress on the regional conflicts as well as more central issues. Kissinger used to remark that linkage was not a theory but a fact of life.[40] This interconnection of events was later proved true by reality—both negatively, when the Soviet invasion of Afghanistan in 1979 doomed the SALT II Treaty, and positively, when progress on the regional issues (especially the Soviet withdrawal from Afghanistan) played a key role in the extraordinary improvement of relations toward the end of the Reagan administration.

But linkage was also a strategy, not merely an observation. Nixon sent his senior officials a letter on February 4, 1969, two weeks after his inauguration, saying he believed in such a strategy: Progress would have to be made on a broad front; the Soviets could not be allowed to use arms control as a "safety valve" to relieve tensions they created in the regions of conflict. Arms control and economic relations were to be slowed down until there was progress on Vietnam and the Middle East.[41]

One point of interest here is bureaucratic. The Department of State, more matter-of-fact in its approach to diplomacy and skeptical that this obviously Kissinger-inspired letter really reflected Nixon's thinking, ignored the presidential letter and charged ahead on arms control and other matters. They got their way on some issues. It was a Pyrrhic victory, however, because it confirmed Nixon's worst suspicions of the disloyalty of the Department of State and decided him on opening up special White House backchannels to the Soviets, relying on Kissinger and Soviet ambassador Anatolii Dobrynin.[42]

Nixon and Kissinger then had the idea of using this special channel to Moscow to try to force an early end to the Vietnam War. A special emissary—Cyrus Vance was sounded out—would go to Moscow, authorized to begin talks on arms control with the Soviets and simultaneously to meet secretly with senior North Vietnamese officials. The U.S. emissary would have a mandate to make significant moves in both areas (and to try to keep them in tandem). The idea was floated to Dobrynin— but the Soviets never replied. Dobrynin, pressed later by Kissinger, intimated that Hanoi had not approved it.[43] The Soviets always pleaded that they had little influence with Hanoi. The North Vietnamese presumably wanted their freedom of action, without Soviet meddling.

This Soviet evasiveness was a smart tactic and, in retrospect, inevitable. The Americans seemed to be on the run—Nixon had already begun a gradual process of unilateral withdrawals—and the Soviets had minimal incentive to spend political capital with their North Vietnamese ally when everyone could see the public pressures pushing us out. The Soviets hid behind the negotiations that had begun the year before in Paris: They always claimed they supported those negotiations and hoped for a solution, and successfully avoided being roped into any greater obligation to us.

Later, in 1972, the Soviets did provide us with invaluable help on Vietnam, but they (and we) stumbled into it.

The sequence of events needs to be recalled. Kissinger and North Vietnamese Politburo strategist Le Duc Tho had been meeting secretly for a year and a half (in yet another backchannel relationship from which the State Department was excluded), but these talks had broken off in January 1972. In February, Nixon made his historic visit to Beijing. At the end of March, the North Vietnamese army launched a major ground invasion south across the Demilitarized Zone; as at Tet in 1968, they apparently hoped for a knockout blow that would shatter the administration's resolve in a presidential election year. Scheduled for May was Nixon's summit visit to Moscow. In between the North Vietnamese invasion and the scheduled May summit, Nixon thus confronted a fateful decision on whether and how to respond to the North Vietnamese escalation. The major option being considered was a dramatic American escalation of the war—resuming the bombing of North Vietnam that President Johnson had halted, plus mining the harbors of Hanoi and Haiphong (in effect a blockade).

As Nixon mulled his decision, Kissinger was sent off to Moscow secretly in April 1972. (I was a member of his team.) Leonid Brezhnev—rather foolishly, as it turned out—offered to assist us in getting the Kissinger-Tho talks back on track. We had no need for the Soviets as a messenger; we had our own channels of communication with the North Vietnamese. But we let the Soviets pass a procedural proposal to Hanoi, which Hanoi accepted. Kissinger and Le Duc Tho met as arranged in Paris on May 2.

The meeting in Paris turned out to be a farce. The North Vietnamese, elated by the military success of their offensive, were at their most arrogant and intransigent. In fact, they played into Nixon's hands, since when he announced the mining and bombing on May 8, he revealed the disastrous encounter in Paris as proof that the United States had no recourse except military action to restore the balance.

The Soviets now faced the mortifying choice of whether to let Nixon proceed to Moscow for a state visit exactly two weeks after he had begun pummeling a Soviet ally. They were embarrassed that the meeting they had set up had turned out so badly. More important, Brezhnev and his colleagues had had, in the week-long discussions with Kissinger in April, a tantalizing look at all they had at stake in keeping U.S.-Soviet relations on a steady course. For one thing, arms control—especially the Anti-Ballistic Missile (ABM) Treaty that reassured the Soviets against any U.S. breakthroughs in ABM technology. Second, Europe—where Willy Brandt's "Eastern treaties" accepting postwar borders in Eastern Europe, awaiting ratification, were hanging by a thread in the Bundestag and the Soviets had to fear that a revival of East-West tensions would doom their whole German policy.[44] Next, economic relations, about which Brezhnev practically drooled as he imagined broad vistas of U.S. investment, trade, and technical assistance for the sluggish Soviet economy. Brezhnev had to contemplate all these potential losses—not to mention leaving the United States in bed with the hated Chinese, whom Nixon had just visited. All of this had to be weighed against the principle of fidelity to a socialist ally several thousand kilometers away who had launched a major offensive at the worst possible time and had embarrassed Brezhnev by pigheaded behavior at a negotiating meeting he had helped set up.

The North Vietnamese were apoplectic during this period, denouncing both Moscow and Beijing for succumbing to "the Machiavellian policy of reconciliation with U.S. imperialists . . . who are now attempting to lure us into the path of compromise."[45] The Soviets nevertheless proceeded with Nixon's Moscow visit in May 1972 as if nothing had happened. While it was a hair-raising experience at the time to wait to learn the Soviets' response to Nixon's escalation, in retrospect Brezhnev's decision is not difficult to understand.[46]

The episode was the epitome of linkage. The Soviets had by then too much of a stake in the American relationship, including positive incentives (such as economic relations and arms control benefits) and the fear of penalties (China, Brandt's *Ostpolitik*). The difference between 1969 and 1972 was that the United States had acquired all this considerable leverage in the interim.

The immediate American gain was that the Moscow summit guaranteed Nixon's Vietnam policy for the remainder of the year. The antiwar critics' assault on him for this major escalation—this reckless act that seemed to put all his other accomplishments at risk—was blown away in an instant by the Soviets' willingness to proceed with the summit. Nixon had a free hand. The U.S. military campaign blunted the North Vietnamese invasion and produced a breakthrough in the negotiations in October; Nixon won reelection by a huge margin. The North Vietnamese felt even more betrayed by the Soviets, and with good reason. All this needs to be borne in mind when reading criticisms of the "naive" Nixon-Kissinger policy toward the Soviet Union.

After the 1973 Paris Agreement, the Soviets curtailed their arms supply to North Vietnam. The U.S. government's own information was that shipment of significant equipment such as antiaircraft weaponry was suspended (no longer needed since U.S. bombing had ended), while ammunition and some logistical equipment continued at modest levels. The Soviets increased economic aid and canceled North Vietnam's debts.[47] Foreign Minister Andrei Gromyko tried to soothe Kissinger over lunch at the Soviet embassy in February 1974 with the assurance that the Soviet interest was to have "quiet" in Indochina. Only as the war heated up again in 1974, and as it became clear that the U.S. Congress was imposing severe constraints on U.S. aid to Saigon, did Soviet-bloc military and economic aid to North Vietnam expand sharply again. But that is another story.

STRATEGIC CONSEQUENCES

Nixon's strategy in Vietnam had two tracks—one, a negotiating track and, two, a policy of gradual unilateral withdrawals of U.S. troops coupled with stepped-up training and equipping of the Army of the Republic of Vietnam (the so-called Vietnamization of the war). The intention was to give the South Vietnamese the maximum chance to survive. While, at a minimum, it was to leave a "decent interval" between the American exit and whatever fate might be in store for the South Vietnamese, the expectation in the Nixon administration—especially after the 1970 operation against the NVA sanctuaries across the Cambodian border—was that, in proper conditions, they could indeed survive.

Kissinger had long been a skeptic of the war's chances of success, and he was even gloomier in the immediate aftermath of the controversial Cambodian operation, when the United States was torn apart by a near civil war; hence, the apocalyptic Spenglerian ruminations that Adm. Elmo Zumwalt says he heard from Kissinger in the fall of 1970 about America's inability to function as a major power.[48] But as the military results of the Cambodian operation became better understood—it virtually ended the NVA threat in the southern half of South Vietnam, the most populous part of the country—Kissinger changed his view, becoming convinced that the South Vietnamese had a good chance to make it if the United States gave them adequate help. Adequate help meant withdrawing our forces in a controlled way and not negotiating any agreement that denied us the ability to continue arming and supplying the South Vietnamese.

For both Nixon and Kissinger, this was a point of principle, both on moral and on strategic grounds. They modeled themselves after French president Charles de Gaulle, who extricated France from Algeria carefully over a four-year period,

> because [in Kissinger's words] he, too, thought it important for France to emerge from its travails with its domestic cohesion and international stature intact. He extricated France from Algeria as an act of policy, not as a collapse, in a manner reflecting a national decision and not a rout.

> Such an ending of the war was even more important for the United States. As the leader of democratic alliances we had to remember that scores of countries and millions of people relied for their security on our willingness to stand by allies, indeed on our confidence in ourselves.[49]

The sticking point in the negotiation with North Vietnam was not some exorbitant American demand. Our own proposal was that we would withdraw *totally* as part of a settlement so long as there was a cease-fire, a return of prisoners of war, and an accounting of those missing in action. We would leave the political future of the country for Hanoi and Saigon to settle by—we hoped—political means. The sticking point in the negotiation was that we were being asked, in addition, to overthrow our own ally on our way out: The North Vietnamese insisted that we agree to decapitate and dismantle the South Vietnamese government and put in its place a tripartite coalition easily dominated by the Communists. (That tripartite coalition would then negotiate formally with the Communists!) This we were not prepared to do.

There was, on the face of it, a moral issue—we were being asked to perform a gross act of betrayal of the non-Communist South Vietnamese. But there was also a strategic issue: A Great Power that allies rely upon cannot stay long in the business of being a Great Power if it makes a practice of ditching its allies under pressure. There was, in addition, the hope that a compromise outcome "with honor" would encourage the American people to see that our international engagement, even in Vietnam, had ultimate validity and purpose and, conversely, the fear that a totally humiliating outcome would have a psychologically devastating impact on the country's willingness to stay engaged.

In other words, the strategic argument for the Nixon policy had little to do with the strategic arguments by which Kennedy and Johnson had gotten us into Vietnam. We were getting out—the only issue was how— but *that* was thought to have strategic consequences.

It was President Eisenhower who first painted the metaphoric picture of dominoes falling one by one (though a similar analysis can be traced back to the Truman administration).[50] Arthur Schlesinger, a critic of the war policy of Johnson and Nixon (but not of Kennedy's), dismissed this mode of analysis as "really dumb." Was it really likely, he asked, that "if we abandon a futile effort in a part of the world where we have no vital interest, other powers will conclude that we will therefore offer no resistance in parts of the world where we do have vital interests?" Likewise, Schlesinger seriously doubted that the subsequent Soviet meddling in far-flung regional conflicts, from Angola to Afghanistan, had any connection to the defeat in Vietnam, "as if such meddling were determined not by local opportunities and vulnerabilities but by events on the other side of the planet." In Southeast Asia, Schlesinger argued, the only dominoes that fell were Communist dominoes falling against each other—China invading Vietnam in 1979 after Vietnam invaded Cambodia.[51]

But this hardly exhausts a serious analysis of what transpired. Even at the regional level, it is no tribute to the health of American policy to say that Thailand and the other potential dominoes of Southeast Asia survived because of a Chinese attack on Vietnam. That is, in fact, what happened: We were simply lucky that China, fearing a Soviet-Vietnamese pincer, filled the vacuum we had left. The United States was a shrunken factor in Southeast Asia after 1975, as we shall see, as demonstrated most poignantly by the meager leverage we were able to muster in the eighteen-year agony to end the protracted war in Cambodia. It was the jockeying among the Communist powers that determined events.

The Thai government drew the same conclusion. It announced in March 1975 that it wanted the twenty-five thousand U.S. troops in Thailand withdrawn within a year, and it sought improved relations with Hanoi. (All U.S. forces, in fact, left Thailand within sixteen months.) According to an internal State Department summary of international reaction, the Thai press reflected disillusion and even alarm at the American willingness to abandon Indochina. The media in the Philippines and South Korea saw the outcome as the United States reneging on a commitment. In Japan, some members of the ruling Liberal Democratic party raised questions about the reliability of the U.S.-Japan Security Treaty. Indochina figured in the Japanese debate over whether to sign the Nuclear Non-Proliferation Treaty; some argued that new reassurances were needed from the United States if Japan was to sign on to such a self-denying obligation.

Beyond Asia, the debacle in Vietnam had its effect on American allies and (we will see in the next chapter) on America's adversaries. Reports came in through diplomatic and other channels of other governments reassessing their ties with us. During Henry Kissinger's shuttle negotiation in the Middle East in March 1975, as he attempted to produce a second Egyptian-Israeli agreement on disengagement of forces in the Sinai, the unfolding collapse in Vietnam had a direct effect. When Kissinger paid a visit to Damascus, Syrian president Hafez al-Asad, a shrewd observer of the balance of power, told Kissinger bluntly of his conclusion that the United States would in the long run abandon Israel, just as it was doing with Vietnam and Cambodia. Sooner or later it would happen, Asad insisted, over Kissinger's denials.[52] This kind of impression was not helpful to Kissinger as he strived to persuade Arab leaders to deal realistically with the State of Israel.

The impact inside Israel was greater. Kissinger was arguing to Israeli leaders, just as he had argued to South Vietnamese leaders two and a half years earlier, that the risks of compromise were manageable and that they could have confidence in American assurances of long-term support. Kissinger awoke in his King David Hotel room on March 18 to see a cartoon by Dosh in the *Jerusalem Post* that portrayed a Southeast Asian scene. In the background, two large areas are in flames, one labeled "Vietnam," the other, "Cambodia." In the foreground, amid similar devastation, a mother smiles sweetly to her child and says " . . . and then came a clever man from America and brought us peace. . . . "

As explained by David Kimche, a longtime senior Israeli intelligence and foreign ministry official, all this played into the hands of right-wing opponents of the Sinai negotiation and led the Israeli government, headed by Prime Minister Yitzhak Rabin, to stiffen its position:

> Even if nothing was said in our negotiations with the Americans, Israel could not but draw disconcerting parallels. The United States appeared powerless—despite assurances given—to sustain her friends and allies in South-East Asia. . . . It may have been a fortuitous coincidence of un-related events, but they made their mark on Rabin and fueled his deter-mination not to make Israel's security dependent on decisions taken in Washington without Israel's participation and assent.[53]

The Egyptian-Israeli negotiations broke down in late March (though they were to be put back together in the late summer). Israeli defense minister Shimon Peres, who in those days was playing the hawk, pointed to Indochina as justifying Israel's refusal to make further compromises in the spring: "In a world going up in flames, with guarantees toppling like so many stacks of cards . . . I am convinced that our decision was the right one." Peres explained that "while small nations were subject to pressures from the big powers, the validity of agreements made by the big powers was limited." He said the "Viet Cong had violated an agreement signed less than two years ago with the United States."[54]

Kissinger was deeply shaken by the trend. Not only Vietnam, Cambodia, Thailand, and the Middle East, but also Turkey (punished by Congress after the Cyprus crisis) and Portugal (turning leftward after its 1974 revolution) appeared to mark a period of shrinking American influence around the world. During his abortive March 1975 Mideast shuttle, a demoralized secretary of state poured out his gloomy assessment to the journalists accompanying him on his aircraft. He was holding one of his regular "background" sessions with the fifteen or so reporters crammed into the small conference area in the mid-section of his specially configured Boeing 707. A "sense of almost fatalistic gloom," one participant called it; it was "an appraisal of the over-all world situation that was the most pessimistic [the reporters] had heard in some time." Kissinger told them, among other things, of Asad's prediction of the eventual American abandonment of Israel.[55]

Back in Washington, Kissinger recovered his public composure. Advice from some of his colleagues in the State Department (in particular a perceptive memorandum from Helmut Sonnenfeldt and William Hyland on April 4) encouraged him to do what he could to limit, not advertise, the damage. It was not in our interest to overestimate the immediate consequences, they wrote. If we were bent on convincing ourselves that we had suffered a monumental setback, others would certainly believe it. (Some friendly governments that were geniunely worried—including the Chinese—were also stressing to public audiences that the Americans were still a force to be reckoned with.) Kissinger took this advice—in part—and the tone of his public remarks became more upbeat. In speeches and interviews in May and June he emphasized that our problems were remediable, that our foreign policy in general had been a success, and that with renewed vigilance and care we could continue our role of world leadership.

In an interview broadcast May 5 on the NBC *Today* show, for example, Kissinger told Barbara Walters:

> I believe that the major objectives which the United States has set itself are dictated by our history, by our values, by our geography. They are unaffected by what has happened in Viet-Nam. . . . If we look at the whole postwar record, we have preserved the global peace. Almost every great initiative in the postwar period has either been initiated by America

or has been carried out with our strong support. If we want to avoid a world of chaos, if we want to achieve a world of progress, the American role is absolutely imperative.

But Kissinger also insisted on a realistic recognition that we had suffered a severe setback. He could not accept the notion that the defeat made no difference. The beginning of wisdom, he was convinced, was to recognize at least that we had a problem. In an address to the St. Louis World Affairs Council on May 12, Kissinger warned:

> [W]e should not treat issues of prestige or credibility too lightly or too ironically. A nation's credibility, the value of its word, enables it to influence events without having to turn every issue into a test of strength. When a country's prestige declines, others will be reluctant to stake their future on its assurances; it will be increasingly tested by overt challenges. Given our central role, a loss in our credibility invites international chaos. There is no question that the trauma America has undergone in the last decade—from the assassination of one President to the resignation of another—has raised many doubts.
>
> We must work hard to maintain our position. And we shall.

This was a wise precaution. The most persuasive proof of the domino theory was not in Southeast Asia but at home—the most important domino to fall being the American people and their willingness to remain engaged in the world. Analyst Earl Ravenal, a dove on Vietnam and a strong advocate of "America First" global retrenchment, explained the phenomenon candidly and brilliantly in *Foreign Affairs* in July 1975. The American people, Ravenal wrote, were so deeply traumatized by the Vietnam failure that they would shun future commitments out of fear of repeating the discredited Vietnam adventure: "[I]t is not Vietnam directly that will inhibit American responses in the future. It is the *structural* similarity of future challenges, as perceived by the American people and their representatives, that will be likely to evoke the same responses or obstructions, hence the same ultimately effective constraints on American power. . . . The reliability of the American response is the first casualty of Vietnam, and particularly of the end game there."[56]

Foreign leaders could only draw the obvious conclusion that American commitments had lost much of their credibility. The United States would be less of a factor anywhere for a significant period of time. Ravenal personally welcomed this retrenchment, but he reserved only ridicule for American liberals who had been insisting that our withdrawal from Vietnam would make no strategic difference except to leave us "healthier."

Singapore prime minister Lee Kuan Yew made the same point in a toast at a White House dinner on May 8, 1975. Lee, a fervent ally of this country, had angled for the White House visit because he wanted to come over here at that painful moment and give his American friends both a pep talk and a warning. He tried to make Ravenal's point more positively, hoping against hope that the damage could be repaired soon: "No better service can be done to non-Communist governments the world over than to restore confidence that the American Government can and will act swiftly and in tandem between the Administration and Congress in any case of open aggression. . . . If the President and Congress can speak in one voice on basic issues of foreign policy and in clear and unmistakable terms, then friends and allies will know where they stand and . . . the world will see less adventurism."[57]

The impact of Vietnam on the home front was not so quickly to be repaired, however. Even to this day we can see the traces of that ferocious national debate and the isolationist impulse that it let loose. The liberals had carried American internationalism since before World War II, and their defection over Vietnam tilted the political system sharply. A thoughtful liberal like Anthony Lake could insist in 1976 that "charges of isolationism, neo- or otherwise, . . . make little literal sense."[58] But, whatever label one used, there was an unmistakable turning inward. The British scholar Alastair Buchan, in a collection of essays pulled together by Lake in 1976, saw Vietnam's direct impact on the world's basic conditions as marginal or indirect but conceded that the most lasting effect of the war would be on Americans' "perception of themselves, of the world, and of the proper role of the United States in it."[59]

Another essayist in Lake's collection, the distinguished sociologist Edward Shils, described the extraordinary social and cultural changes the war had wrought at home. Disrespect for the government grew to the point where it fueled a "general dislegitimation of institutional authority" in American society. All our institutions, from the church to business to the universities, were shaken. Our media absorbed an adversarial philosophy. A great gulf widened between the average American's traditional values and a new counterculture that mocked familiar American attitudes toward everything from religion to business to sex. The traditional leadership groups suffered a "loss of nerve."[60] Shils speculated on the longer-term implications of such a demoralization:

The exercise of authority is inevitable in society, and its more-or-less effective exercise is necessary. In American society great responsibilities have been placed on authority, but there is a deeply rooted tendency not to acknowledge its rightfulness. . . . This tendency, which brings to a high point an old American tradition, was intensified by the disputes about the war. . . . If it does continue, it will keep American society in perpetual disorder, and it will comprise our most memorable and enduring inheritance from the war in Indochina.[61]

Perhaps the most important effect of the revolution at home, for our present purposes, was the structural change it brought in our institutions of government, specifically the shift of power from the president to Congress in foreign policy. After the Vietnam mess and the Watergate scandal, the "imperial presidency" was discredited. The idea that the president should have unrestricted discretion to conduct foreign affairs was dead. The relative deference that Congress was thought to have shown to executive branch prerogatives was repudiated (though it would have been news to Woodrow Wilson and Dean Acheson that Congress was not a crucial factor). In any case, Congress resolved that it would no longer grant the president a "blank check," as many of its members felt it had done in the August 1964 Gulf of Tonkin Resolution, which had paved the way for Johnson's Vietnam involvement. Watergate added impetus, fueling the reaction to unfettered presidential power more generally and also sweeping into office, in the 1974 mid-term elections, a new class of ambitious young members who challenged all authority, including that of their own leadership hierarchy in Congress.

This dimension of our own "cultural revolution" was reflected, first of all, in a vast body of legislated restrictions on presidential power and discretion in foreign and national security policy. Some of the broad categories of this legislation in the 1970s were:

• the restrictions on military action and security assistance in support of Indochina from 1970 to 1975, which denied help to the non-Communist Vietnamese, Lao, and Cambodians resisting the Communist takeover;

• the Tunney and Clark amendments on Angola (1975–76), which prohibited U.S. efforts to block the Soviet-Cuban intervention in the Angolan civil war;

• the embargo on military aid to Turkey after the 1974 Cyprus crisis, which was relaxed by 1978 but which for a time complicated relations with both Greece and Turkey as well as U.S. efforts to resolve the Cyprus problem;

• new congressional oversight of intelligence activities and operations, the product of the bitter critique of intelligence agencies by congressional investigating committees in the mid-1970s;

• Freedom of Information Act amendments, enacted over President Ford's veto in 1974, that took away the executive's exclusive power to determine what documents could be kept secret;

• limits on U.S. military personnel in crisis situations abroad, such as ceilings on the number of U.S. Marines in Lebanon in 1982–84 and on U.S. military trainers in El Salvador;

• the War Powers Resolution of 1973, requiring, in essence, congressional authorization for the deployment of U.S. troops in hostilities abroad beyond sixty days;

• a variety of restrictions based on human rights considerations, which limited or attached conditions to aid to countries said to violate human rights, including denial of aid for police training. As countries such as El Salvador returned to democracy and as cooperation against drugs and terrorism became a major U.S. objective, reversing the ban on police training proved to be a laborious process;

• the Symington-Glenn and Nuclear Non-Proliferation Act regimen of controls on the transfer of nuclear-energy materials, reinforced by restrictions on aid to countries that failed to comply with safeguards. These restrictions have affected relations with major friendly countries such as India, Pakistan, Brazil, Argentina, China, Egypt, and others;

• institutional and procedural changes that deprived the president of discretionary flexibility in trade disputes, making blunt American countermeasures nearly automatic regardless of strategic considerations;

• limits on the discretion the president had to impose economic sanctions or export controls for foreign policy purposes;

• restrictions on U.S. arms transfers, which gave Congress the power to obstruct or attach conditions to large-scale commercial transactions that used to be matters of executive discretion;

• tougher requirements for reprogramming of funds, by which congressional committees could deny the president the flexibility he used to enjoy to reallocate authorized or appropriated funds to support related operations or programs;

• growing use of earmarking of aid funds to compel the expenditure of fixed amounts for countries favored by Congress, while funds for other recipients were squeezed out by the shrinking of aid totals;

• and in addition to the above, the constraints imposed by conservatives: for example, the Jackson-Vanik linkage of most-favored-nation trade treatment to Soviet emigration and restrictions on aid to Mozambique or to land reform in El Salvador.

These broad categories embraced hundreds of statutory provisions (though many duplicated each other). In some cases, there were merely reporting requirements; in other cases, the restrictions could be waived by the president if he made a public certification of some sort. Some restraints were presidential commitments exacted by Congress as the price of support for presidential initiatives. The net result, nevertheless, was a vast network of restrictions and inhibitions—"micromanagement" is the word that presidents like to use—that has transformed the way the nation's foreign policy business is conducted. The 1964 edition of the congressional publication *Legislation on Foreign Relations* was a single volume of about 650 pages. Twenty years later, it had grown into three volumes of more than a thousand pages each.[62]

The centerpiece of the challenge to presidential power was the War Powers Resolution, which had great symbolic importance. It was enacted over President Nixon's veto in November 1973, when Nixon was seriously weakened by the Watergate scandal. The fact of Nixon's veto deprived the resolution of some of the legitimacy that its architects sought: They had hoped that a "compact" freely agreed upon between a president and Congress would have a lasting legal, political, and moral effect. Nixon, however, saw it as unconstitutional, as have all his successors, Democrat as well as Republican.

One irony of the War Powers Resolution is that it was based on a myth.

It was designed to prevent a repetition of the Vietnam involvement; yet the Vietnam involvement would probably have met the criteria of the resolution had it been in effect at the time. President Johnson wanted to avoid Truman's mistake of going to war without congressional authorization; that was the whole point of his asking for the Gulf of Tonkin Resolution. Sen. Arthur Vandenberg, the champion of postwar bipartisanship, had once said that Congress had to be in on the takeoffs if it was to be in on the crash landings. President Johnson, after his Vietnam experience, commented ruefully to Eugene Rostow that he had "failed to reckon with one thing: the parachute. I got them on the takeoff, but a lot of them bailed out before the end of the flight."[63] Retrospectively, critics of the war put all the blame on executive overreaching, forgetting that the Vietnam intervention had considerable congressional and public support when it began. * In this sense, the War Powers Resolution reflected more the political weakness of the presidency as of late 1973 than a solution to a constitutional problem.

A second irony of the War Powers Resolution is that after 1973, in this area, subsequent presidents managed to carve out again some freedom of action—more so than in most other areas of micromanagement. President Reagan's quick military strikes against Grenada in 1983 and Libya in 1986, his low-key commitment to convoy tankers bound for Kuwait in 1987–88 during the Iran-Iraq war, President Bush's operation against the dictator Manuel Noriega in Panama in 1989, and President Clinton's air strike in Iraq in 1993 all dramatized that presidents—if their actions seem successful—can still act unilaterally and flexibly in small-scale operations in the exercise of their power as commander in chief and are not necessarily hobbled by Congress. In none of these cases did Congress invoke the War Powers Resolution to block or limit presidential action, either because the presidential action was popular or because (as in 1987–88 in the Gulf) the risks seemed low and the strategic case for the action was broadly accepted. The resolution in its precise terms proved procedurally unworkable.

Yet there can be no doubt of the limits of presidential freedom of action. The Lebanon affair in 1983–84, when the United States and

---

*Johnson's real problem was that the Gulf of Tonkin Resolution had been voted on in August 1964 in the context of a few limited U.S. retaliatory air strikes. While its literal language authorizing armed force was broader, hardly anyone in Congress imagined it was a vote for a ground war and half a million combat troops. Thus, the resolution was inadequate as a *political* safety net when—a few years later—the war had changed its nature and then become unpopular. A more contemporaneous resolution in early 1965, when the U.S. ground war began, would have provided more political cover. It probably would have passed by a large margin as well.

three European allies sent forces to Beirut, where they became caught up in the Syrian assault on the Lebanese government, led Congress to pass a new resolution—in the name of the War Powers Resolution—granting the president eighteen months' authorization to continue the deployment. Reagan denied he needed authorization but acceded to the bill, anyway, for fear of a cutoff of all funds. In January 1991, as President Bush contemplated Operation Desert Storm against Saddam Hussein's occupation of Kuwait, both houses of Congress debated and passed resolutions of authorization. Bush, like Reagan, denied that he needed such approval. But the congressional votes of support averted a monumental constitutional crisis that would have ensued had Bush launched a full-scale war with one or both houses having disapproved. President Clinton's clumsy and tentative commitments of force in Somalia, Haiti, and Bosnia in 1993, in pursuit of objectives that were not clear to the public, generated a wave of "war powers" resolutions in Congress that were beaten back only because the president backed off from the operations.

Both branches maintain their contrary positions on the point of constitutional principle, yet the constitutional *practice* in the postwar period has evolved into a consistent pattern—a kind of common law on the war powers question: Presidents who get into major, protracted, and costly wars without the cushion of clear and contemporaneous congressional support (like Truman and Johnson) are risking political disaster. They do better if (a) they win quickly (as in Grenada, Libya, or Panama); (b) very few people get hurt (as in the Persian Gulf in 1987–88); or (c) for a bigger war (like Desert Storm) they, in fact, get congressional support. The War Powers Resolution may indeed be a procedural failure, but Congress's assertion of its power since Vietnam is a new—and permanent—political reality.

The Vietnam/Watergate experience also had a lasting effect on the structure of Congress itself. The hierarchy of authority *within* the institution broke down as a wave of reform weakened the leadership, took away the power of committee chairmen, and bred a proliferation of semiautonomous subcommittees. By the early 1990s there were nearly three hundred committees and subcommittees, and more than sixty of them were holding hearings on an ordinary day. At least twelve congressional committees had subcommittees on some aspect of international economic policy, for example. The Department of Defense alone had to answer to more than a hundred full committees or subcommittees on various aspects of its business. Pentagon officials had to write and submit an average of three statutorily mandated reports each day (each of which cost an average of a thousand work hours and $50,000 to prepare); senior Defense Department officials spent an average of three thousand hours per year preparing for and presenting testimony to Congress. Congressional staff (whom some credit—or blame—for the expansion of congressional micromanagement) now numbered twenty thousand professionals—triple the number twenty years before.[64] C. Boyden Gray, the White House counsel under President Bush, liked to joke that when he met a member of Congress at a social function and could not recall the member's name, the safe recourse was to say, "Why hello, Mr. Chairman." The odds were that the person was chairman of something.

The days of dominant figures like House Speaker Sam Rayburn and Senate Majority Leader Lyndon Johnson are long gone. The members develop their own expertise and autonomous fiefdoms, with television magnifying their individual impact. Much weakened is the system's ability to bottle up or withstand assaults by highly motivated interest groups, whether ethnic or ideological. The powerful committee chairmen who used to be able to commit their members to deals with the leadership or the executive branch are also long gone. Under the new rules, committee chairmen can be replaced by their members if the members are sufficiently dissatisfied.

This diffusion of power within a more powerful Congress means that a president has a hard time negotiating with Congress even when he is willing to compromise. The congressional leadership sometimes simply cannot deliver the troops either to a consensus or to a decision. Even worse is the occasional inability of Congress to keep the bargains it has struck. The Lebanon war powers compromise of September–October 1983, already referred to (which granted President Reagan an eighteen-month authorization), came apart after the car bombing of the U.S. Marine barracks in Beirut. The renewed congressional uproar convinced the Syrians that the United States was "short of breath" (as Syrian foreign minister Abdul Khalim al-Khaddam contemptuously told his Lebanese counterpart). Negotiations in pursuit of a compromise in Lebanon fell apart.

THE CREDIBILITY GAP

Since the 1970s, the pendulum has swung back to a certain degree. In new political circumstances, some restrictions have dropped away (like the embargo on Turkey and the Clark Amendment on Angola). Occasionally, new and less restrictive laws have been passed, superseding the old. The proliferation of committees monitoring intelligence activities was rationalized, in the Carter period, into two select committees. If a president manages to forge a bipartisan consensus on the substance of a policy, the remaining procedural requirements are not always an obstacle.

The prospect, however, is for trench warfare over all the many issues of micromanagement—slow, inching gains (or losses) of ground, exhausting battles over a broad front, testing presidential stamina, skill, imagination, and courage over the long term. As before in our history, the will of the American people and the force of events will decide where the balance is struck in each period.

In the 1970s, however, there can be no serious doubt that power had shifted radically away from the president. The impact was visible every day. Indochina fell in April 1975; the congressional investigation of U.S. intelligence activities was in full swing; Congress cut off funds for anti-Communist Angolans at the end of 1975 (a confirmation of Earl Ravenal's prediction). In May 1976, the veteran French statesman Maurice Couve de Murville, who had been Charles de Gaulle's foreign minister, rose on the floor of the French National Assembly and described a world that was "in turbulence as never before." Some pointed to the menacing growth of the Soviet Union to superpower status, he said. That was real, but not really new:

> [T]his instability might well be thought to originate much more in the American crisis caused by the defeat in Vietnam and the incredible Watergate affair. The credibility of the United States throughout the world has suffered a serious blow. Above all, the American people's loss of confidence in its leaders, embodied every day in the systematically negative positions of the Congress in Washington, have led to a sort of paralysis of power. . . .

> Both of these—Soviet power and the American crisis—are true, and spectacular.[65]

Thus, in an ironic turn, one of the high priests of Gaullism lamented the paralysis of the United States on the world scene, because it had let loose a profound destabilization of the international order.

Couve de Murville used the phrase "the credibility of the United States throughout the world." The notion of credibility was much derided in the United States at the time. It was thought to be a synonym for the hyperactive imagination or personal vanity of Nixon and Kissinger. Credibility, of course, featured prominently in the statements and thinking of those two men (see Kissinger's interviews quoted above). It was an intangible concept, hard to document or prove or measure. Simply put, Nixon and Kissinger were convinced that when others doubted the strength of American commitments or warnings or promises, our influence diminished. Allies would be less willing to rely on us; our adversaries, less afraid to challenge us.

Intangible as the concept may be, Couve de Murville understood it. So did others. Years later, in the crisis leading up to the Gulf War of 1991, Iraq's dictator Saddam Hussein was to invoke the retreats in Vietnam (and Lebanon) as encouraging proof that America could be defeated. In a speech in Amman in February 1990, he declared: "Brothers, the weakness of a big body lies in its bulkiness. . . . [W]e saw that the United States as a superpower departed Lebanon immediately when some Marines were killed, the very men who are considered to be the most prominent symbol of its arrogance. . . . The United States has been defeated in some combat arenas for all the forces it possesses, and it has displayed signs of fatigue, frustration, and hesitation. . . ."[66]

A few months later, Saddam invaded Kuwait. As the crisis intensified, America's defeat in Vietnam featured prominently in Iraqi rhetoric. On August 29, Saddam warned the Americans that if they fought Iraq, "it will be a greater tragedy for you than Vietnam. . . . God is on our side. . . ."[67] It was a constant theme in the Iraqi media.[68] Journalist H. D. S. Greenway heard the same from Iraqi officials: "In Baghdad, just before the war broke out, almost every official I met mentioned that the United States could not endure a protracted war, as attested to by the American failure in Vietnam. This impression was reinforced by the Reagan Administration's pullout from Beirut in 1983 after the Marines were bombed in their barracks."[69] In July 1990, when American ambassador April Glaspie had told Saddam that the United States opposed Iraqi military action against Kuwait, Saddam had replied with another oblique but unmistakable reference to Lebanon and Vietnam—citing America's inability to take casualties in a conflict.[70]

Ambassador Glaspie was later criticized for the weakness of her protestations, yet the truth of the matter is that even if she had had more ferocious "talking points" to deliver, *Saddam would not have believed her*. That is the literal meaning of credibility (or its absence). Based on his assessment of American resolve in Vietnam and Lebanon, Saddam ignored the words and judged the strength of the commitment behind them. His assessment was wrong, it turned out, but the price we paid for the loss of credibility was the need to earn it again by war.

For our purposes here, the most important test of American credibility after Vietnam was the reaction of the Kremlin leadership. In 1975, in Moscow, Leonid Brezhnev was drawing his own conclusions about the outcome in Vietnam and its strategic implications.

PART

TWO

THE CORRELATION

OF FORCES

6

LEONID BREZHNEV

No Western official spent more time with Leonid Brezhnev than Henry Kissinger, and I was privileged to be part of Kissinger's team in most of those encounters. While I also attended summit sessions with Nixon and Ford, I saw Brezhnev most often in the many hours and days of meetings that Kissinger held directly with the party general secretary (as he was then) between April 1972 and January 1976. I probably spent over a hundred hours with him. Sometimes it was in the formal setting of his Central Committee office in the Kremlin, or in the informal surroundings of the Politburo's hunting resort at Zavidovo, outside Moscow, or in the hair-down atmosphere of raucous lunches and dinners where he held forth without briefing papers prepared by his aides and, more important, where the stimulus of Georgian wine or Ukrainian pepper vodka added a certain extra force to his personality.

Brezhnev was a man of few apparent intellectual gifts. His grasp of the intricacies of arms control or Third World issues was minimal, and his mastery of many other substantive topics of foreign policy was weak except when fortified by prepared papers. Whenever Kissinger asked him a precise question about, say, an arms control point—or, indeed, when- ever it came time for him to respond to an unexpected Kissinger presen- tation on almost any issue—there would be a huddle on the Soviet side of the table as aides leapt up from both ends and all crowded around the leader to explain to him what the issue was and advise him how to respond.

His strengths, however, were of a different kind. I recall watching the whole Politburo gather during Nixon's 1974 summit in the waiting room behind St. Vladimir Hall, where some important U.S.-Soviet accord was about to be signed. These Soviet politicians were, to all appearances, unimpressive men. They were not politicians in the Western mold— smooth, good-looking, charismatic; they were old, dumpy, crude. They looked more like old-time labor union bosses or Mafia dons. While they were for the most part men of rough working-class backgrounds and limited education, they owed genuine loyalty to the Revolution that had opened the doors of opportunity to men like them. Their careers had advanced in the hardest school of all—the Communist party during the Stalin era. These Politburo leaders of the 1970s were the young men of the 1930s and 1940s who had been vaulted up the career ladder when the generation above them was murdered en masse in the purges. They were then thrust into positions of serious responsibility when a world war engulfed their country. Politics for them was a harder game than fund-raising and sound bites. These were the winners of that game. They exuded power in its raw, unpolished form.

It was from this environment that Leonid Brezhnev had emerged, in the pattern of Stalin and Khrushchev before him, underestimated by his colleagues until he had gained ascendancy by his dogged mastery of the party apparatus and its patronage machinery. The son of a steelworker and a steelworker himself, he had received a technical education at party schools. "[P]oorly educated and not really very literate," is how Georgii Arbatov later described him.[1] The party gave young Leonid Ilyich a series of assignments as a local political boss, in the faraway Urals during the collectivization of agriculture, then in Ukraine, where he worked under Khrushchev. Brezhnev had a reputation in his early career as someone not particularly bright or strong in character. In prewar Ukraine he was nicknamed "the Ballerina," since "anyone who wants to can turn him around." This bit of gossip came from Khrushchev, who recounted it to his son in 1963 as an explanation of why Brezhnev was too weak a personality to be his successor. "He isn't up to the job," the elder Khrushchev concluded.[2] Little more than a year later, Brezhnev proved him wrong.

Arbatov describes Brezhnev's rise thusly:

He was particularly artful in apparat infighting, where he showed sophis-ticated cunning. In the final analysis, he managed to elbow out all his rivals and ill-wishers from the leadership. He did this slowly, without exposing himself to the risk of crises and conflicts and without using bloody repressions as Stalin had done, even without destroying his rivals verbally in public, as Khrushchev was wont to do. He obtained total obedience and submission from his comrades, and even instilled fear in them. Even such people as Andropov, Suslov, and Gromyko feared him; at least, that was my impression.[3]

Soon after Brezhnev's coming to power, a group of advisers were briefing him on a lengthy document when he interrupted them: "It's hard for me to grasp all this. On the whole, to be honest, this isn't my area. My strong point is organization and psychology."[4] This was unfeigned modesty, but shrewdly self-aware: It was his mastery of organization that had put him in power and his insights into human psychology that kept him there.

When I encountered Brezhnev, he was new to foreign policy, and his intuition sometimes served him well, sometimes not. In his talks with American leaders, I saw him resort alternatively to crude cajoling and bullying. When a negotiation reached an issue of crucial importance, however, he did not need his aides' detailed briefing papers: He understood instinctively when the Soviet Union needed to yield to superior strength and when it did not. He could maintain a stonewall, or back down gracefully, with apparent equanimity, usually showing the most acute awareness of where the bargaining advantage on the issue really lay. On other occasions, Brezhnev wore his emotions on his sleeve, openly displaying a raw racial hatred of the Chinese, for example. He would also wax eloquent on his grandiose economic plans, like the new Baikal-Amur Railway across Siberia, for which he was eager to win Western—especially American—aid. On these occasions he probably only increased our appreciation of the leverage we had.

Brezhnev did not have Aleksei Kosygin's administrative genius or Mikhail Gorbachev's law degree, but he was sophisticated in the arena that most counted: He understood power. In his attitude toward the United States there was still a certain awe of our power (which at that time I thought we did not deserve); his bluster masked a residual sense of inferiority. But as Soviet strength grew, the impulse to achieve security by probing for Western weaknesses and exploiting opportunities also grew. His limitations as a domestic leader left a legacy of stagnation—the "era of stagnation" became Gorbachev's code phrase for the Brezhnev period. But that phrase ignores foreign and military policy, in which there was no stagnation.

THE CORRELATION OF FORCES

In the early and mid-1970s, when I witnessed Leonid Brezhnev in action, his interest in the Third World was not intense. In 1972 he was perfectly willing to sacrifice the interests of his North Vietnamese ally when more important Great Power stakes were involved. He showed no sign of Khrushchev's enthusiasm about the leaders, concerns, and prospects of potential allies among the developing nations. On the contrary, Brezhnev would make crude wisecracks to Kissinger about Third World leaders he had encountered, ridiculing their dress and behavior. Once, he told the story of a Muslim leader praying before the photograph of Lenin in the Politburo conference room.

In the early Brezhnev years, Soviet assistance to Third World countries was rationalized, in the sense that it began to be governed more by economic criteria and not just political calculations. Whereas Khrushchev had been willing to incur an economic cost for a political gain, or in the name of a grand ambition to move the recipients rapidly to industrialization, under Brezhnev the emphasis was on realistic projects that could be justified as economically cost-effective. Soviet commentators began to reflect a more realistic view of the important role of agriculture, light industry, and the private sector in Third World development.[5] They were more cautious about prescribing in detail the correct path from colonial backwardness to socialism.[6] Soviet aid policy could be characterized as "businesslike," a word that Brezhnev liked to use in many different contexts. The net outflow of Soviet economic aid in 1973, in fact, was only around 0.03 percent of GNP; new aid had leveled off, while debt repayments were increasing.[7]

Even more important were the indicators of circumspection in the political/military sphere—the fear that revolutionary violence in the Third World might not always serve Soviet interests. In the early Brezhnev years (1964–70), memories of the Cuban Missile Crisis had not faded; in 1969, Soviet commentator I. Shatalov rebuffed (somewhat defensively) the Chinese and other Third World radicals who were still egging on the Soviets to take greater risks: "In the age of atomic weapons, calls to settle scores with imperialism by the military might of the Socialist countries are extremely reckless. They conceal . . . the desire of their authors to evade their own duty of creating a powerful, united, mass anti-imperialist movement."[8]

By the mid-1970s, however, the world was changing. Brezhnev watched the United States and the West undergo what seemed to be a systemic crisis. The American trauma, to which Couve de Murville called attention in the spring of 1976, was compounded by the economic recession in the West produced by the first energy shock, the 1973 quadrupling of oil prices. Brezhnev watched Nixon fall, then Indochina, then Angola. Communist parties were growing in influence even in Western Europe. The all-European summit conference in Helsinki in May 1975, at which the Helsinki Final Act was signed, was still viewed in some quarters as a Soviet success, since it was thought (erroneously) to symbolize Western acceptance of the status quo in the Soviet-dominated Eastern half of Europe.

This was also the era when the Soviets achieved strategic parity. The inferiority of their military position at the time of the Cuban Missile Crisis had been overcome; they had caught up with the United States in overall numbers of long-range ballistic missiles in about 1970—and kept on building. In the mid-1970s they caught up with the United States in the technology of multiple warheads, which, when combined with their superiority in large, heavy land-based missiles, promised to give them a most deadly strategic advantage.

In sum, it was in the Brezhnev era that the Soviet Union definitively achieved superpower status. Part of the Kremlin's interest in bilateral summit meetings with the American president and bilateral arms agreements with the United States was to ratify this status. Foreign Minister Andrei Gromyko had proclaimed proudly in April 1971: "Today there is no question of any importance which can be decided without the Soviet Union or in opposition to it."[9]

Not coincidentally, then, Leonid Brezhnev was in a triumphant mood at the Twenty-fifth Congress of the Communist Party of the Soviet Union in February 1976. His speech of February 24 was marked by the same disconcerting exuberance as Khrushchev's milestone speeches of 1956 and 1961, the same chilling self-assurance that the trend of history was in Moscow's favor in the world at large. "The general crisis of capitalism is continuing to deepen," he proclaimed.[10] As in 1961, the speech's effect was compounded by the West's own self-doubt—indeed, by a self-doubt that had a far more objective basis in 1976 than the Kennedy administration's partisan carping in 1961 about the state of the world as Dwight Eisenhower had left it.

The international situation was positive enough that Brezhnev led off his speech with it. "No impartial person can deny that the socialist countries' influence on world affairs is becoming ever stronger and deeper," he boasted. Successes in the Third World were given pride of place—most prominently (and gallingly) the "glorious victory" of the Soviet Union's ally Vietnam over the "imperialist invaders"; the Soviet people could be proud, he said, of the "considerable aid" they had given to the Vietnamese effort. He also hailed the success of the People's Republic of Angola, which had just defeated its rivals in the Angolan civil war. Brezhnev devoted four paragraphs to a strong expression of overall support for the national liberation struggle. He now stressed, and paid tribute to, the leftward lurch in many of the "liberated" countries' internal policies—the strengthening of the state sector, abolition of feudal landownership, nationalization of foreign enterprises, and development of indigenous cadres. The Soviet Union was duty bound to support this historical process out of its "revolutionary conscience" and "Communist convictions."

Not only did the trend in the Third World strengthen the cause of socialism, but (like Khrushchev) Brezhnev sought to make the case that the strength of the "socialist camp" was of enormous benefit to the Third World. Whereas Khrushchev had worried about the Third World's continuing economic dependence on imperialism, Brezhnev, in an era of Western economic weakness produced by the energy crisis, could boast that the "present correlation of world class forces" was enabling the Third World to "resist imperialist diktat."

A year and a half later, Soviet support for national liberation movements was even enshrined in the new Constitution of the USSR. Article 28 of the "Brezhnev Constitution" of October 1977 in effect converted an ideological commitment into a state obligation:

> The USSR's foreign policy is aimed at ensuring favorable international conditions for building communism in the USSR, protecting the Soviet Union's state interests, strengthening the positions of world socialism, *supporting the peoples' struggle for national liberation and social progress,* preventing wars of aggression, achieving general and complete disarmament and consistently implementing the principle of the peaceful coexistence of states with different social systems.[11] (emphasis added)

The "correlation of forces," alluded to by Brezhnev above, is a concept that came to be associated with him and his era, just as "peaceful coexistence" had come to be associated with Khrushchev. The idea seemed to have an endless fascination in the mid-1970s for Soviet commentators, who undoubtedly saw it as vindicating their policies, their system, and their hopes.[12]

Like most Soviet slogans, it had a Leninist pedigree. In all politics, Lenin wrote in 1918, "one must be able to calculate the balance of forces. . . . This is the core of Marxism and Marxist tactics. . . ."[13] Both Marx and Lenin were acutely aware of the importance of the factor of power in human affairs, though they analyzed international politics more in terms of the power of classes than of nations.[14] Whereas Woodrow Wilson and Franklin Roosevelt had hoped to establish a new world order based on harmony, the heart of Soviet ideology was the notion of mortal struggle. The "correlation of forces" at any given time was the measure of who was winning that struggle.

In the 1970s, Soviet analysts like Georgii Shakhnazarov (who later turned up as a reformist adviser to Gorbachev) were developing complex theories of how to measure the "correlation of forces."[15] In the Soviet lexicon, the idea was broader than Western academic theories of the "balance of power." Whereas the latter sometimes tended to focus on the military balance, the Soviets, in good Marxist and Leninist fashion, sought to factor in the elements of social evolution, economic potential, and political will and cohesion. Also included were the factors cited in Brezhnev's February 1976 speech—the growth of the "national liberation movement" and the new assertiveness of the nonaligned; the divisions among the capitalist powers resulting from the Mideast war and the energy crisis; and the outcome in Vietnam, which raised doubts of American staying power.[16]

This new confidence about Third World trends led to an odd debate among Soviet analysts. Some traditionalists continued to portray imperialism as a vital force and the United States as therefore still dangerous; others pointed more confidently to American setbacks and frustrations.[17] From our point of view it was not much of a choice—between those who saw us as evil (and therefore to be resolutely fought) and those who saw us as weak (and therefore ripe for defeat).

Military strength was centrally important in the Soviet calculation, whatever the academic pretensions about the nonmilitary factors. The Soviets' achievement of strategic nuclear parity, in particular, was seen by their commentators as a decisive shift in the world balance: it deterred imperialist military challenges, shifted the competition to other spheres of political rivalry, and forced the West to negotiate. Thus, Genrykh Trofimenko in 1975:

> To sum it up, the balance of world forces had further shifted in socialism's favour by the early 1970s as evidenced, for example, by the attainment of Soviet-American nuclear and missile parity and the awareness by the USA of its limited possibilities to influence diverse events in the world by means of military forces. This made the US ruling class start a "reappraisal of values" and acknowledge the need "to reconcile the reality of competition between the two systems with the imperative of coexistence."[18]

In 1972, commentator Vadim Zagladin pointed to the impetus that this change in the world situation would give to Soviet foreign policy: "It signifies that the possibilities of the socialist world to influence actively the policy of imperialism are growing. And it follows that the responsibility of socialism to utilize these possibilities is also growing."[19]

Another writer, A. Sergiyev, rubbed the West's noses in it in the spring of 1975, portraying vividly—and not wrongly—the scope of the West's economic problems and political demoralization. Most of the themes cited above appear in Sergiyev's article, which is worth quoting at length:

The high military potential of the socialist countries is among the decisive factors for preserving peace and the peaceful coexistence of states with different social systems. . . . In the new strategic situation the ruling circles of the US monopoly bourgeoisie have failed in their "position-of-strength" policy upon which they had pinned high hopes.

In the early 1970s capitalism was characterised by incessant economic crises and production slumps; unbridled inflation engulfed all the principal capitalist countries; the acute currency crisis became permanent and a crisis in power resources was in progress. . . . There was a powerful up-surge in the early 1970s and expansion of the class struggle waged by working people in capitalist countries, namely, France, Italy, Japan, Brit-ain, the FRG, Portugal, and Greece. The international communist move-ment is, undoubtedly, the most influential political force of our time. . . .

Another mighty international force of our days is the national liberation movement. In the struggle against imperialism it comes out as a natural ally of the international working class and the socialist states. The coin-cidence of interests of the socialist states and the developing countries of Asia, Africa and Latin America in the struggle against imperialism, and colonialism, against war and imperialist aggression creates an objective basis for unity of their action in the world arena in regard to the basic problems, and increases the foreign policy potentialities of progressive forces. . . .

Inter-imperialist contradictions which have particularly intensified in the last few years are among the essential factors that weaken the aggressive imperialist circles. One can observe an ever growing discrepancy of eco-nomic and political interests in the main imperialist "centres of power": the USA, Western Europe and Japan. The inter-imperialist contradictions came out in full when attempts were made to work out a common attitude of the developed capitalist countries for the solution of the monetary and energy crises. . . .

The shifts that are taking place in the world show that imperialism is being forced to retreat.[20]

CONCEPTS OF DÉTENTE

The American strategy toward the Soviet Union in the Nixon-Kissinger period, which eventually acquired the label "détente," did not deny the new strength of the Soviet superpower. On the contrary, that was its premise. It was a strategy to tame the bear. As discussed in the last chapter, the United States sought, by a combination of incentives and penalties (and the tactics of "linkage"), to shape the environment in which the emerging Soviet superpower would have to operate. Nixon and Kissinger, two men who had never before been seriously criticized for naïveté about the Soviet Union, in fact held the most sober view of its potential menace and were attacked at home, through most of Nixon's term, for their intransigent anti-Sovietism.

Harking back to George Kennan's historic 1947 article in *Foreign Affairs*,[21] Nixon and Kissinger saw the paradox of a Soviet state whose internal system was inherently flawed and whose external behavior was nevertheless—or, perhaps, for that very reason—a source of danger to the outside world. A policy of firm and patient resistance to encroachments (containment, as it was called after Kennan), coupled with a willingness to engage more cooperatively whenever Soviet behavior warranted, might not only protect the free world but also, over time, compel a future generation of Soviet leaders to face up to their system's internal contradictions.[22]

In a speech in San Francisco on February 3, 1976, Kissinger sought to place the American policy in historical perspective:

> Historically, the adjustment of an existing order to the arrival of one or more new actors almost invariably was accompanied by war—to impede the upstart, to remove or diminish some of the previously established actors, to test the balance of forces in a revised system. But in the nuclear era. . . . [i]t is our responsibility to contain Soviet power without global war, to avoid both abdication as well as unnecessary confrontation. . . .
>
> The policies pursued by this administration have been designed to prevent Soviet expansion but also to build a pattern of relations in which the Soviet Union will always confront penalties for aggression and also acquire growing incentives for restraint. These goals are well within our capacities. Soviet power is evolving with considerable unevenness. Soviet society is no longer totally cut off from contact with or the influences of the world around it nor is it without its own needs for outside relationships. It is the great industrial democracies, not the Soviet Union, that are the

engine of the world economy and the most promising partners for the poorer nations.

American critics of détente found it morally objectionable to treat with such a repressive regime and even argued that the policy gave the Kremlin a freer hand to tighten its repression. In an address in Washington on October 8, 1973, Kissinger defended the policy, suggesting that the influences of the outside world were bound to have an effect on the Soviet internal evolution as well:

> How hard can we press [for internal changes] without provoking the Soviet leadership into returning to practices in its foreign policy that increase international tensions? Are we ready to face the crises and increased defense budgets that a return to Cold War conditions would spawn? And will this encourage full emigration or enhance the well-being or nourish the hope for liberty of the peoples of Eastern Europe and the Soviet Union? Is it détente that has prompted repression—or is it détente that has generated the ferment and the demand for openness which we are now witnessing?

The Soviets had a different concept of détente. In the developing world, for example, as Khrushchev had told Walter Lippmann in 1958, revolution was part of the status quo, and it was the West that had to adjust to that reality.[23] Neither "détente" nor "peaceful coexistence" meant any Soviet renunciaton of the global ideological mission. As Brezhnev explained in his speech to the Twenty-fifth Party Congress in February 1976:

> It could not be clearer, after all, that détente and peaceful coexistence have to do with interstate relations. This means above all that disputes and conflicts between countries are not to be settled by war, by the use or threat of force. Détente does not in the slightest abolish, nor can it abolish or alter, the laws of the class struggle. . . . We make no secret of the fact that we see détente as the way to create more favorable conditions for peaceful socialist and communist construction.[24]

In the Soviet view, therefore, détente was yet another means by which to induce the imperialists not to interfere with the revolutionary trend of history. In the declaration of the 1969 Moscow Conference of Communist parties, the requirement of policy was said to be a "struggle to *compel*" the imperialists to accept peaceful coexistence.[25] As the then Brezhnev loyalist Georgii Arbatov put it in 1972, "The correlation of forces is not some abstract formula but perceptible reality which *compels* the imperialist powers to adjust to the new situation."[26] Détente and peaceful coexistence were to serve, as Raymond Garthoff has put it, "to make the world safe for historical change."[27]

Thus, peaceful coexistence, détente, and the correlation of forces were all interconnected. The Soviet Union's new strength meant that the United States had to adapt to both the fact of Soviet power and the revolutionary changes in the world that Soviet power was promoting. Whereas we hoped détente would act as a restraint on the Soviets, the Soviets saw it as a restraint on *us*, on our temptation to try to slow the process of history. Whereas we saw détente as a way to manage the Soviets' emergence on the world scene, the Soviets saw it as a way to manage *our* transition to a new and lesser status without undue resistance.

The Soviets dismissed the idea of "linkage" because it implied that they needed relations more than we did. Trofimenko was particularly contemptuous of the Nixon-Kissinger attempt to hold arms control hostage to Soviet Third World conduct: "American leaders pictured a deal along the lines of: We give you the status quo in strategic arms, and you give us the status quo in the Third World."[28] To Trofimenko, such a deal was "out of the question" and "untenable from the very beginning," since Third World peoples were "striving . . . for economic and social liberation from the sway of American and other transnational corporations. . . ." and would always have Soviet support.[29]

In fact, reality would determine case by case whether linkage worked or not. Similarly, reality would decide whose theory of détente would prevail in the end.

In this context, Brezhnev and his colleagues proceeded with their military buildup, which had begun after the Cuban Missile Crisis with the aim of catching up with the United States but which had continued for fifteen years, long after strategic parity had been attained. By the mid-1970s, under Brezhnev, the Soviet Union, through its systematic buildup in several key categories of equipment, had achieved an ability to project its military power overseas that Khrushchev could only have dreamed of:

• For the first time in their history, the Soviets built an oceangoing navy, having previously limited themselves to coastal defense (as well as strategic-missile submarines). In 1960, the Soviets had 160 surface warships and less than nine hundred cargo ships and tankers; by 1979, they had doubled the numbers. They built large numbers of troop ships, freighters, amphibious assault ships, and other vessels capable of projecting power far from Soviet shores. In 1970 and again in 1975, in exercises involving more than two hundred ships, they conducted their first naval maneuvers involving coordinated simultaneous operations in many parts of the world.[30]

• In 1960, the Soviet Union had no long-range military transport aircraft. By the time of the invasion of Afghanistan in 1979, they had some 150 strategic airlift planes to ferry heavy equipment to Afghanistan, including the huge new An-22 turboprops that could carry eighty-eight tons over twenty-five hundred miles. In Angola, from 1975 onward, Soviet long-range aircraft transported, equipped, and maintained a Cuban expeditionary force that reached over sixty thousand combat troops in a theater six thousand miles from the USSR (and six thousand miles from Cuba). Likewise, the Soviets expanded their sealift capabilities, ferrying supplies to such distant destinations as Angola, the Middle East (including in the October 1973 war), Ethiopia, and Vietnam.

• While the Soviets were expelled from Egypt by Anwar Sadat in the early 1970s and lost the use of the port of Alexandria, they were actively accumulating other foreign anchorages and access arrangements (such as Cam Ranh Bay in Vietnam, Latakia in Syria, Aden in South Yemen, Umm Qasr and Basra in Iraq, and numerous ports in the Mediterranean) to support long-range naval operations.

• In 1965, there were less than four thousand military advisory personnel from the USSR and Warsaw Pact countries in the Third World. From 1970 to 1975 the number varied between eight thousand and ten thousand, but by 1979 it had risen to nearly sixteen thousand.[31] (The numbers did not include the East German and Cuban intelligence and security personnel who helped build security services and sustain friendly regimes, especially in Africa.)

• Likewise, Soviet weapons shipments to Third World clients escalated. In the period 1967–73, Soviet military aid agreements with non-Communist developing countries (principally in the Arab world) were estimated by the CIA at some $8.7 billion—more than double the total for the period 1960–66. In the period 1974–79, the total quadrupled, to about $34 billion. Soviet economic-aid agreements in 1965–74 totaled over $6.2 billion, nearly a two-thirds increase over the period 1955–64.[32]

• The use of Cuban proxy troops in Africa seemed particularly ominous. It served Castro's ambition to play a bigger "revolutionary" role on the world stage, but, even more, it gave the Soviets a maddeningly effective instrument of intervention that incurred less of a propaganda penalty than the direct use of Soviet combat personnel would have. (Many of the Cuban troops in Africa, for example, were black.) "The Gurkhas of the Russian empire," UN Ambassador Daniel Patrick Moynihan labeled the Cubans. "It was a brilliant move. . . ." Moynihan later wrote. "The Rand Corporation at its peak of performance could not have invented a Third World weapons system the equal of the Cuban army."[33]

Meanwhile, in the early 1970s, U.S. defense and foreign assistance budgets steadily declined under the impact of the domestic reaction to Vietnam. Congress cut $40 billion from Nixon's defense budget requests and challenged many of his proposed weapons programs.[34] Only glacially did U.S. defense budgets recover, increasing slightly under Gerald Ford, somewhat more under Jimmy Carter, then more sharply under Ronald Reagan, when the extent of Soviet overreaching had become not only evident but intolerable.

In the late 1970s, the new Soviet engagement in the Third World seemed to be paying geopolitical dividends. In Africa, not only had the Soviets' Angolan clients been victorious, but the left-wing military junta in Ethiopia that had taken power in 1974 upon the death of Haile Selassie was by 1977 openly pro-Soviet. It signed a Treaty of Friendship and Cooperation with Moscow in November 1978. Upheavals in Yemen in 1978–79 produced a pro-Soviet regime in South Yemen and pulled the traditionally more moderate North Yemen into a closer relationship with Moscow as well. A coup d'état in April 1978 brought a Communist party into power in traditionally neutral Afghanistan; Afghanistan signed a Friendship Treaty with the Soviet Union in December 1978. In Cambodia, Moscow's ally Vietnam invaded Cambodia in December 1978 to oust the hated Khmer Rouge regime, which had linked itself to China and defied Hanoi's control. In Nicaragua, the Communist Sandinista party held the dominant position in the coalition that had toppled the dictator Anastasio Somoza in 1979.

The Soviets had not instigated these events, but they treated them as natural developments confirming the historical trend. They responded first with their now proven tools of economic and military assistance. As Ethiopia became locked in a clash with Somalia in a dispute over the Ogaden desert, the Soviets transported Cuban troops to Ethiopia from both Cuba and Angola and escalated their arms supply. From the end of November 1977 through February 1978, Moscow airlifted somewhere between twelve thousand and fifteen thousand Cuban troops to Ethiopia, including three combat brigades, and delivered up to $1 billion in weapons and equipment.[35] Cuban and East German personnel appeared in South Yemen. The Carter administration, especially Assistant to the President for National Security Affairs Zbigniew Brzezinski, saw an "arc of crisis," with instability and Soviet influence expanding from the Horn of Africa to the Arabian peninsula to Iran, Afghanistan, and Pakistan,[36] against the backdrop of Soviet clients advancing in other faraway regions as disparate as Central America and Indochina.

Where Khrushchev (following Lenin's advice) had wooed Third World leaders even if they were non-Marxist, Leonid Brezhnev now found himself the proud beneficiary of the coming to power of a new generation of avowedly Communist regimes spread across several continents of the globe. Soviet doctrine moved hastily to catch up with the phenomenon. The Brezhnev era was marked by a new ideological emphasis on "Marxist-Leninist vanguard parties" that were expected to break new ground in political organization in the Third World.[37] It was another tactical innovation of the Brezhnev period, along with the expansion of airlift and sealift, the use of Cuban and East German proxies, and other new instruments for projecting military power.

To some degree, this new focus on Marxist-Leninist parties reflected some disillusionment with the reliability of the bourgeois nationalists. Of Khrushchev's stable of new friends, many had been deposed by the early 1970s, only Cuba had declared its conversion to Marxism-Leninism, and the Egyptian experience (Sadat had expelled Soviet troops in 1972) had shown that arms supply was no guarantee of leverage or permanent alliance. With the windfall of new radical regimes, which the Soviets were now helping to sustain in power, Soviet commentary began to stress the virtue of turning national liberation movements into full-fledged "Marxist-Leninist vanguard parties." Regimes like Angola, Ethiopia, Afghanistan, and South Yemen were advised to reorganize themselves thoroughly along Leninist lines, with a centralized, disciplined party, a broad political organization, a Marxist-Leninist ideology, a centrally planned economy, and a drive to squeeze out the private sector and any political pluralism. The Cubans and East German advisers, who helped organize a disciplined and loyal secret police, were especially valuable in the process of consolidating power. Nicaragua was a different case; it was having difficulty moving rapidly in this direction, and the Soviets seemed disappointed.

Years later, of course, it would become clear how narrowly based all these new regimes were. When the overall climate of global politics later changed, they became vulnerable, but in the mid- and late 1970s the psychological momentum was all in their direction. These new regimes were not only accomplished facts; they and their Soviet patrons could honestly imagine them to be the wave of the future. Their internal opponents were demoralized and in disarray, seemingly abandoned by the West. Beyond the intrinsic significance of the countries involved (and they were, for the most part, strategically marginal), they pointed to an unmistakable trend. An Ethiopian official observed that after watching the Soviet performance in the Ethiopia-Somalia conflict, not a single African government dared to criticize the USSR in public; a Somali official told an American journalist, "We have learned that there is only one superpower."[38]

Fifteen years later, the phrase "there is only one superpower" was tossed about in self-congratulatory fashion to refer to the United States after the collapse of communism, but in the late 1970s much outward evidence pointed in the opposite direction. Whereas the United States was learning the purported "lesson of Vietnam"—that military force was futile—Soviet leaders were learning not that military force was futile but that it worked. As Bruce Porter has put it, they were not only ascending up an "experience curve"; they were ascending up a "confidence curve."[39]

THE BREAKDOWN OF DÉTENTE

From today's vantage point we can clearly see that these Soviet gains were not permanent. Even at the time, there were those who cautioned that the Soviets were not ten feet tall, that there were many potential weaknesses in their position, and that their gains were more the product of opportunism than of a grand design.[40] But most of these potential weaknesses did not become actual until later, when the Soviets' momentum ran out—when the international perception (and reality) of the "correlation of forces" changed. In the 1970s, from the American vantage point at the time, we had lost control over events. The insights of Earl Ravenal and Maurice Couve de Murville were being borne out. Three American administrations—those of Nixon, Ford, and Carter—were humiliated both by Soviet actions and by domestic divisions that complicated, if not paralyzed, the American response.

Nixon and Kissinger, as part of their strategy, had sought to spell out a "code of conduct" of superpower relations in the developing world. Among its key principles was that neither superpower should seek unilateral advantage, that both had an obligation in the nuclear age to exercise restraint. Nixon had spelled out these principles as an American concept in his address to the UN General Assembly on October 23, 1970, and his administration thought it an achievement when Brezhnev agreed to sign a joint document incorporating the same ideas at the May 1972 Moscow summit. It was called "Basic Principles of US-Soviet Relations" and was much mocked later when it became clear that the Soviets—for reasons we have seen—had a more elastic interpretation of what it all meant. The American side, however, had thought it useful to get the Soviets on record subscribing to what, on its face, was a status quo– oriented set of principles incompatible with the more disruptive elements of Soviet Third World doctrine.[41]

To us, the "Basic Principles" were a correct *definition* of the ground rules of behavior, if not a legal contract. They were not thought to be self-enforcing. As Nixon had shown in the Jordan crisis of 1970 and the Mideast war of 1973 and as Ford tried to demonstrate in Angola in 1975, neither of them imagined that we could rely on voluntary Soviet compliance; it was up to us to defend our interests on the ground when challenged—in the name of that set of principles. The Nixon policy at the height of its success (which was probably 1971–72) managed to integrate the incentives and the penalties into a coherent approach that provided important leverage. When the policy was succeeding, it was also overwhelmingly popular in the United States. The domestic reaction to détente came later—after the fact—when the objective circumstances had changed. Circumstances had changed in large part because the administration had lost control of its own policy.

The most dramatic setbacks were on the "containment" side of the equation—the retreats from Indochina and Angola, the reduction in our defense budget, the investigations of our intelligence agencies, and so forth. Congress never permitted the United States to deploy the one anti-ballistic-missile (ABM) site to which we were entitled under the 1972 ABM Treaty. Our leverage over the Soviets in arms control began to weaken.

Simultaneously, Congress imposed, in the Trade Act at the beginning of 1975, the Jackson-Vanik and Stevenson amendments, which denied the Soviets nondiscriminatory trade treatment or significant credit guarantees, respectively. This surprising development represented a significant domestic shift from earlier in Nixon's term when it had been a cardinal principle of the Democrats that East-West trade needed to be enhanced in order to promote peace. Now Right and Left came together to punish the Soviet Union, but not so much for its geopolitical aggression as for its internal repression. While these restrictive amendments impended, they were useful leverage in promoting, for example, Soviet flexibility in permitting Jews and others to emigrate. Once enacted into law, however, they drove the Soviets to repudiate the U.S.-Soviet trade accord of 1972 and to restrict Jewish emigration (which was cut back dramatically). The measures paradoxically decreased our leverage over Soviet behavior.

The new American concern for human rights in the Soviet Union was in part a popular reaction to the Nixon-Kissinger approach, which had focused too cold-bloodedly on the geopolitical issues and mishandled the domestic concerns over human rights that began to be expressed with particular vehemence in 1973.[42] Liberals had long criticized Nixon and Kissinger for alleged amorality linked to controversial events in Vietnam, Chile, and elsewhere (not to mention Watergate); the Right had always been unhappy at the camaraderie with the Soviets (and Communist Chinese) dramatized at the friendly summits. A bloc of liberals who had been to the administration's left over Vietnam moved to its right over Soviet Jewish emigration and suspicions of the Soviets aroused by the Arabs' initiation of the 1973 Mideast war. (These were the neoconservatives.) In the summer of 1973, Soviet human rights champion Andrei Sakharov publicly endorsed the Jackson-Vanik Amendment on Soviet emigration. This opened the floodgates, making it respectable—indeed mandatory—for the American intelligentsia to abandon its long-standing advocacy of East-West trade.

Just as liberal internationalism had carried American global involvement in the postwar period until Vietnam, so, too, the liberal defection over U.S.-Soviet relations (over human rights) was a pivotal event in undercutting the American commitment to détente in the mid-1970s. The center of gravity of American politics shifted to the right on U.S.-Soviet relations—but only on the human rights issues. While the carrots were denied, the sticks were not restored. Thus, the administration lost the ability to carry out its own strategy. The country's "cultural revolution" after Vietnam and Watergate thus claimed U.S.-Soviet relations as its second victim, around the time Indochina fell. Even Ravenal and Couve de Murville had not anticipated this.

This breakdown of America's Soviet policy was a tragedy, for several reasons. In a period of Soviet adventurism, American self-paralysis exacerbated the problem of Soviet irresponsibility and postponed the day when the Kremlin leaders would learn to accommodate themselves to the international system. That day would not come for another decade and a half, after a period marked by considerable international violence. Only dramatic Soviet overreaching in the several adventures of the late

1970s—and a sharp American reaction—restored the international balance.

Jimmy Carter campaigned for the presidency in 1976 promising a 6 percent cut in the U.S. defense budget and simultaneously criticizing the weakness of the Nixon-Ford-Kissinger policy of détente. Carter's was thus a schizophrenic administration, torn between the conciliatory liberalism of Secretary of State Cyrus Vance and the harder geopolitical line of Zbigniew Brzezinski. Carter, at Vance's urging, sought first to unlink the issues, maintaining vocal condemnation of Brezhnev's domestic repression but also negotiating vigorously on arms limitation— until the Soviets' African interventions and then the invasion of Afghanistan forced the president to withdraw his SALT II Treaty from Senate consideration. Linkage was thus proven a reality once again, with a vengeance. The Soviets' irresponsibility in the Third World had succeeded in poisoning even the more central elements of the relationship. Brzezinski remarked that SALT lay "buried in the sands of the Ogaden."[43] With it lay buried the decade's hopes for détente.

These regional conflicts of the 1970s raged until the late 1980s, when their resolution did as much to end the Cold War as their eruption had done to inflame it. The story of these regional conflicts contains many lessons and bears telling in more detail. It is to this we now turn.

7

THE VACUUM OF POWER:
ANGOLA, 1975

The subjects of this chapter and the next, Angola and Cambodia, are about as far apart as any two countries can be, and not only geographically. In the mid-1970s it was not self-evident that either country held any intrinsic strategic interest for the United States. The significance that they then acquired came as new crises emerged in both places that reflected the vacuum of American power. In Angola, the Soviets intervened, and the United States backed away from a confrontation. In Cambodia, the Indochina war continued in altered form after 1975 and took a course that reflected the virtual absence of American influence.

It was in Angola that Leonid Brezhnev brought home to Henry Kissinger a very crude lesson in power politics. Kissinger's visit to Moscow in January 1976 followed by a month the Senate vote that effectively ended American support for the two anti-Communist factions in the Angolan civil war. Kissinger hoped to discuss Angola with Brezhnev, to try to forestall a rout of the anti-Communists by the Soviet-backed Cuban army, but Brezhnev rebuffed him in a crude and humiliating fashion.

When Kissinger and his team arrived at Brezhnev's Kremlin office on the morning of January 21, 1976, they were greeted by a cheery and dapper general secretary. In his blue suit, blue shirt, and red patterned tie, he was a more elegant dresser than in the earlier period of our meetings with him, when he had not yet fully emerged as a world figure. On his lapel were four medals, which we were informed were: Hero of the Soviet Union, Hero of Socialist Labor, the Lenin Peace Prize, and the Joliot-Curie Prize. He was at the top of his form, self-confident and in command. As the two delegations took their seats on either side of the long conference table, the American journalists who had accompanied Kissinger were permitted to take pictures, record the banter, and pepper Brezhnev with questions. The following exchange took place:

> *Reporter:* Will Angola be among the subjects [to discuss]?
> *Brezhnev:* I have no questions about Angola. Angola is not my country.

Kissinger: It will certainly be discussed.

Gromyko: The agenda is always adopted by mutual agreement.

Kissinger: Then I will discuss it.

Brezhnev: You'll discuss it with Sonnenfeldt. That will insure complete agreement.

This was a sarcastic reference to Kissinger's hard-line senior adviser on Soviet affairs, Helmut Sonnenfeldt, whom Brezhnev did not like and who was frequently the butt of his jokes.

After the journalists left the room, Brezhnev opened with a statement avowing his eagerness to complete a new strategic arms limitation treaty (SALT II). Kissinger seconded the sentiments about SALT but raised Angola, saying it was intolerable that a country in the Western Hemisphere (Cuba) should launch a virtual invasion of Africa; Soviet support for this Cuban force was a precedent that the United States had to resist. At the 1972 summit, the two superpowers had pledged to practice restraint. If that principle was breached, Kissinger warned, the prospect sooner or later was for a cycle of action and counteraction that could lead to disastrous results.

Brezhnev responded dismissively that the two sides should be talking first and foremost about SALT and not raise "all sorts of extraneous matters." The Soviet Union had no military presence in Angola. Kissinger came back at him, repeating that the introduction of a Cuban expeditionary force in Angola backed by Soviet arms was a matter we had to take seriously. Brezhnev repeated that the two sides should be talking about strategic arms control, and he steered the meeting in his direction by launching into his substantive presentation of the Soviet position on the subject.

Kissinger tried again the next day. In the late afternoon, during a break in the meeting, as the principals were standing around at one end of the table, Kissinger mentioned Angola. Brezhnev said he did not want to discuss it and walked away.

Kissinger raised the subject again after the formal meeting resumed, asking if the Soviets had a reply to a U.S. diplomatic proposal of two weeks earlier. Brezhnev repeated flatly that the Soviets were playing no role in Angola. Kissinger did manage to have a more extensive discussion of the subject a day later with Gromyko. But the foreign minister, too, evaded any acknowledgment of Soviet responsibility or any willingness to negotiate. Within a month the anti-Communists were routed and the Soviet-backed Angolan Marxists emplaced in power. With the collapse of American leverage had come the evaporation of Soviet interest in paying heed to American opinions on the matter. Thus did Angola become a case history—almost a caricature—of Soviet behavior in the Brezhnev era.

Angola was an unlikely candidate for such intense and high-level jousting between the superpowers. It is a miserably poor country, about twice the size of Texas, on the west coast of southern Africa. Its population in the mid-1970s was about six million.

The Portuguese overseas empire, like the Belgian, won no prizes for enlightened stewardship. For much of its five-hundred-year domination of Angola, Portugal's main interest was to export the colony's population as slaves. Some 3 million of its tribal peoples were shipped to the New World before slavery was outlawed in the 1830s.[1] In the coastal cities, where the Portuguese settled, there grew up an urban, Europeanized mestiço class culturally and ethnically distinct from the much larger black tribal population of the interior, which remained relatively untouched by whatever was evolving on the coast. The Portuguese encouraged the country's ethnic, geographic, and social divisions, however, in order to divide and rule.[2] And long after the other European powers had accepted that colonialism was an anachronism, the lonely Portuguese clung to what they considered their "overseas provinces," as the embodiment of their notion of national grandeur and historical duty. Antonio Salazar, the longtime dictator, declared that "Africa is the complement of Europe, indispensable to its defense, a necessary support for its economy."[3]

Several black nationalist movements developed in Angola in the 1950s and 1960s, and a rebellion against the Portuguese began in earnest in 1961. We shall consider the individual groups more closely below. Each had ties to some outside powers. The CIA had contacts with at least one of them, beginning in the Kennedy period. The Nixon administration maintained the contact but concluded, with respect to southern Africa in general, that the liberation movements were making no headway in their armed struggle. An interagency policy study in 1969, in response to Kissinger's National Security Study Memorandum (NSSM) 39, led to a decision by Nixon to ease the pressures on the white regimes of the region on the assumption that they were "here to stay" for the foreseeable future.[4] Portugal enjoyed sympathy in Washington, moreover, as a loyal and founding member of NATO; the Portuguese Azores were a crucial refueling stop, for example, for our cargo aircraft on their way to resupply Israel in the 1973 war. U.S. military aid to Portugal was not intended to be used in the colonial territories, but reports persisted that much equipment was diverted for use against the guerrilla rebellions.[5]

The Nixon-Kissinger analysis was correct in assuming the military ineffectuality of the Angolan liberation forces. Where the administration went wrong was in missing the demoralizing impact the protracted colonial wars were having on the Portuguese army. It was a revolution in *Portugal* that liberated Angola—a coup against the tired dictatorship in Lisbon in April 1974 by left-leaning army officers whose program included, among other things, liquidating the overseas empire. While other guerrilla rebellions have succeeded (like the Algerian and Vietnamese) by exhausting the political will of the foreign power, the Angolans may be unique in their achievement of getting the foreign army to switch sides.

Portugal's imperial collapse put immediate pressure on southern Africa's remaining white bastions—Rhodesia, South-West Africa (known as Namibia), and the Republic of South Africa. The geographic buffer provided by Portuguese Angola and Mozambique was gone: the white minority-ruled regimes were now strategically more exposed. And they knew it. It was in 1974, in the wake of those developments, that South Africa launched its secret program to develop a nuclear weapons capability—its defiant response to the new pressures it was under.[6] But the historical tide let loose by Portugal could not be stopped by such means. The white regimes were not "here to stay." The nuclear program would be abandoned in the early 1990s by South African President F. W. de Klerk as he was abandoning apartheid itself.

The course of the revolution inside Portugal, however, not the fallout in Africa, was the U.S. government's main preoccupation at the time. By mid-1975, the prospect of a Communist victory in Angola seemed to be only the accompaniment of the dangerous drift toward a Communist outcome in Lisbon.[7] A struggle had developed in Lisbon within the Armed Forces Movement that had taken power in the 1974 coup; far-left officers aligned with the Communist party were locked in political combat with more moderate officers whose political platform included turning over power to a civilian democratic government. Over the next few years, Kissinger was to be deeply troubled by the apparent resurgence of the Communist parties in Western Europe. This was the phenomenon of "Eurocommunism," usually typified by the more moderate line adopted by the French and Italian Communist parties, which were gaining electoral ground in the period. Kissinger regarded the phenomenon as yet another example of the demoralization of the Western democracies in a time of American retreat and Soviet arrogance. Portugal's Communist party remained one of the most incorrigibly Stalinist, which made Kissinger's alarm at the trend in Lisbon all the greater—until late in 1975, when (against Kissinger's expectations) the moderate officers rallied, took over the Armed Forces Movement from the radicals, and set Portugal on the path of democracy.

As far as Angola was concerned, all the coup leaders in Lisbon, of whatever stripe, proclaimed the end of empire, and the date of November 11, 1975, was set for Angolan independence. At the urging of the Organization of African Unity (OAU), the three main liberation movements agreed, in an accord signed at Alvor in Portugal on January 15, 1975, to join in a transitional coalition government to unify the various fighting forces and prepare for a democratically elected government after independence. The coalition soon broke apart as tribal, ideological, regional, and factional rivalries led to an outbreak of fighting within a month of Alvor. It soon escalated into a full-scale civil war.

THE ANGOLAN CIVIL WAR

The most effective of the three liberation groups seemed to be the Popular Movement for the Liberation of Angola (or MPLA, by its initials in Portuguese). The MPLA's leadership was Marxist-oriented, with ties to the Soviet bloc, Cuba, and left-wing political elements in Portugal. Its domestic support came mainly from the Kimbundu, the most urbanized of the country's major population groups, as well as the coastal towns-people in general. Much of its leadership came from the substantial mulatto community, which was a source of friction. The MPLA strived to build a nontribal, socialist national movement, in order to transcend its narrow ethnic base; it was credited with an effective political organization. By mid-January 1976, the MPLA was estimated by scholar Chester Crocker to represent about one-third of the country's population.[8]

The FNLA (National Front for the Liberation of Angola) was led by Holden Roberto, who had reportedly been on a $10,000-a-year CIA retainer, on and off, since the Kennedy administration. Roberto was a kinsman of Zairian president Mobutu's wife. The FNLA was strong in the north of Angola, among the Bakongo, who comprised about 15 percent of the population. It was dependent on Zaire for military support, though it also received material help after 1973 from China.[9]

The third liberation group was UNITA, or the National Union for the Total Independence of Angola, headed by Dr. Jonas Savimbi. Savimbi had studied medicine in Portugal; kicked out of Portugal for his political activities, he then switched to political science, in which he obtained a doctorate in Switzerland. He was a senior colleague of Roberto's in the FNLA but split from Roberto in 1964. Savimbi was no Jeffersonian democrat—none of them were—but he was a charismatic figure and the only major liberation leader who had personally conducted any kind of sustained guerrilla campaign against the Portuguese from within Angola. His credentials as a nationalist and a revolutionary had been blessed by Che Guevara himself.[10]

UNITA's main tribal base was the Ovimbundu of the center and south. It had very little international visibility or support before 1975, except for some small-scale backing from Zaire, Zambia, and China. In 1975, South African forces intervened on its behalf, which weakened its international standing. Estimates of its broad domestic support, however, ranged from 40 to 65 percent of the country.[11] A fact-finding committee from the OAU reported in 1975 that UNITA would likely win at least a plurality and possibly a majority in the free elections to be held under the Alvor accord.[12]

INTERVENTION

As the civil war among these groups escalated in 1975, it drew in an array of outside powers and swiftly became a global, not just a local, concern. Americans, Soviets, Cubans, Chinese, South Africans, Portuguese, Zairians, Zambians, and Namibians all played a role, with the Soviets and Cubans intervening to put the MPLA into power and most of the rest intervening to back UNITA and the FNLA against them.

Who intervened first is still a subject of intense dispute,[13] and that question played a part in the fateful debate in the U.S. Congress at the end of 1975. Critics considered the American involvement illegitimate because it was said to have provoked Communist intervention instead of being a response to it; the Ford administration replied that the critics had their facts wrong. Yet since much of the American involvement was covert, the administration was inhibited about making its version of the facts known until a domestic political crisis had already erupted. I would summarize the sequence as follows.

The international lineup formed even before the Alvor accord, as leftist officers in the new Portuguese military regime (including Adm. Antonio Rosa Coutinho, high commissioner in Luanda, Angola's capital) made sure that weapons were left behind for the MPLA as Portuguese troops withdrew. The "Red Admiral," as he was called, later boasted: "I gave the MPLA the opportunity—otherwise they wouldn't have won."[14] Soviet weapons started appearing in MPLA hands in late 1974. Meanwhile, the Chinese had established their political ties with the opposing FNLA in 1973 and sent arms and 120 military advisers to the FNLA in their camps in Zaire in June 1974. The United States revived its payments to the FNLA's Roberto in July 1974. In January 1975, just one week after Alvor, President Ford approved a $300,000 grant to the FNLA for political organizing (a small printing press, some broadcasting equipment, party badges, uniforms, and so forth).

Around the same time, the Soviets were making a decision to provide thousands of infantry weapons, machine guns, bazookas, and rockets. This matériel began arriving in March, when thirty Soviet cargo planes carried it into nearby Brazzaville, one of the staging posts for shipments into Angola. In April, another one hundred tons arrived by air in Dar es Salaam, Tanzania. As this equipment was arriving in March and April, a further Soviet-Cuban decision was being made to send over two hundred Cuban military advisers to train the MPLA in the use of the equipment.[15] The Cuban advisers arrived in May, followed by a second wave of Soviet deliveries, including mortars and armored vehicles.

The dispute is less over this sequence of events than about their interpretation. To many critics of the American involvement, President Ford's decision in January 1975 to dispense $300,000 to the FNLA for political activities was the pivotal event, antedating (and presumably provoking) the Soviet and Cuban involvement.[16] Yet the record suggests either a parallel evolution of engagement on both sides or else hesitant American decisions on *political* involvement paralleling much bolder Soviet and Cuban decisions to send *weapons* and *military personnel*.

According to William Hyland, who served as the State Department's director of intelligence and research and then as President Ford's deputy assistant for national security affairs during this period, the Ford decision of January 1975 represented a ridiculously small sum, perhaps enough to cause uneasiness in the lower reaches of the State Department but not enough for any significant impact on the ground in Angola. Kissinger's assistant secretary of state for African affairs, Nathaniel Davis, later resigned as our Angola involvement grew, believing it a risky venture that would only lead to an escalation on both sides; Davis was gun-shy, having been badly burned by controversy as ambassador in Chile at the time of the Pinochet coup.[17] Similarly, according to Hyland, Director of Central Intelligence William Colby—burned by earlier controversies about his Vietnam activities and enmeshed in congressional inquiries into the whole history of the CIA's covert actions—was no eager participant in the growing Angola involvement, either.

Ford and Kissinger thus met with bureaucratic resistance and procrastination, accounting for what they both considered a weak and inadequate U.S. response to the growing Soviet and Cuban military intervention.[18] It is hard to imagine, moreover, that Soviet and Cuban decisions to escalate in the spring and summer of 1975 were not also affected by simultaneous events in Indochina, especially the obvious unwillingness of Congress to support continued U.S. engagement in a faraway conflict.

In any event, by July 1975 the MPLA, with its extensive external supplies, was gaining ground fast, driving both the FNLA and UNITA organizations out of Luanda. The leaders of both Zaire (Mobutu) and Zambia (the respected Kenneth Kaunda) appealed urgently to Washington not to allow the minority Marxist MPLA to seize power on the back of Soviet and Cuban intervention. Kaunda visited Washington in April 1975 to deliver this message. President Ford then decided (on July 18) on significant U.S. support for UNITA and the FNLA: In four separate decisions, about $32 million was disbursed between July and November, plus $16 million in Department of Defense surplus weapons. It was over this escalation in U.S. policy that Assistant Secretary Davis resigned. (The scale of this July decision makes even clearer how puny the January subvention of $300,000 for political activity really was.) Around the same time, China and South Africa began to supply arms as well.

The tit for tat continued and escalated. In August, U.S. intelligence finally detected the presence of Soviet and Cuban military advisers and trainers—and now the Cuban combat troops.[19] The MPLA now controlled twelve out of Angola's sixteen provinces, including most of the coast, and had forced UNITA out of several major cities in the center and south of the country.

UNITA then turned for additional help to South Africa, which launched incursions with its own forces into MPLA-held areas. By September-October, although Cuba had sent several hundred military advisers and about seven hundred combat troops, South African intervention and the U.S. equipment turned the tables; the MPLA was beaten back. In October, massive new increments of Soviet and Cuban military assistance began to arrive, however. By November, a few thousand Cuban combat troops had arrived, flown first by the Cuban air force and later by Soviet military transport. They took part in the fighting.

In early November, as Cuban leaders contemplated their major escalation in the level of combat troops, a major question in their minds was whether the United States might intervene effectively to block it. The Cubans are said in authoritative accounts to have concluded that in view of Washington's domestic crises (Watergate, the fall of Indochina, congressional investigations of the CIA), plus the unpopularity of South Africa, an American reaction was unlikely.[20] They calculated better than they knew, for the U.S. government was close to running out of funds.[21]

On Independence Day, November 11, 1975, the MPLA declared itself the government of Angola, in violation both of the Alvor accord and of the OAU's policy favoring a national unity coalition. The Soviets and their allies, but only about one-third of the OAU's membership, recognized the MPLA. Cuban troops totaled about four thousand by December.

Some scholars, including Raymond Garthoff, have supported the thesis that the Soviets were reacting to the initiatives of others—specifically, that the Soviets were responding in 1974 to the Chinese involvement, then in 1975 to the American.[22] The Chinese activity throughout was minimal, however.[23] As for the Soviet involvement, the record suggests that the idea of intervention was more a Cuban idea than a Soviet one, reflecting Castro's attempt to rekindle the revolutionary spirit of Che Guevara and burnish his own image as an international figure.[24] And as Hyland points out, the Cubans first came in when the MPLA was *winning*.[25] Nor was the arrival of the South Africans as decisive a military factor as some have argued. The Cuban military advisers arrived before any South African military involvement as well as before any U.S. arms had been shipped.[26] The South African involvement became a significant political liability, however.

Georgii Arbatov was an eyewitness to some of the Soviet deliberations on Angola at the time. From the vantage point of his contacts with key Politburo figures and advisers, he could see a policy that derived essentially from temptation and opportunism—a policy "loaded with revolutionary jargon and closely intertwined with imperial ambitions." The Soviet military expected to win easily: "The Americans will swallow it," they argued. Arbatov recounts in his memoirs that he had a chance to warn Brezhnev personally that it would be a terrible mistake: While it would succeed in the immediate sense, it would set a bad precedent of superpower military intervention and "undermine the very foundations of détente." But Brezhnev and his key advisers responded to him with incredulity, grumbling about past American policies in other regions for which, apparently, the Americans only deserved their comeuppance.[27] It was as if Brezhnev and his colleagues had no category of thought for the concept of self-restraint, of not seizing an opportunity, of not filling a vacuum.

THE SENATE PULLS THE PLUG

Most of the back and forth on the ground in Angola took place out of the spotlight of public concern in the United States. Our own involvement was still theoretically covert. The appropriate committees of Congress had been briefed on President Ford's decisions, without any significant objection. Kissinger expressed public alarm at the scale and blatant quality of the Soviet-Cuban military intervention. We had considerable African support as well, based on negative reaction to the Soviet-Cuban intervention and on the clearly stated OAU preference for a compromise coalition.

Against this background, Kissinger began in October to sound out the Soviet Union on some sort of political deal to call a halt to the cycle of escalation. A direct correspondence was begun with Brezhnev.[28] A sharp message was sent to Moscow on November 22 expressing astonishment at the Soviets' recognition of the MPLA, contrary to the OAU's wishes, protesting the extent of sophisticated Soviet military equipment flooding into Angola and strongly recommending that the Soviets reexamine their policy. At that point, the MPLA's setbacks should have argued for such a compromise from the Soviet point of view. The United States proposed cessation of all outside military assistance and an internal negotiation under African auspices. According to Kissinger's later testimony, the Soviets' answers were "evasive but not totally negative."[29] They sent messages saying there was no Soviet military presence in Angola. In late November and early December, there were peace feelers from various Soviet diplomats sounding out the U.S. commitment to a compromise. Soviet president Nikolai Podgornii told the British ambassador in Moscow that a coalition was possible. A diplomatic mission to Africa by Davis's successor as assistant secretary of state for African affairs, William Schaufele, backed by letters from President Ford to thirty-two African heads of state, sought to mobilize African support for a compromise. On December 9, Soviet ambassador Anatolii Dobrynin was invited to an Oval Office meeting with Ford at which the U.S. position was forcefully presented.

At about that moment, the Soviet airlift suddenly halted. A Soviet message on December 18 stressed that Moscow had never wanted a civil war in Angola. The message called for an end to all foreign intervention (while refusing to equate its help for the MPLA with our "neo-colonialist intervention"). A deal may have been in reach.

By a quirk of fate, this was the moment when the supposedly covert contest in Angola became the subject of a public uproar. The story of Nathaniel Davis's resignation in July as assistant secretary of state leaked out in a *New York Times* report by Seymour Hersh on December 14; it dwelled at length on Davis's grievances: his principled objection to U.S. arms shipments, his preference for diplomatic solutions, and his frustration with Kissinger's supposedly adamant insistence on a military confrontation with the Soviets.[30] Senate critics of the policy then forced a secret session of the Senate on December 17 to educate the members in the scope of the covert program. The details leaked and fed a rapidly escalating public discussion that left very little still secret.

In the year that Saigon had fallen, the fear that we were walking blindly into another jungle quagmire was widespread—confirming Earl Ravenal's prediction about Americans' likely allergy to anything that looked like a repetition of Vietnam. "If we have learned anything from Vietnam, it is that the United States cannot police the world," said Sen. Edward Kennedy of Massachusetts during the Senate debates.[31] "I am tired, the Congress is tired, the American people are tired of the United States intruding into areas where it should not be," said Sen. John V. Tunney, Democrat of California.[32] On December 17, on the day of the secret session, Senator Tunney introduced an amendment to the defense appropriations bill for fiscal year 1976 banning any use of the funds for any such activity in Angola.

Then specific details of the covert program appeared in a second *Times* story by Seymour Hersh, two days after the supposedly secret session. This piece argued that the Soviets' involvement, far from justifying the U.S. program, was in fact a response to American actions, especially Ford's $300,000 decision in January.[33] This article, too, had an electrifying effect, strengthening the case for the program's opponents.

On December 19 (the day the second Hersh article appeared), the Senate voted twice. A motion (supported by the administration) to table, or kill, the Tunney Amendment was defeated, 58–21. Then a formal vote to adopt the Tunney Amendment won by 54–22.

The administration was stunned, especially by the failure of Senate conservatives to support what it saw as a clear-cut case of resistance to Soviet aggression. Sen. Jesse Helms, Republican of North Carolina, was against the administration on both votes. Sen. Henry M. Jackson, Democrat of Washington, who had been browbeating Kissinger for three years for alleged softness toward the Soviets, voted against the president on the first (crucial) vote and then threw the administration the bone of being "paired against" Tunney on the second vote, after everyone knew the issue had been decided. Barry Goldwater, Republican of Arizona, did not vote on either bill but announced his support for the president on the second one. Bob Dole, Republican of Kansas, recorded no vote on either.

That we were on the same side as the South Africans was a deadly moral handicap. Other liberal arguments were traditional. As for the egregious Soviet intervention (which no one defended), the argument was made that our resort should be to peaceful and not military means. Sen. Hubert Humphrey (D-Minn.) urged "a tremendous diplomatic offensive to get those Cubans out of there, to point out exactly what they are up to. . . ."[34] Georgia governor Jimmy Carter, running for president, called for an end to U.S. military aid; he suggested that "economic aid of a humanitarian nature can be granted to one or more of the Angolan factions but through normal congressional appropriations and not through secret channels of the CIA."[35] Sen. Dick Clark of Iowa was unconcerned even by the prospect of a Soviet victory because it was certain to be short-lived: "The history of Soviet intervention in Africa," he said, "is one of almost total failure. . . . If the MPLA wins, the Soviets will be lucky if they can hang on for a year or two."[36] The Soviets would lose goodwill in Africa, and the United States would gain by its moral example, Sen. Clark believed:

> Even if all efforts to bring an end to foreign intervention in Angola fail, I am convinced that the best way to counter Soviet "influence" there is for the United States to stop its own intervention and to make it clear that we respect the independence of Angola and seek good relations with whatever government comes to power there.
>
> If the Soviet Union then persists in its intervention, it alone will be jeopardizing its relations in that region by interfering in the internal affairs of an independent nation.[37]

Fear of involvement in a foreign conflict was probably the dominant emotion at work, and a powerful one at that. (The House was to approve the Tunney amendment on January 27 by 323–99.) But there was also a painful debate about whether covert action was compatible with democracy. The secrecy of the program was used as a substantive argument against it: Our enemies knew what we were doing, the argument went, so why can't the American people know? To some liberals, the issue was *ad hominem*: The covert military involvement was a symptom of Henry Kissinger's obsession with secrecy, which bespoke his European realpolitik and distaste for American democracy, which was of a piece with the illegality that was rampant in the Nixon administration as demonstrated by Watergate and the secret bombing of Cambodia. "Kissinger's folly," exclaimed Rep. Charles Diggs of New York.[38] London-based Africanist Colin Legum wrote in the *New Republic* that American liberals had talked themselves into the frame of mind that anything Kissinger was involved in had to be wrong:

One gets the impression from this distance that if Kissinger were to say that Angola should be handed over to the Russian sphere of interest, liberals would rise in unison to condemn him for rank appeasement: and if he says that the Russians are indulging in reckless power politics in Angola he will be equally attacked. "Henry can do no right" seems to have become a substitute for objective thinking. Is one right in supposing (as the Russians seem to believe) that the US is to be prevented from playing an effective international role so long as Kissinger is in office? You liberals sometimes make it sound that way.[39]

These personal attacks on Kissinger bore no relation to the subject at hand, which was a policy dispute. The program had been begun covertly in order to provide political protection for the vulnerable neighboring countries that were our necessary partners in the endeavor; quiet involvement also minimized the challenge to either outside power's prestige and left more scope for pursuit of the diplomatic compromise that so many were advocating. This was an intelligence operation conceived in regular procedures in the executive branch and communicated to the requisite committees according to the applicable rules of congressional oversight. Kissinger submitted into the hearing record in January 1976 a listing of nearly forty briefings of more than two dozen senators, 150 congressmen, and over 100 staffers between July and December 1975.[40]

Whether covert action is compatible with democracy is a fair question but a complex one. We will turn to this question again in chapter 14. Our society as well as our political system places a premium on openness. Yet, since our Founding Fathers, secrecy and intelligence activities have been an integral part of our governmental process. It is perfectly possible, moreover, to design procedures of democratic accountability through congressional oversight while maintaining secrecy toward adversaries.

The more interesting problem in 1975 (and we shall see it recur later over Central America) was one of the structural flaws in the procedure of oversight. The Hughes-Ryan Amendments of 1974 had set up a procedure requiring "timely" reporting of covert actions to eight congressional committees (the Foreign Relations, Armed Services, Appropriations, and Intelligence committees in both houses) subject to a pledge of maintaining confidentiality. While the committees' right to veto was not formally accepted, the briefings were an opportunity, at a minimum, for a test of the political waters. At Kissinger's January 1976 Senate hearings, he was pressed hard on the question whether the briefed legislators' silence should have been construed as assent. His answer essentially was that the administration could be forgiven if it concluded after forty briefings that a policy was not overwhelmingly controversial.[41]

The textbook purpose of congressional standing committees is to take on a certain responsibility on behalf of colleagues in the chamber at large. In this case (as with the CIA's mining of Nicaraguan harbors in 1984), the committee members who had been informed of the activities between July and December and raised no strong objection all ran for cover when tendentious leaks occurred and an emotional public debate then raged. The whole issue was simply reopened. The structure of authority (or lack of it) in Congress thus assured that a policy decision legitimately made by a president, properly briefed to the elected representatives in Congress and to which they did not object, could be killed by any opponent of the policy via a selective (or inaccurate) leak to an ideologically sympathetic journalist. One might more appropriately consider *this* inconsistent with our democratic process.

A different criticism of Kissinger's covert approach came from Daniel Patrick Moynihan, then our flamboyant permanent representative to the United Nations. Moynihan, who made vigorous speeches at the United Nations denouncing the Soviets for their neocolonialism in Africa, faults Kissinger for not leading a more forthright public campaign. Kissinger's preoccupation with the back-room style of diplomacy, in this view, coupled with a kind of intellectual as well as physical exhaustion on the part of the administration, forfeited the chance to mobilize domestic and world opinion.[42] The question can be asked whether Moynihan's strategy would have worked, given the depth of the Vietnam trauma. The Ford administration clearly lost control of events with its own strategy, however.

CONSEQUENCES

After the Senate voted on December 19, the Soviet military airlift to Angola resumed on December 25. The force of our moral example of restraint had no noticeable effect—except to encourage Soviet-Cuban escalation: the number of Cuban troops quickly tripled from about four thousand in early December to eleven thousand or twelve thousand by the end of January. The South Africans pulled out; FNLA and UNITA forces retreated into the bush, hoping to be able to sustain a guerrilla war. The "People's Republic of Angola" was proclaimed and later signed a Friendship Treaty with the Soviet Union. Arkady Shevchenko, a specialist in UN affairs in the Soviet Foreign Ministry then contemplating defection to the United States, recounts in his memoir that his leaders in Moscow were "overjoyed" at the lack of American resistance to their intervention in Angola; Shevchenko himself was "dismayed."[43] In June 1976, the Tunney Amendment's cutoff of fiscal year 1976 funds for Angolan operations was converted into a permanent ban by legislation introduced by Dick Clark (the famous Clark Amendment).

Kissinger took the blow hard. The *ad hominem* attacks were coming not only from the Left but now also from the Right as Ronald Reagan launched a challenge to Ford's renomination based in part on an attack on détente. (Ford sheepishly abolished the word "détente" from his policy pronouncements.) The personal attacks during the Angola debate made Kissinger conclude that he was becoming more of a liability than an asset to the country. In late November 1975, Ford fired James Schlesinger, his hard-line secretary of defense, and also CIA director William Colby. Kissinger was seen (wrongly) as the mastermind behind this move, which eliminated two men who had been the source of much frustration for him. The attacks on him only grew worse.

Kissinger was at the point of resignation. He spent much of December agonizing over the matter with his staff and preparing a resignation letter. He was once again in a Spenglerian mood about the future of the free world, and it was not a pleasant period for those of us who worked for him. Then he went to see Ford in early January and offered to step down in order to ease Ford's political burdens. The president refused the offer. As Ford recounts in his memoirs: "I was shocked by the idea. His resignation was something I simply couldn't accept. The country needed him—I needed him—to implement our foreign policy at this difficult time."[44]

Even through all the political storms over Kissinger, Ford remained a staunch admirer of his secretary of state. I suspect that Kissinger knew all along that Ford would react that way. Likewise, Ford was amused that Kissinger hedged his bets by showing him the letter of resignation only in draft.[45]

Kissinger's trip to Moscow in January 1976, as we saw at the beginning of this chapter, was the occasion for a last-ditch effort to resuscitate the Soviet interest in a compromise. Brezhnev and Gromyko admitted only that they had provided fraternal help to the MPLA against the "colonialists," including what Gromyko termed "insignificant" quantities of arms. (Angolan president Neto, in a radio interview at about the same time, spoke gratefully of MiG-21s, T-34 and T-54 tanks, armored personnel carriers, antitank missiles, SAM-7 antiaircraft missiles, rocket launchers, and AK-47 automatic rifles supplied by the Soviets.)[46] A peace settlement was now a matter for the new Angolan government to decide, Gromyko averred. He did not see why any of this should affect U.S.-Soviet relations.

Kissinger disputed all this with a fervor dimmed by his knowledge that, with our leverage gone, his démarches were to no avail. He told the Soviets that they could hardly disclaim responsibility for an intervention based on a massive Soviet airlift and sealift of troops and weapons. He called it a tragedy; he predicted it would undermine the policy of détente in the United States; he predicted that the Cubans might well face a protracted guerrilla war. Kissinger predicted, in short, serious consequences out of proportion to the intrinsic significance of the Angolan conflict.

This was Ford and Kissinger's honest conviction, which they reiterated publicly in the various unsuccessful attempts to head off the Tunney and Clark amendments. The issue for them was not even the MPLA's Marxist orientation but rather the precedent set by the Soviet-Cuban military intervention. In Mozambique, the other major Portuguese African colony that had newly won independence, the United States had quickly recognized the new government led by the Marxist FRELIMO liberation movement—the difference being that FRELIMO seemed to have majority backing and was not being foisted on the country by a foreign expeditionary force. As Raymond Garthoff has put it, "The American stake in the Angolan situation was not *threatened* by the Soviet-Cuban involvement on the other side; it was *created* by it."[47] Likewise, half the countries of the Organization of African Unity, voting in January—even after the winner was clear—continued to insist that only a coalition could legitimately govern Angola. The United States could easily have lived with a coalition government that included the Marxist MPLA; if Alvor had held, there would have been no Angola crisis. But the reality of 1975 was a dramatic projection of Soviet power, at a moment of American weakness, tipping the scales in a local conflict on a continent that had been (since the Congo) free of superpower confrontations.

American abdication, in Kissinger's view, was bound to have larger consequences. As he put it in his testimony on January 29:

Do we want our potential adversaries to conclude that in the event of future challenges America's internal divisions are likely to deprive us of even minimal leverage over developments of global significance? . . .

We are told that by providing money and arms for Angola we are duplicating the mistakes we made in Vietnam. Such an argument confuses the expenditure of tens of millions of dollars with the commitment of U.S. troops. If we accept such a gross distortion of history—if we accept the claim that we can no longer do anything to aid our friends abroad because we will inevitably do too much—then the tragedy of Vietnam will indeed be monumental.[48]

Kissinger's warning to Brezhnev in Moscow the week before he now repeated before Congress. In the long run, he said, a price would be paid by Moscow as well: "When one great power attempts to obtain special positions of influence based on military interventions, the other power is sooner or later bound to act to offset this advantage in some other place or manner. This will inevitably lead to a chain of action and reaction typical of other historic eras in which great powers maneuvered for advantage, only to find themselves sooner or later embroiled in a major crisis, and often in open conflict."[49]

In the next five years, as the Soviets exploited other power vacuums, the chickens would, in fact, come home to roost. Georgii Arbatov describes what he saw from his vantage point in Moscow:

As often happens in politics, if you get away with something and it looks as if you've been successful, you are practically doomed to repeat the policy. You do this until you blunder into a really serious mess. That is what happened in Angola. At the moment we did not expect big troubles, because the Americans were preoccupied with healing the wounds of Watergate and launching a heated election campaign. Of course they protested, and some strong words were used, both through diplomatic channels and in the media. But relations remained more or less intact, and the fact that the Soviet Union became even more suspect and untrustworthy was hidden under the surface of what soon seemed to become business as usual. . . .

I began to worry that our government would remember only the success of the action and the absence of serious international complications. Indeed, my concerns later proved to be justified.

We were unable to resist further temptation to become involved in the complex internal affairs of other countries. After Angola, we went boldly down the path of intervention and expansion that we had beaten so assuredly. It led us through Ethiopia, Yemen, a series of African countries, and, eventually, into Afghanistan.[50]

In the United States, Angola was indeed another knife thrust into the already wounded body of détente. Conservatives who shied away from supporting the administration's policy of counterintervention urged that American grain sales to Moscow or strategic arms limitation talks be halted. This was "a very simple way to get the Communists out of Angola without getting us involved there at all," said Jesse Helms in the Senate debate.[51] Whatever had happened to linkage? conservatives asked pointedly. President Ford was taken aback by critics who blamed *his administration* for "losing Angola." He later wrote: "Instead of getting mad at the Senate, people tended to blame me. Angola was going down the drain, they said, and as President, Ford was responsible. All this led to new questions. Was détente worthwhile, or just another Soviet trick? The public quite understandably found it hard to comprehend why we should have any dealings with the Russians when they were stealing a march on us in Africa."[52]

Kissinger lashed back. He lamented that Congress had deprived the president of both carrots and sticks, killing off trade relations with the Soviets via the Jackson-Vanik Amendment and blocking strong counteraction on the ground via the Tunney and Clark amendments. "We cannot engage in a rhetoric of confrontation while depriving ourselves of the means to confront," he riposted to conservatives in a speech in San Francisco on February 3, 1976.

Kissinger's predicament was partly of his own making. He had badly mishandled his relations with congressional conservatives. He never had a serious conversation with Jesse Helms, for example, on Angola, and Helms's vote for Tunney was in large part an expression of deep distrust of a secretary of state who seemed so obviously to disdain conservatives like Helms. Kissinger's State Department minions also committed the gaffe of asking liberal Republican senator Charles Percy to try to bring along Helms—Percy being one of the few Washington figures that Helms detested even more than he detested Kissinger.[53]

While it was fair to tag some of the hawkish critics with hypocrisy on Angola (and some of the liberal critics with strategic shortsightedness), Kissinger had laid himself open to attack in other ways. The nebulous notion of restraining the Soviets by a "web of vested interests" or "interrelationships" had come from some of Kissinger's own rhetorical enthusiasm in the headier, earlier days of détente. At the time of Nixon's 1972 summit, Kissinger defended the expanding economic and technical agreements with the Soviets as key elements of a strategy to institutionalize cooperation. The theory of linkage, tying trade and arms control to Soviet regional behavior, went back even earlier, to a time (1969) when we were withholding such goodies as explicit leverage. But in 1975, Kissinger and Ford were loath to sacrifice arms control and argued that both it and economic relations were in the mutual interest, not favors we did for the Soviets.

Undoubtedly, domestic politics played a role. Grain sales to the USSR were a boon to the Republican Midwest; achievement of a SALT agreement would have made a difference in Ford's general-election race against Jimmy Carter. (I have been told this by more than one of Carter's foreign policy team.) It was undoubtedly the attraction of a SALT agreement that led Ford to send Kissinger to Moscow in January 1976 in the unpropitious context of the aftermath of the Angola humiliation.

While the conservatives could quote back at Kissinger some of his own more sentimental utterances about the "web of vested interests," they were willfully ignoring his hard-boiled advice about geopolitical combat. As he explained in January 29 testimony: "[T]here is no substitute for a local balance; indirect pressures [like economic leverage] can succeed only if rapid local victories are foreclosed."[54] As the "hero," if you will, of hard-line Nixon policies in Vietnam, Cambodia, Chile, Jordan, and elsewhere, Kissinger had never in his career imagined that a more constructive relationship with the Soviets could be achieved without steadfast containment of their expansionism.

The United States struggled in 1976 to reconstruct a southern Africa policy on the ruins of the Angola fiasco. The South African ambassador to Washington, Roelof ("Pik") Botha, came to Kissinger with a startling proposition from the government of John Vorster in Pretoria. With the collapse of the Portuguese Empire, South Africa's support for the white minority regime of Ian Smith in Rhodesia was no longer physically sustainable. Rhodesia, squeezed by UN economic sanctions, was now landlocked, having lost its Mozambican outlet to the sea. The South Africans were retrenching; they were prepared to deliver Ian Smith to a majority-rule settlement in Rhodesia if Kissinger could deliver a fair negotiation and a moderate black interlocutor.

Thereupon Kissinger seized the high ground, made his first trip to Africa, and delivered an eloquent speech in Lusaka, Zambia, on April 27, committing the Ford administration to majority rule in Rhodesia (and also Namibia and South Africa). It was a way of eating crow seven years after the notorious NSSM 39 study predicting that the whites were "here to stay." It was, more importantly, a way to try to promote moderate outcomes and moderate black leaders—he was trying to boost Kaunda's standing, for example, by making the speech in Lusaka—before the radicalizing effect of the Soviet-Cuban influence in Africa grew. After an agonizing negotiation involving the United States and Britain, South Africa and Rhodesia, Zambia and moderate Rhodesian black exiles, Ian Smith was essentially brutalized by Vorster into accepting a version of majority rule in September. Once Ford lost the November election and Jimmy Carter became president, however, U.S. policy became less concerned with promoting moderates in the same fashion. The compromise with Smith was abandoned, the negotiations fell apart, and the radical Robert Mugabe (whom we, Kaunda, and others had sought to block) inherited power when a final settlement ultimately was reached.

The Soviets learned the wrong lesson from the Angola adventure. It was, as noted, the beginning of an exuberant period in their policy. Arbatov's fear—that his Kremlin masters would grow overconfident and overreach—was borne out. In Angola, exactly as Kissinger had predicted to Gromyko, the Cuban occupying army (which eventually reached over 50,000 troops) became the target of a protracted guerrilla war. The tables would ultimately be turned in Angola, as elsewhere in the Third World. The Soviets would learn at considerable cost the broader lesson that Kissinger had tried to teach—that to every action there would sooner or later be a reaction and that a steep price would someday be paid out of proportion to the initial gain.

8

CAMBODIA AFTER 1975:

FROM WAR TO WAR

One of the more mystifying aspects of Henry Kissinger's secret negotiation in Paris with Le Duc Tho in 1972 was the discussion of Cambodia. As Kissinger's wrangling with the chief North Vietnamese negotiator worked its tumultuous way toward agreement on a cease-fire in Vietnam, Kissinger pressed also for an end to the fighting in both Laos and Cambodia. He warned that continuation of the war in those two countries would almost certainly disrupt whatever settlement was reached in Vietnam. It was also the view of all of us on the American side of the table that it was the North Vietnamese who had brought the war to those neighboring countries and that they now had both the power and the incentive to wind the conflict down throughout Indochina.

Le Duc Tho, whose Politburo responsibilities had included masterminding the revolutionary war in Cambodia, seemed to agree. "The questions of the war in Vietnam and Cambodia are closely linked," he assured Kissinger in late September 1972; "once the war is settled in Vietnam, there is no reason for the war to continue in Cambodia."[1] He committed North Vietnam, in Article 20 of the Paris Agreement, to withdraw its troops from Laotian and Cambodian territory within sixty days and to cease using it for purposes of waging war in Vietnam. He committed Hanoi, in private understandings with Kissinger, to "do its utmost" to deliver its Laotian Communist allies to the negotiating table and to "actively contribute" to the same in Cambodia.[2]

A cease-fire and political compromise were duly achieved in Laos in February 1973, within a month of the Paris Agreement on Vietnam. But on Cambodia, as time passed, Le Duc Tho pleaded his inability to deliver his Cambodian "comrades" (known as the Khmer Rouge*). We were

---

*I.e., "Red Khmer," Khmer being an ethnic designation for Cambodians. The term "Kampuchea" is also occasionally used for Cambodia and was the official designation of the country during the period of Khmer Rouge rule, 1975–78.

skeptical at first, but this turned out to be one of the noteworthy occasions when Le Duc Tho was telling the truth.

As we were later to discover, the dispute between the North Vietnamese and the Khmer Rouge over whether to accept a cease-fire in Cambodia at the end of 1972 was a crucial moment in the growing clash between them that produced the third Indochina war six years later. Khmer Rouge defiance must have been particularly galling to Le Duc Tho, Hanoi's proconsul if not godfather to the Cambodian revolution, all the more so as North Vietnam continued to be a main source of support for the Khmer Rouge military effort; in early 1973, Hanoi was still providing weapons and supplies, military advisers, some direct combat help (like the manning of heavy artillery and rocket launchers), rear-service administrative support, and transport and other logistical assistance.[3] Without Hanoi, the Cambodian Communists would not have gotten anywhere. Now, however, the Khmer Rouge considered a cease-fire a dangerous risk: According to their own later statement, they resisted all such pressures in 1972–73 because "if the Kampuchean revolution had accepted a cease-fire it would have collapsed."[4] They considered North Vietnam's importunings—and its deal with the Americans—a betrayal. (This admission by the Khmer Rouge of their military and political vulnerability in 1973 casts an interesting light on whether the United States and the Cambodian government might not have been able to defeat the Khmer Rouge if we had not labored under the strict constraints imposed by Congress, including the termination of all U.S. military activities later in the year.[5])

We learn from Prince Norodom Sihanouk's memoir that the Khmer Rouge were sufficiently angered by Hanoi's pressures that they asked Hanoi to remove its troops from Cambodia.[6] But the North Vietnamese remained—defying their allies' wishes in addition to violating their explicit commitment to us in Article 20 of the Paris Agreement.

Thus, the war continued in Cambodia, with the United States continuing its limited military and economic assistance to the Cambodian government resisting the Khmer Rouge onslaught. The Cambodian government declared a unilateral cease-fire for a few weeks in the hope of encouraging its adversaries to follow suit. The gesture failed. The United States thereupon shifted its air power from the Vietnamese and Laotian theaters, after the cease-fires there, to bolster the efforts of the Cambodian army. This lasted for only six months, however, as all U.S. air and any other military operations in or near Cambodia were halted after August 15 by legislation that cut off all funding, passed by Congress over Nixon's strong objections. Congress's hope—like the Cambodian government's in attempting a temporary unilateral cease-fire—was that an end to American military action would make a negotiated settlement more likely.

The non-Communist Cambodians fought on, even after the halt to U.S. military operations. In retrospect, it is remarkable that they survived for nearly two years more, which is a testimony to their bravery and perhaps also to the accumulating reports of the unusual viciousness of their Khmer Rouge adversary. In 1971 and 1972, word had begun circulating of the extraordinary brutality with which the Khmer Rouge were governing the civilian population in areas they controlled in outlying provinces of Cambodia.[7] But internationally the Khmer Rouge profited from having Sihanouk as their figurehead leader—he had foolishly thrown in his lot with the Communists after his Parliament deposed him in March 1970.

Thus, many in the United States thought of the Khmer Rouge as a coalition of some kind, embracing "many Khmer nationalists, Communist and non-Communist," eager to be independent of Moscow or Beijing, with whom it was in our interest to treat and whom it would be a mistake to alienate lest we "push them further into the arms of their Communist supporters."[8] These words were written in March 1975 by Anthony Lake, when the administration of President Gerald Ford was seeking emergency military aid for the Cambodian government. The *New York Times* correspondent in Cambodia, Sydney Schanberg, wrote confidently at about the same time that "most non-Cambodian observers" discounted the administration's predictions of a Communist bloodbath. In an echo of past wishful speculations about Mao Zedong, Ho Chi Minh, and Fidel Castro, Schanberg saw the Khmer Rouge, too, as a diverse bloc whose future direction was not yet determined. One Khmer Rouge leader, Khieu Samphan, was described by Schanberg as a Communist but "also a nationalist with a reputation for integrity, incorruptibility and concern for the peasants who is highly respected among non-Communist Cambodians." The brutal behavior of Khmer Rouge forces in areas they controlled was "not . . . widespread," Schanberg wrote, and was mostly the product of the bitter ongoing war; once they won the war, he was confident, "there would be no need for random acts of terror."[9]

Anthony Lewis of the *New York Times* wrote in March 1975 of the continuing war: "Some will find the whole bloodbath debate unreal. What future possibility could be more terrible than the reality of what is happening to Cambodia now?"[10] The *Washington Post* agreed, expressing its editorial support for Congress's view "that the threatened 'bloodbath' is less ominous than a continuation of the current bloodletting."[11] The

Los Angeles Times wrote of "the necessity to withhold any further military assistance for the good of the suffering Cambodian people themselves."[12] Schanberg wrote another piece summing up his view that the "ordinary people" of Indochina had no interest in abstract notions of American credibility. "[I]t is difficult to imagine," he wrote from Phnom Penh on April 13, 1975, "how their lives could be anything but better with the Americans gone."[13]

As with Seymour Hersh's reporting on Angola later in the same year, this version of events in our leading newspapers had its influence on the national debate. The public's patience with the Indochina ordeal had clearly run out long before, but these arguments provided a comforting rationale for our departure. Congress withheld aid to the Cambodian government.

The commentators were right that the Khmer Rouge were nationalist as well as Communist; that is, they were not stooges of any foreign power. But they were nationalists of a fanatic bent more extreme than anything seen since the Nazis. Sydney Schanberg was also right that the Khmer Rouge, when they seized power on April 17, had "no need for random acts of terror." The terror was systematic.

The new rulers of Cambodia stunned the world by the amazing enterprise of emptying the capital city, Phnom Penh, of its entire population. This was deliberate policy, apparently decided upon at a Special Congress of the Khmer Communist Party in February 1975.[14] The man who reportedly presided over that Congress was Khieu Samphan, the reputed moderate. He had written in his doctoral thesis at the University of Paris in 1959 that a new Cambodia had to be based on the "dormant energy in the peasant mass," as opposed to the corrupt cities.[15] Therefore, in 1975 the cities—embodying the urban, modern, Westernized, sophisticated Cambodia—would be destroyed and a wholly new society created.

Phnom Penh was indeed literally emptied; a city of 3 million people was turned into a wasteland. Homes, hospitals, schools, factories, offices, were emptied of their occupants at gunpoint. Columns of fearful Cambodians were marched out of the city—old and young, sick and lame; those that fell by the wayside were shot, if they did not die first of hunger and disease. Upon reaching the wilderness, marchers were forced into communal settlements or in some cases ordered to build new villages in the jungle where none existed.

All officials and soldiers, even low-ranking ones, were liquidated, and for good measure, their families. Then schoolteachers, students, or indeed anyone with eyeglasses or who could read or write, presumed to be intellectuals and therefore bourgeois. Of more than five hundred doctors known to have been practicing medicine in Cambodia before April 1975, only forty were found alive when the Khmer Rouge were driven from power in 1978. All vestiges of modern civilization were targets—Phnom Penh's central market, as well as its cathedral, were razed. Power plants, schools, and hospitals were blown up. Typewriters, radios, televisions, phonographs, not to mention books, were looted, to be destroyed as hated remnants of a culture to be eradicated. Out of a Cambodian population of approximately 7 million at the beginning of 1975, somewhere between 1 and 2 million were killed under the Khmer Rouge.[16] Sydney Schanberg won a Pulitzer Prize for his Cambodia reporting—for his vivid coverage of the emptying of Phnom Penh, in which he had the misfortune to be caught up, and presumably not for his political analysis beforehand.

Relations between the victorious Communist allies in Cambodia and Vietnam after April 1975 proved even more difficult than before. They inherited long-standing disputes over land and sea boundaries between the two countries. Until the seventeenth century, the Mekong Delta area of southern Vietnam had belonged to the Khmer Empire; then it was absorbed by the Vietnamese in an era of expansion that was interrupted by the appearance of the French.[17] The Khmer Rouge, preferring to imagine that the borders they inherited were the discriminatory impositions of French colonialism, now began unilaterally occupying disputed land along the Vietnamese border (and also the border with Thailand). The Cambodians also accused the Vietnamese of trying to interfere in their party affairs, and there was a schism between the two Communist parties.[18] There was the legacy of mistrust from the period of the American war, when Hanoi had tried to push the Khmer Rouge into an unwanted cease-fire in 1972–73, as we have seen. Pol Pot, the paranoid Khmer Rouge leader, claimed Hanoi had tried to bribe his bodyguards to assassinate him.[19]

The roots of the conflict lay deeper in ancient tribal feuds and fears between the Khmer and the Vietnamese that, of course, long antedated the implantation of communism. What communism added to the picture was two ruthless Leninist regimes unconstrained by any popular reluctance to continue a generation of warfare. The Cambodians feared Vietnamese hegemony in the region; they, in turn, provoked the Vietnamese out of nationalist fervor and the bravado of a fanatic leadership. Both faced economic disarray at home resulting from the devastation of war as well as their own destructive policies; both regimes undoubtedly saw political profit in stirring up nationalist resentment against a despised ancient rival in order to distract or discipline a restive population. For Pol Pot, the bloody purges now had an additional justification—to create a new, purified society tough enough to withstand the Vietnamese threat.

The Vietnamese Communist leadership in Hanoi, with which we had had the dubious pleasure of dealing, seemed, in turn, singularly unsuited to a life of peace. When Kissinger and his team visited Hanoi in February 1973, after the Paris Agreement, to initiate a dialogue on future relations, we were shown the cultural sites of the city we had (only a few weeks before) been bombing. I take it for granted that every Asian culture has a fine aesthetic tradition. Yet Hanoi's art museum seemed a motley collection of mother-of-pearl tackiness and imitations of French impressionism; in contrast, Hanoi's history museum portrayed a vivid chronicle of wars and migrations, conquests and defeats, in contests with neighbors to the west (Cambodia) and the north (China). Le Duc Tho, who accompanied Kissinger on this cultural tour—and who had never visited these museums before—reacted in the liveliest manner to every archaeological exhibit by reminiscing to Kissinger about prisons he had been thrown into by the French, in his days as a young revolutionary, in the environs of the dig.[20] This was a society (or at least a regime) that chose to celebrate its struggles, not its aesthetic sensibilities.

In 1978, the Vietnamese began to flex their muscles in the face of what they saw as Cambodian provocations. Disaffected (if not terrified) Cambodian Communists who feared purges by the Khmer Rouge leaders defected to Vietnam and formed the nucleus of a substitute Cambodian Communist regime that Hanoi was to put into power in Phnom Penh soon enough.

The Chinese, who had long-standing ties to Sihanouk, tightened their relations with the Khmer Rouge regime, which the hapless prince continued to lead as an imprisoned figurehead. China supplied arms. Contrary to the Johnson administration's assumption of a North Vietnamese policy sponsored and masterminded by Beijing, the Chinese saw the unified Vietnam as a growing geopolitical problem. Chinese premier Zhou Enlai had made clear to Kissinger in 1973 that China was in no hurry to see Hanoi dominate all of Vietnam, much less all of Indochina. For that reason, Zhou was more than satisfied with the Paris Agreement, which seemed to him to confirm the independence of South Vietnam and to reinforce the independence of Laos and Cambodia.[21] In 1975, Communist China and Communist Cambodia made common cause against the powerhouse that the newly unified Communist Vietnam represented.

The Sino-Vietnamese rivalry, like the Khmer-Vietnamese rivalry, derived from ancient roots and modern provocations. Vietnam's struggle against Chinese domination went back two millennia. Border disputes went back a century and a half. In the modern period, both Vietnam and China contemplated exploring for oil in the Gulf of Tonkin and South China Sea and disputed control over the Paracel and Spratly islands.[22] Much of the brutality of Communist rule in South Vietnam fell on the ethnic Chinese, who comprised a significant proportion of the exodus of "boat people." Hanoi deeply resented how both Moscow and Beijing had betrayed it in unseemly summits with Nixon in 1972 but forgave the Soviets, who were far away (and thus no direct threat) and who came through once again as the most reliable source of economic and military aid.

After some initial hesitation, Vietnam joined the Soviet economic bloc, the Council on Economic Mutual Assistance (CEMA, or COMECON), in June 1978 and in November 1978 signed a Friendship Treaty with Moscow. The Chinese suspected that a secret annex to the treaty provided for Soviet access to bases in Vietnam in exchange for weapons for an invasion of Cambodia.[23] Thus was the Sino-Soviet conflict transplanted with a vengeance to Indochina, no sooner had America's war against communism ended there.

There is no evidence that Hanoi's grievances against the Khmer Rouge included any particular objection to the latter's human rights record.[24] On the contrary. On the second anniversary of the Khmer Rouge takeover of Phnom Penh, in April 1977, Politburo leaders in Hanoi sent the usual public congratulatory message to their Cambodian comrades:

> Following up the great victory won on April 17, 1975, under the leadership of the Kampuchean Revolutionary Organization and in the tradition of ardent patriotism and industry, the heroic people of Kampuchea over the past two years have upheld the spirit of self-reliance and have overcome many difficulties in their resolve to heal the wounds of war, restore their economy and stabilise their living conditions. . . . The Vietnamese people warmly hail these fine achievements of the fraternal people of Kampuchea.[25]

THE THIRD INDOCHINA WAR

This facade of "fraternal" friendship fell away completely in December 1978 when Vietnam sent 150,000–200,000 troops to invade and occupy Cambodia and install its own group of friendly Cambodian Communists in power. Vietnamese vice foreign minister Nguyen Co Thach later confirmed to Rep. Stephen Solarz that Vietnam had intervened not to protect the human rights of the Cambodian people, which Hanoi regarded as an internal affair, but to end the persistent and provocative cross-border raids by the Cambodians.[26] Vietnamese troops captured Phnom Penh within two weeks and soon afterward established the "People's Republic of Kampuchea" under the leadership of Heng Samrin, a former Khmer Rouge.

The Khmer Rouge forces fled westward in disarray but later regrouped and organized a guerrilla campaign against the occupiers, Hanoi's forces being less adept in the unaccustomed role of counterinsurgency than in their previous role as invader in Laos and South Vietnam. In a final irony, the Vietnamese reportedly used U.S.-made aircraft and helicopters in regular missions over Cambodia, dropping 250-pound explosives, antipersonnel "cluster bombs," and defoliants to destroy crops. The Vietnamese seem to have made a point of looting the Cambodian food supply, in part to feed hungry Vietnamese at home, and of blocking or stealing international relief shipments; Vietnam used the deliberate creation of famine as an instrument of war to starve out the Khmer Rouge guerrillas in rural areas.[27] The practice was widely condemned; the *Washington Post* called it a form of genocide.[28]

The international dimension of the conflict then came into play. The Soviets backed their Vietnamese ally in Hanoi and the new Vietnamese-installed government in Phnom Penh, stepping up arms supplies to both. The Chinese continued to back the Khmer Rouge, now in the bush; a "Deng Xiaoping Trail" for Chinese arms deliveries to the Khmer Rouge opened up through Thailand. The Vietnamese complained bitterly that the Chinese "have changed friends and enemies like they change underwear."[29] The new Cambodian war became a proxy war in the Sino-Soviet conflict.

Leonid Brezhnev was never known for his subtlety on the subject of China. In 1973, he had taken Kissinger and then Nixon aside during high-level meetings to urge, with great emotion, that Moscow and Washington join hands against the yellow peril. The Chinese were arrogant, treacherous, subhuman, he insisted. The crude racial anecdotes he told bespoke a fear that must have been genuine; it is hard to see any other explanation for behavior that only confirmed in Nixon's and Kissinger's eyes the utility of the relationship they were forging with China.[30] Having failed to persuade us, Brezhnev later shifted course and attempted to woo the Chinese and end the feud that was so clearly playing into the hands of the United States; the Soviet leader made a number of such overtures to China, in 1976–77 and then again in 1981–82, after Ronald Reagan came into office.

But the Chinese rebuffed all the overtures, considering that the objective menace of Soviet policies and power belied Brezhnev's newly conciliatory words. Beijing treated the Vietnamese occupation of Cambodia as one of the "three obstacles" to a normalization of relations with Moscow. (The other two were the Soviet invasion of Afghanistan and the threatening Soviet military posture on the Chinese border.) In Chinese eyes, these three issues embodied the fundamental geopolitical threat that the Soviet Union posed to China. China stuck to this position firmly for the next ten years, until Mikhail Gorbachev met the Chinese demands in all three areas.

The United States had a weak hand in all this from the beginning, and our lack of leverage is one of the most obvious lessons to be drawn from the whole episode. We had no direct influence in Indochina, having lost the war and seen our Indochinese allies devoured. The Carter administration made an attempt to normalize relations with Vietnam in 1977–78, believing, in Secretary of State Cyrus Vance's words, that "the Vietnamese are trying to find a balance between overdependence on either the Chinese or the Soviet Union" and that it was in our interest to promote this.[31] The effort aborted, partly because of domestic controversy in America—a public not yet ready to reconcile with the erstwhile enemy— and also because of Hanoi's clumsy insistence on war reparations and its failure to account for U.S. missing in action.[32] But, in addition, America's purchase on events was weak. Vance's analysis—that Hanoi might prefer a course independent of both Moscow and Beijing—was not wrong, but America's clout in Southeast Asia at that stage of our history was not so impressive as to outweigh, in Hanoi's mind, the imperatives of geopolitics. China and the Soviet Union, not the United States, were now the principal outside players in the region, and history and geography pushed Vietnam—probably inevitably—to seek Moscow's protection against China.

Gradually, and not coincidentally, the focus of policy on this issue in the Carter administration shifted from the State Department, eager for a reconciliation with Hanoi, to Zbigniew Brzezinski, Carter's national security adviser, who saw Cambodia in the context of the growing Sino-Soviet clash. Seeing Cambodia as the Sino-Soviet proxy war that it was becoming, Brzezinski considered that in the global strategic context U.S. interests lay more with China. Brzezinski had visited China in May 1978 and committed the United States to a strategic partnership. Nixon and Kissinger had masked the growing partnership with China as a "triangular relationship" that in fact worked as leverage on both Moscow and Beijing;

Washington tried to use the triangle to secure better relations with both. This now gave way to a more open alignment with the Chinese against the Soviets.

The shift was, to a great extent, the American reaction to the pattern of Soviet overreaching in the Third World, especially in Angola and Ethiopia/Somalia. Brzezinski's instructions from Carter in May 1978 were to seek a more active Chinese role in resisting these Soviet encroachments. Brzezinski urged the Chinese, for example, to give aid to Jonas Savimbi's UNITA in Angola, since the U.S. government was barred from doing so by the Clark Amendment. Brzezinski asked the Chinese to weigh in diplomatically elsewhere in Africa and the Middle East.[33] At the end of 1978, the United States completed the process of normalizing relations with China, revoking its recognition of the Republic of China on Taiwan. While Vance urged a more balanced posture between Moscow and Beijing, Brzezinski told Deng, on Carter's instructions, that "the United States has made up its mind."[34]

The embrace of China was a Faustian bargain as far as Cambodia was concerned, for it left us indirectly in bed with the hated Khmer Rouge. For Brzezinski, indeed, it was a conscious decision. He told Elizabeth Becker: "I encouraged the Chinese to support Pol Pot. I encouraged the Thai to help the D.K. [Democratic Kampuchea]. The question was how to help the Cambodian people. Pol Pot was an abomination. We could never support him but China could."[35]

This unholy alliance was to haunt our policy for the next fifteen years. We were not alone; our friends in Southeast Asia (the Association of Southeast Asian Nations, or ASEAN, comprising Malaysia, Singapore, Thailand, the Philippines, Indonesia, and later Brunei) were also troubled by Vietnam's invasion of Cambodia and took a similar position. When the world community faced the decision of what to do with Cambodia's UN General Assembly seat, it followed ASEAN's lead and registered its nonrecognition of the Vietnamese-installed regime by continuing to recognize the Khmer Rouge as the holder of the seat. Cyrus Vance agonized over this decision but concluded that we had no choice if we wanted to avoid diplomatic isolation.[36]

The United States may have sought to emphasize its equal revulsion at both the Phnom Penh regime and the Khmer Rouge, but it was an intention without operational content. Our policy was essentially at the mercy of the Chinese. We hesitated even to respond to Prince Sihanouk's request for asylum in the United States in January 1979, preferring to let the Chinese decide whether to take him in.[37] (They took him.) When Chinese party leader Deng Xiaoping visited Washington later in January, he told Carter of his intention to strike a military blow against Vietnam in order to "teach Vietnam a lesson;" he asked for U.S. support. The Carter administration found this highly embarrassing and tried to take a neutral public position. When the Chinese did strike Vietnam, however, in a three-week incursion across the border within two weeks of Deng's triumphant Washington visit, American denials of complicity, while true, rang hollow. Whereas the United States hoped to get the Vietnamese out of Cambodia, as part of a political solution ensuring Cambodian freedom as well as independence, Deng told an astonished Japanese prime minister Masayoshi Ohira in December 1979 that he preferred to keep the Vietnamese bogged down in Cambodia in order to bleed them: "It is wise for China . . . to force the Vietnamese to stay in Kampuchea because that way they will suffer more and more and will not be able to extend their hand to Thailand, Malaysia, and Singapore."[38]

Antiwar Americans like Arthur Schlesinger, who had long debunked the domino theory, noted with satisfaction afterward that America's other allies in Southeast Asia had survived intact after Indochina fell.[39] Thailand emerged unscathed, even flourishing, as did the other ASEAN countries. The real reason, of course, was that China stepped into the breach as the bulwark against Vietnamese or Soviet regional dominance. (Nixon and Kissinger, having brought China into the global game, ironically helped undercut the validity of their own domino theory.) All well and good, except for the price that continued to be paid—especially by Cambodians—for the abject weakness of *American* influence in the service of our own objectives.

Resistance grew in Cambodia to the Vietnamese occupation. The Khmer Rouge were joined by the remnant of the non-Communists who had survived the Khmer Rouge and then the Vietnamese genocide. We and our ASEAN friends helped the non-Communists to organize—the so-called National Army of Sihanouk (ANS, in French) and the Khmer People's National Liberation Front (KPNLF), under the respected politician Son Sann. In 1982, the ANS, KPNLF, and Khmer Rouge, under ASEAN pressure, established a formal coalition and shared the UN seat.

But the non-Communists remained weak. Only the Khmer Rouge, backed by Chinese arms, were an effective military counterweight to the Phnom Penh regime backed by Hanoi and Moscow. The United States could not bring itself to furnish any substantial assistance to the non-Communist Cambodians, who, we could only assume, represented the overwhelming majority of the population. The non-Communist resistance found itself involuntarily in the frightening position of being the junior party in a deadly alliance with the Khmer Rouge. The United

States found itself in the undignified position of asking *China* to provide some arms to Sihanouk and Son Sann (which China did). According to published accounts, the United States began in 1982 to furnish covert assistance, but it was "nonlethal" (that is, no weapons); it began at about $5 million a year and grew to only about $12 million by 1985.[40]

This refusal to give arms guaranteed the continuing military weakness of the non-Communists, which in turn assured that the various Communist antagonists would dominate both the fighting and the diplomacy that surrounded it. By the same token it assured our own lack of leverage over the course of events. All the Communist players—the USSR, China, Vietnam, and their Cambodian clients—acted according to their own strategic necessities, driven by their rivalries. The war turned into a bloody stalemate; Deng's desire to bleed the Vietnamese seemed fulfilled, with no conclusive result so long as Soviet support for Hanoi continued. Progress toward a diplomatic solution was glacial. Diplomatically, the United States deferred to its ASEAN partners, who gave political and some material backing to the non-Communists and indeed preferred that we stay in the background, given the limits of what we were prepared to do.

ASEAN leaders dissociated from China's policy of "bleeding" Vietnam; they wanted a negotiated solution in order to head off a regional crisis. ASEAN countries were also prepared to offer Vietnam an attractive economic relationship if a settlement was reached. But it was ASEAN that shaped the strategy of isolating Hanoi and Phnom Penh, keeping Cambodia's UN seat in the hands of the (deposed) Khmer Rouge regime and trying to unify the opposition coalition, including the Khmer Rouge.[41]

Why the absence of significant direct U.S. support for the non-Communist resistance? Even the Reagan administration, champion of "freedom fighters" around the globe, shied away. The small amount of covert aid has already been noted. In 1985, Congress authorized up to $5 million in overt aid to the Cambodian non-Communists—not a great amount, but it was authorized for either economic or military aid. The administration chose to use the authority for only economic assistance— medical supplies, malaria prevention, training, and commodities—and the program was funded in the early years at only about $3.5 million annually of the $5 million authorized.[42] The pressure for the legislation had ironically come from the Democrats, especially Rep. Stephen Solarz of New York. The special irony was that Solarz had been a member of the congressional "class of 1974," first elected after Watergate, which had proved its manhood by rejecting President Ford's pleas to aid the non-Communists in Phnom Penh in 1975.

The Reagan administration had its critics on the Right who considered its response too timid—all the more so in view of the apparent Democratic support for the idea. Without a more active U.S. policy, they argued, there would be no incentive for Vietnam to negotiate. These critics denounced as "capitulatory rhetoric" the arguments of officials who claimed that chances for diplomacy would be better if the United States avoided a military role.[43]

In those days I was in the State Department heading the Policy Planning Staff and urged on my colleagues in the Bureau of East Asian and Pacific Affairs that the United States do more. But there was in the administration then a profound fear that Congress and the public would react sharply to anything having to do with Indochina; the emotions were thought to be still too raw, the congressional support for the idea too thin. This was not necessarily wrong, and we probably profited from the fact that the administration had not initiated the program. Imagine the reaction if Ronald Reagan had proposed a major reintervention in Indochina! Operational experts also disparaged the fighting ability of the non-Communist forces, which was a fair assessment—but also self-fulfilling if we denied them significant aid.

The Reagan administration, moreover, at least after Alexander Haig left the State Department in 1982, did not share the Nixon-Kissinger-Brzezinski sense of geopolitical partnership with China, which might have led it to see a larger stake in thwarting Soviet-Vietnamese hegemony. Reagan had long been a friend of Taiwan's, not of mainland China. While he visited Beijing in 1984 and kept the relationship on an even keel, he had much less of an emotional commitment to it. Even the younger officials making Asia policy, without the pro-Taiwan history, thought that the Nixon, Ford, and Carter administrations had all gone overboard in their sentimentality about China. There was also a certain sympathy for the concerns of countries like Indonesia—an important and steadfast U.S. ally—which feared Chinese hegemony in Southeast Asia more than Vietnamese. The result, for all these reasons, was a fairly passive American role in Cambodia.

The Sino-Soviet competition heated up. The Soviets' military shipments to Vietnam more than quadrupled from 1978 to 1979, in support of the Vietnamese occupation of Cambodia.[44] They supplied about $2 billion in weapons to Hanoi in 1979 and 1980 and about $750 million per year thereafter, in addition to about $1 billion a year in economic aid.[45] In return for this aid the Soviets gained access to all the superb air and naval facilities bequeathed by the departed Americans. According to Richard Holbrooke, Carter's assistant secretary of state for East Asian and Pacific affairs, in March 1980:

> Soviet ships and submarines call at Danang and Cam Ranh Bay. Soviet long-range aircraft operate out of Danang on an increasingly regular basis. Earlier this month a Soviet frigate made a precedent-setting call at the Khmer port of Kompong Som, thus projecting a Soviet naval presence further into Southeast Asia. Through their increased access to these facilities, the Soviets have significantly enhanced their military capabilities, not only in Southeast Asia and the Southwest Pacific but also in the Indian Ocean.[46]

Soviet officials reacted bitterly to the more brazen American flirtation with China in the Carter period (though they were probably pleased to see the Reagan administration's more arm's-length relations with China). But the Soviets had brought it on themselves, by the hubris of their Third World expansion.

Meanwhile, on the ground in Cambodia, the two groups of Communist thugs—the Khmer Rouge and the Phnom Penh regime (whose leaders were all former Khmer Rouge)—fought it out, and the decent folks trapped in the middle struggled to avoid being crushed. Phnom Penh and its patrons in Hanoi proclaimed their takeover irreversible, confident that they could outlast the resistance.[47]

9

THE SOVIET QUAGMIRE
IN AFGHANISTAN

The Soviet invasion of Afghanistan in December 1979 is one of those events whose significance only grows in retrospect. It produced a major crisis in East-West relations as well as an upheaval in Southwest Asia that has not subsided at this writing. Ultimately, however, its greatest impact was within the Soviet Union itself.

There are Russians who say that "if there hadn't been the Afghan war, there'd never have been *perestroika*"—which is to say that the debacle in Afghanistan was a significant factor in the discrediting of the Soviet system that produced it.[1] Not only Brezhnev's foreign policy but the conspiratorial decision-making process that characterized it—the brutal monopoly of power exercised by the Communist party Politburo—was frontally challenged by the reformers who came to leadership positions in the Soviet Union in 1985. The quagmire that Afghanistan had become was cited over and over as a terrible example of an abuse of power that could never be permitted to happen again and that needed to be prevented by democratization of the political system. It demoralized the military and fostered popular discontent.

Whereas our Vietnam failure prompted a cultural revolution of sorts in the United States, Afghanistan's impact in the Soviet Union went far deeper. The American system has a healthy capacity for self-renewal: leaders change; new political figures come regularly to office with no vested interest in past mistakes; the polity can start afresh, if it chooses, at every election. The Soviet system had no such capacity, and the frustration of Afghanistan was one of the factors that strained it to the breaking point.

THE "GREAT GAME"

Afghanistan, it has been said, is a country without ethnic or geographic cohesion; it was formed not by internal coalescence but by external pressures from the competing colonial powers, especially the Russian Empire pressing down from Central Asia and the British zealously guarding the gateway to imperial India.[2] As happened elsewhere under colonialism, Afghanistan's boundaries, when they were fixed in the late nineteenth century by British and Russian accords, ignored tribal and economic patterns and sowed the seeds of constant instability. Porous borders and tribal irredentism made their contribution to the frequent Anglo-Russian clashes in the nineteenth century, to the pressures from the Soviets in the first half of the twentieth century, to the tensions between Afghanistan and its South Asian neighbors in the postwar period, and to the fears of the spread of Islamic fundamentalism from Afghanistan to the newly independent republics of Soviet Central Asia today.

The colonial rivalry between Britain and Russia over Afghanistan became known as the "Great Game." Neither side would permit the other to win it; both treated Afghanistan as a crucial buffer, but not without repeated incursions, diplomatic assurances to the other (soon broken), and continuing suspicions of each other's ambitions. By the 1830s, Russia had conquered the weak Muslim emirates of Central Asia but found them an unruly lot. As with its Soviet successors 150 years later—and even its post-Soviet successors—one of Russia's motives for its expanding military involvement in the region was its fear of chronic instability. Most accounts of Afghan history cite the famous diplomatic message of Russian vice chancellor Prince Alexander Gorchakov in November 1864. When Russian troops occupied parts of what is now Uzbekistan, Gorchakov notified the European powers of these military steps in a detailed memorandum explaining why Russia had little real choice. In a burst of candor, he admitted that the "greatest difficulty" was "being able to stop":

> The situation of Russia in central Asia is similar to that of all civilized states that come into contact with half-savage nomadic tribes without a firm social organization. In such cases, the interests of border security and trade relations always require that the more civilized state have a certain authority over its neighbors, whose wild and unruly customs render them very troublesome. It begins first by curbing raids and pillaging. To put an end to these, it is often compelled to reduce the neighboring tribes to some degree of close subordination. Once this result has been achieved, the latter take on more peaceful habits, but in their turn they are exposed to the attack of tribes living farther off. . . . The state therefore must make a choice: either to give up this continuous effort and doom its borders to constant unrest, which would make prosperity, safety, and cultural progress impossible here, or else to advance farther and farther into the heart of the savage lands where the vast distances, with every step forward, increase

the difficulties and hardships it incurs. Such has been the fate of all states placed in a similar situation. The United States of America, France in Africa, Holland in its colonies, England in the East Indies—they all were inevitably driven to choose the path of onward movement, not so much from ambition as from dire necessity, where the greatest difficulty lies in being unable to stop.[3]

But there were other motivations. Russian influence in Afghanistan was a way to distract the British and keep them off balance in India. Russian diplomats and statesmen were hopeful that the weaker Britain was in India, the more accommodating Britain would be in Europe.[4] The Afghans in the meantime fended for themselves as best they could, "like a poor goat on whom the lion and the bear have both fixed their eyes," in the words of Emir Abdur Rahman toward the end of the century.[5]

The Great Game did not flag in the new century when the Bolsheviks replaced the tsars. As we saw in chapter 2, the Bolsheviks embraced the erratic Afghan king Amanullah Khan, who found the Soviets a useful source of aid even while he gave sanctuary to the Muslim *basmachi* who resisted Soviet rule in Central Asia. The Soviets preached everlasting respect for Afghan independence, but mutual suspicions ran deep; by the mid-1930s, all the Soviet civilian and military technicians had left, and Afghan-Soviet relations remained distant.[6]

NONALIGNMENT AND ITS PERILS

After World War II, the British left India, but Afghanistan found itself thrust into an even deadlier game. Seeking economic aid and also arms from the United States as a reinsurance of their security, the Afghans were rebuffed by an American government that in the 1940s and 1950s saw Afghanistan as "of little or no strategic importance to the United States" and as inevitably in the Soviet sphere of influence.[7] The Afghans complicated their relations with Washington by their mischievous policy toward their new neighbor Pakistan, occasionally stirring up irredentist feeling among their brother Pushtuns across the Pakistani border. When the Eisenhower administration committed itself to Pakistani security, Afghanistan lost out and turned reluctantly back to the Soviets, hoping to achieve the best accommodation possible with its powerful neighbor.

The Afghans did receive some economic aid from the United States, but this modest token of reinsurance, in the end, proved a dubious blessing. While geography did not give Afghanistan cohesion, it provided some protection. Its inaccessibility, hard terrain, and tough-as-nails tribes-people had helped to spare it the humiliation of direct colonial rule. As Afghanistan entered the modern world, however, it decided, like most other emerging nations, that it needed to develop economically. Afghanistan had always been desperately poor. Economic development, all the experts told it, required first building a physical infrastructure, especially a network of roads to link it up with neighbors. This posed a great dilemma, for previous Afghan rulers had understood that a network of roads for commerce could easily become a network of invasion routes. Abdur Rahman's policy at the end of the nineteenth century has been described as one of "aloofness, isolation and deliberate underdevelopment," precisely intended to hinder the mobility of any troops, Russian or British, that might have their eyes on his country.[8]

Afghan rulers after 1950 nevertheless sought Soviet and American aid for major infrastructure projects. The U.S. Agency for International Development (AID) built the main arterial roads in the southern part of the country, as well as Kandahar airport, and built Kabul airport jointly with the Soviets. The scale of U.S. aid and therefore U.S. political influence remained low, however; Soviet road building in the north brought direct lines of communication from the Soviet Union to the country's core, reorienting trade and gaining not only economic and political influence but strategic access. All of these facilities, especially what the Soviets, but also the Americans, had built, well served the logistical needs of the Soviet invasion force in 1979–80.[9]

At various times the Afghans sought again to escape the grip of Soviet dependency but were usually rebuffed. In 1962, Mohammed Naim Khan, foreign minister and also the younger brother of Prime Minister Mohammed Daoud, visited President John F. Kennedy at the White House and asked for help in developing westward trade routes through the shah's Iran, to lessen dependence on the Soviet Union. Kennedy thought this too expensive and pointedly reminded Naim to improve ties with Pakistan. In any case, Kennedy said, "the United States is a long way off and even though it is very anxious to help it can at best play a limited role."[10]

The story of Afghanistan in the 1970s is the story of a neutral buffer state that made yet another effort to reduce its dependence on the Soviet Union and to move toward truer nonalignment. Again, Afghanistan reached out to the United States and Iran—and this time they responded.

Henry Kissinger visited Afghanistan twice, in November 1974 and August 1976. Daoud and Naim were still in power—Daoud, now the strongman-president who had deposed his cousin the last king, Zahir Shah, in 1973, and his brother Naim, still his closest confidant. Their quiet politeness and avuncular manner masked the brutality of the Afghan political arena in which they had been successful players for decades; their warmth toward their American visitors belied their reputation as leftists as well as the common misperception of a country that relished its isolation and was resigned to living in the shadow of the Soviet Union.

On each of Kissinger's visits we were treated to presidential box seats at Kabul Stadium for a performance of the Afghan national game—*buzkashi*, a rough-and-tumble competition of men on horseback struggling to advance downfield the headless body of a goat. Sort of a down-market version of polo. A great roar rose from the crowd whenever one team or the other made some brilliant maneuver. We Americans marveled at the horsemanship, our awe heightened by stories that up in the mountains the tribesmen played the game without the confines of a stadium or rules of etiquette, usually incurring light to moderate casualties among the players (if not the spectators).

No one would ever call the Afghans a gentle people. Yet young U.S. Foreign Service officers who served in Kabul in those days all came away with a tremendous affection for a proud people who endured enormous hardship—an infant mortality rate of one-third to one-half, life expectancy of fifty years for those who survived childhood—and yet wanted from us nothing more than a chance to buttress their independence, indeed their self-sufficiency.

What made the United States more responsive in the 1970s was an American policy more attuned to the complex geopolitical stirrings of the region. The United States was still conscious of its strategic stake in Pakistan, only recently (in 1971) dismembered in a war with India backed by the Soviet Union; Washington was also conscious of its improving position in the Muslim world following Kissinger's post-1973 Middle East diplomacy. Our regional allies urged us to pay more attention to Afghanistan. The Persian Gulf, also, posed a particular strategic problem. The British having abandoned their protectorate over the lower Gulf in 1971, the United States counted on its friends the shah of Iran and the Saudis to take a greater responsibility for regional security. This led the shah, among other things, to respond more positively to Afghanistan's pleas for westward trade routes. Daoud and Naim, in turn, eagerly assured Kissinger that Afghanistan would desist from its efforts to destabilize Pakistan via Pushtun irredentism.

There are some who charge that the shah's regional ambitions are what destabilized Afghanistan and precipitated the 1978 crisis.[11] Yet the evidence is strong that the new thrust in Afghanistan's policy was an Afghan initiative. As early as 1974, Daoud was turning to pro-Western

Iran, Saudi Arabia, and Kuwait for economic aid. Also in 1974, he sent his brother Naim to Beijing to assure the Chinese (with whom Afghanistan shares a tiny stretch of border) that Afghanistan was neutral in the Sino-Soviet conflict. In 1975, Daoud himself visited the shah in Tehran (receiving a pledge of up to $2 billion over a ten-year period and a quick loan of $400 million on easy terms). In June 1976, President Zulfikar Ali Bhutto of once-estranged Pakistan visited Kabul, and Daoud returned the visit to Islamabad two months later. In the spring of 1978, Daoud visited India, Pakistan, Egypt, Turkey, Saudi Arabia, among other countries; he visited Pakistan again (this time received by Bhutto's successor, Zia ul-Haq). An economic accord was signed with China. The shah of Iran was scheduled to visit Kabul in June 1978, and Daoud announced plans to visit President Carter in Washington.[12]

If pursuit of a more genuine nonalignment was a crime, then Daoud was guilty. It is not plausible to blame the outcome on Iran (which was never in a position to deliver on its ambitious aid pledges) or, even less, on the United States. Nor is it clear that Afghanistan's foreign policy played a significant role in the April 1978 coup d'état in which Communist military officers overthrew Daoud, murdering him, his entourage, and his family, including his brother Naim.

THE APRIL 1978 COUP

Afghan leftists did not get around to forming a Communist party until 1965, when the People's Democratic Party of Afghanistan (PDPA) was established. Within two years it split into several factions, the most important being the radical Khalq group, whose leaders included Nur Mohammed Taraki and Hafizullah Amin, and the more Moscow-oriented Parcham,* headed by Babrak Karmal.

President Daoud, as he broadened Afghanistan's international options in the mid-1970s, was also seeking to consolidate his power at home. He quashed coup plots against him from both the Right and Left; he created a new political party to back him and sought to weaken all rival parties; and he began purging untrustworthy elements from the government and armed forces. In the process he accomplished the extraordinary feat of frightening both Khalq and Parcham into reuniting, in July 1977, in a common desire to get rid of him. In April 1978, when a large, angry crowd at the funeral of a murdered Parchami leader stunned Daoud with

---

*The factions were named, respectively, after their newspapers: *Khalq* ("the Masses") and *Parcham* ("the Banner").

its demonstration of Communist strength, he began preparing a crack-down. He was preempted by a group of Communist officers still en-trenched in the armed forces, who moved against him on April 27.[13] The new regime proclaimed itself the Democratic Republic of Afghan-istan. The "Revolutionary Council" was headed by Taraki (of the Khalq), who became prime minister, with Amin (of the Khalq) and Karmal (of Parcham) as deputy prime ministers.

What role the Soviet Union played in the April 1978 coup is disputed. The origins of the upheaval are almost certainly to be found in the boiling caldron of the domestic feuds in Kabul. Some accounts suggest the Soviets were caught by surprise; from April 27 to 30, TASS continued to refer to the event as a military coup, not as a "socialist revolution," as would be expected if the Soviets had been active supporters.[14] Other accounts suggest that Moscow had advance knowledge of the plot and interposed no objection.[15] What is not disputed is that within a few days Moscow warmly embraced the new regime and immediately began pouring in economic and military assistance and scores of military and civilian advisers to bolster it.

The April 1978 coup is historically interesting mainly as the prelude to the Soviet nvasion twenty months later, but it is intellectually interesting—perhaps even more interesting—for a different reason. The U.S. reaction to it followed a familiar pattern of American thought about international politics. Washington's response cannot be dismissed as a mere aversion to bad news, wishful thinking, or consciousness of the weakness of our position. It was in large part a reflection of a certain philosophy of how to deal with radical regimes in the Third World and with the Soviet role there.

To Secretary of State Cyrus Vance, the key fact was that "we had no evidence of Soviet complicity in the coup"; therefore, "our interests would best be served by letting Afghanistan continue its traditional balancing act between East and West."[16] The United States should not prejudge the ultimate evolution within Afghanistan, Vance thought. The admin-istration thus took at face value the new regime's professions of non-alignment, partly in order to avoid triggering provisions of our law that prohibited U.S. aid for any "Communist" country. Aid continued, in-cluding a Peace Corps contingent and a small military training program. Carter State Department official Anthony Lake later wrote that "a policy of active engagement was pursued in the hope that the new regime would act more like 'national communists' than like Soviet clients. Existing economic aid ties were maintained; Ambassador [Adolph] Dubs met frequently with the Foreign Minister."[17] As Lake indicates, it was an important general principle of this liberal perspective that Third World radicalism was best viewed in terms of its local or regional causes, not through the distorting lens of our global competition with the Soviet Union. [18]

Even National Security Adviser Brzezinski supported the mild reaction to the coup and defended it years later: "What could we have done? [he asked an interviewer] It was an internal coup, there was no evidence of Soviet involvement, and hence there were not grounds for an American protest. The regime was undefined and unconsolidated; there was doubt as to whether it could hold power. As long as we could have *some* influence in Kabul, why cut off aid? It was better to wait and see how things turned out."[19] The April coup is barely mentioned in Brzezinski's memoirs. [20] There were others who had a different view, such as former ambassador to Afghanistan Robert Neumann, who was convinced the new rulers were Communists beholden to Moscow. [21] But in the presence of ambiguity and what seemed like only a marginal impact on the balance of power, the United States tended toward a conciliatory approach.

Lake's thoughtful essay (written in 1985) is one of the best discussions of the American debate over how to deal with radical regimes, particularly leftist ones. There was a strong liberal school that tended to believe that radical regimes, even if avowedly Marxist and "anti-imperialist," were, in fact, highly nationalistic and could be weaned away from the Soviet embrace. Their radicalism reflected indigenous causes, such as social and economic inequities, and could be moderated by a patient American policy of engagement, including assistance for economic development. To lump them a priori with the Soviets was only a self-fulfilling prophecy. We have seen this attitude at work with respect to Communist China, Vietnam, Cuba, the Khmer Rouge, and the Sandinistas. The opposing school of thought, usually identified with conservatives, tended to see the strategic consequences of Soviet-backed radicalism as inherent and inescapable and was less inclined to accept the moral legitimacy of undemocratic, Soviet-backed Marxist regimes in the first place. This school preferred policies of pressure rather than conciliation.

The dirty little secret of both schools of thought, as Lake acknowledged, was that their prescriptions were 180 degrees reversed when governments of the opposite coloration were concerned. In the case of rightist regimes (Pinochet's Chile, apartheid South Africa), it was conservatives who recommended "constructive engagement" and liberals who insisted on unrelenting pressures. [22] Underlying the tactical debate was really a conflict of philosophy about deeper questions of morality, ideology, and global strategy.

The Carter State Department's initial diplomatic response to the April 1978 coup, therefore, aside from trying to maintain decent relations with the new regime, was to consult with our allies and friends in the region and essentially reassure them that we did not see it as a major East-West crisis. A *New York Times* editorial on May 5 described the administration as "rightly unruffled" by the event.[23] Senior U.S. officials acknowledged openly that we did not share with our more worried friends "precisely the same perception of these events or their causes."[24] The *Washington Post* printed a dispatch from a British journalist in Kabul with an extraordinarily benign view of the new regime—in fact, succumbing in almost parodic fashion to the romantic notion, which we have seen so many times before (and since), of the reformist, nationalist quality of the new radical rulers: "Taraki and his Cabinet colleagues are agrarian reformers, intensely nationalist and likely to be formidably opposed to direct Soviet intervention. . . ."[25]

As time went by, Brzezinski's skepticism increased as the Soviet role in the country grew. "Creeping intervention," he called it.[26] In a June 1978 interview, Taraki affirmed his party's position that "the basic conflict of contemporary history" was that between international socialism and international imperialism, represented by the USSR and the United States, respectively.[27] There was no ambiguity about whose side Afghanistan was on. But Washington's conciliatory approach was not seriously reexamined until February 1979, when Ambassador Dubs was kidnapped by dissident radical tribesmen and killed in a bungled rescue attempt—in the presence of a Soviet adviser—in circumstances that suggested not only incompetence but callousness on the part of the Afghan authorities.

Among Afghanistan's neighbors, the April 1978 coup itself had been immediately and profoundly unnerving. A different kind of strategic analysis was being applied there. A former neutral buffer had suddenly become, for all intents and purposes, a Communist regime and Soviet ally, its hollow claims of nonalignment notwithstanding. This was an objective change for the worse in the strategic environment of all of Afghanistan's neighbors, no matter whether the Kremlin had instigated the coup or not. What our friends wanted to hear from the United States was not necessarily a promise that we could undo what had happened but at least a reassurance that we shared their perception that something serious had taken place, calling for heightened vigilance and solidarity.

This was clearly the shah's view. In early June 1978, I accompanied Henry Kissinger on a private visit to Iran for a meeting in Ramsar, an elegant resort on the Caspian Sea. The shah was agitated. To him, the Afghan coup *was* a serious event, with the ominous implication of a stronger Soviet presence in the region—and even more serious was the apparent inability or unwillingness of the United States to perceive it. The shah speculated to Kissinger that the Carter administration, in its eagerness to improve relations with Moscow, had reached some kind of secret understanding with Moscow to divide up the Southwest Asian region into spheres of influence, perhaps even partitioning Iran, as Stalin had attempted to do after the war. It was a paranoid vision. Kissinger did his best to assure the shah that the United States—especially under Jimmy Carter—was psychologically incapable of such a cynical spheres-of-influence policy.

The deeper source of the shah's nervousness was undoubtedly the Islamic resurgence that had already begun in his own country. Yet the American passivity in the face of Afghan events was of a piece with the general American posture as the Islamic revolution unfolded in Iran, contributing significantly to the shah's demoralization as his own crisis enveloped him. He had rested his strategic policy for a generation on the rock of his solid alliance with the United States, and now his external circumstances were becoming unprecedentedly uncertain just as his internal situation was doing the same. The important psychological quality of confidence, on which alliances like this depend, was being shaken by the apparent divergence of strategic analyses, its significance magnified by the shah's Middle Eastern mind-set of intrigue.

The Soviet role in Afghanistan, as noted, grew rapidly. A secret agreement is believed to have been reached in July 1978 to supply another $250 million in weapons.[28] From an estimated 350 Soviet advisers in Afghanistan at the time of the coup, the number doubled in the next two months and reached some 3,000 to 3,500 (including 1,000 military) by May 1979, and 7,200 by December 1979.[29] By June, U.S. officials believed the Soviets had placed their personnel in "virtually" every Afghan ministry and had taken over "key positions" in the defense and security apparatus.[30] The need for Soviet personnel was increased by the large-scale purges of nationalists and Muslims from the civil service, which produced administrative chaos. Taraki and Amin also began removing Parchami leaders from positions of power, sending Karmal away as ambassador to Prague. Many thousands of political opponents were executed.

Taraki and Amin then began a revolutionary policy of modernization to eradicate the country's reactionary culture and wrench it out of its backwardness. Land reform, secularization, and women's liberation were a profound cultural shock; the regime also attempted to impose rigid centralized control over the tribes. As one scholar observed, it almost appeared that the regime, in its doctrinaire fanaticism, "systematically planned to alienate every segment of the Afghan people."[31] Muslim-led tribal rebellions broke out immediately all over the country. The Afghan army, mostly conscripted villagers, was not a reliable instrument of discipline. Desertions escalated, and weapons flowed to the opposition. The tribal rebellion turned into a country-wide guerrilla war.

By the spring of 1979, though neither knew it, the two superpowers were launched on a collision course. In March 1979, a particularly ugly uprising took place in Herat, a major city in the western part of Afghanistan. An Afghan infantry division defected to the rebels, and several dozen Russian military advisers and their families were hunted down, tortured, slaughtered, their corpses mutilated and their impaled heads reportedly brandished on pikes carried through the streets.[32] The Herat massacre provoked a sharp expansion of the number of Soviet military advisers and in the supply of weapons, including armored vehicles and helicopter gunships.

Roughly in parallel with these events, the United States became active. Shaken by the fall of the shah of Iran in February 1979, the dramatic deterioration of U.S.-Afghan relations after the death of Dubs, and the incontrovertible evidence of Soviet dominance, Brzezinski began generating plans for covert support for the Afghan rebels. His memoirs report cryptically on an administration decision in April "to be more sympathetic to those Afghans who were determined to preserve their country's independence" and on consultations he had with Saudi Arabia and Egypt.[33] Other published reports indicate that Saudi Arabia, Egypt, and Pakistan were the principal sources of outside aid to the rebels and that Iran and Libya joined in.[34] (The CIA seems to have provided "nonlethal" aid—that is, technical assistance, communications gear, and medical equipment—between April 1978 and December 1979, but little additional information is available from published sources.)[35] Overruling State Department caution, President Carter, at Brzezinski's urging, in the summer approved a policy of high-level warnings to the Soviets, publicly and privately, that their role in Afghanistan could jeopardize U.S.-Soviet relations.[36]

THE SOVIET DECISION TO INVADE

The political and security situation in Afghanistan eroded at an accelerating rate, and the Soviets found themselves more and more consumed by the task of shoring up the collapsing regime. A Friendship Treaty signed between the two countries in December 1978 only escalated the public commitment of Soviet prestige. The deteriorating security situation bred political dissension within the regime and led the Soviets to send senior emissaries to Kabul to try to whip the Afghan party and government into shape, the better to cope with the insurgency. By the summer of 1979, despite the presence of some four thousand Soviet military advisers, the government was on the verge of losing control of the countryside.

The Soviet decision to launch a full-scale military invasion in December 1979 was based on several factors.

On the face of it, it was to avert the collapse of an allied government. Experts agree that if Moscow had not intervened in this fashion, the regime would have disintegrated.[37] Apprehension that it would be replaced by some kind of anti-Soviet or pro-Western regime was the mirror image of Western anxiety over the implications of the April 1978 coup, intensified by the Soviets' fear of such a presence on their own border. Afghanistan's neutrality having been shattered by the April coup, a year and a half later it was indeed a zero-sum game.

Fear of Western penetration of Afghanistan was a major theme of Soviet public statements at the time. Whether this was a phony excuse, sincere paranoia, or a justified concern is hard to tell. The Soviets were undoubtedly aware that outside aid was coming to the rebels. One theory was that the United States needed Afghanistan as a staging area against the Soviet Union now that the shah of Iran had been overthrown.[38] "An imperialist military bridgehead on our southern border" is how Leonid Brezhnev described the danger in a statement in January 1980. Brezhnev continued: "To have acted otherwise would have meant leaving Afghanistan a prey to imperialism, allowing the aggressive forces to repeat in that country what they had succeeded in doing, for instance, in Chile where the people's freedom was drowned in blood. To act otherwise would have meant to watch passively the origination on our southern border of a seat of serious danger to the security of the Soviet state."[39]

This accusation of American military designs on Afghanistan was, in fact, an old theme in Soviet propaganda and perhaps in Soviet thinking. Khrushchev in his memoirs goes on at length on the subject. At the time of his 1955 visit to Kabul, he says, "it was clear to us that the Americans were penetrating Afghanistan with the obvious purpose of setting up a military base."[40] This reads oddly today, in light of what the declassified U.S. documents of the time tell us about the U.S. government's decision more or less to write Afghanistan off.[41] But it may have been firmly believed. Foreign Minister Andrei Gromyko, one of the handful of Politburo leaders who took part in the invasion decision in December 1979, reportedly explained to his son years later, shortly before his death, that the primary "objective" reason for the decision was "the attempt by the U.S. government to destabilize the situation on the southern border of the USSR and threaten [Soviet] security."[42] The bona fides of this conviction was even given some credence by the parliamentary commission of inquiry that, ten years after the event, investigated the decision to invade and condemned it. The commission reported to the reformed Soviet Congress of People's Deputies in December 1989:

> The overall international situation was, at the time when the decision was made, undoubtedly difficult and was marked by acute political confrontation. Given that situation, there was some idea that certain quarters in the United States of America were intending to take revenge for the loss of their positions following the fall of the Shah's regime in Iran. The facts indicated that such a train of events was possible . . . Elements of armed interference from outside were on the increase, and the Afghan Government had issued appeals for help to the Soviet leadership.[43]

Whatever the political significance of external involvement, however, even a critical observer like Raymond Garthoff considers that the military assistance being supplied from outside at this stage was "minimal."[44]

China (which had taken a whack at Vietnam in early 1979) was another suspected villain in Soviet propaganda on Afghanistan in 1979. In *Pravda* on April 21, Boris Ponomarëv, hard-line head of the Communist party Central Committee Secretariat's International Department, highlighted the mutual security clause of the Soviet-Afghan Friendship Treaty: "This provision of the treaty has special significance these days, when the Peking leaders have committed aggression against the heroic people of Vietnam and are providing direct support to anti-government elements in Afghanistan and outside it . . . "[45] But Garthoff cites evidence that the Chinese were not, in fact, furnishing weapons before the Soviet invasion.[46]

The Islamic factor also played a part. The Iranian Revolution, which so traumatized the United States, shook the Soviets to some degree as well, given their nervousness about its influence in the Soviet Muslim republics and the religious element in the burgeoning rebellion inside Afghanistan.[47]

Despite their confusion about who exactly the strategic villain might be, the Soviet leaders were clearly alarmed. Having extended the reach of their power globally and perhaps stalked by the premonition that they had overreached, they undoubtedly feared a precedent if their ally were to fall. The credibility factor thus worked in their minds as much as it did in ours over Vietnam. This was the same Leonid Brezhnev who, at the time of the invasion of Czechoslovakia in 1968, had given his name to the doctrine of the irreversibility of Communist gains. This was the same Leonid Brezhnev who, as we saw above, pointedly invoked the image of Chile (where a pro-U.S. coup in 1973 had ousted the leftist regime of Salvador Allende) in describing the danger posed in Afghanistan. The East German ambassador in Kabul told the American chargé d'affaires in 1979 that "if the Soviet Union allowed a pro-Soviet communist government in a border state to collapse, it would have an unsettling effect on other border states within the Soviet orbit."[48] It is not excluded that this was later proved correct, given the psychological impact that the Soviets' humiliating withdrawal from Afghanistan in 1988–89 may have had in Eastern Europe.

The issue of credibility had a personal dimension as well. With Brezhnev ailing, a succession struggle was imminent, and no one in the leadership group wanted to look weak. Diplomat Sergei Tarasenko later described the atmosphere: "All these guys, they were cynical, they valued personal interest above the interest of the country. They were positioning themselves well, at least being again on the Politburo when the guard will be changed. And over this period there is a gang mentality: stick together, to be tough, to show that you are a true believer, that you are indeed a Communist, you are Leninist, you do everything to guard the system."[49]

Another factor in the decision was the assumption that international reaction to a full-scale military move would be manageable. Whatever the purported paranoia about the U.S. role, the Soviets were in fact acutely conscious of the generally weakened posture of the United States in the 1970s. "The 'Vietnam syndrome' that the U.S. went through only whetted appetites," wrote a reformist Soviet commentator years later, listing Afghanistan among the misadventures that Soviet policy fell prey to.[50] The aforementioned U.S. chargé d'affaires in Kabul, Bruce Amstutz, is convinced that the Soviets had fresh in their minds not only our Vietnam trauma but our apparent helplessness and preoccupation over the Iranian takeover of our embassy in Tehran the month before.[51] Though others like Raymond Garthoff dispute this analysis,[52] it looks like America's own credibility problem was again rearing its ugly head.

More strikingly, U.S. chargé Amstutz received repeated hints from his East German and Soviet diplomatic colleagues in Kabul in the summer of 1979, as the internal situation deteriorated, that more drastic Soviet intervention might be necessary. Amstutz interpreted these hints as a deliberate signal that the Soviets hoped any such action would not have a negative impact on U.S.-Soviet relations.[53] There is no publicly recorded U.S. reaction to these messages, least of all a U.S. response that might have disabused the Soviets of the notion that the United States would acquiesce. While Brzezinski informed Carter in July (perhaps based on these sources) that the Soviets would probably try to unseat Amin, the national security adviser seems not to have interpreted the overtures in Kabul as any kind of signal. The administration's main concern was the second Strategic Arms Limitation Treaty (SALT II), which it concluded with the Soviets in June. Whether a matter of inadvertence or policy, it is hard to escape the conclusion that American passivity over the course of this period contributed to the Soviets' complacency about the political costs of intervention.[54] Both Brzezinski and Vance acknowledge the point.[55]

The precipitating cause of the decision to intervene was something more mundane and human—the depth of the Soviet leaders' personal revulsion at the behavior of Afghan strongman Hafizullah Amin. Amin and his fellow Khalqi leader Nur Mohammed Taraki had ruled the country together since April 1978 (having sent their Parchami brethren into virtual exile). Amin was long suspect in Moscow for his presumed American connection. He had studied in the United States at Columbia University (Teachers College) and the University of Wisconsin (summer school). In Moscow, this was assumed to make him pro-American or a likely CIA recruit. In my experience, it is rare that indoctrination at elite American universities turns one's politics to the Right; this would have been a first. In any event, Amin failed his doctoral examination at Columbia—unlikely to turn him pro-American. In power, he made no noticeable effort to win the confidence of the United States.[56]

As the internal situation continued to sour, the fraternal partnership of Taraki and Amin turned into a blood feud. Amin gained the upper hand, to the dismay of the Soviets, who considered him responsible for the disastrous policies that were wrecking the country. Fending off Soviet pressures, Amin reportedly did make overtures to Zia of Pakistan; nothing came of this except to inflame the Soviets more. Taraki, whom the Soviets much preferred, stopped briefly in Moscow on September 10 on the way home from a nonaligned summit in Cuba and conferred with Brezhnev on the overall situation; Brezhnev gave Taraki a bear hug at the airport. But within a week, Amin had Taraki arrested and three weeks later had him murdered. To Brezhnev this was a gross political and personal affront.

The KGB's analysis was that Amin's ascension would compound the regime's divisions and the country's instability. The KGB station in Kabul advised Moscow: "The situation can only be saved by the removal of Amin from power and the restoration of unity" in the party.[57] Between mid-September and mid-December 1979, the Soviets made three attempts to assassinate Amin, but all were bungled. One of his cooks, a KGB plant, tried in vain to poison him. KGB defector Vladimir Kuzichkin tells this story:

> Lieutenant-Colonel Mikhail Talybov, an active illegal documented as an Afghan citizen, was selected to carry out the order. He was sent straight to Kabul, where with the help of KGB resources he was infiltrated into Amin's entourage as a cook in the presidential palace. Talybov was given the job of poisoning Amin. But as Misha Talybov told me himself later, it proved to be no simple matter to do this. Amin was so suspicious that he never ate anything completely. He ordered several dishes and ate a little from each one. What was more, his food was tasted by his bodyguards. On several occasions Talybov added poison to the fruit drinks that Amin usually took. But Amin always mixed the drinks, thus reducing the possibility of poisoning.
>
> "I couldn't poison everything in the kitchen," Talybov exclaimed. "The operation had to be discreet."[58]

Had any of the assassination plots succeeded, the Soviets might—at least for the moment—have felt no need to intervene. When the military operation did take place on December 24, 1979, part of its objective was to remove the man the Soviets considered the root cause of the disaster. According to a 1982 magazine interview of Kuzichkin, a few hundred Soviet commandos, plus a team of KGB officers led by the commander of its terrorist-training school, dressed in Afghan army uniforms and driving vehicles with Afghan markings, machine-gunned their way to the presidential palace. Amin was found drinking at a bar on the top floor with an "exceedingly beautiful" young female at his side. Both were shot dead on the spot.[59]

Alas, the one bit of sex that I managed to find for this book to satisfy my publisher turns out to be suspect. The "exceedingly beautiful" female had disappeared completely from the episode by the time Kuzichkin put his recollections in memoir form in 1990: In his later version, Amin was simply "found in one of the rooms" and gunned down in a long burst of automatic-weapons fire.[60] A subsequent eyewitness account from a member of the special KGB commando squad described the group's coming upon Amin's second-floor office; a grenade was thrown into the president's study, after which he rushed out of the room—into a hail of gunfire—dressed in an Adidas T-shirt and blue boxing shorts. Suspicious attire, perhaps, but still no female.[61]

According to the Soviet parliamentary commission of inquiry set up ten years later and recently published Politburo documents, the decision to invade was made in early December by a "narrow circle of people" that excluded most of the membership of the Politburo. That narrow circle included Brezhnev, then president as well as general secretary; Dmitri Ustinov, minister of defense; Yuri Andropov, KGB chairman; Foreign Minister Gromyko; and Central Committee ideologue Ponomarëv. The commission of inquiry found it objectionable that the party Politburo "did not even assemble in its full complement to discuss this matter and make a decision on it," nor did the government or Parliament have a voice. (The commission had to admit that given the political style of the time, if the decision had been presented to these wider forums, it would doubtless have been endorsed.)[62] Later published documents reveal that all the Politburo members were asked to sign a piece of paper attesting to the decisions, but the decisive consensus had already been reached in a smaller group.[63]

Journalist Don Oberdorfer reports a dramatic inside account of the key meeting, from a Soviet source whom he considers reliable and authoritative:

> For the first part of the meeting, the deteriorating situation in Afghanistan was discussed by other top officials in the absence of Brezhnev. Although intervention had been debated from time to time for many months, a crisis point was reached. . . . On the crucial day, after about forty minutes of discussion, consisting mostly of bitter condemnation of Amin, the door opened and Brezhnev shuffled in. According to the Soviet source, who had access to an eye-witness account, the doddering General Secretary, with Gromyko holding his elbow to assist him, shook hands with and kissed all his colleagues. In a whisper loud enough to be heard by others in the room, Gromyko summarized the situation and told Brezhnev that Amin was a terrible man. According to this account, Brezhnev got to his feet, placing his palms on the table in front of him, and said only two words, *neporyadichnii chelovek*, meaning, "indecent person." Spoken in this Mafialike manner, Brezhnev's words about Amin were taken as an order to eliminate him. On December 24, 85,000 Soviet troops began pouring into the country, and three days later Amin was overthrown and killed.[64]

When the war later came to be regarded as a national catastrophe, Soviet citizens were treated to a spectacle of bureaucratic finger pointing and blame shifting. To students of bureaucratic politics in the West, it was a familiar phenomenon. Self-serving leaks to the media, cover-your-rear-end versions of events, and open institutional warfare seem to be among the Free World government practices that Russian reformers learned most easily. The army general who headed the military advisory mission in Afghanistan at the time let it be known ten years later that he had warned Moscow against increasing its military presence in the country but that his KGB colleague was sending back more optimistic reports.[65] Then Oleg Kalugin, a KGB major general who joined the reformers as a member of Parliament, claimed that Andropov had really been opposed to military intervention but had deferred to his friends Brezhnev and Ustinov.[66] But another disaffected KGB source claimed that while its agents in the field were warning against intervention, the KGB in Moscow was sending memoranda to the Central Committee through Andropov "to the effect that they were awaiting us there almost with open arms." He accused Andropov of "purposeful disinformation of the Politburo."[67]

Georgii Arbatov, who helped draft the parliamentary report ten years later, blames the defense establishment.[68] But the professional military leadership insist that they, too, had been against military intervention. Chief of the General Staff Marshal Nikolai Ogarkov, First Deputy Chief of the General Staff Marshal Sergei Akhromeyev, and Deputy Chief of the General Staff (and later Afghan commander) Gen. Valentin Varennikov visited Defense Minister Ustinov together in late 1979 to warn him that a commitment of Soviet troops to combat could not stabilize the situation and would only provoke a nationalist reaction among the population. They recommended that Soviet units only form garrisons in major cities, render "humanitarian aid," and beef up the Afghan army. According to Varennikov's later account of all this, Ustinov overruled them. Dmitri Ustinov was not a military man—he had been the chief bureaucrat running the military-industrial complex when Brezhnev elevated him—and Varennikov was sarcastic: "I do not think we should now blame everything on Dmitri Fedorovich alone. He was simply given the wrong job in 1976."[69]

Brezhnev, Andropov, and Ustinov were, of course, all dead by the time of these revelations. The stolid Gromyko, who outlived them all, never indulged in the self-exculpatory orgy, even though he, too, may have been only a passive player, deferring to the others.[70] As mentioned earlier, he clung until his dying days to the arguments that to him justified the intervention. Yet Gromyko may have been one of the first to have genuine doubts. He reportedly told India's Foreign Minister Narasimha Rao in April 1980 that the Soviets had miscalculated when they went in.[71] Gromyko had been led to believe that the military operation would complete its mission in around three months.[72]

The question of Soviet purposes is not entirely academic. This, too, became a subject of debate in the United States: Were the Soviet motives offensive, posing a threat to the region and the world? Or were they defensive, just sustaining the status quo by propping up a beleaguered ally? Once again, schools of thought have contended as to what reaction was warranted and how America's fundamental interests ought to be perceived. George F. Kennan, for example, deplored the "disquieting lack of balance" in Washington's reaction—the "extravagant" view of Soviet motivations and the resulting "war atmosphere."[73] The Carter administration was later criticized by Raymond Garthoff for its seeming lack of curiosity as to the root motivation of the Soviet action as it rushed to take a series of punitive steps.[74]

One can make a case for the subjectively *defensive* motive of the Soviet intervention. It would follow from this, Garthoff argues, that the United States overreacted. President Carter reversed by 180 degrees his whole policy toward the Soviet Union—withdrawing the SALT II Treaty from the Senate (where it was languishing, anyway); imposing a range of sanctions, from a grain embargo to a boycott of the 1980 Olympics in Moscow; proclaiming in the "Carter Doctrine" a direct U.S. military commitment to defend the Persian Gulf. The Soviets seem to have been caught by surprise by these drastic measures. It is possible that the Kremlin leaders honestly failed to understand the American reaction—or to believe its sincerity—and thus were only reinforced in their fear of American designs on the region.[75]

None of us can finally know the innermost thoughts of the Kremlin leaders who made the decision. Nor is such knowledge ever attainable in the give-and-take of international affairs. Thus, for all the very human (and very American) desire to understand the other fellow's point of view, another school of thought argues for what it would consider an objective rather than a subjective mode of analysis.

In this view, even if the motive was subjectively defensive, the invasion created an immediate strategic problem for all Afghanistan's neighbors—obviously far graver even than the April 1978 coup—and the brazenness of the Soviet action was a serious shock in the wider East-West framework. The analogy with Korea is apt. Had the Soviet suppression of the Afghan resistance *succeeded*, moreover, the result would have been a net forward movement of Soviet power, consolidating its new hold on a former nonaligned buffer. There is no way that neighboring Pakistan could not see this as an enormous change in its strategic situation. Likewise, China and the United States, Pakistan's protectors.[76] Moreover, coming after the string of adventurist moves in Africa and Communist gains in Indochina and Central America, it was bound to reinforce the impression of a Soviet policy that knew no restraints. From the transport of Cuban troops the Kremlin had now graduated to the use of its own troops in outright invasion of a Third World nation.

That the Soviets may have been genuinely surprised at the American reaction is, of course, not a valid excuse for the invasion, nor does it diminish the force of the general perception that the invasion upset the regional balance. After the fall of the shah, the United States legitimately feared a vacuum in the Gulf. A new boldness in Soviet policy in the region could not be taken lightly by any serious American government. It may be true that the invasion was not part of any Soviet grand design or master plan, but rather an improvised response to a threatened loss of position. Nevertheless, the Carter administration (particularly Brzezinski) was correct that the objective consequences—particularly if the Soviets had been allowed to succeed and to pay no price—would have represented a strategic disaster.

The wisest word on the subject of Soviet motivation may be that of a younger George F. Kennan in his legendary "Long Telegram" of February 1946, sent from Moscow where he served as chargé d'affaires and resident Kremlin watcher. At the bottom of the Kremlin's "neurotic view of world affairs," he wrote, was the "traditional and instinctive Russian sense of insecurity. . . . Basically this is only the steady advance of Russian nationalism, a centuries old movement in which conceptions of offense and defense are inextricably confused."[77]

STRATEGIC CONSEQUENCES

In the context of the other events of the 1970s, the very casualness of the Kremlin rulers' decision to intervene in Afghanistan is the best evidence of hubris, of an arrogance of power, an easy assumption that their will could be imposed on any who resisted. It could not be permitted vindication.

The Carter administration responded not only with the various political and economic sanctions mentioned but with a measure that proved more lasting and effective than any of the sanctions. This was a systematic covert program of military and other material assistance to the Afghan resistance forces, who became known as the mujahedin. President Carter signed a secret "finding" to establish a program in intelligence channels with the aim of enabling the mujahedin to harass the Soviet occupying forces (no more ambitious objective then thought attainable).[78] The program was expanded under Reagan and received consistent bipartisan support in Congress—breaking, at least in this instance, the Vietnam-era taboo about covert intervention. According to an account leaked in the summer of 1981:

> A year and a half after Soviet troops marched into Afghanistan, the US Central Intelligence Agency is coordinating a complex, far-flung program, involving five countries and more than $100 million, to provide the Afghan resistance with the weaponry of modern guerrilla warfare. The result is an emerging anti-Soviet alliance—the United States, China, Pakistan, Egypt, and Saudi Arabia—that, in the judgment of American planners, is effectively countering the most blatant Soviet aggression of the postwar era.[79]

The Chinese became the main supplier of Soviet-type arms (any other kind of weapons being a dead giveaway of outside intervention); the Americans and Saudis became the principal paymasters. Before the decade ended, the United States alone had funneled more than $2 billion in guns and money to the rebels.[80]

The Soviet invasion of Afghanistan tipped the political balance in America irreversibly against détente. Not only SALT II but also Carter himself was a casualty. The president's postinvasion admission in an ABC-TV interview that "my opinion of the Russians has changed most [more] drastically in the last week than even the previous two and one-half years before that" was gleefully exploited by the Republicans as a confession of naïveté. (The White House omitted the text of the interview from the official *Weekly Compilation of Presidential Documents* and the annual volume of *Presidential Papers and Addresses*.)[81]

The event helped to consolidate the U.S.-Chinese relationship of which the Soviets seemed to have such fear. Carter's Secretary of Defense Harold Brown was in Beijing in January 1980; his public statements suggested a new coordination of policy. Afghanistan also cemented the U.S. alliance with Pakistan, quelling for a decade Democratic liberals' concerns about Pakistan's authoritarian internal politics and its nuclear weapons program. Five million Afghans fled the country, or about one-third of the population—3 million to Pakistan, 2 million to Iran—in the largest refugee movement in history. Even the Indians, the Soviets' generally faithful friends, were embarrassed.

The nonaligned nations, who usually soft-pedaled Soviet misdeeds (especially when they feared Soviet punishment for complaining), this time reacted with unusual forthrightness. The Arab and Muslim bloc, from moderate Saudi Arabia to radical Iran, were united in their indignation, and their solidarity drove the nonaligned. On January 14, 1980, an emergency special session of the UN General Assembly passed by an overwhelming margin—104 for, 18 against, 18 abstaining—a resolution that "strongly deplore[d] the recent armed intervention" in Afghanistan and called for the immediate, unconditional, and total withdrawal of "foreign" troops.[82] Similar resolutions were passed by the General Assembly every year that followed. The Soviets were usually not named but nonetheless warned countries that a vote for these resolutions would be viewed as an "unfriendly act."[83]

The Soviets were at a geopolitical dead-end unless they could win quickly. But they could not win quickly.

The assault on Afghanistan in December 1979 had seemed an awesome demonstration of military prowess. It had as its centerpiece a swift airborne insertion of high-quality troops and Special Forces units at Kabul airport and airfields around the country. These airborne troops then fanned out and linked up with armored and mechanized troops in motorized rifle divisions to encircle and capture key cities, command and control and communications sites, fortresses, and roads.[84] The Soviets were considered the masters of this kind of airborne assault—they may even have invented it when early Red Army airborne forces pioneered these techniques in the war to suppress the *basmachi* in Central Asia in the 1920s.[85]

But soon the military effort bogged down. After the initial commitment of 85,000 troops failed to do the job, 35,000 more were sent. But this was not enough, and infrastructure deficiencies made it impossible to send more. Amazingly, the Soviet military had made little effort to learn lessons from the American experience in Vietnam. The extraordinary growth of the Soviets' military capability over the previous decade and a half had increased their confidence in their ability to handle new forms of intervention, yet their strategy and tactics had not kept pace. (Whereas Khrushchev in 1961 had warned that so-called local wars had a great potential to escalate to nuclear war (see chapter 4), Soviet military doctrine in the late 1970s had concluded that this was no longer necessarily the case.)[86] They transplanted to the unique physical and political terrain of Afghanistan the strategies and tactics of the set-piece strategic offensive designed for the Central European theater. Indeed, it was a carbon copy of their Czech invasion of 1968. They proved to be inept at combined-arms coordination; their officers on the ground were unable to make independent decisions, adapt tactically to the theater, achieve the mobility and speed they counted on, or gain adequate tactical or strategic intelligence.[87]

Soviet policy drifted. As the war went badly, subordinates on the scene fell prey to the familiar bureaucratic "ailment"—as General Varennikov described it—of "reporting to the center only what would please it, not what was actually happening."[88] And the old man at the center, Leonid Brezhnev, continued to deteriorate physically and mentally. An academic commented on how hard it was to preserve the image of a functioning general secretary, "because the leader could not read to the end of the texts prepared for him."[89]

Meanwhile, the mujahedin's external aid gave them added staying power. Russians confirm now that as early as 1980, many of those involved in Moscow and in Afghanistan were beginning to realize that the war policy was not working.[90] The guerrilla rebellion had spread to all twenty-nine provinces. The Soviet troops, instead of being able to stay in garrisons, were drawn into the main combat role as the Afghan army seemed close to disintegration.

The mujahedin—like the Afghan people—were an uneasy combination of diverse and contentious tribes and factions led by highly individualistic and ambitious chieftains. Elements of the rebels were moderates, or "traditionalists," some loyal to ex-king Zahir Shah, who still lived in exile in Rome. Others were Islamic radicals—anti-Western and anti-American but equally anti-Soviet. Under Iranian influence and the radicalizing effect of the war, the Islamic factor grew in importance in the resistance.[91]

In the early years of the aid program, the United States made a key decision that compounded this problem. Probably wisely, we left it to the Pakistanis to train the mujahedin and directly supervise the military effort; the Americans worked through the Pakistanis. I say "probably wisely" because the Vietnam experience suggested the senselessness of transplanting an unwieldy Pentagon bureaucracy to a faraway theater whose military, political, and cultural features were unfamiliar to us. Far better to work through the Pakistanis, who knew the people and the terrain intimately and could operate in an austere fashion even more unfamiliar to the institution that made famous the $640 toilet seat. The military effectiveness of the mujahedin over the years tends to vindicate this decision.

The price paid was a loss of direct control. Pakistani military intelli-

gence (the Inter-Services Intelligence Directorate, or ISI), which managed the program, had its own favorites among the mujahedin and played
them—namely, the more radical Islamic factions, which, while anti-
Western, were believed to be the best fighters. Nor did their Islamic fervor
disqualify them in the eyes of Pakistani president Zia, who launched an
"Islamization" program at home and who toyed with the idea of Islamic
regional solidarity (Pakistan, Iran, Afghanistan) as a hedge against the
erratic qualities of his American ally. The ISI was not amenable to
operational advice from the CIA.[92] This dilution of U.S. control was to
become troublesome in the late 1980s, when the United States had reason
to take more seriously the possibility of a political settlement. It also
complicated the military effort at that later stage.

THE NEGOTIATING TRACK

A similar complication existed on the diplomatic front, and this had its
comical qualities. From the very beginning, there was a "diplomatic
track," of sorts, but it did not deserve to be taken seriously. The Soviets'
negotiating position, if it can be called that, was that their troops would
vacate Afghanistan once the "outside interference" that caused the insurgency ceased. There was no serious Soviet willingness to withdraw
until the rebellion was defeated. The Soviets and the puppet Democratic
Republic of Afghanistan in Kabul insisted on face-to-face talks between
the Kabul regime and the government of Pakistan: This would have
amounted to de facto recognition of Kabul as well as the delegitimization
of the resistance, since Pakistan was sought as the interlocutor in its role
as the "instigator" of the resistance. Thus, the various mediation efforts
that were made in the early 1980s—by the European Community in
1981, by the United Nations in 1981, and thereafter—got nowhere.

   In late 1981 and early 1982, an agreement was reached on procedure.
The Kabul regime accepted UN mediation, and Pakistan (and its Amer-
ican ally) accepted that Pakistan could engage in talks with Kabul indi-
rectly through the United Nations. The first UN special envoy was the
Peruvian diplomat Javier Pérez de Cuéllar; when Pérez de Cuéllar became
UN secretary-general in 1982, he named Ecuadorian diplomat Diego
Cordovez special envoy. Talks began in Geneva in June 1982.[93]

   The negotiation as it evolved dealt with four topics: the withdrawal of
"foreign" (i.e., Soviet) troops; "noninterference" (which meant ending
outside aid to the mujahedin); international guarantees of whatever settlement was reached; and return of the refugees in "safety and honor,"
in the words of the UN resolutions. Eventually it was decided to negotiate

four separate "instruments," or accords, on these issues. Within these topics the more concrete issues were the timetable for Soviet troop withdrawal; the relationship between it and the obligation to end outside aid to the resistance; and—an issue that was later separated out as too ambitious—an internal political compromise among the Afghan parties.

The Geneva talks had a number of peculiar features. First, the mujahedin were not at the table. The resistance leaders were, in fact, totally hostile to the negotiations, fearing a sellout. But Pakistan held the whip hand for the first few years, relatively eager to settle because of the tremendous burden of the refugees and its fear of Soviet military pressures. Another odd feature of Geneva was the general assumption that it would produce no result. Most outside observers (including myself) shared this low expectation. This became a problem late in the decade when suddenly agreements started to be reached, and the United States was not happy with what it saw.

One reason for our surprise was that Pakistan did not keep the United States fully informed of what was going on in the talks. The State Department had not been overly concerned—since no one expected anything to come out of them. As agreements emerged from Geneva, the Pakistanis told the resistance leaders even less than they told the United States. The United States hesitated to tell the resistance leaders what it knew for fear of antagonizing Pakistan.

Thus, the diplomacy as well as the covert program was under Pakistani control, with little U.S. influence. The poetic justice was that the Pakistani Ministry of Foreign Affairs, which kept us out of the diplomacy, was also excluded by the ISI from influence over the military program. As we shall see, the diplomatic endgame had its Keystone Kops quality.

By 1985, both the war and the diplomacy were in stalemate. The breakthrough would come with the appearance of a new leadership in the Soviet Union without a vested personal stake in the original decision and with the escalation of U.S. military aid to the mujahedin, especially the furnishing of "Stinger" antiaircraft missiles—a decision by Reagan that was actually opposed by much of the U.S. government. In some respects we succeeded in spite of ourselves. The process will illustrate some important lessons about negotiation—when it works, and doesn't work, and why.

10

CENTRAL AMERICA TO 1985

It is in Central America that the United States has been forced most continually to confront the moral dilemmas presented by Third World radicalism. Since Woodrow Wilson and Franklin Roosevelt, North Americans have been torn between their idealism—that is, their anticolonialist heritage—and their strategic preoccupation, namely the responsibility that they considered fell on their shoulders to shield the Western Hemisphere, or the world, from intervention by foreign tyrannies. We debated whether Latin American revolution was a strategic challenge due to communism's inextricable link with Soviet foreign policy, or an indigenous phenomenon fueled by local poverty and legitimate grievances. Our assertions of power either alternated with or were infused with a heavy dose of moral doubt.

The French have the adjective *complexé* ("having complexes"), which perfectly suits the relationship between the United States and Latin America—on both sides. The most salient fact, it seems to me, is (as mentioned in chapter 2) that Latin America started out in the mid–nineteenth century as roughly equal to the United States in the main categories of economic potential but then plunged down a different path, with far different results. The United States not only became a superpower; it became a world power, with global interests and preoccupations, whose every act—of commission or omission, deliberate or inadvertent—impinged on the political and economic life of its weaker neighbors. The coexistence of North and South in the hemisphere thus became a matter of constant delicacy or offense. Enormous intellectual passion was thrown into the task of explaining—not only in a historical sense but in a moral sense—what accounted for the disparity of power.

Marxists posited a theory of colonialist exploitation of the South by the North. A version of this went by the name of "dependency theory," the point being that the United States had become rich by keeping Latin America and the rest of the developing world in a state of economic weakness and political servility in order to exploit their resources.[1] This theory was psychologically satisfying to the self-declared victims but was weak economics and bad history. The United States has for most of the modern period depended relatively little on foreign resources and trade; it is one of the most self-sufficient of all economies. U.S. investment in Latin America is less than 1 percent of U.S. total investment, domestic and foreign. If the wealth of the advanced industrial state depended on the exploitation of colonies, Spain would have vaulted past Britain after 1500 as the world's superpower.[2] And the dependency theory, of course, failed to address the question of why the two countries that started out as equals diverged in the first place.

It has taken a long time for more dispassionate analyses to win favor. Today the most interesting approaches are those of the Peruvian Hernando de Soto, with his microeconomic insights into the syndrome of under-development,[3] and of the Venezuelan Carlos Rangel and Americans like Lawrence Harrison and Michael Novak, with their analysis of historical and cultural factors that account for different attitudes toward economic activity.[4] De Soto stresses that entrepreneurship, the key to development, is a native talent everywhere but that a successful free market cannot develop without the requisite social structure and legal institutions. He thus marks out a middle ground between Left and Right, condemning both the Left's ideological fetishes and the "mercantilism" of the entrenched privileged classes that block the rise of an entrepreneurial middle class in Peru.

Rangel's historical approach begins with the legacy of colonial Spain: "It was Latin America's destiny to be colonized by a country that, though admirable in many ways, was at the time beginning to reject the emerging spirit of modernism, and to build walls against the rise of rationalism, empiricism, and free thought—that is to say, against the very bases of the modern industrial and liberal revolution, and of capitalist economic development."[5]

Rangel, Harrison, and Novak have taken Max Weber's and Joseph Schumpeter's insights into the development of European capitalism and extended the analysis to the Third World, especially the Western Hemisphere. They explore the contrast between North America's Protestant culture of individualism and economic and political pluralism and Catholic South America's tradition of hierarchy, unitary order, moral absolutism, and communitarianism. The South's intellectual heritage, strongly influenced by its religious culture, has been unfriendly to bourgeois individualism and thus to the spirit of entrepreneurship and the values of the middle class as they were celebrated in the Protestant world. Thus, in our own time, Pope Paul VI said in a 1971 encyclical: "Certainly personal initiative must be maintained and developed. But do not Christians who take this path tend to idealize liberalism . . . while easily forgetting that at the very root of philosophical liberalism is an erroneous affirmation of the autonomy of the individual in his activity, his motivation and the exercise of his liberty."[6]

While popes and some Catholic commentators may deny it, this rejection of liberal individualism produces an intellectual culture that is susceptible to contrasting extremes—either perpetuating the feudal social structure that burdened nineteenth-century Latin America or else succumbing to the socialist ideas that took hold in the mid–twentieth century (embraced by Catholic "liberation theology"). Even Thomas Jefferson wondered if Latin Americans were capable of sustaining a democratic tradition. Writing to John Adams in 1818, Jefferson warned that while the Latins would win their independence from Spain, "the dangerous enemy is within their own breasts. Ignorance and superstition will chain their minds and bodies under religious and military despotism."[7]

Lawrence Harrison likes to quote Daniel Patrick Moynihan: "The central conservative truth is that it is culture, not politics, that determines the success of a society. The central liberal truth is that politics can change a culture and save it from itself."[8]

The United States for a long time undoubtedly took advantage of Latin America's political and military weakness to ensure congenial conditions of business access, all the while attributing to itself the most benign of motives. The United States also had a strategic preoccupation with the security of the Panama Canal. The truth of the U.S.-Latin relationship is much more complicated, however, than the mythology on either side— not the least where Nicaragua is concerned. It was Franklin Roosevelt who was president when the first Anastasio Somoza seized power in 1933 and began a half century of dynastic tyranny and corruption; Roosevelt shied away from intervention—out of moral principle.[9] Intervention by the North, whatever the motive (even to oppose tyranny), was understood to touch the rawest of nerves because it dramatized the inequality of power. Yet on many occasions, especially in the Nicaraguan case, we were berated for *failing* to intervene. The more conscious the United States became of the sensitivities, the more it went through a moral wringer.

As noted in chapter 2, the self-assurance with which the righteous Woodrow Wilson had been able to wield American power in Central America in the name of democracy had given way to the modern liberal affliction of self-doubt. A relativistic age stripped away much of the self-congratulation in American thinking about Latin America as surely as

Sigmund Freud was stripping away layers of denial about sex. But (as with Freud) we were not left with the clearest practical idea of what was expected of us.

The ever-wise Walter Lippmann observed in 1927 that Americans were torn between the capitalists who profited from the status quo and the liberals wracked by feelings of guilt. These were the seeds of the ideological division that reached its most acute phase in the 1980s. Lippmann regarded it as a symptom of our immaturity as a great power:

> When something happens in the Caribbean, the only voices heard are those of the oil men, the fruit men, mining men, bankers on one side, and the outraged voices of the Gladstone liberals on the other. The debate is conducted by the hard-boiled and soft-hearted. There is no opinion which is both hard-headed and far-seeing. The effect on policy is bad: the hard-boiled interest works continuously, and the rather amateurish officials in the State Department who are assigned to these duties are unable to cope with it. . . . So usually the situation is developed without the check of public criticism until it reaches a climax where marines have to be used. Then the soft-hearted people roll over in bed and wake up. There is a great outcry about imperialism, and the policy of the government becomes confused and vacillating. After a while the soft-hearted clamor subsides. . . .
>
> There can be no remedy for this until Americans make up their minds to recognize the fact that they are no longer a virginal republic in a wicked world, but they are themselves a world power, and one of the most portentous which has appeared in the history of mankind. When they have let that truth sink in, have digested it, and appraised it, they will cast aside the old phrases which conceal the reality, and as a fully adult nation, they will begin to prepare themselves for the part that their power and their position compel them to play. [10]

Liberal Presidents like Franklin Roosevelt and John Kennedy strived to redress the wrongs by more solicitude for the Latins' self-respect or by more generous economic aid (the Good Neighbor Policy, the Alliance for Progress). It would be a mistake to discount the genuine idealism that infused their approaches and the attitudes of many others in the United States to this day. Latin America in fact achieved remarkable economic growth—5–6 percent a year in the 1960s and 1970s[11]—but the inability of these programs to do much more than scratch the surface of the massive poverty and inequalities only confirmed to Latin American radicals the hypocrisy of the imperialists. American liberals, alarmed at the deepening social crisis and desperation of the Latins, became even more insistent that social reform and U.S. aid were essential to head off radicalism.

Strategic-minded presidents like Eisenhower, Johnson, and Nixon, on the other hand, reacted sharply to Latin American radicalism without feeling excessively burdened by guilt—witness Guatemala in 1954, the Dominican Republic in 1965, Chile in 1970–73. The Nixon administration (at least in the person of Kissinger) marked a transition in conservative thinking away from the concern for business interests, for which Kissinger had contempt, to a more purely geopolitical concern about the spread of pro-Soviet radicalism in a region strategically vital to us. This was Kissinger's preoccupation in the Chile case.[12] The Nicaraguan Revolution, in the context of Soviet aggressiveness in Africa and Afghanistan, took on (in conservative eyes) a special ominous quality: First the Kremlin was sending Cuban troops to Africa, then using its own troops in Afghanistan; now communism was spreading in our own hemisphere.

These conflicting moral and strategic perceptions came into head-on collision over Nicaragua and El Salvador in the 1980s.

THE NICARAGUAN REVOLUTION

The Sandinistas are a Leninist party calling themselves the Sandinista National Liberation Front (or FSLN by their Spanish initials), named after Augusto Sandino, who led an ill-fated resistance against the U.S. Marine occupation of Nicaragua in the 1920s and 1930s. The Sandinistas came to power in Nicaragua in 1979 as the leading group in the broad coalition that toppled the regime of the dictator's son, Anastasio Somoza, Jr. While the Sandinistas' radicalism was no secret, the Carter administration and most of its partners in the Organization of American States (OAS) had come to the conclusion that the protracted political crisis that wracked Nicaragua in the late 1970s could be ended only by bringing an end to the Somoza dynasty. The United States and the OAS smoothed the way for Somoza's peaceful departure in favor of the broad opposition coalition, which represented (along with the Sandinistas) liberal intellectuals, business groups, labor unions, and much of the middle class.[13]

On June 23, 1979, in an unprecedented move, an OAS meeting of foreign ministers formally called for the removal from power of a member government. The OAS resolution called for the "immediate and definitive replacement of the Somoza regime" and for the installation of a democratic government that would include the groups in the coalition that opposed Somoza, guarantee respect for human rights, and hold free elections "as soon as possible."[14] On July 12, the Sandinista-led five-person junta representing the anti-Somoza opposition in exile sent a reply to the secretary-general of the OAS hailing the "historic" OAS resolution of June 23 and pledging to create a "broad-based democratic government," guarantee human rights, hold free elections, and otherwise fulfill the commitments of the resolution.[15]

The Carter administration was suspicious of the FSLN, far preferring to see the moderates in the anti-Somoza coalition gain power. It was well known that Fidel Castro had played a key role in unifying the various Sandinista factions and providing logistical support for the revolution. But once the Sandinista-led junta took over, the administration adopted the course of action we saw attempted earlier in the case of the Afghan regime after the April 1978 coup: to try to maintain influence by maintaining relations. As Anthony Lake has described it:

> After failing to prevent a Sandinista victory in Nicaragua in the summer of 1979 either by gaining reform of the Somoza regime or (at the last moment) by stitching together international efforts at a moderate resolution of the fighting, the Carter Administration concentrated on gaining leverage with the new regime. A $75-million aid program was instituted, after frustrating delays by Congress. The program was designed to: (a) allow the United States to compete on the ground with the Soviets and the Cubans, who were sending a small number of military advisers and thousands of civilian teachers, medical workers, and the like; (b) strengthen the position of the middle class, which had provided much support for the Sandinistas but might also be an important force for economic and political pluralism under their rule; and (c) encourage moderation in Nicaraguan foreign policy, especially with regard to El Salvador. Seeking either to overthrow the victorious new Sandinista government or to sever completely the long-standing ties between its leaders and their friends in Cuba seemed unrealistic.[16]

On September 11, 1979, Deputy Secretary of State Warren Christopher testified to a House subcommittee: "The [Nicaragua] government's orientation, as revealed in its initial policies, has been generally moderate and pluralistic and not Marxist or Cuban." Its leadership, he said, was "very diverse," its foreign policy seemingly friendly to its neighbors and desirous of "close and friendly relations" with us. While some of its influential figures had expressed anti-American views, Christopher said, "over time, we hope that Nicaragua will find a balanced foreign policy."[17]

According to Thomas J. O'Donnell, who was deputy chief of mission at the American embassy in Managua, Nicaragua, at the time, the United States was deluding itself about finding moderate forces within the Sandinista leadership:

> In retrospect, it was inevitable that the Sandinista regime would drift left, but we didn't think so at the time. . . . Ambassador Larry Pezzullo and I were hoping that there was a moderate element that we could identify, and at various times we identified different people. Occasionally even Tomás Borge [a leading radical] sounded like a moderate. But we were never really able to identify the moderate, or to use a better term, the pragmatic factions. . . . Frankly we never really understood the dynamics of the leadership and probably still don't.[18]

Gradually it became clear that the FSLN was moving in the direction we feared—in the manner of the Eastern European Communist parties after World War II, which similarly had come to power at the head of broad anti-Fascist coalitions and which then set about to consolidate their power by squeezing out all their non-Communist coalition partners. An extraordinary document has come to light outlining the FSLN's internal planning in September 1979—less than two weeks after Warren Christopher's hopeful statements. From September 21 to September 23, the National Directorate of the FSLN held a three-day secret assembly, and a report of the session—the so-called 72-Hour Document—was circulated among key party figures in October. The report spoke in classical Marxist-Leninist terms of the FSLN's duty to remain the "vanguard" of the revolution. The document explained the FSLN's alliance with the democratic elements of the bourgeoisie as tactical steps to win power and to "neutralize" both domestic rivals and "Yankee intervention." Internally, "groups opposed to the [revolutionary] process must be crushed!" But the strategy was to move only gradually to more radical steps of economic and social transformation until the party had consolidated its political control, which it would do by such steps as expanding the state sector (and the military) and breaking the economic power of the bourgeoisie.[19]

In foreign policy, the main enemy was, naturally, "the imperialist power of the United States," and the document invoked the principle of "revolutionary internationalism." The party's "guidelines" were a militant program directed against not only the United States but "Fascist" dictatorships in Latin America:

a) Develop political and diplomatic relations which will strengthen our process of military consolidation and economic independence.

b) Stimulate and strengthen the formulation of a national anti-imperialist and democratic policy, both internationally as well as on the continental level, and in the Caribbean area in particular.

c) Contribute to and promote the struggle of the peoples of Latin America against fascist dictatorships [and] for democracy and national liberation.

d) In the Central American region, because of its immediate strategic value, the same principles will apply, emphasizing the need to neutralize, through the proper handling of their internal contradictions, the aggressive policies of the military dictatorships. . . .[20]

The Council of State, a quasi-legislative body representing the entire coalition, was originally to have thirty-three seats, of which the FSLN would have thirteen. When it convened in May 1980, it had been expanded to forty-seven seats, with the Sandinistas and their allies taking all fourteen new seats—giving them a large majority. The democratic opposition, then consisting of the business community, non-Marxist political parties, and others, acceded to the changes—partly at the urging of the American ambassador—on the grounds that the council was intended only to be temporary until free elections were held.[21] Soon the non-Communists in the five-person junta had been squeezed out as well, leaving a junta of three members of the FSLN. The non-Communists who left the junta—Violeta Chamorro, Alfonso Robelo, and (later) Arturo Cruz—were distinguished anti-Somoza democrats who were, for their pains, later excoriated as *Somocistas* when they went into more open opposition to Sandinista rule. In August 1980, Sandinista defense minister Humberto Ortega announced the postponement until 1985 of the free elections promised to the OAS.

In foreign policy, the trend was equally disturbing. Daniel Ortega, Humberto's brother and later the president, was received at the White House by President Carter on September 24, 1979, as head of a delegation representing the new government. Carter offered substantial aid but cautioned against interference in neighboring countries. Clearly, there was a higher probability of American sympathy for the new revolutionary government if its conduct toward its neighbors posed no strategic problems. Unfortunately, the Sandinistas felt compelled to act on their principle of "revolutionary internationalism." They gave priority from the beginning to their ties with Cuba and, to a lesser extent, the rest of the Soviet bloc. The Cubans sent thousands of advisers; the Nicaraguans sent students to Cuba. Even Omar Torrijos, the Panamanian strongman and friend of the Sandinistas, became alarmed at the degree of Cuban influence and urged them to be more sensitive to their neighbors' fears.[22]

The Soviets did not engineer this outcome, but they exploited it. As early as January 1980, ideologist Boris Ponomarëv wrote of the Nicaraguan Revolution in the same category as the Afghan, Ethiopian, and Angolan revolutions.[23] Also in January 1980, revolutionary Nicaragua abstained on the UN General Assembly resolution, passed overwhelmingly, deploring the Soviet invasion of Afghanistan. In March 1980, an agreement was signed in Moscow establishing party-to-party ties between the FSLN and the Soviet Communist party. In the same month, Cuba made large-scale deliveries of Soviet weapons to Nicaragua, including antiaircraft and antitank guns and artillery. By the end of 1980, Nicaragua's armed forces had grown to twice the size of Somoza's National Guard.

Whatever the Soviets did or did not do to instigate the revolution, Nicaragua was a strategic windfall. The implications of the spread of revolution in Central America were articulated in stark terms by the Kissinger Commission, a bipartisan group appointed by President Reagan in 1983–84 that included distinguished Democrats like Lane Kirkland of the AFL-CIO, lawyer Robert Strauss, and San Antonio mayor Henry Cisneros as well as Republicans Kissinger, Nicholas Brady, and William Clements:

The ability of the United States to sustain a tolerable balance of power on the global scene at a manageable cost depends on the inherent security of its land borders. This advantage is of crucial importance. It offsets an otherwise serious liability: our distance from Europe, the Middle East, and East Asia, which are also of strategic concern to the United States. . . . To the extent that a further Marxist-Leninist advance in Central America leading to progressive deterioration and a further projection of Soviet and Cuban power in the region required us to defend against security threats near our borders, we would face a difficult choice between unpalatable alternatives. We would either have to assume a permanently increased defense burden, or see our capacity to defend distant troublespots reduced, and as a result have to reduce important commitments elsewhere in the world. From the standpoint of the Soviet Union, it would

be a major strategic coup to impose on the United States the burden of
defending our southern approaches. . . .[24]

It was the same strategic judgment that had led Walter Lippmann to
support President Lyndon Johnson's intervention in the Dominican Republic in April 1965. Lippmann, of course, was the perceptive critic of
postwar U.S. overextension, as we saw in chapter 2. At almost the same
moment, in fact, Lippmann was severely criticizing Johnson's escalation
in Vietnam, which in his view was a classic example of a commitment
far outside the area of America's vital interest. By the very same geopolitical token, however, Lippmann considered it "normal, not abnormal,
for a great power to insist that within its sphere of influence no other
great power shall exercise hostile military and political force."[25] Some
critics of U.S. policy in Central America in the 1980s were fond of
invoking Lippmann as the scourge of interventionism, conveniently forgetting that it was the one region of the developing world in which he
took a relaxed view of U.S. involvement.[26]

The strategic concern in Washington was borne out by the Sandinistas'
decision in mid-1980 to provide weapons, ammunition, and training to
the Communist guerrillas seeking to overthrow the government of El
Salvador. In September 1980, the Carter administration warned privately
that continued Nicaraguan aid to the Salvadoran guerrillas would jeopardize U.S. aid to Nicaragua. Managua replied that it was not involved.
In October and November an airlift of supplies for the Salvadoran guerrillas began from a new airstrip twenty-three miles northwest of Managua.
In November, an umbrella organization uniting the Guatemalan Communist guerrillas was also established in Managua.[27]

I need to stress here that all the developments I have just described
occurred under Jimmy Carter, before Ronald Reagan appeared on the
scene and while the United States was continuing to provide economic
help to the new revolutionary government. By January 1981, the Carter
administration had provided $118 million in direct bilateral aid to Nic-
aragua, plus U.S. support for $262 million from the international de-
velopment banks, and for the refinancing of $500 million in private bank
debt.[28] Before it left office, the Carter administration suspended the bilateral aid, disappointed that its hopes for a normal relationship with the
post-Somoza government—which it had helped put into power—had
been dashed.

To critics like Jeane Kirkpatrick, the Carter posture toward the Sandinistas smacked of a defeatist view that America was on the wrong side

of history and that Marxist revolution was inevitable and perhaps even preferable to the status quo.[29] The Carter administration's own post-mortems dwell on whether the outcome could have been avoided. But for State Department official Anthony Lake, for example, the decision to disavow and replace Somoza was not open to doubt. Lake's regret, rather, was that his administration had missed an earlier opportunity to overthrow Somoza during the crisis of June 1978, when the Sandinistas might not have been strong enough to dominate the democratic opposition.[30]

The dilemma of U.S. policymakers in 1978, however, was even more profound: Somoza was then much more entrenched and harder to dislodge, meaning that a much more determined political assault on him was required, for which there was little domestic support in the United States. Lake's intuition in 1978 that this was the moment to install a moderate alternative came up against not only some conservatives' strong sympathy for Somoza but a more widespread reluctance to see the United States get into the business of overthrowing authoritarian governments around the world that were not hostile to us. This would be a rather ambitious assignment and an ironic outcome after all the Vietnam-era angst about excessive American interventionism abroad.

President Carter, in fact, shared this reluctance, out of moral conviction. Exactly as FDR had refrained in the 1930s from U.S. intervention to block the Somoza dynasty at the beginning, so Carter in the 1970s thought unilateral U.S. action would be wrong. According to Robert Pastor of his NSC staff, Carter "basically decided we were not going to do it alone, that the age of U.S. unilateralism was past."[31] Carter instructed his diplomats to launch a series of consultations with Latin governments, which undoubtedly only added to complications and inhibitions. For Carter, moral consciousness produced paralysis.

Given the dynamics of revolution, moreover, forcing a moderate succession in 1978 in the hope of blocking the radical ascendancy would necessarily have been a speculative gamble. Breaking the back of the existing structure could just as well have accelerated the radical trend instead of slowing it down—as happened with Diem in South Vietnam in 1963 and with the shah of Iran in 1979. Nor would the Sandinistas have cooperated had we moved against Somoza in 1978. Both Somoza and the FSLN shared an interest in postponing the day of reckoning, Somoza for obvious reasons and the FSLN to radicalize the situation further in order to gain ascendancy in the opposition.[32] In short, the Carter administration would have faced an impossible dilemma had it tried to act on the intuition of some of its members in 1978, and it is easy to see why it shied away.

The Carter administration then found itself, in 1979, impaled on the other horn of the dilemma in its futile attempt to woo or moderate what was, in its essence, an implacably hostile anti-American regime bent on destabilizing Central America.

THE REAGAN ADMINISTRATION

The Carter administration's liberals wrestled with the key question of how to strengthen the democratic center in Central America against extremists of both the Right and Left. They may have come up with the wrong answer, especially in their bouts of wishful thinking about the Sandinistas, but it was the right question. The Reagan administration's conservatives floundered on Central America until they managed to come up with their own answer to that question.

Ronald Reagan as president was a more enigmatic figure than most of his detractors or his supporters realized. The stories about his lack of interest in intellectual matters are true. His eyes sometimes glazed over in complex discussions. When he finished reading from his five-by-eight-inch cue cards in an official conversation, the conversation often drifted off aimlessly. The jokes he cracked in important meetings in the Situation Room or with visiting heads of state were sometimes apt, sometimes a tactic to hide his uncertainties. There are stories of his being sent a policy-options memorandum with boxes for him to check to mark his choice and of the memo coming out of his office with all the boxes checked (though I think Richard Nixon did the same thing once in a distracted moment).

Reagan's strengths lay elsewhere, and I do not mean just his Hollywood-nurtured ability to deliver a speech with feeling or to walk into a room with a tall, commanding stride. He did have a remarkable physical presence in a room, which reflected an inner composure as well as whatever Hollywood had taught him. But Reagan also had an innate political shrewdness and knew his country's mood. His reticence in meetings was often simply a case of keeping his cards close to his chest. More than that, few presidents have left the imprint of their philosophy so firmly stamped on their country or their times. Ronald Reagan could not have done this without embodying something of substance. Some of his critics alternated between denouncing him for his ideological views and rigid convictions, on the one hand, and insisting (usually after one of his election victories) that the American people had voted only for a genial man with a smile. They could not have it both ways.

He was an unashamed believer in American exceptionalism. America was great and good and had a moral mission to be the "shining city on a hill" and "the last best hope of man on earth."[33] Whereas Jimmy Carter had often contrasted American ideals with American actions, Reagan never doubted his country's sincerity. Whereas Jimmy Carter had sought, in the post-Vietnam era, to teach America its limits (as during the Iran hostage crisis), Reagan rejected the defeatism that that seemed to imply and sought to restore the country's faith in its limitless possibilities. He forthrightly declared in 1982 and 1983 (to the dismay of many of our Soviet "experts") that the system of our adversaries was both evil and doomed. Reagan's sunny patriotism spoke to Americans who were fed up with their country's being pushed around by the Iranians or being taken advantage of by the Soviets in the Third World. Jimmy Carter, in a sense, was an interruption of the country's recovery from the Vietnam trauma, and the foreign policy embarrassments of Carter's presidency only assured that, after him, our recovery would burst forth with a vengeance.

Similarly, in domestic policy, Reagan's passion to reduce the burden of government on the economy came at a time when, fifty years after the New Deal, all Western societies were discovering that bureaucracy, regulation, and taxation were beginning to stifle the entrepreneurial sources of growth. At the Bonn economic summit in May 1985, all the leading industrial democracies voiced this conclusion.[34]

The intellectuals' mockery of Reagan was thus misplaced. The philosophy he embodied coincided with the historical moment to powerful effect. Reagan understood a number of basic things well—in my view, the most important things—and had the courage of his convictions. He was totally impervious to what the editorial boards of the *New York Times* and *Washington Post* thought—a truly liberating quality for a conservative president. Nixon had been constantly tortured by the liberal criticism, struggling stoically to overcome it.

All this being said, Reagan entered office on January 20, 1981, facing a Central America crisis he did not want. It was a crisis at home as well as in Central America.

Reagan's policy in the region, so often pictured as bellicose and malevolent, was actually quite hesitant and confused.[35] For all the accounts of the policy as intransigent and militaristic and of Reagan as an anti-Communist Rambo,[36] his administration came close to conceding the consolidation of the Sandinista regime, and this was in part a reflection of his strong personal reluctance to inject U.S. troops into another jungle war. Reagan's memoirs also reflect a genuine sensitivity to Latin fears of the "Great Colossus of the North."[37] His administration was split between those much more eager than he to intervene and those more eager than he to accommodate the Sandinistas. The contradictions would bedevil the policy well into Reagan's second term, as well as plunge him into a monumental political scandal.

An early blowup was inevitable. The 1980 Republican platform deplored the "Marxist Sandinista takeover of Nicaragua" and vowed to "support the efforts of the Nicaraguan people to establish a free and independent government."[38] The Sandinistas, in turn, interpreted Reagan's election in November as a kind of declaration of war and opened the floodgates of arms for the Salvadoran rebels before Reagan had even entered office. As journalist Christopher Dickey has put it, the hardliners on both sides had begun to fulfill each other's prophecies.[39]

In early January 1981 the Communists in El Salvador launched their "final offensive," in a (failed) attempt to topple the government, and the Carter administration finally obtained irrefutable evidence of the Nicaraguan regime's blatant arming of its Salvadoran comrades, belying Managua's repeated assurances. (The Reagan administration published much of the evidence in a "White Paper" in February 1981, which, while it was nitpicked by critics in minor aspects, was confirmed by all later evidence.[40] A year later, the chairman of the House Intelligence Committee, Democrat Edward Boland of Massachusetts, vouched for the "persuasive evidence" the U.S. government had accumulated.)[41]

The incoming administration, in two of its early acts, increased military aid to El Salvador by $25 million, including another two dozen military trainers, and formally terminated the U.S. aid to Nicaragua that Carter had suspended. Reagan was thereupon nearly overwhelmed by a firestorm of panic that he was plunging the country into another jungle war. The first question posed to him at his first news conference on January 29, 1981, was "how do you intend to avoid having El Salvador turn into a Vietnam for this country?" Walter Cronkite began his first interview with the new president (March 3) with the question "Do you see any parallel in our committing military advisers and military assistance to El Salvador and the early stages of our involvement in Vietnam?" A Gallup poll taken in March reported that two out of three informed Americans believed El Salvador could become "another Vietnam."[42]

Whereas the Carter administration had wrestled with the liberals' dilemmas, the Reagan administration found itself enmeshed in conservative ones. Reagan and his team believed fervently that the Soviet Union was on the march in the Third World and needed to be stopped; they believed the 1980 election had expressed the public's insistence that there be an end to Soviet gains abroad. Yet in Central America the administration found it almost impossible to sustain support, especially congressional support, for forceful measures.

The new secretary of state, Alexander Haig, saw Vietnam parallels of a different kind—which led him to advocate a *stronger* policy that would avoid the incrementalism that marked our early misguided entry into Vietnam. Haig, who carried scars from wounds he received in combat in Vietnam, later wrote:

> Very nearly the first words spoken on this subject in the councils of the Reagan Administration made reference to the danger of "another Vietnam." Indeed this danger existed, if Reagan repeated the errors of the past and resorted to incrementalism. To start small, to show hesitation, was to Vietnamize the situation. To localize our response was to Vietnamize the situation. Such a policy, in my view, could only lead us into the old trap. . . .[43]

Haig urged Reagan, in effect, to blockade Cuba—"going to the source," as he sometimes put it:

> There could not be the slightest doubt that Cuba was at once the source of supply and the catechist of the Salvadoran insurgency. Cuba, in turn, could not act on the scale of the rebellion in El Salvador without the approval and the material support of the U.S.S.R. I believed that our policy should carry the consequences of this relationship directly to Moscow and Havana, and through the application of a full range of economic, political, and security measures, convince them to put an end to Havana's bloody activities in the hemisphere and elsewhere in the world.[44]

Yet Haig was met by a president and White House and cabinet colleagues who wanted no part of an escalating Caribbean crisis, fearing the political risks and preferring to concentrate the president's prestige in the first year on his economic program. White House advisers James Baker, Michael Deaver, and Edwin Meese, strongly backed by First Lady Nancy Reagan, argued against military involvement in Central America. Mrs. Reagan's concern was to dispel the image of her husband as a warmonger; for the same reason she became an ardent advocate of a détente with the

Soviets. Defense Secretary Caspar Weinberger and the Joint Chiefs of Staff were opposed to any military engagement without a clear prospect of victory and of popular support at home. They mocked Haig's "thunder machine." Weinberger, in his memoirs, barely treats Central America at all except to get in his digs at Haig.[45]

In the final irony, it was the rejection of Haig's more muscular options that led the administration to come up with what it thought was a lesser, more discreet option. This was the covert CIA program of pressure on Nicaragua, which turned into an insurgent army (dubbed the "counter-revolutionaries," or Contras) which itself, in turn, created a monumental political crisis.

As Haig's influence in the administration waned (compounded by his gaffe—"I am in control here"—after the assassination attempt on Reagan in March), U.S. policy floundered. The rhetoric, especially from Haig, continued to be militant, but the Sandinistas saw through it. To Arturo Cruz, Jr., a young Nicaraguan then working in the Foreign Ministry, it was clear that the regime saw the Reagan administration increasingly as a "paper tiger."[46] In an unguarded moment, Lenin Cerna, the aptly named chief of Sandinista state security, expressed confidence in a Radio Sandino interview that the United States "won't dare invade Nicaragua directly because such an act would be very costly politically."[47] In August, Humberto Ortega referred to the revolution explicitly as Marxist-Leninist: ". . . our revolution has a profoundly anti-imperialist character, profoundly revolutionary, profoundly classist; we are anti-Yankee, we are against the bourgeoisie . . . we are guided by the scientific doctrine of the revolution, by Marxism-Leninism."[48]

The United States seems to have turned to covert action because other options were unavailable or too extreme. Modest financial support had been quietly provided to the democratic opposition leaders in the Carter administration, but it was not for military activity; it was to try to keep the moderates alive as a political force.[49] Now the question was whether to support a military force in the field—and no one in the administration really liked the idea. CIA director William Casey overcame his own initial reluctance because "there was no other way to do it," according to a CIA officer's account to Christopher Dickey.[50] It was a "lowball option, a small operation not intended to overthrow [the Sandinistas]" but to "harass" them, recalled Thomas Enders, Haig's assistant secretary of state for inter-American affairs.[51] On November 1, 1981, Casey met with Argentine military leaders and worked out a plan to train about a thousand anti-Sandinista Nicaraguans and a special force of about five hundred other Latin Americans; the Nicaraguans would harass Cuban and Sandinista military targets in Nicaragua, and the other force was to interdict the arms flow to the Salvadoran guerrillas.[52]

On November 16, the proposal was presented to Reagan at a meeting of the National Security Planning Group (a gussied-up National Security Council meeting) in the Situation Room in the West Wing basement. It was part of a package agreed to by all the key agencies—State, Defense, CIA, the Joint Chiefs of Staff—that included additional U.S. open military aid for El Salvador and Honduras, $250–$300 million more in economic aid to Central America and the Caribbean, and other steps of military training, intelligence gathering, and public information. Enders made the pitch for the covert-action plan. But Reagan's reaction was "skeptical"; he doubted the paramilitary effort would succeed in pressuring the Sandinistas, and according to Enders, he was "profoundly averse to violence." Even after modifications were made to the covert plan to minimize civilian casualties and reduce direct U.S. participation, Reagan still did not agree to it and made no decision at the November 16 meeting.[53]

A week later, Reagan signed National Security Decision Directive 17 approving the overt measures of economic and military aid to Central American and Caribbean neighbors. But before signing the intelligence "finding" to authorize the covert-action plan, he dispatched Haig on a secret and rather bizarre diplomatic mission—a meeting with the vice president of Castro's Cuba, Carlos Rafael Rodriguez, in Mexico City—to see if some understanding might be reached. Haig went reluctantly, and the encounter found no meeting of the minds. (In his view, it was because of the weakness of the U.S. posture.)[54] Reagan, satisfied that he had exhausted the alternatives, signed the finding on December 1, 1981. According to press accounts, $19 million was congressionally authorized for covert aid in Nicaragua in fiscal year 1982 and again in 1983, with another $10 million taken from CIA discretionary accounts in fiscal year 1983.[55] Haig regarded the whole program as a "cop-out."[56]

Casey briefed the two congressional intelligence oversight committees but did so in a way that left ambiguity and confusion over the program's objectives. Some legislators came away with the impression that the target was the Cuban military support structure in Nicaragua and the flow of arms to El Salvador, while others understood that there was a political objective of moderating the conduct of the government in Nicaragua.[57] State Department officials had convinced themselves that the insurgents would be a "bargaining chip"—to be traded away in exchange for an end to Sandinista support for neighboring insurgencies—but none of this was reflected in Casey's briefings.[58] Meanwhile, according to Contra sources, the CIA was telling them that the goal was the overthrow of the regime and that the more limited rationales were for congressional consumption.[59]

The confusion about motive was a ticking time bomb. In December 1982, House Intelligence Committee chairman Edward Boland pushed through an amendment to the 1983 Department of Defense Appropriations Act (the first of many significant Boland amendments) to prohibit any U.S. support for groups "for the purpose of overthrowing the Government of Nicaragua. . . ." It was the liberals who opposed this, preferring to ban all programs outright; the administration was satisfied, since all parties clearly understood that it permitted any activity that had any other rationale.[60] Probably at that stage, given the small scale of the program, the CIA in good faith could say it was operating within the prescribed limits. (Probably it was the Contras in the field who were being misled.) Casey even said in public that he thought the Contras had "no chance" of overthrowing the Sandinistas.[61]

The debate had a surrealistic quality to it: Would the CIA be violating the law if its operations had a limited aim and the Sandinista regime cracked under the pressure anyway? As time went by, critics began to attack the program, *inter alia*, for its inability to promise conclusive results—a disingenuous criticism, since the only truly conclusive result had been prohibited by law.[62] No doubt the administration would have loved to see the Sandinistas fall, but in truth it was content with whatever degree of pressure it could mobilize—the more the better. This was a perfectly sensible strategy and consistent with the law. But charges of bad faith began to fly in all directions—proving the error of papering over fundamental policy differences by ambiguous or too clever statutory compromises.

The administration paid a price, moreover, for the covert nature of the program: The details inevitably leaked as the issue became more controversial, but the administration felt inhibited from making its case. (It was also still divided.) Reagan, the "Great Communicator," was publicly silent on the topic of the Contras until the middle of 1983, leaving the way open to the critics to gain the upper hand in the debate.[63]

At the initial stage in late 1981, the intelligence committees reacted badly to the intellectual confusion about the program's purposes, but they took no steps to block the covert aid, partly because the growing repression in Nicaragua was losing the regime American supporters. The precariousness of the legal and political compromise was dramatized, however, by the first-class uproar that occurred in 1984 over the mining of Nicaraguan harbors. This had been intended as economic pressure—they were only "firecracker" mines designed to scare off other nations' commerce with Nicaragua. (Richard Nixon called the whole idea "Mickey Mouse.")[64] The myth persists that the committees were not informed in advance of the mining; they quite definitely were.[65] But just as in the Angola case in 1975, the committees ran for cover when the CIA's cover in the operation was blown and a controversy erupted. Sen. Patrick Leahy was cynical about his colleagues' performance: "[T]here were senators who voted one way the week before [Leahy told the *New York Times*] and a different way the following week, who knew about the mining in both instances. And I think were influenced solely by the public opinion. And I think that's wrong and that's a lousy job of legislative action."[66]

All this pointed up again some of the problems in the congressional oversight process. One was Bill Casey's cagey approach to briefings, which turned his mumbling speaking style into an instrument of policy. (He has been described as the only CIA director who didn't need a secure telephone for secret conversations, since his voice was already scrambled.) But there were human problems on the other side, too—distinguished members of our national legislature who were sometimes briefed on important matters at a time of day when they were not at their best. A senior conservative senator from Arizona who later complained of not being informed was thought by Bob Woodward to have been "well med-icated" on cocktails when the information first reached him; a senior liberal senator was briefed on the matter by a staff aide but "forgot."[67]

The administration felt put upon over the mining issue, but it ignored two fundamental problems—one, the dubious wisdom of the mining idea in the first place and, two, the growing congressional rebellion against the covert policy. By the summer of 1983, the Contra army had grown to about seven thousand men—about the same number as the Sandinistas had had in the field in the rebellion against Somoza—and by 1984 they were operating deep inside Nicaragua. But the Democratic House was voting on a regular basis to terminate the Contra program, and by 1984 (after the revelations of the mining) the Republican-controlled Senate was getting cold feet as well.

THE CONTROVERSY

Central America was beginning to divide this country as no other issue since Vietnam. Demonstrations, marches on Washington, media dissent, campus teach-ins, prayer vigils, civil disobedience, guerrilla graffiti, protests by Hollywood stars—many of the manifestations of the Vietnam era were repeated, indeed with many veterans of the anti-Vietnam movement reappearing, a little older and grayer, trying to get the old juices flowing.[68] "I feel like the ghost of teach-ins past," quipped Prof. Kenneth Boulding of the University of Colorado.[69] Young journalists, too, relished the chance to make their reputations as their elders had done in Indochina. Browse through my endnotes for this chapter and you will find an armful of books (a small fraction of the total number) by journalists who had covered Central America.

Opposition came from many sources. As the controversy developed, it was caught up in the perennial struggle between the president and Congress for control over foreign policy. When the CIA became involved in covert programs, deep-seated American ambivalence about such unseemly instruments of policy came to the fore again. But, much more so than in, say, Angola, there was ideological passion and a bitter clash between conservatives who saw Soviet-inspired revolutionary regimes in our neighborhood as a moral and strategic threat and liberals who saw the issue in terms of indigenous poverty, discontent, and military repression.

According to Frank McNeil, a Foreign Service officer who quit in protest over Reagan administration policies: "More than poverty, it was oppression, violations of fundamental human rights, and systematic corruption that precipitated the crisis of legitimacy and fueled the upheaval. Insurgencies are at root political wars. . . ."[70] According to a congressional staff aide in 1981 who opposed military assistance to El Salvador in its struggle with the Communist insurgency: "Military assistance was not the answer, because the problems were political and political problems were only made worse by the provision of military aid."[71]

In an echo of some of the more radical themes of the Vietnam era, some critics argued that our involvement in Central America not only was misguided or risky but that it was immoral. We were the bad guys, standing against "the tide of history," as Sen. Christopher Dodd put it in a speech in April 1983.[72] Even if Central American communism was an unfortunate development, the United States did not have the moral standing to oppose it by force because of our own heritage of complicity in perpetuating the rightist regimes and unjust conditions that were the source of the upheaval. "We have unclean hands," proclaimed Rep. Vic Fazio (D-Calif.) during the 1986 congressional debate over funding for the Contras.[73] The more simplified versions of Latin American history became commonplace: The United States was responsible for creating and sustaining the Somoza dynasty, acting out of arrogance and greed for its business interests.[74] Therefore, a revolutionary upheaval was inevitable—due to our own policies—and we had no right to stand in the way, no matter what the imperfections of the revolution.

Other traditional themes were common. The Soviet military buildup in Nicaragua was a *response* to the U.S. covert program, asserted Rep. Lee Hamilton of Indiana,[75] getting the sequence of events startlingly wrong. As we have seen, the Nicaraguan military buildup and large-scale weapons deliveries from Cuba and the Soviet Union began in 1980, long before the Contra program, though they grew faster as the conflict escalated in later years. But the view was widely held that whatever was bad about Sandinista policy was the result of—not a justification for—U.S. policy. It was Reagan's belligerence that "has pushed the Sandinistas further away from the negotiating table and into the willing embrace of the Soviets," said Rep. Michael Barnes (D-Md.).[76] As Sandinista repression grew, it, too, was blamed on the United States. According to Rep. Jim Moody (D-Wisc.), Reagan's policy "plays right into the Sandinistas' hands," giving them "an excuse to continue domestic repression, press censorship, tight economic controls, and the unpopular military draft."[77]

The principle of ideological *duty* that impelled the FSLN to consolidate its monopoly of power and promote revolution had no place in this analysis. In the 1986 House debate, doubts were even expressed about whether the Sandinistas' Leninist ideology should be taken all that seriously or whether its repressive tendencies were any worse than those of some other countries. Rep. Les AuCoin of Oregon: "We know the Sandinistas are no Boy Scouts but neither are some other governments. South Africa has a repressive system. So does South Korea."[78]

To Rep. George Brown of California, having a Marxist regime in Nicaragua was no great problem: "There are Marxists, including Communists, in the governments of many of our allies. Some of these governments are our friends—one even controlled by Socialists."[79] This seemed to be a confused reference to France, where socialist president François Mitterrand had brought four Communists into his first cabinet in 1981 as part of a (successful) strategy to neutralize and weaken the French Communist party. When these words were spoken (1986), it was fatuous as an analogy to Nicaragua, where the process had already worked in deadly fashion in reverse.

As for the remedy proposed, the critics' answer (as in Angola) was to abjure violence and seek conciliation. Diplomacy and power were seen as alternatives, not as mutually reinforcing. Democratic House leader Jim Wright later explained: "Everyone with whom we talked believed . . . that a show of friendship by the United States would influence political developments for the better."[80]

The role of the churches was important in the national debate over Central America, perhaps even more so than on Vietnam. The Protestant National Council of Churches provided a goodly share of collection-plate monies to radical groups. The Catholic church was particularly pivotal. During much of the Vietnam era it had been a conservative force backing the war effort, its anticommunism a natural response to Communist persecution of the large Catholic population in Indochina. In Latin America, where the church historically had been a bulwark of the social status quo, it was now going through a traumatic transition; nuns and priests began to see their mission more as a ministry to the poor and disfranchised, and a radical Catholic doctrine of "liberation theology" developed. Popes in Rome were uneasy at this militancy, especially the Polish-born John Paul II, who knew that Marxist radicalism was more a source of tyranny than of liberation. His pronouncements, including encyclicals, a speech in Puebla, Mexico, in 1979, and a letter to the Nicaraguan bishops in 1983, sought to rein in the political activity and doctrinal enthusiasms of these radicals:

> This idea of Christ as a political figure, a revolutionary, as the subversive man from Nazareth, does not tally with the church's catechesis [the Pope declared at Puebla]. By confusing the insidious pretexts of Jesus's accusers with the very different attitude of Jesus himself, some people adduce as the cause of his death the outcome of a political conflict and nothing is said of the Lord's will to deliver himself and of his consciousness of his redemptive mission.[81]

Church authorities tried to hew to a sane middle course, calling for democracy and peace and opposing the excesses of both political extremes. This only made them prime targets of rightist brutality in El Salvador and of Sandinista repression in Nicaragua.

The impact in the United States, however, was less balanced. It reflected the emotionalism of the nuns and priests in, especially, El Salvador and the lay groups on the Left that they linked up with at home. Rightist goons had murdered San Salvador's archbishop Oscar Romero in March 1980 and then four American Maryknoll missionaries in December. The Maryknolls became even more radical opponents of the Salvadoran government even as that government struggled to evolve in a moderate direction; they became influential molders of opinion, fiercely opposing any U.S. military aid or any strong U.S. measures against the Sandinistas. The Speaker of the House, Thomas P. ("Tip") O'Neill, Jr., of Massachusetts, had an elderly aunt and many acquaintances in the Maryknoll order, and he affirms in his memoirs that they, more than anyone else, shaped his thinking on Central America; they were his "special source."[82] Perhaps it was also relevant that Miguel D'Escoto, Sandinista foreign minister, had been a Maryknoll priest until forbidden to perform priestly duties under John Paul II's directives ordering priests to remove themselves from politics.

Other views of the Maryknolls are less kind. Geraldine Macias worked as a Maryknoll in Nicaragua until convinced that the FSLN had betrayed the revolution's good intentions; in the *National Catholic Register* in 1983 she expressed her frustration at U.S. church groups' naïveté and ignorance about the harsh realities of Communist Nicaragua.[83]

As with the Vietnam War, it is hard to believe that the broad mass of the American public accepted the argument that America was evil. Most likely, the strongest force at work was a visceral fear of a Vietnam-like quagmire. Yet the more radical participants in the debate—including some groups actively supporting the Salvadoran Communist FMLN (Farabundo Martí National Liberation Movement) or working with the Sandinista leaders and some veterans of the old anti–Vietnam War movement—had their impact. They played on these fears and worked hard to demonize the people and governments the administration was trying to support in Central America. (One such group was the Committee in Support of the People of El Salvador, or CISPES, linked to the FMLN. In 1988, it received a grant of $5,000 from the New World Foundation, chaired by Hillary Rodham Clinton.)[84]

Finally, the Democratic Congress itself was a complex mix of motives. The opposition banner was taken up by the Democratic caucus for political as well as philosophical reasons: It was an issue on which the otherwise invincible Reagan seemed vulnerable. How else to explain the conversion of conservative Texas congressman Jim Wright to a more militant position the closer he advanced to the Speakership? While some of the most vocal Democrats were driven by ideology, the party leadership seems to have adopted a posture of opposition partly because of the pressure from the Left and partly because of the opportunity it offered to trip up the president.

On the other side of the barricades was the Reagan administration, itself divided between those who cared enough to send the very best of U.S. military power directly into downtown Havana or Managua and those who saw other national priorities or preferred other means. The administration accepted the traditional view that economic progress was a key to Central America's future and wholeheartedly embraced the Kissinger Commission's strong recommendations (an $8 billion aid program over five years); the administration ironically found the Democratic Congress the main obstacle to the full funding of this program. In addition to the pressures from the Left, there were pressures from the Right. Rep. Newt Gingrich (R-Ga.), for example, a former history professor, sent the White House his frequent proposals for a more aggressive strategy to embarrass the congressional Democrats for their coddling of Leninists. The administration shied away from this.

The Soviet threat was an argument with some public resonance, and it was featured in all of Reagan's pronouncements. Whenever the possibility arose of advanced Soviet weapons, like MiG jet fighters, coming to Nicaragua, there was a vigorous bipartisan reaction—the Democrats then being triggered more by the positive memories of the Cuban Missile Crisis, when a Democratic president courageously blocked a Soviet military power play, than by the negative reflexes of Vietnam. Strong warnings against Soviet meddling were included in the bipartisan Kissinger Commission report and in Bush's Bipartisan Accord of March 1989. By the same token, the Sandinistas' ties with Moscow were always an embarrassment to the Democrats. Daniel Ortega visited Moscow triumphantly in April 1985, just after the House of Representatives had defeated Reagan's Contra aid bill; the chagrin was sufficient to help force another vote in June, which Reagan won.[85]

Reagan had allies in these battles, including a remarkable and crucial ally on the Democratic side—the AFL-CIO. American labor leaders like George Meany, Jay Lovestone, and Irving Brown had retained a fervent anticommunism from the 1930s, when American Communists had attempted to capture the American labor movement. With gusto and organizing genius, these leaders had helped the free trade unions in the devastated countries of postwar Western Europe to resist the Communist-led unions financed by Stalin. In 1962, the AFL-CIO founded the American Institute for Free Labor Development (AIFLD) to help democratic labor unions survive and compete in a Latin America newly threatened by Castroism. This endeavor was the natural partner of a Kennedy administration that still embodied in many ways the last hurrah of unapologetic liberal anticommunism. By the 1980s, labor's effective efforts in this area under Lane Kirkland found a new ally in Ronald Reagan. Reagan awarded Irving Brown a Presidential Medal of Freedom, the nation's highest civilian honor, shortly before Brown died. The alliance between Reagan and labor was symbolized also by the prominence in his administration of neoconservatives—individuals, many of them with close ties to labor, who retained their anticommunism as well as much of their liberal tradition but felt abandoned by a Democratic party that had drifted leftward after Vietnam. The radical Left never ceased to vent its spleen against the treachery of the AFL-CIO in Central America. [86]

Liberal journals like the *New Republic* became a forum for articles critical of the Sandinistas for their internal repression as well as for their links with Moscow. [87] This took some courage in intellectual circles. Other allies included Cuban-American organizations known for their anticommunism and some American Jewish groups concerned by the Central American Communists' intimate links with Libya, Iran, the Palestine Liberation Organization (PLO), and other Middle East radicals. [88]

Neither side in the debate was able to test its theories. The Reagan administration rejected the accommodationist course that was urged upon it, considering it appeasement of an implacable enemy; its opponents in Congress gradually tightened the legislative restrictions on what they saw as a reckless policy. Each side thwarted the other, as had happened in Vietnam. No wonder, then, that the crisis in Central America deepened, and the president's battle with Congress grew only more bitter.

THE NEGOTIATING TRACK

The Reagan policy was thus caught between intense pressures from the Left, especially in Congress, and pressures from the Right, reflected in the convictions of many key officials inside the administration. Between the hammer and the anvil, the administration struggled to forge a coherent regional strategy.

The initial focus of the Reagan policy—and of the controversy—was not Nicaragua but El Salvador. Reagan and his administration were accused of condoning right-wing death squads, which was a caricature. [89] Vice President George Bush visited San Salvador in December 1983 and made a dramatic speech denouncing the death squads as "murderers," "reactionary," "cowardly," "terrorists," and "the best friends the Soviets, the Cubans, the Sandinista comandantes and the Salvadoran guerrillas have." [90] Frank McNeil, otherwise a strong critic of the administration, notes that the death-squad killings and human rights abuses abated for a number of years after the Bush visit. [91]

Reagan's policy in El Salvador was rescued from much of its torment in May 1984 when, under U.S. pressure, a free election was held that brought to power José Napoleón Duarte, a revered Christian Democrat whose hatred of the extreme Right dated back to the early 1970s, when an earlier election victory was stolen from him by the military and he was imprisoned and tortured. Controversy over El Salvador substantially ebbed in the United States with Duarte's election. But the very fact of his election could be cited by the Reagan administration in defense of its regional strategy—which was to replace dictatorial governments with democratic governments that would put the death squads out of business. The administration sometimes laid itself open to charges that it did not aggressively anathematize, or gear its whole policy to the pursuit of, individual military officers linked to atrocities. But its approach was to view human rights as, at bottom, less a juridical matter than a matter of political structure. George Shultz wrote later:

> The governments of El Salvador, Honduras, and Guatemala contained and tolerated many unsavory characters. Still, serious people in those governments were engaged in a stalwart effort to move toward democracy and the rule of law. The American left would have us leave those governments to struggle on their own and not worry whether communism came to prevail. The American right would have us support the anti-Communists no matter how outrageous their behavior.[92]

The whole arrangement in El Salvador was shaky. The military remained torn between its moderate and extremist wings, and the brutal war that the Communists waged against economic and civilian targets exacerbated hardships, humiliated the moderate government, and contributed to a vicious spiral of polarization and violence on all sides. Whence the administration's program of economic and military aid and its preoccupation with halting the flow of outside arms that fueled the insurgency.

Congress, as we have seen, had a different approach. Congressional Democrats continued to fight against any, especially military, aid to El Salvador and relented only on condition that the aid be formally linked to the U.S. president's ability to certify on a regular basis that progress was being achieved in such areas as human rights, economic reform, free elections, peace negotiations, and investigation of the murders of the American nuns in 1980. The aid, in the end, continued, but not without a wrestling match with Congress every year that only added to the humiliation of the democratic government we were trying to support, as if it were South Vietnam.

As far as the broader regional conflict was concerned, Haig's November

1981 meeting with Cuba's vice president exemplified that Reagan himself was not averse to diplomacy. As congressional pressures continued to mount on our Nicaraguan policy, it became politically essential that the United States participate in diplomatic efforts for regional peace. Here the administration found its efforts challenged by the conservatives.

Late in 1981, Haig's aide Thomas Enders attempted a direct dialogue with the Sandinistas. Enders was a six-foot-six-inch Yale-educated New England patrician Foreign Service officer with a fiery Italian wife and a domineering style. He was brilliant, loyal, energetic, and eager to plunge into negotiations despite the political risks. In the summer, long before any covert-action program, Enders persuaded Haig—and even conservatives like Sen. Jesse Helms—that such a diplomatic effort was warranted; if it failed, his argument went, stronger options could always be considered later.[93] So Enders visited Managua in August and proposed a deal: Essentially, the United States would accept the legitimacy and finality of the Nicaraguan Revolution and normalize relations with it, provided it ended its military supply of the Communist insurgencies in neighboring countries.

Weeks went by without any response from the Nicaraguans. Enders peppered them with suggested texts of agreements and of statements and reassurances the United States would make when and if such agreements were reached. But there was still no response. The U.S. overture seems to have triggered a major debate within the Sandinista leadership. On October 7, Daniel Ortega delivered a blistering attack on the United States at the UN General Assembly,[94] which Enders interpreted as signaling the outcome of the internal debate and the Sandinistas' rejection of the American overture.

The power of "revolutionary internationalism" was too great. Tomás Borge, one of the most militant of the *comandantes*, proclaimed at a military ceremony on July 19, 1981: "This revolution goes beyond our borders. Our revolution was internationalist from the moment Sandino fought in La Segovia. With Sandino were internationalists from all over the world. . . ."[95] Bayardo Arce, another of the *comandantes*, declared in a secret speech to the Nicaraguan Socialist party in May 1984: "We cannot cease being internationalists unless we cease being revolutionaries. . . . It is impossible even to consider this."[96]

Thus, the deal, which seemed to Americans a reasonable compromise, went to the heart of the Sandinistas' image of themselves and of their reason for being. In their internal policy, as a Leninist vanguard, they saw it as their *duty* to effect the revolution and to deny power to rivals who did not share their ultimate goal. Power sharing in a democratic process was not what they were about: If they had been social democrats, they would have been Social Democrats. But they were not. In foreign policy, too, their duty was revolution. Indeed, they had to fear that as long as they remained surrounded by countries aligned with the United States, their own revolution's survival would be in jeopardy (despite their contempt for American policy in the short run). Their fear of encirclement was inherent in their knowledge that their very existence challenged the hemispheric order. Their militancy made it self-fulfilling.

Thus, the negotiating efforts were doomed at this stage—exacerbating, in turn, the domestic controversy in the United States. Journalist Roy Gutman has written a highly regarded critique—*Banana Diplomacy*—whose main thrust is that the Reagan administration bungled many opportunities for a compromise with Managua.[97] He cites Enders's arrogant personal style with the Nicaraguans and, even more, the pressures against Enders from conservatives inside the administration (Kirkpatrick, Weinberger, Casey, Judge William Clark), who, indeed, relentlessly harassed the diplomatic efforts that Enders (and his successor Langhorne "Tony" Motley) persistently pursued in subsequent years.

George Shultz found the internal squabbling as frustrating as Haig had—a "swamp," he later called it.[98] In early 1983, Enders and Shultz developed a proposal to work with Mexico on a regional settlement; the conservatives insisted on an NSC meeting with Reagan at which they could air their complaints about Mexico's untrustworthiness. (The Mexicans' tilt toward Nicaragua was, in fact, a major problem.) Reagan sided with the conservatives.[99] "We can no more negotiate an acceptable political solution with these people," said Pentagon official Fred Iklé in a speech (referring to the Salvadoran Communists), "than the social democrats in revolutionary Russia could have talked Lenin into giving up totalitarian Bolshevism."[100]

Shultz persisted in developing diplomatic ideas, to the conservatives' annoyance. CIA director Casey once needled him: "George, don't be a pilgrim." "What's that?" Shultz asked. "An early settler," Casey cracked.[101] Shultz, not amused by this aspersion cast on his firmness as a negotiator, peppers his memoirs with tart epithets describing his conservative tormentors—"mischief-making," "ineptitude," "blundering," "grappling for control"—applied principally to Judge Clark and the NSC staff.[102]

But Shultz was no slouch at bureaucratic maneuvering, either. The conservatives were furious at his ability to go directly into the Oval Office on several occasions and secure the president's go-ahead, end-running the obstruction from other agencies that would have resulted from a more open deliberative process. Shultz managed to get Reagan's approval of a quick Shultz stopover in Managua on June 1, 1984, for a dramatic airport meeting with Daniel Ortega. Shultz frequently managed to develop diplomatic plans without letting word get to the other agencies that he knew to be hostile. This only allowed the latter's suspicions to fester. Jeane Kirkpatrick later remarked: "[S]ince he didn't keep anybody informed, Casey or Cap or anybody, everybody felt free to develop their own fantasies, as in a Rorschach [ink-blot] test," of what Shultz was up to.[103]

Conservative suspicion came from many sources. There is in one part of the American psyche (the right side of the brain?) an instinctual nervousness about international negotiations. It appears as a constant fear that our striped-pants diplomats (whose interest in things foreign is suspect to start with) are likely to be taken in by wily foreigners. Will Rogers is said to have cracked, "America never lost a war and never won a conference." Kissinger used to quote this sardonically when he was under fire over détente with the Soviets.

But the suspicion of treating with an adversary comes also from our moral streak, and it is not limited to the Right. There is the fear that even sitting down with a morally objectionable foe implies approbation. Thus, even (and perhaps especially) if we have no practical policy for eliminating the despised reality, at least we can withhold our blessing; indeed, we must. From 1917 to 1934 we refused to establish normal diplomatic relations with Soviet Russia. In the same tradition in the more recent period have been the pressures to downgrade relations with apartheid-ruled South Africa or post-Tiananmen China. It is often a substitute for an effectual policy.

On Central America, the conservatives failed to appreciate that any president who would confront an adversary needs to appeal to a public that wants to know that all peaceful alternatives were exhausted first. Reagan himself explicitly endorsed many of Haig's, and later Shultz's, diplomatic ideas and always shrank from the more extreme measures proposed. It would be "lunacy" to invade Nicaragua, the president told Shultz in January 1986 (and Shultz recounted to us at a staff meeting). Some thought all the diplomacy a betrayal of Reagan's true vision, but they misread their complex leader. A few years later, when conservatives continued to agitate for more support for the Contras, Reagan complained to his chief of staff Kenneth Duberstein: "Those sonsofbitches won't be happy until we have 25,000 troops in Managua, and I'm not going to do it."[104]

Nor did the conservatives figure out how to marry up the negotiations and U.S. power. In July 1983, the Defense Department, briefly overcoming Secretary Weinberger's usual reluctance to wield military force, convinced the president to approve a plan for stepped-up military pressures on Nicaragua. These consisted of an ostentatious six-month air, sea, and land exercise in Honduras and off both the Atlantic and Pacific coasts of Nicaragua, including what could be interpreted as preparation for a blockade. The plan aborted, however, when Shultz—who learned of the orders only when they leaked to the *New York Times*—went into the Oval Office and threatened to resign.[105] Such a policy of pressures against Nicaragua might have been useful as negotiating leverage if only it had been formulated with some such strategy in mind instead of in the vacuum of gratuitous posturing lacking credibility.

Yet the conservatives also sensed correctly that the negotiations the State Department was urging—in the absence of significantly greater American leverage in some form—could not possibly have succeeded. The deal that Enders was seeking in 1981 would have represented a rather significant concession of our acceptance of the Nicaraguan Marxist-Leninist regime in exchange for pledges of a cessation of arming guerrillas, which it is 100 percent certain the Sandinistas would have violated. The chutzpah with which the Sandinistas continued to repeat barefaced lies denying their involvement in arms supply was discouraging, not to say breathtaking. The United States would have been bound by any restraints it formally accepted; the Sandinistas, far less so.

Nor were the Nicaraguans even interested in a serious negotiation. Arturo Cruz, Jr., working in the Nicaraguan Foreign Ministry in 1982, was involved in the diplomatic preparations: "[P]art of my job was to draft papers on negotiations with the United States, based on three principles: that the negotiations process was a tool to buy time for the revolution; that the negotiator we chose had to be weak, so they could not make any decisions; that our negotiating strategy had to be based on the dynamic of American fears and anxieties so that we could take advantage of American dissension over Central America."[106]

Latin American nations launched mediating efforts, however, that forced the United States to engage in diplomacy simply to ensure that the mediators did not present us with even more one-sided compromises favoring Nicaragua. A group of nine Western Hemisphere nations (including the United States) met in San José, Costa Rica, in October 1982 and developed a set of principles for a comprehensive regional settlement— arms reductions; multilateral and bilateral negotiations among countries and internal democratization within countries; an end to all external aid to all insurgencies. Three months later, a separate group of four Central and South American nations (Mexico, Colombia, Panama, and Venezuela) convened on the Panamanian island of Contadora and launched a diplomatic process along the same lines. The so-called Contadora process become the main multilateral forum for the next few years.

The routine of the diplomatic stalemate was interrupted in October 1983 by the U.S. military operation on the Caribbean island of Grenada. This was triggered by the violent collapse of a brutal Cuban-backed Communist regime on the island, threatening civil war.[107] A group of neighboring island nations, the Organization of Eastern Caribbean States, pleaded for U.S. intervention to shield them from Cuban intervention or spreading violence. (They had no military forces of their own.) There was also a contingent of American students at a local medical school. The United States landed troops, drove out the Communists and the Cubans, turned the country over to its civilian politicians via a free election, and then withdrew.

Grenada is interesting for its impact both in the United States and in Central America. At home, critics pounced on it as classic North American arrogance and interventionism, confirming the worst fears of Ronald Reagan's cowboy mentality. The New York Times, astoundingly, saw it as the moral equivalent of Afghanistan: "Simply put, the cost is loss of the moral high ground: a reverberating demonstration to the world that America has no more respect for laws and borders, for the codes of civilization, than the Soviet Union."[108] Yet the American public cheered it overwhelmingly, especially when the rescued students kissed the airport tarmac and thanked Reagan when they reached home.

The Normandy landing it was not, but the Grenada operation broke the Vietnam-era taboo in America against the use of military force. That was its true significance. Many in the media and Congress, still in the mind-set of Vietnam, were stunned by the outpouring of public support. But no one could have expected this in advance, and it took special courage on Reagan's part to proceed with it two days after the terrorist car bombing of the barracks in Lebanon that killed nearly 250 U.S. Marines. Certainly Grenada was minor-league, but what would it have said about our psychological condition as a superpower if we had been afraid to do even that?

The Soviets huffed and puffed about American aggression. The U.S. government found it hard to take the Soviet reaction seriously, however. Moscow television, broadcasting a solemn TASS statement on the affair, helpfully displayed for its viewers a large map of the Iberian peninsula, with Granada, Spain, prominently highlighted.[109]

Closer to home, Grenada had a shock effect on Cuba and Nicaragua. They feared they might be hit next. Nicaragua immediately made overtures to the United States for talks, hinting at a willingness to discuss security issues. Some critics think this another lost opportunity.[110] On its face, Grenada had restored some of the psychological balance whose absence had precluded successful negotiations previously. This was Shultz's view, and he authorized another negotiating initiative.

Enders's successor, Tony Motley, and his deputy Craig Johnstone came up with a four-step plan of reciprocal moves by Nicaragua and the United States over a ninety-day period. In the first phase, Nicaragua was to send the Cuban military contingent home and close the radio command-and-control facilities for the insurgencies in neighboring countries. In return, *inter alia*, the United States would reduce its military presence in the region and its opposition to international economic aid for Nicaragua. Free elections inside Nicaragua were to be held in the last phase of the process, along with termination of U.S. aid to the Contras.[111] In any event, as word got around town of the Motley plan, this, too, was argued out in front of the president in a stormy NSPG meeting on June 25, 1984.

A record of the June 25 NSPG meeting has been published, and it offers a vivid picture of the internal debate.[112] Weinberger and Kirkpatrick urged the president to drop the bilateral dialogue with the Sandinistas that Shultz had begun in his quick Managua airport meeting with Daniel Ortega; they urged a lower-key posture of endorsing the multilateral efforts of the Contadora group. Ambassador Kirkpatrick told the president that she thought the administration had not done enough to win congressional support for the Contras: "If you showed your commitment and the administration's commitment with more activity it would be a positive factor in Congress. . . . We have not made the impression that if the Congress cuts off the Contra funding this is of major importance to the administration." The previous November, Congress had legislated a $24 million cap on funding for the Contras—an amount that was just then running out. Mrs. Kirkpatrick argued that a negotiating effort in the absence of Contra funding would be a risky exercise without leverage: "[T]he coincidence of our undertaking this bilateral negotiating effort at the same time as the Congress fails to support funding for the Contras is enough to totally unravel our entire position in the region."

Shultz responded that the United States had to show our Central American partners and our Congress that we were willing to negotiate. We had made negotiating moves toward the Soviet Union in order to put the Soviets on the spot after they had walked out of the Geneva arms talks: "Similarly, in Central America, . . . [a]n essential ingredient in [our] strategy is that we can say, if Nicaragua is halfway reasonable, there could be a reasonable negotiated solution. . . . It is essential to have something like that going on or else our support on the Hill goes down."

Reagan sided with Shultz on the general principle of continuing the bilateral talks to show Congress that we were making the effort and so as not to let the Sandinistas "off the hook": "If we are just talking about negotiations with Nicaragua, that is so far-fetched to imagine that a communist government like that would make any reasonable deal with us, but if it is to get Congress to support the anti-Sandinistas, then that can be helpful. . . . [T]he press is eager to paint us as having failed again, and we don't want to let Nicaragua off the hook." In August, a somewhat watered down version of the four-step plan was presented to Sandinista representatives in Manzanillo, Mexico, by Ambassador Harry Shlaudeman, the formidable and relatively hard-line career diplomat who served then as the U.S. special envoy.

My own view, which I expressed to Shultz hesitantly at various stages of the process, was somewhere between his and Mrs. Kirkpatrick's: I was convinced that in the absence of leverage, we risked being saddled with a negotiated outcome that could have been a disguised formula for permitting the consolidation of Sandinista power. I was not against negotiation per se (having participated in Kissinger's diplomatic endeavors, many of which were similarly attacked), but my instinct told me we had a weak hand.

The initiative, in the end, failed from every point of view. It had no impact in the Congress, which in October 1984 passed the second Boland Amendment: "During fiscal year 1985, no funds available to the Central Intelligence Agency, the Department of Defense, or any other agency or entity of the United States involved in intelligence activities may be obligated or expended for the purpose or which would have the effect of supporting, directly or indirectly, military or paramilitary operations in Nicaragua by any nation, group, organization, movement or individual."[113] This amendment, attached to the 1985 Defense Department authorization, was a more sweeping prohibition than the 1982 version, which had banned only actions "for the purpose of overthrowing the Government of Nicaragua." It was part of the price paid for the mining episode. The most that the administration was able to salvage in 1984 was a bargain with the Congress allowing the administration to come back after February 28, 1985, and seek appropriations again through an expedited procedure.

With Nicaragua, the four-step plan was an even greater failure. The Sandinistas flatly rejected any democratization provisions, even deferred ones. But they also rejected the State Department's central idea of an end to their support for revolutions in Central America.

This result was inevitable. The core of the negotiating problem was that the Sandinistas *could not* unlink their foreign conduct from their internal system; the two were bound together inextricably by ideology and practical strategy.[114] A "trade-off" that essentially conceded their internal system in exchange for amelioration of their external conduct was, paradoxically, a nonstarter on both sides. Both sides feared it as a demoralizing surrender of principle—and we feared they would cheat, anyway. We can consider ourselves fortunate that they turned it down whenever some variant of it was offered, in 1981 or in 1984. Harry Shlaudeman told Robert Kagan later that "the chances of a really stable agreement with the Sandinistas were nil, regardless of the Reagan administration's position."[115]

Roy Gutman's critique of the administration's negotiating strategy misses the point in an even more fundamental way, however. He shares Enders's skepticism about the relevance of democratization in Nicaragua. ("Get serious. There is no chance for democracy in Nicaragua," Enders had snapped in 1981 to NSC staffer Constantine Menges. Motley's expressed view was exactly the same.)[116] But as the years went by, the United States put increasing emphasis on Nicaraguan democratization, invoking the OAS's original 1979 insistence on democracy, free elections, and human rights. To Gutman, this was contrived (since Enders's earlier conversations with Managua had conceded the point) and also a calculated effort to torpedo serious negotiation (since the Sandinistas obviously regarded their system as nonnegotiable). Gutman attributes the shift to the ascendancy of the hard-liners in the administration, now reinforced by having one of their number, Judge Clark, as the president's national security adviser.[117]

But the shift also reflected the fundamental reality that the internal structure of Nicaragua *was* the core issue. Enders's haughty personality was not the problem. (Motley was a much more congenial fellow.) A young revolution in its militant, exuberant phase was simply not going to renounce its "internationalist" duty. Hence, the conservatives' instinctive mistrust of a diplomacy that had no convincing strategy behind it, even if the State Department could argue that nothing concrete was being given away. Shultz, in the end, was being ill served by his subordinates, who persisted in coming up with badly thought out initiatives that were bound to leave him exposed to conservative challenge.

And so the diplomacy proceeded in Reagan's first term, since the administration found it politically impossible to reject negotiations out of hand and the State Department, even in the absence of leverage, was institutionally incapable of refraining from exploring whether our interests might not possibly be protected in some yet undiscovered negotiating scheme. As in the Afghan negotiations in Geneva, elaborate documents were worked out in the Contadora group; these documents spelled out reciprocal obligations, including the U.S. obligation to end Contra aid and reduce military support for Honduras and El Salvador (much too stringent for our taste) and the Sandinistas' obligations to halt interference in other countries (too weak in their verification and enforcement, in our view). Unlike the Afghan case, the United States here had some voice in the proceedings and was usually able to mobilize the front-line nations facing Nicaragua (El Salvador, Honduras, Guatemala, and sometimes Costa Rica) to insist on tighter and more balanced provisions. The United States thus avoided any agreements that would have done harm. The diplomacy continued, always with formal (but unenthusiastic) U.S. support, producing no result.

It would take a few more years for American policy to straighten itself out—to marshal its leverage and also to put it in the service of a coherent political objective that gained domestic and international support.

PART

THREE

RESOLUTION

11

THE REAGAN DOCTRINE:
A MEMOIR

Robert C. ("Bud") McFarlane, who succeeded Judge William Clark as national security adviser in October 1983, recalls that there was no well-thought-out strategy or concept behind the new policy that began to be enunciated on his watch in early 1985 and that became known as the "Reagan Doctrine"—the systematic support of guerrilla forces fighting against Third World Communist dictatorships. Reagan never gave McFarlane any instruction or uttered any word that such a strategy should be developed. There was no National Security Study Directive (NSSD) asking for an interdepartmental review of the subject, nor any National Security Decision Directive (NSDD) in the president's name setting forth a new policy—the procedures commonly followed for major initiatives. "Not one nano-second" went into any analysis or planning, McFarlane has scathingly recounted.[1]

Our specific policies in the various regional conflicts—Central America, Afghanistan, Angola, Cambodia—continued to be buffeted, moreover, by the controversies in this country and the contradictions within the administration. Liberals generally chafed at covert military actions, and conservatives feared any negotiation as a potential sellout of the resistance forces.

Yet, despite all this, the United States found itself, by the summer of 1985, supplying substantial aid to anti-Communist insurgents in all the regions mentioned and articulating a rationale for what amounted to a remarkable new activism. Ten years after the fall of Indochina, another important Vietnam-era taboo had been decisively broken: The United States was dramatically reengaged on the ground in the hardscrabble geopolitical contest with the Soviets on several continents.

History works in strange ways. The aspiration for such a reengagement had long animated Reagan and some of his followers, but the process of turning it into a broad policy was to see its share of confusion, clumsiness, and dumb luck. It all came together because, beneath the surface disarray, something fundamental was happening in the world that made it so. If the Reagan Doctrine is at one level an example of the unimpressive way American policies are sometimes developed, it is at another level a case study of how historical forces and purposeful leadership sometimes converge to produce major international changes.

DEFINITION

It was columnist Charles Krauthammer who first pinned the label Reagan Doctrine on the administration's policy of support for anti-Communist rebels. In an essay in *Time* magazine in the spring of 1985,[2] Krauthammer called attention to a vague and little-noticed passage in Reagan's State of the Union address of February 6, 1985: "[W]e must not break faith with those who are risking their lives—on every continent, from Afghanistan to Nicaragua—to defy Soviet-supported aggression and secure rights which have been ours from birth."

Krauthammer argued that this signified a dramatic departure in American policy—"overt and unashamed American support for anti-Communist revolution." The basis for this policy was "justice, necessity and democratic tradition." Whereas the Truman Doctrine had set forth the basic postwar philosophy of containment of Soviet aggression and the Nixon Doctrine had adjusted it to emphasize bolstering allies instead of carrying the entire military burden ourselves, Reagan, said Krauthammer, was going on the offensive; the new doctrine, unlike its predecessors, "supports not the status quo but revolution."

In particular, the new American strategy was a direct challenge to the Soviet doctrine that had come to be associated with Leonid Brezhnev since he had ordered the invasion of Czechoslovakia in 1968 to keep it in the Soviet camp—the idea that Communist gains, once made, could not be reversed. On the contrary. Unjust, undemocratic, illegitimate Communist regimes maintained in power by Soviet guns were no longer off-limits to the "democratic militance" of a revived, self-confident America.

Krauthammer was then, and would continue to be, a more eloquent and sophisticated spokesman for the policy than anyone in the administration. Over the course of 1985 and 1986, in further essays in the *New Republic*, he expanded on the concept and defended it against its growing legion of critics.

The Reagan administration, in fact, consciously avoided proclaiming any new "doctrine" in the president's name—for a number of reasons. For one thing, it always seemed a bit immodest for a president to proclaim that a pronouncement of his warranted elevation to the pantheon of

Monroe and Truman. Better to let others catch the significance and award the designation. Thus, Carter's powerful enunciation of America's stake in the Persian Gulf in 1980 earned the description Carter Doctrine from the press. Nixon's White House public relations tigers were crude enough to push for the label Nixon Doctrine from the moment he had enunciated his new approach while on a trip to the Pacific in July 1969, but there is little doubt that he would have earned it, anyway.[3]

A more practical reason for shying away from the label "doctrine" is the reaction it tends to elicit from critics, especially academics. There are intellectuals who delight in pouncing on any such pretensions in their political leaders and in analyzing any "doctrine" to death. No policy is a juicier target for intellectual criticism than one that can be labeled "doctrinaire"; all the logical weaknesses in its exposition can be nitpicked, and the very proclamation of a doctrine can be said to imply a mindless dogmatism that is bound to get our foreign policy into trouble somewhere by not doing justice to the complexity of the real world[4]—academics relishing, of course, the chance to turn the tables and make this sort of criticism of the practical men running our public affairs.

It is what I call the "academic fallacy" to attribute such power to the words of a presidential speech and such discipline to the U.S. government. It is not that words are unimportant (especially for as ideological a president as Reagan) but that academics tend to assume that once a passage is uttered in a speech, it becomes a sacred text, slavishly invoked and followed by a government bureaucracy that, as if on automatic pilot, is incapable of adapting rationally and prudently to complex situations as they arise (or of resisting presidential decisions they don't like). As we shall see, Reagan's pronouncements provoked fears among some intellectuals that they were a mandate for an indiscriminate global plunge into guerrilla conflicts that would soon exhaust us. Thus, any "doctrine" risked becoming a straw man.

THE CONVERGENCE OF FACTORS

While the Reagan activism in the Third World had its beginnings in the first term (the Contras, the Afghans, Grenada), the doctrine did not reach its full flowering until the second term. It was the same Reagan presidency (and paradoxically it was more ideological in the first term), but many factors had to come together before the full impact of the new policy was felt.

There was, first, the long-standing disposition of American conservatives since John Foster Dulles to seek the rollback, not only the containment, of Soviet communism. A group of young conservative policy experts who brainstormed national security issues in the late 1970s in day-long sessions at Washington's Madison Hotel (the "Madison Group") developed the general notion of a strategy to exhaust the Soviets; their principal focus was a U.S. military buildup, though some in the group hoped to reverse the Nicaraguan revolution as well.[5] Dr. Fred C. Iklé, then an academic strategist and former Ford administration arms control official, led a Republican advisory council in 1978 that urged military aid for Africans resisting Cuban intervention.[6] The 1980 Republican platform demanded "self-determination and genuine independence" for what it termed "the new captive nations of Africa and Latin America threatened by the growing dominance of Soviet power."[7] As far back as 1968, scholar Constantine Menges had written papers at the RAND Corporation on the thesis that newly implanted Communist regimes were vulnerable to a determined strategy of democratic insurgency, and he renewed the suggestion in 1980 while serving as an informal adviser to the Reagan campaign.[8]

The broad strategy of maximizing pressures on the Soviet system and exploiting its vulnerabilities was enshrined in an important internal directive, NSDD-75, signed by Reagan in early 1983. Its focus, though, was on economic pressures and military competition, more than on the Third World.[9]

The general aspiration of rollback was expressed in various public pronouncements in Reagan's first term. Secretary of State Haig spoke in Berlin on September 13, 1981, of the "democratic revolution" and its universal applicability. In a major address on June 8, 1982, in London's Westminster Hall, the president hailed the inevitable triumph of democracy and the growing crisis of totalitarianism. In a prescient passage, Reagan pointed out the systemic crisis the Soviet Union was going through (which was three years before Mikhail Gorbachev came to power):

> . . . I believe we live now at a turning point. In an ironic sense, Karl Marx was right. We are witnessing today a great revolutionary crisis—a crisis where the demands of the economic order are conflicting directly with those of the political order. But the crisis is happening not in the free, non-Marxist West but in the home of Marxism-Leninism, the Soviet Union. It is the Soviet Union that runs against the tide of history by denying human freedom and human dignity to its citizens. It also is in deep economic difficulty. The rate of growth in the national product has been steadily declining since the 1950s and is less than half of what it was then. The dimensions of this failure are astounding. . . .

What we see here is a political structure that no longer corresponds to its economic base, a society where productive forces are hampered by political ones. The decay of the Soviet experiment should come as no surprise to us. Wherever the comparisons have been made between free and closed societies—West Germany and East Germany, Austria and Czechoslovakia, Malaysia and Vietnam—it is the democratic countries that are prosperous and responsive to the needs of their people.

As against this crisis in the East, Reagan at Westminster hailed the vitality of the democratic idea, including in the developing world: "In India, a critical test has been passed with the peaceful change of governing political parties. In Africa, Nigeria is moving in remarkable and unmistakable ways to build and strengthen its democratic institutions. In the Caribbean and Central America, sixteen of twenty-four countries have freely elected governments. And in the United Nations, eight of the ten developing nations which have joined the body in the past five years are democracies."

The Communist world was not immune to this trend:

Some argue that we should encourage democratic change in right-wing dictatorships but not in Communist regimes. To accept this preposterous notion—as some well-meaning people have—is to invite the argument that, once countries achieve a nuclear capability, they should be allowed an undisturbed reign of terror over their own citizens. We reject this course.

As for the Soviet view, President Brezhnev repeatedly has stressed that the competition of ideas and systems must continue and that this is entirely consistent with relaxation of tensions and peace. . . . We cannot ignore the fact that even without our encouragement, there have been and will continue to be repeated explosions against repression in dictatorships. The Soviet Union itself is not immune to this reality. Any system is inherently unstable that has no peaceful means to legitimize its leaders. In such cases, the very repressiveness of the state ultimately drives people to resist it—if necessary, by force.

While we must be cautious about forcing the pace of change, we must not hesitate to declare our ultimate objectives and to take concrete actions to move toward them.

Among the recommendations Reagan made at Westminster, one was for the creation of a National Endowment for Democracy—to support democratic parties, free labor unions, independent media, and other institutions of pluralism in Eastern Europe and the developing world. This was a way to carry out overtly some of the political action that the CIA had been involved in after World War II (working with the American labor movement) in Western Europe. This endowment soon came into being with bipartisan congressional support.

When Reagan harped on an ideological theme, it represented a powerful personal conviction; it was not just a script fed to him by his conservative speechwriters. It is true that his writers, especially Bently Elliott and Anthony Dolan, were passionate keepers of the flame. But I know from my own exposure to the process of drafting Reagan's speeches that the president took an intense interest in the themes and texture of his major addresses and that he and his writers shared a firm belief in the power of ideas.

One of Reagan's favorite themes was his conviction that communism was a spent force. He stated it most provocatively to the National Association of Evangelicals in Orlando on March 8, 1983 (the speech in which he also called the Soviet Union an "evil empire" and "the focus of evil in the modern world"): "I believe that communism is another sad, bizarre chapter in human history whose last pages even now are being written. I believe this because the source of our strength in the quest for human freedom is not material but spiritual. And because it knows no limitation, it must terrify and ultimately triumph over those who would enslave their fellow man."

To the Irish Parliament in Dublin on June 4, 1984, Reagan declared: "Those who think the Western democracies are trying to roll back history are missing the point. History is moving in the direction of self-government and the human dignity that it institutionalizes, and the future belongs to the free." Indulging in a little revolutionary romanticism, stimulated perhaps by his Irish ancestry, Reagan in Dublin defended the right of Central Americans to resist communism—and expanded it into a "worldwide struggle" that embraced those fighting for freedom everywhere:

> The people of Nicaragua and El Salvador have a right to resist the nightmare outside forces want to impose on them, just as they have the right to resist extremist violence from within whether from the Left or Right. The United States must not turn its back on the democratic aspirations of the people of Central America. . . .
>
> Let us. . . . offer the world a politics of hope, a forward strategy for freedom. . . . Those old verities, those truths of the heart—human freedom under God—are on the march everywhere in the world. All across

the world today—in the shipyards of Gdansk, the hills of Nicaragua, the rice paddies of Kampuchea, the mountains of Afghanistan—the cry again is liberty.

But an aspiration alone is not a policy. The rhetorical fervor of Reagan's first term could not alone have accomplished more than creating a mood. Even Grenada, which tantalized as a precedent for reversing Communist gains, was not part of any global plan. Other factors were yet to come into play.

The second significant factor in the emergence of the Reagan Doctrine was the *fact* of the growing Soviet weakness that Reagan described. Soviet policy in the Third World was running out of steam in the late Brezhnev years. The Soviets had essentially overreached in the 1970s and were unable to consolidate their gains in the 1980s. Indigenous resistance developed in several of their new Third World clients—Angola, Ethiopia, Nicaragua, Cambodia, as well as Afghanistan (not to mention the crisis in Poland). As Brezhnev aged and the Politburo aged with him, a decrepit Kremlin leadership was starting to lose its grip.

In 1983, when I first joined the State Department as a senior member of the policy planning staff, I took part in regular meetings with members of the CIA's National Intelligence Council. These were the agency analysts in charge of drafting national intelligence estimates and keeping track of broad trends; they were natural soul mates of the policy planning staffers whose job similarly was to think ahead and spot trends. The vice chairman of the National Intelligence Council then was Charles Waterman, and I remember vividly a meeting in 1983 that we hosted at the State Department for him and some of his colleagues when one of the topics was a phenomenon on which our CIA friends had done a paper: after decades in which the West and its allies had been targets of Communist guerrilla insurgencies, now, suddenly, almost all the guerrilla wars going on in the world were rebellions *against* Communist regimes. It was an extraordinary reversal of fortune, whose scope had not been brought home to me until then. Certainly some of these insurgencies had outside help (especially Afghanistan and Nicaragua), yet—as critics always used to lecture the U.S. government during the Indochina war—no such uprising could sustain itself with such persistence without an indigenous base.

In May 1984, a brilliant young Harvard-trained Sovietologist named Stephen Sestanovich, then serving on the National Security Council staff, published an article in the *Washington Post* calling attention to the signs that Moscow was feeling the strain of its Third World involvement. Soviet scholars—and even Brezhnev's successor, Yurii Andropov—were expressing disillusionment with the weak economic performance of clients who were becoming more of a burden than a strategic gain. Third World "socialism" was turning out to be a disappointment.[10] At the NSC, Sestanovich and his mentor, strategist Donald R. Fortier, along with others, spotted this Soviet overextension in the developing world as a major strategic vulnerability.

A third factor was an important evolution in Central and South America. In Reagan's first term, most of the public focus was on the controversial war in El Salvador, while the Contra program for Nicaragua—still ostensibly covert—drifted in and out of the public debate. But by May 1984 the United States had used its influence with the moderate-leaning junta in El Salvador to ensure a free presidential election; as we saw in chapter 10, this election was won by José Napoleón Duarte, a legitimate democrat and human rights champion whose international credibility was unimpeachable. Suddenly, the Left's assault on Reagan's El Salvador policy lost much of its force. The Central America debate then shifted more to the issue of the Nicaraguan resistance, which fit into the worldwide pattern of anti-Communist insurgencies.

In parallel with this shift was the democratic trend in Latin America as a whole, which Reagan and others in the administration pointed to with increasing enthusiasm. Rightist military regimes were ceding power to civilian governments all over the hemisphere. In 1979, only about one-third of the population of Latin America had been living under civilian democratic rule; by the middle of the 1980s the figure was over 90 percent—an extraordinary evolution that the architects of John Kennedy's Alliance for Progress could only have dreamed about.

Of course, the trend toward civilian rule had many causes. In Argentina, the junta (which had been collaborating with Bill Casey in Nicaragua) had been discredited by the 1982 Falklands debacle. Elsewhere, the global recession had so depressed Latin economies that the military were happy to dump the seemingly hopeless mess into the hands of the hapless civilians, who were more likely to get U.S. help. The model of Spain's and Portugal's successful transition to democracy in the 1970s was also influential in Latin America. But there can be no doubt that U.S. policy was welcoming and backing this democratic trend, not resisting it.

This last was not a minor matter. While some liberal critics continued reflexively to denounce U.S. support of right-wing military dictatorships and reactionary plutocrats, the Reagan administration's consistent support for Duarte in El Salvador was a clear sign that the United States was now backing the democratic center in Central America against the extremes of both Left and Right. Some conservative critics in the United States were in fact quite uneasy. Sen. Jesse Helms considered Duarte's land reforms dangerously socialistic. Henry Kissinger, long a critic of Wilsonian crusading, signed on (as chairman of the 1984 Kissinger Commission report) to the policy of aiding the democratic center; yet privately he grew nervous when the administration extended its human rights pressures to the Philippines in 1986 and South Korea in 1987, undercutting rightist leaders without any clear picture of what was to follow, risking (in his view) another Iran or Nicaragua.

The Wilsonian streak in the Reagan policy was the mark of the neoconservatives, who insisted on the promotion of democracy as the other side of the coin of the strategic challenge to the Soviets. Elliott Abrams, as Reagan's first assistant secretary of state for human rights and humanitarian affairs, had been the author of a memorandum, which was leaked to the *New York Times* in November 1981, insisting that the United States could not play favorites in its human rights policy. Our struggle with Soviet communism was at root a moral one, the memorandum argued, and our credibility depended on our being committed to democracy in the case of rightist regimes as well as leftist.[11] Abrams moved over to become head of the Inter-American Affairs bureau in July 1985 and applied the policy faithfully in his new domain. Not only was this a central feature of our Central America policy, but with Abrams as a prime mover, the administration put relentless pressure on Chilean dictator Augusto Pinochet until he stepped aside in favor of free elections in 1988–90.[12] This was blatant Yankee interventionism, rivaling anything seen since the first third of the twentieth century. But it had almost universal international and domestic approbation.

Thus, the Reagan State Department institutionalized the practice, begun under Carter and Vance, of making human rights a part of America's diplomatic agenda. The Foreign Service's enthusiasm for harassing rightists should not be doubted, which only exacerbated conservative suspicions of the State Department. It also led to some embarrassed hesitations in 1988 when the rightist candidate in El Salvador, Alfredo Cristiani, won a free election to become Duarte's successor. Cristiani's bona fides as a democrat was questioned, unjustly, in fashionable Washington.

Whoever deserves the credit—and surely it belongs to the Latin Americans themselves—the democratic trend in the region had profound significance. Among its practical consequences was a key change in the political lineup in Central America: Nicaragua, instead of being the lone champion of anti-imperialism in a region dominated by "Fascist" dictatorships (as it fancied itself in 1979), now found itself the lone dictatorship in a region of democracies. Not only was El Salvador now inarguably democratic, but Honduras and Guatemala were acquiring civilian governments by mid-decade and joining the trend. (Costa Rica had long enjoyed democratic rule.) The diplomacy of Central America was thus transformed in a way that put the Sandinistas on the defensive on precisely the issue they wished to avoid—namely, the nature of their domestic system.

The final factor in the emergence of a new American policy was the 1984 election in the United States itself. Whereas Reagan's victory in 1980 (along with Republican capture of the Senate) had been a political shock to the Democrats, it could have been blamed on a discredited Carter presidency. The 1984 result seemed to confirm a deeper political and cultural revolution. The Reagan landslide in 1984 reflected how different a country it was from four years, or especially ten or fifteen years, before. The economy was embarked on the longest peacetime expansion in history. While later critics were to lament the ballooning federal budget deficit and a purported climate of "greed," future economic historians are likely to remember also that the 1980s saw the creation of 19 million new jobs, a surge in U.S. manufacturing exports, and the revolution in supercomputers and microelectronics, which transformed the technological base of the Free World's industrial system. Western economic principles as well as political principles seemed to be enjoying vindication. It was a heady moment.

As his biographer Lou Cannon put it, Reagan "sought to restore national self-confidence by transferring his own self-confidence to his countrymen."[13] The 1984 Olympics in Los Angeles (though the Soviets and their allies boycotted the games in retaliation for 1980) saw an outpouring of national pride. American flags were everywhere. Reagan's campaign commercials trumpeted that it was "morning in America."

In foreign policy, Reagan's 1984 reelection victory confirmed his success in repairing much of the psychological damage of Vietnam. Grenada (while a minor military episode) and the various covert programs under way (while some were controversial) bespoke a country that was no longer traumatized. Certainly Vietnam's effects still lingered (and do to this day), but the contrast with a decade earlier was overwhelming. The year that George Orwell had chosen for his dark vision of a totalitarian future turned out instead to betoken the resilience of the country and the reinvigoration of its international commitment.

All this had its impact on one pivotal group of people—Democrats in Congress. On June 20, 1985, Rep. Stephen Solarz published an article in the *New York Times* under the blunt title "It's Time for the Democrats to Be Tough-Minded." Implicitly criticizing the persistence in his party of McGovern-style pacifism and notions of American guilt, Solarz called for more forthright Democratic support for defense spending and resistance to Soviet aggression:

> Despite our long and honorable tradition of anti-Communism, Democrats have tended in recent years to refrain from forthrightly expressing our view of the inherent immorality of the Soviet system. . . . Whatever the reasons for our reticence, we have enabled our opponents to contend that our proposals to reduce East-West tensions are based on illusions about the Soviet Union. By appearing to yield the moral high ground, we have lost political ground as well.
>
> Democrats need to recognize that Soviet repression and Communist tyranny are not a distant memory but a living nightmare. It is a nightmare in the alleys of Afghanistan, for the peasants who have seen their loved ones murdered and land destroyed; in the jungles of Southeast Asia, to the villagers killed or crippled by yellow rain; in the prisons and labor camps of the Soviet Union, for the dissidents and refusniks yearning for freedom; in the streets of Poland, to the supporters of Solidarity, whose dreams of democracy were crushed by martial law.
>
> But a resolute anti-Communist policy for the Democrats requires more than simply denouncing Communist tyranny. It means, for a start, being just as vigorous in advocating legitimate defense spending as we are in denouncing Pentagon waste. . . .
>
> It means resisting Communist expansionism in the third world by providing arms and aid to non-Communist forces, such as those in Afghanistan and Cambodia, resisting Communist invasion and occupation of their countries.[14]

The 1984 election therefore seems to have had in Washington the political impact on our foreign policy that the 1980 Reagan election had had on domestic economic policy. Whereas the (mostly southern) "boll weevil Democrats" in Reagan's first term had tipped the congressional balance in his favor on his tax cuts and economic program, so in the second term a swing bloc of centrist Democrats tilted toward Reagan on a number of these Third World campaigns. Like Solarz, they had concluded that it was a deadly mistake to seem to be defending Communists against Ronald Reagan all the time.[15] The Vietnam syndrome was now a political liability, not a dominant trend. (These "swing" Democrats were voting, more often than not, in defiance of their party's congressional leaders, who clung to a more orthodox liberal position on many defense and foreign policy issues.)

The swing Democrats sometimes hedged, picking and choosing among the various insurgencies. Solarz championed the Afghans and the Cambodians while disparaging Jonas Savimbi in Angola and the Nicaraguan Contras.[16] But the rising tide lifted all boats. Suddenly the votes appeared, in the summer of 1985, to repeal the ten-year-old Clark Amendment and permit the United States to support Savimbi and his UNITA insurgency. Five million dollars was authorized openly for the Cambodian non-Communist resistance in fiscal year 1986.[17] As a public debate intensified over support for the Nicaraguan Contras—now overt—the administration managed to wangle only $24 million from Congress for fiscal year 1984 and $27 million in fiscal year 1985; Congress was to authorize another $100 million in the summer and fall of 1986.[18] Aid to the Afghan rebels increased dramatically, from a reported $280 million in fiscal year 1985 to $470 million in fiscal year 1986, plus an additional $25 million in fiscal year 1986 for overt civilian cross-border assistance, Department of Defense transportation costs, and political/media training for the mujahedin leadership.[19]

Thus, the centrist Democrats deserve their share of the credit for turning the Reagan Doctrine into an operational reality. Without them, the expanded aid programs simply would not have been possible, and the doctrine would have remained a rhetorical flourish, not a *policy* being implemented around the globe.

BIRTH OF A DOCTRINE

If the Reagan Doctrine's conception came from the Reaganites' early aspirations, in the fertile environment of a transformed American polity, its actual birth in early 1985 was a labored and even painful process. As indicated earlier, there was no plan or definite expectation as Reagan's second term began. But, driven in part by tactical considerations, the administration felt its way and began articulating its aspirations more boldly. Both Ronald Reagan and George Shultz began to give the anti-Communist insurgents—the "freedom fighters"—a more prominent place in their speeches. The reason had a lot to do with the upcoming congressional vote on Contra funding. It was, in essence, an attempt to elevate the Contra debate to a higher plane of discussion, putting it in the context of a broader global phenomenon and indeed an American tradition. To put it another way, it was an attempt to get the glow of the popular cause (the Afghans) to rub off onto the unpopular one (the Contras).

In an address in New York on January 9, 1985, CIA director William Casey called attention to the vulnerability of the Soviets' newly won client states. "[T]he tide has changed," Casey proclaimed:

> There are over 100,000 Soviet troops in Afghanistan, 170,000 Vietnamese troops in Cambodia, and 40,000 Cuban troops in Africa. This is worldwide military aggression directly and by proxy. That and the horror of it is the bad news. The good news is that the tide has changed. Today in Afghanistan, Angola, Cambodia, Ethiopia, and Nicaragua, to mention only the most prominent arenas, hundreds of thousands of ordinary people are volunteers in irregular wars against the Soviet army or Soviet-supported regimes. Whereas in the 1960s and 1970s anti-Western causes attracted recruits throughout the Third World, the 1980s have emerged as the decade of freedom fighters resisting Communist regimes.[20]

In the White House, with the president's encouragement, his speechwriters looked for occasions to reaffirm the theme of the democratic tide and communism's vulnerability. The NSC staff, especially Don Fortier and Steve Sestanovich, cultivated the idea of a strategy against the Soviets. On January 24, some preliminary thoughts were inserted in remarks by the president to a gathering of Western Hemisphere legislators brought to Washington by the bipartisan Center for Democracy. Reagan focused on the Contras but made a more generalized pitch that all the various groups struggling against Communist dictatorship deserved our help: "I think it behooves all of us who believe in democratic government, in free elections, in the respect for human rights, to stand side by side with those who share our ideals, especially in Central America. We must not permit those heavily armed by a faraway dictatorship to undermine their neighbors and to stamp out democratic alternatives at home. We must have the same solidarity with those who struggle for democracy as our adversaries do with those who would impose Communist dictatorship."

A similarly vague call to action—the one spotted by Krauthammer—was inserted into the president's State of the Union address on February 6, 1985: "We must stand by all our democratic allies. And we must not break faith with those who are risking their lives—on every continent, from Afghanistan to Nicaragua—to defy Soviet-supported aggression and secure rights which have been ours from birth. . . . Support for freedom fighters is self-defense and totally consistent with the OAS and UN Charters. . . . I want to work with you [Reagan told the Congress] to support the democratic forces whose struggle is tied to our own security."

Meanwhile, in the State Department, I was nervous about the Central America strategy being pursued by my colleagues in the Latin American bureau and was increasingly convinced that without congressional approval of the Contra program our entire Central America strategy—diplomacy and all—was doomed. Without leverage over the Sandinistas, our diplomacy would do no more than ratify Sandinista ascendancy in Central America while pushing Shultz closer into target range of conservative attack. I was thinking of urging him to make Nicaragua and the Contras a priority topic of his own upcoming speeches.

Out of the blue I received some ideas along the same lines from Mark Palmer, then a deputy assistant secretary of state in the European bureau. Palmer had helped to author Reagan's 1982 Westminster speech and its proposal of a National Endowment for Democracy; he was a man of broad intellectual interests, creativity, and Wilsonian passion. With his dapper bow tie and gregarious manner, he served later as American ambassador in Hungary during the democratic revolution of the late 1980s, an unabashed champion of that revolution. Palmer phoned me in mid-January with an idea for a speech—placing the contemporary fighters against Communist tyranny in the context of America's traditional support for those resisting repressive governments, harking back to Simón Bolívar and the Polish patriots of the nineteenth century. I mentioned Palmer's idea to Shultz and took Mark up on his offer to jot some ideas on paper. In the meantime, on January 23, I sent Shultz a memorandum proposing that he devote an upcoming speech, at the Commonwealth Club of San Francisco, to the topic. "Thus the issue of covert action can be tackled on a higher moral plane," I argued. Shultz agreed on January 26.

Mark produced about eleven pages of speech material a few days later. It filled in the historical background and offered some useful rhetorical points. The issue of support for anti-Communist resistance fighters, Palmer wrote, had to be addressed in the framework of basic principles—our traditional support for democracy. As for providing arms to resistance movements, why not? It was absurd that the forces of dictatorship felt free to do what they wished in subverting others while the democracies were unilaterally inhibited. I showed Mark's material to Shultz and also sent him an outline of my own, melding Mark's ideas with some of my own into the skeleton of a major speech. Shultz liked my outline; he took a copy with him to a lunch at the White House on January 25 and later invited me into a meeting in his office with Casey, McFarlane, and others and asked me to hand out copies. My paper undoubtedly reinforced the existing sentiment to stress the same theme.

The job of the policy planning staff of the State Department is not limited to speechwriting. The staff has been the birthplace of major policy initiatives and the locus of key advisers to the secretary of state. Only two members of my staff of about twenty-five were assigned the speechwriting duty. The staff's main assignment is to play a role in the secretary's deliberations on policy. A wise secretary of state values his policy planners as the source of a second opinion, challenging the recommendations that the regional and other operational bureaus hope the secretary will rubber-stamp; thus, we helped Shultz to know what his real choices were and to avoid becoming a prisoner of any of the bureaus. Our job was not just to second-guess tactics, however, but to add a special perspective—to think about strategy, about problems over the horizon, about global trends that cut across the regional compartments into which the department is divided. My staff and I played a role in several key issues, from the Libya problem and the Arab-Israeli peace process to Third World debt and Soviet provocations in the Berlin air corridors.

This is not to belittle the importance of the secretary's speeches, especially those of a thoughtful secretary eager to shape the public consciousness. Shultz engaged with Weinberger, for example, in a significant public debate about the use of force—its morality and efficacy—triggered by Shultz's frustration at the Pentagon's virtual insubordination while our military forces were engaged in Lebanon.[21] It was my idea that he speak out on the subject after I heard him pour out his frustrations in staff meeting after staff meeting, and I worked with him on the major speech he delivered to the Trilateral Commission in Washington on April 3, 1984. My staff and I helped produce further speeches Shultz delivered on the general subject of the use of force and specifically on the need for more vigorous measures to combat terrorism.[22]

Shultz's address to the Commonwealth Club of San Francisco on February 22, 1985, is one of the seminal statements of the Reagan Doctrine. The principal draftsman was Robert W. Kagan, a bright young member of my staff who later went to work for Elliott Abrams in the Bureau of Inter-American Affairs. The Central America section of the speech was the handiwork also of Luigi Einaudi, resident intellectual downstairs in the Inter-American bureau who later served as a distinguished U.S. ambassador to the OAS.

In this speech, Shultz, like Haig and Reagan, hailed the "democratic revolution." Shultz cited not only the resistance forces in Afghanistan, Cambodia, Nicaragua, Ethiopia, and Angola but the Solidarity trade union in Poland, other dissidents in Eastern Europe and the Soviet Union, and advocates of peaceful democratic change in places as far afield as South Africa, Chile, South Korea, and the Philippines. It was no longer possible, he said, for skeptics to imagine that the aspiration for representative government was a culture-bound luxury of the advanced West, that more statist structures were required to hasten economic development, or that advocacy of Western values was somehow ethnocentric or arrogant.

Shultz invoked the nineteenth-century American tradition of support for Bolívar and the Polish patriots, as Mark Palmer had suggested. He pointed to the remarkable advance of civilian democratic institutions in Latin America. Then he bore in on the phenomenon of anti-Communist resistance movements. These insurgencies, Shultz said, were a challenge to the Brezhnev Doctrine—there was no longer reason for us, or anyone else, to accept the legitimacy of tyrannical rule:

> So long as Communist dictatorships feel free to aid and abet insurgencies in the name of "socialist internationalism," why must the democracies, the target of this threat, be inhibited from defending their own interests and the cause of democracy itself?
>
> How can we as a country say to a young Afghan, Nicaraguan, or Cambodian: "Learn to live with oppression; only those of us who already have freedom deserve to pass it on to our children."

Shultz outlined a number of general principles: the United States needed to support democracy and human rights against tyrannies of the Right as well as the Left. We needed to provide economic and security assistance to friendly democratic governments against the variety of threats they faced. "What we should do in each situation must, of necessity, vary. But it must always be clear whose side we are on. . . ."

With this background, Shultz concluded with a strong plea for support for the armed resistance in Nicaragua:

> The democratic forces in Nicaragua are on the front line in the struggle for progress, security, and freedom in Central America. Our active help for them is the best insurance that their efforts will be directed consistently and effectively toward these objectives.
>
> But the bottom line is this: those who would cut off these freedom

fighters from the rest of the democratic world are, in effect, consigning Nicaragua to the endless darkness of communist tyranny. And they are leading the United States down a path of greater danger. For if we do not take the appropriate steps now to pressure the Sandinistas to live up to their past promises—to cease their arms buildup, to stop exporting tyranny across their borders, to open Nicaragua to the competition of freedom and democracy—then we may find later, when we can no longer avoid acting, that the stakes will be higher and the costs greater.

The U.S. goal, Shultz said, was a change in Nicaraguan behavior—a reduction of the Sandinista military threat and campaign of regional subversion and a recommitment to the pledges of democratic pluralism made to the OAS in 1979: "We will note and welcome such a change in Nicaraguan behavior no matter how it is obtained. Whether it is achieved through the multilateral Contadora negotiations, through unilateral actions taken by the Sandinistas alone or in concert with their domestic opponents, or through the collapse of the Sandinista regime is immaterial to us. But without such a change of behavior, lasting peace in Central America is impossible."

Thus (in Kagan's and Einaudi's subtle formulation) did Shultz deftly finesse the chronic issue of whether or not the Contras' goal was to overthrow the Sandinista regime.

Shultz included a general point about the strategic relationship with the Soviets. Like Reagan he cited the Soviets' internal weaknesses and speculated that the "correlation of forces" was tilting against them. But the main thrust of the speech was the focus on democracy, which appealed strongly to Shultz and also reflected writer Bob Kagan's neoconservative vocation.

THE DIPLOMATIC TRACK

If we are tracing the birth of the Reagan Doctrine, two other key documents must be mentioned. One was the president's speech at the UN General Assembly later in the year, on October 24, 1985. The idea of devoting this speech to the regional conflicts seems to have originated with Bud McFarlane, who wanted to be sure that these issues got on the agenda of the Geneva summit with Gorbachev scheduled for a few weeks later. McFarlane asked his staff to work with State on a diplomatic initiative. I was consulted during the drafting (as was Mark Palmer), but the process turned into another typical tug-of-war between State, which wanted a serious-looking proposal, and the conservatives (including CIA director Casey, White House speechwriter Ben Elliott, and NSC staffer Constantine Menges), who mistrusted almost anything that the State Department was involved in. Menges recounts that he and Casey intervened more than once to try to block the proposal; this failed. But after another direct appeal by Casey to Reagan, some of its language was toughened.[23]

In the event, Reagan in his UN speech strongly condemned the Soviets and their clients for waging unjust wars of occupation and repression in Afghanistan, Cambodia, Ethiopia, Angola, and Nicaragua. No conservative in the administration could have complained of this thrust:

> All of these conflicts—some of them under way for a decade—originate in local disputes but they share a common characteristic: they are the consequence of an ideology imposed from without, dividing nations and creating regimes that are, almost from the day they take power, at war with their own people. And in each case, Marxism-Leninism's war with the people becomes war with their neighbors.
>
> These wars are exacting a staggering human toll and threaten to spill across national boundaries and trigger dangerous confrontations. . . . During the past decade these wars played a large role in building suspicions and tensions in my country over the purpose of Soviet policy. This gives us an extra reason to address them seriously today.

Then Reagan proposed that talks begin first among the warring parties in each country. In a second stage, these internal negotiations would be reinforced by a U.S.-Soviet dialogue aimed principally at the withdrawal of foreign troops and a halt to outside supply of arms. Third, as peace and "democratic reconciliation" took hold, the United States promised generous economic aid to help rebuild the shattered countries and promote their return to the family of nations.

This October 1985 Reagan initiative did not bear immediate fruit, but it had significance nonetheless. The internal tug-of-war reflected the heightened fear of conservatives that the State Department would sell out any gains the "freedom fighters" made. Leaving aside the *ad hominem* mistrust of the State Department, it has to be acknowledged that any pursuit of diplomatic compromise inevitably has an unnerving effect on the morale of those fighting; no one on the battlefield really wants to die for a compromise outcome or to be the last to die before a cease-fire is declared. Thus, unless conducted with extreme care and solicitude for the morale of one's allies in the field, diplomacy *can* be dangerous—and can also be manipulated by one's opponents for that very purpose. (The North Vietnamese understood this game very well.) Our early Central America diplomacy indeed had as its unannounced goal (at least in State) the idea that we might ultimately trade away our support for our friends in some deal over their heads. And as a U.S.-Soviet dialogue developed on these issues, it gave rise to further fears among our clients that their fate might be decided not only over their heads but—worse—as part of some larger global superpower trade-off. Nicaragua-for-Afghanistan "deals" were in fact being bruited about in the public prints and even hinted at by the Soviets.[24]

Our diplomats had a habit of plunging into a negotiation for its own sake without always being sensitive to these concerns, which not only was impolitic but also put at risk the very leverage that underpinned their diplomacy. Conservatives were not completely wrong in their suspicions. Reagan tried to reassure them in his February 4, 1986, State of the Union address that our goal was not just to help the insurgents fight but to help them win: "You are not alone, freedom fighters. America will support. . . . with moral and material assistance, your right not just to fight and die for freedom but to fight and win freedom. . . ."

Yet Reagan was right in his UN speech to proclaim the necessity of a diplomatic track. Diplomacy is an indispensable part of any sensible strategy. Few of the "freedom fighters" we were supporting had a realistic expectation of military victory; what they were fighting for (or were entitled to) was a fair share of political power—Savimbi made this point often—a fair share that had been denied them by the Leninist regimes dominating their countries and propped up by Soviet arms. Moreover, to maintain international support (not to mention congressional support) for our new policy, it was essential that the United States demonstrate that it had a political objective and was not just fueling a war for its own sake.

The terms that Reagan announced in his UN speech hardly gave away the store. He made clear that U.S. aid to the anti-Communist resistance forces would continue until "definitive progress" had been made in negotiations—which, presumably, *we* would define. Moreover, initial talks among the warring parties in each country would have had the immediate effect of winning the Contras, the mujahedin, UNITA, and the others equal status with the Communist regimes they were opposing—a major political victory. For this reason, there was little chance the Soviets and their clients, at that stage, would accept the "offer."

The balance of forces on the ground was only beginning to shift. The Soviets and their clients did not yet feel under sufficient military pressure to concede the legitimacy of the armed rebellions against them; this would take a few more years. Yet the United States was now confident enough of the trend that it could safely risk a venture into diplomacy—legitimizing a diplomatic track that eventually would pull it (as well as the Soviets) into hard trade-offs. As the balance of forces was gradually restored on the ground over the next few years, the conditions for fair and fruitful diplomacy would come into being.

A U.S.-Soviet dialogue on these issues had, in fact, already begun. After Reagan's reelection, the Soviets had come back to the arms reduction talks in Geneva. Shultz and Gromyko met in January 1985 and agreed not only to resume the arms talks but also to pursue discussions on a range of other issues.

While Shultz was eager to get arms talks back on track, he was at first wary of putting stress on the regional conflicts as well. He was profoundly dubious of the "linkage" philosophy of Nixon and Kissinger, which held that arms control talks could not succeed outside of the overall context of relations. Shultz delivered a speech at the RAND/UCLA Center for the Study of Soviet International Behavior in Los Angeles on October 18, 1984—with Kissinger in the audience—virtually repudiating "linkage." I had tried to talk Shultz out of this but only managed to soften his text. He passionately defended the negotiations he was conducting, especially in arms reduction, which he believed were in the overriding national interest despite the Soviets' propensity to do things "abhorrent to us" or threatening to our interests in other areas:

> The U.S.-Soviet relationship, of course, is a global one. We impinge on each other's interests in many regions of the world and in many fields of endeavor. A sustained and sound relationship, therefore, will confront the fact that the Soviets can be expected periodically to do something abhorrent to us or threaten our interests.
>
> This raises the question of linkage. Should we refuse to conclude agreements with the Soviets in one area when they do something outrageous in some other area? Would such an approach give us greater leverage over Moscow's conduct? Or would it place us on the defensive? Would it confirm our dedication to fundamental principles of international relations? Or would it make our diplomacy seem inconsistent? Clearly, linkage is not merely "a fact of life" but a complex question of policy.
>
> There will be times when we must make progress in one dimension of the relationship contingent on progress in others. We can never let ourselves

become so wedded to improving our relations with the Soviets that we turn a blind eye to actions that undermine the very foundation of stable relations. At the same time, linkage as an instrument of policy has limitations; if applied rigidly, it could yield the initiative to the Soviets, letting them set the pace and the character of the relationship. . . .

Shultz's deeper reasons for rejecting "linkage" were not analytic at all, but bureaucratic. His speech was an expression of pure frustration; he was sick and tired of the conservatives in the administration invoking all other sources of political tension as reasons to call a halt to arms control. Thus, Weinberger had tried to use the Soviet shootdown of the Korean airliner in September 1983 and the killing of an American major in East Germany in March 1983 as arguments to suspend arms talks.[25] Reagan sided with Shultz: ". . . George is carrying out my policy," he confided to his diary in November 1984, vowing to meet with Weinberger and Casey to "lay it out to them."[26]

In August 1984, as the State Department began discreet internal planning for a resumption of the U.S.-Soviet dialogue after our election, Shultz had asked me why I was so insistent on including the regional issues. I responded in a memorandum, on August 17, pointing out the variety of reasons, strategic and tactical: There was no long-run hope for decent relations, including in arms reduction, without Soviet restraint in the Third World, I wrote; the linkage was a reality. Moreover, I argued that U.S.-Soviet discussions of these issues were an effective forum in which to get across the terms on which we insisted for settling these conflicts, as well as a potentially useful channel for eventual negotiation once the balance of forces was restored on the ground and real bargaining began. Shultz, as noted, remained fearful of "linkage" as a concept, but he actively promoted U.S.-Soviet discussions on regional issues from 1985 onward.

STRATEGIC RATIONALE

The other major document of the Reagan Doctrine was a little-noticed White House statement published on March 14, 1986. This was an eight-page printed essay in the president's name entitled "Freedom, Regional Security, and Global Peace." Nowhere did it use the phrase Reagan Doctrine, but that is what it was a statement of—and perhaps the definitive one. This, too, was the handiwork of Sestanovich and Fortier, though I had a small part in its drafting. It was, among other things, an attempt to respond to critics of the Reagan Doctrine with a thoughtful analytic statement of what the policy was and what it was not.

The March 1986 document, first of all, explained our strategic stake in the various regional conflicts—especially what they told us about Soviet conduct. The pattern of Soviet adventurism over the previous fifteen years had wrought enormous human misery as well as exacerbating international tensions; these issues could not be regarded as "peripheral to other issues on the global agenda." (Linkage was back!) The United States, working with others, had the ability to help ease or resolve these conflicts. The document noted, as part of the global resurgence of democracy and pluralism, the phenomenon of armed resistance to Communist tyranny: "We did not create this historical phenomenon, but we must not fail to respond to it." The tools of American policy, the statement went on, included traditional and conventional instruments of economic and security assistance to friendly governments but also prudent support for resistance movements, geared to a political strategy that looked to diplomatic solutions:

> The form and extent of support we provide must be carefully weighed in each case. Because a popularly supported insurgency enjoys some natural military advantages, our help need not always be massive to make a difference. But it must be more than simply symbolic: our help should give freedom fighters the chance to rally the people to their side. . . . There can be no regional peace in Central America—or wherever Soviet client regimes have taken power—so long as such aggressive policies face no resistance. Support for resistance forces shows those who threaten the peace that they have no military option, and that negotiations represent the only realistic course.

Where Shultz's San Francisco speech of February 1985 put most emphasis on the democratic revolution, the more interesting passages of this March 1986 document dealt with the Soviet problem. The statement emphatically denied that our strategy was to "bleed" the Soviets, as some had charged (and as Deng Xiaoping was content to do in Cambodia); the American goal was, rather, to bring these conflicts to a decent end— and, more fundamentally, to convince the Soviets that adventurist policies were now doomed to failure. As Sestanovich had foreshadowed in his *Washington Post* article in May 1984, the Reagan document took note of the Soviets' evidently growing disillusionment with their Third

World involvement. Now, as the Soviets were clearly reassessing many of their policies under their new general secretary, Mikhail Gorbachev, it was precisely the moment for us to make as clear as possible the costs of their Third World mischief making and thereby spur their reappraisal:

> Our goal, in short—indeed our necessity—is to convince the Soviet Union that the policies on which it embarked in the 70s *cannot work*. We cannot be completely sure how the Soviet leadership calculates the benefits of relationships with clients. No one should underestimate the tenacity of such a powerful and resilient opponent.
>
> Yet there are reasons to think that the present time is especially propitious for raising doubts on the Soviet side about the wisdom of its client ties. The same facts about the democratic revolution that we can see are visible in Moscow. The harmful impact that Moscow's conduct in the developing world had on Western readings of its intentions in the last decade is also well known. There is no time in which Soviet policy reviews and reassessments are more likely than in a succession period, especially when many problems have been accumulating for some time. General Secretary Gorbachev himself made this point last year when he asked American interviewers whether it wasn't clear that the Soviet Union required international calm to deal with its internal problems.

In sum, the March 1986 White House document was a moderate, decidedly undoctrinaire, and careful statement of the policy, designed to calm the fears that it was a commitment to mindless global crusading. It also contained, moreover, a remarkably frank exposition of the strategy that lay behind the new policy—the explicit geopolitical challenge to the new Soviet leadership that would be pressed by the administration over the next few years.

CRITIQUES

The Reagan Doctrine came in for its share of criticism of both its morality and its efficacy. It was challenged from the Left, from the "realist" center, and from the Right. It was denounced for being dangerously provocative, on the one hand, and for being ineffectual, on the other.

On the liberal side, there were thoughtful observers like columnist Stephen S. Rosenfeld, who worried that the risks were likely to grow as the administration was impelled by ideology to go further and further.

Especially with a new leader in the Kremlin, in his view, Moscow's response was unpredictable.[27] Other critics like Selig Harrison warned starkly that U.S. support for the Afghan rebels posed "grave risks" of a major confrontation with the Soviet Union.[28]

Harvard professors Stanley Hoffmann and Michael Walzer and New York senator Daniel Patrick Moynihan questioned the policy's consistency with international law. The United States was in the humiliating position of being hauled before the International Court of Justice by Nicaragua on charges connected with the 1984 mining of Nicaraguan harbors. Instead of being a champion of international order, we were espousing a theory that justified the wanton overthrow of governments. To Senator Moynihan, that we were only emulating the Communists' past practice was not an adequate excuse; we were only "debasing our own conduct in the course of resisting theirs."[29]

Charles Krauthammer set upon these arguments with great relish, turning some of the Left's own familiar moral rhetoric against it. How often had we heard from liberals that U.S. policy was always defending an unjust status quo against the forces of progressive change? Why did liberals' tolerance of all sorts of "liberation struggles" against colonialism suddenly evaporate when faced with a struggle against Soviet colonialism? To oppose the Reagan policy in the name of "order" was "a profoundly reactionary position."

The idea that the United States was always on "the wrong side of history" was discredited most of all, Krauthammer argued, by recent history itself—the brutality of Communist or other radical regimes that had replaced friendly regimes in Cuba, Vietnam, Cambodia, Iran, and now Nicaragua.[30] Krauthammer could have gone on to quote Senator Moynihan's own blasts against Soviet neocolonialism in Angola when Moynihan had been President Ford's UN ambassador[31] (which read quite well in retrospect) or Professor Hoffmann's 1981 warnings that the United States had better get ready for the tide of leftist revolution in the Third World in the 1980s[32] (which read today as an ironic commentary on liberal myopia—and inconsistency).

From another direction came criticism from the "realists." Robert W. Tucker was perhaps the most eminent of those whose dislike of U.S. interventionism harked back to Walter Lippmann's critique of both Wilsonianism and containment. Tucker published an essay in 1985 criticizing the Reagan Doctrine on two grounds: He deplored the moralism of the impulse to propagate democracy around the globe, and he feared it was a blueprint for American overextension. Such a universal doctrine seemed to embody no limits:

Admittedly, the proponents of the Reagan Doctrine do not propose to act consistently on the basis of this view of legitimacy. The claims of doctrine, they acknowledge and even insist, are to be subordinated to the requirements of prudence. But will this always prove possible? Having proclaimed a new vision of international order, a vision that makes democratic forms and processes the centerpiece of that order, will it prove possible to reconcile the claims of the new order with the claims of prudence? Or will not a policy obedient to prudence appear as a betrayal of the new order and of the value—freedom—it enthrones?[33]

The new doctrine, Tucker observed, went far beyond containment in its open espousal of the rollback of existing Communist regimes. He doubted the administration could long maintain domestic support for such a policy—pointing to the controversy over Nicaragua as proof. And in the meantime the doctrine, "if taken seriously, may well prove destructive of existing international order." If it truly undermined significant Soviet strategic positions, it risked major confrontation; if it did not, it was not that significant a policy.[34]

To this "realist" criticism, the Reagan administration could only respond by insisting on the prudence of its conduct. The March 1986 White House statement was intended as a reassurance that situations were considered case by case and that what I call the "academic fallacy" was not borne out by the facts: The administration was not on automatic pilot. The fear of overextension was also answered by another point made sharply by Krauthammer. Having been on the receiving end of so many guerrilla insurgencies in the past, we should have learned that it is the governments that are the *target* of such rebellions, and their backers, who risk exhaustion, not the insurgents and their supporters:

Consider the current warning that the Reagan Doctrine is economically ruinous and militarily dangerous. It is, in fact, in purely economic terms astonishingly cheap. Aid to the *contras* is now $27 million, and the administration wants $100 million. Even at that level it amounts to three-hundredths of one percent of the defense budget. Nor is the threat of "overextension" any greater. Reagan Doctrine intervention in Afghanistan and Nicaragua (and Angola, if aid is now "covertly" to go to UNITA) confronts Soviet expansionism without the expenditure of American lives and without any direct threat to the Soviet Union. If these are the consequences of universalism, then it ranks as one of the most cost-effective tools of American foreign policy.[35]

Efforts were made to measure the cost-effectiveness of the U.S. strategy. In his New York speech in January 1985, CIA director Casey estimated that the Soviets were spending $8 billion annually to finance counter-insurgency in these countries.[36] Two Soviet writers in 1988 conceded the point, citing an $8 billion figure for Afghanistan alone:

> The USA skillfully exploits the fact that in "low-intensity conflicts" it is much cheaper to support guerrillas than the government. . . . The USSR spent on military operations in Afghanistan five billion rubles annually, while the USA spent not more than one billion dollars annually on its support for the Afghan antigovernmental forces, or almost six to eight times less. According to Western estimates, approximately the same ratio of American and "induced" Soviet expenditures exists in conflicts involving Nicaragua, Kampuchea, Ethiopia, and Angola.[37]

Others estimated the Soviets' total annual costs of counterinsurgency at anywhere from $12 to $20 billion.[38]

To be fair to my friend Professor Tucker, he acknowledged at the end of Reagan's term that the policy had turned out more successfully than he expected: "The administration's success in dealing with the Russians has been due to a combination of luck and Reagan's instinct, which was right in the end.

"The policies pursued . . . had a marked effect on the Soviets. . . . Those measures persuaded them that the bid for supremacy they were making in the late 1970s could not succeed and indeed was dangerous. . . ."[39]

Yet, for all those who feared the administration was going too far, whether liberals or "realists," there were others who disparaged the Reagan Doctrine for its ineffectuality. The lack of any coherent planning at the beginning of 1985 was noted at the beginning of this chapter. There are scholars who discerned the tactical considerations—particularly, the push for Contra funding—that drove the policy and who concluded therefore that the doctrine deserved to be taken less seriously[40] or even that the policy masked a period of American decline more than an era of American resurgence.[41]

Other arguments were made as to why the policy would not work.[42] There were doubts that Soviet behavior would be much affected by our actions; it was believed that the Soviets could match any American escalation on the ground and would never accept defeat. Governments we were threatening, moreover, would only be thrown further into the Soviets' arms. The controversial American use of military and covert means was thought to alienate other Third World countries. Doubts were expressed about the capabilities of the guerrillas: Could any of them really win? If their prospects were so dim, these were poor places to try to demonstrate our resolve.[43] There was concern that our European allies would not long tolerate U.S. policies that could provoke the Soviets. (There was particular distaste in Europe for our Central America policy,[44] though behind the scenes, especially among the Social Democratic governments of southern Europe; there was also a burgeoning disillusionment with the Sandinistas.)[45] Pointing especially to the growing congressional and public uneasiness about Central America, critics, in short, doubted that the United States could sustain a global policy of sufficient leverage to achieve the goals set out for it.

These constraints on U.S. policy were real enough. In the period 1985–87, the administration could point to no diplomatic success, only to a series of festering conflicts in which our "freedom fighters" were at least managing better to survive.

Liberal charges of the policy's ineffectuality were ironically mirrored by conservative fears. Ambassador Jeane Kirkpatrick, after she left office, was concerned that the policy was handicapped because much of it was carried out covertly instead of being openly explained and defended.[46] Angelo Codevilla, a conservative intelligence specialist, warned in 1986 that the policy was running aground because it was being undermined within the administration.[47]

Codevilla's article was a perceptive description of the bureaucratic infighting, noting not only the conservative suspicions of the State Department but the splits within some of the other departments. While CIA director Casey was one of the champions of the new policy, the working level of the CIA was populated by more cautious types who were dubious of the operational capabilities of the insurgents we were supporting. Codevilla speculated that these lower-level CIA officials had been traumatized by the Nicaraguan mining episode, by the congressional investigations of the CIA in the 1970s, or by Director Stansfield Turner's purge of the operational side of the house in the Carter years. In the Defense Department, similarly, there were champions of the policy on the civilian side (most importantly Fred C. Iklé, under secretary for policy), as against the more cautious personalities within the uniformed military.

Codevilla was especially dismissive of the whole idea of a diplomatic track, whether its goal was to seek compromise solutions or to moderate

Soviet behavior. Liberal critics were convinced that the goal of raising the costs to the Soviets was unattainable; Codevilla did not think it was good enough. For conservatives, there was no political objective morally or strategically valid except helping the anti-Communists win.

While some liberals and conservatives both disparaged the policy as ineffectual, a contrary view came even more ironically from a surprising direction—the radical Left. Writing in the *Nation* at the end of 1985, Michael T. Klare found the Reagan administration's policy more impressive than that.[48] He pulled together a number of the themes, policy shifts, and practices of the Reagan administration and saw a common thrust—the Defense Department's new military doctrine and command structures for so-called low-intensity conflict; the bolder policy of "active defense" against terrorism, heralded especially in Shultz's speeches (drafted by my staff); and the policy of military support for anti-Communist insurgencies. He saw in all this a "comprehensive government effort to devise a persuasive rationale for military intervention." All these policies, Klare lamented, were gaining impressive congressional and public support, and the Vietnam-era taboos against interventionism were fading away. He pointed to Solarz's *New York Times* Op-Ed article of June 1985. Indeed, soon after Klare's article, the campaign against terrorism furnished the (very popular) justification for Reagan's air strikes against Libya in April 1986, Reagan's next military action after Grenada.

A few years later, another radical analyst, Fred Halliday, a Marxist at the London School of Economics, wrote a book on the U.S.-Soviet competition in the 1980s, making a similar point in the wider perspective of superpower relations.[49] A significant shift in global politics had taken place, he was convinced. Halliday saw "socialism on the defensive" in the Third World—that was the title of one of his chapters—and viewed Gorbachev's response to Reagan as a strategic retreat that threatened to leave the Soviets' Third World clients orphaned. The United States had succeeded brilliantly in its policy of raising the costs to the Soviets:

> If in the 1970s the Soviet Union had appeared to be gaining ground in the third world as a result of the upheavals taking place there, the reverse was true of the 1980s. . . .
>
> Whatever Soviet officials believed about the legitimacy of the movements involved, and of Soviet aid to them, the fact was that the price of such support in east-west terms rose considerably. After many other disputes, détente came to an end in 1979, amidst the turmoil of Afghanistan,

and from the early 1980s onwards US support for opposition forces within Soviet third world allies began to take its toll. The Afghan intervention was the most obviously costly, and, within the USSR, controversial of these commitments: but the overall policy, dating back to Khrushchev's period, of backing third world revolutions and nationalist movements as part of a global rivalry with the USA appeared to be increasingly difficult. . . .

Soviet "new thinking" was an attempt to lessen the degree of western pressure in order to enable the USSR to concentrate its efforts upon internal restructuring, on *perestroika*. It was, therefore, a defensive strategy, an attempt to reduce conflict in the name of common human values and to lessen the degree of military confrontation in the third world.[50]

In Halliday's judgment, moreover, there were even more profound implications: "With the uncertainties in eastern Europe and Soviet claims that the Red Army would not intervene to crush serious opposition, it was becoming more and more evident that new opportunities for challenging the communist parties in power, with western encouragement, were opening up. The 'reversibility' of communism was now on the agenda."[51] A Soviet defeat in Afghanistan, he thought, could even have "demonstration effects" on Eastern Europe and "implications for the USSR itself."[52] Halliday wrote all this in 1988.

I have to confess that reading the Klare article in early 1986 was a tonic. Witnessing all the bureaucratic wrangling at close hand, I knew that no "comprehensive government effort" was ever as efficacious, or even as attainable, as the paranoia of the Left would have it. We were more impressive than we deserved to be. Today, however, rereading Klare and Halliday after the passage of time and in the perspective of Soviet history as it later unfolded, I find it hard to avoid the conclusion that these outside-the-mainstream analysts more clearly discerned the shift in the global "correlation of forces" that many liberals and conservatives, perhaps too close to events, missed. Conservative Reagan watchers were demoralized by all the bureaucratic compromises they witnessed; liberal intellectuals felt too much of a stake in dismissing the significance of a Reagan presidency that they simultaneously ridiculed and feared.

Despite all the criticisms, in other words—and despite all the internal confusions that were there for all to see—it *was* a very different American policy, because it was a very different America. There is no way this could not have its impact on Soviet policies.

It is to this that we now turn. The Soviet Union was undergoing its own revolution. American policy did not cause it, but undeniably played a role in its unfolding. We will attempt to analyze the origins of the Soviet transformation, particularly in foreign policy, and to trace the interaction of the two sides. Contrary to some predictions, regional conflicts began to ease, not to explode into crisis. The Cold War in the Third World was about to end.

12

THE GORBACHEV REVOLUTION

The first time Ronald Reagan and Mikhail Gorbachev set eyes on each other was a cold, wintry morning in Geneva on Tuesday, November 19, 1985. Reagan, the seventy-four-year-old elder statesman nearing the twilight of his career, waited inside the ornate doors of the meeting site, the nineteenth-century Château Fleur d'Eau, for the arrival of the fifty-four-year-old rising star of international politics. The world watched anxiously on television. Reagan's staff waited anxiously too, wondering how the old man would handle the encounter.

Some aides like me, watching on television from a State Department staff office in a nearby hotel, worried that an informal "get-acquainted" summit like this had an inherent risk of turning out badly. Most of the summits that I had seen at close hand, especially in the Nixon era, involved considerable preparation—not only in the sense of big briefing books but some prior understanding between the parties on the substantive outcome so that there would be no surprises. This time, there was no such understanding.

Our government was in its usual disarray. The Defense Department had leaked to the press a stiff memorandum that Weinberger had sent to the president warning against concessions on arms control, especially any concessions on the president's Strategic Defense Initiative (SDI, or what the media called "Star Wars"). Shultz was furious at the Weinberger letter and the leak; Weinberger was furious that he had not been invited to Geneva and that the summit communiqué was being drafted behind his back.[1] A clever Soviet diplomacy could embarrass Reagan by whip-sawing us with unexpected proposals (as indeed happened at Reykjavik a year later). Moreover, God knows what Gorbachev's briefing papers had told him about Reagan and his presumed intellectual limitations in extended conversation.

The long black Soviet Zil limousine drew up to the president's villa, and the young, cocky Moscow University law graduate got out, still bundled up in a heavy overcoat, scarf, and hat. To the world's amazement, the old man, coatless, scarfless, and hatless, bounded down the steps to offer the young Soviet a smile and a vigorous handshake in the chill winds, then steer him by the elbow back up the steps into the villa. It was marvelous one-upmanship.

Perhaps it was an appropriate symbol. The Geneva summit went well for the American side. Reagan engaged Gorbachev more than adequately in general discussions of personal political philosophy. Reagan conceded nothing on SDI or arms control but gained politically by the very demonstration that even he, the reputed warmonger, could achieve peaceful relations with the other nuclear superpower. And within six years' time, the cocky technocrat-politician, for all his youth and intellectual energy, had presided over the collapse of his foreign and domestic policy, indeed of his country. Reagan lived to see the Berlin Wall come down (he had insisted it should in a Berlin speech on June 12, 1987) and even to see his most controversial characterization of the Soviet Union endorsed by a democratic Russian foreign minister on American television. It was a mistake to call it "the Union of Soviet Socialist Republics," said Andrei Kozyrev cheerily just after the failed coup of August 1991. "It was, rather, [an] evil empire, as it was once put. . . ."[2]

Gorbachev certainly changed history. No one can deny him historical and moral credit for the transformation he wrought, even if it went far beyond his intentions and his conception. I know from my own years in Washington that history is not just the product of impersonal forces. On the contrary, the human element—the courage and intellectual qualities of individuals or their all-too-human absence—can determine the course of events. Lyndon Johnson's brooding insecurities, Richard Nixon's tenacity and suspiciousness, Ronald Reagan's ideological certitude and self-confidence—how can anyone gainsay that these qualities influenced decisions and choices that were made? And so much hangs on presidential decisions. From that vantage point, no outcome in world affairs is ever foreordained. Nevertheless, historians will have before them for a long time to come the task of sorting out how much Mikhail Gorbachev was the cause and how much he was the effect of what was happening in the 1980s.

He came into power in March 1985 sure in the conviction that the Soviet system had to be changed. "We could not go on living like that," he later put it simply, declaring that this was the "first conclusion" he drew for himself at the moment that power fell to him.[3] His reform program (which he called *perestroika*, or "reconstruction") consciously repudiated the old Soviet style of governance—its ossified ideology, its stultifying centralized economic bureaucracy, the coercion with which the country's political life and East European empire were maintained, and many of its misguided foreign adventures. But his vision, even until the bitter end of his rule, was never of a Western-style constitutional democracy and free market but of a more benign, reformed Communist political and economic structure that would work better because he had put it on a less coercive basis. He hoped for a new version of communism that would inspire the voluntary effort and willing cooperation of its people—a planned economy that would be more efficient because it was somewhat more decentralized and flexible, a political process that would bolster the Communist party's leadership role by being somewhat more participatory and open to free expression.

In Eastern Europe, similarly, his avowed aim was to replace the coercive relations of the past with a more voluntary basis for bloc unity. It was the "Sinatra Doctrine," a Soviet spokesman cracked, each satellite's leadership now being enabled to say, "I'll do it my way."[4] Gorbachev sought to replace old-line party bosses with Communist reformers like himself, seeing this as the perfect answer to the satellites' chronic problems of economic performance, internal legitimacy, and relations with Moscow. Such reform Communists would feel themselves natural partners of the reform leadership in the Kremlin, making common cause against the hard-liners in all their countries.

The flaw in this vision, of course, was that when the factor of coercion was removed, there was nothing left that Soviet or Eastrn European peoples had much interest in. Given a free choice, they didn't want a benign form of communism; they wanted the real thing: democracy and independence. They couldn't wait to throw the regime out—an unsurprising anti-incumbent reaction after a forty-year (or seventy-year) record of criminality and incompetence unmatched by any political party in world history. Thus, Gorbachev's vigorous pursuit of change was enough to delegitimize the old system and sap its strength but not to save it. He let loose a process of demoralization and political unraveling he could not stop.

To his everlasting credit, he let this process run its course. There were outbursts of bluster, to be sure—peremptory presidential decrees, sporadic threats to use force against the Baltic republics*—but, overall, Gorbachev refrained from systematic (or effective) resort to the brutality of the Soviet past. On this point he stood his moral ground, and for that he may even deserve the Nobel Peace Prize he received. Only in a Soviet leader,

---

*Evidently applying a "Nancy Sinatra Doctrine": "These boots are made for walkin' . . . all over you."

however, could it be considered an exemplary act to refrain from murdering one's own people.

He was justly praised for his tactical brilliance as well. He maneuvered between the zealots of reform and of repression, splitting the difference between their programs, convincing each side that he was shielding it from the excesses of the other. He thus maintained a balance between them that averted a civil war, while the undercurrents inexorably flowed in the direction of change. When a reactionary coup was attempted in August 1991, the hard-liners had been too much weakened and the trend of democratization in the society had become too strong for the putsch to succeed. That was his achievement. But when the hard-liners were defeated, his balancing act was over.[5]

Gorbachev was replaced by a less sophisticated man for whom he had contempt, Boris Yeltsin, who saw more clearly than he that any hope of prosperity and legitimate rule could begin only with repudiation of the socialist command economy and of the Communist party that kept it in place. Gorbachev had clung too long to a naive vision of socialism that meant in practice, at that stage, a retrograde position, no longer a vision of reform.

In foreign policy, Gorbachev and his colleagues, especially his foreign minister Eduard Shevardnadze, had a clearer perception than they had in domestic affairs. While on many issues they could be as self-interested and wily as any past Soviet leaders, there was a trend of moderation that eventually became undeniable. To concentrate on their internal crisis, they needed a respite abroad—what Lenin had called a "breathing space." Whatever the long-term motive, the changes they brought about were concrete enough and far reaching enough to be of enormous benefit to the international system. Long before the post-Communist leadership under Yeltsin commenced the most significant reductions of the Soviet military machine, and even before the dramatic collapse of Soviet power in Eastern Europe in 1989, a transformation of Soviet foreign policy had already become evident in the Third World. It was here, in a sense, that the end of the Cold War began.

ANTECEDENTS

Leonid Brezhnev's legacy at home was an economy in stagnation; abroad, an ambitious foreign policy that had overreached. The energy shocks of the 1970s disguised the underlying economic realities: The West reeled under the blow of the oil cartel's energy price hikes, but over time the power of the cartel weakened, and real prices plunged in the 1980s; the

Western economies were in fact on the threshold of the "Information Age"—the revolution in microelectronics and supercomputers that demonstrated again their resilience and genius at innovation and dissemination of technology. The Soviet Union, meanwhile, was an oil exporter; the rise in prices was a great boost to its foreign-exchange earnings. It could import Western technology and finance a military buildup and venturesome foreign policy. But when the artificial boost in oil prices came to an end in the 1980s, the essential backwardness of the Soviet economy remained—the utter inability of its rigid bureaucratized structure to adapt to the postindustrial age. Gorbachev summed it up in a blunt statistic in a speech in February 1988, revealing that if one discounts the oil price rise and Brezhnev's artificial stimulation of the alcohol industry (!), the growth rate had been stagnant over twenty years.[6] It was not much different from the point that Reagan had made about Soviet economic performance in his June 1982 Westminster speech.

As the 1980s began, Brezhnev's foreign policy was running out of steam as well. The hubris of Brezhnev's report at the Twenty-fifth Party Congress in February 1976 was notably absent from the old apparatchik's subsequent appearance at the Twenty-sixth Party Congress in February 1981. By then, Poland and Afghanistan were festering crises; détente lay in tatters, and Ronald Reagan was in the White House. Instead of exuberance about the "correlation of forces" and the trend of "national liberation," the starting point of Brezhnev's 1981 report was an admission that the previous five years had been "rough and complicated." The aggressiveness of U.S. imperialism had "increased acutely"; some newly independent states were following the capitalist path; some of the socialist-oriented states were developing "in difficult conditions." Brezhnev touched upon phenomena that were highly ambiguous from the Soviet point of view, such as the Iranian Revolution and the nonaligned's focus on North-South economic relations, which lumped the USSR together with the West in the category of the wealthy North.[7]

The new unease about the Third World was revealed even more dramatically in scholarly work that elaborated on the doubts that had crept into the 1981 Brezhnev speech. In 1982, a book appeared called *Socialist Orientation in the Liberated Countries* by a group of authors so eminent in the party secretariat and academic institutes that it had the color of an official document: Karen Brutents and Rostislav Ulyanovskii of the central committee secretariat's international department; Yevgenii Primakov, director of the prestigious Institute of Oriental Studies (later a close Gorbachev adviser and head of the post-KGB Russian foreign intelligence service); and Anatolii Gromyko, son of the great man and director of the African Studies Institute. The socialist orientation of developing countries, these authors conceded, was not, after all, irreversible. What Khrushchev had feared was now the reality: Not only did many developing countries continue to be economically dependent on the capitalist world; they were integrated into it. The problems of economic, social, and political underdevelopment were profound and sometimes intractable. The phrase "socialist orientation" was deliberately used to distinguish these Third World nations from truer cases of "socialist development"—a way of distancing the Soviet Union from responsibility for their fate.[8]

Brutents wrote in *Pravda* a few years later: "The postcolonial period of the liberation struggle's development, when anti-imperialism continued to draw strength primarily from the problems, emotions, and memories of the colonial days . . . is coming to an end." And he warned that the "readiness of the developing countries to play an active part in the struggle against imperialism should not be taken for granted."[9] Other scholarly commentary elaborated on the problems with the nonaligned movement. The movement's criticism of the Soviets over Afghanistan was an alarming case of its acting truly nonaligned instead of as an anti-imperialist cohort. Islamic fundamentalism after the Iranian Revolution, for all its useful anti-Americanism, raised the danger of a virulent new source of anticommunism not only in the Middle East but also potentially in the Muslim republics of Soviet Central Asia. The Third World's trumpeting of a "New International Economic Order" was a call for a massive transfer of wealth from the rich North to the poorer South. When first unveiled in 1974, the idea received Soviet support as a "progressive" (i.e., anti-Western) principle, but, as suggested, Moscow glumly changed its tune when its own Third World clients invoked the slogan as an argument for concessional economic arrangements with their Soviet patron.[10]

Another eminent scholar, Georgii Mirskii, lamented the ideological blinders that had hindered earlier Soviet analysis of Third World complexities:

Years passed before we understood the significance and influence of the middle classes, the intelligentsia, the bureaucracy and the army, which indeed had been understood earlier by Western scholars. And years passed before we sufficiently realized what enormous weight can be attributed to traditions and non-class-related social institutions like tribalism, the deeply rooted dividing lines in Asian and African societies according to ethnic, religious, caste and clan lines, which ultimately are laid down in a lasting system of patronage-clientele relations which push class contradictions to the background. These class contradictions are unmistakenly present but come to the fore in specific, indirect, hidden and unclear forms.[11]

What all these analysts were conceding in their dry, jargon-filled prose was an extraordinary moral defeat. The prospects for socialism in the Third World were far less promising than once imagined; the self-image of a Soviet regime that had long sought vindication in the spread and success of its ideas worldwide was badly tarnished. Third World experience, in its variety and complexity, was mocking Marxist-Leninist certainties about the laws of historical development. The hopes of the 1960s (or the 1920s) that the former colonial countries would be a reliable ally against the Western powers were evaporating. The Third World was becoming a burden as much as an asset to Soviet foreign policy. And these economic and political analyses did not even begin to address the military quagmires in which Soviet clients now found themselves mired in various regions.

ANDROPOV AND THE "FINNISH SCHOOL"

In November 1982, Brezhnev died and was replaced by Yurii Andropov, a longtime party secretariat functionary who had been, since 1967, head of the KGB. Andropov remains to this day an enigmatic figure, praised by some Russians as a man of intellect and openness of mind and yet stained indelibly by his role in the 1956 suppression of Hungary, where he was ambassador, and in the Brezhnev-era suppression of dissidents in which he obviously played a central role as head of the KGB. Even when he was in the top job—a brief interlude of barely over a year, until February 1984—rumors circulated in the West that the gaunt and ascetic-looking Andropov enjoyed jazz and other decadent pursuits and was a closet liberal. All this invited ridicule, given the unreformed nature of the Soviet dictatorship as it then was. But as time passes, a complex picture of the man indeed emerges.

Georgii Arbatov's recent memoir paints a portrait of a man of genuine talent as well as (he says) human qualities. Arbatov himself was one of a group of youngish academics, of a self-proclaimed reformist bent, whom Andropov took under his wing. Arbatov sings his praises as a political figure who stood out among his Politburo colleagues in his intellectual curiosity, his lack of interest in enriching himself and his family, and his personal courtesy. Andropov apparently put people at ease and appreciated Arbatov's opinions. "I know of no instance when he intentionally committed any base act for its own sake,"[12] writes Arbatov—a hilariously ambiguous but appropriately Soviet commendation, since it allows for whatever base acts may have been committed for other reasons. More convincing, perhaps, is Fyodor Burlatskii's less romanticized description of a man with a precise steel-trap mind, a "penetrating and firm gaze," and extraordinary self-discipline. Yet Burlatskii, too, testifies to the loyalty that Andropov inspired in his subordinates.[13]

Skepticism aside, Andropov now seems clearly to have been a central figure in a small community of high- and mid-level Soviets who understood, through much of the post-Stalin period, that the system was deeply flawed. Some, like Burlatskii, had worked closely with Khrushchev and were punished in the Brezhnev era for their reformist enthusiasms. Others in the group, like Arbatov at his Institute for the USA and Canada and *Izvestia* commentator Aleksandr Bovin, kept their heads down and made their moral compromises as eager public spokesmen for the Brezhnev-era policies that they later denounced.

The godfather of the group was not Andropov but really the venerable Otto Kuusinen, the Finnish-born Old Bolshevik who served on Stalin's Politburo but who gathered together a group of bright young staffers in the late 1950s when he was assigned the task of drafting a new official textbook on Marxism-Leninism in the wake of Khrushchev's de-Stalinization. Andropov returned from Hungary to the party secretariat and recruited for his friend Kuusinen the likes of Burlatskii and Arbatov, Bovin, Georgii Shakhnazarov, Oleg Bogomolov, and Gennadii Gerasimov (the latter three also prominent under Gorbachev). Various accounts suggest that these men remained in loose contact with each other even when Khrushchev was deposed and the Brezhnev "era of stagnation" cast its dark shadow over any who would attempt intellectual or political experimentation.[14]

For our purposes here, Andropov's significance is that he went public, as general secretary, with a sophisticated and decidedly skeptical view of the Third World—and in a way that attracted the attention of Reagan administration officials. Addressing a plenary meeting of the party's central committee on June 15, 1983, he sarcastically called into question the ideological credentials of various Soviet clients and suggested that supporting them might be too expensive. They were, essentially, on their own, he said:

> It is one thing to proclaim socialism as one's goal and quite another thing to build it. A certain level of productive forces, culture, and social consciousness are needed for that. Socialist countries express solidarity with

these progressive countries, render assistance to them in the sphere of politics and culture, and promote the strengthening of their defense. We contribute, to the extent of our ability, to their economic development as well. But, on the whole their economic development, just as the entire social progress of those countries, can be, of course, only the result of the work of their peoples and of a correct policy of their leadership.[15]

This stern lecture was accompanied by the extraordinary admission that the Soviet commitment to the Third World had to be subordinated to the USSR's concerns about its deteriorating relations with the West: "The threat of a nuclear war overhanging mankind causes one to reappraise the principal goals of the entire communist movement," he declared. The heightened tensions with the Reagan administration in 1983 (the Strategic Defense Initiative; the political warfare against NATO's deployment of new missiles in Europe) were an argument for Soviet caution on other fronts of the Cold War, he seemed to be saying.[16]

Andropov stressed at the same time that Moscow was not in the business of "exporting revolution." This repeated the familiar formula of Brezhnev and Khrushchev before him—except that the second half of the usual formula (the determination to block the "export of counterrevolution") was not repeated. The other shoe didn't drop. The sharp-eyed Stephen Sestanovich, who wrote his *Washington Post* article a year later on the new trend in Soviet thinking, noticed also that the official May Day slogans for 1983 omitted the traditional list of Soviet Third World clients to whom the party usually swore undying affection and loyalty. Sestanovich was convinced that the Soviets were "feeling the pinch" of their Third World economic, political, and military commitments.[17] Expert Charles Wolf, Jr., summed up the findings of a 1984 RAND Corporation study:

In constant 1981 dollars, using official exchange rates, costs of the Soviet empire rose from about $18 billion in 1971 to $24 billion in 1976 and about $41 billion in 1980, an annual growth rate of nearly 9% for the decade. As a proportion of published CIA estimates of Soviet GNP, the costs of empire rose from about 1.1% in 1971 to about 2.7% at the end of the decade, averaging 1.6% over the period. As a ratio to Soviet military spending, they rose from 9% to 19% during the decade, averaging almost 13%.

The picture is even more striking if these data are expressed in rubles rather than dollars. . . . Expressed thus in rubles, which the Soviets use for the bulk of their economic activity, the costs of empire rose from 1.8% of Soviet ruble GNP in 1971 to 3.6% in 1976 and 6.6% in 1980, averaging 3.5% for the decade. As a ratio to Soviet military spending, in rubles the costs rose from 14% in 1971 to 28% in 1976 and 50% in 1980, averaging 28%. The annual average growth rate of the ruble costs of empire was more than 16% for the decade.[18]

Another factor deserves to be noted briefly: The competition with China in the Third World seems to have fizzled as well. The Chinese proved even less able to sustain a significant political, economic, or military involvement in Africa, for example, and this motivation for the Soviet commitment waned correspondingly. A 1985 congressional report summed up the decline of Chinese influence in the 1970s:

> Chinese military support for liberation in southern Africa was revealed as largely inconsequential. In the last half of the decade, Chinese arms sales to sub-Saharan Africa were just $140 million.

> By the end of the 1970s, the Sino-Soviet competition in Africa was nearly over. Beijing could not match Soviet arms shipments to the region, and China's economic aid programs declined sharply after a $400 million credit was extended for the construction of the Tanzania/Zambia Railroad. Chinese economic aid of $2.445 billion to sub-Saharan Africa in the two decades from 1959 to 1979 was double that of the Soviet Union. But by 1979, Chinese aid to sub-Saharan Africa was a mere $40 million a year, while the USSR and Eastern Europe extended $185 million. USSR, too, had reduced its economic aid and began to rely increasingly on military and security ties to African states for influence. In turn, Africa turned to the West for large-scale aid and occasionally to China for lower cost projects in light industry and agriculture.[19]

THE COMING OF GORBACHEV

Andropov died of kidney disease in February 1984. The mystery of what kind of ruler he would have been if he had dominated the scene for several more years will never be solved. He might well have launched himself down the path that his protégé Gorbachev pursued, though probably in a more controlled fashion. My guess is that he would have pulled back more brutally when the party's grip on power became directly threatened. Perhaps Andropov could have squared the circle of combining political control from the top and more enthusiastic voluntary popular participation. If the West's faith in the autonomy of human nature has any validity, however, the experiment would have been doomed, just as Gorbachev's was.

In any case, when Andropov died, the old guard was not quite ready to yield power. By then, Mikhail Gorbachev was the leading candidate of the younger generation, but his generation had to wait a little longer, for the old guard picked Konstantin Chernenko as the next general secretary. Chernenko had been Brezhnev's office manager and flunky; he was not a major figure in his own right but a placeholder and intellectual cipher. (I had taken many pictures of Brezhnev with my Pocket Instamatic during my travels with Nixon, Ford, and Kissinger. Years later, as I looked at the photos, I spotted Chernenko in some of them. But no one had bothered to introduce him to us or had taken him seriously in our presence.) Chernenko's health was so poor on his accession that after Vice President George Bush met him at Andropov's funeral, Bush cracked to the U.S. embassy staff on his departure from Moscow: "See you again, same time, next year!"[20]

Bush was right: The Chernenko interlude postponed the moment of generational change by little more than another year. During the several years of successive decrepit leaders, all the Soviet Union's problems had festered. Its economy stagnated and fell further behind the West; the war in Afghanistan stalemated; East-West relations drifted. Chernenko was frequently ill, and the young aspirant Gorbachev was often asked to preside at Politburo meetings. When Chernenko died, the old-timers had run out their string, and Gorbachev was the natural successor. He was named general secretary on March 11, 1985.

The sudden emergence of a young, energetic, and sophisticated leader had the effect in the West of a glass of cold water in the face—exhilarating, but a bit of a shock. Vice President Bush and Secretary of State Shultz, in Moscow for the third funeral in two and a half years, came away strongly impressed by the man's self-assurance. "He performs like a person who has been in charge for a while," Shultz told journalist Don Oberdorfer, "not like a person who is just taking charge."[21]

The shock effect was magnified by the fact that there was nothing particularly benign about his initial moves. What we seemed to be dealing with was a more vigorous—and therefore tougher—generation of Soviet opponents. "Comrades, this man has a nice smile, but he's got iron teeth," Andrei Gromyko is reported to have said, endorsing him before the Politburo.[22] It is not likely that Gromyko or the other Politburo heavies, old or young, chose him with an expectation that he would do anything other than reinvigorate the Soviet system in order to assure its effectiveness at home and abroad. His record as a longtime party loyalist and careerist, with close and extensive KGB connections, gave little reason to suspect he was a closet revolutionary.[23] And probably he was not.

Gorbachev's first moves in domestic policy were not particularly imaginative or even reformist. Before he developed *perestroika*, he experimented for a year and a half with *uskorenniye* ("acceleration"), which was a clumsy attempt to drive the existing system harder. There was a crackdown on alcohol use (which earned him the resentment of the workers for whom alcohol was a respite from the grimness of Soviet life); there was a reemphasis on discipline (including even a celebration of Stalin's Stakhanovite "shock-worker" campaign) and a reliance on other hortatory measures. Since quality control was known to be a serious weakness of Soviet manufacturing, Gorbachev responded in classic Soviet fashion: He created a new bureaucracy to supervise the quality of production in the rest of the bureaucracy. This just brought Soviet industry to a virtual halt for a few months until managers and local party bosses figured out how to circumvent the new superagency.

In the political realm, there was no perceived letup in human rights abuses or emigration restrictions for the first two years.[24] A crackdown on the black market led to new police measures. Dissident Anatolii Marchenko died in prison in December 1986. There was no sign of a willingness to abridge the Communist party's monopoly of power, enshrined in Brezhnev's 1977 Constitution.

Nor did Gorbachev's early steps in foreign policy contain any pleasant surprises. In his inaugural speech to the central committee, he spoke in conventional terms: "The Soviet Union has always supported the people's struggle for liberation from colonial oppression. Today our sympathies are on the side of the countries of Asia, Africa and Latin America that are following a path of strengthening independence and social renovation."[25]

As Gorbachev shook hands with or conferred with dozens of visiting world leaders at the Chernenko funeral (including Bush and Shultz), the Soviet press treatment of some of his Third World encounters was revealing. Nicaraguan president Daniel Ortega received special attention, as did the Ethiopian strongman Mengistu Haile Merriam. At Andropov's funeral the year before, Ortega had received less favorable treatment, and the Ethiopian had not been received at all.[26] TASS reported that Ortega and Gorbachev both "condemned resolutely" the American policy of interference in Central America, which was creating "a dangerous seat of tension there."[27] A month later, another TASS statement on Nicaragua condemned "imperialist diktat" and the U.S. policy of "aggression and intervention."[28] Cuban defense minister Raúl Castro was greeted warmly by Gorbachev at the funeral and also spent time, presumably not only for condolences, with the Soviet defense minister and other senior Soviet officials.

The most dramatic encounter at the Chernenko funeral, however, was Gorbachev's brief but menacing conversation with Pakistan's president Zia ul-Haq, whose country was the prime sanctuary and funnel of arms for the anti-Soviet Afghan guerrillas. Gorbachev and Gromyko gave Zia an earful, according to TASS, about the "aggressive actions" being conducted from Pakistani territory, which "cannot but affect in the most negative way Soviet-Pakistani relations." A signal was sent to us as well, not only about Afghanistan but about Central America. Soviet sources leaked pointedly to Dusko Doder of the *Washington Post* that Moscow was considering "unspecified actions" against Pakistan if President Reagan "continues his military pressure on Nicaragua." U.S. military action against Nicaragua would "provoke a serious effort to topple the Zia government," Doder was warned.[29] The threatening words to Zia were accompanied by a step-up of Soviet military operations inside Afghanistan and along the Pakistani border in the attempt to cut off the flow of weapons to the mujahedin. Similarly, Daniel Ortega returned to Moscow at the end of April for more extensive talks with the new Soviet leadership and further proffers of Soviet moral, political, economic, and military support.

Thus, Gorbachev's initial moves showed no particular promise for an improvement of East-West relations. Nor can it be said that the Reagan administration's hopes to alter Soviet behavior showed any sign of being borne out. The initial Soviet reaction to the Reagan Doctrine was one of indignation, not capitulation.

Reagan corresponded with Gorbachev throughout 1985, suggesting a summit meeting (which took place later that year in Geneva). Reagan's letters raised the issue of the conflicts in the Third World, complaining of Soviet policies in Central America and elsewhere. Gorbachev replied testily in June:

> [W]ith regard to third world countries, we impose neither our ideology, nor our social system on anybody. And do not ascribe to us what does not exist. If the question is to be raised without diplomatic contrivances as to who contributes to the international law and order and who acts in a different direction, then it appears that it is precisely the U.S. that turns out to be on the side of the groupings working against legitimate govern-

ments. And what about direct pressure on the governments whose policy does not suit the U.S.? There are enough examples of both on various continents. . . .[30]

The subject of regional conflicts came up, briefly, at the Geneva summit. As Gorbachev described it afterward in his November 21 news conference, he had rejected the president's tendency to see the "hand of Moscow" in every conflict. The two sides should work together and, above all, refrain from interfering in the internal affairs of other states. He took a dig at Western policies on the Third World debt problem. The Soviet leader was rather patronizing:

> Tension, conflicts in some regions, even wars between various states in some part of the world or another, have their roots both in the past and in the current socio-economic conditions of those countries and regions. To present the whole thing as if these contradiction knots have been born of the rivalry between East and West is not only erroneous but also extremely dangerous. I said this to the President and the American delegation.
>
> If today, for example, Mexico, Brazil and several other states are unable to pay not only their debts but even the interest on those debts, one can imagine what processes are going on in those countries. The situation may become strained and lead to an explosion. Will they then again talk about the "hand of Moscow"? But you simply cannot come out with such judgments on such issues in so irresponsible a manner before the entire world. These banalities still occur in some places, but they are inadmissible, particularly at meetings such as the present one. . . .[31]

Reagan wrote Gorbachev after Geneva, reiterating the importance of the regional conflicts. The president expressed continuing concern with Soviet policies but offered American cooperation to promote solutions, especially one that would include Soviet withdrawal from Afghanistan:

> Regarding another key issue we discussed, that of regional conflicts, I can assure you that the United States does not believe that the Soviet Union is the cause of all the world's ills. We do believe, however, that your country has exploited and worsened local tensions and conflicts by militarizing them and, indeed, intervening directly and indirectly in struggles arising out of local causes. While we both will doubtless continue to support

our friends, we must find a way to do so without use of armed force. This is the crux of the point I tried to make.

One of the most significant steps in lowering tensions in the world—and tensions in U.S.-Soviet relations—would be a decision on your part to withdraw your forces from Afghanistan. I gave careful attention to your comments on this issue at Geneva and am encouraged by your statement that you feel political reconciliation is possible.

I want you to know that I am prepared to cooperate in any reasonable way to facilitate such a withdrawal and that I understand that it must be done in a manner which does not damage Soviet security. [32]

This provoked an even angrier response from Gorbachev on Christmas Eve, 1985, essentially accusing the president of promoting terrorism:

Let us see the world as it is. Both of us offer such assistance. Why apply a double standard here that Soviet aid is a source of tension and American assistance is good will? Better to be guided by objective criteria. The Soviet Union will help lawful governments which ask us for aid because they have been and are being subjected to external armed interference. But the U.S., and such are the facts, inspires action against governments and arms anti-social, and in essence, terrorist groups. Looking at the matter objectively, it is specifically such external interference which creates regional tension and conflict situations. Were there no such activities, I am sure tensions would be reduced and the prospects for political settlements will become much better and more realistic.

Unfortunately, developments are proceeding in another direction. Take for example, the unprecedented pressure and terror to which the government of Nicaragua, which has been lawfully elected, has been subjected. I will be frank—the things the U.S. has done lately make us wary. It seems that just now a shift [in U.S. policies] is exacerbating regional problems. Such an approach does not facilitate finding a common language and complicates the search for political solutions.

With regard to Afghanistan, one gets the impression that the United States side intentionally fails to notice the open door leading to a political settlement. [33]

There was a constant stream of alarmed articles in 1986 in the authoritative foreign ministry journal *International Affairs* denouncing what was called American "neoglobalism." (The disparaging epithet seems to have been helpfully suggested first by Anthony Lewis of the *New York Times.*)[34] The United States had committed open aggression in Lebanon and Grenada and was fostering aggression elsewhere, wrote one analyst; U.S. reengagement in regional conflicts reflected a new strategy of "indirect aggression or tactics of 'undeclared wars' " in furtherance of Washington's "hegemonistic plans."[35] The new doctrine of interventionism enunciated by George Shultz was denounced by another writer as "blatant chauvinism" and as a "whitewash [of] counterrevolution."[36] The Soviet Union was duty bound to oppose the new "imperialist policy of brute force and diktat" that the Reagan Doctrine represented, wrote a third.[37] It was a "doctrine of international brigandage," wrote a fourth.[38]

In March 1986, when the United States was in the midst of a confrontation with Libya in the Gulf of Sidra, Gorbachev, in a dinner speech in honor of the president of Algeria, denounced U.S. policy as showing the "imperial bandit face of neoglobalist policy." Neoglobalism, he said, meant "complete disregard for the commonly recognized norms of international relations, encroachment on the sovereignty of states and the . . . futile attempt to deny the peoples the right to organize their lives as they see fit."[39] After the U.S. bombing of Libya in April 1986 (in response to blatant Libyan involvement in terrorist attacks on Americans), the Soviets canceled a meeting at which Shultz and Shevardnadze were to choose a date for the next summit. That the Soviet Union would continue to invest so much prestige in one of the most unsavory of its clients was not a good omen.

Yet beneath all the intemperate language there was a defensiveness and a plaintive tone—the protestation (in Gorbachev's dinner remarks) that "we will never consent to difficulties faced by the peoples on the path of progress being used by external forces for exploiting and reactionary goals. . . ."[40] The Reagan Doctrine's more offensive posture in Third World conflicts was having an impact. A Warsaw Pact meeting in June 1986 reaffirmed the principle of noninterference in countries' internal affairs as "today . . . more imperative than ever before."[41] The shoe was now on the other foot, and it was hurting.

Reality was bound to impose itself. Despite the anti-imperialist fulminations, the first flush of a new leadership in office in fact provided a congenial atmosphere for the intellectual ferment that had already become fairly intense under Andropov. Moreover, as Gorbachev undertook more systematic economic reforms, he decided he needed the intelligentsia as allies against the entrenched party and economic bureaucrats. Thus, he introduced *glasnost* ("disclosure," or "openness"), which en-

couraged the nation's journalists and intellectuals to criticize and pub-
licize more vigorously the flaws of the existing system, including foreign
policy. The intellectuals, being the most fickle of all classes in any society,
turned on him a few years later for not going fast enough, and in the
end their devastating exposure of the system's evils contributed mightily
to its loss of legitimacy and its collapse.

In foreign affairs, however, the rethinking had a more immediate and
fruitful evolution. The intellectual experts on foreign policy—the *insti-
tutchiki*, the reform-minded journalists and commentators—were unleashed. Gorbachev mobilized them and over the course of a year
developed the main lines of a new foreign policy, which was formally
unveiled at the Twenty-seventh Party Congress in February 1986. "New
political thinking" was the label proudly attached to it, and it became
the foreign policy counterpart of economic *perestroika*.

Three principal factors were at work. One was the obvious need to
concentrate on the internal crisis. In an interview in *Time* in the fall of
1985, Gorbachev said it openly: "[S]omebody said that foreign policy is
a continuation of domestic policy. If that is so, then I ask you to ponder
one thing: If we in the Soviet Union are setting ourselves such truly
grandiose plans in the domestic sphere, then what are the external conditions that we need to be able to fulfill those domestic plans?"[42] Yevgenii
Primakov, who by then had become a Gorbachev adviser, wrote in *Pravda*
in 1987: "The organic link between our country's domestic and foreign
policy has perhaps never before been as clear as it is now." Primakov
cited the country's poor economic performance in the preceding decade,
with the gap between American and Soviet national incomes increasing
instead of decreasing.[43]

Second, it followed from this that the Soviet Union needed a fundamental improvement of relations with the West. "Peaceful coexistence," said Primakov in the same article, could no longer be treated as
just a tactic to win temporary respites from Western pressure. Moscow
needed to shift the East-West competition away from the military to the
political realm:

Until comparatively recently we regarded peaceful coexistence as a breathing space interrupted by those who are trying for the umpteenth time to
stifle the first country of victorious socialism. That situation also persistently
dictated the need to once more increase combat capability as the only
practical way of ensuring the country's security.

Today such assessments and interpretations are clearly inadequate and inaccurate. Even though the improvement of the Soviet Union's defense capability is as important as ever, political means of ensuring its security are now coming to the fore.[44]

While Primakov attributed the change to the dangers of thermonuclear war, it was also, as Stephen Sestanovich later wrote, a strategy for cutting the costs of competing. Primakov was saying, in effect (in Sestanovich's words), that it was time for the Soviets to overcome their "inordinate fear of capitalism"—a paradoxical recommendation, since at the same time they were denouncing its new "bandit face."[45] But the Soviet Union simply had no choice.

The third factor was the growing disillusionment with the whole enterprise of revolution. This was demonstrated in February 1987 when Ali Salim Al-Beidh, South Yemeni Socialist party leader, visited Gorbachev and was treated to a stunning public lecture on the shortcomings of revolutions both in the Third World and at home. The official announcement reported:

> The talks dealt with the experience of revolutionary struggle, including both negative and positive experience, the general principles of revolution and mostly with the fact that a correct policy is a policy that takes careful account of the realities. . . . The basic flaw of all revolutions was that they advanced tasks that could not be fulfilled at a given moment, which inevitably led to . . . discrepancy between words and actions.[46]

The Soviets came up with an elaborate new intellectual construct, with appropriate quotations from Marx and Lenin to back it up, but the essence of the matter was the virtual dismantling of much of the traditional ideology. Where Brezhnev and all his predecessors had argued emphatically that "peaceful coexistence" applied only to relations among states and not to the (intensified) ideological struggle, the new party program, approved by the Twenty-seventh Party Congress in 1986, dropped the idea. "[W]e deemed it no longer possible," Gorbachev wrote later, "to retain in it the definition of peaceful coexistence of states with different social systems as a 'specific form of class struggle.' "[47] The notion of a permanent struggle underlying all political relations was thus simply abandoned; in the nuclear age such a doctrine of perpetual conflict was now said to be inappropriate.

Instead of expectations about the imminent "crisis of capitalism," there were realistic assessments of its durability. Instead of an "international socialist division of labor" (reflecting the autarky of the socialist bloc and its pretensions of economic superiority), global "interdependence" was now the watchword—the common interest of all nations in trade and cooperation. Gorbachev now proposed a "comprehensive system of international security," which included a host of conciliatory themes: nuclear and conventional arms reduction; a new Soviet military doctrine that was said to be only "defensive"; a willingness to help settle regional conflicts; a new devotion to the United Nations; and expanded international cooperation on economic, environmental, and humanitarian concerns.[48]

The most bourgeois of notions, "interdependence" is a Wilsonian vision of fundamental harmony, of a Kantian world in which nations adhere to international norms of behavior that reflect the common aspirations and interests of mankind. "Common human values" was a favorite Gorbachev phrase. Despite all the attempts to give it a proper Leninist pedigree (Brest-Litovsk and all that), there is no honest way to describe it except as the negation of the Marxist-Leninist philosophy of the mortal struggle between two systems, of the violent revolutionary triumph of socialism over imperialism.

I was cynical about these rhetorical changes at the time. I had helped write dozens of speeches for Henry Kissinger in the mid-1970s about the virtues of "interdependence." It had become a cliché. At that earlier time, in the wake of the OPEC oil price gouge and the beginnings of the "North-South dialogue," the United States was arguing self-interestedly—but not only self-interestedly—that the Third World could never gain by impoverishing the industrialized West. The world economy had grown too interdependent for even the oil producers to think that they could gain in this manner in the long run. Third World radicals, of course, rejected the idea of interdependence as a self-serving recipe for perpetuating Western economic dominance; they egged on the oil producers as a kind of (unlikely) vanguard of Third World ascendancy.

For the Soviets now to adopt the Western view that the Third World—and the Second and the First—were really, after all, part of one big happy global family was, to me, too good to be true. I assumed the Soviets were simply reciting to Americans what we wanted to hear, to dull our reactions (just as the Soviet campaign against the horrors of nuclear war usually had the self-serving strategic purpose of stirring up Western public opinion against U.S. or NATO defense programs). The fine hand of Anatolii Dobrynin, the wily former ambassador to the United States, was evident in some of the formulations.[49]

There was much to be skeptical about in the new Soviet policy. Gorbachev still pressed his propaganda campaign for the denuclearization of Europe, undermining NATO defense strategy; his theme of a "common European home" called into question the legitimacy of the American presence on the Continent. Soviet officials crowed that they were depriving the West of the "enemy image," thereby softening Western positions. Gorbachev's claims of a "defensive" military doctrine were not substantiated in any way by Soviet military budgets or dispositions until two or three years after the pronouncements. As for the Third World, as late as the end of 1987, I gave a talk at a seminar in Washington pointing out that the Gorbachev record was decidedly mixed: He was still clinging to and arming unsavory radical clients in the Middle East like Syria, Libya, and the PLO; the self-serving quality of other moves in the direction of Israel and Arab moderates also seemed too obvious.[50]

It was, ironically, Anthony Dolan, Reagan's chief conservative ideologist and speechwriter, who eventually persuaded me that the rhetorical changes meant something. To Tony, ideas counted, and rhetoric in its Aristotelian sense went to the heart of human motivations. As Tony, champion of the New Right, taught me, ideology was what galvanized a movement; it was the moral bond between a leader and his followers. In the Soviet system, it was the marching order for the troops—the army of lower-level officials—and for the population that the party had the job of continually mobilizing. A change in the ideology—especially the wholesale dumping of the idea of mortal struggle with the West—sent an unmistakable new signal to the cadres and was not easily reversible. Indeed, Yegor Ligachev, Gorbachev's chief hard-line challenger in 1987–88, complained that the abandonment of the philosophy was sowing confusion: "We proceed from the class nature of international relations. Any other formulation of the issue only introduces confusion into the thinking of Soviet people and our friends abroad."[51]

Thus, to Dolan, Gorbachev's new line had to be more than a tactic. Tony—who had continually berated me for my association with the ill-fated "détente" policy of the 1970s—was now on my left, arguing over many a friendly lunch that I should take Gorbachev more seriously. As time went on, it was clear that Tony's thinking paralleled Reagan's.

The degree to which ideology was being challenged, at least in the intellectual circles around Gorbachev, was brought home to me most dramatically a few years later. In July 1989, a conference was held in Moscow commemorating the bicentenary of the French Revolution. The smug French, who should have been smart enough to avoid any association of their revolution with the Soviets' in the first place, were undoubtedly jolted to hear Aleksandr Yakovlev, perhaps Gorbachev's closest intellectual adviser, condemn both:

> When today we are tortured by confusion about how the country and the Leninist party could have accepted the dictatorship of mediocrity and tolerated the Stalin years and rivers of innocent blood, we cannot fail to see that the reasons which provided fertile ground for authoritarianism and despotism included an unhealthy faith in the possibility of expediting sociohistoric development, and an idealization of revolutionary violence going back to the middle of the 19th century and the very roots of the European revolutionary tradition.[52]

A central element of the new Gorbachev foreign policy, just as of the new domestic policy, was a critique of Soviet history. The rewriting of history was an old Soviet practice; now it was being done honestly. Not only scholars but also senior leaders—especially Foreign Minister Shevardnadze—began to acknowledge that past leaders like Stalin and Brezhnev had made major blunders; Soviet foreign policy had created massive problems for the Soviet state, and those leaders had to bear a substantial share of responsibility for the Cold War and for the breakdown of "détente" in the 1970s.

In a July 4, 1987, speech, Shevardnadze blasted a Soviet foreign policy that had been "out of touch with the fundamental vital interests of the country."[53] Gorbachev, in his November 2, 1987, speech on the seventieth anniversary of the Bolshevik Revolution, spoke in general terms of "errors," of failing to make use of "opportunities opening up," of reactions to Western actions that were "not always adequate."[54] These first acknowledgments were unspecific and sometimes euphemistic, but more was to come.

One of the first detailed critiques was by Vyacheslav Dashichev, a historian and Europeanist at the Institute for the Study of the Economics of the World Socialist System, in the liberal weekly newspaper *Literaturnaya Gazeta* (edited by Fyodor Burlatskii) in May 1988. Dashichev scathingly described the historic "miscalculations and incompetent approach of the Brezhnev leadership" that had provoked the West into responding:

[A]s the West saw it, the Soviet leadership was actively exploiting détente to build up its own military forces, seeking military parity with the United States and in general with all the opposing powers—a fact without historical precedent. The United States, paralyzed by the Vietnam catastrophe, reacted sensitively to the expansion of Soviet influence in Africa, the Near East, and other regions.

All this was interpreted in the West as a further increase in the Soviet threat. The extreme right-wing political circles that came to power in the United States and the other NATO countries turned sharply away from détente toward confrontation. The Soviet Union found itself faced with unprecedented new pressure from imperialism. . . .

It is our conviction that the crisis was caused chiefly by the miscalculations and incompetent approach of the Brezhnev leadership toward the resolution of foreign policy tasks. . . . Though we were politically, militarily (via weapons supplies and advisers), and diplomatically involved in regional conflicts, we disregarded their influence on the relaxation of tension between the USSR and the West and on their entire system of relationships. [55]

Dashichev continued his critique in a June 1988 interview. Brezhnev's aggressive campaign in the Third World succeeded in driving all the world's other major powers into a coalition against the USSR, he wrote. The West built up its military programs (including the Strategic Defense Initiative), and the Soviets were bankrupted in the attempt to follow suit:

[W]e launched an offensive against imperialism's positions in the Third World in the mid-seventies. We attempted to expand the sphere of socialism's influence to various developing countries which, I believe, were totally unprepared to adopt socialism. And what came of all this? A sharp clash of political contradictions with the Western powers (and that was not all—even China opposed our actions in the Third World). Détente was derailed, and we came up against a new and unprecedented explosion of the arms race.

The United States wanted to use it to push us back against a wall, to corner us, to create economic, social, and political difficulties. It adopted the form of the SDI and the inflation of military budgets beyond belief, and we naturally tried to follow suit. This proved that our foreign policy was not cost-effective. In other words, our foreign policy actions made us shoulder the steadily growing burden of military expenditures and moral costs.[56]

Shevardnadze continued the reassessment with an important address to a meeting at the Foreign Ministry on July 25, 1988. He recited a list of past Soviet mistakes, which he blamed on the previous conspiratorial style of government, which had now given way to *glasnost*:

> Serious damage was inflicted on [Soviet diplomacy] and by implication, to the country, by administrative-command methods, disregard of special, professional knowledge, and an undemocratic secretive willful style of taking decisions affecting millions of people, the priority of military over political means of countering imperialism, and the inability to see through its manoeuvering to draw us into an arms race fraught with economic attrition for the USSR.

Shevardnadze listed as mistakes not only the costly arms race but also the feud with China, the long-standing Soviet underestimation of the European Community, the 1983–84 walkout from the Geneva arms talks after NATO INF deployments, and the Soviet decision in 1977 to deploy SS-20 INF missiles in the first place. He, like Dashichev, repudiated the traditional Soviet defense doctrine that the USSR had to be as strong as any possible coalition against it (which had, of course, magnified the insecurity of all individual countries near the Soviet periphery).[57]

REASSESSMENT OF THE THIRD WORLD

One of the surprising features of Gorbachev's report to the Twenty-seventh Party Congress in February 1986 was the minimal attention it had devoted to Third World clients, in contrast to all the Brezhnev reports. It contained no separate section on the Third World and made scarcely any mention of individual allies or friends—except Afghanistan, which was described, in striking terms, as a "bleeding wound." The party program adopted by the Congress devoted only one brief paragraph to the "socialist-orientated" countries.[58] The tone and vocabulary with which the Third World was discussed were starkly different than before. The exuberance, the optimism about the course of history, were all gone. The Gorbachev report contained the familiar disavowal of the "export of revolution"—and also followed Andropov in omitting or downplaying the traditional duty to fight "counterrevolution" (which was buried in a section on counterterrorism). Third World friends were no longer viewed as such an important revolutionary force or as such a factor in the demise of capitalism. Instead of an internationalist duty to stand by them in their liberation struggle, there was a feeble expression of "profound sympathy for their aspirations."

The new policy put more emphasis on those developing countries that were traveling the capitalist road than on Brezhnev's "Marxist-Leninist Vanguard Parties." There was still an opportunistic, Khrushchev-style hope that these countries might be weaned away from the West—but without the Khrushchev-era illusions about their "socialist" character. Classical foreign policy calculations about state relations were supplanting ideological theories. The new party program said wistfully:

> [T]here are also real grounds for cooperation with young states that are traveling the capitalist road. These grounds include a common interest in the preservation of peace, the strengthening of international security, and the termination of the arms race. They include the sharpening contradiction between the interests of the peoples and the imperialist policy of diktat and expansion. They include the understanding by the young states of the fact that political and economic ties with the Soviet Union facilitate the strengthening of their independence.[59]

Gorbachev accordingly put renewed stress on relations with India, which he visited in November 1986. Major military and economic cooperation agreements were signed. In October 1986, Shevardnadze visited Mexico, and the Mexican foreign minister, Bernardo Sepulveda (who drove the Reagan administration crazy over Central America), received a lavish reception in Moscow in May 1987. Shevardnadze visited Brazil, Argentina, and Uruguay in September 1987. Moscow began wooing moderate Arabs that it had traditionally shunned—Saudi Arabia, Oman, and the United Arab Emirates—and strived to restore economic relations with Egypt, rescheduling a large tranche of Egypt's debt.[60]

Disillusionment with Third World involvement was only growing, however, stimulated by the revelations of *glasnost*. Soviet foreign-aid projects in the Third World were now the subject of media exposés. Instead of the traditional encomiums to momumental aid projects and fraternal relations, the Soviet media told horror stories of waste, fraud, and corruption. Steel mills had been built without first determining where the necessary raw materials could be obtained; canneries were built in locations where, it turned out, the migrating tuna appeared offshore only every three years. A Soviet-built oil pipeline was dedicated in a grand ceremony while an oil truck hidden nearby pumped oil into it to provide a flow—since the line had not been completed on schedule. Nepotism, bribery, and cronyism were rife in the selection of the personnel who received the much-sought-after plum of the chance to work abroad.[61] The same breast-beating and self-criticism that Americans had gone through with *The Ugly American* thirty years before was now a staple of Soviet public discourse.

The most favored among the traditional clients continued to receive enormous amounts of aid. According to U.S. estimates, Soviet military and economic aid from 1979 to 1987 to Vietnam and Cambodia totaled nearly $29 billion; to Afghanistan, nearly $9 billion; to Angola, over $8 billion (1975–1987); and to Nicaragua, over $3 billion. From 1983 to 1987, Cuba received nearly $11 billion, not counting over $22 billion in price subsidies on oil and sugar.[62] This generosity to Stalinist clients continued to pose problems for U.S. foreign policy and to play into the hands of those (like me) who were still skeptical of Gorbachev's foreign policy. But these aid commitments now became controversial at home. Traditional Communists and nationalists valued these allies and resisted the idea of leaving them in the lurch. (Notions of the Soviet Union's "credibility" as a great power were bandied about—not wrongly.) But others challenged the costs of sustaining these pathetically performing radical deadbeats—costs that included not only money but problems in relations with the West.

Izvestia in March 1990 gleefully published a breakdown of the 80-billion-ruble ($137.6 billion) foreign debt owed to the USSR: Half was owed by "socialist countries"—the likes of Cuba, Mongolia, Vietnam, North Korea, and the East Europeans. The other half was owed by other developing countries, and the bulk of that by losers like Syria, Iraq, Afghanistan, Ethiopia, Algeria, Angola, South and North Yemen, Libya, and Nicaragua (pluss49India and Egypt).[63]

Reformist writers argued that humanitarian objectives should replace Cold War ideological objectives in the Soviet foreign aid program and that the preoccupation with military aid was a disgrace.[64] Others questioned the costs and benefits of Soviet arms transfers.[65] Altogether it was a debate familiar to the American scene in the same period, except that in the Soviet Union it became part of a debate about a much more serious economic crisis. The eminent reform economist Nikolai Shmelëv addressed the Soviet Parliament in June 1989 and complained of the billions of rubles squandered in faraway places like Latin America: "[B]afflingly, we spend a considerable proportion of this sum on, for instance, paying four times the going rate for Cuban sugar (compared with the world price), and we pay in hard currency. This source alone would be enough to keep the consumer market in balance for the few years we need in order to turn ourselves around somehow and really embark on the road of reform."[66]

Andrei Kozyrev, later Yeltsin's foreign minister, was an obscure crew-cut diplomat in his thirties burrowing away in the Soviet Foreign Ministry on UN affairs. In the fall of 1988 he wrote an article in the ministry journal bitterly attacking the Third World policies inherited from Brezhnev. The radical regimes that Brezhnev had collected as clients turned out to be dictatorial and worthless and wasted vast amounts of Soviet aid, Kozyrev argued. Like Dashichev, he lamented that Moscow's support for them had increased international tensions and harmed relations with the West. All together, the losses were "enormous"—and not only financial:

> [P]rofiting by foreign assistance and wielding "arch-leftist" anti-imperialist rhetoric, some regimes in those countries were in no rush to tackle the problems of hunger or backwardness, relying on the force of arms to pursue domestic or external policies, thus instilling no faith in the "progressive non-capitalist" path of development. Their attempts to run the economy by administrative-system methods, reliance on military aid from abroad, and neglect for democratic freedoms necessarily resulted in the polarization of political forces. Virtually all those regimes are involved in protracted and bloody conflicts with their opposition. . . .
>
> Unfortunately, there are no data concerning the price paid by the Soviet Union for providing assistance to those countries. . . . Furthermore, it is important to stress that aid itself is only the tip of the iceberg. Our direct or indirect entanglement in regional conflicts brings about enormous losses, exacerbating overall international tensions, justifying the arms race and hampering mutually beneficial economic ties with the West.[67]

Andrei Kolosov, identified as a "political analyst," wrote a similar piece later in the same journal, stepping up the official criticism of Soviet clients and the policy of supporting them. (I later heard that this was the nom de plume of an aide to Deputy Foreign Minister Vladimir Petrovsky.) In the eagerness to plant the "banner of anti-imperialism," he wrote, Moscow had militarized these relationships and only pushed these regimes—and the Soviet Union itself—further into the miasma of tyranny, bankruptcy, and conflict:

[W]e waged an outright war in Afghanistan, we were deeply enmeshed in several acute regional conflicts (and we encouraged socialist developing countries to take part in them), and we promoted the creation of regimes in different parts of the world that tried, under the banner of anti-imperialism, to implement in their own conditions the administer-by-command model and therefore counted on us in everything. The specifics of these regimes, the militarist bent typical of our domestic and foreign policy, and the backwardness of the Soviet civilian economy that was strongly manifest even then made for the fact that military cooperation and arms deliveries were the heart of our relations with developing states "friendly" to us. Their militarisation only pushed them even farther into participation in conflicts and into authoritarian rule and worsened the situation in the economy that was rapidly falling apart as it was, as a result of the application of our scheme. The "allies" demanded more and more resources, became more deeply involved in conflicts, and increasingly strengthened in everyone's eyes the association between Soviet policy and instability, authoritarianism and economic failures.[68]

Afghanistan loomed large in the agonizing reappraisal. Gorbachev had bluntly told one of his hosts on a Canada visit in 1983 that Afghanistan was "a mistake."[69] When Reagan mentioned the subject to Gorbachev at their Geneva summit in November 1985, the latter seemed to distance himself from it. Reagan later recounted: "When I brought up the Soviet invasion of Afghanistan, Gorbachev responded that he had known nothing about it personally until he heard a radio broadcast, suggesting that it was a war he had no responsibility—and little enthusiasm—for."[70]

In his speech to the Twenty-seventh Party Congress on February 25, 1986, as mentioned, Gorbachev said that "counterrevolutionaries and imperialism have turned Afghanistan into a bleeding wound."[71]

By the time Soviet troops left Afghanistan in February 1989, after more than nine years of war, the officially admitted toll was over thirteen thousand Soviet dead, over thirty-five thousand wounded, and over three hundred missing in action. (The real toll may have been higher.) The economic cost was at least 60 billion rubles (nearly $100 billion at the official exchange rate). The Soviets dug deep into their reserves of gold and diamonds to finance the war.[72] The young journalist Artyom Borovik, who wrote candid articles covering the war for the magazine *Ogonëk*, described the domestic impact of Afghanistan in terms reminiscent of America in the 1960s, when the war "came home":

With a mere wave of Brezhnev's elderly hand they were thrown into a country where bribery, corruption, profiteering, and drugs were no less common than the long lines in Soviet stores. These diseases can be far more infectious and dangerous than hepatitis, particularly when they reach epidemic proportions. . . . It often seems to me that war and violence had crossed the border into our country.

In Afghanistan we bombed not only the detachments of rebels and their caravans, but our own ideals as well. With the war came the reevaluation of our moral and ethical values. In Afghanistan the policies of the government became utterly incompatible with the inherent morality of our nation. Things could not continue in the same vein. It is hardly coincidental that the ideas of *perestroika* took hold in 1985—the year the war reached its peak.[73]

Soviet press coverage in the age of *glasnost* stirred up popular discontent over the exemption from military service of the children of influential party members. Returning war veterans were bitter that they were not treated as heroes, like veterans of past wars; the press reported on atrocities committed by Soviet troops. There were anguishing stories of the veterans' problems of readjustment to civilian life. A demoralized military exhibited problems familiar to the Vietnam-era U.S. military; not only drug addiction but lack of discipline, sensitivity to public criticism, desertion, draft evasion—and a reluctance to get involved in any further military adventures.[74] Marshal Sergei Akhromeyev, Gorbachev's senior military adviser, conceded to American interviewers that Afghanistan had left "a scar on the body of our society."[75] The demoralization of the armed forces was a factor in their extraordinary passivity in 1989, when the Soviet empire crumbled in Eastern Europe. The prospect, at least for a time, was an "Afghanistan syndrome" in Soviet society that would discredit distant engagement—as was apparent in the 1990–91 Gulf crisis, when popular opinion expressed itself passionately against any military involvement.[76]

As Borovik indicated above, it was no accident that the reform impulse of *perestroika* took hold at the height of the Afghanistan ordeal: The system was discredited, far more profoundly than Vietnam affected the United States. To Andrei Sakharov—who had been sent into exile in Gorkii in 1980 because of his protests over the invasion—Afghanistan demonstrated "the danger posed to the world by a closed, totalitarian society."[77] And Sakharov's martyrdom itself turned into a kind of moral "bleeding wound." The American system, with its capacity for self-renewal, rebounded after Vietnam, drawing on its own moral resources and democratic resilience. Yes, there was a reaction against excessive secrecy in government and a struggle over accountability between Congress and the president. But in the USSR the very core of the system was held to blame—the arbitrariness of dictatorial rule, the party's monopoly of power, and the complete absence of accountability. The parliamentary commission of inquiry in 1989 condemned most of all the undemocratic manner in which such a decision could be made. The "Afghanistan syndrome" led to serious consideration of a Soviet version of our War Powers Resolution, requiring parliamentary approval for any future commitment of troops abroad.

But even more, it fueled the revulsion against the essence of the system itself. Many an autocracy has been discredited and undermined by failure in war. This one should be added to the list.

IMPACT OF THE WEST

This brings us to the question of what impact Western actions had on the transformation in Soviet policies, externally and internally. Claims that the Reagan and Bush administrations "won the Cold War" were a feature of recent presidential election campaigns. Others denied, on the contrary, that Western policies had anything to do with what transpired, attributing it to internal forces in Soviet society. Still others—count me among them—give credit to a variety of factors, internal and external.

Our main task here is to look at the question of Western impact on Soviet *foreign* policy. That impact is easier to trace, and less speculative, than the impact on the Soviet internal system. However, as Afghanistan indicates, this is not beyond the realm of possibility, either.

The conceptual changes in Soviet foreign policy, especially in the Third World, began essentially under Yurii Andropov. His skeptical remarks to the June 1983 plenum antedated Gorbachev's "new thinking"— and also the Reagan Doctrine. The first disillusionment with the Third World came, then, largely from the inherent weaknesses of socialist theories and real-world clients. The economic burden began to outweigh the political gains of Brezhnev's great adventures of the 1970s.

American policy, as it became bolder under Reagan, had, as we have seen, only an irritating effect on the Soviets at first. They protested about neoglobalism, yet often with a plaintive tone that expressed a certain nervousness. Andropov had told the June 1983 plenum that the risks of confrontation with the imperialists argued for caution. Yevgenii Primakov made the same point in an essay in June 1988, condemning such reckless tendencies as "Trotskyism" and "adventurism and ultra-revolutionary ideas," which would risk world war on behalf of Third World clients: "If mankind were drawn into an all-embracing thermonuclear catastrophe, none of the national or social liberation movements would have any value."[78]

The Reagan administration made the regional issues a more central topic of the U.S.-Soviet diplomatic agenda beginning in 1985. The White House was caught up in the enthusiasm of the Reagan Doctrine; Shultz at State had supplied much of the rationale for the doctrine in his San Francisco speech of February 1985. The litany of U.S. policy toward the USSR in those days was our four-part agenda—arms reduction, the regional conflicts, human rights, and economic and other bilateral relations. We argued—correctly—that the unhappy experience of the fate of "détente" in the 1970s showed that the U.S.-Soviet relationship could not survive on arms control alone if the political elements of the relationship were going sour.

The regional issues became part of my portfolio as head of policy planning at State. It was a classic subject for the policy planning staff—a topic of broad importance that cut across the different regional bureaus' lines of responsibility. The Soviet specialists, housed in the European bureau, were usually familiar with Soviet internal affairs, NATO matters, and arms control but usually had no special knowledge of the Middle East or Central America or southern Africa or Southeast Asia. The bureaus that handled those issues, in turn, were usually not intimately conversant with the Soviet angle. In my days with Kissinger I had been directly involved in his regional negotiations (especially the Middle East, Indochina, and southern Africa) as well as following closely the Soviet Union's policy in all these areas.

The regional dialogue with the Soviets proceeded on several levels. The issues came up at summits, whether Gorbachev liked it or not. The Soviets much preferred to focus on arms control, which offered them opportunities to agitate against Western defense policies, instead of the regional issues on which they were then on the defensive. Gorbachev once exploded at Shultz for trying to raise the regional issues—ironically, in view of Shultz's own discomfort with "linkage."[79] But they eventually stopped fighting it. At Geneva in November 1985, Reagan raised Afghanistan with Gorbachev with some passion, expressing particular indignation at photos he had seen of Afghan children maimed by Soviet bombs and mines—including wooden toys booby-trapped to explode.[80]

(The NSC staff and CIA tried in vain to get one of the toys in time for Reagan to show Gorbachev.)

The summit in Reykjavik in October 1986 was dominated by arms reduction, but even here Reagan raised the topic: "I brought up Afghanistan and the continuing Soviet subversion of Third World countries, to which he listened but did not respond."[81] A U.S.-Soviet working group stayed up all night at Reykjavik debating the non-arms-control issues; I led the discussion for the American side on the regional conflicts, with Primakov as my interlocutor. By then I had moved back to the National Security Council staff and was a deputy assistant to the president for national security affairs.

The regional topics also featured regularly in the frequent meetings between Shultz and Shevardnadze. Afghanistan tended to dominate, and it was in this channel that the United States received the first serious hints that Gorbachev had decided to withdraw. Experts' meetings were also arranged—that is, regular talks between our assistant secretaries of state in charge of particular regions (Latin America, East Asia, Africa, Middle East) and their counterparts from the Soviet Foreign Ministry. These produced boring meetings with the Soviets but panic within the State Department. The European bureau wanted new diplomatic initiatives in order to advance U.S.-Soviet relations, while the other regional bureaus were not eager to legitimize the Soviet role in their regions and did not want the European bureau bargaining away their chips. Assistant secretaries like Elliott Abrams and Paul Wolfowitz (Latin America and the Far East, respectively), who were suspicious of the Soviets, asked me what this was all about and wanted my help and mediation. While I was still at State, I was almost always able to dissuade Shultz from badly thought out diplomatic overtures in this forum.

Finally, there were the so-called super-regional talks covering all the issues. These were led on our side by Michael Armacost, under secretary of state for political affairs (the third-ranking official at State), accompanied by me. Armacost, a distinguished career diplomat with extensive experience dealing with East Asia and the developing world, was a pivotal figure in the department on these issues because of his expertise and his rank, which gave him an overview of our policy. I accompanied him because at the NSC I had the same kind of overview portfolio as I had had at State and I was the logical one to represent the NSC. Our Soviet counterparts were at the deputy foreign minister level—first Anatolii Adamishin, a soft-spoken and capable professional (of reformist inclinations) who visited Washington in August 1986, and then the formidable Yulii M. Vorontsov, whom we met in Moscow in March 1987, in Geneva in November 1987, and in Moscow again in August-September 1988.

Yulii Vorontsov, as we shall see in later chapters, usually had something noteworthy to present—either a concession or a threat—which made our conversations with him always interesting. He was a tough personality who had served in Washington as Dobrynin's deputy during the Kissinger era. In the era of "new thinking" he combined the smoothness and polish of the Gorbachev generation with some of the bullying qualities of the old. He could be charming but was no friend of the West. On his Mideast travels he spread disinformation about U.S. policies to undermine our position. He acted as proconsul in Afghanistan when Soviet troops were leaving and deserves a Stalin Prize for helping stiffen the Kabul regime's morale during that difficult time. He won the plums of ambassador to the UN, where he served creditably during the 1990–91 Gulf crisis, and then ambassador to Washington. When Yeltsin replaced Gorbachev and kept Vorontsov on, I believe it was a sop to the hard-liners still in the system (who once attempted to make him foreign minister in place of the dovish Kozyrev).

It took a few years for the regional dialogue to bear fruit. As I had predicted to Shultz in August 1984, the discussions were a useful forum for communicating our positions and would become a valuable channel for real bargaining once conditions on the ground ripened. It vindicated Reagan and Shultz's desire in 1985 to have a diplomatic track—especially when we were successfully marshaling leverage on the ground. Conservative fears of sellout were not borne out by anything that I witnessed in these channels. If the Reagan policy deserves credit for helping end these conflicts in ways satisfactory to American interests, part of the credit must go to the diplomatic track—to the willingness to settle once a Soviet negotiating partner displayed a serious willingness to do so as well.

In December 1988, George Kennan was asked in a television interview how much American and Western policies could claim to have caused the changes in the Soviet Union. "Only marginally," he replied, going on to say that the main cause of the Soviet transformation was "the realization on the part of many intelligent people in the Soviet Union in these recent years of the fact that the whole system was going down hill, that it was no longer competitive. . . ."[82] While Kennan was focusing on the Soviets' internal changes, it is nonetheless an odd answer from the father of containment theory, who had written presciently in July 1947 that a patient and firm Western policy of blocking Soviet adventures abroad would eventually force the Kremlin to turn inward to confront the reality of its internal weaknesses.[83]

Similarly, Strobe Talbott, then a columnist, argued at the beginning of 1990 that

> . . . Gorbachev is responding primarily to internal pressures, not external ones. The Soviet system has gone into meltdown because of inadequacies and defects at its core, not because of anything the outside world had done or not done or threatened to do. Gorbachev has been far more appalled by what he has seen out his limousine window and in reports brought to him by long-faced ministers than by satellite photographs of American missiles aimed at Moscow. He has been discouraged and radicalized by what he has heard from his own constituents during his walkabouts in Krasnodar, Sverdlovsk and Leningrad—not by the exhortations, remonstrations or sanctions of foreigners.[84]

Talbott invoked the writings of the later Kennan, the elder statesman Kennan who had preached in vain against the excessive militarization of U.S. containment policy and urged conciliation:

> It is a solipsistic delusion to think the West could bring about the seismic events now seizing the U.S.S.R. and its "fraternal" neighbors. If the Soviet Union had ever been as strong as the threatmongers believed, it would not be undergoing its current upheavals. Those events are actually a repudiation of the hawkish conventional wisdom that has largely prevailed over the past 40 years, and a vindication of the Cassandra-like losers, including Kennan.
>
> If Kennan's view and his recommendations had prevailed, the world would probably at least still be where it is today, beyond containment, and perhaps it might have arrived there considerably sooner and at less expense.[85]

The force of the internal pressures in Soviet society is undeniable, as are the inherent weaknesses on which much of its Third World policy ran aground. Yet it seems forced and artificial to claim that Western actions had no significant impact, even on Soviet foreign policies. The new Soviet leadership took the Reagan challenge seriously; they did not dismiss the Reagan policies as ineffectual and meaningless, as some American critics did. We saw how Andropov pointed to the need for caution abroad and how Primakov stressed the need for coexistence with the West in the nuclear age—at the height of Reagan's challenge. In 1988, two Soviet academics writing in an official journal explicitly cited American counterpressures as an argument for a foreign policy retrenchment.[86] The Soviets were squeezed between both forces, their internal weaknesses and a Western policy they acknowledged as more formidable than before.

Gorbachev, not long after he came into power, acknowledged this himself. On October 15, 1985, explaining the need for a new party program, he said: "It has been necessary to work out a new understanding of the changes in the correlation of forces that are occurring. . . ." There was a "very dangerous shift" in the policies of the imperialists, he said, in seeking military superiority and suppressing liberation movements. It was "imperative to take a realistic view" of the interests of the various forces at work. The new party program would demonstrate the party's "ability to take into account the changing situation in due time, face the reality without any bias, objectively appraise current events, and flexibly react to the demands of the moment."[87]

"Realistic" was a compliment that Moscow often bestowed upon Western leaders who were conciliatory; they were praised for having accommodated to the objective factors of history that Moscow embodied. We are entitled to return the compliment, especially when it is echoed in Gorbachev's own analysis.

In all the Soviet critiques of the Brezhnev foreign policy that have been cited above, from Shevardnadze on downward, a recurring theme is that the Brezhnev policy had harmed Soviet interests by increasing international tensions and harming relations with the West. That is another way of saying that Soviet policies had provoked a Western reaction. Brezhnev had precipitated an arms race that, in the end, Moscow could not afford, said Shevardnadze and Dashichev. In the Third World, it was Brezhnev's adventurism—not U.S. neoglobalism (pace Anthony Lewis)—that was responsible for plunging the Soviets into protracted regional conflicts that contributed to the breakdown of détente. This was precisely Brezhnev's "miscalculation," in Dashichev's words—a policy that caused "enormous losses," in Kozyrev's account.

But it was a miscalculation *because the West reacted.* It harmed relations with the West because the West made an issue of it. It raised international tensions because somebody fought back. The price was too great—and we had deliberately raised that price. By these accounts it is demonstrable that the West's response was a principal reason for the Soviet reformers' repudiation of past Soviet policies. Had there been no counter from the West, these policies would have been less costly and less disadvantageous. Had the West not committed itself to match the Brezhnev military buildup, there would have been no arms "race" and the Soviets would have strengthened their position at less cost. In the regional wars— Afghanistan, Angola, Cambodia, Nicaragua—had there been no resistance, it goes without saying that Brezhnev's policies there, too, would have been successes, not failures.

This is not to deny the internal evolution or the credit that goes most of all to those courageous Soviet critics and reformers who saw, independently, the financial and moral bankruptcy of the previous course. But it is enough to document the impact of a revived West and, in particular, of the challenge that the United States posed to the Soviets directly in these regional conflicts at the very time that Gorbachev came to power. As Sestanovich had suggested in 1984 and as the White House statement made explicit in March 1986, the United States deliberately raised the costs to the Soviets in the Third World at exactly the moment when they were reassessing all their policies for a multitude of reasons. And if the preceding discussion of Afghanistan has any validity, the ultimate impact was not limited to Soviet foreign policy alone.

13

BEGINNING OF THE END:
AFGHANISTAN

Between 1988 and 1992, the new Soviet leadership liquidated almost all its Brezhnev-era military commitments in the Third World. The breakthroughs came in what is, by historical standards, rapid succession. In April 1988, a set of agreements signed in Geneva committed the Soviets to begin withdrawing all their troops from Afghanistan on May 15 and to finish by the following February 15—the pledge that Lieutenant General Gromov fulfilled by his theatrical march across the Amu Darya Bridge. In December 1988, an accord was signed in New York requiring the withdrawal of all Cuban troops from Angola within two and a half years. This deadline, too, was met. Later diplomacy brought about a Vietnamese troop withdrawal from Cambodia in 1989, a free election in Nicaragua in 1990, and political settlements in both El Salvador and Cambodia in 1992 and 1993.

The much-maligned "negotiating track" bore fruit.

GORBACHEV AND AFGHANISTAN

As noted in chapter 9, the negotiations on Afghanistan that were organized in Geneva under UN auspices sputtered along after they began in June 1982. At Brezhnev's funeral in December 1982, Andropov assured President Zia of Pakistan that the Soviet Union wanted to leave Afghanistan "quickly" but that Pakistan had to cease support for the resistance. Zia interpreted this as a sign that Andropov was groping for a way out.[1] But clearly Andropov did not want the Soviet Union to suffer a defeat, impairing its international credibility. At a Politburo meeting in 1983, Andropov was adamant: "Our main opponent here is American imperialism. . . . That is why we cannot make any concessions."[2] Neither Pakistan nor its allies were prepared to accept the Soviet terms, however. Not only did these terms represent a dishonorable concession to an illegitimate Afghan regime, but as a practical matter Pakistan, while it was groaning under the burden of 3 million Afghan refugees, knew full well that the refugees would never go home as long as that illegitimate regime remained in Kabul.

The Geneva talks convened for a second round in April–June 1983. By then, Andropov and his colleagues had permitted the negotiators—the Kabul regime and the Pakistani government, with Diego Cordovez as the UN-designated intermediary—to work on drafts of a "comprehensive" settlement. The texts even envisaged the withdrawal of Soviet troops. Cordovez, ever the optimist, crowed that the texts were "95 percent . . . ready."[3] The problem, of course, lay in the conditions that the Soviets continued to insist upon for their withdrawal—namely, the immediate cutoff of outside support for the resistance, with no such cutoff for the Kabul regime. The Pakistanis also complained publicly that one of the key issues—what kind of government would prevail in Kabul once the Soviets departed—was not even being addressed in Geneva at all.[4]

Positions hardened during 1983. The Americans were wary of the drafts when they saw them and distrusted Cordovez for his overeagerness. The Soviets hinted in May that they might offer a specific timetable for withdrawal as part of the agreement, but no such timetable materialized in the negotiation.[5]

In February 1984, when Chernenko succeeded Andropov, Soviet policy hardened further. At Andropov's funeral, Chernenko gave Zia the cold shoulder and granted a long audience to Afghan Communist leader Babrak Karmal. (Funeral diplomacy deserves a book of its own.) There was no movement in the Soviet position in the next round of Geneva talks in August 1984. Meanwhile, on the ground in Afghanistan, the Soviets experimented with new and more effective counterinsurgency tactics, particularly with special operations forces (*Spetznaz*) and more vigorous use of helicopter gunships and combat aircraft, which seemed to succeed in at least keeping the resistance at bay. Su-25 fighter-bombers were introduced to provide close-in firepower, supplementing the Tu-16 high-altitude bombers. Soviet airborne units launched raids deep behind mujahedin lines. The Soviets also seemed to be making headway in professionalizing and putting spine into the Afghan army and in recruiting some local militias to align themselves with Kabul.[6]

It is highly likely that Gorbachev, as a key figure by then in the Politburo, played an important role in this decision to escalate. When he came to power formally in March 1985, Afghanistan was one of those issues on which his opening moves were no great boon to mankind. He threatened Zia at Chernenko's funeral. Gen. Mikhail Zaitsev, a World War II hero and former commander of Soviet troops in East Germany, was sent to Afghanistan to step up the military pressure. Soviet forces continued their escalation of combat operations inside Afghanistan and along the fifteen-hundred-kilometer border with Pakistan; inside Pakistan, virtually every major city became the target of either aerial bombardment, artillery shelling, or incidents of sabotage in the next two years.[7]

The mujahedin gave as good as they got. From 1984 onward, they were receiving more and better weapons from outside. Instead of old Lee-Enfield rifles, they now had automatic AK-47s, heavy machine guns, and artillery rockets. In 1984, they took some daring new steps: specially trained units began targeting the Soviet high command, killing fourteen senior officers that year; other rebels brought the war over the border into Soviet territory, infiltrating anti-Soviet propaganda and broadcasting via clandestine radio into Soviet Central Asia.[8] By early 1985 the mujahedin were able, for the first time, to lob rockets into Kabul and by July to overrun a major government base, at Peshghowr in the Panjsher Valley in the northeast. The Soviets protected the cities and their own forces but could not regain territory, even with their new tactics and firepower.[9]

In the second half of 1985, the first glimmers began to appear of an evolving Soviet policy. In June, in the UN negotiation, the Soviets informed Cordovez that they were now prepared to include a bilateral protocol with Kabul spelling out a withdrawal timetable—one of the crucial missing elements in Cordovez's "comprehensive" texts—and they were prepared to be a guarantor of the whole package if the United States did the same.[10] In July, the central committee of the Communist party instructed the Soviet media to begin limited coverage of the Afghan war, which had been forbidden since 1979.[11] At his Geneva summit meeting with Reagan in November, Gorbachev seemed to distance himself from the Afghan mess in a way that struck both Reagan and Shultz as significant (see chapter 12). During the summit, one of Gorbachev's key advisers on Third World issues, Yevgenii Primakov, told reporter Don Oberdorfer in an interview: "We are ready to withdraw from Afghanistan but we need some guarantees. . . . [W]e want to withdraw," Primakov said, but in proper form and in a way that "saves our face."[12] On November 27, 1985, in the first public statement on the Afghan war in eight months, Gorbachev reported to the Supreme Soviet that he had stressed to Reagan in Geneva that Moscow wanted a political solution: "We want friendly neighbouring Afghanistan to be an independent nonaligned state; we are for the establishment of a practice of guaranteed noninterference in Afghanistan's affairs. The question of withdrawal of Soviet troops from that country will thus also be resolved. The Soviet Union and the government of Afghanistan are wholly for this."[13]

Gorbachev, in short, was trying out his own two-track policy. He encouraged his military to go all out to improve the situation on the ground as best they could, but simultaneously he explored a political track. According to what an authoritative Soviet source later told Oberdorfer, Gorbachev told his military he would give them two years to win the war; if they could not succeed, he would have other options.[14] The Soviets thus continued in their public and private statements to hint at their eagerness to withdraw and to find a political solution, and they permitted more movement at Geneva at least on subsidiary issues.

The terms on which they insisted were still unacceptable to the other side and permitted us to remain skeptical of their intentions. In October 1985, the Politburo had secretly reaffirmed the goal of ensuring a "friendly" government in Kabul.[15] Yet Gorbachev was preparing his people, his Afghan Communist allies—and also his Kremlin colleagues— for a shift in policy. Domestic pressures against the war were growing; the UN General Assembly continued to pass critical annual resolutions by overwhelming margins. Inside the Politburo, Gorbachev would read out to his colleagues letters he had received from mothers, from soldiers, even from generals serving in Afghanistan, that all asked the questions Why are we there? Why are the Afghan people not with us? How can this be our "internationalist duty" when we are destroying villages and killing civilians and seeing terrible things happening?[16]

Facing a monumental economic, social, and political crisis at home, Gorbachev wanted nothing more than to put Afghanistan behind him. However, like American presidents in a similar situation (especially liberal ones), he had to move carefully, not wanting to add diehard pressures on Afghanistan to the hard-line pressures he would inevitably evoke by his domestic reforms. As time went on, he consolidated his political position, but events in Afghanistan did not make things easier: He was forced to make the painful bite-the-bullet decisions in Afghanistan even as he was plunging ahead with the most controversial of his internal reforms.

In February 1986 came Gorbachev's famous comment about Afghanistan as a "bleeding wound." The comment was hailed in the West as a great turning point, but the excitement it provoked may have been more than it deserved; after all, he did not say that the Soviet Union was "bleeding," only that the nefarious West had put poor Afghanistan into such a condition. He still demanded a one-sided cutoff of rebel aid. Nevertheless, he conveyed the tone of a government that was hoping to get out, not investing more of its prestige:

[C]ounterrevolutionaries and imperialism have turned Afghanistan into a bleeding wound. The USSR supports that country's efforts aimed at defending its sovereignty. We would like in the very near future to return to their homeland the Soviet troops who are in Afghanistan at its government's request. An agreement has been reached with the Afghan side on a schedule for their staged withdrawal, as soon as a political settlement is reached that will ensure a real cessation of armed intervention from outside in the internal affairs of the Democratic Republic of Afghanistan and will reliably guarantee its non-resumption.[17]

As UN mediator Cordovez shuttled from Moscow to Kabul to Islamabad in March, he discovered that Moscow and its Afghan allies had indeed, as Gorbachev said, agreed on a specific timetable for Soviet withdrawal once a political settlement was reached: The figure was four years. The Pakistanis rejected this as totally unacceptable, insisting that three to four months was more than sufficient to remove the Soviet troops that had taken only three weeks to arrive.

In April 1986 came a crucial battle on the ground in Afghanistan. The Afghan army, with Soviet direction and backing, laid siege with ground forces and helicopters to Zhawar Fort, one of the most important resistance strongholds, a bare ten kilometers from the Pakistani border. After two weeks of determined fighting and heavy artillery bombardment, they drove the mujahedin from the base. It was a major victory for the Soviets and Afghans—until the mujahedin retook it within a week. The outcome was a significant deflation of Soviet and Afghan morale. Never again during the war were they able to mount another offensive action of the same intensity.

In May 1986, Afghan party boss Babrak Karmal was replaced by Najibullah, head of the secret police. While to Western eyes it seemed a simple matter of putting in someone tougher, in truth it was another reflection of the more complex game Gorbachev was playing. An active diplomacy was bound to be unnerving to the Afghan Communists; unlike some in the U.S. State Department, the Kremlin never lost sight of the need to secure the base while attempting a war of maneuver. Karmal, though not as fanatic as Taraki and Amin, was one of the veterans of the original 1978–79 revolution; he had shown signs of resisting the new Gorbachev line that touted Soviet withdrawal and political accommodation. Unlike Karmal, Najibullah seemed up to the task of holding the regime together while it navigated the turbulent waters of possible compromise.

"National reconciliation" became the watchword, and it translated into efforts to broaden the base of the regime and attract more adherents by downplaying its ideological fervor. A few non-Communists were appointed to minor posts. Relinquishing Communist control was not part of the plan, however. Najibullah was subtle enough, loyal enough—and brutal enough—to take on the difficult assignment. That he remained in power until April 1992—more than three years after Soviet troops had left—was a tribute to his skill (as well as to the $300 million a month in aid the Soviets continued to provide him).

The thought occurred to me that the Kremlin's America watchers— especially Arbatov and Dobrynin—had reviewed with great care the Nixon-Kissinger policy of trying to strengthen the South Vietnamese militarily while simultaneously seeking a negotiated outcome. The pitfalls of this course were apparent. Nixon, starting with a high base (540,000 troops), began a process of gradual unilateral withdrawals; it eased the domestic pressures—but at the price of whetting appetites for further withdrawal. By such an approach one sacrifices some of one's freedom of action in addition to heightening the demoralization of one's ally.[18]

Gorbachev tried out the idea of a token unilateral withdrawal in a way that was clearly meant to avoid the risks the United States had run in Vietnam. It turned out to be too clever by half. In Vladivostok on July 28, 1986, he announced a unilateral withdrawal of six Soviet regiments— one armored, two motorized rifle (infantry), and three antiaircraft artillery regiments. This was a step, he said, "to speed up and give further impetus to a political settlement."[19]

On the contrary, it was a fiasco. U.S. intelligence monitored the Soviet redeployment and noticed a number of things. First, the armored regiment that withdrew with elaborate ceremony on October 15 was an under-strength unit that had never seen combat; additional tanks were sent *into* Afghanistan to bring the unit up to strength for the withdrawal parade. As for the motorized rifle regiments, two fresh regiments with inferior equipment entered Afghanistan to occupy the bases of better equipped units, which dispersed; these newly arrived, inferior units then returned ceremoniously to the USSR as part of Gorbachev's "withdrawal." Finally, the three air defense regiments that pulled out—half of Gorbachev's "withdrawal"—were forces that had played no role whatever in the war, given that the mujahedin had no air force.

The State Department publicized all the details,[20] and it is not known what happened to the careers of the planners in Moscow who had thought up such an incompetent ploy. There were no further Soviet unilateral withdrawals until the Geneva accords.

U.S. POLICY

American policy in Afghanistan benefited from an extraordinary degree of bipartisan support. The pressures, if anything, came from congressional figures on both sides of the aisle wanting an even stronger policy. In such a political climate, the outcome in Vietnam would have been far different. The Reagan administration was bombarded by congressional resolutions calling on it to do more to "render effective material aid to the freedom fighters" (as proposed in 1982 by Sen. Paul Tsongas [D-Mass.] and Rep. Don Ritter [R-Pa.]); a version of it passed in 1984.

Sen. Gordon Humphrey (R-N.H.) and Rep. Charles Wilson (D-Tex.), and their staffs, were the most active in harassing the administration to provide more aid.[21] In 1985, Humphrey created a congressional task force, with twenty-six members from both parties, which conducted public hearings on political, strategic, and other aspects of the war. Critics kept an eagle eye on the Geneva negotiations and raised a protest whenever the administration seemed to be about to put the mujahedin at risk. They kept up pressures on the State Department and Agency for International Development to set up and fund the open humanitarian assistance program (educational, medical, and food supplies) that Congress proposed and mandated beginning in 1986. Congressional pressures and backing also ensured the more than doubling of the covert military assistance, from a reported $250–$280 million in fiscal year 1985 to $630 million in fiscal year 1987.[22]

There were critics, to be sure, but they were lonely voices. Selig Harrison of the Carnegie Endowment was concerned that the United States was cynically "fighting to the last Afghan" and was not trying hard enough in the negotiations[23]; he dismissed as "wishful thinking" the idea that the Soviets were getting bogged down there.[24] Further on the left, Richard J. Barnet and Eqbal Ahmad argued that the Soviet move in Afghanistan was defensive and limited and that the American motive was really to pay back the Soviets for our humiliation in Vietnam.[25] Sen. Charles Mathias, a moderate Republican from Maryland, held up passage on the Tsongas-Ritter resolution for two years because he thought it might endanger the diplomatic effort to find a solution.[26]

The dominant view, however, shared by a large majority of both Democrats and Republicans, was that expressed by Rep. Stephen Solarz. While he disparaged the Contras and Savimbi, Solarz was a staunch supporter of the Afghan resistance. Unlike Mathias, he was convinced that helping the Afghans would promote a negotiated settlement, not prevent it:

If the Soviets are to pay for their occupation and even contemplate withdrawal, and if they are to be deprived of a platform from which to threaten Pakistan or the Persian Gulf, it will be largely because the *mujahedeen*, as the Afghan resistance forces are known, sustain their nationalistic and religious struggle. Diplomatic pressure for a settlement has played a role, but is an insufficient means to achieve U.S. ends. The United States and other countries that share America's strategic concerns should therefore provide a range of assistance to the *mujahedeen*.[27]

DIPLOMACY

By 1985, at Soviet suggestion, the Geneva negotiations had reduced the complex issues to four separate but interlocking documents, or "instruments." One was a set of pledges of nonintervention and noninterference in Afghanistan's affairs; the second embodied international guarantees of a settlement; the third governed the voluntary return of the refugees. The fourth—and trickiest—addressed the key issue of Soviet troop withdrawal and its relationship to the other obligations. It was the first three instruments whose agreed content Cordovez was able to celebrate early; it was the last one that remained incomplete—and crucial.

The delicacy of the issue in U.S. politics was dramatized in late 1985, when the question arose of whether the United States would join an ultimate settlement as one of the international guarantors. As the negotiations percolated in Geneva, diplomatic pressures developed on the United States to declare itself on the point; Cordovez had already obtained Moscow's concurrence and thus put Washington on the spot. The State Department hesitated; then it offered a confidential oral concurrence by a low-level official. Cordovez asked for something more formal.[28] Deputy Secretary of State John C. Whitehead then announced it, after the Geneva summit, in a speech before the World Affairs Council of Washington, D.C., on December 13, 1985:

The United States has firmly supported and continues to support a negotiated withdrawal of Soviet troops. In this connection, we have informed the Secretary-General in writing of our willingness to play an appropriate guarantor's role in the context of a comprehensive and balanced settlement. We have also conveyed our readiness to accept the draft guarantees instrument that Mr. Cordovez has presented to the parties and to us, provided that the central issue of Soviet troop withdrawal and its interrelationship to the other instruments were resolved.

It created a mini-uproar, as conservatives in Congress protested that the United States was agreeing to a pig in a poke. The way the Geneva instruments were constructed, the United States seemed to be promising to end its "interference" in Afghanistan's affairs (meaning to terminate aid to the resistance) without even knowing when the Soviets were prepared to withdraw.[29] It was later charged by the conservatives that the decision had been made by the rogue elephant State Department without Reagan's knowledge or consent.[30] (The facts on this point are a bit murky, but it is known that Shultz had briefed Reagan on the issue earlier, and it is highly likely that the president either did accept or would have accepted Shultz's recommendation.)[31]

As usual, the conservatives' fear was overblown, but they had a point. In the abstract, it should have gone without saying that the United States would participate in guaranteeing any settlement reached; the promise to do so was no big concession, since our final assent could be withheld until a settlement was reached that was satisfactory to us. In other words, we were not agreeing to guarantee anything unless we liked its final terms.

The problem lay in the bizarre structure of the negotiations. The official parties to the Geneva talks were, in theory, the government of Pakistan and the government of the Democratic Republic of Afghanistan. But this was a totally artificial construct. The Kabul government's legitimacy was very much in dispute (which is why Pakistan still insisted on only indirect talks with it, through a UN mediator). The Soviets, who had created the problem, were not a party, nor were the mujahedin. This artificiality came from the necessities and inhibitions of UN diplomacy. The UN, by its nature, was equipped only to deal with disputes between sovereign governments (hence, Pakistan and the Kabul regime); the UN had no categories, at least in those days, for thrusting itself into mediation of a civil war, let alone joining in a procedure to overthrow a member government. Nor, because of the Soviet Union's superpower status, could the UN deal with the matter as an issue of simple aggression. Thus, inevitably, the Geneva negotiation turned into a trade-off of Soviet withdrawal in exchange for a cutoff of outside aid to the rebels, the trade-off that the Soviets themselves offered (though it was originally Cordovez's idea[32]).

This trade-off was a false equation not only from the moral point of view but also for practical reasons. The cutoff of outside aid would be an instantaneous act; the Soviet troop withdrawal would be a process that, in the best of circumstances, would unfold over a period of time. But the Geneva documents—as they had already been negotiated—required that the aid cutoff be simultaneous with the *commencement* of

Soviet withdrawal. (Recall that the Soviets' first offer of a specific time-table, in early 1986, would have extended the withdrawal over four years!) This was gross negligence on someone's part, because the mujahedin would obviously remain at risk if their aid was cut off while any significant number of Soviet troops remained in-country.

The fact is, the United States was peculiarly diffident in expressing its views on the evolving texts, and Pakistani diplomats did not always keep the U.S. State Department fully informed. In August 1984, indeed, Pakistan accepted Cordovez's formula on the cutoff of rebel aid without U.S. advance knowledge or concurrence.[33] Some of these undesirable developments were allowed to occur because neither Pakistani nor American diplomats thought the Geneva negotiations would ever produce any significant result. The Pakistanis were constantly responding to Soviet and UN pressures not to obstruct; they did not want to give the Soviets a propaganda advantage by seeming to block progress. Therefore, they went along with Cordovez's importunings. In any negotiation, mediators tend to put pressure on the side most likely to yield. Thus, Pakistan was induced to accept a formula that left the mujahedin's survival in jeopardy.[34]

When I moved to the White House as a deputy assistant to the president in the spring of 1986, I convened a meeting in my office with the State Department experts handling Afghanistan. My NSC colleagues Steve Sestanovich and Shirin Tahir-Kheli were concerned at the way the negotiation was developing. Our colleagues from State openly admitted their unhappiness with the structure of the Geneva instruments and with the way the Pakistanis often plunged ahead without giving us much of a chance to object. But our State friends also comforted themselves with the thoughts that (a) nothing was likely to come of this negotiation, anyway, and (b) the risks to the mujahedin could be reduced if we insisted on the shortest possible timetable for the Soviet exit. (Pakistan, as noted, was then insisting on a rapid, three-to-four-month pullout.)*

I remained uneasy. I shared the diplomats' view that the Geneva negotiation was unlikely to produce a solution. More likely, I thought, the war would drag on, and the outcome—or lack thereof—would be determined by cruder factors than the niceties being haggled over in

---

*The State Department was not a monolith. The views in question were held by the Near East bureau. But the office of Legal Adviser Abraham Sofaer wrote scathing critiques of the Geneva documents, and Dr. Zalmay Khalilzad, an Afghan-American I had brought onto the policy planning staff, was an unerring source of analysis and advice during this period.

Geneva. Therefore, we on the NSC did not make a big fuss over the tactics or the terms, merely urging our State colleagues to keep a closer eye on the talks. We were wrong in our assessment, however, not realizing what should have been easy to predict: that the Soviets, if they ever decided to pull out, would welcome the face saving that Geneva would provide. A year and a half later, the Geneva chickens would come home to roost and nearly cause a crisis in U.S.-Soviet relations.

A second thorny issue in the negotiations, from the NSC staff's vantage point, was the role of the mujahedin. They were only in the early stages of forming a unified political organization, a seven-party coalition in exile based in Peshawar, Pakistan. The Pakistanis made a point of keeping them even less well informed than us, preferring to preserve their own freedom of action in the diplomacy without any complicating pressures or obstinacy from their Afghan clients. The United States hesitated to brief the mujahedin representatives on all we knew because we feared antagonizing the Pakistanis. We confined ourselves to giving aid and advice to the Peshawar alliance on how to organize an office, deal with the media, and be the very model of a modern revolutionary movement.

Pakistan's concerns were not frivolous. In addition to wanting to preserve diplomatic flexibility, it feared building up a powerful Afghan exile organization on its soil; it was acutely conscious of the negative example of the Palestine Liberation Organization (PLO) and the explosive "state within a state" that the PLO had built first in Jordan and then in Lebanon, shattering the stability of those countries. Since it was handling the arms supply and training, Pakistan understandably wanted control over the political agenda as well. The CIA and State Department went along with this, seeing no reason to complicate life for the courageous Pakistanis, who were carrying the multiple burdens of the war effort, the refugees, and the risks of Soviet wrath.

Those of us on the NSC staff were concerned that this was not a sustainable policy. From the president's point of view, this country had a commitment to the "freedom fighters" and could not just look the other way if Pakistan someday decided to cut a deal with the Soviets against the wishes of the resistance. In addition, strengthening the rebels' *political* role was an effective way to add to the pressures on the Soviets. If it also constrained the Pakistanis' diplomatic freedom of action somewhat, this was not a bad thing, since our Pakistani friends already seemed a bit too freewheeling for their own good. Building up the rebels' political role was a hedge against the risks of Geneva.

My NSC colleagues therefore came up with the idea of inviting the leadership of the Peshawar alliance to Washington for a highly publicized laying on of hands by President Reagan. The Pakistanis blanched, the State Department muttered dark forebodings, but the meeting took place. Dr. Syed Burhanuddin Rabbani, head of one of the moderate factions, was (by rotation) the chairman of the exile organization when, together with the leaders of three of the other factions, he paraded, in turban and traditional robes, into the Oval Office on June 16, 1986. Reagan gave them a pep talk—his talking points having been drafted by the NSC staff—assuring them that the United States regarded the resistance alliance as a party in its own right, that we would keep them informed of developments and never sign an agreement behind their backs or contrary to their interests. The State Department had initially gagged at what it saw as extravagant pledges but went along in the end with what should have been seen as unexceptionable expressions of America's obligation. A presidential press statement after the meeting made these pledges our public policy (though none of this was ever published in the *Department of State Bulletin*):

Your goal is our goal—the freedom of Afghanistan. We will not let you down.

Like the Afghan people, we hope for a negotiated end to this war. Year after year, UN resolutions have called for a total and rapid withdrawal of Soviet troops and for self-determination for the Afghan people. Let us renew that call today. Only an agreement that has the support of the Afghan people can work. This is a fact of life, and it is why the role of the resistance alliance is crucial. The diversity of the alliance, its roots in the faith and traditions of Afghanistan, shows that the alliance is the true representative of the Afghan people.

The rebel leaders came downstairs afterward to the Situation Room where State and NSC officials peppered them with respectful questions about the state of the war. With their beards and colorful dress they seemed out of place in that famous meeting room, but they shamed us with their modesty and bravery—these seemingly unsophisticated men whose brothers were fighting the mighty Soviet war machine to a stalemate and at a terrible human cost. The sheikhs then trooped over to Langley, where they had a presumably more useful conversation about their military needs.

THE STINGER DECISION

Robert Dilger was a fifty-four-year-old retired air force colonel who owned an electronics store in Xenia, Ohio, and tinkered with inventions in his workshop. In 1986, hearing of the Afghans' problems, he developed, using the parts from several guns, an eight-foot-long, portable 30-mm antitank gun that he believed could be used easily by Afghan and other guerrillas fighting the Soviet Union and its clients. He may not have read all the literature on the Reagan Doctrine, but he was one of its champions in spirit. In 1986 he peddled the idea and the plans around official Washington, presenting them to people at the CIA and to Vincent Cannistraro, who dealt with intelligence policy matters on the NSC staff. Vince treated him politely, humored him, and kept a copy of the plans, which he later showed me—an amusing sidebar, he thought, to the bureaucratic infighting that had been going on in the U.S. government on the subject of new weapons for the mujahedin. The CIA's reaction to Dilger's sales pitch is not known, but can be guessed.

In retrospect, it is probably good that the U.S. government did not leap at Colonel Dilger's idea. On August 19, 1986, he and a friend were driving in his friend's pickup truck in Arlington, Virginia, with a home-made prototype and twenty rounds of ammunition in the back of the truck, when they stopped at a gas station. While his friend got out to pump the gas, Dilger went to the back to load a shell in order to show how it worked. The gun accidentally discharged, firing a high-velocity nine-inch shell through the body of the truck into a gasoline pump, blowing up much of the gas station and wounding four people with shrapnel. The two were arrested.[35]

Fortunately, by this time the United States had come up with a better idea—the Stinger antiaircraft missile.

During the war, the Soviets (like the United States in Vietnam) had come to rely on air power for their counterinsurgency effort. This led the United States, from the earliest days of the Afghan program, to provide the rebels with some antiaircraft capability. In the early years, in accordance with traditional tradecraft, the CIA's watchword was "plausible deniability"; it was thought prudent to provide weapons that were not U.S.-made and that therefore could not be traced obviously to the American source of supply. We provided Soviet-designed and Chinese-made heavy machine guns, the British-made "Blowpipe" surface-to-air missile, and, most important, Soviet-designed, SA-7 shoulder-fired, surface-to-air missiles purchased clandestinely in Eastern Europe. These weapons were initially quite effective. Soviet fighters and fighter-bombers had to fly higher to avoid the missiles, sacrificing the accuracy of their bombing. Helicopters, such as the Mi-24 gunships and troop-carrying Mi-8s, adopted nap-of-the-earth tactics, flying fast at treetop level to avoid the SA-7s; they then became more vulnerable to the heavy machine guns. The rebels learned to direct their gunfire at the choppers' weak spots— the Mi-24s' main rotor and tail boom, and the Mi-8s' thin armor.[36]

As in all wars, the contest of wills was also a contest of brains. The Soviets developed countertactics. The SA-7 is a heat-seeking missile, so the Soviets installed baffles on the helicopters to cool engine exhaust and cover plates for the engine intakes; they used decoy flares to fool the missiles. Their fighter-bombers (faster than helicopters) began using nap-of-the-earth tactics. These changes reduced aircraft losses considerably. Meanwhile, the mujahedin began to exhaust their supplies of Blowpipes and SA-7s and also complained that, for some reason, a significant proportion of the SA-7s they were given were not functioning properly.[37]

By late 1985, the U.S. government faced a dilemma. President Zia of Pakistan told a visiting delegation of sympathetic congressmen in mid-1985 that the mujahedin needed some better missiles, perhaps the U.S.-built Stinger. The thirty-five-pound Stinger was more capable than the SA-7 by every measure. Its range of five kilometers was twice that of the SA-7, its warhead more lethal. Its infrared seeker was more effective in all kinds of weather than the SA-7's heat seeker and better able to distinguish between real targets and flares; it also did not have to be aimed so precisely at an aircraft's heat source. Nor did the operator have to sit in place and keep the target in his sights until impact (risking counterfire), which was the case with the SA-7.

With the new, more aggressive Soviet offensive strategy of 1984–85 and the more intensive use of fighter-bombers and gunships, the mujahedin had a monumental problem. But Zia's suggestion of the Stinger set off a monumental battle within the U.S. government.[38]

The political foundation for an American response had been laid in March 1985, when Reagan had signed NSDD-166, a directive stating a clear policy of seeking to defeat the Soviet occupation of Afghanistan and force a Soviet withdrawal. (President Carter's original directives and intelligence findings of 1980 had had the less ambitious goal of "harassment" of the Soviet forces.)[39] But implementing the policy in the U.S. government, as usual, was another matter.

Support for the Stingers came from several sources. Fred Iklé, under secretary of defense for policy, was a crucial supporter, as was Michael Pillsbury, who worked at various times in the Pentagon and for conservative Republican senators pressuring the administration on Afghanistan.

Sen. Orrin Hatch (R-Utah) and Rep. Charles Wilson kept up steady pressure. NSC staffers, including Vincent Cannistraro and Christopher Lehman, also played a pivotal role.

Opposition came from surprising directions. The idea that American military leaders were warmongering Cold Warriors is a myth; in most situations they reacted like a bureaucracy. In this case, the Joint Chiefs of Staff were reluctant to draw down inventories of a valuable U.S. weapon and also feared that its technology might fall into the wrong hands. Even more vociferous opposition came from working levels of the CIA—ironically, in view of Director Casey's passionate advocacy of the Reagan Doctrine. But never underestimate the power of working-level officials to obstruct a presidential decision they disagree with. CIA officials argued, first of all, that plausible deniability would be lost if U.S. weapons were furnished. Perhaps in the back of their minds was the fact that the Pentagon would be involved if U.S. equipment was introduced and they would have to share bureaucratic control. CIA officials also insisted that the Stinger was too complicated to be operated by illiterate Afghan tribesmen; they claimed disparagingly that the rebels' problems with the SA-7 were the result of poor maintenance and skills and would only be worse with the more advanced Stinger. They even claimed (clearly incorrectly) that Zia was against the move. The CIA representatives dragged their feet in interagency deliberations on the matter, took no action, and, in the end, delayed the delivery of Stingers by over a year.

What decided the issue was the vigorous entry of the State Department on the pro-Stinger side. If the department's performance on the diplomatic track left something to be desired, its crucial role in the bureaucratic battle over Stinger redeems its honor. The Near East bureau was nervous about introducing American weapons. But Ambassador Morton Abramowitz, an unusual combination of physical and intellectual energy, a liberal and a man of some moral passion, was at that time the director of the Bureau of Intelligence and Research and therefore took part in interagency deliberations on intelligence matters. Abramowitz concluded from a visit of his own to Pakistan in September 1985 that there was no alternative to Stingers. He persuaded his close friend, the usually cautious Mike Armacost, under secretary of state for political affairs. Armacost was the pivotal person in the department on these issues—he and Mort persuaded Shultz—and thus the balance in State was tipped, and with it the balance in the government.

After a lengthy series of interagency meetings, the opposition was worn down. The Joint Chiefs' fears of compromising sensitive U.S. technology were blunted when it was discovered that much of Stinger technology had already been betrayed to the Soviets.[40] The CIA's claims that Zia opposed the move were easily refuted. Their claims that the Stinger was beyond the capacity of the Afghans to handle were also refuted. For one thing—embarrassing to the CIA—there were suspicions that the rebels' problems with the SA-7s were due not to lack of skill but to sabotage by the Polish suppliers from whom the CIA was (clandestinely, it thought) buying the missiles.[41] And while the bureaucratic wrangling over Afghanistan continued, all agencies were agreeing, separately, on a shipment of fifty Stingers for Jonas Savimbi in Angola. (In CIA, this was dealt with by a different group of people.) Savimbi's men received the missiles in April 1986 and by July were claiming eight out of ten direct hits against Cuban and MPLA aircraft.[42] The CIA's objections thus suffered a direct hit as well.

Reagan decided the matter in April 1986—or thought he did—ordering the delivery of Stingers to the Afghans. The CIA procured fifty of them from the army but then left them sitting in a warehouse in Virginia with the argument that the Soviets had been seen testing new antimissile defenses that had to be investigated. The army dutifully conducted further tests and determined that the Stinger could overcome these defenses.[43] The missiles then finally arrived in Pakistan in the summer of 1986. Even without fancy high-tech training simulators and hundreds of hours of indoctrination, the mujahedin mastered the equipment. On September 26, 1986, they tried out the system near Jalalabad airport and blew up three Mi-24 helicopter gunships coming in to land.

The Stingers transformed the war immediately. According to a U.S. Army study after the war, 340 of them were fired in combat, and 269 aircraft were downed. Even if the figures include some exaggeration, there can be no doubt that the weapon's effectiveness forced another shift in Soviet tactics. Soviet combat aircraft again had to fly higher to avoid risks; Soviet ground troops began deriding the pilots as "cosmonauts" because they flew so high.[44] Soviet supply flights were grounded or inhibited. The resistance learned to lie in wait for aircraft along known routes and to set traps by staging ground ambushes that drew in close-support aircraft. They regained almost unrestricted freedom of movement for their own forces and supplies on the ground.[45]

While the military impact was what was intended by U.S. planners, the political impact proved to be even greater than anticipated. The Soviet military, having been given two years by Gorbachev to show if they could win the war, were stymied—just at the decisive historical moment. A Soviet military historian's 1990 postmortem acknowledged:

Helicopter gunships were the most formidable weapon for use against the dushmans.* However, with the appearance of different portable surface-to-air missile systems such as, for example, the American "Stinger" or the English "Blowpipe" in the weaponry of insurgent detachments, there was a sharp increase in the number of helicopters lost. . . .

It was becoming increasingly obvious to the Soviet command that it would not succeed in completely routing the insurgents by military means. . . .[46]

The symbolism of a major U.S. political commitment—embodied in crossing the "plausible deniability" threshold—must also have had its impact on Kremlin thinking. And the new U.S. commitment was not limited to Stingers. According to journalist Steve Coll in the *Washington Post*, the CIA began in 1985–86 to supply

. . . extensive satellite reconnaissance data of Soviet targets on the Afghan battlefield, plans for military operations based on the satellite intelligence, intercepts of Soviet communications, secret communications networks for the rebels, delayed timing devices for tons of C-4 plastic explosives for urban sabotage and sophisticated guerrilla attacks, long-range sniper rifles, a targeting device for mortars that was linked to a U.S. Navy satellite, wire-guided anti-tank missiles, and other equipment.[47]

A cumulative $2 billion worth of U.S. weapons and aid went to the mujahedin in the 1980s, according to Coll—an amount matched by Saudi Arabia and supplemented by aid from China. Arms supplies rose to sixty-five thousand tons annually by 1987. According to French observer Olivier Roy: "Hundreds of truckloads of material in the south, and thousands of horses in the north (including Tennessee mules airlifted from the US to Pakistan), permitted a continuous flow of weapons into Afghanistan."[48] Chinese mules were brought in by truck. Cross-border raids by the mujahedin into the Soviet Union itself became more brazen, with commandos firing volleys of rockets, assaulting border posts and airfields, laying mines, and knocking out power lines and power stations inside the territory of the USSR.[49]

---

*Dushman is a traditional and derogatory Russian term for Central Asian rebel tribesmen.

DIPLOMACY AND ITS SURPRISES

Soviet body language suggested a yearning to get out, but as far as the U.S. government could tell, the Soviets were still unable to come to grips with a decision to risk defeat. At the Reykjavik summit in October 1986, in my talks with Primakov, we simply exchanged stock formulas. But a month later, in November 1986, a group of visiting Americans from the unofficial "Dartmouth" exchange program was stunned to hear a senior Soviet say: "We know we have to get out, but we don't know how to get out. Please help us."[50] Even more surprising to the Americans was to be praised by the same official after they went on Soviet television themselves and criticized Soviet policy. "The Soviet people have to start learning that we have to get out of Afghanistan, and we can't go on television to say it," he told them.[51]

A decisive Politburo meeting was held in Moscow on November 13, 1986—seven weeks after the first Stinger kill. According to the minutes of the meeting, Gorbachev told his colleagues: "We have been fighting in Afghanistan for six years now. If we don't change approaches, we will be fighting there for another 20 or 30 years. . . . We must finish this process in the swiftest possible time."[52]

Andrei Gromyko, the lone Politburo survivor of the original decision of 1979, backed up Gorbachev: "The situation is worse today than it was six months ago. . . . We must be much more active in searching for a political solution. Our people will breathe a sigh of relief if we undertake steps in this direction." Chief of Staff Marshal Akhromeyev reluctantly acknowledged both the political and the military failure: "We control Kabul and the provincial centers, but we have been unable to establish authority. . . . We have lost the struggle for the Afghan people. . . . We have deployed 50,000 Soviet soldiers to seal the border but they are unable to close all channels through which arms are being smuggled across the border."

Despite the remonstrations of KGB chief Viktor Chebrikov that more should be done to choke off the arms supply, the consensus was as Gromyko declared: "Today, our strategic goal is to end the war." Najibullah and his top colleagues were summoned to Moscow in December and were told (according to other accounts) that the Soviets were planning to withdraw within one and a half to two years—thus, at the latest by the end of 1988.[53]

The United States was unaware of the Politburo decision, but the signals to the Dartmouth group were sufficiently intriguing to prompt us to initiate another high-level consultation. In March 1987, it was decided to send Mike Armacost to Moscow for another round of "super-regional" talks with Yulii Vorontsov. I was to accompany Mike. There had been a tendency since Reykjavik for the world's attention to focus on arms control, and we needed, at a minimum, to bring the regional conflicts back onto the table.

The NSC staff arranged for Armacost and me to be called in for a sendoff meeting with the president—an unusual move but a useful reinforcement of the president's line. We met in the Oval Office on March 11. Reagan (prepped by the NSC staff) gave us a tough pep talk, stressing that the regional issues were a stumbling block to everything we were trying to accomplish in U.S.-Soviet relations; they included cases of outright Soviet aggression. We had to make this clear to the Soviets.

On the way to Moscow, Mike and I met in a London hotel with Pakistani foreign minister Yaqub Khan. Yaqub was one of the most colorful figures of modern diplomacy. He was a soldier by profession, having been military governor of East Pakistan in 1971 when President Yahya Khan launched the disastrous crackdown in the province—which then became independent Bangladesh after a bloody civil war and Indian invasion. Yaqub had refused Yahya's orders and was put under house arrest. Subsequent Pakistani leaders respected not only his integrity but his erudition (he spoke Russian, French, Italian, and several other languages) and his diplomatic charm. He was Pakistan's ambassador in Washington in the 1970s when I first met him. He took me to lunch occasionally at the Jockey Club and impressed me enormously by instructing the waiters in voluble Italian.

In London in March 1987, we compared notes on the status of the Geneva talks—an attempt at closer coordination than had been achieved in the past. On the question of the timetable for Soviet withdrawal, the Soviets and Afghans had come gradually down to a figure of eighteen months; the Pakistanis in turn had allowed their long-standing counterproposal—three to four months—to grow to six to seven months. Mike and I were nervous about this and told him so: in any negotiation, when two sides come within range of each other and one side says eighteen months and the other side says six, the negotiation is almost inevitably on a slippery slope toward the midpoint of twelve—yet one year was much too long a period given the risks to which the mujahedin would be subjected once outside aid was cut off on day one.

We also chatted with Yaqub about possibilities for compromise on Afghanistan's future political arrangements, a key topic not covered by Geneva. There was speculation (encouraged by the Soviets) that ex-king Zahir Shah might give up his comfortable exile in Rome to return as a compromise figurehead. In London, we left the issue open, but I cautioned that we could be more creative on political compromise *after* the Soviets had made a clear and convincing decision to get out on a satisfactory schedule. We had to keep the pressure on Moscow.

This London meeting was our effort to stiffen the Pakistanis against the incessant pressures coming from the UN mediator and the Soviets. Consultation between allies, in short, had to mean coordination of policies as well as the sharing of information.

In Moscow on March 16, Mike met first alone with Vorontsov, ostensibly to talk about the schedule for the visit. Vorontsov was in character, however, and stunned Armacost by referring pointedly to Nixon's "Christmas bombing" of Hanoi in December 1972—suggesting that the Soviets, too, could be brutal (presumably to Pakistan) while they exited from their equivalent of Vietnam. Mike reacted sharply that this was not acceptable.

Shevardnadze received Mike and me, on March 17, in an overheated, small meeting room in his outer office—from which he excused himself periodically for what he said were phone calls from Gorbachev. Armacost was polite but firm. When Shevardnadze expatiated on Najibullah's program of broadening his political base—"national reconciliation"—Armacost told him flatly that Najibullah's policy was a failure and that Najibullah would have to step down if peace was to be achieved. Shevardnadze seemed taken aback by Mike's blunt statement of what was, indeed, the truth.

We left Moscow in March with the conviction that the Gorbachev leadership, despite all the hints to visiting journalists and academics, had not yet bitten the bullet about quitting Afghanistan. The ham-handed threats of a "Christmas bombing," the illusions about Najibullah's domestic success, were a bad omen. But the fighting was intensifying in 1987, and 1987 was the year in which the Stinger's impact was being felt even more with every passing day, neutralizing the strategy by which the Soviet military had once thought to win the war.

In July, Najibullah and his top colleagues were summoned to Moscow again. Gorbachev seems to have made clear, as he had done on earlier occasions, that the Soviet Union was looking for a way to get out and the Afghans had better be prepared. Two days after meeting with Najibullah, Gorbachev went public with one of his bluntest statements: "In principle, the question of the withdrawal of Soviet troops from Afghanistan already has been decided," he told the Indonesian newspaper *Merdeka*. He continued, however, to demand a guaranteed halt to outside "interference."[54]

Shevardnadze visited Washington in September 1987 for his regular meeting with Shultz. Their diplomatic dialogue had developed into a personal friendship and a shared conviction that an extraordinary transformation was taking place in U.S.-Soviet relations.[55] Not without reason are Shultz and Shevardnadze given much credit for the concrete work that gave content to that transformed relationship—the steps in arms reduction, the improvement in human rights conditions in the USSR, the expansion of bilateral relations, and the progress that was soon to be made in the regional diplomacy. This time in Washington, on the second day, Shevardnadze asked for a private conversation with the secretary, and the two retired with their interpreters to the small inner sanctum behind the secretary's formal office. "We will leave Afghanistan," the foreign minister abruptly declared: The political decision had been made; the troops could be out in a year.

Suddenly, there seemed to be what lawyers call a "date certain," and Shultz considered this a breakthrough. In deference to Shevardnadze's wishes, Shultz told only the president and a few other key officials; the two ministers even spent two hours in a larger meeting with all their advisers just after their tete-à-tete, reciting the standard formulas on Afghanistan while keeping secret the dramatic news Shevardnadze had just brought. Shultz told the press afterward that it was "the most thorough and searching discussion" of Afghanistan that he and Shevardnadze had ever had. But he did not elaborate.[56]

Word spread in the administration despite the secrecy. My colleagues and I on the NSC learned that Shevardnadze had given such a promise to Shultz, though we were never clear about how explicit it had been, and we continued to look—in vain—for concrete evidence of such a decisive change in Soviet policy on the ground or in the negotiation.

Clues accumulated, but only gradually. Armacost and I had another meeting with Vorontsov, this time in Geneva in mid-November. It was at this meeting that the Soviets, for the first time, told us they were willing to separate the military from the political issues—that is, to unlink their troop withdrawal from any requirement that there be a prior political settlement in Kabul. As with Le Duc Tho's similar concessions to Kissinger in Paris on October 8, 1972 (which I suspect Vorontsov and his old boss in Washington, Dobrynin, had not forgotten)[57], the unlinking of the military issues from the more intractable political ones made an agreement on troop withdrawal in the Geneva context more likely. Vorontsov's move was a mixed blessing, because it brought to the fore all the latent problems of the Geneva process. So matters rested until the Washington summit of December 1987, when Ronald Reagan proved that he was smarter than his diplomats.

As the summit approached, the administration was taking a burst of criticism from congressional conservatives for its decision two years earlier to offer to guarantee the Geneva accords. The White House therefore invited resistance leaders to Washington for another visit and further reassurances; Reagan gave them another Oval Office pep talk on November 12. Then, in an interview with network television anchors on December 3, Reagan was asked whether it was really his administration's policy to end aid to the resistance upon the commencement of Soviet withdrawal. He answered with the resounding equivalent of a "Hell, no!":

I don't think we could do anything of that kind, because the puppet government that has been left there has a military, and it would be the same as what I'm arguing about with regard to the freedom fighters in Nicaragua. You can't suddenly disarm them and leave them prey to the other government—and this is p-r-e-y, not p-r-a-y. No, the people of Afghanistan must be assured of the right of all of them to participate in establishing the government they want, and that requires more than just getting his forces out of there.

Thereby he single-handedly undid all the damage done in the Geneva process by three years of diplomatic clumsiness.

There was panic in the State Department. Reagan had forgotten that he himself had approved the decision to guarantee, they argued; the United States had long since acquiesced in the Geneva trade-off (a cutoff of aid on the day the Soviet withdrawal began); this was a slap in the face to a Soviet leadership that had told us it was committed to withdrawing. When the summit began, Primakov was in Washington for the usual summit working-group talks on regional issues, this time with Richard Solomon, my successor as State's policy planning director, and me, along with other experts on both sides. Primakov took me aside during a break and complained bitterly about Reagan's remarks. Could I assure him, he implored, that the United States still stood by the Geneva process? Yes, I said, trying to be as vague as possible; we stood by Geneva. What I did not tell him, and did not yet fully realize, was that we were about to redefine what Geneva meant.

By then, Gen. Colin Powell had become Reagan's national security adviser, succeeding Frank Carlucci, who had succeeded John Poindexter. Powell, like Carlucci and Brent Scowcroft, lived up to the classical model of the honest broker in that job. Loyal first and foremost to his president, he conducted himself in a way that won the trust of the cabinet secretaries, who by law are the president's principal advisers. He pushed no personal agenda; rather, he ensured that all the cabinet views were accurately reflected in the president's deliberations. Powell was not able to break bureaucratic deadlocks if the president was unwilling to (often frustrating for Shultz), but he showed an extraordinary political savvy (in the best sense), tact, and personal integrity that made it no surprise to me when he went on to even more important responsibilities.

At one of our regular morning senior staff meetings in the Situation Room, one of my NSC colleagues reported to Powell that the State Department wanted to "walk the president back to where the policy was." "Wrong!" said Powell with a smile; we were going to "walk" the policy to where the president was. He knew that Ronald Reagan was not going to let the United States sign any agreement that put the Afghan "freedom fighters" at risk.

With Reagan's strong backing, the NSC staff spent the next month bringing the State Department along—a painful process—on a formula to improve the "symmetry" of the Geneva instruments by adding supplementary conditions without which we considered the bargain unequal. At the end of December, NSC staffers Robert Oakley, Nicholas Rostow, and I collaborated on a memorandum for Powell listing such requirements as a "front-loading" of the withdrawal (i.e., ensuring that the bulk of Soviet troops left early in the time period), a stand-down of Soviet military activities, ironclad prohibition of Soviet reintervention, and a Soviet cutoff of military aid to the Kabul regime to parallel our cutoff of the resistance. Except for the last point, they were not new demands. Armacost and Oakley went to Pakistan early in the New Year to confer with Zia, who completely shared our president's view that improved "symmetry" in some form was essential. After much thrashing about—with Reagan adamant and the State Department still reluctant—the two governments eventually decided that symmetry of military supply was the most important requirement, along with front-loading of the withdrawal. The Soviets were so informed.

Gorbachev let it be known that he considered the shift in the U.S. position a betrayal.[58] He complained bitterly to a visiting group of American senators and academics that he felt "embarrassed and incensed" that the United States was now demanding further concessions.[59]

The Soviets had grounds, perhaps, to feel put upon. We had added new conditions to Geneva in the name of "symmetry" just when the Soviets were approaching the crucial moment of decision. But two points must be made. First, no major country can be tricked into agreeing to what it considers an unequal bargain. The Geneva process—which gradually, as I predicted, gravitated toward a one-year timetable for Soviet withdrawal—left the mujahedin badly exposed if their outside supply was terminated on the first day. This arrangement no longer reflected the balance of forces on the ground, where the resistance, especially since the arrival of Stingers, had gained a much stronger position. A negotiating formula first agreed upon in 1985—though never by the resistance—no longer reflected reality in 1987. The tide on the battlefield had turned. It was inevitable, almost as a law of nature, that the final negotiation would adapt to the new reality, not the other way around.

The second point is that, even with all the hints, the Soviet decision to bite the bullet was not evident to us by any tangible measure until February 1988, and it is at least as possible to argue that the stiffening of the American position ensured this Soviet decision as to argue that it was an unfair turning of the tables. The sequence of events suggests strongly that when the Soviets saw there was no longer a possibility of winning an advantage over the mujahedin through the Geneva texts, they and their allies finally faced up to the decision that was required of them.

On February 8, 1988, an official Soviet statement in the name of Gorbachev announced a Soviet commitment to withdraw, in the context of the Geneva accords, by the following February 15 (i.e., the twelve-month timetable).[60] The commitment was not totally unconditional, since the Soviets insisted that the Geneva accords be signed, but the date certain and the categorical quality of the announcement removed any doubts—including my own—that this time it was for real. Mike Armacost had had running bets with various CIA officials who doubted the Soviets would ever leave Afghanistan; a few hundred dollars changed hands after February 8.[61]

Gorbachev's was an unusual statement—a text read by an announcer (not a televised speech by the man himself), a statement in the name of Mikhail Gorbachev but invoking the collective views and position of the "Soviet leadership." It must have been the focus of intense wrangling as to whose head would be on the block. The Soviet media began a shrewd campaign to head off recriminations or stab-in-the-back theories or a backlash from the military: articles appeared praising the performance, honor, dignity, and glory of the Soviet armed forces; they had done their duty in a difficult assignment, subject to limits imposed by the politicians, and they had not been defeated. The blame was spread around but particularly laid at the door of the political leadership that had made the decision nine years earlier to intervene.[62]

Gorbachev's calculation proved right, in the short run. There was no backlash—only a demoralization that proved more profound in the end than Gorbachev or anyone else could have imagined.

The Geneva accords were signed in April 1988, but not without some further pulling and hauling between the NSC and State. Shultz had announced in January the formal U.S. position on "symmetry": We offered the Soviets either "negative symmetry," in which we would terminate military supply to the resistance and the Soviets would terminate similar aid to the Kabul regime, or else "positive symmetry," under which we would feel we had the right to continue to aid the resistance so long as Moscow aided Kabul. After intensive negotiations, the Soviets essentially accepted neither. The Soviets did let Shultz know, however, that they would not torpedo U.S.-Soviet relations even if the United States clung to its insistence on the right to arm the resistance. And even this was communicated to Shultz not by explicit assurance but by indirection; there is not one sentence in any record of any conversation in which any Soviet assured us we had their permission to arm the mujahedin. Yet by their winks and nods and general statements of interest in U.S.-Soviet relations, an "understanding" of sorts could be thought to have been reached: The United States intended to make a *unilateral* statement of its right to continue to arm the resistance so long as Moscow armed Kabul, and we had reason to expect that the roof would not fall in.

The problem was not simply the elusiveness of this "understanding" but the degree to which it left Pakistan exposed. We, a guarantor of the accords, were being let off the hook, but Pakistan—through which all the aid we provided was funneled—was not. The Soviets never relinquished, even by winks and nods, their right to punish Pakistan severely if Pakistan continued to funnel aid to the resistance after signature of the accords.

Despite remonstrations from Colin Powell, Shultz was determined to sign, anyway, with the unilateral statement. Since the president tended to go along with Shultz, Powell's leverage was limited. With me, Rostow, Oakley, and our Soviet specialist Fritz Ermarth harassing him, Powell did his best to keep Armacost's and Shultz's feet to the fire during their long private sessions with the Soviets. But Shultz continued to tinker on his own with the wording of the statement even on the flight to Geneva.[63] On April 14, before he signed the instrument on international guarantees committing us to support the cessation of outside "interference," the secretary read the following: "The obligations undertaken by the guarantors are symmetrical. In this regard, the United States has advised the Soviet Union that the U.S. retains the right, consistent with its obligations as guarantor, to provide military assistance to parties in Afghanistan. Should the Soviet Union exercise restraint in providing military assistance to parties in Afghanistan, the U.S. similarly will exercise restraint." In the same statement, however, Shultz stressed that the *Soviets'* commitment to withdraw by a date certain was "central to the entire settlement" (i.e., unconditional) and "essential to achievement of the settlement's purposes," including the end of outside involvement.

The Soviets never criticized the American statement. They did, however, as some of us had predicted, unleash their fury at Pakistan. They intensified their bombing attacks on resistance bases in Pakistan, particularly in November. But Zia held firm. No more than on previous occasions did the Pakistanis buckle under this military pressure. Moscow occasionally threatened to slow down its withdrawal, but this was a bluff. The withdrawal continued—"front-loaded," as the Geneva accords required, with half the troops and equipment out by August 15.

In the end, therefore, Shultz was proved right and we NSC cynics wrong. The Geneva accords were the fig leaf that the Soviets needed to withdraw their troops unilaterally, and the elusive "understanding" on "positive symmetry"—in reality a unilateral U.S. assertion of the right to continue rebel aid—was tolerated by a Soviet leadership that had already had enough of Afghanistan. Their troop withdrawal proceeded on the promised schedule, until General Gromov's march across the bridge on February 15, 1989.

ENDGAME

From the strategic point of view, the Soviet troop withdrawal transformed the nature of the Afghan problem, though it did not completely resolve it. Without a doubt, it was a courageous decision by Gorbachev and the most convincing proof that he represented a renunciation of Brezhnev-era policies. The more skeptical I had been beforehand, believing that the Soviet rulers were incapable of such a risky and humiliating retreat, the more I had to acknowledge that something significant had taken place.

There were those—including a prominent allied leader, who expressed such a view in my presence—who wondered if we really wanted the Soviets to leave, knowing that it would only feed the adulatory frenzy that was surrounding Gorbachev in the West; it would strengthen Gorbachev's hand, particularly in Europe. My view was different—that the departure would be universally recognized as a strategic setback for the Soviets, having a healthy effect on international perceptions of the global "correlation of forces." Syria's ruler, Hafez al-Asad, a key Soviet client, vented his nervousness publicly. Responding to an interviewer's question, he grumbled: "I think they [the Soviets] thought it was a good thing. . . . An outside observer might see things in an opposite way."[64] More concretely, the Soviet departure meant an end to the threat to Pakistan and the Gulf posed by the Red Army's thrust in 1979.

It also meant that Afghanistan's continuing turmoil was to that degree reduced to a problem of local and not global significance. That was certainly the view of the Bush administration, which came into office at the beginning of 1989 when a number of regional conflicts were heading toward solution. Europe, not wrongly, seized its attention. The Bush team, in any case, consisted of more pragmatic men whose emotional and ideological commitment to the "freedom fighters" was much less than that of their Reaganite predecessors. This pragmatism may ironically have complicated chances for resolving these regional conflicts.

There was unfinished business in Afghanistan, in my view—the Communist regime of Najibullah, which had been installed by Soviet power. Not only was it a regime without legitimacy, still facing a determined country-wide rebellion by its people, but in a sense it still embodied a strategic problem: The defeat of the Soviet aggression was not complete as long as the political fruit of that aggression still survived. The U.S. government correctly took the position that while many forms of political compromise were possible, a Communist-dominated regime in Kabul was still unacceptable.

In early 1989, however, this problem was confidently thought to be about to solve itself. This particular fruit of aggression was thought to be sufficiently overripe to fall of its own weight soon after the Soviet departure. The CIA, to its credit, made no predictions of Najibullah's imminent demise, erring (as many of us thought) on the side of a more cautious estimate—that it might take a year to eighteen months for the drama to play itself out. As for the rest of us, I attended interagency meetings at the beginning of the Bush administration that dwelt on such questions as how to convert a covert military assistance program into an overt program of economic aid in the middle of a fiscal year, with all the legislative, technical, and tradecraft implications attached thereto. Those questions were addressed as a matter of urgency, since we thought the rebels' victory was at hand. Outside the CIA, the consensus in the policy community on February 15, 1989, was three months. The U.S. government pulled its chargé d'affaires out of Kabul in the expectation of an imminent and bloody final siege of the capital.

This was, of course, a howling miscalculation. Kabul's spine proved stiffer than we imagined, the war continued to be a stalemate, and the final crisis was delayed for over three years. This unexpected result was the product of a number of factors, including some mistakes by the Bush administration and some of the Reagan administration's chickens coming home to roost.

One important factor was the Soviet military assistance that accompanied the withdrawal of troops. We should have seen the parallel (as surely the Soviets did): Just as the United States had done for South Vietnam between October 1972 and January 1973, the Soviets poured in large quantities of new equipment both before the February 15, 1989, deadline and afterward. In addition, about $1 billion in military equipment and installations were left behind.[65] Our interlocutor Yulii Vorontsov, a deputy foreign minister, had been given the concurrent assignment of ambassador to Kabul to stiffen the Afghans; he did so brilliantly, assuring them that the Soviets still backed them and bullying the local diplomatic corps. His masters provided the staggering amount of $250–$300 million a month in weaponry after February 15—$3 to $4 billion a year—including new systems such as hundreds of SCUD-B surface-to-surface missiles and more advanced aircraft. The U.S. commander with jurisdiction over the theater, a certain Gen. H. Norman Schwarzkopf, declared a year later that the amount of Soviet matériel flooding to Afghanistan was "absolutely unbelievable."[66]

The United States stepped up its supplies to the resistance after the Geneva accords in April 1988 but seems, incredibly enough, to have slowed down its program toward the end of the year.[67] The incoming Bush administration confirmed the policy community's assessment that Kabul was likely to fall quickly. There were logistical problems, compounded by inertia and overconfidence, which continued until the late summer of 1989, when congressional pressures and mujahedin difficulties pushed it to reopen the flow.[68] By early 1990, a year after the Soviet withdrawal, the military situation had frozen once again into a stalemate.

At the same time, the regime's enhanced firepower was matched by another new advantage—the fact that the departure of the Soviet combat troops changed the *political* nature of the war. As Olivier Roy put it: "[T]he Soviet withdrawal undermined the common ground among the Mujaheddin. No longer were they waging *jihad* [holy war] coupled with a war of national liberation against non-Muslim invaders, but civil war, in which traditional social segmentation was now superseding the ideological dimension."[69]

The United States and Pakistan made an attempt not only to hold the rebel factions together but to promote their formation of an alternative government to take over once Kabul fell. The hopefully named Afghan

Interim Government, based in Peshawar, was a failure. It was too much weighted in favor of certain of Afghanistan's diverse ethnic and linguistic groups and underrepresented others; it suffered from the onus of being seen as a Pakistani-U.S. creation, just as the Kabul regime was shedding some of the onus of its Soviet provenance.[70] The fatal weaknesses of this umbrella organization left power on the ground in the hands of the field commanders and also ensured that military strategy in the endgame would fall victim to the growing rivalry and disarray among the factions.

The regime, too, was factionalized. There was constant coup plotting in Kabul (which generally received less publicity than the disarray on our side), and there was an aborted mutiny in Kabul in March 1990. Eventually, this took its toll on Najibullah and his grip on power. The disarray among the mujahedin, however, was the principal factor delaying their victory.

The most important split was between the so-called fundamentalists, mainly the faction led by Gulbuddin Hekmatyar, and the so-called traditionalist factions. The Pakistani Inter-Services Intelligence (ISI) directorate, which managed the program, funneled a disproportionate share of the weaponry to Hekmatyar because it considered his group the best fighters (which they were probably not).[71] He was a clever, ruthless, single-minded opportunist, opposed to any political compromises or to sharing power with his fellow rebels.[72] Yet Zia was partial to Hekmatyar, looking with favor on the idea of a fundamentalist Islamic Afghanistan that would be a natural ally of the "Islamized" Pakistan that he thought he was creating. Zia told Selig Harrison in the summer of 1988: "We have earned the right to have [in Kabul] a power that is very friendly to us. We have taken risks, as a frontline state, and we will not permit a return to the prewar situation, marked by a large Indian and Soviet influence and Afghan claims on our own territory. The new power will be really Islamic, a part of the Islamic renaissance which, you will see, will someday extend itself to the Soviet Muslims."[73]

All this had perverse effects. The resistance laid siege to Jalalabad in March 1989, shortly after the Soviet departure. Jalalabad, in eastern Afghanistan, was close to the ISI supply line and in the fundamentalist-controlled part of the country. The assault failed for many reasons, but one was the fundamentalists' bloodthirsty reputation for killing surrendering government troops; wavering defenders understandably decided in this case to stand and fight rather than surrender. A few months later, a resistance force led by traditionalist factions laid siege to Kandahar. This attack failed, too, for a variety of reasons—though these factions believed that for political reasons they were not given adequate supplies by their

ISI quartermasters. Partly as a result of this kind of self-induced paralysis, *no* major city fell to the resistance until over two years had passed after the Soviet troop withdrawal.

Zia had died in a mysterious plane crash in August 1988, which killed also the American ambassador, Arnold Raphel, one of the brightest stars of my generation in the Foreign Service. (He was succeeded by Bob Oakley.) Zia's departure did not change the policy of the ISI, which shared his Islamic vision and persisted in its preference for the fundamentalists. The United States began to express mild demurrers in diplomatic channels, but this was never translated into effective pressure in intelligence channels. The CIA, in fact, had its own quiet contacts with Hekmatyar.

The divergence of interest between Pakistan and the United States on this point is instructive. Allies never totally agree; all collaborations are a convergence or overlapping of interests, not an identity. We are always presented with the need to decide our priorities. Just as the congressional liberals put aside for the duration their concerns over Pakistani human rights problems and nuclear proliferation to bolster Pakistan while it was the bulwark of the struggle, so the administration had to swallow hard as Zia skewed the arms allocation because the Pakistanis had been otherwise doing a highly effective job of running the war. Zia shared our strategic concerns about the Soviet Union; he was also quite pro-American. For decades, fearful of the Soviet-Indian "pincer," Pakistan had relied on the United States and China. But the United States, too, can be a difficult ally. We always seemed to be on the verge of disengaging from the world (as evidenced by our shrinking foreign-aid budget), and the restlessness in Congress over Pakistan's nuclear program and its lack of Western-style democracy was never completely absent from U.S. policy.

Pakistan paradoxically, therefore, had an interest in simultaneously working with us, shielding itself from our pressures and hedging against an uncertain future in which we might end up abandoning it or turning on it. Thus, perversely, our pressures on Pakistan to halt its nuclear program may only have confirmed in Pakistani eyes the necessity of the nuclear option as the ultimate guarantee of Pakistan's survival. Zia undoubtedly also saw salvation (in more ways than one) in an Islamic grouping of states that could band together against outside pressures, whether from the Soviet Union or India or the West. This might seem shortsighted from our vantage point—Zia and his people were too Western oriented to find real soul mates in the likes of Iran or the egregious Hekmatyar—but it was a strategic alternative, of sorts, for a country that had been dismembered by India in 1971, was continually threatened by India and the Soviets, and still felt highly vulnerable.

Many Pakistanis were worried by Zia's favoritism toward Hekmatyar. One of them was the foreign minister, Yaqub Khan. At a dinner in his honor at the Pakistani embassy in May 1987, Bob Oakley and I listened as he complained gloomily of how our two countries' intelligence services seemed to be collaborating to put the worst elements in power in Kabul. As with Churchill's remonstrations to FDR during World War II, he thought it was time to start fighting the war with an eye to the postwar political conditions we were shaping.

As time passed, the U.S. Congress became even more restless. Liberals who had supported the aid program for the resistance as long as the Soviet army was occupying the country began to question the rationale. Rep. Anthony Beilenson, chairman of the House Intelligence Committee, proclaimed as early as May 1989 that the rebels no longer deserved U.S. support.[74] Sen. Bill Bradley of New Jersey declared in June that the time had come to work harder for a negotiated settlement, not only to end the killing but to give a boost to Pakistan's new Harvard-educated democratic leader, Prime Minister Benazir Bhutto.[75] Claiborne Pell, chairman of the Senate Foreign Relations Committee, urged that we persuade the Soviets to join us in terminating outside military aid mutually.[76] Even Representative Solarz was restless. When an administration official testifying before his subcommittee said that the Afghan game was in the fourth quarter and we needed to stick with it, Solarz complained that this was "the longest fourth quarter in creation." But Solarz favored continuing aid.[77]

Congressional conservatives, meanwhile, pressed the Bush administration hard from the other direction. They badgered Brent Scowcroft, the president's national security adviser, complaining vociferously about the hiatus in military aid, and (successfully) insisted that the U.S. program be continued, not terminated. The administration asked Congress for a reported $280 million authorization in fiscal year 1990.[78] Conservatives joined liberals in wanting to stem the flow of aid to Hekmatyar while stepping up aid to the others.[79] As Secretary of State James Baker began to engage the Soviets in discussions of some kind of political solution, a high-powered bipartisan group of senators, led by Majority Leader Robert Byrd and Minority Leader Robert Dole, cabled Baker in Moscow in February 1990 to warn that any compromise that left Najibullah in power even in a transitional government was unacceptable.[80]

Nonetheless, objective reality was bringing the United States and Soviet Union closer together. At Baker's session with Shevardnadze in Wyoming in September 1990 and at Bush's summit with Gorbachev off the coast of Malta in December, the superpowers came together in espousing a UN proposal for a transitional coalition under UN supervision. The U.S. strategic interest still required that the Communist leadership in Kabul be removed to complete the symbolic defeat of the Brezhnev enterprise. But this did not rule out an accommodation between other elements of the Kabul government and the more moderate elements of the resistance. The United Nations continued to be mistrusted by the resistance and by American conservatives, but it could also be the vehicle in this case for wearing down the Kabul regime. We now seemed to have the stronger hand and the psychological advantage. We also had reason to want to see the fighting end soon lest its prolongation further radicalize and polarize the situation and add to Hekmatyar's strength.

The Soviets, too, were feeling the pressure, and as early as April 1990 their diplomats began to hint that "negative symmetry" (which they had rejected two years earlier) wasn't such a bad idea.[81] They also feared Islamic extremism as a danger in Soviet Central Asia and as a radicalizing factor in the whole Middle East at a time when they had no interest in new regional crises. They decided that they, too, had an interest in a rapid end to the Afghan civil war. Yet they could not bring themselves to ditch Najibullah.

What broke the impasse was two major events that delivered a body blow to radicalism generally in the Middle East—the Gulf War and the collapse of Communist power in Moscow. When the world community went to war against Saddam Hussein in early 1991, the egregious Hekmatyar announced his backing of Saddam. This was infuriating to the Bush administration and was too much even for the Saudis, who were (aside from us) the other main source of funding for the mujahedin. Overcoming their habitual timidity about facing down radicals, the Saudis pulled on the reins. The Bush administration decided to omit Afghan funding from its fiscal year 1992 budget while leaving open the possibility of resumption.[82] We and the Saudis thus found the courage to squeeze the ISI to shift the direction of the arms supply. (The Saudis seem to have resumed some support after an interval, however.)[83]

The abortive August 1991 putsch in Moscow sealed Najibullah's fate. Andrei Kozyrev, by then foreign minister of Boris Yeltsin's democratic Russian republic, declared shortly after the coup that Najibullah was the main obstacle to a compromise:

Everything has long been ready for settlement in Afghanistan—only our support of Najibullah has prevented it. . . . By supporting extremist forces in Kabul, we are also creating a foundation for extremists in opposition. Remove Najibullah, and the extremists in Peshawar will also go. Then moderate political forces from both sides will agree among themselves. If the mujahedin take Kabul by force, however, then there will be an extremist regime along our borders.[84]

This drastic shift was still not totally reflected in a Soviet policy still run by Mikhail Gorbachev. But the new Soviet foreign minister, Boris Pankin, quickly reached an agreement with Baker on "negative symmetry," which brought events a step closer to the same result. Baker and Pankin signed a joint statement in Moscow on September 13 calling for an early cease-fire and transitional coalition government and announcing the termination of their weapons deliveries respectively to the resistance and to Kabul as of January 1, 1992. The Americans were now confident that the rebels' stockpiles and the dynamics of the situation would produce the collapse of Kabul (as indeed it did). Not without reason did a liberal Moscow newspaper refer to Najibullah, after the Baker-Pankin accord, as "another casualty of the August revolution."[85]

On November 15, 1991, Pankin received a delegation of the Afghan resistance in Moscow—headed by the same leader, Burhanuddin Rabbani, who had met with Reagan in 1986—which was an extraordinary demonstration of the Soviets' new stance. By March 1992, with the arms cutoff in effect, Najibullah was announcing generously that he would step down as soon as a UN peace plan took effect. Events did not wait on such niceties, however. The psychological dam broke a month later, when, in April 1992—fourteen years after the Communist coup in Kabul and four years after the Geneva accords—the regime's army cracked under the pressure. Resistance forces advanced on Kabul, government forces this time defected to the rebel side, and Najibullah took refuge in a UN office in the capital.

It was implausible that a Communist regime in Kabul would very long outlive the Communist regime in Moscow whose creature it was. The disarray of its opponents prolonged its life, but not forever. With the fall of Kabul came the necessary and ignominious end of Brezhnev's adventure, the disastrously arrogant overreaching that had made its own contribution to discrediting everything Brezhnev represented. The United States, by arming the rebels, had forced the Soviet leadership into hard choices. We shaped the balance of forces on the ground and pursued a political strategy that offered the Soviets a face-saving way out; it was met in turn by an intelligent and courageous Soviet leadership that responded rationally to the political and military calculus with which it was presented.

History has not ended for the Afghans, however. Selig Harrison quotes horrific statistics compiled by the United Nations as of 1990:

[N]early 1 million dead; 535,000 disabled veterans; 700,000 widows and orphans; one-third of all villages destroyed; two-thirds of all paved roads unusable; 26 types of deadly mines strewn over the countryside, largely unmapped; and a refugee exodus of 5.9 million people to Pakistan, Iran, and the West—including 1 million children born and brought up in camps who have never known their homeland. Out of 11.7 million people left in the country, some 25 percent—or twice the prewar average—are now in cities and towns. More than 2 million "internal refugees" have fled to urban centers for protection. With much of the countryside depopulated, agricultural production has plummeted. Annual production of wheat, the country's staple food crop, has declined by 54 percent.[86]

As the various political and tribal factions continue to maneuver at this writing, peace has not finally arrived. Warlordism reigns in the country-side under the guerrilla commanders as the politicians who returned from exile in Pakistan struggle still to produce a unified administration. Gul-buddin Hekmatyar continues to disrupt.

Afghanistan will never again be what it was. Many social changes are probably irreversible—a generation of young Afghans educated under secular rule, of young women jealous of rights they were granted. The country has fractured along regional and ethnic lines and is doomed to a future of prolonged instability and violent unrest.[87] Its turmoil has begun to spill over into the now-independent Muslim republics of Soviet Central Asia, and it remains another factor of unpredictability in a volatile region. The needs of the Afghan people for outside aid, for relief and reconstruc-tion, have grown. Yet in a post–Cold War world eager to put such memories behind it, a world now overcrowded with needy claimants, the Afghans' voices are not easily heard above the din of the continued turmoil inside the shattered country.

14

OUT OF ANGOLA

The departure of the last Cuban soldiers from Angola, airlifted out on May 25, 1991, was not the occasion for the international hoopla that greeted General Gromov on the Amu Darya Bridge. (All they got was a lengthy welcome-home speech from Raúl Castro.) But it had a similar symbolic meaning. Angola had been Brezhnev's first overreaching after the American defeat in Indochina; it had, in a sense, launched the Soviets on the course that plunged them into Afghanistan. By the end of 1988, however, Angola had become another Soviet enterprise brought to a conclusion, like Afghanistan, after the United States engaged itself more directly in the military struggle on the ground and coupled this with an intelligent diplomacy.

In some ways, Angola is more interesting than Afghanistan, because the domestic debate in the United States over Angola better reflected the hesitations that lay just beneath the surface of the Reagan Doctrine. The powerful bipartisan support of our Afghan involvement was exceptional. The tug-of-war between liberal opponents of the Angolan resistance and its conservative champions; Congress's anguish about our covert military involvement; the conservative mistrust of the State Department's diplomacy—were more typical. Whereas the Contras were condemned and the mujahedin hailed, Jonas Savimbi's UNITA seemed precariously poised on the fault line of American ambivalence.

The Angola conflict suffered from being enmeshed with other domestic controversies over southern Africa—especially the agony of South Africa itself. It was not an accident that the region was a focal point of American emotions, hopes, and pressures from many directions. Chester Crocker, the professor who became Ronald Reagan's assistant secretary of state for African affairs, wrote later:

> Southern Africa is a beautiful region, magnificently endowed with human and natural resources, the potential economic engine of a continent, and a place whose web of racial and civil conflict tears at our hearts, urging

us to engage ourselves. But at another level, southern Africa can become, as former Ambassador to Pretoria Ed Perkins put it, a sort of "political vending machine" into which we insert our coins to receive moral hygiene or instant ideological gratification. Featuring almost every form of odious human behavior—racism, brutal oppression, Marxism, authoritarianism, terrorist violence, organized butchery of unarmed villagers and gross official corruption—the region became a moralist's theme park.[1]

The United States left the field in Angola in 1975 because of the controversy over South African involvement and the clumsy U.S. covert program, but owing more fundamentally to this country's sheer unwillingness to contemplate plunging into another jungle war in the same year that Indochina fell. Following the congressional cutoff of U.S. aid to the anti-Communist forces in December 1975, South Africa pulled out its forces as well.

The war did not end, however. The MPLA regime proved incapable of consolidating its political position or broadening its support. This should not have been surprising, in view of the tribal divisions among the contending parties and the OAU task force's earlier estimate that UNITA would have won at least a plurality and possibly a majority in the elections scheduled in the Alvor agreement.[2] The Cuban troop presence escalated, from ten thousand in November 1975 to fifteen thousand in 1976 to thirty thousand in 1981 (later to reach fifty thousand and perhaps more), contrary to the expectations of some American legislators who thought the U.S. covert involvement had been the cause of the Soviet/Cuban intervention.

UNITA maintained its tribal base and some of its military potential in the southern portion of the country. South Africa resumed some arming and training of UNITA guerrillas, less in the hope of winning the Angolan civil war than as a way of keeping the victorious MPLA regime off balance. Undoubtedly, this reinforced the MPLA's dependence on the Cubans. But the MPLA had formed an alliance with its fellow radicals of SWAPO (the South West Africa People's Organization), enabling SWAPO to conduct guerrilla operations into South African–occupied Namibia from Angolan bases. Cross-border violence was increasing in both directions, and the regional conflict festered.

LINKING ANGOLA AND NAMIBIA

When the Reagan administration came into office in 1981, it launched an unexpectedly active diplomacy in southern Africa, if only to prevent the caldron from boiling over. It managed to cobble together leverage on Angola even in the absence of an ability to give material support to UNITA (still barred by the Clark Amendment). Secretary of State Alexander aig decided, in effect, to seize Namibia as a diplomatic hostage.

Namibia, known in history as South-West Africa, had been a German colony before World War I. There was a Bismarckstrasse in its capital, Windhoek, and even a Goeringstrasse, named for Hermann's father, who had been a colonial administrator. The League of Nations awarded it to South Africa as a Mandate territory after the war, and it was continued as a UN Trusteeship after World War II—until South Africa began applying some of its discriminatory racial policies to the territory. In 1966, the UN General Assembly declared South Africa's Trusteeship of Namibia at an end and asserted UN supervision over the territory pending preparations for independence.

Even the Nixon administration joined in the international community's pressure on South Africa to vacate Namibia. In 1970 it backed a UN Security Council resolution declaring South Africa's continued occupation illegal; it reaffirmed the U.S. embargo on arms transfers to South Africa, with specific reference to South African military operations in the territory, and formally discouraged American investment in Namibia. One of the first major policy matters I dealt with after I joined Kissinger's National Security Council staff was helping shepherd these Namibia issues through the interagency process and to Nixon for his decision. Basically, Nixon's personal sympathies were with the South Africans; he hated to give in to liberal pressures, and he grumbled at the pressures from inside his own administration to take punitive measures. But he had no realistic choice except to yield to political necessity and take at least some steps to vindicate the legal position he had inherited from his predecessors. Reluctantly, he did the right thing.

Kissinger did, as well, when he negotiated with the South Africans over Rhodesia and Namibia in 1976, after the fiasco in Angola. The collapse of the Portuguese Empire having rendered Rhodesia strategically (as well as morally) indefensible, South African prime minister John Vorster told Kissinger that he would squeeze Ian Smith to accept majority rule in Rhodesia if Kissinger could organize a transition that put moderate blacks in power. This Kissinger was attempting, with British prime minister James Callaghan and Zambian president Kenneth Kaunda as partners, when Jimmy Carter's election intervened to put Kissinger out of business.

It was in the same period that Kissinger pressed the South Africans to move closer to eventual independence for Namibia. There, too, the South Africans indicated they were willing to make major concessions provided that SWAPO guerrillas were not given power; they had conceded the eventual right of Namibia to independence and were seeking (with little success) to organize the Namibian whites and non-SWAPO blacks to compete with SWAPO politically. In September 1978, during the Carter administration, the South Africans were driven further to acquiesce in UN Security Council Resolution 435, which called for transferring power to the people of Namibia through free elections under UN supervision.

Implementation of Resolution 435 remained stalled, however. This was the Reagan administration's opening: It pledged its support for early implementation of 435 *provided* that Cuban troops left Angola.

This linkage was highly controversial, but it was more than a clever diplomatic tactic. South Africa's ultimate willingness to pull out of Namibia depended significantly on whether or not an independent Namibia would be bordered on the north by a radical MPLA-led Angola sustained by Cuban troops and giving sanctuary to SWAPO guerrillas. The linkage between Angola and Namibia thus had a practical reality. Looked at more positively, it represented an expansion of our southern African diplomatic agenda and an arguably more realistic approach to the settlement of both problems. It was a conscious application of the linkage theory of Henry Kissinger, on whose staff Haig and Crocker had both served.[3]

This diplomatic linkage of Angola and Namibia was opposed, however, by America's European allies, by many black African governments, and by critics in the United States, who all predicted it would doom any negotiation. Not surprisingly, the approach was rejected outright by the Angolan government when Crocker visited there in 1981. Even the South Africans hesitated at first, not certain whether linkage weakened the pressures on them to implement Resolution 435 (which it probably did in the short run) or strengthened the pressures (which it did in the longer run); they were basically reluctant to risk either withdrawal from Namibia or abandonment of UNITA. By 1982, however, the South Africans went along. Crocker attempted to organize a negotiation among the various parties in 1982–83. South Africa and Angola discussed terms for a cease-fire; the United States and Angola discussed possible conditions for Cuban withdrawal. But there was no result. Violence continued, with South Africa launching offensives against SWAPO sanctuaries in Angola and the Soviet-backed Angolan army (FAPLA, or the People's Armed Forces for the Liberation of Angola) conducting periodic offensives against UNITA-held territory in the southeast.

The United States stuck to its position on linkage nonetheless. This was highly unusual. Normally, American diplomacy eventually gives way to the pressures that inexorably build. Even with a policy less controversial than holding Namibia hostage, if an adversary does not respond favorably in a short time, critics take it for granted that it is we who must modify our negotiating position to break the deadlock. It is the Soviets, over the years, who excelled in cold-blooded stubbornness, cleaving to long-standing concepts (like the call for a European Security Conference) decade after decade, figuring that they would lose little by maintaining their version of what was desired and that ultimately the impatient democracies would be worn down. Too often they were right. Now it was Crocker who clung Gromyko-like to the linkage policy for nearly four years.

Then an amazing thing happened: Instead of America's being sent to eternal damnation for defying the prevailing wisdom, the Angolan regime accepted the U.S. position. In November 1984—not coincidentally the month of Ronald Reagan's reelection—the MPLA threw in the towel. It issued a policy document, its "Plataforma," which, after vehemently denouncing linkage, went on to demand that South Africa implement Resolution 435 on Namibia in return for a withdrawal of Cuban troops from southern (but not northern) Angola. These precise terms were not likely to be accepted; a *total* Cuban withdrawal had to be part of any ultimate deal. But it was like the old story of the tycoon and the starlet. When he asked if she would sleep with him for $1 million, she thought a moment and said yes. When he then offered her twenty dollars, she recoiled: "What do you think I am?" He replied: "That we've already established. Now we're just haggling over the price." For the next four years, the Angola/Namibia diplomacy proceeded on the basis of linkage, and the interconnection between the two issues was treated by the international community as the most natural thing in the world.

Chet Crocker was an unusual diplomat in many ways. He was an academic specialist in African affairs from Georgetown University and the Center for Strategic and International Studies; in 1970–72 he had put in a stint on Kissinger's NSC staff, where I first met him. To all outward appearances he was the classic mild-mannered professor—soft-spoken, bespectacled, balding at a young age, with a wry smile and shy sense of humor. But as the point man for the Reagan administration's Africa policy he showed other qualities in abundance—physical stamina, diplomatic brilliance, personal charm, and political courage—through eight long years of nearly continual controversy.

As Crocker recounts with great vividness in his memoir,[4] it was his fate to be set upon by both the Left and Right. The liberals, most prominently the Congressional Black Caucus, objected not only to the linkage of Namibia and Angola but even more to the policy of "constructive engagement" with South Africa. The Reagan administration took the position that a just evolution in South Africa could best be encouraged by maintaining that country's exposure to outside influences; it also believed that the strongest force against apartheid was the country's economic advance, which was empowering the black work force and creating, inevitably, a black political leadership. Thus, the administration resisted calls for economic sanctions, which it thought would only harden the whites in their isolation. This position was criticized as morally obtuse by liberals, even though they applied exactly the same reasoning to left-wing regimes, from Cuba to Nicaragua to Vietnam, arguing that sanctions only hardened attitudes. In the end, the Reagan administration was pushed by Congress into tightening economic sanctions on South Africa in 1985 and 1986, and these may indeed have spurred the willingness of the white community to contemplate drastic change. But the administration's historical analysis also had a sound basis—and the sanctions campaigns always came most disruptively in the middle of Crocker's efforts to engage the South Africans constructively on the Angola/Namibia issues.

Crocker paid a price among liberals for being the chief spokesman for these "racist" positions despite his extraordinary diplomacy that eventually produced the major breakthroughs in both Angola and Namibia. And yet, despite the scars he bore for his manful defense of "constructive engagement" and linkage, he was also the object of chronic suspicion among conservatives, who worried that his diplomacy put the Angolan "freedom fighters" at risk. I had my own occasional disagreements with Chet, as I shall discuss, but these never dimmed my admiration for his skill, tenacity, and courage.

REPEAL OF THE CLARK AMENDMENT

Once linkage was agreed, the negotiation focused essentially on two things: (1) persuading the South Africans that Namibia was no longer tenable and (2) persuading the MPLA, the Soviets, and Cuba that military victory over UNITA was impossible and that the Cuban presence only guaranteed constant South African pressures. This persuasion took a long time.

UNITA never expected to win a military victory; what it sought was a share of power to which it felt the Alvor accords entitled it. As the negotiation process unfolded—without its direct participation—UNITA sought to demonstrate its presence and dramatize its claim. Between March and October 1984 it carried out military operations all over the country, breaking out of its southeastern base to attack a provincial capital in the center, a diamond mine in the north, oil pipelines in Cabinda in the far north, power stations in Luanda, and rail yards in a major port. [5]

The Angolan regime and its Soviet and Cuban backers thereupon geared up in 1985 for a major offensive that it hoped would finish off UNITA once and for all—a drive against UNITA's home base in the southeast. Beefed up by a large delivery of new Soviet weapons, FAPLA armored brigades totaling four thousand men came close to taking Jamba, Savimbi's capital, in October. South African intervention turned the tables, however, demonstrating that Pretoria would not allow UNITA to be defeated. A South African Defense Forces (SADF) mechanized unit reinforced UNITA on the ground, and South African air force jets badly mauled the Angolans. But the Angolan air force chief proclaimed his government's undying determination to eliminate Savimbi: "We have to go over to the offensive and liberate the territory occupied by UNITA and cut off its supply lines from South Africa." [6] In March 1985, Mikhail Gorbachev reaffirmed Soviet "solidarity" with the Angolan regime against "the aggressive designs of South Africa's racists, who are supported by international reaction." [7]

The other crucial development of 1985 was the repeal of the Clark Amendment and the gradual reengagement of the United States in direct support of Savimbi. This came about by the usual tortuous path, which sometimes seems the only way the U.S. government can make important decisions.

The essence of the matter is that the administration of Ronald Reagan, champion of the freedom fighters, did not actively seek repeal of Clark, while the U.S. Congress, which had lately specialized in denying presidents flexibility in overseas interventions, repealed it anyway. In Congress, this was another example of how the balance had been tipped by the sweeping results of the 1984 presidential election. The conservatives were energized, and moderate Democrats were concluding, as we have seen, that their party could not afford to be postured forever as anti-anti-Communist.

In the Senate (which the Republicans still controlled), conservatives Steven Symms and Jim McClure of Idaho and Malcolm Wallop of Wyoming began a new push for repeal of the Clark Amendment in the spring and summer of 1985. Symms had visited Savimbi in his jungle capital the year before and was determined to restore U.S. aid. Even though the conservatives had done little to affect the congressional battle in December 1975—or perhaps with a guilty conscience because of it—they had adopted Savimbi as a cause ever since. The Republican Senate had voted before, in 1981, to repeal Clark, but the Democratic House had blocked it. Majority leader Robert Dole—with an eye on his own prospects for the presidential nomination in 1988—was happy to oblige the conservatives once again.

In the House, the dynamics were somewhat different. Republicans Jack Kemp of New York and Trent Lott of Mississippi raised the issue. The most important bloc on African issues, however, was the Congressional Black Caucus, backed by liberals on the African Affairs Subcommittee of the House Foreign Affairs Committee. While some prominent American black intellectuals (like Bayard Rustin) strongly opposed the Soviet/Cuban intervention as a new form of colonialism,[8] the established black leadership was strongly pro-MPLA and anti-UNITA, out of either a reflexive pro-leftism or an allergy to anyone connected with South Africa.[9] They were the champions of the Clark Amendment. But suddenly the Black Caucus confronted a worthy adversary—the Cuban-Americans, who were passionately anti-Castro and had decided it was time to frustrate Fidel's military adventures in Africa.

Prompted, apparently, by the National Security Council staff, a delegation from the Cuban-American National Foundation went to see Rep. Claude Pepper, the veteran Florida Democrat revered by his party for his longtime championing of health care and other important liberal causes. Pepper had many Cuban-Americans in his district; he was not sure where Angola was and asked his visitors to point it out to him on a globe. When they explained that 35,000–40,000 of Castro's troops were propping up a fellow revolutionary regime, Pepper became an ardent advocate of repeal.

Like Senator Dole, Pepper was in a position to pay more than lip service. As chairman of the powerful House Rules Committee, he could help make it happen. On June 11, 1985, the Republican Senate voted 63–34 to repeal the Clark Amendment, and the Democratic House did the same on July 10 by the overwhelming vote of 236–185, with sixty Democrats voting with the Republicans.

The Reagan administration was essentially passive during all this. Its principal spokesman on African issues, Chet Crocker, took no formal position for or against repeal, but his body language said no: "U.S. officials" were said to consider UNITA "an internal Angolan problem and not part of the equation in seeking a southern African peace settlement."[10] Crocker told the New York Times that the administration had "no plans" to provide aid to UNITA.[11] These statements had their tactical utility in deflecting the MPLA reaction to the repeal of Clark, but they also were seen in Washington as reflecting Crocker's preference.

After Clark was repealed, Pepper and Kemp then introduced a bill to begin a modest $27 million program of nonlethal assistance to UNITA. In October, Crocker drafted a classified letter that Shultz signed and sent to Rep. Robert Michel, the House Republican leader, saying that the legislation was "ill-timed and will not contribute to the settlement we seek. I feel strongly about Savimbi's courageous stand against Soviet aggression, but there are better ways to help. A determined effort on our part to pursue the negotiation is a good approach."[12] Shultz's letter leaked and ignited an uproar. Michel wrote a forceful letter back to Shultz arguing that U.S. aid to UNITA was "not only a geostrategic but a moral necessity. . . . I cannot see how we can argue that aid to the democratic forces in Nicaragua helps the chance of negotiations while aid to UNITA somehow damages the negotiating process."[13]

Shultz recognized immediately that his letter to Michel had been a mistake. It was one of the rare occasions I saw him angry at what his staff had gotten him into. As on Central America, his subordinates had led him down a path that exposed him to attack from the conservatives. Shultz bobbed and weaved, stressing in public that "we support the freedom fighting of Jonas Savimbi and UNITA" but quietly suggesting that the Pepper-Kemp bill might not be the best way to go about it.[14]

The objection to the Pepper-Kemp bill was in large part a matter of its overtness. In terms that the master geopolitical street fighter Henry Kissinger would have understood, Crocker argued that an open program of aid was a more blatant challenge to the prestige of the Angolans, Cubans, and Soviets, forcing a public reaction (such as walking out of the talks, which the Angolans did), while a covert program of aid could be effective without this disadvantage. This was what Shultz meant by saying in the letter to Michel that there were "better ways to help." It was, I believe, Shultz's principal motivation in discouraging open legislation like Pepper-Kemp. Reagan himself bought the argument, blurting to the press on November 22: "We all believe that a covert operation would be more useful to us and have more chance of success right now than the overt proposal that has been made in the Congress."[15]

But in the back of Crocker's mind I suspect was something more. In his exhausting effort to nurture delicate negotiations between the MPLA and South Africa, he was acutely conscious of the short-term disruption that U.S. aid for UNITA would cause. Perhaps he was too close to the negotiations to face the prospect with equanimity. Crocker also became convinced that his Angolan interlocutors could be weaned away from their Soviet/Cuban connection by positive inducements; he dangled before them the prospect of eventual U.S. diplomatic recognition if there was a political settlement.[16] The State Department for the same reason resisted labeling Angola (or Mozambique) as "Communist" countries, which by law would have excluded the possibility of economic aid. This approach made more sense with Mozambique, which, while led by self-proclaimed Marxists, posed no geopolitical threat to any Western interest and seemed to be more genuinely nonaligned and interested in ties with the West. (For the same reason, despite conservative pressures, the Reagan administration did not support an anti-Marxist rebel group, RENAMO, against the Mozambican government.) But hopes of weaning the MPLA away from its Communist patrons—without whom it might not have been able to remain in power—were less realistic.

On the issue of aid for Savimbi, Crocker's hesitation soon enough encountered a powerful pro-Savimbi force—his boss, George Shultz. Shultz knew full well that *his* boss, Ronald Reagan, was committed to helping anti-Marxist resistance movements in general and UNITA in particular; Shultz had enough trouble with conservative sniper fire on arms control and Central America and saw no reason to invite more on other issues. In a speech on April 16, 1985—in language drafted by my staff—Shultz had denounced the Clark Amendment for shielding an illegitimate Marxist regime from its own people and for, in effect, enacting the Brezhnev Doctrine into American law. However, the Heritage Foundation unleashed a full-scale attack on Shultz in the fall of 1985, accusing him of betraying Reagan's policies. Angola and Mozambique were prominently featured in the critique.[17]

More important than this conservative attack was Shultz's own philosophical understanding that the leverage of aid to UNITA would ultimately reinforce our efforts to negotiate a Cuban withdrawal from Angola. Shultz had learned a painful lesson from his experience in Lebanon.

In 1982, U.S. Marines had been deployed in Beirut with the humanitarian mission of protecting the Palestinians after the Israeli invasion. After Shultz negotiated a peace agreement between Israel and Lebanon in May 1983, Syria declared war on both the agreement and the Lebanese government. The political ground shifted under our feet, and the marines became targets for the Syrian-backed forces assaulting Beirut. The United States labored mightily to negotiate a compromise in 1983–84, but the Syrian pressure was relentless. Shultz urged Reagan to authorize use of our naval firepower off the coast to bolster the Lebanese. This was blocked, however, by Secretary Weinberger, who considered Lebanon a hopeless mess and wanted out. After terrorists blew up the marine barracks, congressional pressures escalated as well. The Syrian foreign minister gloated to his Lebanese counterpart that the Americans were "short of breath," and the negotiation died. The marines were pulled out ignominiously in February 1984.

Shultz remained convinced that a stalemate in the U.S. government had doomed the peace agreement he had negotiated.[18] He poured out his frustrations so frequently to his staff that, as mentioned in chapter 11, I persuaded him to deliver a speech on power and diplomacy and how the two must go together. This he did, before the Trilateral Commission in Washington on April 3, 1984. I had helped in the drafting, and it is one of my collaborations with Shultz of which I am proudest. In the course of a broad philosophical discussion of the political, military, constitutional, and moral issues involved in the use of force, he declared:

> Certainly power must always be guided by purpose, but the hard reality is that diplomacy not backed by strength is ineffectual. That is why, for example, the United States has succeeded many times in its mediation when many other well-intentional mediators have failed. Leverage, as well as goodwill, is required. . . .
>
> Sometimes, regrettable as it may be, political conflict degenerates into a test of strength. It was precisely our military role in Lebanon that was problematical, not our diplomatic exertion. Our military role was hamstrung by legislative and other inhibitions; the Syrians were not interested in diplomatic compromise so long as the prospect of hegemony was not foreclosed. They could judge from our domestic debate that our staying power was limited. . . .
>
> The lesson is that power and diplomacy are not alternatives. They must go together, or we will accomplish very little in this world.

I was in a meeting between Shultz and Chet Crocker in October 1985, in Shultz's private office, when Shultz applied this lesson to Angola. Frustrated by Chet's reluctance, he spoke emphatically: The repeal of Clark was a *good thing*; Savimbi was *our man*; helping him would *strengthen* our diplomacy, not weaken it. Chet had done brilliantly in making something out of nothing; now we had more cards to play.

But despite Shultz's clarity, the first assistance program for Savimbi developed in the interagency process under Chet's leadership involved only nonlethal items—medicine and clothing, communications gear, tactical advice. I recall another meeting with Shultz a short time later in which Chet explained the virtues of proceeding slowly. I grumbled, Shultz nodded resignedly, and the program went forward in the modest manner Crocker preferred.

Chet assured me after the second meeting that this was only the beginning of the program and that more could come later, incrementally. This indeed happened. Yet Crocker clearly always had one eye on his MPLA and liberal audience. In testimony to the Senate Foreign Relations Committee on February 18, 1986, he pronounced for the first time what became the official euphemism for the covert program: "We intend to be supportive of UNITA in an effective and appropriate manner." However, he went out of his way to assure his audience that this did not change our devotion to peace: ". . . I want to categorically state here that the basis and goals of our policy remain unchanged: We seek negotiated solutions that will bring independence to Namibia and withdrawal of Cuban troops from Angola. Such a solution opens the way for Angolans to reconcile and achieve peace." This was unexceptionable so long as we remained conscious of the value of simultaneously maintaining pressure on the Soviets, Cubans, and MPLA to compromise.

The push to aid Savimbi ran into its share of controversy. The House African Affairs Subcommittee, a center of liberal opposition, held public hearings on the question in October–November 1985 and in April 1986, as did the House Intelligence Committee in March 1986. Critics pointed to a variety of dangers, summed up by Solarz:

Aiding UNITA, the United States simply increases Angola's dependence on the Cubans. Rather than allowing UNITA to overthrow the Angolan government, Cuba would most likely dispatch more troops to Angola to shore up the Luanda regime. The result would be a new stalemate at a higher level of violence. . . . Angola would be unlikely to return to the negotiating table. South Africa would have every incentive to use and prolong the Angolan conflict, both to avoid a Namibia settlement and to gain maximum benefits from a de facto strategic alliance with the United States.

This alliance greatly damages America's position in Africa. . . .

The final reason for not aiding the Angolan insurgents concerns UNITA itself. Even with U.S. assistance, the movement has little chance of overthrowing the regime in Luanda. And even were its prospects brighter, UNITA would be unlikely to bring a new birth of freedom to Angola. Savimbi's background and beliefs belie the feverish attempts of his American supporters to paint him as an African James Madison. He has described his own political philosophy as Marxist, with a preference for the Chinese system. . . . In this continuing struggle, the American interest would be served best by urging national reconciliation instead of siding with one ethnic group against the other.[19]

These arguments had been made in 1975 against the Ford administration. But the Reagan administration in 1985 had a significant advantage over its predecessor. The intervening decade had demonstrated by experience what Ford and Kissinger had argued in the abstract: American restraint had not been met by Soviet restraint but by Soviet/Cuban escalation in Angola and by Soviet intervention in Ethiopia, South Yemen, and then Afghanistan. Shultz stressed the Soviet angle in his speech of April 16, 1985:

> Today, there are about 30,000 Cuban troops in Angola, along with East European advisers. Soviet aid in the region has been almost exclusively military. Our adversaries have no constructive stake in the region, seeing, rather, in instability their best chance to expand their influence. When the Soviets and Cubans intervene in a part of the world far from their borders, we had better pay attention. Such intervention threatens African independence as well as the global balance. The peoples of Africa deserve better than the bankruptcy—economic, political, and moral—of the Soviet model.

Chet Crocker, once suitably braced by Shultz, could be an eloquent spokesman for the value of leverage in diplomacy. In his Senate testimony of February 18, 1986, he affirmed that "our ability to respond diplomatically and in other ways has been measurably strengthened by the repeal of the Clark Amendment," and stressed that "diplomacy requires to be effective a degree of pressure that drives the parties toward a political compromise." Crocker said that he, too, was concerned about military escalation, but he placed the onus on the MPLA and its outside backers: "This past year we have seen the MPLA government, strongly backed by Moscow and Havana, pursue such an escalation. They sought to reverse 2 years of UNITA gains and deal a body blow to that movement. They failed. It is important in our view that they continue to fail. . . . We share Dr. Savimbi's belief that there are no military solutions in Angola." To the arguments about UNITA's unsavory ties to South Africa, the administration and its supporters had the plausible reply that UNITA's dependence on South Africa was the product of the cutoff of U.S. aid and that if the United States resumed its aid, South African influence would be replaced by our own.[20]

The controversy turned into a battle of public relations between backers of the two sides. According to Fred Bridgland (then a pro-Savimbi observer):

Both the MPLA and UNITA hired prestigious lobbying firms to present their case to the capital's powerbrokers. UNITA took on Black, Manafort, Stone and Kelly on a contract of $US 600,000 a year. The move was made after several years of urging by one of Savimbi's main bankrollers, the Saudi Arabians. The company had good relations with CIA Director William J. Casey. And Christopher J. Lehman, a specialist assistant to President Reagan and, at 37, the younger brother of Navy Secretary John F. Lehman, left the White House staff to orchestrate the Savimbi campaign for Black, Manafort.

The MPLA paid a similar amount to Gray and Co., another PR firm with close ties to the White House. Robert Gray, the firm's founder, had been chairman of Reagan's first inaugural committee. Furious right-wingers accused Gray of turning "pink" as he appointed Daniel Murphy, a retired four-star admiral who had served as deputy director for the CIA and as a top aide to Vice-President George Bush, to look after the MPLA's account. After years spent keeping an eye on Communists, Admiral Murphy now advised MPLA representatives visiting the US to wear conservative suits and ties to contrast with Savimbi's preferred Maoist-style suits and Guevara-type uniforms. Murphy hired a former employee of the Gulf corporation, which exploits Angola's oil reserves and pays royalties which sustain the MPLA's war against UNITA. The new man from Gulf quickly told reporters that Savimbi had lied about his academic credentials, though his doctorate dissertation, entitled "The Implications of Yalta for the Third World," can be consulted in the library of Lausanne University. To the *Wall Street Journal*, Admiral Murphy explained his new job with Angola's MPLA government this way: "Their image problem is that they're a bunch of Communists who have a bunch of Cubans there."[21]

Conservative pressures on Gray and Murphy eventually forced them to drop the MPLA account like a hot potato. Hill and Knowlton took it over.

The U.S. program for Savimbi developed surprising momentum. Reagan himself disclosed his intention to provide covert military aid, in the remarks quoted earlier, in a session with journalists after returning from the Geneva summit. Congress was notified in mid-December of a $15 million program.[22] Reagan received Savimbi ostentatiously in the Oval Office in January 1986. As with the Afghan mujahedin, this meeting, arranged by the NSC staff, was a way of sending a signal to the State Department as well as to the Soviets and their clients. In September 1986, when House liberals, led by Lee Hamilton, tried to kill the program, they were soundly rebuffed, 220–187. Centrist Democrats like Dennis DeConcini of Arizona in the Senate and Dave McCurdy of Oklahoma in the House added crucial weight to the pro-UNITA side. Over the next three years, as on Afghanistan, bipartisan groups of senators and representatives would bombard Reagan and Shultz with letters insisting on more military or diplomatic support for UNITA.

Within the executive branch, as the war escalated, UNITA's champions at the Pentagon and NSC staff pushed for the provision of Stinger antiaircraft missiles. In this case (unlike Afghanistan), the State Department was reluctant, but also unlike the Afghan case, the working level of the CIA was supportive of rather than apoplectic over the idea. As recounted in the previous chapter, fifty Stingers arrived in Angola in the late summer and early fall of 1986 and were put to effective use. TOW antitank missiles were also provided.

OVERT VERSUS COVERT

The controversy over aid to UNITA took a surprising turn. While opponents questioned the merits of providing aid, a second debate broke out in 1986 over whether such aid should be provided openly instead of through covert CIA channels. Some critics purported to oppose only the secrecy of the program. In this debate the political bedfellows rearranged themselves in unpredictable ways.

As the Reagan Doctrine went into high gear also in Nicaragua and Afghanistan, this was a debate that clearly went far beyond Angola, and even beyond the Reagan Doctrine. It reflected an innate American discomfort, on both the Left and Right, with clandestine activities.

The *Federalist Papers* speak of intelligence operations (at least intelligence gathering),[23] and our Founding Fathers engaged in secret operations without noticeable inhibition.[24] The Lewis and Clark expedition was designed as a covert military operation into foreign-held territory, funded by a secret appropriation.[25] Yet our twentieth-century tradition is dominated by Woodrow Wilson, whose principle of "open covenants, openly arrived at," while it had specifically to do with discouraging secret treaties, soon took on a more general meaning as a fundamental commandment of openness in a democracy. Intelligence was an unsavory business. Henry Stimson, FDR's secretary of war, closed down a U.S. secret intelligence service before World War II with the legendary comment that "gentlemen don't read other people's mail."

In 1975–76, in the aftermath of Vietnam and Watergate, dramatic investigations were held in the Senate and House (the committees chaired by Frank Church and Otis Pike, respectively) digging into alleged assassination plots, intelligence blunders, domestic spying, and other misdeeds. There is no point defending whatever genuine misdeeds were uncovered; nevertheless, the emotion accompanying the exposés was reminiscent of the Gerald Nye committee of the 1920s, which determined that arms merchants had dragged us into World War I. The subliminal message fifty years later was that only such sinister, undemocratic forces could explain foreign policy problems we had gotten into; in both cases there was a rebellion against the hard traditional practices of international politics, an attempt to cleanse American policy from unsavory influences and to reinforce its moral foundations. It was these congressional investigations of the 1970s that gave birth to the modern procedures of congressional oversight, now exercised by two select committees with power to review (though not necessarily to veto) sensitive executive branch activities in this field.

Opposition to the very idea of covert action remains a durable strain in our political thinking. The American Civil Liberties Union has long argued that it is unconstitutional and incompatible with democracy. In the words of Morton Halperin: "[C]overt operations are fundamentally incompatible with a democratic society. . . . [C]overt operations are used by our Presidents to avoid the public and congressional debate mandated by the Constitution, a debate which is particularly crucial when questions of war and peace are at stake. Granting officials the authority to conduct covert operations inevitably leads to abuses of power, as it did in the Iran-contra affair."[26] Prof. Allan Goodman of Georgetown University argued that the paramilitary dimensions of covert action should be scaled back, shifted out of the CIA, and handed over to the Defense Department to manage. Other forms of covert activity, he suggested, "are ineffective instruments of foreign policy and spawn doubts about the moral character of the U.S. government."[27] Recent experience leads to the paradoxical conclusion that Americans may today be far more comfortable with fighting a major war like Desert Storm than with indulging in clandestine paramilitary activities.

There is a strong case, of course, that such practices are fully consistent with the Constitution.[28] It was the passionate conviction, moreover, of my friend Miles Copeland, a flamboyant longtime CIA veteran, that covert action is the indispensable recourse when open, declared warfare is dangerous and "political action" in the classical intelligence sense can do a job better.[29] Covert action is what Theodore Shackley, another CIA veteran, called "the third option": It is often the middle ground between abandoning the field altogether and escalating to full-scale war.[30]

Henry Kissinger argued the point in congressional testimony on Angola in January 1976:

> We chose covert means because we wanted to keep our visibility to a minimum: we wanted the greatest possible opportunity for an African solution. We felt that overt assistance would elaborate a formal doctrine justifying great power intervention. . . . The Angola situation is of a type in which diplomacy without leverage is impotent, yet direct military confrontation would involve unnecessary risks. Thus it is precisely one of those grey areas where covert methods are crucial if we are to have any prospect of influencing certain events of potentially global importance.[31]

Part of the argument had to do with the practical fact that U.S. covert actions in the last twenty years have usually involved small third-world countries that were our partners—Pakistan in the case of Afghanistan; Zaire in the case of Angola; Honduras, El Salvador, and Guatemala in the case of Nicaragua—and that felt highly vulnerable to retaliatory pressures the more their role was publicly exposed. Donald Fortier, the thoughtful young NSC strategist who later became deputy assistant to the president for national security affairs (until he died tragically of cancer at age thirty-nine), made the point this way in a speech in 1985:

> Covert action is carried out for the most part in cooperation with somebody else, some friendly government that is often both weak (sometimes in fact with no army of its own), anxious (as it watches the modern military machine that its neighbor is acquiring with the Soviet Union's help), and fearful of the cost of open dependence on us (given political cultures that sometimes make the image of such dependence easily manipulable by adversaries of the regime).
>
> *Our need to cooperate with a partner in this fashion limits what we can do.* If our partner is too unsure of himself to oppose an aggressive neighbor openly, then our help has to be given in a way that protects him. We have to be sensitive to his weaknesses and vulnerabilities. Since increasing the

security of such states is one of the goals of our policy in the first place, it would make no sense to pursue that goal in a way that *diminishes* their security instead.[32]

Even after the identity of the neighboring country becomes known—which has happened in almost every case—it makes a great deal of difference whether the disclosure is a press report or a confirmation by the U.S. government. The question is constantly asked: Our adversary knows, everyone else knows, so why can't the American people be told? But in the former case, that of a press report, a vulnerable ally can still evade acknowledgment; the prestige of the opponent is less engaged; the whole business is still taking place in a netherworld of plausible deniability and quiet political shadowboxing. In the latter case, to the contrary, official confirmation by the U.S. government closes off all political escape routes, forces the opponent to react publicly in ways he might not otherwise feel compelled to do, and invites an escalation of pressures; it is not just an acknowledgment of an already known fact but a fresh political act with specific consequences. This may seem a subtle point, but in the real world of foreign policy it can mean the difference between failure and success.

In connection with allies, there was also the additional problem of a peculiarity of American law: An open request for military-assistance funds for an ally for use across its borders or transfer to a third party would have been contrary to existing U.S. foreign-assistance legislation.[33] We had reached the point in our nation's history when major decisions of this kind would be made not by strategists but by lawyers and accountants.

The prospect of being forced to operate openly has been known to inhibit the executive branch's willingness to proceed with a program. In 1989, during a public debate over whether to give military aid to the non-Communist resistance in Cambodia, President Bush's national security adviser, Brent Scowcroft, as well as his deputy (later CIA director) Robert Gates were reluctant for a number of reasons to support a CIA program; one of their reasons was a belief that an openly publicized CIA program was a bad precedent and bad tradecraft.

Perhaps Kissinger's strongest argument for a covert program for Angola had been diplomatic—that keeping an operation quiet, because it posed less of a challenge to the prestige of either side, also maximized the chances for political compromise: "[O]ne reason we did not want to make this an overt action is precisely to avoid a public confrontation and to permit a solution of it without bringing it to the point of open confrontation. . . . "[34] He was convinced from his conversations with Soviet ambassador Dobrynin that some sort of deal was in the making before the unilateral U.S. aid cutoff and that the nonpublic nature of the mutual jockeying on the ground facilitated the diplomacy. Similarly, the Reagan administration's allergy to open congressional resolutions on aid to the Afghan resistance (like Tsongas-Ritter), as well as to calls for open aid for the Contras or UNITA, was produced in large part by this line of thinking. Quiet diplomacy between East and West was a factor for restraint in the nuclear age, most especially where local confrontations were threatening to get out of control. Openness might be more satisfying and more straightforward, but the job of statesmen was not to be cheerleaders but to contain international conflicts and produce peaceful outcomes.

This line of reasoning did not sit well with either liberals or conservatives. The call for openness came, first of all and most naturally, from members of Congress who opposed aid for Savimbi. Lee Hamilton, for example, insisted that the president was resorting to covert means as a way "to circumvent a public debate in Congress on a significant foreign policy decision"[35]; this was an attempt to cast doubt on the democratic legitimacy of what was being undertaken, despite the well-established ground rules of accountability through the intelligence committees. In another context (Cambodia), Sen. Robert Byrd of West Virginia argued dramatically that without public debate over aid for the Cambodians we were only inviting another Vietnam: "Surely we have learned from our experience in Vietnam, if nothing else, that if we are to succeed in a new policy toward that region, it cannot be achieved through secret policy-making, secret military programs, secret arms transfers, or secret deals."[36]

These men can be suspected of harboring the hope that an open debate would kill the whole program they objected to. That result could have been produced by, for example, tying the executive branch up in knots over whether an open program was worse than no program at all, or even feasible, given the insecurities of allies collaborating with us, or, alternatively, by a protracted controversy in Congress and the media in which fears about the program could be cultivated.

Strikingly, however, demands for openness came also from ardent supporters of the Reagan Doctrine. "Covertness is crippling," wrote conservative analyst Gregory Fossedal, " . . . to an enterprise the essence of which is building solid, lasting public support."[37] Sen. Malcolm Wallop complained in 1984 that administration policymakers liked covertness because it was a way of evading the need for more forceful action—"a substitute for policy itself, while thus avoiding or deferring a clear policy choice." He criticized President Ford for not making the case in 1975 for *open* aid to the anti-Marxist forces in Angola: "This reticence only implied that the Administration was unsure about both the effectiveness and the moral legitimacy of the requested authority. . . . " And Wallop vigorously rejected arguments about "facilitating negotiations"—he thought this a woefully inadequate objective that risked betraying the resistance groups we were supporting. In Angola, Afghanistan, and Nicaragua, he wrote, victory should be the goal: "[T]he victory of the anti-Soviet forces is so preferable to its alternative, both in terms of our interests and from a moral standpoint, that U.S. officials should have no difficulty in espousing it publicly. In a democracy no action, however covert, ought to be undertaken unless, if need be, it can be confidently defended in public."[38]

Thus, the debate turned out to be another incarnation of the American ambivalence about the manner of our international involvement. Covert action was defended by its advocates as indispensable; its detractors scorned it as unacceptable—the Left condemning it as too much and the Right as too little. Covert action turned out to be controversial not only because of its unsavory associations and behind-closed-doors procedures but because it embodied the intersection of power and diplomacy. Liberals disliked the military component of policy, seeing it as inconsistent with negotiation; conservatives feared any negotiation, preferring military victory. Both sides joined in a rebellion against the reality that often some combination of the two is required—that sometimes limited rather than unlimited aims must be sought, that leverage and diplomacy go together and neither makes sense without the other. The neater alternatives may be simply unavailable. Short of all-out war—a rare enterprise—this is a reflection of the complexity of the world. Indeed, if one deprives oneself of the intermediate range of tools, one risks being confronted with the starker choices of all-out methods or yielding to an adversary.

Iran-Contra, as noted, reopened the controversy. Even though Iran-Contra was, if anything, a rogue NSC operation bypassing or manipulating regular intelligence procedures, Congress took its revenge by tightening oversight over the regular procedures. But even so, a grudging national consensus seems to have developed in the late 1980s that covert methods were still a necessary part of the national arsenal. The liberal Twentieth Century Fund sponsored a 1992 Task Force on Covert Action and American Democracy; it urged a "minimalist" approach of using covert action only as a last resort, and only according to strict accountability.[39] Two of the wisest commentators on the subject, W. Michael Reisman and James E. Baker, also stressed accountability and legality: "An act accomplished covertly should be overtly lawful."[40] But they acknowledged in less clothespin-on-the-nose fashion that the need for such methods is likely to survive even with the end of the Cold War:

> The United States may, as a moral matter, simply decide to eschew all covert action of certain kinds. But this would not, we believe, lead all other actors, whether from weakness, desperation, or rational calculations, to refrain similarly from such actions. On the contrary, the absence of a manifest retaliatory capacity might even encourage adventurism. Like the strategy of maintaining an arsenal of hideous weapons to deter others from using them, a covert capacity may deter noxious covert activities, pending universal, effective agreement to outlaw them. . . . [S]ome form [of this activity] is likely to continue, driven by the dynamic of political and economic competition and the emergence of new competing versions of public order, for example, some strains of Islamic fundamentalism which endorse covert terror as a legitimate political instrument.[41]

Drafters of the 1991 Intelligence Authorization Act, in order to assure greater accountability, sought to require advance notice to Congress of all covert actions except for extreme cases in which such notification could be delayed up to forty-eight hours. While many of the procedures and definitions were tightened in the final legislation, Bush and the Republicans were able to carve out a residual sphere within which Bush reserved his constitutional prerogative, though he pledged in a letter that he would "anticipate" to delay notification in exceptional cases no more than "a few days."[42]

Thus, the president retained the initiative and a residual flexibility in the law. Congress continues to accept the legitimacy of covert action, even though its individual members frequently rebel. Politically, nevertheless, Iran-Contra exacted its price. Future presidents would pay a much stiffer political, if not legal, penalty for any repetition of the machinations of Iran-Contra—presidential findings not written down or not communicated at all to Congress; attempts by the NSC staff to act on its own and bypass the CIA's obligation of congressional consultation. Thus, the prospect was for continued use of covert methods in a turbulent world, ongoing tension between Congress and the president, and continued national schizophrenia on the wisdom and morality of the practice.

POWER AND DIPLOMACY IN ANGOLA

In 1986, in response to the U.S. decision to resume military supply to UNITA, the MPLA authorities broke off contact with Crocker and withdrew from any active participation in the diplomacy. On the face of it, it vindicated Solarz's warning that such an American intervention would doom negotiations and destroy America's credentials as a mediator. Yet the Angolan leadership, even if they had not been Marxist in their training, would have had to adapt, as all policymakers do, to the objective realities around them. Despite new infusions of Soviet equipment and the assurances received on two visits to Moscow by Angolan president José Eduardo dos Santos, a small-scale FAPLA offensive against UNITA in the 1986 dry season fizzled out. The Americans seemed increasingly to hold key cards, which made a permanent cutoff of contact with Washington counterproductive.

As if to confirm the improvement in the U.S. bargaining position, various African countries urged the Angolans to return to the table. In April 1987, after the active mediation of Congolese president Denis Sassou-Nguesso, Angolan officials resumed their contact with Crocker in a two-day session in Brazzaville. In an even more striking development, the Cubans, in a secret contact in July, made known to the United States their desire to join the negotiation under U.S. auspices.[43] The American strategy of bolstering Savimbi while working for a negotiated settlement was beginning to pay off.

Crocker patiently put together the building blocks of a negotiation. In Brazzaville and in two later visits to Luanda in July and September, he worked on bringing the Cubans into the negotiation and on the question of whether total and not just partial Cuban withdrawal could be on the agenda. He made some headway. Even though the propositions were all abstractions, Crocker was building against the day when the sides would be ready for significant political moves; at that point the groundwork would have been laid and the negotiating process already in place. But the diplomacy was interrupted by a new explosion of fighting.

Real progress in the diplomacy in 1987–88 closely followed the course of the battle, in what was almost a caricature of the thesis of this book. Even while talking to Crocker, the Angolans devoted most of their effort in 1986 to preparing a new offensive against UNITA, this time a major drive that took place in August–September 1987. Further military confrontations took place in the winter of 1987–88 and the summer of 1988. The end result was to convince the Angolans' backers finally that UNITA simply could not be defeated, and to convince the South Africans finally that it, too, could not afford a continuing ordeal of escalation and attrition. Only after this process of continually testing the balance of forces on the ground exhausted itself did the principal breakthrough occur, in the fall of 1988.

The 1987 Angolan dry season offensive saw an unusual degree of direct Soviet involvement. In April–May 1987, Soviet military transport aircraft, including giant An-124s, made around-the-clock deliveries to forward bases with what was estimated to be $1 billion in new weaponry. A Soviet general planned and directed the assault, which comprised ten thousand troops and three hundred to four hundred tanks and other armored vehicles. On August 14, this force moved out from its forward base of Cuito Cuanavale toward Mavinga, where UNITA was believed to have ten thousand to fifteen thousand well-trained troops plus another fifteen thousand to twenty thousand irregulars. The capture of Mavinga would put Jamba, Savimbi's capital, in jeopardy.[44]

Once again, South Africa stepped in to prevent UNITA's defeat. In mid-September, a large SADF contingent of two mechanized brigades and two artillery squadrons (three thousand men) crossed into Angola and blocked the Angolans some fifty kilometers from Mavinga. The Angolans, who apparently did not expect South African intervention on so large a scale, were decisively beaten back in two separate battles; their losses were estimated at between one thousand and two thousand dead, more than twice that number wounded, plus several hundred armored vehicles abandoned or destroyed.[45]

South African military commanders attributed their success to two weapons—their G-5 155-mm howitzer, with a thirty-five-kilometer range, and the Stinger antiaircraft missile in the hands of UNITA, which (just as in Afghanistan) forced the Angolan helicopter gunships and MiG-23 fighter-bombers to work at high altitudes where they could do little damage to either UNITA or SADF ground forces.[46] The impact of the Stinger was not as decisive as in Afghanistan, but it contributed to the core reality that UNITA was not going to be easily defeated by military means.

It had an impact first on Fidel Castro, who, as we saw, initiated contact with the United States in July 1987. In a speech a year later he acknowledged the Mavinga disaster and (by implication) blamed the Soviets: "I believe that history one day will tell everything: what mistakes were made and why. I will only say that Cuba had no responsibility for those mistakes."[47]

The scale of the setback and the dissension with the Soviets clearly had changed Castro's thinking. The Cubans admitted to over two thousand dead over the course of their thirteen-year involvement.[48] In January 1988, they had sent a representative for the first time to take part in Crocker's dialogue with the Angolans (ostensibly as a member of the Angolan delegation); the Cubans explicitly signed on to linkage, indicating that they were prepared to negotiate *total* withdrawal of their forces from Angola in return for Namibian independence under UN Security Council Resolution 435. In March 1988, Angola and Cuba presented to Crocker a detailed proposal for the total withdrawal of Cuban troops in four years. This timetable was not likely to be accepted, but (as in Afghanistan) it was a start.

The South Africans had been bloodied as well, however. Their dead and wounded from warfare and malaria in the 1987 campaign may have been 150—for them, a high number.[49] The UN Security Council voted unanimously on November 25, 1987, to "condemn" South Africa's "illegal entry" into Angola and demanded an immediate withdrawal. For the first time, Angola authorized the recently reinforced Cuban brigade to begin patrolling in southern Angola and to engage South African forces there.[50] The stage was set for some dramatic confrontations.

For the South Africans were not ready to fold. They were the next to go on the offensive. The Pretoria government of P. W. Botha was under domestic pressure as a result of the bloody fighting in the fall. Some critics spoke out against the Angolan war; others cried out for victory. Botha's response was to try to inflict a decisive riposte against the strategic prize of Cuito Cuanavale, the staging base for so many Angolan offensives against UNITA's home territory. The town contained an important airstrip as well as a forward radar station.

For four months in 1987–88, a South African force of four thousand troops, including tanks and artillery, plus eight thousand UNITA troops, besieged Cuito Cuanavale. As a major battle raged, several thousand Cuban reinforcements arrived, initially to take up defensive positions. In mid-January, as SADF forces were threatening to annihilate three nearby FAPLA brigades, Castro ordered his forces to attack the South Africans. This Dunkirk-like rescue (as Castro called it) broke the siege. The South Africans tried two further assaults in February and March 1988 but then subsided.[51] They had lost several aircraft and tanks—hard to replace, given the global embargo against military sales to South Africa.

Having blunted the South African offensive, Castro decided to raise the ante. "It was necessary," he later explained, "to change [the] correlation of forces."[52] Fresh troops arrived from Cuba starting in December 1987, and in March 1988 he ordered a force of fifteen thousand men to head south to the Namibian border to threaten South Africa's traditional sanctuary. The Cubans were asked by the South Africans for assurances that they would not cross the border into Namibia; they refused to give any such assurances. Nervous U.S. officials warned the Cubans that they were "playing with fire."[53]

Crocker picked this moment to resume his dialogue with South Africa. In March 1988, he met in Geneva with then Foreign Minister "Pik" Botha, who responded with derision to the Angolan/Cuban offer of withdrawal stretched out over four years. President P. W. Botha, watching the Cuban military moves, dug in his heels publicly and declared defiantly: "We are staying in Angola until the Cubans leave."[54] But, like the Angolans and Cubans, the South Africans thought it prudent not to block Crocker's diplomatic efforts. In view of the increasing American role on the ground with UNITA and the ambiguous military situation, it was wiser to keep their options open and not alienate the United States.

In early May 1988, Crocker achieved another procedural breakthrough: He organized an extraordinary meeting in London of representatives of South Africa, Angola, Cuba, and the United States. Not only diplomats but the chiefs of military staffs were in attendance. The discussions were overshadowed, however, by the military situation. It was at the London meeting that the South Africans asked the Cubans for assurances that Cuban forces would not enter Namibia and were refused. At a June meeting in Cairo, the South Africans demanded that the Cuban troops (then numbering some forty-five thousand or more) vacate Angola in seven months, the same time span in which they were obligated to vacate Namibia under Resolution 435.

The powder keg was in place; all it needed was a spark. The Cubans had six mechanized infantry regiments and a regiment each of artillery, tanks, and antiaircraft on the Namibian border; they backed this up with three newly built forward air bases for fighters and bombers, giving them air superiority over the South Africans. On June 27, a few days after the Cairo talks had ended, a SADF reconnaissance unit thirty kilometers north of the Calueque Dam in the southwest surprised a Cuban armored unit and opened fire—without instructions, SADF officials later said. The SADF force mauled the Cubans, killing 150, and provoked an immediate Cuban retaliation via an air strike against the Calueque Dam, which killed twelve South African soldiers. (The dam, along the Cunene River, controlled the water supply for nothern Namibia.)

Despite the small numbers involved by the standards of other conflicts, this clash had a tremendous dramatic impact. Inside South Africa—which was not used to taking significant casualties—it provoked new opposition from church leaders and others against the Angolan war.

Cuban air power—which Castro continued to augment through the summer—turned out to be a trump card. By September, there were fifty MiGs based at the forward airfields within striking distance of SADF's bases in Namibia. The South Africans, cut off from international military aircraft purchases and with only a small aircraft industry of their own, had reached the limits.

After the Mavinga, Cuito Cuanavale, and Calueque battles of 1987–88, Cuba and South Africa reached the same conclusion: Both sides had seen the limits of what could be achieved by warfare; both saw the dangers and costs of continuing it. Each side, paradoxically, could also claim a certain degree of victory in the blows it had inflicted on the other. Crocker's moment had come.

In July, at secluded Governors Island in New York, the four governments (the U.S., South Africa, Cuba, and Angola) met again and agreed on a general statement of "principles for a peaceful settlement in southwestern Africa." It was a balanced package of mutual concessions: from South Africa, a promise to provide a date certain for Namibian independence according to Resolution 435; from Cuba and Angola, a promise to provide a timetable for the phased, total withdrawal of Cuban troops from Angola; from all sides, a commitment to end outside intervention; and an invitation to the UN Security Council's permanent members to be guarantors of a settlement (thereby opening a role for the Soviets).

The Soviets—even in the heyday of Gorbachev's "new thinking"— had been surprisingly unhelpful. Deputy Foreign Minister Anatolii Adamishin and Foreign Ministry Africa specialist Vladillen Vasev were the officials whom Crocker made a regular practice to consult and keep informed—in London in late April 1988, in Lisbon in May, in late May and early June at Reagan's Moscow summit, and in late July and early August in Geneva. The Moscow summit joint statement of June 1, 1988, affirmed the importance of "constructive interaction" between the United States and the Soviet Union to promote peaceful solutions of regional conflicts. Yet the Soviets continued to insist on termination of U.S. aid to UNITA as a precondition to Cuban troop withdrawal, which Crocker firmly rejected.[55] Crocker found the Soviets wary of American dominance of the process. Adamishin had told him in mid-1987: "You are playing too many roles." Crocker also believed that the military and intelligence bureaucracies in Moscow and the Communist party ideologists continued to exert influence.[56]

But in the year of Gorbachev's fateful decision to pull out of Afghanistan, it would have been absurd not to treat the Brezhnev adventure in Africa as an even more obvious candidate for early liquidation. By 1988, the realities on the ground showed no prospect for military victory. With their Angolan and Cuban allies willingly participating in a U.S.-led negotiation that promised a balanced compromise, the Soviets eventually came around. Enough was enough, especially in a part of the world where their strategic interest was minimal.

America's dominant role in the diplomacy was not without other grumbling detractors—European powers that had had a role in earlier efforts but were now relegated to the sidelines; radical Africans who mistrusted the United States.[57] But the United States uniquely had influence with South Africa and, once again, with UNITA (after resuming aid), and therefore it had leverage with *all* sides in a way that Moscow, the Europeans, the United Nations, and others did not. As Anwar Sadat figured out in the Arab-Israeli dispute, America's close ties with one side did not automatically disqualify it from mediating; on the contrary. Thus were disproved a number of naive academic theories about what effective mediation depends on as well as the arguments that aid for UNITA would doom our diplomatic role.

SAVIMBI AND THE U.S. POLITICAL SCENE

Crocker's brilliant progress toward a negotiated withdrawal of Cuban troops coupled with independence for Namibia did not ease his domestic problem. It only heightened anxieties. The respective factions in the United States continued their pressures—the liberals hammering away at the relationship with South Africa and UNITA and urging diplomatic recognition of the MPLA regime, the conservatives hammering at the MPLA and worried that UNITA's interests were not adequately protected in Crocker's negotiation. Nor did the critics confine themselves to vocal pressures in Washington. They visited the region and advised their respective friends to hang tough and not cave in to Crocker. They pushed for U.S. economic sanctions on South Africa, Namibia, and Angola without regard to the impact of such measures on Crocker's negotiations. In the fall of 1988 the talks were suspended as both sides waited to see whether Democrat Michael Dukakis—known to be hostile to UNITA— defeated George Bush in the presidential election.[58]

Crocker's problem with the conservatives lay in the anomaly of his asymmetrical relationships with Savimbi and with the MPLA regime. Savimbi, of course, was not a direct participant in the talks, while the MPLA regime was. As in Afghanistan, this heightened fears that the negotiating process might itself elevate the status of the regime at the expense of the resistance movement we were theoretically—and not only theoretically—supporting.

Crocker continued to dangle in front of the MPLA the prospect of diplomatic and economic relations once a political accommodation with UNITA was reached; this was a clever tactic, except that it tended to blur an important point. If the MPLA regime was illegitimate, the beneficiary of U.S. diplomatic relations should not be a broadened version of it but a *different* government entirely. The United States continued to oppose the Angolan regime's membership in the World Bank and the IMF, but its dealings with the regime drained its protests of credibility. This undoubtedly contributed to the willingness of all the other Bank/Fund members to vote Angola in, anyway, in the summer of 1989, over U.S. objection, long before the MPLA had fulfilled the U.S. condition. It reminded me of the vain U.S. attempt to postpone China's admission to the United Nations in October 1971 after the Kissinger visits to Beijing.

The United States was also in the peculiar position that the number-one economic supporter of the MPLA regime was an American oil company, Gulf/Chevron, which continued to operate in Angolan territory (especially the enclave of Cabinda in the north) throughout the civil war. Oil revenues, principally from Gulf/Chevron, sustained the regime and helped finance the Soviet/Cuban expeditionary force, yet the United States took no steps to ban the company's operations. The formal U.S. position toward investment in Angola was to discourage it, but without penalties. Periodic efforts by Congress to impose formal economic sanctions on Angola were resisted by the administration. At one point in May 1987, as a review of southern Africa policy was proceeding in the interagency system, I managed to include in the options paper a consideration of a stronger warning to U.S. companies that investment in Angola was inconsistent with U.S. foreign policy. Even Crocker did not object to such an option at that point. But Carla Hills, outside counsel to Gulf/Chevron, made a strong pitch in June to Frank Carlucci, then national security adviser, that the company's presence served American interests: It reduced our dependence on the Persian Gulf; forcing the company out would do nothing to get the Cubans out; European or Japanese firms would quickly step in. On Carlucci's recommendation, Reagan decided to oppose new restrictions.

I used to ask my colleagues periodically why UNITA didn't attack, or at least threaten to attack, oil facilities. It stood to reason that tightening the economic pressure on Angola would compound the political benefit we had achieved by providing military aid. I thought, at a minimum, that if Gulf/Chevron could be urged to leave, the threat of UNITA military action could serve quite adequately to discourage the Europeans or Japanese from coming in. I was told, however, that Savimbi did not have the desire or the capability to challenge the oil operations. I found out subsequently that this was not true. The thought had indeed occurred to him, but he was restrained by fear of the political backlash in America if he struck at a U.S. company, particularly one that was operating in Angola with the blessing of the U.S. government.[59]

The most troublesome political problem was the exclusion of Savimbi from the negotiating table. The argument for his exclusion was that this negotiation focused on the external issues of Cuban troop withdrawal and Namibian independence; on these problems, the governments represented were the relevant players. The internal issue—so-called national reconciliation among the Angolan factions—was a proclaimed goal but a separate topic to be negotiated on a separate track. South Africa presumably could be counted upon not to sell out UNITA's interests, and a successful negotiation would, after all, ensure the removal of the very Cuban force that had put the MPLA into power at UNITA's expense.

Crocker was disingenuous to claim later that the only "relevant leverage" we had was on the external issues[60]—UNITA was at least as effective pressure on the MPLA regime as on the Cubans—but he is probably right that parallel negotiations on the internal and external issues would have posed insurmountable difficulties. The more readily attainable goal of withdrawal of Cuban troops might have been delayed indefinitely. Just as in Afghanistan and Cambodia, an accord on removal of outside military forces was the precursor and precondition of a negotiation on an internal settlement.

The price Crocker paid, however, was that his course inevitably left Savimbi dangling and left him (Crocker) treating ostentatiously with the MPLA regime as if it were a legitimate government when our formal policy was that it was not. Our lips said no, no, no, but our eyes said yes, yes, yes. For purposes of managing his enormously complex negotiation on Cuban troop withdrawal and Namibian independence, Crocker wanted to avoid being seen as "coming out and flatly 'taking sides' " in the civil war,[61] but he bent over so far backward to avoid embracing Savimbi that he was easily seen as leaning the other way.

Thus, it was predictable that Savimbi and his backers in the United States would be perpetually insecure; it was built into the structure of the negotiations. Crocker should have done more to compensate for this factor, because it was not inevitable that the pro-UNITA forces would lose confidence in him to the degree that they did. The procedure also increased Savimbi's incentive to be obstreperous in order to ensure that his interests were not ignored. His guerrilla movement was active in all of Angola—"UNITA has this country tied in knots," a European diplomat commented[62]—and Savimbi had considerable leverage of his own. Crocker made a point of consulting personally with Savimbi on a frequent basis, and Reagan (and Bush) invited him to the Oval Office periodically. (The substantive consultation with him was far better than in the case of the Afghan mujahedin.) This did not substitute, in Savimbi's mind, for the occasional military action or press conference outburst—"Dr. Crocker is playing into the hands of my own enemies," he once angrily proclaimed—by which he reminded all the others that no deal could be achieved without his consent.[63]

Savimbi's most important leverage, however, came from his congressional support, which continued to grow. A joint resolution was passed *unanimously* in June 1987 condemning the Soviet/Cuban military buildup, denouncing human rights violations by the MPLA, and insisting on an MPLA-UNITA agreement ensuring free and fair elections. On May 12, 1988, Chairman Dante Fascell, ranking Republican William Broomfield, and ten other members of the House Foreign Affairs Committee wrote to Reagan before his Moscow summit urging "pressure on the Angolan Marxist regime to accept the offer of their domestic opponents and agree to a cease-fire, hold peace talks, form a government of national reconciliation, and allow free and fair elections." A similar letter came from Dennis DeConcini and thirty-seven other senators. House Republicans wrote to Reagan protesting the exclusion of UNITA from the agreement Crocker was negotiating.[64] Jonas Savimbi visited Washington in June 1988 and received a public pledge from Reagan on June 30 that "[t]he United States believes that true peace in Angola can only result from national reconciliation, and that UNITA has a rightful role in such a process." In return, Savimbi expressed public support for the negotiations.

Savimbi's supporters, however, and undoubtedly Savimbi himself, were uneasy about what Reagan's pledges did not include: They still left UNITA outside the negotiating hall and still failed to insist on free elections. Reagan's pledges were, in this case, Crocker's handiwork—the NSC staff having been defanged after Iran-Contra and deprived of its ability or inclination to embellish them independently. Savimbi's public relations advisers earned their fees this time, however, as the UNITA leader spent considerable time on Capitol Hill, wooing liberals with an eloquent presentation on his eagerness for a negotiated compromise with the MPLA leading to free and fair elections. He candidly explained that his ties with South Africa were only the product of necessity in view of the massive Soviet and Cuban military involvement. A simultaneous Washington visit by MPLA foreign minister Lt. Col. Pedro de Castro Van Dunem ("Loy") failed to impress; he insisted in his Hill conversations that UNITA controlled only 1 percent of the country and that no Cubans were in southern Angola. Black Caucus member Louis Stokes—then chairman of the House Intelligence Committee—knew better.[65] UNITA's public relations firm Black, Manafort clearly bested the MPLA's firm Gray and Company in that round.

In September–October 1988, as the pace of Crocker's negotiations quickened, so did the congressional anxiety about Savimbi's exclusion. Gov. Michael Dukakis's lead in the presidential opinion polls during the summer heightened conservative nervousness. On October 12, Henry Hyde and twelve other House conservatives wrote to Reagan insisting on a "simultaneous" resolution of the internal political conflict in parallel with any agreement on the external issues. Minority leader Bob Michel added his own similar letter on October 19. An extraordinary collection of fifty-one senators signed on to another DeConcini letter on October 14, warning against a "poorly negotiated agreement." This group, which ranged from Jesse Helms and Malcolm Wallop to Christopher Dodd and William Proxmire, called for a direct MPLA-UNITA negotiation and synchronization of this process with the Cuban troop withdrawal and Namibian independence. They also insisted on continuation of U.S. military aid to UNITA until the entire process was completed.[66]

In an ironic twist on the U.S. linkage strategy of 1981, Savimbi's congressional backers then found a new way to hold Namibia hostage. The administration had requested authorization to reprogram up to $150 million from other accounts to help pay the U.S. share of UN peace-keeping costs. The success of East-West diplomacy in the *annus mirabilis* 1988 had generated or was generating political accords in Afghanistan, the Iran-Iraq war, the western Sahara, and Angola/Namibia; the United Nations was replenishing its funds for the many peacekeeping assignments it was about to undertake. Savimbi's backers in Congress, however, linked their Angola concerns to the UN legislation. In an October 13 letter to Shultz, the bipartisan duo of Fascell and Broomfield declared: "Any use of these authorized funds to support a process which does not include a total Cuban troop withdrawal and reconciliation leading to free and fair elections in Angola would, in our view, be directly contrary to the intent of this legislation." This linkage delayed the bill and contributed to its demise in that congressional session. Colin Powell, then the president's national security adviser, wrote to DeConcini on October 21 assuring him that U.S. support for UNITA was solid and that it "has not been, and will not be, a bargaining chip in the negotiations for Cuban troop withdrawal from Angola."[67] Conservatives who had often disparaged congressional interference in foreign policy were now quite willing to consider its possible virtues.[68]

These were powerful humiliations for Crocker, who was on the verge of an extraordinary accomplishment—the December 1988 accord signed in New York that ensured total Cuban troop withdrawal over the following two and one-half years, linked to a schedule for Namibian independence. The United States launched a major push for a direct MPLA-UNITA negotiation *after* the New York accords were signed, which helped mollify Savimbi and his supporters. And, most important, U.S. military aid to UNITA continued.

Crocker had walked the high wire in a crowded circus, spotlights glaring, with a raucous audience half-cheering him on, half-jeering him. That he reached the other side was a tribute to his essential brilliance as well as to his intestinal fortitude. Nobel Peace Prizes have been awarded for less than he achieved. Perhaps he had lost his balance on occasion; perhaps the congressional pressure, from the repeal of Clark onward, had helped ensure that UNITA's interests were not neglected. While the basic structure of the negotiation was justified—the South Africans did not complain that it was not—the tone of his respective relationships with the MPLA and with UNITA contributed to the appearance of imbalance. He seemed more spontaneously responsive to the sensitivities of the one than the other. He acknowledged that U.S. aid to UNITA strengthened his hand diplomatically, but he was uncomfortable with it nevertheless.

The New York ceremony in which the agreements were signed, at the United Nations, was a bizarre event, as befitted the irreconcilable elements Crocker had managed to reconcile. Chas. Freeman has described the scene:

As a Soviet deputy foreign minister looked on approvingly, U.S. Secretary of State George Shultz presided over the signature by the foreign ministers of Angola, Cuba and South Africa of interlocking treaties accomplishing the removal of foreign forces from southwestern Africa. The three ministers made speeches. The Angolan managed a polite dig at South Africa and the United States. The Cuban was polemically sarcastic about both, and took a barely disguised swipe at the Soviets as well. The South African wound up with remarks that, inter alia, declared his country's solidarity with Third World resentment of Western domination of the global economy. . . .

Diplomats and generals from Angola, Cuba, South Africa, the Soviet Union, the South West African People's Organization (SWAPO) and the neighboring African states raised their glasses to the historic achievements of an American mediation effort that they had spent nearly a decade denigrating and obstructing.[69]

Crocker remained uncelebrated by the Reaganites, nor was he rehired by the Bush team, which made a point of either dismissing or reshuffling most significant members of the Reagan administration. I proposed to Colin Powell that his name be included on the list of those whom Reagan would, in the end, recognize in his farewell "Honors List." Upon Powell's recommendation, the president awarded Chester Crocker the Presidential Citizens Medal (a step below the Medal of Freedom, usually awarded to cabinet members), the second-highest civilian award the president can bestow.

Under the New York accords, the Cubans were to redeploy their forces northward, away from the Namibian border, pulling all their forces back to the 13th parallel in mid-Angola by November 1, 1989—the date for Namibian elections. The South Africans were to reduce their military presence in Namibia to a token fifteen hundred men by July 1989 and vacate Namibia by the November 1, 1989, date for Namibian elections. Half of the Cuban contingent was to be gone from Angola by November 1, 1989, two-thirds by April 1, 1990, the rest by July 1, 1991. (The Cubans beat the deadline by a few months.) Namibia became independent, fulfilling Resolution 435, when a government was formed—dominated by SWAPO but under a seemingly democratic constitution—on March 21, 1990.

All sides took risks in this process. As with the Geneva agreement that removed Soviet troops from Afghanistan (not to mention the 1973 Paris Agreement on Vietnam), the settlement of the external military issues left Angola's internal civil war, alas, continuing. The global strategic significance of the conflict was reduced, with the most important dimension—the Soviet/Cuban intervention—eliminated; the stakes for the parties in the region remained high. Soviet and Cuban prestige, South Africa's sense of its vulnerability, the American commitment to UNITA, Angola's and Namibia's future course—were all still hanging in the balance when Reagan and Crocker left office.

BLEEDING ANGOLA

The United States kept its word to Savimbi to pursue a further negotiation on "national reconciliation," the optimistic term for a political settlement inside Angola. The MPLA and UNITA reached an agreement, on May 31, 1991, on a cease-fire and free elections, and elections were held in September 1992. The breakdown of that process further illustrates some of the harsh realities of trying to resolve international conflicts.

After the New York accords, both sides paused to reassess. The MPLA faced the future without Cuban backing, UNITA without South African backing. America's long-term willingness to underwrite UNITA was questionable, as was the Soviet Union's with respect to the MPLA. As George Bush and James Baker replaced Ronald Reagan and George Shultz and career diplomat Herman Cohen replaced Chester Crocker, conservatives, nervous about the "pragmatic" qualities of the new team, pressed Bush, as president-elect, to reaffirm U.S. support for Savimbi. This Bush did on January 6, 1989, in a press statement pledging to continue covert aid until peace was achieved. The program was estimated in press reports to be in the range of $50–$60 million annually, half for weapons.[70]

Angola faced a depressing economic picture. Manufacturing output in 1989 was at half the level of 1973; commercial agriculture, on which three-quarters of the population depended, had collapsed.[71] Yet there was great reluctance within the MPLA to contemplate ending the war by a political compromise with the hated Savimbi. Some MPLA figures, like President dos Santos, were thought to be moderate, others more pro-Cuban or pro-Soviet or otherwise more hard-line. According to one school of thought on negotiations, this argued for U.S. gestures toward the MPLA to reward and reinforce the moderates; according to another school of thought, only a change in the objective facts on the ground would overcome the resistance of the hard-liners. U.S. policy was pulled in both directions.

The Bush administration was careful to insist (in terms more categorical than Crocker usually used) that "until national reconciliation is achieved, it will be premature to talk about U.S. recognition of *any* government in Angola."[72] At crucial moments as the war continued, it stepped in with needed support for Savimbi, filling the logistical gap left by the departing South Africans. But the United States kept open a diplomatic dialogue with the MPLA—and especially with the Soviets, who were now thought to exert a more constructive influence. Soviet military assistance to Luanda reportedly declined from $1.2 billion in 1987 to

$800 million in 1988.[73] Secretary Baker soon developed the same kind of warm relationship with his counterpart, Eduard Shevardnadze, that George Shultz had had.[74] The Bush team was also more focused on Europe and arms control, the central issues of the East-West relationship, and was impatient more than it was impassioned on the regional issues.

This led to changes in the tone of American policy that were unnerving to Savimbi's supporters. "The Reagan Doctrine is no longer operative in its purer form," an unnamed U.S. official told Lally Weymouth; the United States was "no longer supporting Savimbi to stand up to the Soviets" but rather was contemplating "how to lean on the Soviets to break the logjam" in negotiations between UNITA and the MPLA.[75] And either through design or clumsiness, the Bush administration—almost exactly as in Afghanistan—was believed to have cut back deliveries of weapons to Savimbi in the second half of 1989, as if declaring the game over.[76]

Liberal critics took the opportunity to reopen the question of why we were aiding Savimbi at all when the earlier justification—the Cuban military presence—no longer applied. In June 1989, the Reverend Jesse Jackson called for a halt to aid for Savimbi and for recognition of the MPLA.[77] In September 1989, thirty-two members of the House and two senators invited MPLA leader dos Santos to visit Washington and pushed for establishment of liaison offices in Washington and Luanda as a prelude to full diplomatic relations. Mrs. Robert F. Kennedy, widow of the late senator, was recruited in a campaign, involving liberal groups like the United Church of Christ, that denounced Savimbi as a gross violator of human rights. "Americans should be clear about what we are doing in Angola," Mrs. Kennedy stated. "It is a conscious policy of UNITA to target civilians, to lay waste to the countryside. . . ." The United States was prolonging the war and the suffering.[78] Rep. Howard Wolpe, chairman of the House Africa Subcommittee, argued that continuing military aid to Savimbi "would only slow recent movement toward a compromise. . . ."[79]

Even some conservatives expressed disillusionment with Savimbi. William F. Buckley, Jr.'s National Review published a scathing critique of Savimbi by Polish intellectual Radek Sikorski, who recognized a disturbing totalitarian streak in the way Savimbi ran UNITA: "UNITA's structure is overtly Leninist, based on the same concept of democratic centralism—with a Congress, a Central Committee, and a Politburo nominally in charge of the party—but these institutions are mere appendages to Savimbi's personal rule."[80]

At various stages in 1990, House liberals attempted again to engineer a floor debate on the covert aid program. The charismatic South African leader Nelson Mandela, visiting Washington after release from his twenty-seven-year incarceration, joined the chorus, saying he "strongly condemn[ed]" U.S. and South African backing of Savimbi.[81] (Mandela, a throwback to an earlier era of Third World radicalism, embarrassed some of his American supporters by also expressing his admiration for Fidel Castro and Yasir Arafat.)

The post–New York phase of the negotiation began in January 1989 with a proposal by the MPLA for reintegration of UNITA into the existing Luanda government, minus Savimbi, who was to go into temporary exile.[82] This proposal essentially asked for the decapitation and peaceable surrender of an adversary who had not been defeated and still controlled a large proportion of the country's territory. Under pressure from the United States and some of his African backers, Savimbi came up with a counterproposal in March—a cease-fire, a pledge of noninterference with the economically crucial Benguela Railway, and nationwide free elections in two years leading to a government of national unity. Savimbi was willing to volunteer the additional concession that he need not take part personally in such a coalition government but would be content to remain leader of his party. Since the MPLA was not yet ready to go even that far, however, the negotiation lay dormant.

The next stage was the search for a mediator. For the internal negotiation, the United States was not seen as the most appropriate, so others were sought—preferably an African. Zaire's president Mobutu Sese Seko emerged as the selection of a group of African countries. It was a surprising choice, since Zaire was known to be a principal backer and staging area for aid to UNITA, but perhaps on the same principle that Sadat had applied to U.S. support for Israel, the MPLA understood that Mobutu would have influence with Savimbi and the United States. Mobutu also wanted the boost to his prestige at a time of mounting criticism in the West of his abysmal record as tyrant and despoiler of his country.

Mobutu proved that honorable intentions, if such they were, are not enough in a mediator. He provided a textbook case of how not to mediate. On June 22, 1989, he convened a summit of twenty African heads of state and other leaders in the resort town of Gbadolite in northern Zaire. It was a lively and hopeful occasion, highlighted by the first face-to-face meeting—and public handshake—between José Eduardo dos Santos and Jonas Savimbi. The only formal agreement reached was a commitment to an immediate cease-fire and establishment of a committee to oversee its implementation. The cease-fire took hold, but broke down soon afterward because of complete confusion about other understandings that Mobutu claimed had been agreed upon.

It was as if Mobutu had read some of the more imaginative accounts of Henry Kissinger's negotiating methods and mimicked the misinformation he had read. One of the clichés about Kissinger was his alleged deceptiveness in telling both sides in a negotiation different things. No criticism could have been more off base. No agreement can ever be reached by trickery. Nor can any agreement last twenty-four hours if there are inconsistent understandings of its precise terms. What any mediator has to do is persuade each side of the reasons why *it* will benefit from the agreement; thus, it is inevitable—and absurd to imagine otherwise—that the mediator makes a different pitch to each side in terms of what evolution it can work for and what it will gain. He can tell Arabs that an interim agreement will help get Israelis used to the idea of relinquishing control; he can tell Israelis that the agreement will help lock the Arab party into a posture of resolving the conflict by political rather than military means. If the negotiation succeeds, it is because both propositions are true.

Every agreement involves a gamble by both sides about the future. If the long-run intentions of both sides remain incompatible, the deal will probably break down sooner or later. But even an agreement in which both sides' hopes are compatible involves two sides with different interests who will, moreover, have to justify the agreement before their respective peoples.

Mobutu simply told dos Santos and Savimbi two different accounts of what the other had agreed. He assured Savimbi that he was being treated as an equal participant, on a par with the ostensible leader of the Angolan government, and that dos Santos had agreed to this. He assured dos Santos that Savimbi had secretly agreed to integrate UNITA into the MPLA and to go into temporary exile from Angolan politics. Apparently, neither of these accounts was true. Mobutu told other leaders at Gbadolite that Savimbi had agreed to these things, which leaked out and drove Savimbi—with some justification—to charge betrayal.[83]

Mobutu's behavior was puzzling. There are reports that he was intimidated by MPLA military threats against Zaire. In any circumstances, however, a mediator in Mobutu's situation is often tempted to step up the pressure on the side over which he has more direct leverage, which seems the easiest target. The Israelis often felt they were the victims of such a temptation under American mediation. It is an impulse to be resisted, since by hypothesis it bears only a haphazard relation to the merits of whatever issue is in dispute. Or perhaps Mobutu fell in with the Politically Correct sentiment in Africa, which had largely accepted the MPLA after its 1975 victory. His ambition to ingratiate himself with African or American liberal sentiment might have caused him to lean as he did. In any case, the tactic failed. The cease-fire collapsed, with Savimbi again seeing military action as his way to regain respect, or to use better diplomatic phraseology, to remind all parties that nothing could be settled without his consent. Luanda's power-supply facilities were blown up on June 29, a week after the Gbadolite fiasco. Mobutu's fantasies of winning a Nobel Peace Prize or of matching the success of his friend Kissinger were blown away as well.

The Bush administration intervened at this point to get the negotiations back on track. The president invited both Mobutu and Savimbi to meet with him (separately) in Washington in October 1989. He assured both that we loved them and won from Mobutu a promise to resume participation in the UNITA supply program (which the Zairean had terminated in a huff) and from Savimbi a commitment to return to the negotiating table. Savimbi and Mobutu had a reconciliation meeting in the south of France later in October.

The MPLA, however, true to type, had decided on one more effort to test the balance of strength on the ground. With the South Africans gone from Angola and on their way out of Namibia, with Savimbi's relations perhaps still strained with Mobutu, UNITA seemed more vulnerable than ever. It became clear that the MPLA would make no serious bid for compromise until it had tried one more time for a military victory. The Soviets unhelpfully increased supplies to FAPLA again—by an estimated \$1.2–\$1.5 billion worth of armaments in the preceding two years—and encouraged a new offensive (which the Cubans reportedly opposed).[84]

On December 23, 1989, FAPLA forces sallied forth from Cuito Cuanavale southeastward to launch what they called the "Final Offensive" against Mavinga, the key UNITA logistics base that stood between FAPLA and Savimbi's capital in Jamba. As FAPLA forces besieged the town, the State Department was driven to protest the "massive" level of Soviet assistance, including "a substantial number of Soviet military advisers at the front line."[85] By mid-January 1990, UNITA's situation was desperate. Cut off from South African logistics support (though the South Africans had left behind significant supplies), UNITA was running short of vehicles, antitank weapons, and especially fuel. On February 6, dos Santos proclaimed, somewhat prematurely: "This victory . . . demonstrated the old thesis presented by the leadership of our country, according to which UNITA and their so-called liberated zones were just a fiction maintained only by the army of Pretoria."[86] Not the language of national reconciliation.

UNITA sent emissaries to Washington in mid-February, including Savimbi's vice president, Jeremias Chitunda, to appeal for help. The rebel delegation went home satisfied, telling audiences they were receiving "effective and appropriate" assistance (the approved U.S. government euphemism)—a reported emergency airlift of oil, gasoline, and antitank missiles.[87] The FAPLA offensive stalled at the end of its long supply lines; UNITA withstood the offensive and leapfrogged it by recommencing attacks on urban and other targets in the MPLA's backyard in the north, including the capital, Luanda. By April, the MPLA was again proclaiming its interest in direct talks. The MPLA now proposed for the first time the idea of elections in which other "independent" candidates could participate. While it still ruled out any competing political parties like UNITA that could challenge its monopoly of power, the MPLA was clearly starting down a slippery slope.

The Soviets had not distinguished themselves in the whole affair, with their irresponsible fueling of the "Final Offensive," but again the hard reality on the ground imposed itself. On March 19, 1990, Baker and Shevardnadze met in Windhoek during the celebrations of Namibia's independence and pledged renewed efforts to push for "national reconciliation" in Angola. Portugal, the former colonial power, eventually emerged as the agreed mediator and handled the task with a professionalism that had eluded Mobutu.

The decisive struggle now was within the MPLA Central Committee, where political compromise with UNITA meant a wrenching psychological adjustment. Multiparty elections meant a different kind of Angola in which the MPLA played a different kind of role as a political party. Dos Santos managed to push through the required changes, moving toward democracy by traditional Leninist methods of purging or isolating the more recalcitrant of his comrades.

All this had its effect in Washington. Liberals in Congress failed in October 1990 in yet another attempt to terminate UNITA aid—it was a "cold-war anachronism," said Rep. Ronald V. Dellums[88]—but the handwriting was on the wall. The House passed by one vote a Solarz Amendment to the Intelligence Authorization bill that stipulated an end to UNITA aid if the MPLA accepted compromise. (The bill died for other reasons.) On a visit to Washington, Savimbi was told by some of his key supporters that negotiations were the only solution and that his aid was unlikely to continue into fiscal year 1992.[89]

In April and May 1991, the parties haggled over details. On April 28, the MPLA Party Congress formally renounced Marxism-Leninism, called its new ideology "democratic socialism," and endorsed a multiparty system. With communism having collapsed in Eastern Europe, its African devotees were less eager to keep the faith. On May 31, in Lisbon, in another elaborate ceremony attended by various foreign ministers and other characters who probably did not trust each other enormously, Savimbi and dos Santos signed the documents. The United States and the Soviet Union committed themselves to halt lethal military supply, though other forms of support were permitted to continue.

The election campaign began hopefully for Savimbi. He made a triumphal return to Luanda on September 29, greeting forty thousand to fifty thousand cheering supporters at the airport after similarly enthusiastic greetings in three other provincial capitals. Dressed in an olive-drab military uniform, maroon beret with four general's stars, and a revolver slung from a cartridge-studded belt and carrying a white-handled walking stick, he was a striking figure.[90] It was not hard to see why the MPLA had so feared his political impact and why he was favored to triumph again in the elections scheduled to commence in September 1992.

But things went sour again. As the cease-fire seemed to hold and the election campaign progressed, liberal congressmen took yet another run at terminating the U.S. covert-aid program, even though it was now confined to nonlethal supplies. Mervyn Dymally of the House African Affairs Subcommittee and twenty-eight other Members sent a letter to Bush on December 2, 1991, arguing that our "partiality toward UNITA" was inconsistent with the "spirit and letter of the Peace Accords and respect for Angolan law." It was a criticism whose logic had (fortunately) escaped all the parties to Chet Crocker's lengthy and successful previous negotiation. The congressmen's letter was circulated in Washington by Hill and Knowlton, acting as the new public relations representative of the Angolan regime (Gray and Company having manifestly failed in its previous efforts).[91]

More serious were the charges of Savimbi's treatment of some of his own colleagues. His authoritarian style was well known. One of his closest longtime comrades, Pedro "Tito" Chingungi, was murdered, allegedly by Savimbi's men because of his emergence as a possible rival. These kinds of charges, often circulated by UNITA's enemies,[92] gained credibility in 1992 even among Savimbi's erstwhile admirers.[93] Savimbi reacted by blaming the killings on the CIA.[94] Gratitude was evidently not his strong suit, either.

The charges remain hotly disputed, and the murder could have been the product of other intrigues in the UNITA camp. In any case, Savimbi's emerging reputation as less than a saint undoubtedly contributed to his disappointing showing in the September 1992 elections. Dos Santos had managed to soften his own image. Instead of winning a majority or plurality in the presidential race amid the regime's economic debacle, Savimbi won about forty percent to dos Santos's just under 50 percent. There were other possible explanations for the result, including a woefully inadequate UN election-monitoring operation. The United Nations allowed the MPLA to organize the elections, dominate the media, and curtail voter registration in the rural areas, which were UNITA's strongholds. An October 16 document of UNAVEM II (the UN Angola Verification Mission) concluded that "there were irregularities discovered in the electoral process, which could have affected the overall outcome of the voting. In some cases, the volume of votes lost or gained by each candidate could, taken nationally, be significant as to distort the final results."[95] UN special envoy Margaret Anstee confided to a UNITA official that she had never witnessed a more unfair election, even in Latin America,[96] while publicly she pleaded that the United Nations had been given only a "marginal role" and an inadequate mandate.[97]

Nevertheless, a weary United Nations and U.S. government hurried to declare the results "generally free and fair." This haste was a major mistake. The civil war broke out again—Savimbi resorting to his time-honored way of venting his grievances. Both South Africa and the United States dissociated themselves from Savimbi's conduct; he had no prospect of support from even the Bush administration, let alone the Clinton administration, whose Africa policy was much more in line with the views of the Congressional Black Caucus. The regime lashed back with a vicious military attack on UNITA headquarters in Luanda, killing Savimbi's vice president, Jeremias Chitunda, and members of Savimbi's family.

The Clinton administration then tried a new tack: It essentially switched sides, extending diplomatic recognition to dos Santos in May 1993 and in July even lifting its ban on nonlethal military sales to Luanda. But this approach had no better success. Savimbi and UNITA were in control of some three-quarters of the country's territory. The new phase of the civil war took a terrible human toll. The Clinton team, whatever its distaste for Savimbi, came around inevitably to the traditional strategy of trying to promote a balanced negotiation.

Equally inevitably, sooner or later, somehow or other, these two large factions of Angolans would have to learn to coexist. Neither could defeat the other. The United States by its earlier support of UNITA had proved its point: that the MPLA, installed by Soviet and Cuban arms, had neither the legitimacy nor the possibility to rule alone by suppressing such an enormous number of its fellow citizens by force. The artificial outcome of 1975 could not have stood. The turbulence of the final stages tended to confirm Kissinger's gloomy dictum that no civil war in history ever ended in a coalition government. For Angola to be history's first such triumph was a tall order; it would be more remarkable in its success than in its failure.

It was all together an achievement for the United States to have brought about the removal of all outside military forces and to have brought the conflict so close to a final resolution. In the process, certain lessons about negotiation were also vindicated—that leverage and diplomacy are not incompatible but intimately connected; that America's success as a mediator did not require abandoning its friends; that restoring a balance of forces on the ground was almost always a precondition for the success of negotiations. A covert program, instead of being the mark of Satan, helped produce a constructive result. A strong policy toward the Soviets, instead of provoking an escalating Cold War conflict, magnified the incentives for compromise. Another misbegotten Soviet adventure from the 1970s ended, playing its role in the extraordinary evolution of the Soviet Union.

Outside powers were perhaps reaching the limit of how much they could help bleeding Angola bind up its wounds. For better or worse, this tragic country was now reduced to its own historical dimensions.

END OF THE
CENTRAL AMERICA CRISIS

Central America seemed the most explosive, the most intractable, and ideologically the most heavily laden of the regional conflicts of the Reagan era. Yet by February 1990 the crisis ended in Nicaragua, and a peace treaty ended the war in El Salvador in January 1992. This, too, is a story that illuminates the realities of negotiation—partly by negative example—as well as the emotion and volatility of American attitudes toward engagement in such conflicts.

At one level, the mid-1980s were dominated by the continuing struggle in the U.S. Congress over aid to the Nicaraguan resistance (the Contras). But at another level it was a contest between the Sandinistas and the Contras over democratic legitimacy; each side struggled to burnish its credentials. In the process, both sides confirmed the centrality of the issue the Reagan administration had raised—internal democratization as the key to peace in Central America.

A TALE OF TWO ELECTIONS

In the summer of 1984, the Sandinistas agreed to hold the long-promised election, to test or prove their popular support in Nicaragua. It was a risky course. Humberto Ortega, Daniel's brother and the Sandinista defense minister, has admitted that it was a decision made under pressure. In the first half of 1984, the Contra army, having reached the number of seven thousand to eight thousand men, was making surprising headway. Instead of conducting only sporadic raids from Honduran territory, its guerrilla forces moved deep into Nicaragua in record numbers—and remained there. Meanwhile, the Soviets, to whom the Sandinistas turned for military help (which came later in the year), were weakened by decrepit leadership in the Chernenko era. Ortega later told Robert Kagan: "In 1984, I pointed out that the correlation of forces in the world was very difficult for the socialist camp. . . . We had elections in 1984 because we began detecting that the Soviet Union was not strong. . . . [I]n addition, we had the counterrevolution [the Contras]. The elections were a tactical tool, a weapon. They were a bitter pill that had to be swallowed." The war against the Contras was "very, very hard," he said.[1]

Some Sandinista leaders, like Humberto Ortega, claim they were also thinking of a genuine opening to the middle classes.[2] But the purely tactical motive was probably dominant (as, in fact, Ortega expressed it to Kagan). It was not in the nature of Leninist regimes to subject themselves to unpredictable processes of popular approval such as free and contested elections; the vanguard of history always preferred to find its vindication in other, more abstract sources.

On its face, Humberto's rationale confirms much of the rationale for U.S. policy: Our pressures were forcing the Sandinistas to take risks. Another irony in Humberto's rationale was its implicit contrast with the thinking in the State Department and in other circles critical of the U.S. insistence on democratization. The objection often heard was that the Sandinistas were unlikely to show flexibility over their domestic system but were more likely to compromise on their external conduct, such as their ties with Moscow and Havana and their export of revolution. This was the premise of Thomas Enders's diplomacy in the early 1980s. Yet a speech delivered by *Comandante* Bayardo Arce before a secret meeting in May 1984 suggests a different line of reasoning in Managua. It turns out that only in the area of domestic politics were the Sandinistas willing to take a risk—thus the decision to hold elections (which they, of course, assumed they would win). Their foreign policy was too much a matter of their "internationalist" duty:

> Imperialism asks three things of us: to abandon interventionism, to abandon our strategic ties with the Soviet Union and the socialist community, and to be democratic. We cannot cease being internationalists unless we cease being revolutionaries.
>
> We cannot discontinue strategic relationships unless we cease being revolutionaries. It is impossible even to consider this.
>
> Yet the superstructure aspects, democracy as they call it, bourgeois democracy, has an element which we can manage and even derive advantages from for the construction of socialism in Nicaragua.[3]

The election was a "nuisance," Arce admitted, forced by U.S. pressures. But it was also a way to consolidate the revolution:

> [T]he elections, viewed from that perspective, are a nuisance. . . . But from a realistic standpoint, being in a war with the United States, those

things become weapons of the revolution to move forward the construction of socialism. . . .

We believe that the elections should be used in order to vote for Sandinismo, which is being challenged and stigmatized by imperialism, in order to be able to demonstrate that, in any event, the Nicaraguan people are . . . for Marxism-Leninism. . . .

[W]e are going to use the outcome to legitimize the revolution. . . .[4]

With this philosophy underlying their decision to call an election, it is not surprising that the campaign fell far short of League of Women Voters standards. The coalition of still-surviving democratic opposition parties, called the Coordinadora Democratica, began insisting on such guarantees as free access to the media for all parties, greater scope for independent political activities by unions and churches, and an election for a constituent assembly, not just for president (which is what the Sandinistas had announced). With even greater bravado, the democratic politicians in the Coordinadora openly identified their cause with the armed resistance in the field and asked that the exile groups be included in the political process.[5] The Sandinistas stonewalled.

At this point, the Democratic leadership of the U.S. Congress intervened. Majority Leader Jim Wright, House Intelligence Committee chairman Edward Boland, Reps. Lee Hamilton and Stephen Solarz, and six other Democrats addressed a letter on March 20, 1984, to President Daniel Ortega stressing the importance of a free and fair election. While this goal was unexceptionable, the letter, addressed to "Dear Commandante" [sic], became a notorious "Exhibit A" in the conservatives' case against the extraordinary antiadministration maneuvering of the opponents of our Central America policy. The letter's signers—all avowed opponents of Contra aid—forswore any desire to interfere in negotiations, which they acknowledged were the province of the executive branch.[6] Yet the ingratiating tone and phraseology of the letter came close to suggesting a desire to make common cause with the Sandinistas against the administration:

As Members of the U.S. House of Representatives, we regret the fact that better relations do not exist between the United States and your country. We have been, and remain, opposed to U.S. support for military action directed against the people or government of Nicaragua.

We want to commend you and the members of your government for taking steps to open up the political process in your country. . . . We support your decision to schedule elections this year, to reduce press censorship, and to allow greater freedom of assembly for political parties. Finally, we recognize that you have taken these steps in the midst of ongoing military hostilities on the borders of Nicaragua.

We write with the hope that the initial steps you have taken will be followed by others designed to guarantee a fully open and democratic electoral process [including, specifically, participation by exile groups in the election]. . . .

If this were to occur, the prospects for peace and stability throughout Central America would be dramatically enhanced. Those responsible for supporting violence against your government, and for obstructing serious negotiations for broad political participation in El Salvador would have far greater difficulty winning support for their policies than they do today.[7]

The "Dear Commandante" letter demonstrated the Democratic leaders' sincere hopes that a fair election, whatever its outcome, would end the crisis—if not by a change of regime, then by a legitimation of the Sandinista leadership that could be used in Congress to kill the Contra program once and for all. For all the little digs at the administration that peppered the text, the letter also placed a significant burden on the Sandinistas. The Coordinadora now had gained some international legitimacy, and too heavy-handed a resort to the proverbial "advantages of incumbency" could backfire against the regime. To guarantee their own victory, as the Sandinistas intended, now posed some risk of undercutting the congressional liberals who were indeed in a sense their allies; however, to open up the campaign posed a risk to their power beyond any intention they had had in announcing the election.

The Reagan administration's attitude toward the election, though, was also ambiguous. It did not trust the Sandinistas to run a really fair contest and feared most of all a stolen Sandinista victory that *appeared* to the world as an authentic popular mandate. International gullibility on this score was not to be discounted. Conservatives thus hoped that the election would somehow abort. The State Department tended, on the other hand, to want to see the election play out as a test of the Sandinistas' good faith. State probably shared the congressional Democrats' hope that a decent outcome would help end the Contra program one way or another.

The same dilemma fell hardest of all on the shoulders of Arturo Cruz, the distinguished Nicaraguan economist and politician who was chosen as the Coordinadora's candidate for president. Cruz had the most legitimate democratic credentials imaginable, having served two jail terms as a political opponent of Somoza's and having been a member of the Sandinista-led post-Somoza junta and president of the Central Bank for ten months in the new government. This did not prevent the regime from disrupting his campaign with brownshirt tactics and from denouncing him as a *Somocista* when he afterward joined, for a time, with the resistance political leaders in exile.

Cruz accepted the nomination reluctantly, but at State Department urging. He understood full well that the Sandinistas' control over the levers of power reduced his charges of a fair contest—the issue being not merely one of an honest count on election day but of a free and open campaign allowing the opposition to organize and to make its case effectively. He held out the possibility that he would back out of the race—formally refuse to register his candidacy on the day required—if the Sandinistas refused to work with the Coordinadora on the various guarantees it had asked for. The regime made a few concessions on electoral procedures but none on the more basic institutional changes that were sought. The Sandinistas' obduracy in these matters increased noticeably after the House of Representatives's decisive votes against the Contra aid program at the beginning of August.[8] While causation cannot be proved, these votes, which lifted the pressures on the regime, spoke louder, probably, than the solicitous entreaties of the "Dear Commandante" letter.

Bayardo Arce, in his secret speech in May, had indicated that at the proper time the Sandinistas' *turbas divinas* ("divine mobs") would be let loose to work their will in the political campaign.[9] When Cruz spoke at a closed-door election rally in early August in his hometown of Jinotepe, he drew a large and enthusiastic audience. When he traveled to the next meeting, in Matagalpa, the mobs were ready. As his supporters exited the theater where he spoke, the mobs harassed them and roughed them up. In Chinandega, where a large public rally was scheduled, a gang of youths rampaged onto the sports ground at 5:00 A.M., tore down the structures and banners, and dispersed the rally's organizers. When Cruz came into town for his appearance, the authorities blocked traffic from the surrounding areas to impede attendance. When he began to speak at the platform (which his supporters had rebuilt), a mob of up to three hundred, carrying stones, sticks, and machetes, surrounded the field and began intimidating the crowd; they broke windows and punctured the tires of cars. The police made no effort to restrain the mob—instead, state security men took photographs of those who were attending Cruz's rally. Finally, the crowd itself—seven thousand strong—found its courage, turned on the *turbas*, and drove them back.[10]

As Roy Gutman later recounted: "One of the most striking facts about the Chinandega rally was that no one in Washington seemed to know about it. No U.S. reporter was present."[11] The Sandinistas censored all reporting of the incident in *La Prensa*. But the episode emboldened Cruz, who was seeing how widespread his support was, and unnerved the Sandinistas for the same reason.[12] On September 18, a peaceful indoor meeting in Léon was surrounded by another threatening mob of about six hundred, which struck Cruz with a stone as he left, pulled his hair, and spat on him; the police watched for a while and then escorted him out of town. In the town of Boaco on September 20, Cruz was meeting with friends at a restaurant when the mob came; the vehicle he left in was seriously damaged and narrowly escaped. In Masaya on September 22, a mob of about 150 hanged and burned Cruz in effigy, pelted his car with stones, and broke the windshield.[13] The Sandinistas were giving new meaning to the concept of "negative campaigning."

In the end, Cruz backed out of the race when negotiations broke down over guarantees of a fair election. He had also asked for a postponement of the date—from November to January—to allow more time to organize; his request was denied.

On November 4, 1984, Daniel Ortega won reelection with over 60 percent of the recorded vote against a number of candidates of small opposition parties. But instead of embarrassing Ronald Reagan two days before the U.S. presidential election, which had been the hope, the Nicaraguan vote fizzled. It conferred no legitimacy. Word had gotten through in the U.S. press of the *turbas divinas* and their activities, making a deep impression and forcing Reagan's opponents to take a harder line, at least rhetorically, against the Sandinistas. Sen. Edward Kennedy had inserted into the *Congressional Record* a powerful article by Robert Leiken reporting on the egregious behavior of the Sandinista leadership and its thugs.[14] Democratic presidential nominee Walter Mondale had even called for a "quarantine" of Nicaragua if the FSLN did not halt its support for Communist insurgencies in neighboring countries.

The Sandinistas gained in the short run. Some gullible folk saw the election as open enough. Even those Democratic congressional leaders who were aghast at the electoral excesses were not sufficiently aghast to back the Contras. Fiscal year 1985 began in October 1984 with passage of the second Boland Amendment, prohibiting the expenditure of appropriated U.S. funds for paramilitary operations in Nicaragua. The mining was a factor. But the Sandinistas had also tried a ploy on the diplomatic front: In September they announced their readiness to sign the latest draft of the Contadora agreement—a draft that the United States found wanting in several respects. The Sandinistas almost certainly knew the United States would turn it down and thus took little risk. Congressional Democrats blamed the resulting stalemate in the negotiations on the administration and considered this another basis for denying the controversial paramilitary program.

But the other presidential election held in November 1984—Ronald Reagan's—turned out to have a greater impact. As we have seen, the Reagan victory tipped the balance on a host of issues. Cynthia Arnson, a critic of Reagan's Central America policy, described the political impact this way:

> Of the fourteen seats Republicans picked up in the House, eight were from the South. What looked like a surge of Republican victories in a traditional bastion may have put many Southerners on the defensive, regardless of comfortable margins of victory in their own districts. "They see a wave of people changing parties down there, officeholders," commented House Speaker Tip O'Neill, "and they're deeply concerned about that." Southern Democrats accounted for the bulk of those who switched their position on contra aid.
>
> One aspect of Reagan's landslide victory was particularly relevant to the issue of contra aid—that during his first term the president was consistently more popular than his policies. . . .
>
> "I don't think there was ever a lot of support . . . for the contras," observed a Senate Republican aide, "except you had a very popular president say, 'I want it, I need it.' " Or, in the words of a House Democratic switcher, "Nationally, there is basic opposition to this [contra] policy. The thing that overrides [it] is Reagan's deep personal appeal."[15]

The administration, of course, saw in Central America one of the main applications of the new Reagan Doctrine. Indeed, one of the purposes of the doctrine was to lift the tone of the debate from a nasty brawl over covert arms to Nicaraguan guerrillas to a more elevated philosophical discussion of American support for those resisting tyranny around the globe. As for Nicaragua policy, the administration was simultaneously trying to shift the focus from the Contras, whose provenance and moral qualities were still a subject of dispute, to the misdeeds of the Sandinistas, so recently and vividly dramatized by their election campaign. The Reagan team, fresh from their own electoral victory, geared up for a new request to the Congress for Contra aid in 1985.

The Sandinistas played into Reagan's hands, cracking down on the democratic opposition after the election as if to punish them for their presumption. On their periodic pilgrimages to Managua, Democratic legislators grew tired of being lectured by the Sandinistas on the U.S. responsibility for all their problems. Arnson records the pungent view of an anonymous congressman: "What one Democratic member called the 'Ortega ass-hole factor,' the sense that dialogue was fruitless and communication impaired, began to take hold. 'Personal factors are very important,' he said. 'Why go out on a limb for a jerk?' "[16]

Arturo Cruz, who had won wide admiration in this country for his courageous effort, declared in January 1985 that it would be a "terrible political mistake" for the United States to cut off arms to the resistance before the Soviet bloc ended its aid to the Nicaraguan regime.[17] Two months later, Cruz signed a joint political document with resistance leaders Adolfo Calero and Alfonso Robelo—linking himself with their cause and lending them his credentials as a champion of democracy. They called for pluralism, democracy, and a mixed economy. To moderate Democrats like Rep. Dave McCurdy of Oklahoma, the new political posture of the Contras made a difference: "These people were not talking overthrow. They were talking some opening of the political process."[18]

Wanting to "overthrow" the Sandinista government was still taboo, since the first Boland Amendment of 1982. But Reagan sometimes complicated matters with his off-the-cuff rhetoric. In a news conference on February 21, 1985, he said the goal of the Contras was to "remove" the Sandinista regime "in the sense of its present structure, in which it is a Communist totalitarian state"—not to overthrow it but to make it "say 'Uncle' " and open up the government. A week later, on March 1, he told a conservative gathering that the Contras were "the moral equal of our Founding Fathers and the brave men and women of the French Resistance."

The Nicaraguan rebel movement, while not quite achieving that level of sainthood, had made some progress in broadening its base and cleaning up its act. The State Department estimated in 1988 that of approximately sixteen thousand resistance fighters, fewer than two hundred had ever served in Somoza's National Guard; one-fifth of the officers were former Sandinistas. Most of its political leadership—not only Cruz—had good anti-Somoza credentials; it set up a human rights monitoring organization within the ranks. Most of the rebel fighters were rural youths between the ages of eighteen and twenty-two, drawn from the peasantry and the Miskito Indian tribes alienated by the clumsy brutality of Marxist policies (not unlike Afghanistan). A high official of the Nicaraguan Foreign Ministry published a book in 1991 admitting this. Alejandro Bendaña, who had been a frequent guest on U.S. television spreading the glib Sandinista line, was more honest in his reflections years later. He shocked some of his compatriots with the admission that no Nicaraguan government had been as inimical to the peasants' interests as the Marxist regime acting in their name. The Contra army grew, he acknowledged, not because of sophisticated recruitment campaigns in the countryside but because of Sandinista policies. It was, Bendaña noted ironically, the first genuine peasant revolution in Latin America backed by the United States.[19]

The president's effort was set back in April when someone leaked to the *New York Times* a classified document that had accompanied his request for covert aid. The document included a sentence that "direct application of U.S. military force . . . must realistically be recognized as an eventual option, given our stakes in the region, if other policy alternatives fail."[20] This was taken to be confirmation of the administration's obsession with military solutions and of its secret determination to send in the marines. In fact, it meant something very different—a point that even George Shultz often made, that to deny help to the resistance would be a risky policy in its own right: "For if we do not take the appropriate steps now to pressure the Sandinistas to live up to their past promises—to cease their arms buildup, to stop exporting tyranny across their borders, to open Nicaragua to the competition of freedom and democracy—then we may find later, when we can no longer avoid acting, that the stakes will be higher and the costs greater."[21]

On April 23, the Republican-controlled Senate voted 53–46 to approve covert aid. The margin was disappointing. Ten Democrats, mostly southerners, voted yes, while nine Republicans, mainly from the East and Northwest, voted no—even after a last-minute switch by the administration to seek only humanitarian aid. Speaker Thomas P. O'Neill had used the powers of his office to complicate the administration's lobbying efforts, moving up the House vote to the same day as the Senate's. The House then defeated the administration by an impressive margin—248–180. But the next day, a Republican proposal for $14 million in humanitarian aid through the Agency for International Development (rather than the CIA) lost by the surprisingly close margin of 215–213. A number of moderate Democrats worried afterward that the absence of *any* kind of aid for resistance left the Democrats in an untenable position.

So precarious was the political balance over this issue that within two months the House had reversed itself. On June 12, a McCurdy proposal for $27 million in humanitarian aid passed by 248–184. What tipped the scales was the announcement—which became known in Washington the day after the House defeat of the aid bill in April—that Daniel Ortega was to visit Moscow. The timing could not have been worse. The liberals had been arguing for years that Managua's relationship with Moscow was the product of Reagan's obtuse policy; now, after the Democrats had "improved" U.S. policy to encourage negotiations and reconciliation, Ortega was off consolidating his ties with his principal arms supplier. "I took it as an intentional slap at the Congress and a slap at those of us who had gone out on a limb . . ." said Rep. Butler Derrick of South Carolina. "He embarrassed us, to be perfectly truthful," admitted Speaker O'Neill.[22]

The Democrats were now, not to put too fine a point on it, scared. Said one House leadership aide, "The real issue was, 'I don't want to be responsible for having [the Contras] exterminated.' "[23] Pointing to the Democrats' November 1984 election debacle, Rep. Dan Daniel, Democrat of Virginia, warned on the House floor: "If we now fail to oppose the spread of communism in this hemisphere, and we are once more perceived to be soft on defense and communism, then we could be shut out completely in the next election."[24]

The administration and its opponents groped for compromises. A consensus was confirmed in favor of humanitarian rather than lethal aid, and many echoed the words of liberal Republican senator David Durenberger of Minnesota: "My only position is, don't do it through the CIA."[25] Such was the mistrust of Casey's CIA that new procedures were invented so that the aid would be provided through a new Nicaraguan Humanitarian Assistance Office (NHAO—pronounced "know-how" by the cognoscenti) based in the State Department. George Shultz's preoccupation during much of this period was that this new supervisory body not be located at the NSC, where it would mean "Ollie North running around Central America screwing up our foreign policy" (in Mike Armacost's words at a June 6, 1985, staff meeting I attended in Shultz's office). Shultz really did not want the office in State, either—not liking his department involved in covert programs—but it was preferable to the alternatives.

What finally clinched the June turnaround—the overwhelming House vote on June 12, 1985, for $27 million in humanitarian aid—was a letter Reagan signed and sent to Democratic representative McCurdy (and also to Republican House leader Bob Michel) on June 11. The letter assured McCurdy and the centrist Democrats that the administration favored negotiated solutions in Central America and that its overriding goal was to promote democracy:

> My administration is determined to pursue political, not military, solutions in Central America.

Our policy for Nicaragua is the same as for El Salvador and all of Central America: to support the democratic center against the extremes of both the right and left, and to secure democracy and lasting peace through national dialogue and regional negotiations. We do not seek the military overthrow of the Sandinista government or to put in its place a government based on supporters of the old Somoza regime. . . .

I take very seriously your concern about human rights. The U.S. condemns, in the strongest possible terms, atrocities by either side.[26]

The letter to McCurdy had, in fact, been drafted by McCurdy himself, together with lobbyist Bruce Cameron. McCurdy later said: "I dictated letters to Bud McFarlane that came back with the President's signature."[27] The aid passed.

DEMOCRACY IN NICARAGUA

The Reagan letter to McCurdy sealed the 1985 bargain between the administration and the centrist Democrats. Democratization in Central America turned out to be the goal that unified the broad coalition Reagan was able to put together, with McCurdy and his colleagues playing the swing role that ensured a majority—against the determined opposition, it must be said, of the Democratic congressional leadership. The Sandinistas, too, choked on it, but the goal of democracy had the effect in Congress of easing fears that the United States was promoting *Somocismo* in Nicaragua or death squads in El Salvador and Guatemala. Moderate Democrats found they could support the president without shame. The administration's approach was of a piece with its support for Duarte, who had won a free election in El Salvador the year before, and for free elections and civilian governments in the hemisphere generally.

Meanwhile, the reemphasis on democracy took on fresh importance in the Central American negotiations as well. The idea had been a part of the Contadora discussions all along, but the Sandinistas now found themselves the odd man out in an increasingly democratic region and under increasing pressure internationally. A summit meeting of the five Central American presidents in Esquipulas, Guatemala, in May 1986, concluded by noting the "frankness" of exchanges and the profound differences between Nicaragua and its neighbors on the meaning of democracy.

The Reagan administration could by 1987 point to seven countries in the hemisphere in which military strongmen had been replaced by elected civilians during its tenure: Honduras and Bolivia (1982), Argentina (1983), El Salvador (1984), Brazil and Uruguay (1985), and Guatemala (1986), plus the civilian government freely elected in Grenada in 1984 after the U.S. overthrow of the Communist regime. By the State Department's count, 91 percent of the population of Latin America and the Caribbean lived in nations committed to democratic principles, as compared to less than one-third a decade before.[28] The administration continued to press Congress for economic aid for the newly democratic governments of Central America, as recommended by the bipartisan Kissinger Commission in January 1984, but usually found Congress the stingy party.

Ronald Reagan, of all people, had broken with the long past in which the United States, especially under conservative presidents, had embraced rightist regimes in Latin America. The McCurdy letter only captured what was already an ideological thrust. No one could doubt the anti-Communist energy that helped drive the philosophy—it was proving a potent weapon against the Sandinistas—but there was ample consistency.

In April 1985, Tony Motley resigned as assistant secretary of state for inter-American affairs. His successor, Elliott Abrams, was sworn in in July. He played no direct role in the McCurdy letter, but his appointment was a confirmation of its philosophy. A former Democrat himself—a disciple of Henry M. Jackson and Daniel Patrick Moynihan—Abrams, like others who called themselves neoconservatives, had not so much traveled a road away from traditional liberalism as he had watched his party drift away from traditional liberalism toward the Left. He was one of those Democrats who saw no reason to be ashamed of being anti-Communist; nor did he have any affection for right-wing tyrannies. Not by coincidence had he spent the early years of the Reagan administration as the assistant secretary of state in charge of human rights policy, aggressively—and evenhandedly—championing human rights against dictatorial regimes of both the Left and Right. In October 1981 he had written a memorandum to Secretary of State Haig explaining why an evenhanded policy was essential:

A human rights policy means . . . hard choices which may adversely affect certain bilateral relations. At the very least, we will have to speak honestly about our friends' human rights violations and justify any decision wherein other considerations (economic, military, etc.) are determinative. There is no escaping this without destroying the credibility of our policy, for otherwise we would be simply coddling friends and criticizing foes. Despite the costs of such a human rights policy, it is essential. While we need a military response to the Soviets to reassure our friends and allies, we also need an ideological response. Our struggle is for political liberty. We seek to improve human rights performance whenever we reasonably can. We desire to demonstrate, by acting to defend liberty and identifying its enemies, that the difference between East and West is the crucial political distinction of our times.[29]

In Abrams's view, democracy was the best guarantee of human rights. Human rights became not just a juridical issue—the rescue of hardship cases—but a question of governmental structure. Abrams was one of the Americans most responsible for the unrelenting pressure put on Chilean dictator Augusto Pinochet, which led Pinochet to call a plebiscite in 1988 (which he lost) and to step down in 1990. In many corridor conversations, in fact, I harassed Elliott about the dangers of producing another Iran—pushing out a pro-American dictator without any certainty of what worse horrors might not replace him. In the end, the strength of the Chilean democratic parties—whose resuscitation was a concomitant of the policy of pressure on Pinochet—vindicated Abrams's effort.*

Abrams was controversial because he was a combative, unapologetic defender of U.S. policy who found it congenitally difficult to show respect for those, particularly McGovernite liberals, for whom he had no respect. In dealing with Congress, one possible strategy—the usual strategy of government officials—is to cultivate, to defer, to ooze cooperation. Another strategy—much harder to pull off—is to confront and to challenge, seeking to mobilize political pressures that frighten Congress into backing away. As we have seen, the Reagan administration fluctuated between the two. Abrams, in any case, provoked the bitter enmity of the Left and the anti-Contra Democratic leadership—even as the policy was, in ironic fact, the foundation of a bipartisan majority. But his enemies lay in wait.

Within the administration, Abrams did a great service to George Shultz, putting the secretary on a surer footing bureaucratically. Conservative sniping at Shultz on this issue came to an end, because Elliott was less frightening to the conservatives and because his Latin-American bureau was no longer the fount of constant but unthought-out diplomatic

---

*No one more deserved to be part of the U.S. delegation to the inauguration of the democratically elected successor, Patricio Aylwin, in March 1990. The Bush administration, out of timidity in the face of the controversies that swirled around Abrams, omitted him from the list.

initiatives that risked unpredictable consequences. The conservatives did not all love Abrams—his zeal against Pinochet and his own pressures on the Contras to democratize left them uneasy—but he served Shultz and the president effectively until Iran-Contra wounded him badly. Shultz, to his great credit, stood by him.

Abrams gave enormous impetus, as noted, to a major effort by the U.S. government to get the Contras to improve their democratic credentials. Even after the Sandinistas bungled the 1984 election and cracked down on their domestic opponents, the resistance would be in no position to capitalize on these mistakes, either in Nicaragua or in the U.S. Congress, unless it were demonstrably a moderate organization led by true democrats and conducting itself accordingly. It was a tall order for a beleaguered guerrilla organization, in the midst of a civil war, perpetually fearful of being strangled by its fickle patron, Uncle Sam. It was also reminiscent of the futile efforts of John Kennedy to unify the Cuban exiles before the Bay of Pigs or his all-too-successful efforts to squeeze Ngo Dinh Diem in Vietnam because of his inadequacies.

But the Reagan administration's efforts had better results—especially when reinforced by material support. Bud McFarlane warned Contra leader Adolfo Calero in early 1985 that the resistance had to develop a moderate political program and leadership and that it could count on only a year or two of congressional support. [30] Washington's influence first helped unify the military and political organization of the resistance— UNO (the United Nicaraguan Opposition)—in 1985–86, combining the forces of the FDN (Nicaraguan Democratic Force) in the north with those of ARDE (Democratic Revolutionary Alliance) and FARN (Nicaraguan Revolutionary Armed Force) in the south. The FDN, founded in 1982, included former members of Somoza's National Guard but also former Sandinista officials and militiamen; ARDE and FARN were led by ex-Sandinistas. One of the founders of UNO was Arturo Cruz, who had earlier associated himself with ARDE.

In 1987, at administration urging, the resistance was further reorganized into the RN—the Nicaraguan Resistance, including not only UNO but also the Southern Opposition Bloc (BOS), the political group led by the liberal Alfredo Cesar. The RN was headed by a seven-member political committee consisting of Adolfo Calero and Aristide Sanchez of the FDN; Alfonso Robelo (ARDE); Alfredo Cesar (BOS); Pedro Joaquin Chamorro (son of Violeta and former editor of *La Prensa*); Azucena Ferrey (a Social Christian and anti-Somoza activist); and a rotating representative of the YATAMA command of the Atlantic coast Miskito Indians. The resistance set up internal procedures to monitor its forces' human rights practices—perhaps the first guerrilla band in recent history to do so—procedures whose leverage came from the fact that U.S. support was conditioned on such an effort. As with the anti-Castro exiles in 1960–61, the groups with ties to the old regime included some of the best fighters and thereby tended to have the sympathy of the CIA personnel trying to field the best fighting force. It was the State Department—the liberals' favorite whipping boy Elliott Abrams—that fought hardest to squeeze out *Somocista* influence and ensure a democratic orientation.

The guerrillas were increasingly effective, with bases on both coasts and in the center of the country. Doubling in size, they reached their peak of around sixteen thousand men by 1987. Their effectiveness drove the Sandinistas to the most brutal of Vietnam-style counterinsurgency techniques. In 1985, for example, in an effort to "drain the sea" of peasant supporters, the regime cleared the population from the border zones where the resistance was establishing a popular base, relocating them in camps and creating "free-fire zones" in the vacated areas; they resettled some 180,000 peasants inland, according to their own admission. By the end of 1987, the State Department estimated that some 250,000 Nicaraguans had been forcibly resettled to prevent their recruitment by or support for the resistance.[31]

The Sandinista style of governance had established itself quite early in the rural areas. In December 1981, in remote Correntada Larga, state security rounded up a reported sixty-seven unarmed *campesinos* suspected of organizing opposition; they were taken out in small groups and either hanged or shot. On April 10, 1982, in Murra in Nueva Segovia, seventeen evangelicals of the Assemblies of God were ordered to dig their own graves, after which their throats were slit as they prayed. At an army base in Wiwili in 1983, eleven people were massacred. At San José de Bocay in 1985, nine people, including children aged five and two, were murdered and thrown into a common grave. In the first year after the Sandinistas were removed from office in 1990, nine confirmed mass graves like these were located in various parts of the country—the work of the army or state security—and other killing fields were waiting to be exhumed.[32]

In Managua, the capital, there was a more genteel but equally determined crackdown on the civilian political opposition, including the Catholic church. An expanded state of emergency was declared on October 15, 1985. The church radio, *Radio Católica*, was closed down in October; the distinguished independent newspaper *La Prensa*, in December. The new Sandinista-drafted constitution was no sooner promulgated in early 1987 than President Ortega invoked its emergency powers to suspend whatever civil liberties it purported to recognize. Even in the absence of an emergency, the constitution defined individual rights narrowly in the context of "the collective security" and provided no checks and balances to Sandinista control over the structures of government. The tightly run process of the draft constitution's consideration by the electorate was protested in vain by the opposition political parties.[33]

The Sandinista secret police force (the General Directorate of State Security) numbered about four thousand men—ten times as large as Somoza's. Under the state of emergency, the regime also cracked down in October 1985 on the Catholic church's Commission for Justice and Peace, a group that monitored religious and civic rights; security police occupied the commission's offices, expelled the staff, and confiscated all materials and files. A month later, the regime attempted to censor publications of the Permanent Commission on Human Rights, a private body that had been formed in 1977 to monitor the Somoza regime and that had been blowing the whistle on Sandinista repression.[34]

The Nicaraguan army had reached a total of sixty-two thousand by 1985, plus about the same number of reserves and militia—a total force ten times as large as Somoza's and nearly as large as the forces of Honduras, El Salvador, Guatemala, and Costa Rica combined. Over three thousand Cuban, Soviet, and East-bloc military advisers helped train the Nicaraguans in the use of the sophisticated Soviet equipment that poured in (some $1.1 billion estimated in 1986–87). By 1985 the Sandinistas had a tank inventory of some 340, growing numbers of advanced Soviet artillery, and some five to eight Mi-25s, the export version of the famous Mi-24 helicopter gunships that were the principal Soviet counterinsurgency attack weapon in Afghanistan. Soviet military deliveries to Nicaragua grew from 850 metric tons in 1980 to 18,000 in 1984.[35]

MILITARY AID FOR THE CONTRAS

Against this backdrop, in February 1986, the Reagan administration decided to go for broke, seeking $100 million in *military* aid for the resistance. "You can't fight attack helicopters piloted by Cubans with Band-Aids and mosquito nets," Reagan told reporters on February 18. On March 16, in an address to the nation, he painted a dramatic picture of Soviet/Cuban/Nicaraguan beachheads in Central America, "just two days' driving time from Harlingten, Texas." Patrick J. Buchanan, the White House director of communications, was given space in the *Washington Post* to argue that, by blocking Contra aid, "the national Democratic Party has now become, with Moscow, co-guarantor of the

Brezhnev Doctrine in Central America. . . . With the vote on contra aid, the Democratic Party will reveal whether it stands with Ronald Reagan and the resistance—or Daniel Ortega and the communists."[36]

The excessive rhetoric backfired, as the House voted down the request on March 20; McCurdy's bloc of swing Democrats voted with the party leadership.[37] Yet the Democratic opponents of Contra aid did not distinguish themselves by the sophistication of their arguments, either. The democratic resistance was dismissed as "a band of cut-throat mercenaries" by Rep. James Weaver of Oregon.[38] U.S. policy was "brutal, illegal, and ineffective," said Rep. Gerry Studds of Massachusetts.[39] It was a "war against the Nicaraguan people," Rep. James Oberstar of Minnesota was sure.[40] It was "a guarantee for more bloodshed," said Rep. Peter Kostmayer of Pennsylvania.[41] The familiar arguments were made (as we saw in chapter 10): that it was U.S. policy that forced the Sandinistas into the arms of the Cubans and Soviets; that Sandinista repression was another result of U.S. policy; that the true enemies in Central America were hunger, poverty, and disease; that we needed, instead, to try harder for a diplomatic solution; and that in view of the discreditable history of U.S. policy in the region over the decades, we had "unclean hands" (as Rep. Vic Fazio put it).[42]

But the price paid by the Democratic House leadership for the swing bloc's support was a pledge to allow McCurdy and his followers to offer an alternative aid package of their own. The Democrats' vulnerability was played up by a heavy-handed Sandinista military incursion into Honduras soon after the negative vote; it looked to be a repeat of the blunder of Ortega's trip to Moscow the year before. Ortega was a "bumbling, incompetent, Marxist-Leninist communist," a twice-embarrassed Speaker O'Neill exploded.[43] Many months would go by before Reagan's final success, but the momentum was clearly with him.

Ambassador Philip Habib, the seasoned professional diplomat who had succeeded Harry Shlaudeman as the special envoy for Central America, created a mini-uproar in April 1986 when he signed a letter to three Democratic members of Congress stating that the draft Contadora treaty, as it stood, "requir[ed] a cessation of support of irregular forces and/or insurrectional movements from the date of signature." This set off alarm bells among conservatives—it was an exact replay of the clumsy Geneva negotiation on Afghanistan—fueling fears that either the administration's interpretation of Contadora or else Contadora itself was a trap for the resistance. Habib was a tough-minded character born in Brooklyn and one of the great personalities of the Foreign Service, but his diplomatic career had been mostly in East Asia, not Central America. Constantine

Menges of the NSC staff, alarmed at the letter when he saw it, passed a copy to Rep. Jack Kemp, who demanded that Reagan fire Habib. (Instead, at Shultz's insistence, Menges himself was fired.) Abrams, who had cleared off on the original letter, stepped in and disavowed its wording.[44]

Yet the most significant fact about all this was that the political pressure in the Habib flap was coming from the conservatives, not the liberals. Influential members of Congress now blamed the Sandinistas for the negotiating impasse. The three Democratic congressmen to whom Habib later wrote his letter (Michael Barnes, Jim Slattery, and Bill Richardson) visited the Contadora sessions in Panama and reported back to a Washington news conference on April 8 that "Nicaragua is being intransigent, that the Sandinistas' commitment to peace is suspect."[45] This sudden inspiration on the part of liberal congressmen was, if nothing else, a proof of the shifting political climate in Washington.

Administration opponents of the Contadora treaty took the opportunity to go on the offensive. Dr. Fred Iklé, the under secretary of defense for policy and a leading champion of the Reagan Doctrine, released a twelve-page Defense Department report entitled "Prospects for Containment of Nicaragua's Communist Government," assessing the risks of a Contadora treaty that left the Sandinista regime intact and included inadequate verification measures to prevent Nicaraguan violations. Tracing the history of Communist treaty violations, especially in Korea and Indochina, the report concluded that such a peace treaty would face the United States with an *increased* military problem of ensuring the security of Nicaragua's neighbors; the potential costs ranged as high as $1.5 billion for expanded military assistance and $7.2–$9.1 billion annually for the expanded U.S. military role in the region.[46] The State Department regarded the Iklé report as either a slight to its diplomatic efforts or a blow to the prospects for agreement. Under Secretary Armacost publicly repudiated it—even though it had been cleared by an interagency committee that included State.[47]

Negotiations proceeded in Congress toward a compromise. McCurdy came up with a package of $30 million in humanitarian aid and $70 million in military aid. He proposed a parallel $300 million in additional economic aid for the region's democracies. This Contra program was now too big to be run out of a State Department office like the previous year's humanitarian aid (and it was also a military program), so it was decided to create yet another new body—this time an interagency group chaired by the State Department—to supervise CIA's implementation, ensure policy guidance, and be accountable.

The Democratic leadership sought at all costs to delay an up-or-down vote, fearing Reagan would win.[48] Reagan intensified his personal lob-bying with swing voters over the summer, inviting into the Oval Office for a pep talk legislators who had never seen the sanctum sanctorum. With the bit between his teeth, this president—so often dismissed by detractors as "unengaged"—kept up the pressure and exploited all his political strengths. Michael Barnes conceded: "The guys in the middle just got tired of being beaten up on both sides. They knew Reagan was going to come back and back and back on this. He was obsessed by it. . . . He just wore everybody out."[49]

A key vote took place in the House on June 25, 1986, when the McCurdy package of $100 million for the Contras passed by 221–209. In October it was enacted as part of the (fiscal year) 1987 continuing resolutions.

The Sandinistas reacted in a brutal way. First, they shut down *La Prensa* again. A few days later, they moved again against the Catholic church—preventing Monsignor Bismarck Caballo from returning to Nic-aragua after a trip abroad and expelling Bishop Pablo Antonio Vega of Juigalpa from the country after forcibly removing him in a helicopter and depositing him on the Honduran border. To the Contras' opponents in the United States, the episode could be cited as proof that U.S. support for the resistance was provoking Sandinista repression. Yet the shock effect in the United States was such that there was no further receptivity to Sandinista excuses. "By these incremental steps, the pluralist revolution seems hopelessly betrayed," lamented the *New York Times*, seeing the Sandinistas on the "road to Stalinism."[50] Pope John Paul II, who happened to be on a Latin American tour at the time, called the expulsion of Bishop Vega "an almost incredible act."[51]

The administration moved rapidly to set up the new, squeaky-clean supervisory body required by the legislation. A senior interdepartmental group was created, staffed by the State Department and chaired by Under Secretary of State Armacost. I was the NSC representative for the first few months, in my capacity then as a deputy assistant to the president for national security affairs with a broad portfolio to monitor foreign policy issues. At meetings in November and December, the group was briefed by CIA Central America Task Force director Alan Fiers on the status of the program. The impression we were left with—and I think not wrongly—was that the Contra forces were gaining strength so rapidly that only the speed of the supply of weapons was limiting the growth of recruitment. Not only the matériel but the psychological impact of the dramatic U.S. commitment was changing the balance of forces on the ground.

IRAN-CONTRA: BASTARD CHILD OF THE REAGAN DOCTRINE

Between October 1984, the date of the second Boland Amendment, and August 1985, the effective date of the $27 million in humanitarian aid, the United States had provided no appropriated funding at all to the Contras, and until October 1986, no appropriated military aid. The year 1985 was a difficult one for the Contras in the field, as supplies became less reliable and the Sandinistas' military performance improved. The first Soviet Mi-25 helicopter gunships arrived in October 1984—the month of the second Boland Amendment. The Contras' difficult struggle in this interim was a common theme of the administration's appeals to the public and Congress. They were "close to desperate straits," Reagan declared in a briefing of the press on April 4, 1985. What he did not reveal was that, in the interval, he and his colleagues in the executive branch had resorted to other means. To an administration ideologically committed to supporting "freedom fighters," the denial of appropriated funds did not mean the end of the matter. Reagan secretly directed his national security adviser, Bud McFarlane, to hold the Contras together "body and soul."[52]

The administration resorted to other means that it was convinced (with varying degrees of justification) were legal and that were meant as "bridging" funds to sustain the Contras until another attempt could be made to win funding from Congress.[53] First, it solicited some $34 million from other, friendly, wealthy governments. This was certainly legal, and the cup passing was done by Reagan himself with Saudi king Fahd and, on the orders of George Shultz, by Elliott Abrams with the government of Brunei. Second, the White House raised about $2.7 million from various conservative individuals and groups that were persuaded by NSC staffer Lt. Col. Oliver North and others to donate directly to the Contras. This was legally questionable, depending on what exactly North's official involvement was. Third, North and some associates came up with the idea of skimming off excess profits from their secret arms sales to Iran for the benefit of the Contras. This turned into a legal and political firestorm when it was disclosed by Atty. Gen. Edwin Meese in a hastily convened White House news conference on November 25, 1986.

The main lesson to come out of this affair is the primacy of the law in the conduct of our government's business. Other lessons relate to the role of the NSC (an institution I have a certain affection for, having served there a dozen years under four presidents) and the authority of Congress (an institution still groping to define its role in the national security area). The episode opened a whole series of questions about presidential accountability to Congress—questions whose answers, however, may be even more elusive now than they were before Iran-Contra.

I had known of the secret arms sales to Iran and opposed them. (I had known nothing of the diversion of funds to Central America.) Nevertheless, however wrong I thought their actions, in human terms it was a chilling experience to watch many close colleagues badly hurt and some destroyed in a storm of public scandal. Oliver North was a man of undoubted energy and charm. He prodded a sluggish bureaucracy with ideas—almost all unwelcome, not all crazy. He was the classic workaholic who made himself indispensable; he was always willing to stay up all night to finish a job when others were willing to leave it to him. Under close supervision, he did yeoman work—in the 1985 interception of the *Achille Lauro* terrorists or the Libya bombing of April 1986. Unsupervised, however, Oliver North was a risk taker, a man tempting fate, flying high in an ethereal zone somewhere between reality and fantasy.

My boss at the NSC, Vice Adm. John Poindexter, was a striking contrast—a shy man, a brilliant physics Ph.D. and top Annapolis graduate, a straight arrow. "Unlike North, Poindexter was not someone who relished power or saw covert action as a sport," Michael Deaver has written.[54] At an NSC staff meeting just after the Iran story broke, Poindexter assured the staff that once the American people knew the whole story, they would applaud what had been done. He believed it. He was clearly out of his element in that job from the beginning; the national security adviser's job requires finely honed political skills that he did not possess. He preferred concentrating on the back-room work of substance and management; he hated the "political" work of dealing with Congress and the press, which has been an inescapable part of the job since Kissinger's day. This excess of scruple only left him without allies and friends when trouble hit. He was no match for the wily chief of staff, Donald Regan, in internal White House politics, let alone the deadly thicket that Ollie North led him into. The Iran initiative was not Poindexter's idea, but he followed through on it in a lapse of strategic judgment; the Contra activities that North plunged into he failed to restrain, in a lapse of (at the very least) political judgment. Poindexter properly took responsibility for what had transpired and saw his career destroyed, without the support group of cheering fans and the lecture fees that provided a safety net for North—and even the prospect of a political career.

The Iranian dimension of the "Iran-Contra" affair was bizarre enough. It began as an attempt to develop a new strategic relationship with Iran. Alarmed by Soviet efforts to woo the ayatollahs, some on the NSC staff came up with the idea of initiating secret contacts. As an earnest of our interest in better relations, we were prepared to transfer a small quantity of defensive weapons, such as TOW antitank missiles. We sought from the Iranians, as an earnest of their interest (of which we thought we had indications via the Israelis), help in securing the release of some of the American hostages held by Shi'ite fundamentalists in Lebanon.

My friend Michael Ledeen, then a consultant to the NSC, had told me in 1985 of the contact with Iran through the Israelis. I told him it was crazy. When I joined the NSC staff in early 1986, I was briefed by Admiral Poindexter, Don Fortier, and Oliver North. I told them it was crazy. My objections were mainly strategic: in the bitter Iran-Iraq war that had been raging since 1980, Iran was on the verge of victory; Iranian domination of the Gulf would be a strategic disaster for the West. Therefore, I considered it essential to stick by our official policy, which was to support our moderate Arab friends in helping Iraq resist and to seek by various means to *deny* weapons to Iran. I considered the fears of Soviet inroads in Tehran exaggerated, and I simply did not think the objective convergence of interest existed for a U.S. rapprochement with a militant, ideological, anti-Western Iran.

The Iranians, it is even clearer in retrospect, were simply diddling us to get the weapons. Our "strategic relationship" with them was a mirage. Operationally—especially when in early 1986 the technical arrangements were put in the hands of so dynamic a "fixer" as Ollie North—all that was really happening was the occasional arms shipment and the occasional hostage release. I wrote a memorandum to Poindexter on May 22, 1986, warning that the policy seemed to be degenerating into an arms-for-hostages deal.[55] He did not include me in important deliberations after that point.

In the subjective intent of the senior U.S. participants, including the president himself, I have no doubt that the *policy*—that is, the strategy, the objective, the purpose—was a good-faith quest for a strategic relationship with Iran, not a mere trade of arms for hostages. That is why Ronald Reagan persisted so long in the conviction that his "policy" was not arms for hostages, and he was speaking honestly. On this point, both Reagan and his accusers may have fallen victim to semantic confusion. In all my discussions with my NSC colleagues, the arguments were always in terms of a breakthrough toward some transformed strategic situation in the Gulf (though I disputed it). The supersecret presidential finding signed by Reagan on January 17, 1986—which a staff aide hand-carried to my office at Poindexter's instruction to show me—listed release of hostages as the third "purpose" of the exercise, after (1) the establishment of a more moderate government in Iran and (2) the hope of obtaining significant intelligence about the region. [56] McFarlane attempted (in vain) to have a broad strategy discussion with the Iranians during his secret visit to Tehran in May. The problem was, as I noted above, that the transfers of hostages and arms, intended as subordinate steps, ended up being all that was really going on. The policy was not meant as arms for hostages, but it degenerated into that as the mirage of a new strategic relationship evaporated in the desert haze.

When the secret dealings with Iran first leaked in a Beirut newspaper in November 1986, there was considerable indignation in the American press—the Ayatollah Khomeini being Americans' least favorite foreign statesman—but the criticism and the debate did not break down along partisan or ideological lines. The media turned the affair into a full-blown "scandal" only when the highly ideological Central America issue was introduced. Instantly, the battle lines formed in the familiar pattern. On the face of it, the administration had sought to circumvent the policy of Congress and the laws it had passed in the period when it had sought to constrain U.S. support for the Contras. And by shady means, to boot. The administration was bound to pay a huge price for its circumvention of legal restraints—the flouting of arms export control procedures; the unwritten or undisclosed presidential findings; the use of the NSC staff to bypass CIA channels that would have required congressional disclosure. The revelations came exactly one month after the appropriation of $100 million in Contra aid and became the perfect weapon in the hands of those who still wanted to kill it.

This is not the place for a full-scale exhumation of the controversy. The political and legal case against the policy is made with full force in the majority report of the joint Senate-House committee that held televised hearings on the matter in 1987[57] and in the final report of Lawrence Walsh, the independent counsel. [58] There are also exhaustive examinations by Theodore Draper and others. [59] The arms transfers to Iran (even indirectly through the Israelis) are criticized as foolish as well as violations of laws requiring notification to Congress of such transfers. The bypassing of congressional consultation, the circumventions of the Boland Amendments' restrictions, and the alleged attempt to cover it all up afterward are held to be not only violations of law but also an abuse of power with serious constitutional implications.

As for the administration's defense of its actions—there really wasn't any. The White House, particularly under the influence of Chief of Staff Donald Regan and his successor, Howard Baker, decided to blame everything on Poindexter and North and let them fend for themselves. North was summarily fired; Poindexter was pushed to resign. Throughout, there was virtually no attempt to defend the legality or propriety of *any* of the efforts to aid the Contras except on the rare occasions when Reagan's own conduct was inescapably at issue. (White House press secretary Marlin Fitzwater stepped forward briskly with a good legal argument when the subject arose of Reagan's solicitation of King Fahd.)[60] It was left to the Republican minority on the joint congressional committee to mount a more comprehensive rebuttal. The minority report sought to demonstrate that the president had scope for the exercise of discretion in these matters under the Constitution, especially in the gray areas and loopholes left in statutes like Boland, which, on close inspection, represented imprecise compromises.[61] The joint committee split along partisan lines—a clue to the political warfare over Central America policy that underlay the debate.

Was the diversion of funds to the Contras illegal? The ironic answer is: We shall never know. The judicial proceeding that took over from the congressional investigation, under the direction of Lawrence Walsh, ended up shining surprisingly little light on the core issues of the scandal. The indictments of North and Poindexter on the more interesting substantive counts—brought under the rubric of a broad conspiracy to defraud the United States—all fell away because of legal complications either in pretrial proceedings or on appeal. North was convicted only on the charges of making false statements to Congress, destroying official documents, and accepting an illegal gratuity (a security system for his home). And even these convictions were later overturned.

The more central substantive counts were dropped, first of all, because of the impossibility of trying them without the admission into evidence of large numbers of sensitive secret documents that the government was unwilling to declassify. When faced with the broad conspiracy charges, North prepared a broad defense that included reference to other intelligence activities of the U.S. government in the fields of covert action and counterterrorism in which he had been involved and which formed the policy context in which (he argued) his actions had to be judged. Trial judge Gerhard Gesell accepted the general legitimacy of North's proposed defense and the broad discovery of documents that it inevitably required. The thousands of documents that North sought, however, included some of the most sensitive of the "family jewels" of the U.S. government— records of legitimate intelligence activities that were legitimately kept secret. Government lawyers consulted in advance with the leaders of both parties in Congress and with the chairmen of the intelligence committees—including the liberal Louis Stokes on the House side—and they all concurred that the material included vital national secrets that were simply not releasable.

The prosecution of the broad charges was thus bound to fall apart because of this classified material. In the end, Judge Gesell dismissed the two main counts on January 13, 1989, over a separate but related issue having to do with the attempt to sanitize the smaller number of documents that prosecutor Walsh himself wanted to use; Gesell ruled that edited documents were not acceptable as evidence. At the beginning of the investigation, the Justice Department had offered Walsh the benefit of its technical expertise on the exceedingly tricky handling of cases involving secret documents; Walsh had rejected the help because he did not trust any lawyers in the Reagan Justice Department.

The other counts against North and Poindexter fell away because of the "taint" of trial evidence by the congressional hearings that had been held. Key Iran-Contra figures had testified in the hearings under a grant of limited immunity from prosecution, which barred the use of their hearing testimony in any trial proceeding against them. After North's conviction, on appeal, the U.S. Court of Appeals for the District of Columbia in July 1990 remanded the case to the trial court for a more extensive examination of whether the trial had been tainted by the testimony of witnesses who had themselves been influenced by the hearings.[62] The trial court ended up dismissing all remaining counts for this reason.

It would seem natural to conclude that the collapse of the principal indictments was a historical accident, the result of technicalities in the law and its heavy procedural bias in favor of defendants' rights. But it was no accident. For the problem with secret documents was a direct result of the degree to which North's actions in question were intertwined with legitimate ongoing intelligence activities. The judicial process proved ill suited to dealing with issues so intimately interwoven with foreign and intelligence policy. And the problem of the "taint" of the congressional hearings was no accident, either. The judicial process could hardly proceed unscathed through a political controversy so highly charged that it had been played out in dramatic public hearings that transfixed the country through the summer of 1987. The legal issues were bound up in a political battle of the titans—a struggle between Congress and the executive branch, between Republicans and Democrats, and between liberals and conservatives, over Central America policy. Even the independent counsel's operation, moreover, was constantly accused of being politicized, from the ideological animus its lawyers openly displayed toward Elliott Abrams to the Democratic political activist chosen by Walsh in 1992 to prosecute former Defense Secretary Caspar Weinberger to the counts in the Weinberger indictment handed down four days before the 1992 presidential election.[63]

In the end, most of the convictions that Walsh won, whether by trial or plea bargain, were against secondary figures like Abrams or CIA officers Clair George or Alan Fiers, who were more the victims of Oliver North than they were his cohorts. Most of the convictions involved making false statements to, or withholding information from, Congress; these individuals had either felt trapped by their sense of bureaucratic obligation to shield, or, alternatively, felt compelled to try desperately to dissociate from, misdeeds on the part of North of which they almost certainly disapproved. Robert McFarlane, a more central actor, also pleaded guilty to counts of making false statements to Congress. Abrams, like McFarlane, accepted a plea bargain because a trial would have bankrupted him. Abrams's trial judge was so unimpressed by the government's case that he imposed no sentence, instead asking Abrams only to perform 100 hours of community service and pay fifty dollars in court costs.

Lying to Congress cannot be defended. The criminal statutes applied in these cases, however, had historically been applied in other kinds of cases of false statements to federal investigators, never before to the interaction between the executive and legislative branches.[64] Officials are now on notice that the traditional maneuvering with Congress can subject them to criminal penalties if they are not scrupulous; perhaps this is appropriate—so long as it is borne in mind that the relation of the executive to Congress is not one of subordination in this area, any more than in any other area. This is the clear import of two hundred years of constitutional law on executive privilege and the separation of powers.[65] Executive-legislative relations, including in congressional hearings, are inherently political; policy and political battles between the branches will always be with us. Congress now has a new weapon in its hands.

From the perspective of this book, the most interesting aspects of the Iran-Contra affair are these political and institutional implications. First of all, the affair originated in yet another breakdown of the comity by which our complicated system of separation of powers works, when it works. Democratic senator David Boren, then chairman of the Senate Intelligence Committee, summed up the fundamental problem perceptively in early 1987:

With each new breakdown of bipartisan consensus and trust comes a new list of congressional restrictions on the executive branch. With new restrictions come new initiatives by the White House aimed at evading what are viewed as unwise limitations upon the prerogatives of the commander in chief. Executive evasions breed more congressional distrust and the cycle continues, paralleling the arms race in its destructive and irrational escalation.[66]

Just as with Vietnam and Watergate, the Iran-Contra affair had lasting institutional effects. That withholding information from Congress can now be a criminal offense for executive branch officials is an important shift in the balance of power between the two branches—poetic justice, perhaps, and certainly an ironic outcome of a ploy intended to advance executive prerogatives.

Among the other ironies, however, is that Congress made no attempt to legislate changes in the National Security Council structure or staff, recognizing its statutory and constitutional status as part of the executive office of the president. The Tower Board—the bipartisan investigative board composed of former senator John Tower, Gen. Brent Scowcroft, and former senator and secretary of state Edmund Muskie—strongly recommended against tinkering with the presidential office by statute,[67] and Congress agreed. The Reagan administration, under Poindexter's capable successor, Frank Carlucci, instituted a number of internal reforms in early 1987, such as hiring a senior legal adviser[68]; Colin Powell and Brent Scowcroft, who followed in the national security adviser's job in the Republican era, maintained the reputation for scrupulous conduct.

I can testify from my personal experience on the NSC staff for four years after Iran-Contra that the scandal had its chastening effect: No one had any inclination thereafter to try exotic schemes or to conduct a private foreign policy. The NSC staff's proper job is coordinating policy deliberations and advising the president; it is simply an ineffective as well as inappropriate vehicle for *executing* operational decisions. It has no business, certainly, operating behind the president's back (as apparently North and Poindexter did on the diversion of funds), and its suitability to implement presidential policies behind the backs of the State and Defense departments is also highly problematic. In rare circumstances, like Nixon's sensitive diplomacy with Moscow, Beijing, and Hanoi, a case can be made—but the president in such a situation takes a heavy personal burden on his own shoulders. A president also has every right to overrule what his cabinet secretaries recommend (as Reagan did with Shultz and Weinberger over arms for Iran and as many other presidents have done)— but he had better know what he is doing.

As the NSC pulled in its horns after Iran-Contra, Congress took its institutional revenge on someone else—the CIA. This meant, first of all, more continuous oversight over covert actions. It also meant—especially after Casey's retirement in February 1987 and replacement by the less flamboyant Judge William Webster—a CIA that was institutionally tamed, if not demoralized, and much more deferential to Congress than ever before. The CIA's new situation—after first Vietnam and now Iran-Contra—was summed up in a striking pronouncement by Robert Gates, Webster's deputy (and later successor), in a speech in September 1987. Gates pointed out the surprising fact that the CIA's intelligence product was now freely available to Congress:

> Virtually all CIA assessments go to the two Congressional Intelligence Committees. Most go also to the Armed Services, Foreign Relations, and Appropriations Committees. In 1986, CIA sent some 5000 intelligence reports to Congress and gave many hundreds of briefings. All this is new in the last decade or so. As a result, and thanks to their staffs, many Senators and Representatives are often better informed about CIA's information and assessments on a given subject than the policymaker. And that intelligence is often used to criticize and challenge policy, to set one executive agency against another, and to expose disagreements within an Administration.[69]*

This development, plus Congress's increasing control over the CIA's budget, left the CIA, according to Gates, "poised nearly equidistant between the Executive and Legislative branches":

> The oversight process has also given Congress—especially the two intelligence committees—far greater knowledge of and influence over the way CIA and other intelligence agencies spend their money than anyone in the Executive would dream of exercising: from expenditures in the billions to line items in the thousands. . . . Congress may actually have more influence today over our priorities and how we spend our money than the Executive Branch.
>
> The result of these realities is that CIA today is in a remarkable position,

---

*This chicken came home to roost for a Democratic president in 1993 when conservative senators obtained a CIA psychological profile of exiled Haitian president Jean-Bertrand Aristide and leaked it to discredit the Clinton administration's policy of attempting to restore Aristide to power.[70]

poised nearly equidistant between the Executive and Legislative branches. . . .[71]

The notion of the CIA's "equidistance" between Congress and the executive was indeed "remarkable" and created a minor uproar when Gates put it forward. Its consistency with the 1947 National Security Act, which founded the CIA—or with the Constitution of the United States—may be doubted. The Constitution vests the executive power in the president; the CIA was created by law as a provider of advice to the National Security Council, a body of the president's cabinet that advises *him*. Gates hastened to insert the word "involuntarily" into the clause when he adapted the speech as an article in *Foreign Affairs*,[72] but his original point was well taken as a description of where a turbulent political evolution had brought us.

THE UNDEAD: THE CONTRAS AND CENTRAL AMERICAN DIPLOMACY

While the $100 million appropriated for the Nicaraguan resistance continued to be dispensed over fiscal year 1987, the scandal, coupled with the Democrats' recapture of the Senate, shattered the administration's long-term hopes. Reagan's public approval rating dropped 21 percent, to the lowest of his presidency, and the sharpest drop ever recorded. Half the public was convinced he was lying, and two-thirds now trusted Congress more than the president "to make the right decisions on foreign policy."[73]

Oliver North made a dramatic presentation in the televised hearings in July, rallying the "silent majority" with his charisma; it raised hopes in some quarters that the administration might yet salvage future military aid for the resistance. But it was now a dispirited administration—wounded, gun-shy, depopulated of most of its more ideological champions, dominated by men like George Shultz and former senator Howard Baker (Regan's replacement as White House chief of staff), who saw conciliation of Congress as the best strategy now. Elliott Abrams remained, manfully protected by Shultz but also severely weakened because of a tangential connection with some of North's schemes for privately funded supply of the Contras.

It was a paradoxical moment of both strength and weakness in the U.S. bargaining position. On the ground in Nicaragua, the Contras were coming into their own; the $100 million in U.S. aid meant training, weapons, equipment, and logistical support as they had never had before. The Sandinista regime was reeling under the pressure. Yet the longer-term prospect for the resistance was clouded by the transformation of the political climate in Washington. In the mind of some in the State Department like special envoy Philip Habib, this was the moment for a diplomatic initiative—when we knew our bargaining position was at its peak. But the unfolding Iran-Contra scandal absorbed, and distracted the attention of, the U.S. government. The administration, so soon after its success in winning the Contra aid, was again groping for a strategy.

An important diplomatic effort was launched, but it was by Costa Rican president Oscar Arias. On February 15, 1987, he called together the presidents of his fellow Central American democracies—El Salvador, Honduras, and Guatemala—and unveiled a proposal. It included an immediate region-wide cease-fire; an immediate halt to outside military or financial support for insurgent forces (U.S. support for the Contras, Sandinista support for the Salvadoran Communists); the opening of internal dialogues between governments and unarmed opposition groups; amnesties; regional talks on reduction of armaments; and a calendar for democratization, including early restoration of press freedom and free elections according to the constitutions of each country.[74] The other three presidents reserved judgment on Arias's plan, conscious of the risks. The four agreed, however, to present the plan to Daniel Ortega at a subsequent Central American summit to be scheduled.

Like most peace plans for Central America, it had its pluses and minuses from the U.S. perspective. As in Afghanistan or Angola, the United States was uneasy about relinquishing its main leverage—its aid to the rebels—on Day One, while waiting for the uncertain implementation (and weak verification) of the Communist regime's obligations. From the Sandinistas' point of view, the Arias Plan continued Contadora's uncomfortable emphasis on opening up the internal political process. In any case, Arias's plan immediately filled the negotiating vacuum; it became the dominant concept in the diplomacy, propelled by Arias's energetic salesmanship and by the plan's utility to Democrats who opposed Contra aid. The more the administration's misgivings became evident, the more Arias was lionized in Congress at the administration's expense.

Arias's motives were a mixture of sincerity and calculation. He was a true democrat, representing a nation with a long democratic tradition. He also wanted the Contra war to end, because he feared an escalating regional crisis. He closed down an airstrip in northwest Costa Rica that the CIA was using to supply the Contras.[75] But while his opposition to the Contras won him applause in Congress, his premises were much closer to those of the Reagan administration. Costa Rica had supported the Sandinistas against Somoza in 1979 but had been disillusioned by their totalitarian bent. Costa Ricans "feel they have been betrayed. We feel they lied to us," Arias had told Roy Gutman in 1985.[76] In other words, he shared the Reaganites' premise that a change in the internal structure of Nicaragua was the key to peace. Even more: Arias confided to other American friends that he really wished the United States had gotten rid of the Sandinista problem by more drastic means. "You lack the guts to do what needs to be done," he reportedly said, "to intervene militarily and depose the Sandinistas."[77]

In early 1987, when Arias launched his initiative, the upheavals in Washington made a decisive U.S. action of this kind even more implausible. In such a circumstance, to Arias, the growing strength of the Contras was enough to cause a regional crisis but not enough to solve his problem. Thus, the urgency of his diplomacy. To a U.S. administration that complained of the plan's inadequacies, he was saying in effect: "This is my second-best choice, too, but your unwillingness to get rid of the Sandinistas by military means leaves me no alternative." This irony was lost on his congressional admirers and probably also on the Norwegian Nobel committee that awarded him the Peace Prize for 1987.

Arias's admirers in Congress, particularly Jim Wright of Texas, the new House Speaker, wanted to invite him to address a joint session of Congress, a courtesy frequently extended to foreign heads of state. The administration refused to consent, which only added to Arias's allure. He addressed an open meeting of the House Democratic Caucus instead.[78]

This was only a minor example of Wright's determined effort to take control of Central America policy away from the president—a fascinating piece of U.S. constitutional history that deserves further study in its own right. Through his frequent trips to Central America and meetings with regional leaders, Wright presented an alternative U.S. foreign policy opposed to Contra aid and eager for a settlement with Managua. He met frequently with Sandinista leaders and representatives without informing the administration. He encouraged Arias to proceed with his plan despite the administration's misgivings; he put pressure on Honduras to go along with Arias rather than the administration, threatening to block Honduras's foreign aid otherwise: "Democrats have been in power since 1954," Wright told a group of visiting Honduran military officers. "The members of the Appropriations Committee are amenable to helping you. We would look with very great disfavor on anything that slowed the peace process."[79]

The message conveyed to our allies was simple, and it was repeated by Democratic party whip Tony Coelho at a lunch with Central American ambassadors in August 1987: "The administration will be in office seventeen more months. The Speaker will serve ten years."[80] When national security adviser Colin Powell made an official trip to Central America in January 1988 to meet with leaders on President Reagan's behalf, Wright sent his majority leader, Tom Foley, and whip, Tony Coelho, to another lunch with Central American ambassadors as a "counterweight" to Powell's trip; they warned the Central Americans that the executive branch was "only part" of the U.S. government and that it was Congress that "appropriated money and decided who got aid, not the White House."[81]

Even the equable George Shultz lost his patience at one point in 1987 and lashed out at Wright at a White House meeting for undercutting U.S. foreign policy. Wright was shaken, and Shultz probably made a mistake in letting Wright off the hook publicly as easily as he did. On November 17 he and Wright held a joint news conference to mark a truce between the two sovereign entities—just like the joint news conferences Shultz customarily held with a visiting head of state or foreign minister after a hard day of negotiation. Wright conceded some points about democracy in Nicaragua and constitutional proprieties at home, but came out looking statesmanlike. Shultz later found out to his chagrin that a group of House Republicans and swing Democrats had been planning a revolt against the Speaker over his ethical lapses and his Central America shenanigans but that the news conference concordat with Shultz had torpedoed it.[82]

During 1987, amid the brouhaha of the Iran-Contra hearings, the administration set about in a low-key way to explore the possibilities for renewed Contra aid for fiscal year 1988. Another conciliatory letter on the theme of democracy was being negotiated, like the Reagan letter to McCurdy in 1986, this time with Rep. Jim Slattery, Democrat of Kansas. The negotiating process (with both Nicaragua and Congress) then took a sudden and bizarre turn. At the beginning of August, I was in a hospital bed in Boston recovering from surgery when I got an anguished call from Arnaud de Borchgrave, editor of the *Washington Times*, saying Reagan had agreed to cut off aid for the Contras. What was going on? No, no, I groggily assured Arnaud, the administration was proceeding as it had the year before; I was familiar with the internal discussions. Turn on your TV set, Arnaud suggested, not impressed by my utility as a knowledgeable source.

In the few days I had been absent, Tom Loeffler, a former Texas Republican congressman acting as adviser to Chief of Staff Howard Baker, had had the idea to approach his fellow Texan Jim Wright and propose a deal. The plan thus originated on the political side of the White House and not from any of the administration's Latin America experts (though

Shultz, Abrams, and NSC staffer José Sorzano were brought in late in the process). Secretary Weinberger tried to persuade Reagan and Shultz it was a bad idea. Announced to a stunned world on August 5, the plan included a call for an immediate cease-fire, suspension of outside resupply to insurgencies, regional security negotiations, internal dialogue, and early elections. It also called for completion of the negotiation with Nicaragua by September 30, and if the deadline were not met due to actions by Nicaragua, the parties "would be free to pursue such actions as they deem necessary to protect their national interest."

The so-called Wright-Reagan Plan had some redeeming features—tight linkage between the Sandinistas' obligations and our own; stringent verification procedures; strong language warning off the Soviets from establishing military bases in Central America and demanding an end to Nicaragua's "subversion or destabilization of duly elected governments in the hemisphere." Thus, it was refreshingly free of the "moral equivalence" that characterized most of the multilateral Central American diplomacy, equating the Sandinistas' subversion in the region with the efforts by the United States and its friends to oppose it. Humanitarian aid to the resistance was not barred.[83] Administration defenders of the deal pointed to the obligations it placed on the Sandinistas and the improved prospects for wooing the moderate Democrats to vote for military aid if the Sandinistas failed to meet the September 30 deadline.[84]

On the other hand, the administration was declaring a moratorium on its lobbying for any new Contra military aid unless and until it was in a position after September 30 to prove that the Sandinistas were the obstacle to a negotiated settlement. This was Arnaud's (and my) concern. The Sandinistas would easily be able to make cosmetic changes or else back off from the more overt forms of repression for a brief period and thereby complicate Reagan's ability to start up the aid ever again. If a policy is controversial, declaring a moratorium on the policy wins a temporary respite, but the political cost of starting up again is always higher than expected. Lyndon Johnson found this to be the case with Vietnam bombing halts; and before him, Kennedy, with nuclear-testing moratoria. The Wright-Reagan Plan left the fate of Reagan's policy too much in Daniel Ortega's hands, and I could easily have given Ortega ideas on how to use the plan to confound the administration that authored it.

The most serious effect of Wright-Reagan, however, was on our Central American allies who had stood firmly until then and had not leaped to accept Arias's plan because of the risks they perceived from an agreement with weak verification provisions and other problems. The long-awaited

Central American summit was to begin in Guatemala City on August 6—the very next day after the Wright-Reagan initiative—the first formal summit-level discussion of the Arias Plan in a meeting that included Daniel Ortega. Almost always in the past, before a meeting of our Central American friends among themselves or with the Nicaraguans, the State Department made a point of keeping our friends fully briefed on our thinking, bolstering the resolve of the Hondurans and Salvadorans who had the most to lose from a risky settlement. This time, the sloppy and furtive procedures by which Wright-Reagan was generated left our friends unbriefed. In the vacuum, they panicked. Salvadoran president Duarte later told Jack Kemp that he "could not sleep all night" after hearing of the Wright-Reagan initiative.[85] Whatever the specific elements in the Wright-Reagan text that might have been sold to our friends as beneficial, the moratorium on Contra aid seemed to relieve the military pressure; the whole procedure in Washington did not inspire confidence, especially after the Iran-Contra debacle and with the Democrats back in control.

The upshot was that our Central American allies were panicked into an immediate endorsement of the Arias Plan—exactly the opposite of the administration's intentions. Paradoxically, the Sandinistas, who faced risks themselves in the Arias Plan's democratization provisions, also lost their balance; they, too, accepted the plan, feeling the brunt of the military pressure from the Contras and fearing to be isolated at such a moment among the Central Americans. Speaker Wright quickly abandoned the plan that bore his name and endorsed Arias's too. (As Shultz later said of Wright, "[H]e could smile at you while he cut your throat.")[86]

Over the next two years, the Central Americans hammered out details of the Arias Plan. The accord at Guatemala City (sometimes called "Esquipulas II") dealt with cessation of outside military supplies to insurgencies; "free and democratic elections" were to be held in each country according to existing constitutional provisions—but these were to be delayed until after the 1988 elections for a region-wide Central American Parliament, a pet project of Guatemalan president Vinicio Cerezo.[87]

The Nicaraguans—advised by sympathetic House Democrat David Bonior[88]—came up with some conciliatory gestures, such as a formal lifting of the state of emergency, release of some political prisoners, permission for some exiled opponents to return, and agreement in principle to a dialogue with the resistance. Some of these steps—especially the last—were important; insurgent movements always gain in legitimacy from being included in a national dialogue. But the negotiating process was only beginning. While Wright-Reagan had fallen by the wayside, Reagan's political concession of a moratorium on military aid was in effect de facto; the Sandinistas' conciliatory gestures—as I predicted—made it less and less realistic that Reagan would be able to rally support for Contra military aid again.

Sandinista behavior still left a lot to be desired. The day after the Guatemala accord, sixteen members of the Nicaraguan Confederation of Trade Union Unity were arrested and imprisoned. A week later, police with cattle prods, egged on by *turbas*, broke up two peaceful opposition rallies. On September 21, Nicaraguan vice president Sergio Ramirez said it was "absurd" to believe the Sandinistas would demilitarize and that "only those who are not in their right minds would think of requesting the surrender of the revolution."[89] *Radio Católica*, shut down in 1985, was about to reopen in October 1987 but was then denied permission to broadcast. *Turbas* harassed peaceful demonstrations of the human rights group January 22 Movement of Mothers of Political Prisoners. Police detained members of the Social Christian party and Social Democratic party as they attempted to organize.

House Democrats, perhaps understandably nervous about the prospects for democracy now that the Contras' military pressure was bound to diminish, passed a "sense of the House" resolution on December 8, 1987, insisting that the Nicaraguan regime reform itself in order to assure free and fair procedures in advance of any elections. The resolution (which passed overwhelmingly, 346–58) insisted on a variety of political and institutional changes—ensuring freedom of expression, association, assembly and movement, religion, and education; allowing the return of exiles; abolishing arbitrary police practices and tribunals; allowing complete freedom of the press and access to broadcast media; guaranteeing the right to strike and independent labor unions' right to publish; lifting restrictions on the church; and assuring Indian and Creole rights.[90] It was a good list—far more rigorous than what the Arias Plan required—and it was helpful leverage over the Sandinistas in the ensuing diplomacy.

In a sense, with the definitive cutoff of military aid to the Contras, the burden of proof for political good conduct was shifted in our public debate from the Reagan administration to the Sandinistas.[91] Doubts about the Sandinistas—and fears about colluding in the extermination of the resistance forces and their families—led Congress to approve several more installments of nonlethal aid. Esquipulas II permitted outside financial aid only for "repatriation," "relocation," and "reintegration" of paramilitary groups "into normal life." The administration argued that keeping the rebels and their families alive during the complex political process that was supposed to unfold was a means to those ends, and it managed to win the point.

The resistance remained intact, though the fighting subsided. Amazingly, they did not disband, or flee as refugees; their numbers did not shrink. Direct contacts between the regime and the resistance were organized in the fall of 1987 under Cardinal Obando y Bravo's aegis; a formal cease-fire was agreed at a meeting in Sapoa, a town near the Costa Rican border, in March 1988. But less than a week later, *La Prensa* was forced to close again temporarily when the regime cut off its supply of newsprint. A month later, Sandinista riot police wielding rubber truncheons dispersed striking workers; opposition workers distributing leaflets were arrested. Sandinista television denounced Violeta Chamorro, publisher of *La Prensa*, as a war criminal. On July 10, in Nandaime, without provocation, security forces attacked an opposition rally with tear gas, beatings, and arrests. The next day, *Radio Católica* was shut down again indefinitely, and *La Prensa* was ordered closed for fifteen days.

Interior Minister Tomás Borge warned the opposition that his police would use "institutional violence" to suppress activities considered provocative by the government. "We can be flexible and tolerant," he explained, "but not to the point of killing the revolution. That would not be tolerance; it would be stupidity."[92]

BUSH, BAKER, AND THE 1990 ELECTIONS

The Bush administration offered many contrasts with its predecessor. Among the contrasts most apparent to those of us who straddled both administrations were two factors that showed up vividly in Central America policy—the downplaying of ideology and the remarkably frictionless cooperation within the government. I have commented earlier on the Bush team's lack of emotional commitment to the Reagan Doctrine and the cause of the "freedom fighters" that so animated Reagan personally. Aside from Vice President Dan Quayle, the new administration had no ideologues in top positions—or even in key mid-level positions—and, in any case, inherited most of the regional conflicts at historical stages at which they had lost much of their strategic significance, with external troops already on their way out of Afghanistan, Angola, and Cambodia.

The Bush administration was also extraordinarily free of public or even significant private disarray—a word that, the reader will note, has appeared with repetitive frequency in earlier chapters. This was a reflection of a knowledgeable, activist, hands-on president who asserted his authority on a daily basis and never let bureaucratic disputes harden into the deadlocks that so often paralyzed the Reagan administration, as in arms control or Lebanon; nor was there the wild internecine warfare that had plagued Central America policy or that dogged Al Haig and George Shultz through much of their diplomatic endeavors. The Bush team— Secretary of State James Baker, Secretary of Defense Dick Cheney, Joint Chiefs of Staff chairman Gen. Colin Powell, CIA directors William Webster (a holdover) and his successor Robert Gates, and Assistant to the President for National Security Affairs Brent Scowcroft—worked together remarkably well. There were indeed policy differences on a variety of subjects—Gates was definitely more hard-line than the others in his views of the Soviet Union—but the differences were handled in a mature manner. In large part this was because the teacher (the president) was paying sufficient attention that the pupils in the sandbox never had the chance to start throwing sand at each other. On a basic issue like the use of force, which had paralyzed the Reagan administration—recall the great battle of the speeches between Shultz and Weinberger in 1984—the Pentagon, while still reluctant, was more responsive to presidential wishes with Cheney in charge. Witness the successes of the 1989 Panama operation against Noriega and Desert Storm in the Gulf in 1991.

Baker, quintessentially a political animal, quickly took charge of Central America policy, with the principal aim of rendering it politically harmless to his boss. It was an explosive issue that had nearly ruined Reagan—much as Baker had warned as early as 1981 when he was part of Reagan's original White House staff. Baker used to insist that Mike Deaver go quickly into the Oval Office and debrief Reagan any time CIA director Casey had been in alone with the president. Deaver recalls that Baker "was like a dog with a bone. He would say that the crazies want to get us into war [and that] we cannot get this economic recovery program going if we get involved in a land war in Central America."[93] Even after Reagan's landslide reelection, Baker told Lou Cannon that Central America was still an issue that could undo the president in his second term.[94] My own view is that the hesitancy of the policy in the first Reagan term contributed to its festering into the second, and that Baker thus ironically contributed to the persistence of the problem that so worried him.

In any event, at the beginning of the Bush administration, Baker's political instincts produced a more successful result—the Bipartisan Accord unveiled with much fanfare at the Bush White House on March 24, 1989. Bush and Baker, along with Speaker Jim Wright, Senate majority leader George Mitchell, and an array of the rest of the congressional leadership from both parties, reached an agreement on Central America policy that was a much smarter arrangement than the Wright-Reagan fiasco of a year and a half earlier.

The essence of the 1989 Bipartisan Accord was a political strategy on which Congress and the president found common ground, focusing on the Nicaraguan presidential election, which was now scheduled for February 25, 1990 (according to an agreement reached among the Central Americans in February 1989). This was the correct focus for U.S. policy, for any remaining hopes for moderating Sandinista behavior internally or externally depended on whether political pluralism could take root there. The Bipartisan Accord stressed the centrality of democratization throughout the region and the importance of peace agreements "based on credible standards of compliance, strict timetables for enforcement, and effective, ongoing means to verify both the democratic and security requirements of these agreements."[95] Humanitarian aid would continue to flow to the resistance at current levels (about $4.5 million a month) for the purpose of preparing their voluntary reintegration into normal life as permitted by Esquipulas.

The accord also, like Wright-Reagan, insisted, in strong language, on an end to Nicaragua's "subversion and destabilization of its neighbors" and to "Soviet-bloc military ties that threaten U.S. and regional security"; it called the Soviet Union's continued support for Central American subversion a "direct violation" of the Esquipulas agreement. It ended with a cryptic but ferocious-sounding warning:

> The U.S. Government retains ultimate responsibility to define its national interests and foreign policy, and nothing in this accord shall be interpreted to infringe on that responsibility. The United States need not spell out in advance the nature or type of action that would be undertaken in response to threats to U.S. national security interests. Rather it should be sufficient to simply make clear that such threats will be met by any appropriate constitutional means.[96]

The warning was a way to hint at other kinds of leverage that might be brought to bear. Neither the new administration nor the congressional leaders had any stomach for threatening a resumption of military aid to the Contras; the more general warning was meant to substitute but sounded even more ominous, whether intended or not. How credible it was, however, is an open question.

The reality was that the military pressure of the Contras was being dropped as an instrument of U.S. policy. It was, in fact, long dead in the Congress, and Bush and Baker surrendered nothing by conceding it. They were making the best possible bargain with Congress on a strategy to maximize all the available *nonmilitary* pressures that could be brought to bear. One element was to increase the diplomatic pressure on Mikhail Gorbachev to cut his links with Nicaragua—Soviet military aid still running at $500 million a year even in the enlightened era of "new thinking." Beyond this, the administration managed to get Congress to sign on to a document that would have brought some satisfaction even to the Reagan administration—a guarantee that the resistance would be kept alive; a call for the strictest verification; the ominous (if unspecific) warnings; plus the very fact that this was Congress and the president sticking to a common policy for the first time.

Oscar Arias visited Bush in the White House on April 4, 1989, and, in the spirit of the thing, told reporters afterward that he agreed that humanitarian aid to the resistance was appropriate until democratization of Nicaragua was complete.[97] He said the same thing in August and thereby helped undercut the continuing efforts of congressional liberals to cut off all funds.[98]

There were some problems with the accord—including the small matter that it was unconstitutional. By a side deal, the administration agreed that the congressional leadership and key committees would be empowered to review the continued Contra funding in mid-November 1989 and, in theory, terminate it if they chose. The Supreme Court in 1983 had declared such a legislative veto an unconstitutional procedure.[99] White House counsel Boyden Gray was of this opinion, but Baker was not deterred.[100] Fortunately, no one attempted to sue anybody over the issue, and Congress made no attempt to exercise the authority that the accord purported to grant.

The practical effect on the ground in Nicaragua was to shine a very bright international spotlight on the February 1990 election. A replay of the 1984 fiasco would be, without any question, a political disaster for the Sandinistas. With the Arias Plan now adopted—and the congressional liberals having won their argument that U.S. policy needed to abandon the Contra war—a continuing Sandinista policy of repression would be left shorn of all excuses. Specifically, the full panoply of election monitoring was about to unfold—bipartisan observers from Congress, international observers by the score (including former president Jimmy Carter), world media hordes, all zeroing in on the election's fairness.

A new instrumentality of international political pressure was evolving here. In less controversial situations like Namibia (or even Cambodia), free elections under international supervision were becoming a routine part of UN peacekeeping functions. An improvised version of the evolving techniques had helped undermine Philippine dictator Ferdinand Marcos in 1986 by denying him his ability to rig an election. In Panama in May

1989, Noriega's attempt to do the same accelerated the political crisis that ended in the U.S. military operation at the end of the year to remove him. The Sandinistas were now about to pay a price for their international celebrity, because the world spotlight would cramp their style enormously.

On February 14, shortly before the Bipartisan Accord, the five Central American presidents met in the resort of El Tesoro, El Salvador. In return for planning for the voluntary repatriation of rebel groups, the four democratic presidents exacted from Daniel Ortega a commitment to reforms of the electoral and other laws to allow full freedom of expression, assembly, and political organization. But Ortega's manner of fulfilling these pledges was typical. The Sandinista-controlled National Assembly steamrolled through a reform law in April that dashed the hopes of the fourteen opposition democratic parties. A five-member Supreme Electoral Council, supposed to represent all parties, included three Sandinista members and representatives of other parties as chosen by the government. Exiles or expatriates could not vote by absentee ballot but only if they returned home. Access to state-dominated television was rationed to thirty minutes per day for all opposition parties *together*. Any foreign financial support had to be shared 50 percent with the Supreme Electoral Council. The OAS was invited to send observers, but monitoring by local diplomats (e.g., the U.S. embassy) was restricted, and foreign polling firms were banned from operating in Nicaragua. Some of these restrictions were eased under international pressure, but only partially and grudgingly.[101]

The democratic parties grouped in the United Nicaraguan Opposition (UNO) nominated Mrs. Violeta Chamorro as their presidential candidate to oppose Daniel Ortega. She and her supporters were to face some of the same harassment as Arturo Cruz in 1984. A bipartisan group of observers under the aegis of the Center for Democracy—including Democratic National Committee leader Peter Kelly, Republican National Committee chief of staff Mary Matalin, former Mondale aide Robert Beckel, and Center president Allen Weinstein—witnessed a display of Sandinista brownshirt tactics in December 1989 in Masatepe, where an UNO rally addressed by Mrs. Chamorro was attacked by *turbas* wielding rocks and machetes, killing a participant.[102] Nearly two hundred national and local legislative candidates from the opposition had been intimidated into resigning; some three hundred Nicaraguans being trained as neutral poll watchers quit under personal threat. Jimmy Carter protested the fact that congressionally appropriated funds to support voter registration and poll watching were blocked by the regime. "It takes great courage to be an UNO activist in Nicaragua, as much as it took to be a Solidarity organizer or a Charter 77 signer in Czechoslovakia," concluded the *New*

Republic in February 1990 after summing up this record of Sandinista tactics.[103]

Arias told Bush at the end of July 1989 that he was convinced the Sandinistas would lose if a fair campaign and vote could somehow be assured. But others were less confident—either because of a lesser opinion of Mrs. Chamorro or because of a lesser opinion of the Sandinistas. I, a member of the latter school, wrote to Scowcroft on July 27 urging that we put more pressure on Gorbachev to squeeze the Sandinistas to clean up their act and take steps to "delegitimize" the election results in advance if we feared a stolen election.

The administration duly kept the pressure on Managua, though with a certain clumsiness that contrasted with the more ideologically motivated campaigns of the Reagan administration. With great effort, it had managed in October 1989 to persuade Congress to appropriate the not-mind-boggling sum of $9 million—some for voter registration and training election monitors, some for voter education, and some ($1.8 million) in direct campaign support for UNO. Congressional liberals had fought against even this, and the Sandinistas of course denounced it as "CIA intervention." The money was to be administered not by the CIA but openly by AID and channeled through the National Endowment for Democracy. Yet AID's lawyers were so hypersensitive in the wake of Iran-Contra that the funds eventually appropriated went through four layers of auditing before they were dispensed. No wonder that the money did not start to flow into the hands of its recipients until mid-December—a bare two months before the election. The lawyers and accountants were satisfied; whether the result bore any relation to a coherent foreign policy was another matter.

The Sandinistas struck a blow for progressive thought on January 18 when their party paper *Barricada* blamed the delays in the funding for UNO on the " 'Jew-Style' with which the U.S. Congress manages the taxes of the taxpayers." This was accompanied by insinuations about the ethnic background of some of the individuals from the bipartisan U.S. groups that worked with the National Endowment for Democracy. The State Department denounced the slurs as "contemptible" and pointed the finger at the Nicaraguan government for "doing everything in its power to block monies designed by Congress to help level the playing field for the opposition."[104]

What with the red tape on the U.S. side and the Sandinista obstruction, probably less than 10 percent of the $9 million got through. Photocopying machines and telephones meant for UNO were held up at customs for months and were seen being delivered to opposition headquarters the day after the election.[105]

The widespread expectation was that the Sandinistas were going to win, through fair means or foul. Daniel Ortega boasted to the press on election day that it was "impossible" that he could lose.[106] "The Sandinistas have no credible opposition," agreed the left-wing *Nation*.[107] Secretary Baker told the Senate Foreign Relations Committee on February 1, 1990: "If we determine that it is free and fair . . . and we determine that they have indeed stopped their support of subversion in neighboring countries or in other places in Latin America, then we'd be prepared to normalize our relations with that government."[108] These were stiff requirements, but the administration's body language (at least as read by the press) told of a readiness to wash its hands of the whole Central America mess as an unwelcome inheritance from the Reagan era. The Reagan crusade would not be continued. "Baker has been very cautious about committing himself on how we might react" to a Sandinista victory, said one official. "As long as [the election] is within the limits of civility, we will probably learn to live with it," said another.[109] "This city is so tired of this issue that it is seeking ways to live with it regardless of who wins the election," a senior official was quoted as saying.[110]

The fatalism was reinforced by opinion polls in Nicaragua. An ABC/ *Washington Post* survey the week before the election showed a three-to-two Sandinista lead; Peter Jennings intoned that this demonstrated "the failure of U.S. policy" (presumably meaning that it proved the Sandinistas had popular support). Both ABC and NBC predicted a Sandinista victory "by a wide margin." Ted Koppel's *Nightline* on February 23 was devoted to the issues of normalizing relations after the expected Sandinista victory.[111]

The results, of course, were dramatically different. Mrs. Chamorro won on February 25 with an official margin of 55 percent to 41 percent (with the actual Sandinista total believed by some other Central Americans to be ten points lower).[112] UNO also won a strong majority in the Parliament. The Bush administration, having washed its hands of the whole issue a few days earlier, now woke up and quickly claimed credit, attributing Chamorro's success to its own repudiation of Reagan's militaristic policies.[113]

The Sandinistas' electoral defeat was most overwhelming in the rural areas, where the peasants had long since come to despise them (and to back the Contras). Rep. Stephen Solarz, one of those who never lost confidence in Mrs. Chamorro's chances, was contemptuous of U.S.

pollsters who had thought Nicaragua was just another Iowa.[114] Naive Americans, with little understanding of the pervasive fear in totalitarian societies, assumed that what they were being told was the reality.

One preelection polling team—obviously not working for ABC News—had conducted a revealing experiment. They had conducted three hundred interviews in the Managua area, asking the same questions with only one variable—the color of the pens the interviewers were holding. One-third of the pollsters carried pens with the Sandinista colors and slogans; one-third had pens with UNO's campaign colors and logo; the other third had pens with neutral colors and no emblems. To interviewers carrying UNO pens, the respondents gave their opinions as 56 percent for Mrs. Chamorro, 44 percent for Daniel Ortega. Interviewers holding the Sandinista pen reported 63 percent responses for Ortega. The enigmatic neutral pen elicited 62 percent for Ortega—probably representing the same caution from a populace not used to sharing its private opinions with strangers.[115] The experiment might simply show the tendency of respondents to humor their questioners—except that the UNO pen holders got a result very close to the final voting result.

The intensity of the outside attention had so cramped the Sandinistas' style that the electorate of 1.7 million Nicaraguans did not fear for their safety; the intimidation factor was neutralized. They trusted the secret ballot and took their opportunity, accomplishing the still rather courageous feat of throwing the Leninist bums out.

ASSESSMENT

On the face of it, the voters' rejection of a political party with such a record of criminality and economic disaster (30 percent unemployment, 33,700 percent inflation) needs little further explanation. But questions arise: Why did a totalitarian regime take such a risk and let itself be thrown out? What was the effect of U.S. policies? Why is it that after a generation of leftism a Latin American electorate voted overwhelmingly for a candidate who openly took aid from the United States, was photographed with President Bush, and refused to denounce the U.S.-funded armed insurgency as many urged her to do?

Some on the hard Left, like Alexander Cockburn, denounced the outcome, somewhat incoherently, as the result of U.S. military and economic "terror" against a "brainwashed" population.[116] Aside from these diehards, the outcome was welcomed in all quarters in the United States; the only debate was over who should get credit. Conservatives naturally paid tribute to the Contras and the Reagan Doctrine. The Bush administration was conspicuous in its nonadherence to this view; it essentially joined the traditional critics of U.S. policy who attributed the result explicitly to the abandonment of Reagan's military approach and the adoption of the Arias diplomacy.[117] Democratic majority leader George Mitchell was sure that it was "when the United States turned from promoting war to promoting peaceful democratic process in Nicaragua [that] we helped make this result possible."[118] The *New York Times* even gave some credit to the Sandinistas: "[I]f President Daniel Ortega guessed wrong about the outcome, so did his detractors who claimed that the Sandinistas were incapable of conducting a truly free election."[119]

This was all an evasion. It is absurd to deny that U.S. military and economic pressures over a decade had their impact on Sandinista decisions, including the decision to accept Esquipulas and risk another election in 1990. The Sandinistas have admitted as much to the Cubans,[120] just as Humberto Ortega admitted something similar with respect to the 1984 election. Alexander Cockburn had it almost right—except that it was not a U.S. campaign against the Nicaraguan *people* to brutalize them into submission but a campaign to press the regime to permit the Nicaraguan people to exercise a choice.

The analogy to Eastern Europe in the late 1940s still seems apt: The FSLN was a Leninist party that came to power as leader of a broad anti-Fascist coalition and then proceeded to squeeze out all its non-Communist partners. The difference between postwar Eastern Europe and contemporary Central America, however, was that while the East European Communist parties, in the shadow of Stalin, were free to complete the job, the FSLN, in the shadow of the United States, was not. The jaws of the crocodile were never permitted to close. The armed resistance in the field so preoccupied the regime that it never consolidated its power.

The armed resistance was far more important than the economic pressure; a number of Communist regimes still survive in the face of economic isolation, having never had difficulty imposing hardships on their people. It was also the spur to the international political pressure that forced the Nicaragua regime to permit some limited breathing space for a civic opposition at home—the church, *La Prensa*, democratic parties, labor groups. Most of that international political pressure—particularly the frenetic diplomatic activity—was clearly prompted by the military crisis that well-meaning democrats like Oscar Arias wanted to dampen. In tyrannies where all resistance has been extinguished, the international community's record of remedial action, or even of caring, is rather bleak.

444 MORE PRECIOUS THAN PEACE

Whatever credit is owed to this diplomatic pressure, then, it was the armed resistance that forced the diplomatic pressure that produced the political opening.

Even after Congress cut off military aid, the sixteen-thousand-man Contra army had remained surprisingly intact, in much of the interior of the country, as a kind of internal hemorrhage and as a symbol of the depth of the country's discontent. In the end, the United States kept the Contras alive long enough to extract from the diplomatic process and from the Sandinistas a crucial political quid pro quo—a sufficiently free election in which the core issue of Nicaragua's destiny would be addressed.

The Bush administration gave credit also to the Soviet Union and to its own diplomatic efforts with Mikhail Gorbachev. The Soviets had long been an uncooperative party, even though not a major contributor to the Central American conflict. In the spring of 1988, Costa Rican president Oscar Arias had appealed publicly to Gorbachev to halt arms shipments to Communist guerrillas in El Salvador and Guatemala. Astonishingly, he received no reply over a long period and then was sent a boilerplate message through the Soviet Foreign Ministry insisting that no Soviet weapons were going to those insurgents. Arias was offended and appalled, and in a Washington speech he lambasted the Soviets:

> It is quite obvious that they are supporting Fidel Castro who is also supporting the guerrillas in El Salvador as well as in Guatemala. And it is also true that unless they decide to cut that support we'll [not] be able to reach peace. . . . I also pointed out [to Gorbachev] that his refusal to stop sending arms to the region would make clear before the whole world that the new political position proclaimed by the Soviet leader to humanity is not true and you can't trust it to construct the history of peace.[121]

Arias hoped the United States would raise the issue with Moscow at a high level.

This the Reagan administration did, and the Bush administration sought to do so even more systematically. Bush, Baker, and Scowcroft (unlike Shultz) resorted self-consciously to Kissinger-style linkage. Baker proposed to Bush that they "subject the Soviets to Chinese water torture on this subject. We'll just keep telling them over and over—drop, drop, drop—that they've got to be part of the solution in Central America, or else they'll find lots of other problems harder to deal with."[122] As Gorbachev prepared to visit Cuba in early April 1989, Bush sent him a toughly worded message on March 27 insisting that improved U.S.-Soviet relations depended on an end to Moscow's arming and financing of Havana and Managua:

> It is hard to reconcile your slogans . . . with continuing high levels of Soviet and Cuban assistance to Nicaragua. There is no conceivable military threat that justifies that assistance. And now, at a point when we are clearly charting a new course, your assistance is almost certain to be used to undercut [our] diplomatic effort. . . .
>
> A continuation of [this] practice in this region of vital interest to the U.S. will . . . inevitably affect the nature of the [U.S.-Soviet] relationship. . . .[123]

Bush's hand was strengthened by the equally tough language in the Bipartisan Accord of three days earlier.

But the Soviets essentially stonewalled Bush just as they had stonewalled Arias. Gorbachev went to Havana and later claimed he could not get a word in edgewise as Fidel Castro filibustered with his litany of complaints against the United States. (The United States was just starting up the exile TV Marti broadcasting from Florida; Castro denounced the "provocation" and "aggression against the sovereignty of our airwaves.")[124] Gorbachev replied in May to Bush's letter, lamely urging Bush to normalize relations with Castro and claiming that, in any case, the Soviet Union had stopped sending arms to Nicaragua in 1988. It was an almost insulting reply: The administration knew that Soviet weapons were still flowing. But it comforted itself with the thought that Gorbachev had now implicitly promised to stop.[125]

The idea of using linkage was not wrong; the Soviets were continuing to subsidize Nicaragua to the tune of almost $1 billion a year in economic and military assistance. But there were a number of problems. One was that we were not linking very much to Soviet compliance with our demands; no thought was given, for example, to postponing the first Bush-Gorbachev summit until we saw how the Soviets (or Nicaraguans) behaved. I made such a suggestion to Scowcroft in late July, without really expecting such a drastic step to be taken by a team that essentially did *not* place the regional issues all that high on the U.S.-Soviet agenda.

A second problem was that our linkage was almost always cast in terms of arms supply and hardly ever in terms of pressure on the Sandinistas to ensure a fair election on February 25, 1990. The latter was the real issue and indeed the focus of our Central America strategy. I was convinced that the Soviets could easily terminate their weapons flow—since the Contras' weapons had been cut off since 1987—and then be off the hook with us, without having done anything that made a difference on the ground. Why they would claim they already had, and lie to us, was and remains incomprehensible to me. But I assumed that at some point they would indeed halt the flow, since it was not a strategically significant concession at that stage. Far better, I suggested to Scowcroft at various points, to hold the Soviets accountable for the Sandinistas' electoral behavior as well and thus keep them on the hook to exert pressure on Managua over something that really counted.

The third problem, as noted, was Gorbachev's inability to tell the truth—and the difficulty the Bush administration seemed to have in noticing. Five months after Gorbachev's May 1989 letter claiming that Soviet arms supplies had ended, an unmarked plane crashed in El Salvador carrying 24 SA-7 antiaircraft missiles intended for the FMLN guerrillas. In a long, self-serving leaked account in *Time* magazine of how brilliantly they handled the Soviets, Baker's aides called attention to the Soviet freighter *Vladimir Ilyich* that set sail for Nicaragua in November 1989 with four new Mi-17 helicopter gunships. Bush and Gorbachev were said to have had an acrimonious exhange on the subject at their storm-tossed summit off Malta in December—and the *Vladimir Ilyich* then turned around and headed back to Leningrad.[126] This was hailed as a victory. Reading the fine print of the *Time* article, however, one cannot help but notice what else happened: The *Vladimir Ilyich* set sail again at the end of January and delivered its cargo of helicopters.[127]

The administration was also much pleased with the joint statement between Baker and Shevardnadze on Februrary 10 that pledged both superpowers to "respect the results of free and fair elections." Yet, given the general expectation that the Sandinistas would win, this was more an American concession than a Soviet one. Whenever bearded on the issue of democracy in Central America, the Soviets unfailingly declared their devotion to implementation of Esquipulas—again, a cheap concession, since they expected their allies to win and to be legitimized by the process. There is no evidence of any pressure by Moscow on the Nicaraguans to halt their thuggish electoral practices, and no evidence of a real halt to Soviet arms supply to Nicaragua until the Sandinistas' electoral defeat.

However, the Soviets undeniably did play a role in the democratic electoral outcome. Soviet economic hardships at home, changes in foreign-aid policies, and parliamentary pressures in the new Supreme

Soviet in Moscow all pointed to a grim prospect of declining Soviet economic support for both Cuba and Nicaragua. Even more, the collapse of Soviet power in Eastern Europe in the second half of 1989 sent a demoralizing signal: If Gorbachev felt no commitment to save collapsing Communist allies so close to home, how little must be his commitment to a small ally far away? Whatever gamble the Sandinistas thought they had been running in 1987–88 when they agreed to the election was now a far, far chancier thing. But for the people of Nicaragua, Eastern Europe was a gloriously hopeful signal: The aura of the invincibility and irreversibility of Communist power was evaporating. Instead of the intimidating, self-confident Leninist vanguard of 1979, the Sandinistas were beleaguered holdouts of an internationally discredited doctrine. Thus, the Soviets indeed aided our diplomacy, but much more by their collapse than by the evasions that so beguiled our diplomats.

Postelection Nicaragua was not to be without its serious problems, economic and political. Daniel Ortega told a cheering crowd that the Sandinistas would try to continue governing "from below"—that is, through their control of the army, security forces, and many civilian institutions.[128] But the discrediting of Communist ideology was bound to have far-reaching psychological effects in Latin America. The bubble of revolutionary illusion was burst. Octavio Paz, the eminent Mexican author, wrote:

> The Nicaraguan election has dealt the all-but-final blow to Marxist-Leninist revolution as an alternative in this hemisphere. It initiates the closing episode of the tumultuous era that began in 1959 with the Cuban Revolution and will conclude with the fall of Fidel Castro.
>
> Thankfully, this part of the world, like Eastern Europe, has finally given up Marx for Montesquieu. . . .
>
> The Sandinista defeat, like the defeat of the Marxist left generally, is the defeat of fantasy. The communist remedy to social injustice proved worse than the malady.[129]

The socialist model of economic development was discredited by the *perestroika* of Gorbachev himself and by the economic crisis of every country that persisted in applying that model. The temptation to play the nonaligned card in foreign policy was also a casualty; the collapse of Moscow as the rival pole of international politics left the West dominant.

But rather than an abject submission to U.S. power, the response in Latin America seemed to be a healthy outgrowing of its complexes about the United States. Paz wrote:

> Significantly, the Sandinista defeat can also be read as something of a defeat for the anti-gringo sentiment that has plagued Latin America long past its historical reality. After all, the Nicaraguan people elected the candidate openly endorsed by the President of the United States, George Bush, who was a key supporter of arming the Contras. . . . The abandonment of anti-gringo sentiment, which is evident across Latin America, will be a key factor in confronting the problems of a Central America at peace.[130]

A Latin America of democracies had daunting economic and social problems, but also accountable governments and the prospect of productive links with an international economy that was built—now unapologetically—on market principles. Political and economic ties with the United States were, for the first time in generations, relatively uncontroversial. A dramatic reflection of this was the North American Free Trade Agreement (NAFTA), the U.S.-Canadian free trade zone broadened by a 1992 treaty to embrace an eager Mexico. Other Latin American countries lined up to seek their own bilateral free-trade arrangements with the United States. All this made economic sense. What was extraordinary was that it was so long in coming. The Western Hemisphere is a natural trading community, and what hindered it in the past was the Latins' inability to come to terms with their economic dependence on the United States because of ideological obstacles—the false socialist alternatives, the flirtation with nonalignment, the chip-on-the-shoulder resentments of the Colossus of the North. Mexico had long been the most prickly. NAFTA thus symbolized the collapse of ideology, which freed the Latins to act in their rational economic self-interest, to turn their complementarity with the United States into an advantage. The controversy that NAFTA ignited in the United States showed it was hardly a one-sided U.S. imposition. Latin America had found a new political maturity. The deflation of the fashionable anti-Americanism was another of the positive by-products of the end of the Cold War.

The last holdouts may be in the United States. A hilarious account of the April 1991 Congress of the Latin American Studies Association tells the tale. This gathering of U.S. academic specialists on Latin America had the good fortune to be addressed by three Soviet academics who described the "new thinking" in the Soviet approach to Latin America. While Soviet government policy still left a lot to be desired, as we have seen, academic thinking in Moscow had already come a long way, repudiating the Brezhnev era in wholesale fashion. Vladimir Stanchenko of the Institute of World Economy and International Relations took the floor. An eyewitness (Mark Falcoff) watched the reaction:

Reading his paper in excellent American-accented English, Stanchenko tore into the entire course of Soviet policy in Latin America for the last three decades. It was no secret, he confided to the audience, that since the Cuban revolution the Soviet Union sought to exploit unrest in Latin America as a way of "weakening U.S. interests and constraining Washington's global position." This is what led both Soviet military planners and ideologists to establish a military and naval presence in Cuba (which he called "a hostage to Soviet military power"). Later on, euphoric with the "strategic parity" achieved with the United States after Vietnam, Brezhnev purposely increased tensions in the region as a way of "harassing the sleeping giant, the United States." Among other things, Brezhnev used "the dictatorship in Cuba" to manage and direct Third World movements and also to advance Soviet interests in the English-speaking Caribbean (Grenada and Guyana), a region to which he, Brezhnev, "attributed great importance."

As for Central America itself, Stanchenko observed that there would be "little doubt" of a Soviet involvement through Cuba: Nicaragua's military build-up under the Sandinistas, as well as arms, assistance, and advice to the FMLN and "other Marxist groupings," bore witness to Soviet involvement. In effect, until recently Soviet policy in Central America "has contributed unnecessarily to the deterioration of relations with the United States," while working to impose "totalitarian regimes" in hapless Third World countries.

There it was—everything down to the T-word! When Stanchenko finished, it seemed as if all the air had been sucked out of the room. Hands rose rapidly. "What you are saying," gasped one woman, "is what the Right in the United States has been saying for some time"—which, as far as it went, was certainly a valid observation. Another demanded to know if Stanchenko had been born before 1959—surely not all of these events in the region began only when the Soviets put their hands into the pot. Then one man in the first row stood up and said, "When President Reagan called the Soviet Union 'the evil empire,' some of us tried to explain to our classes that the Soviet Union wasn't like that at all. Now, however, we hear voices from the Soviet Union repeating arguments of the extreme Right in the United States." Then, moving in for the kill, he said, "Don't you people have something of a problem of credibility? Why should I believe you now? Were you telling the truth before, when you wrote in a very different vein?" (Scattered but determined applause.)

Stanchenko assured the audience that he had indeed been born before 1959—"that's why I know more about some of these things than many of you here." As to his own credibility, he informed the audience that he had only begun to publish since *perestroika*. "Other colleagues may have written the opposite." Nonetheless, he went on, he could very specifically affirm that Soviet arms shipments to the region occurred before Ronald Reagan came to power in the United States. "Either you believe the facts— or you don't believe the facts."

Perhaps the most characteristic response came not from the hard Left but from the soft. "I am concerned about the United States as an international police force for hire, and the Soviet Union not able to do anything about it," one voice from the back of the room wailed. "What will it mean for world peace?" Wasn't the Cold War, with all its warts, better at least in that way? Stanchenko didn't think the Cold War was all that good for world peace. There were discontented rumbles as the session broke up; the speakers were surrounded by angry academics. When Stanchenko finally broke free to go to lunch, he was heard to remark to an American colleague, "Well, I have to tell the truth, don't I? What else can I do?"[131]

16

CAMBODIA: THE DEADLY
GAME OF PEACE

For those who bear the memory of America's agony in Indochina, the number fifty-five thousand has an unforgettable resonance: It is the approximate number of Americans killed in action in Indochina from 1961 to 1975. By an ironic twist of history, it is also said to be the number of Vietnamese troops killed in action in Cambodia in the nearly eleven years of invasion and occupation from December 1978 to September 1989.[1] The Cambodian quagmire indeed became, as was often said, "Vietnam's Vietnam."

While Vietnam's invasion in 1978 achieved its immediate objective of driving its erstwhile Cambodian Communist allies from power, guerrilla war persisted with an intensity that denied Hanoi its longer-term objective, namely, to install a friendly regime in Phnom Penh that could sustain itself without Vietnamese military support. The Khmer Rouge—and the non-Communist resistance forces that emerged under the leadership of Prince Norodom Sihanouk and Son Sann—tapped into ancient Khmer hatreds of the Vietnamese and resistance to their dominance. Hanoi only intensified nationalist animosity by sponsoring the large-scale immigration into Cambodia of ethnic Vietnamese, in what looked to some like a classic enterprise of colonization.[2]

The resistance forces set up guerrilla bases near the border with Thailand, the country through which outside arms were funneled to them. The Vietnamese were doomed to a replay of the dismal cycle that the United States went through in its own earlier effort of counterinsurgency: Every dry season, they launched large-scale offensives against guerrilla concentrations; in the rainy season, the guerrillas had the advantage over a conventional army because of their greater ease of movement. In 1984–85, the Vietnamese undertook a major dry-season campaign against the guerrilla coalition's base camps just inside the Thai border and succeeded in driving the resistance forces out of the bases into Thailand. While this denied the resistance the chance to claim a "liberated zone" inside the country, it also posed to the Vietnamese another classic dilemma: The guerrillas could retreat to sanctuaries just over the Thai border, from which to launch future attacks, while their pursuers were inhibited from attacking the sanctuaries for fear of the political onus of attacking sovereign Thailand. The guerrillas even gained, in a sense, by being freed up from the static tasks of defending base areas for the more useful business of small-unit forays against Vietnamese fixed positions inside Cambodia. The Vietnamese found themselves in a reactive role, struggling to seal the porous border and (with more success) to protect their towns and troop positions.[3]

The war, in fact, stabilized. The guerrillas proved unable to penetrate very deep into Cambodia; the Vietnamese occupiers gradually lost their enthusiasm for large-scale counterinsurgency operations and rested on their laurels after the success of 1984–85. The guerrillas had little prospect of winning power; the Vietnamese occupiers faced a long-term drain on their resources but were buttressed by Soviet aid. Between January and July 1989, for example, eleven Soviet cargo ships delivered an estimated fourteen thousand tons of military supplies to the Cambodian port of Kampong Saom, including 100 T-54 tanks, armored vehicles, and heavy artillery; the Soviets also provided 16 MiG-21 fighter planes.[4]

The United States continued to give political support to the resistance Coalition Government of Democratic Kampuchea (CGDK), which comprised three elements—the National Army of Sihanouk (ANS), Son Sann's Khmer People's National Liberation Front (KPNLF), and the dreaded Khmer Rouge. This was the anti-Vietnamese coalition formed in 1982 under pressure from Cambodia's ASEAN neighbors. The United States had no direct relations with Hanoi or Phnom Penh (except occasional communications with Hanoi over the lingering problem of U.S. POWs and MIAs), maintaining an economic embargo against both Hanoi and Phnom Penh and hiding behind ASEAN's skirts diplomatically. It went along with ASEAN in denying the Phnom Penh regime UN representation, treating Cambodia's seat as the rightful possession of the exile coalition. The United States gave minimal amounts of direct aid to the non-Communist resistance—$5 million a year in open aid for "humanitarian" supplies like medicine and tents and, by 1989, a reported $20–$24 million a year spent by the CIA on mostly "nonlethal" items like training, uniforms, some vehicles, rice and canned fish, political offices (in Tokyo, Bangkok, Bonn, and Paris), and two radio transmitters.[5] In early 1985, Thailand and Singapore urged the United States to start providing military aid to the resistance, but Washington resisted the entreaties. The non-Communists received most of their military supply from China, which was also furnishing much more substantial weaponry to the Khmer Rouge.

The Khmer Rouge, estimated at thirty to forty thousand strong, were far and away the most potent of the resistance forces. Sihanouk's ANS claimed an effective strength of eighteen thousand, and the KPNLF, twelve thousand, but U.S. officials doubted the numbers and fighting capability of both. Both were plagued by poor military leadership, corruption, black marketeering, defections to the government side, and factional squabbles and occasional clashes between the two.[6]

American policy was thus haunted by a terrible contradiction. It—correctly—rejected the legitimacy of the Phnom Penh regime that had been imposed by force; in the geopolitical realm it tilted, reasonably enough, against the Moscow-Hanoi-Phnom Penh axis. It adopted (again, reasonably enough) a policy of pressure on the Vietnamese occupation in order to force Vietnamese withdrawal and to promote some kind of negotiated solution. But the economic sanctions and UN niceties could accomplish only so much; the most significant pressure was the military pressure of the Khmer Rouge—the genocidal fanatics who could easily be viewed as the main long-term threat to the Cambodian people—backed by the Chinese, who, as we have seen, were more interested in bleeding Vietnam than in ending the Cambodian civil war.[7] The weakness of America's direct role on the battlefield weakened the non-Communists in the resistance and simultaneously weakened our own leverage in the diplomacy in pursuit of our own view of a decent outcome.

The dilemma was inherited from the Carter era, when the United States was driven by the ominous pattern of Brezhnev's Third World adventurism to tilt further toward the Chinese. Presidential adviser Zbigniew Brzezinski had gone so far as to encourage the Chinese to build up the Khmer Rouge to resist the Vietnamese invasion.[8] It was a dilemma that reared its ugly head at the 1989 Paris Conference on Cambodia, when a proposal to criticize Khmer Rouge "genocide" proved—amazingly—difficult for the United States to accept because the U.S. and ASEAN diplomatic strategy at that time was to step up the pressure on Cambodia's current tormentors, the Vietnamese. The controversy only played into Hanoi's hands. Even when the United States was willing to utter forthright verbal condemnations of the Khmer Rouge (which it did frequently), it could not escape the question of what political outcome it envisioned for Cambodia if its diplomatic efforts on behalf of the resistance coalition ever bore fruit.

The story of U.S. policy in Cambodia is thus the story of another painful and protracted effort to reconcile our geopolitical and moral imperatives. The one policy that might have squared this circle—substantial military aid, from the beginning, to build up the non-Communist resistance into an effective, democratic alternative—was blocked by inhibitions in both the executive branch and Congress about reintervention in Indochina, scene of the historic agony from which we had only recently (and, evidently, not fully) recovered. All of which serves as an object lesson in how a policy of avoiding all risks can often sharpen one's dilemmas, not ease them. Having lost the war, we found that our policy preferences in the subsequent diplomacy were not paid enormous heed. Having abandoned the decent Cambodians in 1975 and being still unwilling to back them decisively, we found that the remnant was barely able to hold its own in a new environment dominated by two rival groups of Communist thugs.

DIPLOMATIC MANEUVERS

All civil wars, as we have seen in this book, are enormously difficult to resolve through compromise. They tend to be winner-take-all affairs. Diplomacy over Cambodia, however, has been a challenge qualitatively different from the other cases—a Sisyphean struggle to reconcile the irreconcilable, to find a basis for compromise including a group that is dreaded by all the others as an unassimilable embodiment of absolute evil.

Diplomatic efforts were stalemated for several years, at every level. The Vietnamese and their clients in Phnom Penh continued to assert that the new situation was irreversible, yet the international community continued to reject it as illegitimate. UN General Assembly votes on the Cambodian question continued by huge margins to reject the Vietnamese occupation and to hold Cambodia's UN seat for the resistance coalition. The General Assembly had never in recent times been known for its vocal opposition to Communist aggression. But just as on Afghanistan the Afro-Asian majority was swayed by the Arab and Muslim bloc, so on Cambodia the key factor was the political weight of ASEAN plus Sihanouk's personal standing among the nonaligned. The stalemate among the Indochinese parties was reinforced most of all by the Sino-Soviet rivalry, as China and the Soviet Union seemed adamant in their material and political support of their respective clients.

In the mid-1980s, the environment began to change. A first sign was a major speech by Mikhail Gorbachev on July 28, 1986, in Vladivostok, the Soviet Union's easternmost major city, a stone's throw from the

Chinese border. Gorbachev stressed the Soviet Union's eagerness to play a constructive political and economic role in the Asia-Pacific region; he offered new diplomatic initiatives, aimed principally at wooing China. The "three obstacles" that the Chinese had long cited as standing in the way of a Sino-Soviet reconciliation—the Soviet military threat along the border; Afghanistan; and Cambodia—were all addressed.

On the military issue, Gorbachev proposed bilateral talks with China on a mutual reduction of forces. On Afghanistan, rather clumsily, he announced the token troop withdrawal that (as we saw) turned out to be a fake, but he reiterated his eagerness for a settlement. On Cambodia, Gorbachev essentially called upon China and Vietnam to patch up their quarrel on the basis of the status quo: "Through its suffering that country has earned itself the right to choose its friends and allies. It is impermissible to try and draw it back into its tragic past, to decide the future of that state in the distant capitals or even in the United Nations."[9] He hinted cryptically that the Soviet Union might give up its naval base at Cam Ranh Bay if the United States gave up its military presence in the Philippines—a bargain the United States was unlikely, at that period of history, to accept. While the specifics on the Cambodian and Afghan issues were not impressive, the overall tone of Gorbachev's Vladivostok speech (and of an important interview he gave to an Indonesian newspaper in July 1987)[10] was of a new diplomatic activism on Asian regional issues. He reached out to ASEAN and others, showing a moderate face and a subtlety that contrasted favorably with Brezhnev.

Of the three "obstacles" to normalization with China, Gorbachev had the most flexibility on the military issue, on which the Soviet Union could act unilaterally to reduce its threat to China. His acceptance of the "zero option" eliminating SS-20s in both Asia and Europe in the negotiation with the United States on intermediate-range nuclear missiles was another important gesture in this area. On Cambodia as well as Afghanistan he had recalcitrant clients to worry about, and in 1986 he was only at the beginning of a process. By 1988, however, significant progress had been made on the issue of border deployments with China and on settling Afghanistan. Only Cambodia remained.

We are not yet privy to Gorbachev's discussions with his Vietnamese allies, but his eagerness for a rapprochement with China was palpable. On February 7, 1989, Eduard Shevardnadze and Chinese foreign minister Qian Qichen met in Beijing and focused on the remaining obstacle— issuing a nine-point communiqué on Cambodia, the first Sino-Soviet statement ever issued on the subject. It spoke of Vietnamese troop withdrawal under international supervision, an end to outside military aid to all factions, a ban on foreign bases in Cambodia, an appropriate role for the United Nations, and an international conference on Cambodia "when the conditions for this are ripe."[11] It was clear that if Hanoi could be made to commit to withdrawing its troops from Cambodia, Gorbachev would be within reach of a triumphant summit visit to Beijing, matching—and to a degree canceling out—Nixon's historic accomplishment of 1972. It would represent a tremendous geopolitical payoff for the Soviet Union, vindicating Gorbachev's "new political thinking" as a brilliant stroke of Soviet foreign policy.

Up until then, Hanoi had toyed with withdrawing some troops but had never bitten the bullet of total withdrawal. Like the Afghan, Angolan, and Nicaraguan Communist regimes, the Vietnamese insisted first on an end to foreign support for the insurgents. Like the Afghan regime (indeed, like the North Vietnamese during their 1969–72 negotiations with the United States), the Vietnamese insisted also on a prior political settlement in Cambodia—that is, a settlement confirming the legitimacy of their client. Between 1982 and 1986, Hanoi had announced symbolic withdrawals that turned out to be only disguised troop rotations—apparently having received technical advice from the same geniuses in the Kremlin who had devised Gorbachev's fake troop withdrawal from Afghanistan in 1986. In 1987 and 1988, however, as the war stabilized, Hanoi attempted its own version of the U.S. "Vietnamization" policy— "Khmerization," if you will—building up Phnom Penh's army to take on more responsibility for the country's defense. Hanoi's troop strength in Cambodia, once estimated at between 170,000 and 200,000, was believed to have dropped to 120,000 in 1987. In May 1988, Vietnam announced it would pull out another fifty thousand by the end of the year and also move its army headquarters out of Cambodia. By the end of 1988, its troop strength in Cambodia was estimated to be somewhere between fifty thousand and seventy thousand.[12]

On April 5, 1989, obviously under pressure from their Soviet comrades, Hanoi and Phnom Penh went further, announcing that all remaining Vietnamese troops would be withdrawn from Cambodia by the end of September 1989. This pullout was still theoretically conditioned on an end to "foreign interference," but the linkage to a prior political settlement was gone.[13] Gorbachev made his triumphal entry into Beijing in May 1989—only to have it spoiled by the international attention focused on the pro-democracy demonstrators in Beijing, some of whom (to Gorbachev's discomfiture as much as his hosts') invoked his name as an anti-Communist symbol.

There were many factors behind Hanoi's decision to pull out. For one thing, the Politburo in Hanoi, never known for its public-spiritedness, clearly calculated that the Phnom Penh regime was doing better on its own and that the guerrillas were unlikely to topple it. In addition, the ASEAN front was weakening. Thailand, led after August 1988 by Prime Minister Chatichai Choonhavan, was one of Asia's prosperous "economic tigers" and was growing restless under the strain of being the main sanctuary for the Cambodian insurgents; it watched the Sino-Soviet rapprochement and wanted Southeast Asia to enjoy the same respite from tension so that Indochina could be turned, in Chatichai's words, "from a battlefield into a marketplace." Thai businessmen and even military leaders (some heavily involved in cross-border smuggling) were eager to end the war and do business.[14] Chatichai made himself, in Lally Weymouth's wry words, "the Oscar Arias of Southeast Asia, a sort of freelance peacemaker."[15] The net result was that Hanoi would only profit from anything it could do on Cambodia to break out of its diplomatic isolation.

The negative incentives, however, must have been at least as powerful as the positive ones. Isolation in international forums had its harmful political and economic effect. But the most powerful pressure on Hanoi was undoubtedly the public defection of its Soviet backer: The message coming from Moscow to all of Moscow's Third World clients was that Soviet patience was wearing thin; the USSR was not prepared to continue aid indefinitely if equitable political solutions were available. Most important of all, the Soviet Union was determined to reach a rapprochement with China for big-league geopolitical reasons and could no longer afford to let Vietnam stand in the way. It must have been a bitter pill for Hanoi to swallow. Exactly as Leonid Brezhnev had subordinated his commitment to Vietnam in 1972 to the overriding U.S.-Soviet relationship, so did his successor Mikhail Gorbachev subordinate it to Sino-Soviet relations in 1988–89.

From the American point of view, the progress on Cambodia was welcome news. It was also the product of forces at work in which the United States had played no major part.

Diplomacy on Cambodia proceeded fitfully, in step with these developments. In August 1987, after years of denouncing Sihanouk as a Chinese "lackey," the Phnom Penh regime issued a statement calling for national reconciliation and dropping its demand that the "Pol Pot clique" be eliminated before it would consider talking to the coalition. Toward the end of the year Sihanouk broke ranks and met alone near Paris with Hun Sen, Phnom Penh's prime minister. Sihanouk and Hun Sen agreed that Cambodians, in the first instance, should resolve Cambodia's problems, but their talks foundered over issues that would continue to prove difficult—Vietnam's unwillingness at the time to commit to total troop withdrawal; the coalition's insistence that the Phnom Penh regime be dismantled during the internationally supervised transition to a reconciliation government; Phnom Penh's insistence that it remain dominant in the run-up to new elections and its unwillingness to share power in any significant way with Sihanouk or anyone else, particularly the Khmer Rouge.[16]

The Khmer Rouge, for their part, continued to display the tendencies of their past, particularly in their brutal treatment of Cambodian refugees at base camps under their control along the Thai border. They never acknowledged or renounced the inhumanity of their period of rule; they would admit only to unspecified "errors." Yet, in the summer of 1988, the Khmer Rouge presented a moderate face in the diplomacy. Whatever their ultimate goals (and few had any illusions), the Khmer Rouge declared their support for "national reconciliation" and for a four-party provisional coalition government that would conduct elections under UN supervision. This was widely believed to be the result of Chinese pressure.[17]

The Malaysians had earlier come up with the idea of an informal meeting of all the Cambodian parties, modeled after the Afghan "proximity talks," that allowed communication to take place under outside auspices without compromising any side's formal position about the status of the others. Fearful of a Sihanouk–Hun Sen private deal favorable to Vietnam, ASEAN revived the idea of a multilateral gathering, and in July 1988 Indonesia succeeded in organizing such a meeting in Bogor, near Jakarta. It was first referred to as a "cocktail party," to highlight its unstructured nature, until Muslims objected to the decadent irreverence; it was then referred to, more soberly, as the Jakarta Informal Meeting (or JIM).

The 1988 JIM brought together the four Cambodian parties for the first time—Phnom Penh's prime minister, Hun Sen; Khieu Samphan, the supposedly moderate Khmer Rouge leader; Son Sann of the KPNLF; and Sihanouk's son Norodom Ranariddh. Sihanouk waited on the sidelines. Later, he, and then representatives of Vietnam, Laos, and ASEAN, joined the discussions. Hun Sen proposed that Sihanouk be the largely figurehead chairman of a largely symbolic national reconciliation council but still refused any serious power sharing. Sihanouk conceded that the Phnom Penh regime need not be totally dismantled in advance of elections. The Khmer Rouge dragged their feet, fearing a gang-up against them, and boycotted the preparations for the next JIM.

In January 1989—as the Sino-Soviet rapprochement accelerated—China and Vietnam held direct talks on Cambodia for the first time:

Dinh Nho Liem, Vietnam's deputy foreign minister, visited Beijing for the first such visit in ten years. Around the same time, Thai prime minister Chatichai, impatient at the slow progress in creating an Indochinese "marketplace," hosted Hun Sen on a visit to Bangkok, where the Phnom Penh leader was wined and dined by eager Thai businessmen and politicians. This move angered ASEAN's other members (and the United States), who were adhering to the strategy of keeping the pressure on Phnom Penh to agree to power sharing. In the wake of this diplomatic windfall, indeed, Hun Sen dug in his heels at the second JIM in February 1989, and no progress was made.

The issues in the negotiation took various forms at various stages, but they boiled down to certain essentials. Hanoi, Phnom Penh, and their Soviet backers continued to try to trade the Vietnamese troop withdrawal for a cutoff of external aid to the resistance. ASEAN, the coalition, and the United States, meanwhile, insisted that a settlement had to be "comprehensive," that is, resolving the internal political conflict as well as the military issues. We feared any solution that let the Vietnamese off the hook after their withdrawal, while their client still blocked internal compromise. We, ASEAN, and the coalition also insisted on a real turnover of power to some new collective body in Phnom Penh in advance of any new elections—preferably under UN aegis. We also pressed for a multiparty system. Phnom Penh refused any diminution of its control in the interim before elections; it refused to accept a multiparty system or any role for the United Nations, which it considered biased against it.

The role of the Khmer Rouge continued to be a big sticking point. The coalition proposed a quadripartite arrangement among the four Cambodian parties, which Phnom Penh rejected because it would be outvoted three to one. Phnom Penh would consider only arrangements that were, at most, two-sided (government versus opposition) and on occasion also sought to exclude the Khmer Rouge totally. ASEAN, the resistance, and the United States sought to keep the pressure on Hanoi and Phnom Penh until they agreed to serious power sharing and a serious role for an international supervisory body to monitor the transition to an elected new government. Hanoi and Phnom Penh always tried to keep international pressures focused on the role of the hated Khmer Rouge.

AMERICAN DILEMMAS

Some form of compromise among the four Cambodian parties seemed inescapable if peace was to be achieved. This was an uncomfortable conclusion for U.S. diplomacy, for it meant, among other things, treating the Khmer Rouge as a party without which a settlement was not possible. This policy soon came under attack at home.

The Bush administration found itself, first of all, bitterly (and unfairly) accused of wanting to bring the dreaded Khmer Rouge back into power. Critics could not understand how the United States could put priority on defeating the Phnom Penh government rather than on defeating the Khmer Rouge. "We are still playing games with [the Khmer Rouge]," Rep. Chet Atkins of Massachusetts protested. "It's a goddamn outrage."[18]

Former senator and secretary of state Edmund Muskie visited Cambodia toward the end of 1989 and returned home arguing for a "fundamental redirection of U.S. policy." The Phnom Penh regime seemed moderate; it "was a communist government in form, but it also included many non-communists, from earlier regimes. It did not appear monolithic; it did demonstrate pragmatism." The Khmer Rouge were the main threat, Muskie argued.[19] Reporter Elizabeth Becker, too, argued that Hun Sen's "newly reformed" regime in Phnom Penh deserved our support against the Khmer Rouge. "He has opened up the country, revived nationalism and won the confidence of the population," she was convinced, especially after the Vietnamese announced their decision to withdraw.[20]

American policy was "idiotic and ruinous," summed up columnist Mary McGrory. She attributed it to a "hang-up" about the Vietnam War that made administration officials stubbornly resistant to any reconciliation with the nasty North Vietnamese who had defeated us.[21] Elizabeth Becker agreed that it was time to "finally get over the Vietnam War and normalize relations with Hanoi."[22] A clinical psychologist who had served as a medic in Vietnam appeared on an ABC News panel to argue that reconciliation with Hanoi was essential if we were to recover from the traumas of the war: "I think that as a nation, our healing is bound up with that relationship that has been destroyed and has never had a chance to be knitted back again."[23]

At the same time, the small amount of aid that the United States was giving to the non-Communist resistance was challenged as objectively helping the Khmer Rouge, since the non-Communists remained militarily weak and any erosion of Phnom Penh's control would arguably benefit mainly the Khmer Rouge.[24] Accusations were made that material help we provided to the non-Communists found its way into Khmer Rouge hands. This was the thesis of an overwrought ABC News documentary in April 1990, though the assertion was flatly contradicted in the aforementioned panel discussion immediately afterward by Rep. Stephen Solarz, who said he was familiar with all the intelligence.[25] Non-Communist forces in the field were also accused of coordinating military moves with the Khmer Rouge and increasingly relying on them—which was probably true but was clearly a function of their lack of support from us. Just as U.S. aid to Jonas Savimbi in Angola reduced his dependence on the South Africans and U.S. aid to the Contras diminished the influence of the *Somocistas*, the answer to the problem of the non-Communists' subordination to the Khmer Rouge was more U.S. assistance, not less.

Thus, the Bush administration's diplomatic posture and policy on the ground were both under assault. [26] It was urged by its critics to abandon the war against Phnom Penh and Hanoi and, indeed, to join with them to block the Khmer Rouge. Bush's policy of backing the non-Communist resistance was not without serious drawbacks and risks. The non-Communist ANS and KPNLF never showed promise as an independent fighting force; as noted earlier, they suffered from failures of leadership and discipline. Our trying to ride two horses—opposing both Phnom Penh and the Khmer Rouge—was a risky gamble: How could we possibly overthrow the one without removing the main barrier to the dominance of the other? But the administration's true calculation was never well articulated, and the alternative proposed by its critics proved, under examination, to be no real alternative at all.

The American strategy was, in essence, a gamble on Sihanouk. Erratic as the prince seemed to be ("mercurial" was the word always used), he was widely believed to retain a large base of popularity inside Cambodia as well as unique standing among all the interested powers. The United States sought a political deal because in cease-fire conditions the non-Communists' military weakness would be less decisive and Sihanouk's international and domestic prestige would turn into greater political leverage for the non-Communists—who presumably represented the majority of the country—against both Hanoi and the Khmer Rouge. "The best way to prevent the Khmer Rouge from returning to power is to shift the conflict from the battlefield to the ballot box," wrote Representative Solarz in defense of the policy. [27]

The flow of outside weapons to the Communist forces—from the Soviets to Hanoi and Phnom Penh and from China to the Khmer Rouge—could be halted *only* in conditions of a compromise political settlement. Neither Moscow nor Beijing would cut off its client from arms supply unless the other side did the same; each was apparently willing to do so if the other did, because in their pursuit of Sino-Soviet rapprochement they were both willing to put the Cambodian issue on ice if it could be done on some fair basis. Obviously, neither Moscow nor Beijing would accept a settlement that excluded its principal client.

The key to a political compromise was to get the Phnom Penh regime to turn over a substantial share of power—not to the Khmer Rouge but in reality to *Sihanouk*, who all agreed should preside over whatever compromise structure emerged.

A tilt in U.S. policy toward Phnom Penh and Hanoi *before* a political deal would not block the Khmer Rouge. On the contrary, it would guarantee continuation of the war and of Chinese arms aid to the Khmer Rouge (as well as Soviet aid to Phnom Penh); the non-Communists would continue to be ground up between the two Communist forces in an ongoing war. *After* a quadripartite political deal, on the other hand, it was highly likely that in the new political setup the shrewd Sihanouk would be able, if need be, to tilt toward Hanoi sufficiently to outmaneuver the Khmer Rouge. Sihanouk claimed he lost forty members of his family to the Khmer Rouge terror; he needed no instruction in what they represented.[28] His 1987–88 bilateral initiatives with Hun Sen represented exactly the kind of maneuvering he was capable of, keeping the Khmer Rouge at bay. But Sihanouk—and the Bush administration—understood that the best hope for the survival of the non-Communists was to *stop the war* and turn the military contest into a political one in which the non-Communists' advantages would be maximized. U.S. aid to the non-Communists would never turn them into military tigers, but it would strengthen their political clout as well as help assure their survival as long as the war continued.

Switching sides as the administration's critics proposed—siding with Phnom Penh immediately against the Khmer Rouge—was a formula for torpedoing the diplomacy and prolonging the war, with no better prospect of a decent outcome. The Khmer Rouge would fight. Outside arms would continue to flow to the two Communist sides; the good guys in the middle would continue to be chewed up. The Phnom Penh regime was also a weak reed for us to lean on, lacking legitimacy (many of its leaders being former Khmer Rouge themselves). It was not so self-evident that Hun Sen's "newly reformed" regime—while it was less murderous than the Khmer Rouge—had "won the confidence of the population." The critics were well intentioned, but for all the risks of the administration's approach, their recommendation was not an effective formula either for a political solution or for ending the Khmer Rouge threat.

The Bush administration stuck to its guns on the diplomatic front, which took some courage. With the lonely backing of Stephen Solarz and amid much congressional and liberal grumbling, it continued to support the various efforts to broker compromise among the four Cambodian parties. Then the administration went even further: In 1989 it made an unprecedented bid for congressional support for overt *lethal* military aid to the non-Communist resistance and nearly got it.

FROM THE ROBB AMENDMENT TO THE PARIS CONFERENCE

Because of the persistence of Stephen Solarz (then chairman of the House Foreign Affairs Subcommittee on Asian and Pacific Affairs), the House of Representatives had consistently endorsed humanitarian aid to the non-Communists, usually by wide margins. In early 1989, the Bush administration boosted the annual request to $7 million (up from $5 million). Republican representative Bill McCollum of Florida initiated a separate program authorizing the provision of excess (nonlethal) Department of Defense stocks and administrative and transportation expenses. About half a million dollars was authorized under the McCollum program in fiscal year 1989.[29] House-passed bills usually authorized both economic and military assistance, but the Senate usually struck the latter.

The Senate, while it usually went along with nonlethal expenditures, was a hotbed of restless opposition. Liberals like Robert Byrd, Alan Cranston, John Kerry, and Claiborne Pell were averse to any new U.S. intervention in Indochina. Then, in July 1989, Sen. Charles Robb of Virginia, a Democrat and Vietnam veteran, submitted an amendment that would put the Senate, too, on record as favoring lethal aid.

The arguments against it were as passionate as they were familiar. Senator Pell preferred that U.S. policy "emphasize diplomatic initiatives currently under way."[30] Like him, Senator Cranston feared that any military aid would "derail the fast-moving peace process." Cranston also feared that military aid was a "slippery slope" that would lead to a repetition of our Vietnam ordeal. Senator Byrd worried about the risk of the aid's falling into the hands of the Khmer Rouge, and he vowed to block the move in the appropriations process—a potent threat, since he was chairman of the Senate Appropriations Committee. It was especially amusing to hear Senator Cranston dredge up old anti-American comments by Sihanouk and denounce the prince as an America-hating tool of the Chinese Communists, unworthy of U.S. support. In 1970–75, when Sihanouk was an opponent of U.S. policy (and uttering these statements), he was the darling of the liberals; now that he was the white hope of U.S. government policy, the liberals looked eagerly for excuses to ditch him.

Sihanouk was also on record as having told the press on May 13 that he did not need U.S. military aid because he was getting plenty from China. This featured prominently in the critics' arguments: Why help the man if he doesn't even want it? The problem was, Ranariddh was telling the U.S. government privately that the non-Communists very much needed U.S. arms, precisely to reduce their dependence on the Chinese and reclaim some independence of action. As the controversy unfolded in the United States, Sihanouk was doing what America's tormented allies often do: He hedged publicly against the possibility of not getting the military aid to preempt an embarrassing rebuff. It was a good example of why America's friends often preferred being helped quietly, through covert channels, instead of being dragged through public humiliations like this.

All in all, the liberal arguments reflected most of all the familiar, visceral aversion to intervention, especially in Indochina. The liberals managed to discover in themselves a passionate hatred of the totalitarian Khmer Rouge and clearly relished seeming to be more anti-Khmer Rouge than a Republican administration. Perhaps there was a twinge of guilty conscience for their role in the abdication of 1975; perhaps there was another motive, which we have already seen: A year later, when Secretary Baker did make some moves in the direction sought by the critics, Stephen Rosenfeld wrote in the *Washington Post*: "The expressed relief, or much of it, may have had less to do with new prospects in Cambodia than with the feeling that it is past time to set matters straight with Vietnam."[31] For some veterans of the old antiwar movement, Cambodia continued to be—dare I say it?—a sideshow to their larger goal of a grand reconciliation between Washington and Hanoi, symbolizing a kind of absolution if not vindication for their ancient cause. An objective clinical psychologist might have concluded that both sides were having trouble exorcising the ghosts of the Vietnam War. If some of the Republicans were still fighting the old battles, so were some of the Democrats.

The arguments for arming the Cambodians were made on the Senate floor by, among others, Republican John McCain of Arizona, a former prisoner of war in North Vietnam: "[I]f we are going to have a lasting peace we must have a strong and viable non-Communist resistance force." Senator Robb, sponsor of the amendment, insisted that the aid was important leverage for those opposing the Khmer Rouge. Democratic senator Joseph Lieberman of Connecticut answered the "slippery slope" argument:

> I am reminded as I listened to the debate this evening of a story Mark Twain once told about the cat who jumped up on the hot stove and was burned and as a result never jumped up on the stove again whether it was hot or not.

Mr. President, we are wiser than that cat. We are all very much aware, and you can feel it in the air in this Chamber tonight, of the tragedy that was our involvement in Southeast Asia once before. But this is a different time and a different circumstance.

A pivotal role was played in the Senate deliberations by Vice President Dan Quayle, a former member of that body. It was Quayle who gave life to the Robb Amendment in the first place by assuring Robb of administration support. An unashamed conservative in a government of pragmatists, Quayle was the one senior figure ideologically attuned to the music of the Reagan Doctrine. Though his colleagues had shifted the focus of U.S. policy to more conventional issues like arms control and Europe, Quayle believed in America's moral obligation to follow through on its commitment to the "freedom fighters" until satisfactory settlements were reached. He spoke out eloquently on behalf of the mujahedin, the Contras, and also the Cambodians, making their case in both moral and geopolitical terms, leaving to Bush and Baker the calculations of domestic political strategy.

Quayle's fate, even more than the case with most vice presidents, was to get no credit for many of his useful labors while his every embarrassment made the front pages. His was a consistent voice in support of the resistance movements, and in the Cambodia case he made a significant difference. Both Scowcroft and his deputy (and old CIA hand) Bob Gates were highly uneasy about a request for lethal aid; they disparaged the fighting qualities of the non-Communists and disdained the whole idea of an open debate about a covert program. But the president was persuaded to go for it.

In May, Quayle traveled on a diplomatic mission consulting with Asian and Southeast Asian allies. By June 22, when he spoke at a conference in Washington, he was in a position to declare the administration's decision to strengthen the resistance:

By strengthening the Non-Communist Resistance, we would be *increasing* the prospects for a successful political, *negotiated*, outcome; by doing nothing, we would increase the likelihood of continued civil war and the potential for a return to power by the murderous Khmer Rouge. Unless Sihanouk is strong enough militarily and politically, he will not be able to hold the center of the Cambodian political stage long enough to ensure a free and fair election. . . . [O]ur assistance to Prince Sihanouk is designed to make it possible for him to be *independent* of the Khmer Rouge *without* becoming a prisoner of the Vietnamese sponsored puppet government. . . .

President Bush noted in his Inaugural Address: "No great nation can long afford to be sundered by a memory." Similarly, *no great nation can long afford to be paralyzed by a memory. We must not permit the Non-Communist Resistance in Cambodia to become the last casualty of the Vietnam war.*[32]

Quayle worked energetically on the Senate floor into the late evening of July 20, buttonholing his former colleagues as they debated the Robb Amendment. When the roll was called in the wee hours, the amendment carried by the surprising margin of 59–39.

There was no need to pass a bill or reconcile differences in language between the two houses of Congress; with both houses now on record favoring lethal aid, that should have been a sufficient political signal for the intelligence committees to endorse such a program. But it was not to be. There was a further legislative hurdle: Where reserve funds do not exist and a reprogramming of already appropriated funds is needed, permission of the Appropriations Committees is required. There sat Senate Appropriations chairman Robert Byrd in the catbird seat, blocking the aid as he had vowed. Before the administration could develop any momentum to overcome this obstacle, the Paris Conference intervened.

France, the former colonial power in Indochina, had often tried to inject itself into Indochina diplomacy—perhaps to redeem its colonial past by modern acts of peacemaking, perhaps to one-up the Americans, perhaps to demonstrate its skills polished over three centuries of statecraft. Probably all of the above. When, in April 1989, Vietnam announced it would pull out by September, French president François Mitterrand stepped forward and proposed a peace conference in Paris for the end of July. On the surface it must have seemed an appropriate moment for a diplomatic initiative. In reality, the French had no plan. The moment when diplomatic movement could be expected would be *after* the Vietnamese withdrawal was completed in September and after the parties had had a chance to test the new balance of forces on the ground. Before then, it was highly unlikely that any of the key parties would make big concessions or take big risks. The Paris Conference was thus more a product of French vanity than of any strategy.

The conference, which took place at the end of July and beginning of August 1989, brought together nineteen nations with an interest in Cambodia plus the four Cambodian parties. It produced no significant progress.[33] This should not have been a surprise, and indeed it was no surprise to the American delegation. Richard H. Solomon, assistant secretary of state for East Asian and Pacific affairs, told a press briefing afterward that the nineteen nations at the gathering might meet again "some months down the road when perhaps the realities on the ground have given people a clearer sense of the real balance of forces that are fighting." He expected the war to continue, "for a period of military testing."[34] The Americans were actually satisfied that they had kept the need for a "comprehensive" settlement high on the agenda—that is, not letting Vietnam off the hook after its troop withdrawal but insisting on a political compromise in Phnom Penh (as well as military provisions that would give us a handle on the Khmer Rouge). Secretary of State Baker made a forceful speech in Paris on July 30 and ensured that this principle was reflected in the final communiqué. Baker also made a point of condemning the Khmer Rouge in the strongest terms and explaining the American attitude toward their role in the peace process:

> The United States strongly believes that the Khmer Rouge should play no role in Cambodia's future. We are prepared, however, to support Prince Sihanouk should he deem it necessary to accept the inclusion of all Khmer factions in an interim coalition or an interim authority. . . . There must be safeguards that Pol Pot and other Khmer Rouge leaders responsible for mass murders will never dominate Cambodia again.
>
> We also cannot accept a continuation of the present regime in Phnom Penh, which was established through Vietnamese aggression.

Nonetheless, the Paris Conference turned out—unexpectedly—to be a disaster for U.S. policy. By the time its aftereffects were felt, it had demoralized the U.S. government, doomed any chances for U.S. lethal military aid for the non-Communists, and revived with new vigor the critics' charges that U.S. policy was helping the Khmer Rouge.

During the Paris proceedings, American officials had to suffer Sihanouk at his most erratic. They came away suffering from what I called "Snooky Shock" ("Snooky" being a mildly affectionate but not totally respectful nickname given to Sihanouk over the decades by frustrated American officials). Sihanouk made no effort in Paris to distance himself from his Khmer Rouge coalition partners. When Phnom Penh attempted to insert a clause in the communiqué insisting that there should be no return to the Khmer Rouge "genocide" of the past, Sihanouk blocked it. It was a public relations disaster, to put it mildly. Critics condemned our ally Sihanouk and focused on the role of the Khmer Rouge as the controversial issue that wrecked the conference (which is exactly why Phnom Penh had pressed the genocide issue in the first place). "[I]t was largely because Prince Sihanouk insisted on such a Khmer Rouge role that the Paris Conference broke down," asserted the *New York Times* in an editorial, warning the administration that going ahead with lethal aid for the non-Communists would be a terrible idea in such circumstances.[35] U.S. officials came home from Paris depressed, even bitter at the temperamental prince whose leadership role we had been championing.

It was easier for those of us watching from afar in Washington, not having to witness Sihanouk's performance firsthand, to see the method in his madness. And our officials, once the "Snooky Shock" wore off, understood perfectly well. Dick Solomon delivered a speech in Los Angeles on September 8 that, while it conspicuously omitted the usual lavish praise of Sihanouk, gave credit to Sihanouk's power-sharing proposals and slammed Hun Sen and the Vietnamese for *their* intransigence. In Sihanouk's eyes, the tactical necessity in Paris had been to continue squeezing Hanoi and Phnom Penh; he (and we) had to resist rising to the bait of an untimely battle with the Khmer Rouge, letting Hanoi off the hook. In Sihanouk's calculation, the confrontation with the Khmer Rouge was bound to come in due time—but preferably *after* a political settlement in which the two Communist forces were cut off from arms supply and the non-Communists were put in a more pivotal position.

Nevertheless, the failure of the Paris Conference was trumpeted in the media. It was unfairly viewed as a failure of *our* policy (when in fact its convening had no part in our strategy), and it was seen as further discrediting Sihanouk, on whom our policy indeed depended. In September, Vietnam announced the completion of its withdrawal from Cambodia—though it was widely believed that at least a thousand Vietnamese troops had remained, integrated into Phnom Penh's army, and that other Vietnamese units returned afterward.[36] Despite the controversy over Hanoi's new deception, the disillusionment after Paris was such that media and congressional pressures continued to mount on the Bush administration to change its policy. The administration did not bend, but it lost heart. It made no further effort to salvage lethal aid for the non-Communist resistance.

THE UN PLAN

The failure of the Paris Conference had the positive result, at least, of impelling the international community to consider new steps to break the deadlock among the Cambodian parties. Soon there emerged the idea of a UN body to administer and enforce a settlement. Credit usually goes to Representative Solarz, who promoted the idea in the fall of 1989, and Australian minister of foreign affairs and trade Gareth Evans, who presented a formal proposal in November. The Australians sent a diplomatic and military survey team to Cambodia to assess the requirements and published a detailed 153-page blueprint in February.

The idea filled the policy vacuum to such a degree that by January it already had the backing of all five permanent members of the UN Security Council (the "Perm Five"), who issued a joint declaration on January 16, 1990, calling for "an enhanced UN role" directly administering free elections and assuring internal security during the transition period.[37] By August 1990, the Perm Five had negotiated a "framework document" for a comprehensive settlement based on the Australian recommendations. It involved a Supreme National Council comprising the Cambodian parties and embodying Cambodian sovereignty and unity; a plan for free and fair elections organized and conducted by the United Nations; a UN Transitional Authority in Cambodia (UNTAC) to perform this function by taking control of all governmental agencies that could affect the outcome of the elections; a cease-fire and cessation of outside arms supply to the contending factions. Opposing military factions were also to be regrouped, then disarmed and demobilized.[38]

That the Chinese and Soviets both endorsed the UN plan was significant evidence of their mutual desire in 1990 to wrap up the Cambodian affair and get on with their more important business together. In November 1989 the Soviets had reportedly told Hanoi they were cutting back military aid by one-third, and in January 1990 they announced they were pulling most of their military assets out of Cam Ranh Bay.[39] China's support for the UN plan actually came as somewhat of a surprise in view of the plan's uncomfortable implications for the Khmer Rouge. Yet China now had an additional incentive to cooperate—its desire to break out of its diplomatic isolation following the bloody June 1989 crackdown in Tiananmen Square. And China and Vietnam were being brought together by the increasing consternation with which they both watched the Gorbachev experiment in Moscow lead to the collapse of Soviet power in Eastern Europe. China and Vietnam, ancient enemies, now shared the ideological bond of wanting no such experiments in democratization in their own countries. A breakthrough meeting of top-level Chinese and Vietnamese party and government officials took place in September 1990 in Chengdu, Sichuan Province. Here the Vietnamese reportedly committed themselves to press Phnom Penh to cooperate with the UN plan and accept Sihanouk as leader of an interim government.[40]

The idea of UN control was much more attractive than sharing power with the Khmer Rouge. It calmed the congressional pressures for a time. Yet the difference between this and our earlier negotiating position was not as great as it seemed. No such interim arrangement could possibly come into being unless and until all four Cambodian parties agreed to it, which implied some modus vivendi and acceptance of the balance of forces among them. Given the many specifics that remained to be agreed, it still would require, in the end, a quadripartite deal on the allocation of power—including the Khmer Rouge—just as was implied by the administration's previous policy.

ENDGAME?

The United States now played a more active role in the Cambodia diplomacy, promoting a UN-based solution in the negotiations among the Perm Five in New York. Paradoxically, however, the domestic pressures did not abate. Baker was always acutely sensitive to domestic pressures, and in July 1990 the U.S. government was pushed into a significant shift. The spring of 1990 had seen former senator Muskie's campaign against the policy and the tendentious Peter Jennings documentary on ABC News; these had their effect on Congress. The administration was persuaded that any form of continued U.S. assistance to the non-Communists, even nonlethal, was doomed in Congress unless it yielded to the pressure. The Senate Intelligence Committee voted on June 28 to cut off covert aid, and Senate concurrence in the $7 million in overt aid (passed by the House) was in doubt.[41]

Meanwhile, on the ground in the region, Thai prime minister Chatichai again showed Thailand's restlessness about the guerrilla base camps inside its borders. Announcing in March 1990 that "we consider our duty done," Chatichai proposed moving the refugees to "neutral camps" under UN auspices, thereby ending the guerrillas' military sanctuary.[42] Yet the Khmer Rouge also seemed to be gaining ground in the war, advancing toward the major town of Siem Reap and claiming they were in striking distance of the capital, Phnom Penh.[43] While the press accounts of imminent Khmer Rouge breakthroughs proved false (as had often been the case in the past), they contributed to the panic about the implications of the Bush administration's policy.

Therefore, in July 1990, Baker decided on a policy shift—tilting in the direction of Hanoi and Phnom Penh by agreeing to talk directly with

Hanoi on the subject of Cambodia and by withdrawing diplomatic support for the coalition's UN seat because of the Khmer Rouge participation. The economic embargo on Phnom Penh was eased to permit humanitarian assistance. The decision leaked to the *Los Angeles Times*, and Baker confirmed it to reporters in a joint news conference he was holding with Soviet foreign minister Shevardnadze after their meeting in Paris on July 18. Baker acknowledged that congressional pressures were a major factor in the decision: "[I]n the absence of the bipartisan policy approach, I think it will be ever more difficult to continue to generate the funds that we need from the Congress to continue this support to the Non-Communist Resistance."[44]

Our ASEAN allies were caught by surprise; they were also angered by the unilateral breach in the agreed-upon policy, which had been to maintain the pressure on Hanoi. Singapore prime minister Lee Kuan Yew, a principal architect of the policy, described himself tactfully as "puzzled" by the U.S. move; ASEAN diplomats were more voluble in criticizing the move as likely to undercut Sihanouk, prolong the war, and encourage Phnom Penh to resist concessions.[45] Sihanouk's son Prince Ranariddh said it would force the non-Communists to tilt closer to China.[46]

U.S. critics of the previous policy, however, were not mollified. The new policy "does not go far enough," said Sen. John Kerry.[47] Chet Atkins said it was "only a first step and will not make any difference until or unless Secretary Baker is willing to terminate" aid to the non-Communist resistance.[48] Senate majority leader George Mitchell generated a letter to the president on July 24, signed by sixty-six senators, asking the president again to "reexamine" American policy toward Cambodia.[49] On September 5, Baker backed down again, promising to open a dialogue with Phnom Penh as well as with Hanoi. In the end, the Bush administration did manage to keep funding alive for the rebels a little longer. Its opponents were held off, perhaps by the well-timed concessions by Baker, perhaps by the diplomatic progress being made at the United Nations or by the distraction of the Iraq crisis, which began two weeks after Baker's original announcement.

As for the impact of the move on the Cambodia diplomacy, it is hard to assess. Some considered it a "welcome step forward," since it opened the way, for the first time, to a direct dialogue with Vietnam.[50] China was stunned by the move, particularly as Baker (probably accidentally) seemed to be announcing it in a joint news conference with Shevardnadze. The appearance of U.S.-Soviet collusion on a geopolitical issue on which the United States and China had been collaborating for a dozen years against the Soviets was undoubtedly a shocker. State Department officials (themselves not enthusiastic about the move) expressed to me privately the hope that it would scare the Chinese into reining in the Khmer Rouge, which would in the end reassure everybody else.

The same officials assured me that Hanoi was still under pressure from the decline in Soviet aid, the reduction of the Soviet naval presence in the region, the Sino-Soviet rapprochement, and Vietnam's internal economic disaster exacerbated by its international isolation. On the other hand, I could see a contrary trend: Hanoi and Phnom Penh were gaining ground internationally. The French, who had normalized relations with Vietnam in 1989, moved toward normalizing relations with Phnom Penh, under the influence of the Hillary Clinton of the Elysée, Mitterrand's activist/ideologue spouse, Danielle Mitterrand. Japan was doing the same, attracted by the business opportunities in Indochina and the strategic opportunity of a partnership with Vietnam as a counterweight to China. In the negotiations, Hanoi and Phnom Penh continued to resist sharing power—even with the United Nations. And it probably did not help that the administration was so fearful of congressional pressures that it withheld disbursement of some of the appropriated funds for the resistance until four House Republicans wrote an angry letter to Assistant Secretary Solomon on April 17, 1991.[51]

The major breakthrough occurred in the summer of 1991. The Cambodian parties met again, this time in early June in Jakarta and two weeks later at the Thai beach resort of Pattaya. Sihanouk was accepted as head of the quadripartite Supreme National Council that was called for under the UN peace plan, and it was agreed that all four parties would return to Phnom Penh to set up the council there under a UN umbrella. In principle, foreign arms supply was to stop, the United Nations was to step in to manage the transition to free elections, and talks were to proceed on regroupment, disarmament, and demobilization.[52] Many thorny issues remained unresolved. But the pressures for a settlement had reached their peak. The Soviets and Chinese were impatient with sponsoring a war that was going nowhere; China and Vietnam both had an increasing incentive to improve their bilateral relations as well as to reduce their international isolation.

One important clue to what was going on was an internal political shake-up in Hanoi. Foreign Minister Nguyen Co Thach, a smooth and impressive operator who had been Le Duc Tho's chief aide in the secret talks with Kissinger in the early 1970s, was sacked as foreign minister by a party congress in June 1991. Thach was considered too anti-Chinese, at a moment in history when Hanoi and Beijing were doomed to reach an accommodation on Cambodia. Indeed, he was blamed for trying to scuttle the deal struck at Chengdu. His successor, Nguyen Manh Cam, a former ambassador in Moscow, was thought to be an advocate of broadening Hanoi's diplomatic options in the wake of the decline in Soviet aid. The change was widely hailed as opening the way to an improvement in Sino-Vietnamese relations. [53]

The good news was that these developments among the Communist powers were pushing Cambodia closer to a political solution. The bad news was that the non-Communists' voice in this—including Sihanouk's—was still weak. Cambodia was moving toward a "red solution"— a solution brought about by all the Communists cutting a deal among themselves. Such an outcome would put into question the seriousness with which key provisions of the UN plan would be implemented, like truly free elections, disarmament of the rival armies, and an effective UN administrative role in the country. [54] With a weak UN presence, Phnom Penh would have the "advantages of incumbency" in any election, and the Khmer Rouge would maintain their power in the field. The losers would be the non-Communists—and the Cambodian people. In a red solution, the Phnom Penh regime, of which the Bush administration's critics were so fond, would ironically have consummated the deal with the Khmer Rouge that Sihanouk and the non-Communists were wrongly accused of. The UN solution, which attracted such international support, would have been undercut by our failure to sustain the independent democratic forces in Cambodia that had the most stake in it.

The diplomacy accelerated. In a second meeting at Pattaya in late August, convening as the Supreme National Council under Sihanouk's chairmanship, the four parties reached unanimous agreement on key military provisions (supervision of the cease-fire; termination of outside military aid), the relationship between the Supreme National Council and UNTAC, elements of a new constitution, and a flag and national anthem. [55] These breakthroughs were incorporated in an Agreement on a Comprehensive Political Settlement of the Cambodia Conflict and associated agreements, which were signed by all parties at a dramatic reconvened session of the Paris Conference on October 23, 1991.

The Paris ceremony was an emotional moment. It implied, at long last, an end to Cambodia's agony. As the cameras whirred and flashbulbs flashed, the four bitter Cambodian enemies affixed their signatures to the agreement in the French government's International Conference Center on Avenue Kléber, the same setting in which I had witnessed, eighteen years earlier, the signing of an earlier Paris agreement—on Vietnam. Perhaps because of the precedent, elation was hard to come by in the context of a Cambodian enterprise even more fragile than that Vietnam accord that had so raised hopes, only to dash them. President Mitterrand articulated the world's unease: "A dark page of history has been turned. Cambodians want peace, which means that any spirit of revenge would now be as dangerous as forgetting the lessons of history."[56]

What had tipped the scales in favor of peace was the extraordinary evolution of relations among the Communist powers in the summer of 1991—the pressures bringing Vietnam and China together, signaled by the removal of Nguyen Co Thach at the June party congress and, even more, by the August putsch attempt in Moscow. Hanoi now faced the prospect not merely of declining Soviet aid but of the disappearance of its Soviet patron from the face of the earth. It concentrated the mind wonderfully. Within days of the Paris agreement, Vietnam's party chief, Do Muoi, and prime minister Vo Van Kiet paid a historic four-day summit visit to Beijing to complete the process of normalization of relations.

Like all negotiated agreements, the accord on Cambodia involved compromise. The interim Supreme National Council, under Sihanouk's ostensibly neutral chairmanship, consisted of six representatives of the Phnom Penh government and five from the resistance factions (i.e., close to the two-sided arrangement favored by Hanoi and Phnom Penh). But on the most important issues—power sharing and the role of the United Nations—Phnom Penh seemed finally to have made the major concessions.

The negotiating breakthrough was its acceptance of an intrusive UN presence that would run the Cambodian government during the interim period. The interim period was to last until a constituent assembly, chosen by free elections under UN supervision, approved a new constitution and then turned itself into a legislative assembly that in turn formed a new government. Elections were later set for May 1993. During the interim period, UNTAC was to take direct control of the government functions of foreign affairs, national defense, finance, public security, and information. It was also to monitor the cease-fire, withdrawal of all foreign troops, cessation of outside military aid, return of the half million refugees (350,000 in Thailand alone), and the regroupment, disarmament, and demobilization of military forces—70 percent of which were to be demobilized by the time of the elections. A UN Advance Mission in Cambodia (UNAMIC) arrived in Phnom Penh in November 1991.[57]

Signature of an agreement that included the Khmer Rouge was received in the United States with less than deafening applause. The accord was even denounced by the same critics who had disapproved of the Bush administration's strategy all along. It was unusual for liberals to denounce a peace agreement, especially one administered by the United Nations, and in disapproving of an accord already signed by all the other Cambodian parties, they were being more royalist than the prince. They blamed international pressures for forcing an unsatisfactory deal on the Cambodians. The Cambodians "could not have come up with a peace plan more dangerous or more dicey than the one the world forced on them," wrote Mary McGrory.[58] "We should have ignored the Khmer Rouge, isolated them and China," argued Rep. Chet Atkins.[59] Hun Sen, Phnom Penh's prime minister, was dispatched to Washington in March 1992 for the ironic task of lobbying among his liberal admirers in defense of the agreement. I watched him at a Washington meeting of the Council on Foreign Relations—the heart of the Washington establishment— working hard to convince the crowd he had not sold out.

The accords had their American defenders. Most notable among them was Elizabeth Becker, a longtime critic of the Bush policy. She welcomed the strong involvement of the international community, seeing it as an important safeguard, and she saw the new arrangements as an opportunity to outmaneuver the Khmer Rouge in peacetime conditions.[60]

Once UNAMIC was deployed in Cambodia, President Bush, on January 3, 1992, lifted the U.S. economic embargo against Cambodia and also lifted the U.S. veto on aid to Cambodia by international financial institutions. The United States also set up a diplomatic office in Phnom Penh accredited to the Supreme National Council. According to a "road map" outlined in April 1991 by Assistant Secretary Solomon, the United States was prepared to contemplate incremental steps of normalization of relations with Vietnam, in parallel with implementation of the Cambodia accords and progress on accounting for our MIAs.

The critics nonetheless pointed to risks in the Cambodia agreement that were as real as they were deadly. The administration's gamble was now to be put to the test. The premise was that turning the contest into a political one would put Sihanouk and the non-Communists in a pivotal position, enabling them to outmaneuver the Khmer Rouge (and also to counterbalance Hanoi's Cambodian clients). Better to have the Khmer Rouge inside the tent pissing out, as Lyndon Johnson would have said, than outside the tent pissing in.

The gamble lay in the fact that the Khmer Rouge were perfectly capable of discerning this strategy. They could be under no illusions about the new lineup. The real options they faced were, as a State Department official was quoted as saying, "to reign or to perish"—to come out on top in a new mortal struggle or to see themselves slowly strangled by the coalition of their opponents and their erstwhile allies.[61] Soon enough,

Sihanouk was maneuvering actively with the Phnom Penh forces to isolate the Khmer Rouge, just as the Bush administration had always counted on. On November 16, Sihanouk was publicly calling for war crimes trials for the Khmer Rouge leaders—the same people whom he had shielded from charges of genocide at the 1989 Paris Conference.[62] A week later, he was openly colluding with Hun Sen, the Phnom Penh prime minister, announcing that he and Hun Sen would form a bipartite government with his son Ranariddh as deputy prime minister; a military alliance between the two factions was signed.[63]

A few days later, Khieu Samphan returned to Phnom Penh for the first time in thirteen years, in his capacity as Khmer Rouge representative on the Supreme National Council. An angry mob of some ten thousand Cambodians who remembered the Khmer Rouge terror stormed his villa. Bloodied by the mob and cornered in a closet, he had to be rescued by the regime's police and evacuated to Thailand. Hun Sen apologized and took responsibility for what was probably a government-sponsored demonstration that got out of control.[64]

Yet the Khmer Rouge still represented a dangerous beast—thrown on the defensive, perhaps, but not yet tamed. In 1991, it was estimated that they still fielded twenty-five to thirty-five thousand troops in main-force battalions, plus the same number of "civilian" cadres and political operatives who could be armed. They controlled only three of Cambodia's twenty-one provinces but held pockets of territory everywhere else. The Chinese claimed to have cut off new weapons shipments in 1990, but large stocks remained. Most ominously, the Khmer Rouge were on their way to becoming economically self-sufficient and therefore less vulnerable to outside pressure; they now controlled the cross-border smuggling into Thailand and pocketed profits from the gem mining and logging concessions they hired out to Thai businessmen and military officers.[65]

In this inhospitable environment, the United Nations set up its Transitional Authority in Cambodia (UNTAC), the most ambitious peacekeeping operation in the UN's history. Learning a lesson from the woefully understaffed operation in Angola, UNTAC comprised over fifteen thousand military personnel, thirty-five hundred police, one thousand civilian administrators, and other volunteers. The military force included twelve battalion-sized units deployed throughout the country.[66] UNTAC had its problems; its civilian administrators arrived late and were never able to take full control over the government institutions it was charged with running. It ended up governing through the officials of the Phnom Penh government whom it was supposed to supplant.[67] This threatened to skew the elections in Phnom Penh's favor and contributed to the Khmer Rouge's decision to boycott the elections.

Nonetheless, the elections of May 1993 were a success. An extraordinary 90 percent of Cambodian voters turned out, defying the Khmer Rouge boycott. Sihanouk's party, run by his son Ranariddh, won 46 percent of the vote in a stunning upset of Hun Sen's People's party. Ranariddh and Hun Sen quickly joined in a two-party coalition to form a solid front against the Khmer Rouge. The Khmer Rouge seemed seriously weakened by the process—"For them, the election was like holding a crucifix to Dracula," wrote William Shawcross.[68] Many Khmer Rouge troops defected, and their numbers shrank. The United Nations quickly folded its tents and went home.

Perhaps too quickly.[69] The hopes for a decent outcome continued to rest, all too precariously, on Norodom Sihanouk. A new constitution restored the monarchy, and at the age of seventy, he ascended again to the throne he had first held as a youth under French tutelage. We had to hope that Sihanouk's electoral victory would gain time for the non-Communists to parlay their pivotal position into a durable political force. Without Sihanouk, there was no strategy. If he should disappear from the scene, the weight of the non-Communists would shrink once again— Ranariddh being no replica of his father. The two Communist factions might well either resume fighting or cut a deal, as they chose. The U.S. and ASEAN strategy could work with Sihanouk, but it was not clear it could survive him.

Thus, the Cambodia settlement remained an extremely fragile arrangement. The United States, having achieved its strategic objective of countering Soviet influence and ending the Vietnamese occupation, had a moral responsibility to see the conflict through to a stable and defensible outcome. Yet the moral ambiguities of the diplomacy had been too painful; the fears of reintervention in Indochina, too paralyzing. America's anxiety about the peace settlement—and the continuing danger that the decent people of Cambodia would once again be either terrorized by the Khmer Rouge or ground up between two gangs of Communist thugs— were to a considerable degree the result of its unwillingness to bolster its friends militarily. In Afghanistan, Angola, and Nicaragua, it should have been evident that U.S. support for anti-Communist resistance movements was not an obstacle to a fair political outcome; it was the precondition for it. The same was even more true in Cambodia. We denied ourselves leverage, and not only the administration's goals but even those of its critics were jeopardized.

However the Cambodia drama plays itself out, it—like Afghanistan, Nicaragua, and Angola—has been reduced to its local dimensions, no longer a political football in a big-power contest. This was some consolation for the long-suffering Cambodians, who continued to face a danger the peoples of those other countries did not. But the Cambodian election nevertheless marked the end of an era in international affairs. These four regional conflicts were the product of the Brezhnev era, of the period of Soviet overreaching, which spawned resistance movements that, in the end, rolled back Communist strategic gains. These conflicts were all being wound down as a new day in East-West relations dawned. History has moved on—perhaps cruelly in view of the legacy of destruction and continuing fear left behind.

It remains to discuss one other crucial area of regional conflict, long featured on the East-West agenda and also transformed by events—the Middle East. This conflict posed different issues but taught some of the same lessons.

PART

FOUR

THE FUTURE

17

THE COLD WAR IN THE
MIDDLE EAST

The conflicts in Afghanistan, Nicaragua, Angola, and Cambodia wound down, reflecting in their way the transformation of the East-West rivalry at the end of the 1980s and beginning of the 1990s. An even more vivid reflection of this change, however, took place in the Middle East. In 1956, the United States had unintentionally bolstered Nasser and raised the curtain on three and a half decades of Soviet-backed radicalism in the Arab world. In the Gulf crisis of 1990–91, the United States intervened decisively to deflate Nasser's heir, Saddam Hussein, while the Soviets looked on uncomfortably from the sidelines. The Gulf War marked a historic reversal of superpower fortunes.

This reversal did not come about by itself. In September 1956, during the Suez crisis, John Foster Dulles had expressed the sanguine opinion to President Eisenhower that the new tie between Egypt and the Soviet Union would, over the long run, not last. He told the president "that I did not believe that any such partnership was durable. I pointed out that where countries were physically adjacent to the Soviet Union and where Soviet troops were there to sustain a pro-Soviet government, the people had little recourse. However, that was not the case where a country was not adjacent to the Soviet Union and where Soviet military power was not available to support the government."[1]

Dulles's prediction turned out to be right, but history does not bestow its favors gratis. The unraveling of the Soviet position in the Middle East came about through a complex evolution, through wars, crises, confrontations, and high-stakes diplomacy, in some of which I had the privilege to take part. It was more than a decade and a half before the Soviet-Egyptian link was broken and another decade and a half before the Soviets were out of business as a supporter of Arab radicals (which really came only with the collapse of the Soviet Union itself). American policy played a role in that evolution—an American policy that consciously sought to undo the blunder of Suez.

BREZHNEV'S BLUSTER

Despite his success at Suez, Khrushchev's exuberant courting of Third World nationalists was looked upon by his successors with a jaundiced eye. It was costing the Soviet Union a considerable amount of money, and the payoff was in many cases unclear. Four o Khrushchev's favored Third World partners were overthrown in a short span of time between 1965 and 1968—Ahmed Ben Bella in Algeria, Sukarno of Indonesia, Kwame Nkrumah of Ghana, and Modibo Keita in Mali. Brezhnev and Kosygin, in the early years of their rule, were more tight-fisted in their disbursal of economic aid and more interested in getting concrete quid pro quos in return for economic and military assistance. As Soviet naval strength grew, for example, Moscow badgered the Egyptians for naval and air support facilities, which Nasser refused to grant until after the 1967 war, when he desperately needed more Soviet arms aid.[2]

Nonetheless, by the mid-1960s the Soviets could still count Nasser as one of their best allies in the Third World.[3] Egypt remained a strategic prize. Nasser was a leader of the so-called nonaligned, a thorn in the side of the West and, in his adventure in Yemen in the early 1960s, a threat to the oil-rich conservative Gulf monarchies on which the West depended.

Gradually, the Soviet posture in the Middle East grew bolder once again. A pivotal event was the February 1966 coup in Damascus, an upheaval within the ruling Ba'ath party that brought into power a Marxist faction spouting revolutionary slogans dear to the hearts of Central Committee ideologues in Moscow. The Syrians looked to Moscow for aid and inspiration, and the Soviets' self-confidence seems to have been bolstered by this appearance of a new "socialist" ally. The Soviets quickly established party-to-party ties with the new Syrian leadership—a special sign of intimacy—and extended a $132 million loan. Thus began a partnership that lasted twenty-five years, such that, even in the era of "new thinking," Soviet foreign minister Eduard Shevardnadze could call Syria in 1989 "the Soviet Union's leading partner in the Near East."[4] In the 1960s, the Syrian developments fostered in Soviet minds the dream of forming a broad anti-imperialist front with Egypt, Syria, Algeria, and Iraq. In November 1966, Egypt and Syria signed a mutual defense treaty.[5]

The Syrians proved a mixed blessing as an ally, however, from the beginning. They seem to have been responsible for a step-up of Palestinian terrorist attacks on Israel, through Jordan. By the spring of 1967, Israel was warning on a regular basis that it blamed Damascus and would retaliate; tensions mounted dangerously. Syrian strongman Nureddin al-Attassi denounced the Israeli claims (in good Leninist rhetoric) as part of an "imperialist-Zionist-reactionary conspiracy" and vowed undying support for the Palestinian "commandos, sons of the occupied territories, who have a natural right to return to and liberate their homes."[6] Recall that, in those days, "occupied territories" referred to the territory of Israel *within* its pre-June 5, 1967, borders.

What happened next was an extraordinary display of superpower recklessness. Moscow, deeming itself Syria's principal protector, warned Egypt that an Israeli attack on Syria was imminent, which led Nasser to expel UN peacekeeping forces from the Sinai and reoccupy it with Egyptian troops. Syria and Israel both mobilized, and Egypt then declared a blockade of the Strait of Tiran. Israel lashed out in early June and defeated Egypt, Syria, and Jordan in six days, occupying large stretches of Arab territory.

While most of the blame for the 1967 war lay in Egyptian bravado and self-delusion, the irresponsibility of the Soviet role is evident. The Soviets passed "intelligence" to a visiting Egyptian parliamentary delegation in late April and early May that the Israelis were planning a strike against Syria and had massed eleven brigades in the north for the purpose. Reports along the same lines were conveyed to Nasser in Cairo by the Soviet ambassador and by Syrian intelligence.[7] There was, in fact, no Israeli preparation at that point for an attack on Syria. (The Egyptian parliamentary delegation that had received the phony information in Moscow was headed by Assembly Speaker Anwar el-Sadat, who never forgot the Soviets' contribution to the 1967 debacle.)

Declassified U.S. intelligence reports reveal the scale of the Soviet miscalculation and something of the Soviet motivation. A mid-level Soviet official acknowledged in June 1967 that Moscow had overestimated the Arabs' military ability and had egged them on in their hostility to Israel. The reason, according to the Soviet official, was

> that the USSR had wanted to create another trouble spot for the United States in addition to that already existing in Vietnam. The Soviet aim was to create a situation in which the U.S. would become seriously involved, economically, politically, and possibly even militarily and in which the U.S. would suffer serious political reverses as a result of its siding against the Arabs. This grand design, which envisaged a long war in the Middle East, misfired because the Arabs failed completely and the Israeli blitzkrieg was so decisive.[8]

The 1967 war turned the Arab-Israeli confrontation, even more than it had been, into a direct superpower confrontation. The Arabs, licking their wounds, became more dependent on the Soviet Union even as they complained about Soviet actions—the misleading reports beforehand, the lack of adequate backing in the crisis. As noted earlier, Nasser relented after 1967 and gave the Soviets what they sought—virtual control over seven air bases and preferential access to four harbors in the Mediterranean and one in the Red Sea. Through massive arms deliveries, the Soviets rebuilt the Syrian and Egyptian military forces.

Similarly, Israel turned to the United States, and Washington soon became its major arms supplier. Before the 1967 war, France had performed that function, and the United States held back, reluctant to risk damage to its Arab ties, especially in the Gulf. In fact, the focus of U.S. interest in the Middle East in those days was much more the Gulf than the Arab-Israeli conflict.[9] But French president Charles de Gaulle was outraged in 1967 that Israel had struck preemptively, contrary to his advice, and he abruptly terminated a military relationship that had been especially close ever since the shared ordeal of Suez. The drama of 1967 impelled the United States into a more direct role, diplomatically and otherwise. Just before Lyndon Johnson left office, he agreed in principle to the first Israeli request for a major U.S. weapons system—F-4 Phantom jet fighter-bombers—and it was during the Nixon administration that America's strategic partnership with Israel was forged.

Diplomatic efforts began hopefully. The UN Security Council had hammered out, over the course of the summer and fall, the famous Resolution 242, adopted unanimously on November 22, 1967. This resolution was a delicate balancing act. Its preamble spoke of the "inadmissibility of the acquisition of territory by war," and its operative paragraphs called for "withdrawal of Israeli armed forces from territories occupied in the recent conflict." But the resolution also called for termination of states of belligerency and for every state's "right to live in peace within secure and recognized boundaries free from threats or acts of force."

The climate for negotiation, nevertheless, turned out to be quite uncongenial. While the Soviets contributed to and voted for this balanced statement—which remains to this day the cornerstone of the peace process—they did not wait long to demonstrate once again their propensity to make mischief. The resolution was deliberately ambiguous about the extent of Israeli withdrawal required: "It called for "withdrawal . . . from territories occupied"—the word "all" or even a definite article "the" in front of "territories" being conspicuously and consciously omitted in the

English text. Yet the Soviets immediately adopted the Arab claim that 242 required total Israeli withdrawal. The Soviets and Arabs were certainly entitled to seek total withdrawal in any negotiation in the framework of 242, but it was stretching things to claim that the resolution *meant* that when those who took part in its drafting knew full well that it did not.[10]

The Soviets had also—foolishly, as they later admitted—severed diplomatic relations with Israel during the heat of the June crisis. Meanwhile, as the Soviets made themselves in effect the lawyer for the Arabs, Arab leaders, meeting at a summit in Khartoum in August 1967, declared that they would accept no peace, no recognition, and no negotiations with Israel. Resolution 242 also called for appointment of a special representative of the UN secretary-general to travel to the region and promote a negotiation; Gunnar Jarring, Swedish ambassador in Moscow, was given this thankless task. The United States, preoccupied by the Vietnam War and the presidential election, avoided active involvement during 1968. The Jarring effort went nowhere.

When Richard Nixon came into office, he was confronted with two new diplomatic initiatives. The Soviets had proposed bilateral talks with the United States, and the French had proposed four-power talks among the United States, USSR, Britain, and France. Nixon was not eager to rebuff the French—he was a great admirer of de Gaulle—or even the Soviets at the very beginning of his term. Despite the misgivings of his national security adviser, Henry Kissinger, and his own skepticism that any diplomacy would achieve anything, Nixon approved the State Department's recommendation that the United States participate.

Kissinger's memoirs describe in detail the differing perspectives of the White House and State Department in Nixon's first term and Nixon's own doubts.[11] In this situation, as in so many others, the department tended to respond reflexively to any problem with a desire to talk that exceeded any sense of strategy; it sent one of its most energetic and capable diplomats, Assistant Secretary of State Joseph Sisco, to join the four-power talks in New York and to conduct the two-power dialogue with Soviet ambassador Anatolii Dobrynin in Washington. Kissinger's view was that the basic conditions for a breakthrough did not exist, given Arab intransigence and the unhelpful Soviet position; he feared that the tendency of the diplomacy, in both forums, would be to increase pressures on the United States to deliver Israel to a settlement involving total or near-total withdrawal, a position the British and French were drifting toward as well. How we were to accomplish this result was never realistically explained. It looked like a one-sided and unproductive process leading us down the path toward a crisis with our Israeli ally and a domestic political crisis to boot.

Nixon was receptive to Kissinger's skeptical arguments in 1969–70 but did not want to deny his old comrade, Secretary of State William P. Rogers, a field to play in, especially since other key issues—Vietnam, arms control, China—were being pulled under White House control.[12] I remember a major brawl that erupted over the wording in a presidential foreign policy report in February 1970, which Kissinger and his NSC staff were drafting. Kissinger wanted the Middle East section to avoid euphoria about the diplomatic prospects so as to reduce the commitment of Nixon's prestige; an early draft referred to the Arab-Israeli problem as "intractable." To Kissinger's professorial mind this seemed self-evidently accurate. But it generated howls of protest from the State Department, which thought it was defeatism and inconsistent with the U.S. commitment to the diplomacy. In the end, a typical bureaucratic compromise produced the following banality: "It [the Arab-Israeli conflict] has serious elements of intractability, but its importance requires all concerned to devote their energies to helping to resolve it or make it less dangerous."[13]

The State Department was essentially having its way despite Kissinger's guerrilla warfare against it, and Rogers had already unveiled a formal and comprehensive U.S. peace proposal on December 9, 1969. It called for peace within secure and recognized boundaries, as Israel sought and as Resolution 242 required, but spoke of Israeli withdrawal in terms implying a near-total pullback to the 1967 lines, with only "insubstantial alterations."

On the ground, unfortunately, the situation was deteriorating once again. The 1967 war having displaced even more Palestinians and radicalized them further, Arab leaders were unable or unwilling to halt the Palestinian commando raids, particularly through Jordan. Egypt shelled Israeli positions from across the Suez Canal. Israel responded with retaliatory air strikes by the freshly purchased F-4 Phantoms. It was a new phase of the Arab-Israeli conflict, dubbed the "War of Attrition."

The tragedy for the peace process was that in a period when a Labour Government in Israel in fact had a certain flexibility, or at least fluidity, in its position on how much territory it would want to retain in any negotiation, the Arabs were completely out of sync. The shock of the 1967 humiliation left no room for moderation in those early years (even though in later years the memory of 1967 did contribute in large measure to the readiness to settle, particularly in Sadat's mind). In the era of Nasser, moreover, it is hard to imagine that a sufficient degree of trust existed on either side. Toward the end of his life (he died in September

1970) Nasser may have been groping toward a diplomatic solution, but his credibility was zero. Later, when Arab attitudes moderated considerably in the late 1970s and 1980s, a Likud government had come to power in Israel with a less flexible approach, especially on the Palestinian issue.

The irony is that the period 1970–72 may well be, despite all this, the seminal period of recent Middle East history. If you ask most students of international affairs (particularly young ones) how the peace process began, they may recall Sadat's stunning visit to Jerusalem in 1977 and the Camp David peace treaty between Egypt and Israel. More knowledgeable observers (or more middle-aged ones) may remember that the October 1973 war generated a burst of unprecedentedly productive diplomatic activity—the Kissinger shuttles—that laid the foundation for Camp David. It is too little appreciated, however, that the conditions that produced the post-1973 diplomacy were, in fact, shaped *before* the 1973 war—in an American policy that consciously sought to alter, in particular, the superpower context.

The Soviets played a major part in fueling the War of Attrition. As in the case of their invasion of Afghanistan, one can endlessly debate their motive: Was it offensive or defensive? To some degree they were reacting understandably to Israeli pressures on their Egyptian client. But overreaching was the bane of Brezhnev's policy generally, as we have seen in this book, and the Middle East was no exception to the pattern.

Israel's deep-penetration raids into Egyptian airspace extended as far as the suburbs of Cairo, deeply humiliating to both the Egyptians and their Soviet backers. Nasser flew in a panic to Moscow in January 1970. The upshot was a Soviet decision to send SA-3 antiaircraft missiles manned by Soviet crews and protected by Soviet combat aircraft flown by Soviet pilots. Soon there were fifteen thousand Soviet military personnel in Egypt. Nixon's foreign policy report of February 18, 1970, referred to above (and drafted by Kissinger and his staff), pointedly warned against the deepening Soviet military involvement:

One of the lessons of 1967 was that the local events and forces have a momentum of their own, and that conscious and serious effort is required for the major powers to resist being caught up in them. . . .

The activity of the Soviet Union in the Middle East and the Mediterranean has increased in recent years. This has consequences that reach far beyond the Arab-Israeli question. The United States . . . would view any effort by the Soviet Union to seek predominance in the Middle East as a matter of grave concern.[14]

Kissinger's view was that the balance of forces in the region was being dramatically tipped by the unprecedented Soviet military intervention. There was no difference whether its motive was offensive or defensive; the extraordinary presence of Soviet troops—flying combat air patrols over the Suez Canal and manning the missile batteries against Israeli planes—was a disproportionate weight in the scales in Egypt's favor that backstopped Arab intransigence in the political sphere. Kissinger was skeptical that any sensible diplomacy could proceed in such an environment, and he was borne out by what happened next.

The United States decided, at the urging of the State Department, to "exercise restraint"—the usual advice of the well-meaning. Israel's request for additional fighter aircraft to counter the Soviet escalation was deferred; Rogers went ahead with a new U.S. diplomatic initiative, negotiating a ninety-day standstill cease-fire that was to take effect at midnight on August 7, 1970. It turned out that in the weeks between Egypt's acceptance of the Rogers proposal and its entry into force, substantial elements of the Soviet-manned air-defense complex moved closer to the canal—and the movement continued into the wee hours of August 7/8 after the standstill was to have come into effect. (Kissinger was never able to understand why our State Department negotiators had chosen midnight as the benchmark for the agreement, given the difficulty of reconnaissance in those days to monitor effectively in the darkness. The answer was that they had provided for no real-time monitoring at all, so the time of day made no difference.)[15] As late as September, Soviet missile construction was continuing—in blatant violation of the standstill provision.

It was a cynical performance, which convinced Kissinger and Nixon that the Soviets were not only untrustworthy but bent on entrenching themselves militarily in the Middle East.[16] The Israelis, feeling they had been had, walked out of the diplomatic discussions. The United States, sheepish that its pressures on Israel had produced such an outcome, sold new arms to Israel. On August 14, Nixon decided on a new $7 million package of equipment to counter the Soviet air defenses—Shrike radar-suppressing missiles, cluster bombs, and sophisticated electronic gear—and on September 1, he approved the sale of eighteen more F-4s.

As if this were not enough excitement for the year, September 1970 was "Black September"—the month of King Hussein's crackdown on the forces of the Palestine Liberation Organization (PLO) who were hijacking airplanes and flying them to Jordan, flaunting their power in defiance of Jordanian authority. The king's military suppression of the PLO on September 16 provoked a Syrian armored invasion of Jordan two days later. In view of the close military links between Syria and the Soviets, Kissinger saw this, too, as a token of Soviet irresponsibility. When he bearded Dobrynin on the subject a week later, he received the extraordinary explanation that (1) the Soviets had not known in advance of the Syrian intention to invade and (2) in any case, the Soviet military advisers had left their Syrian units before the latter crossed the border into Jordan![17] The Jordan crisis was resolved, as King Hussein's army beat back the Syrian invaders. Intense diplomatic pressure on the Soviets had been reinforced by the movement of three U.S. aircraft carriers to the eastern Mediterranean and by secret and not-so-secret joint military planning between Israel and the United States.

What the actual degree of Moscow's responsibility was, we may never know. There were many, including in the State Department, who were decidedly skeptical that the Soviets had any significant hand in it.[18] But Nixon and Kissinger *chose* to treat Moscow as one of the parties responsible for the crisis. Whatever the truth of Moscow's foreknowledge, the purpose was to maximize the Soviets' incentive to exert whatever influence they had to bring the crisis to a rapid conclusion. The Soviets were sufficiently energized by Washington's threats that they pressed the Syrians to reverse course. It was also, in the end, a chance for the United States to redress the psychological balance in the Middle East that had been tipped by the introduction of Soviet missiles and combat forces into Egypt.[19]

During the eventful summer of 1970, Kissinger let slip a revealing expression of the administration's strategy. He was with Nixon at San Clemente, the summer White House, on June 26, when he gave a briefing on foreign policy to the usually bored White House press corps. He woke them up with a startling statement that the U.S. objective was to "expel" the Soviets from the Middle East. As he later described the briefing:

> The Soviet Union's original intentions in sending combat personnel into the Middle East were irrelevant, I said. Even if they had been sent to shore up Nasser, their continued presence represented a strategic threat that had to be dealt with: "We are trying to get a settlement in such a way that the moderate regimes are strengthened, and not the radical regimes. We are trying to *expel the Soviet military presence*, not so much the advisors, but the combat pilots and the combat personnel, before they become so firmly established [emphasis added]."[20]

While all hell broke loose at the time—with the State Department complaining bitterly that Kissinger was sabotaging their delicate diplomacy—it accurately reflected his thinking and Nixon's.

The Soviets during the Brezhnev period seemed eager to avoid another war, but not so eager to spend political capital with their clients to help produce peace. Another war, in their estimation, could only spell trouble for them: Their clients would lose, waste a lot of good Soviet equipment (which they would want replaced immediately), all the while complaining about the inadequacy of Soviet backing and of the Soviet equipment. A durable peace, on the other hand, would be no blessing for the Soviet Union, either. Its natural clients in the Middle East were the more radical Arabs—Nasser, the Syrians, the PLO, the Iraqis. To persuade them to compromise would require great pressure, earning their wrath and ingratitude. A condition of peace, moreover, would strengthen the moderates in the region—countries like Jordan, Saudi Arabia, and others who were clients of the West and whose position would be enhanced by a settlement that satisfied or defused the pressures of the aggrieved Palestinians. It would remove a major obstacle to America's relations with the Arabs.

The American image in the Arab world was basically benign. We were free of direct responsibility for colonialism; the U.S. presence in the region consisted of universities in Cairo and Beirut, a naval medical unit in Egypt, quite modest military deployments, and the mutually profitable involvement in the oil industry. I was with Kissinger a few years later in Algiers in a meeting with President Houari Boumedienne, whose ideology of international affairs was pure Third World Marxism, ostensibly skeptical of American motives in the Middle East. But Boumedienne welcomed Kissinger's shuttle diplomacy, hoping it would succeed. Most of all, he waxed eloquent about the prospects he could see for U.S.-Algerian cooperation in developing Algeria's oil and gas. No other country had the technological capability in this field that the United States had; when a Palestinian settlement made the United States more politically acceptable, there was no limit to the role it would have in the Arab world, he told Kissinger, puffing proudly on his Cuban cigar.

The Soviets' position in the Middle East was thus a mass of paralyzing contradictions. On the one hand, their military presence and their irresponsibility were a dangerous combination. Their direct role in encouraging and training terrorists, which many in the West had debated, has been confirmed by the opening of Soviet archives.[21] On the other hand, their political position in the Middle East was actually weak. Their allies did not trust them, constantly complaining of the inadequacy of their support, suspecting that they were inhibited by fear of the American reaction. The Soviets could deliver weapons, but they could deliver no progress in reclaiming Arab territory taken by the Israelis. Only the United States had the possibility of influencing Israel—a possibility that we would exercise only under proper conditions of a balanced negotiation and a fair settlement. Thus—as Anwar Sadat figured out—the United States held most of the cards.

The idea that the United States should work cooperatively with the Soviet Union on the Middle East was nevertheless part of the conventional wisdom in those days. American liberals and Europeans criticized Kissinger for his recklessness, Cold War myopia, and all-around obtuseness in trying to exclude Moscow. Yet so long as the Soviet Union delivered nothing but trouble, joint efforts with the Soviets did little but confuse the Arabs into thinking they had a protector who would shield them from the hard compromises they would have to make to recover their territory. To Kissinger, the Soviet Union was part of the problem, not part of the solution.

Over the next year, the State Department continued its labors to get a negotiation going. Anwar Sadat had succeeded Nasser in September 1970; he was almost universally expected to be only a transitional figure, and he was still consolidating his position during 1971 when Secretary Rogers attempted to interest him in the idea of an interim agreement with Israel—a partial disengagement of Israeli forces from the Suez Canal. This effort went nowhere. Sadat's intentions in those days were obscure, if not confused. He expressed a desire for peace, but his rhetoric and terms were generally as unorthodox as Nasser's. Whatever his preferences, Sadat was not yet in a strong enough position to accept anything less than a commitment to total Israeli withdrawl—especially when the Israelis mischievously insisted that any interim disengagement include a reciprocal *Egyptian* withdrawal westward from the Canal toward Cairo.

The impasse was confirming Kissinger's analysis that the Middle East was not yet ripe for a diplomatic breakthrough. Whenever the State Department pushed too hard to commit Nixon's prestige or to turn up the heat on Israel, Kissinger usually persuaded Nixon to get the department to back off. It was a calculated strategy to send a message to the Arabs that reliance on the Soviet Union was a fundamental mistake:

> Within the Arab world we needed to strengthen the moderates as against the radicals, the governments associated with the West as against the clients of the Soviet Union. I therefore opposed, as a matter of principle, any concessions to Egypt so long as Nasser (or Sadat for that matter) relied on

anti-Western rhetoric buttressed by the presence of Soviet combat troops. And I saw no point in proceeding jointly with the Soviet Union so long as Moscow's position was identical with the Arab program. Sooner or later, I was convinced, either Egypt or some other state would recognize that reliance on Soviet support and radical rhetoric guaranteed the frustration of its aspirations. At that point, it might be willing to eliminate the Soviet military presence—"expel" was the word I used in a much criticized briefing on June 26, 1970—and to consider attainable rather than utopian goals. *Then* would come the moment for a major American initiative, if necessary urging new approaches on our Israeli friends.[22]

Nixon's Moscow summit in May–June 1972 was a milestone. Sadat had been publicly and privately pushing his Soviet ally to weigh in with the United States to force a break in the deadlock. Sadat had grandly proclaimed 1971 to be the "year of decision," only to see that year pass humiliatingly without any movement. He saw the Nixon visit to Moscow as another opportunity.

By this time I had become Kissinger's principal special assistant and confidant in Middle East matters. I accompanied him to secret meetings with Mideast visitors in Washington—meetings that Nixon authorized but the State Department was not to know about—with such figures as Israeli prime minister Golda Meir, Jordan's King Hussein, and Israeli ambassador Yitzhak Rabin. Kissinger was also discussing the Middle East occasionally with Ambassador Dobrynin. In Moscow, I accompanied Nixon and Kissinger in their May 26 summit session on the Middle East with the Soviet leadership.

It was an eerie occasion, the lonely three of us Americans on one side of a long, elegant table in the spectacular St. Catherine's Hall in the Grand Kremlin Palace. On the other side, Brezhnev had brought out his full team—Prime Minister Aleksei Kosygin, President Nikolai Podgornii, Foreign Minister Gromyko, Ambassador Dobrynin, special adviser Andrei Alexandrov-Agentov, interpreter Viktor Sukhodrev, and others. We were treated to a barrage of bitter criticism of Israeli intransigence and stern warnings that the Middle East was a powder keg that called for joint action by the superpowers. Nixon coolly demurred; when pressed further, he suggested that Kissinger and Gromyko continue the discussion afterward. Two days later, Kissinger and Gromyko spent an afternoon at the Foreign Ministry at Smolensk Square negotiating both the wording of the Mideast portion of the summit communiqué and a private set of "general working principles" on which the Soviets hoped to get formal agreement. The U.S. side essentially stonewalled on both.

The communiqué language, as eventually agreed, was a set of soothing banalities about "normalization of the Middle East situation" and a "military relaxation"—the opposite of the sense of urgency that Sadat wanted. The "general working principles" on which Kissinger labored with Gromyko spoke in the most abstract terms of a comprehensive settlement, Israeli withdrawals, whatever border "rectifications" might be agreed voluntarily by the parties, and so forth.[23] The "principles" paper was the occasion for some Kissingerian deviousness at my expense. As he recounts in his memoirs, his strategy in the long meeting with Gromyko was to stretch it out so that no final agreement would be reached in Moscow on any new document:

> The most serious obstacle to my delaying tactics came from my own staff. In order to waste as much time as possible in my meeting with Gromyko, I made Gromyko repeat some of his formulations over and over again so that I could "understand them better." Peter Rodman, who was keeping the record for our side, obviously considered this an aspersion on his reliability, and kept interrupting me to hand me the precise text of Gromyko's proposal, which he had written down verbatim the first time it had been put forward. My repeated elbows in his side would not deter Peter each time we came to a new "principle" on Gromyko's list. I raised so much cain with him afterward over his excess of zeal that never again would either he or Winston Lord hand over a document to me in front of another delegation during a negotiation—even when I asked for it. . . . In later years, an occasional request by me to Lord or Rodman for a document would send them both into paroxysms of laughter, which must have left the head of state or foreign minister I was negotiating with dumbfounded at the apparent total breakdown of discipline on my supposedly browbeaten staff.[24]

When Anwar Sadat read the Moscow communiqué, it was a "violent shock," he recorded in his memoirs.[25] The Soviets kept him waiting for a month before giving him a full briefing on the summit conversations, only to confirm that nothing significant had occurred. Also in June, Saudi defense minister Prince Sultan reported to Sadat his assessment, after conversations with Nixon and Kissinger, that the United States would not press Israel for concessions as long as the Soviets were in Egypt.[26]

On July 18, 1972, the Egyptian president stepped forward with a geopolitical bombshell perhaps as significant as Nasser's nationalization of the Suez Canal sixteen years earlier: He terminated the mission of the fifteen thousand Soviet military personnel in Egypt and reclaimed all Soviet military installations and equipment set up in Egypt since 1967; the Soviet personnel were to leave within a week. Sadat's bitter disillusionment with the Soviets was one of his main reasons for the move. He wrote to Brezhnev on August 30: "The American claim that the United States, and the United States alone, is capable of finding a solution has been increasingly vindicated, even after the Moscow meeting."[27] Kissinger's message was getting through, loud and clear.

Even before the Moscow summit, Sadat had begun angling for a secret high-level channel to the White House, bypassing the State Department.[28] But no substantive communication had yet passed through that channel, and the United States had no advance warning of Sadat's dramatic lowering of the boom on the Soviets. It came as a complete surprise to Kissinger, who was departing with his staff on that very day for Paris for one of his secret sessions with Le Duc Tho. As he and I were riding in the White House car that morning to Andrews Air Force Base, I asked him about it. He was puzzled; he could not understand why Sadat would take such a step without any assurance from us that we would respond. Even though it represented the fulfillment of his San Clemente dream— to expel the Soviet military from Egypt—Kissinger found its circumstances bizarre. The master strategist had not yet met the bold, underestimated visionary who was already determined to end Egypt's conflict with Israel.

Thus, the American strategy had worked brilliantly. There was one rather large glitch of which we were not yet aware, however, to put it mildly—namely, that Sadat was also planning a war if his overture to the United States did not rapidly bear fruit. Another key reason for kicking the Soviets out was his desire to have freedom of action to prepare for a war that he assumed the Soviets (partly out of fear of the Americans) would try to hamper.[29]

The dialogue with the Americans, for which Sadat was so eager, proved disappointing. In the second half of 1972, Kissinger was consumed by the speedup of the Vietnam negotiations with Le Duc Tho and never found time for the meeting he promised to hold with Mohammed Hafiz Ismail, Sadat's national security adviser. We spent weeks at a time in Paris, or on visits to Saigon, attempting to bring the Vietnam ordeal to a conclusion. Only in late February 1973 did the first meeting with Ismail take place, at a CIA safe house at a secret location outside of New York City. At this session, and a subsequent session in Paris in May (tacked on to another negotiating session there with Le Duc Tho), the discussion proved sterile. To us, the Egyptians, while unfailingly cordial, were sadly wedded to obtaining an immediate Israeli commitment to the 1967 borders and unwilling to entertain interim or other approaches. To us, this was unrealistic. To Sadat, this impasse only demonstrated that "[i]t was impossible for the United States (or, indeed, any other power) to make a move if we ourselves didn't take military action to break the deadlock."[30] After the trauma of the October war, in one of his meetings with Kissinger, he complained: "[Y]ou didn't take me seriously—and this is the outcome."[31]

Yet even the wording of Sadat's complaints confirms that the United States was his principal audience, the superpower he wanted to engage. Despite the Egyptians' bravado during the 1973 war, they had no serious expectation of regaining any significant amount of territory by military means. (That was one reason why U.S. and Israeli intelligence, making the same analysis, assumed Egypt would not attack.) Egypt's war plan consisted essentially of a well-practiced crossing of the Suez Canal, after which its forces were to hang on for dear life.

In other words, Sadat's strategy was political, not military: It was to light a fire under the United States. It was a war fought not to win but to create an international crisis that the United States would have to respond to. It was to shake the Americans out of their comfortable smugness about the status quo and push them into the active diplomacy they had promised in 1972 but failed to deliver. Clausewitz would call it a proof of his dictum that war is the continuation of policy by other means; Freud might call it a cry for help. In its perverse way, and at great human cost, it was the mirror image of Kissinger's strategy and a vindication of it. Throughout the war, Sadat was in insistent contact with the White House through the CIA backchannel, discussing the terms of a future peace negotiation as well as the terms for ending the immediate war. The country that was airlifting arms to his enemy was still the country he wanted to play the decisive role in the region afterward.

When Kissinger and Sadat met and talked for the first time, in Cairo on November 7, 1973, it was as if to resume a conversation begun on July 18, 1972, the day Sadat announced his expulsion of the Soviets. The Jewish-American secretary of state whose career had been devoted to European issues and strategic arms control, not the Middle East, and the flamboyant revolutionary born in a poor village in the Nile Delta had already nurtured the bond of a common strategy. Egypt's reversal of alliances had opened the door to a U.S.-sponsored mediation.

In their very first meeting, Sadat told Kissinger he was ready to end the conflict with Israel.[32] Sadat's problem was that he did not know how to do it. He was essentially putting himself in our hands. Kissinger and he had long hours of intense conversation alone, leaving the staffs of both leaders to mill around and get better acquainted with one another in the garden in the autumn air. Kissinger reverted to his role as teacher, telling Sadat what he knew about Israel's hopes and fears and the need to change Israel's psychology so that the Jewish state could contemplate a retreat from occupied land. When he explained to Sadat the virtues of proceeding step by step, beginning with an interim agreement separating the two sides' forces along the canal and a limited Israeli pullback, Sadat surprised Kissinger by accepting readily.

The war had unlocked possibilities that would not have existed without it. The kind of interim accord that the United States believed offered the best chance for starting the Israelis down the path of withdrawal and that Egypt had been afraid to accept beforehand, Sadat now accepted—without any guarantee of how far it might lead. The national pride regained in the war, plus the faith he had in the United States, made it possible now, reinforced by Kissinger's explanation that it had the best chance of working. More comprehensive plans promised more, but this was something Kissinger thought he could deliver.

The war had also reinforced Arab disgust with the Soviets. Soviet arms supplies came by ship, while the Americans had launched the dramatic airlift to Israel. UN Security Council Resolution 338, which had imposed the cease-fire, had called for negotiations "under appropriate auspices," which Kissinger and Gromyko had agreed meant U.S.-Soviet auspices. But Sadat wanted only the Americans.

Sadat, of course, knew that he had now acquired a kind of moral leverage over the United States. Whereas the American strategy had been to frustrate Arabs who relied on the Soviet Union, the United States now had a large stake in demonstrating that an Arab country that had turned to us would gain something from it. We now had to show the Arabs that such a turn actually paid off. It was unnerving for the Israelis to watch the U.S.-Egyptian relationship develop, but it was the inevitable implication of the earlier strategy—once an Arab leader came to us and presented himself as an independent actor and not a Soviet pawn. The Israelis were soon enough to discover that Egypt's reversal of alliances went hand in hand with an Egyptian policy whose commitment to peace was genuine.

GROMYKO'S DINNER

The United States went through the motions of launching its diplomacy in cooperation with the Soviets, as promised to Moscow during the negotiations over the cease-fire. But the multilateral conference convened in Geneva with the Soviets and some of the Middle East parties on December 21, 1973, turned out to be only a cover for what was to follow. Sadat, as noted, wanted Kissinger to be the intermediary in an Egyptian-Israeli negotiation on a separation of forces along the Suez Canal. Direct political talks between the two sides were still anathema to the Arabs in those days. In December and January, Kissinger shuttled back and forth between Egypt and Israel as the two sides hammered out an agreement, which was signed formally by the two military chiefs of staff at Kilometer 101 in the Sinai on January 18, 1974.

The accord was technically only a military agreement on the separation of two armies that had been left dangerously intermingled on both sides of the canal at the end of the war. It reaffirmed and strengthened the cease-fire. But its political meaning was clear. Israel's forces pulled back to a line about twenty kilometers east of the canal, and its armaments were limited in another zone of about thirty kilometers. Egypt's armaments were similarly limited on its side. But it was the first step of an Israeli withdrawal from Sinai—a "first step," as the agreement stated, "toward a final, just and durable peace according to the provisions of Security Council Resolution 338. . . ."[33]

While helping negotiate this accord, Kissinger was also having his first encounters with the redoubtable President Hafiz al-Asad of Syria, whom he met for the first time in Damascus on December 15, 1973. Asad, the former air force commander who had come to power in a coup after the fiasco of Syria's invasion of Jordan in September 1970, was at the beginning of an extraordinary two decades and more of brutal dictatorial rule. The contrast with Sadat could not have been more striking. Sadat, while one of Nasser's original revolutionary cohorts, was, after all, Egyptian—cosmopolitan, resilient, supple—and he was fluent in the English he had polished in British prisons. Asad was an ascetic, suspicious, little exposed to the outside world, much more an elemental force exuding raw power. Yet, it turned out, Asad, too, wanted a disengagement accord with Israel—and he, too, wanted Henry Kissinger to negotiate it for him.

For Asad as for Sadat, it was a wrenching decision to sign an interim agreement with Israel without any guarantee of an ultimate return to the 1967 borders. That the Israeli army was camped in the outskirts of Damascus at the end of the 1973 war, however, had a certain persuasive effect: Syria badly needed a disengagement agreement that would pull the Israelis back. What is astonishing in retrospect is how Asad made Kissinger sweat over an agreement that Syria needed so badly. But the Syrian was a master of cold-blooded negotiating brinkmanship—convincing us all that he did not care that much if the negotiation broke down, thereby extracting that much more leverage over us. The same pure force of will was making Syria into a formidable factor in the Middle East. By most objective measures Syria was weak; it was not very formidable in size or resources and was a caldron of ethnic divisions kept barely under control by the ruthlessness of Asad's 'Alawite minority.[34] Egypt was the natural leader in the Arab world in terms of physical strength. But Asad (like de Gaulle) turned the power of personality, single-mindedness, and nationalist fervor into a political force.

After a few preliminary shuttles, we returned to the area at the end of April 1974 naively expecting to finish the job in a week or two; we ended up staying thirty-four days, as the negotiation turned into an excruciating test of wills and skills with a master opponent. (The Israelis, led by Golda Meir, were not exactly pushovers, either.) A Syrian-Israeli disengagement accord was finally signed on May 31 in Geneva.[35]

For the purposes of this book, there is one moment during the Syrian negotiation that stands out like a flash illuminating the position of the Soviet Union in the Middle East. Syria was, of course, Moscow's closest ally in the region. Kissinger trod warily on this terrain. He made clear that we welcomed the chance to deal directly with Syria and did not treat Syria as anybody's pawn, but at the same time he was careful not to disparage the Soviet Union or say anything that (he could only assume) would be reported back to Moscow.

What none of us yet fathomed was the depth of contempt the Syrians had for the Soviets. Asad, like Sadat, felt let down during the war; Asad, like Sadat, was more impressed by how the United States had stood by its Israeli ally and was therefore inclined to want to latch on to a good thing with us. Asad, like Sadat, was using the Soviet Union as a source of equipment but of little else, turning now to the United States as the power better able to deliver diplomatic progress. The geopolitical opening for the United States in the Arab world was becoming something even greater than we had imagined. As long as Israel offered us some flexibility—always a big "if"—we were in a position to parlay it into a pivotal role of influence and to magnify the split between Moscow and its erstwhile clients.

Midway through the Syrian negotiation in May 1974, Soviet foreign minister Gromyko started angling for a visit of his own to Damascus to create the impression of a Soviet role in the great endeavor. Kissinger told Asad that it was a Syrian decision whether or when to receive the Soviet dignitary: "One, I will not see Gromyko in Damascus; two, I will not come to Damascus if Gromyko is in Damascus; three, except for that, you are a sovereign country and I will not tell you what to do so long as my other two points are understood. What you do with Gromyko is up to you."[36]

Asad decided to put Gromyko off until the negotiation was finished. But as the negotiation dragged on, seemingly interminably, even he began to feel the heat. He told Kissinger somewhat apologetically that he had agreed to let Gromyko come on May 27, thinking (as we all did) that our business would be over by then. Then new complications and haggles arose; Gromyko's visit was rescheduled for May 28, and he flew into Damascus that afternoon. From Jerusalem that same afternoon, however, Kissinger cabled Asad that he needed to see him yet one more time. In the early evening of May 28, Kissinger and Asad met again in Asad's office and ironed out some of the remaining points.

As the American team (Kissinger, Sisco, me, and our interpreter, Isa Sabbagh) politely prepared to leave, knowing that Gromyko was waiting to see Asad, Asad insisted we stay for dinner. He brought his inner circle together—Foreign Minister Abdul Khalim al-Khaddam, Defense Minister Mustafa Tlas, Army Chief of Intelligence Hikmat al-Shihabi, Air Force Chief Najd Jamil. It was a jovial dinner, with Tlas reciting nonsense poetry for children that he wrote as a hobby and the top leadership of the Syrian police state cracking jokes and treating us as their bosom buddies. It was an intimacy I cannot believe was vouchsafed to many outsiders. Kissinger, who had arranged to pay a courtesy call on Gromyko before leaving (violating another of his earlier "points"), protested to Asad that Gromyko was waiting for him. "It is all right," Asad replied coolly; "you are eating his dinner." As a gesture to the Americans with whom he had shared a grueling month, he had served us the dinner meant for Gromyko. Kissinger paid his brief courtesy call on Gromyko at the latter's guest house, at midnight, on our way to the airport.[37]

America's position in the Middle East had, in the twenty-odd years since Suez, been rebuilt. There were many paradoxes. The closeness of our relationship with Israel—indeed, our indispensability as Israel's economic and military backer—turned out to be crucial leverage in support of our position in the Arab world, not the insurmountable obstacle to America's Arab relations, as some had long feared. It made the Arabs come to us. The period of Leonid Brezhnev's ascendancy and the frenetic military buildup and global geopolitical boldness he represented was also the period of a humiliating Soviet setback in the Arab world—the undoing of Suez and the drift of even some radical Arabs toward Washington. In the period of the much-mocked U.S.-Soviet "détente," Egypt had been detached from the Soviet camp, and Syria wooed, in a geopolitical coup almost as significant as China's new alignment with the West just before.

The only disappointment was our European allies, who—their backs broken at Suez—had hewed thereafter to a weak policy in the Middle East. After 1967, like de Gaulle, they treated Israel as the guilty party and cultivated their ties with the Arabs. The energy crisis of 1973, which many of them blamed on America's support of Israel (though the price hike had other causes), led them to distance themselves further from American Middle East policy.[38] Even the success of the U.S. mediation did not totally mollify them; it confused them.

For Europe's Middle East policy was not so much based on an analysis of the issues as it was a function of Europe's vulnerability to Arab oil, and terrorist blackmail. It was not a policy but a psychological condition. Where we sought to mediate between Arabs and Israelis, the Europeans reflexively positioned themselves somewhere between us and the Arabs (just as the nonaligned usually positioned themselves between us and the Soviets). Over the years, for example, Europeans ostentatiously embraced the PLO long before the PLO had accepted any of the basic premises of the peace process (Resolutions 242 and 338) or renounced terrorism. At a meeting in Venice in 1980 the European Community called for a PLO role and Palestinian "self-determination," a code word for an independent PLO-run state. Even the pope received Yasir Arafat. This was not helpful during the long period when U.S. strategy toward the PLO was the same as it had been toward Egypt—to make clear that it would get no consideration at all from us so long as it was wedded to radical policies and Soviet backing.

The pivotal position of the United States nevertheless survived. When Sadat formally reopened the Suez Canal in June 1975 (it had been blocked since the 1967 war), he insisted that a U.S. aircraft carrier lead the first ceremonial convoy of ships through the waterway. He relished rubbing the Soviets' noses in it. Gradually, the United States replaced the Soviet Union as Egypt's main military supplier. On September 1, 1975, a second Egyptian-Israeli agreement was reached through Kissinger's shuttle mediation. This brought about a more significant Israeli withdrawal in the Sinai, coupled with more elaborate security provisions, including U.S. manning of monitoring stations; the second Sinai accord also included unprecedented political commitments by both sides, such as a pledge not to go to war, a commitment to continue to negotiate toward a final peace, and even permission for Israeli civilian cargoes to use the Suez Canal. It was the foundation for Camp David.

The U.S. position in the region survived even the Carter administration's blunder of October 1, 1977, when Cyrus Vance and Gromyko announced an initiative calling for a comprehensive settlement, resumption of the Geneva conference, and renewed "joint efforts" by the two superpowers. For Anwar Sadat, this was another shock. He had risked assassination by pro-Soviet elements in Egypt in 1971 as well as his whole foreign policy in kicking the Soviets out in 1972; his eagerness to bring the Soviets back into the region was not overwhelming, no matter how logical it seemed to a Democratic administration far away in Washington. And he was profoundly wary of a "comprehensive" negotiation that would give the Syrians a veto.

Sadat later told Kissinger of his dismay. The Vance-Gromyko communiqué was one of the reasons for Sadat's next daring leap into the unknown—his heroic visit to Jerusalem in November 1977 for the first face-to-face contact ever between Egyptian and Israeli leaders.* Part of Sadat's motive was to break the psychological impasse, the stranglehold of fear and suspicion that he understood (partly as a result of Kissinger's tutoring) gripped the Israelis. But another motive was to grab the ball back from the crazy Americans and restore the diplomacy to the bilateral Israeli-Egyptian context in which it had rested before. Once the Carter administration recovered from *its* shock at this move, Egypt and Israel joined in a request to the United States to resume its valued role as sole mediator. President Carter performed admirably in the arduous three-way Camp David negotiations of September 5–17, 1978, which produced the outline of a peace treaty, a total Israeli withdrawal from Egyptian territory, and the framework for a transitional period of autonomy for the Palestinians in the West Bank and Gaza. Sadat's historic gamble at the beginning of the decade had started the region on the path to peace.

THE GORBACHEV REVOLUTION IN MIDEAST POLICY

To Brezhnev's successors, it was obvious that his policy in the Middle East was a failure, as much so as his adventures in the Reagan Doctrine

---

*Carter administration policymakers, such as William Quandt, dispute that this was Sadat's motive, pointing out that Sadat had played along with the U.S. diplomacy for some months. Quandt's own account, however, suggests that Sadat had assumed that the United States had a well-conceived strategy to use the Soviets to rope in the Syrians. When Sadat saw that the strategy was empty, he bolted.[39]

cases and here in a much more strategic region of the world. Thus, "new thinking" came to be applied to Soviet Middle East policy in the 1980s. The Soviets diversified their relations in the region beyond their traditional radical clients; they seemed less resentful and obstructionist toward U.S. diplomatic endeavors. Nevertheless, a competitive element remained in Soviet policy as well as a natural solicitude for a region that was (as they always reminded us) close to their own borders. These contradictory impulses were evident most of all in the 1990–91 Gulf crisis and will likely be a permanent feature of Russian policy over the long term.

The Soviets learned something from failure, but they learned it the hard way. They had attempted to blackmail recalcitrant clients by withholding new weapons; this failed to restore their influence. They tried this tactic with Egypt after the 1972 explusion but ended up resuming arms sales to Egypt after less than a year, without any change in Egypt's policy. They suspended arms deliveries to Damascus similarly in 1976 after Asad started brutalizing Moscow's other client, the PLO, in Lebanon. It had no effect on Asad, and the Soviets resumed the arms flow lest they lose all influence in Damascus.[40] The Arabs were their own masters, rediscovering their freedom of action—associating more with the United States when we had something to offer, all the while using the Soviets as a convenient warehouse for weapons.

After Camp David, the Soviets thought once again that they had an opening. Egypt was shunned as a pariah in the Arab world after its peace treaty with Israel, and a new "rejectionist front" of diehards like Syria, Iraq, Libya, and others was forming. All were clients of the Soviet Union, to one degree or another, and Moscow joined the chorus of those denouncing Sadat's treacherous "separate deal" and its American sponsors. "Accords of treason" was the way Gromyko described Camp David in a 1979 meeting with Arafat—an "imperialist-Israeli-Sadat conspiracy"— and he egged on the Arabs to unify against Sadat.[41]

After Camp David, moreover, the U.S.-run peace process bogged down. With a less flexible Likud government in Israel and with the PLO still insisting on a Palestinian state, negotiations over the Palestinian issue went nowhere. The United States sought in vain to construct what Secretary of State Alexander Haig called a "strategic consensus" among likeminded friends, including Israel and the moderate Arabs. But such overt acknowledgment of common interests was not yet possible for the Arabs in the face of radical pressures. (Many years later, after the Gulf War and collapse of the Soviets, it was conceivable.)

The Soviets attempted to exploit the diplomatic impasse by a strategy aimed at securing a role for themselves in any negotiations. Their chosen vehicle was the idea of an international conference on the Middle East, in form a revival of the Geneva conference that had met once after the October war. The United States and the Soviet Union were to be co-chairmen again (although in later variants the five permanent members of the UN Security Council were to be the sponsors). All the key Arab parties were to be brought together into this conference, including Syria (which had boycotted the 1973 meeting) and, most problematically, the PLO, as "sole legitimate representative of the Palestinian people." A detailed Soviet proposal was put forward in July 1984,[42] and the Soviets persuaded the United States to join in preliminary bilateral talks. The Soviets lobbied hard in the Arab world for such a conference and even began hinting to Israel that diplomatic relations would be restored if such a conference were convened. The ubiquitous Yulii Vorontsov, then Soviet ambassador in Paris, made this pitch to his Israeli counterpart in a private meeting in July 1985.[43]

I considered such an international conference a terrible idea and spent much of my time in government persuading my superiors that it was.

For one thing, only the United States had the moral influence or the tactical sensitivity to move the Israelis. The Camp David approach, focusing an initial negotiation on a transitional phase of autonomy for the Palestinians, was the only approach with a chance of working, especially as long as the Likud was in office. The Soviets, the Syrians, and the PLO all rejected this procedure, which meant that enhancing their influence in the process promised no progress for anyone. As long as the Soviets resisted realistic positions and refused to spend political capital with their clients for significant compromise, we had every incentive to continue to block a Soviet role in the diplomacy. Indeed, it was essential.

The Syrians were the other principal champion of an international conference, and, like the Soviets, they did so for reasons that conflicted with our view of the best interests of the peace process. Syria insisted on a conference partly to humor its Soviet patron and partly to ensure that its own interests were not ignored—another way of saying that it would use it to block any moderate Arab who sought to emulate Sadat and sign a "separate deal" or "partial solution" with Israel. This was the deliberate negation of the step-by-step approach that the United States had determined was the only one that had a chance of working.

A cliché of the period among many experts on the Middle East was that the diplomacy had to be "comprehensive," that is, embracing all fronts—the Sinai, the Golan Heights, the West Bank and Gaza, and

Jerusalem.[44] The storm in the Arab world that followed the Egyptian-Israeli treaty was thought to confirm the unwisdom of step-by-step diplomacy. An international conference would be the ultimate embodiment of a "comprehensive" negotiation, bringing all the various parties and issues together in one forum.

The flaw in this proposition was that it was based on a misunderstanding of how Arab-Israeli negotiations actually worked. No one could doubt that the ultimate *outcome* of the Middle East peace process had to be comprehensive, in the sense of resolving all the outstanding issues. But the negotiating *procedure* need not, and could not, embrace all issues at once. Contemplating major concessions on several fronts simultaneously would be more than the Israeli political system could handle. A multilateral forum would maximize Syria's ability to block other Arabs from seeking compromise with Israel. It would mean holding up the attainable while waiting for the unattainable. The only successful negotiations—Kissinger's three shuttle accords, Camp David, and later the Oslo Israeli-PLO accord—were conducted separately. The Geneva conference of 1973, which was for many years the only model of an international conference, did no harm—but only because, as we have seen, its results were precooked: Egypt, Syria, and Israel had already agreed that they wanted the follow-up to be American-sponsored negotiations on disengagement.

After the Gulf War, the multilateral conference at Madrid in October 1991 proved equally harmless—indeed, highly successful—because the defeat of Iraq and the collapse of Soviet power had weakened Syria, the PLO, and other radicals. I was concerned about a conference even then,[45] but the Bush administration's gamble was vindicated: Madrid was the ceremonial occasion for the launching of historic face-to-face talks among the parties, including Palestinian-Israeli negotiations based on the phased approach that the Palestinians had finally agreed to.

Between 1984 and 1991, however, these conditions simply did not exist. The parties were so far apart that bringing them all together would compound the impasse, not resolve it. I continue to believe it was correct for the United States to resist the Soviet importuning for a conference. If anything, we were too solicitous of Soviet feelings and too shy about rejecting the idea outright. Instead of discrediting it as a fraud on the Palestinians (since it had no chance of producing a result), Secretary of State Shultz chose to allow various discussions on the subject to go forward. An able U.S. diplomat, Wat Cluverius, was assigned to shuttle between Jerusalem and Amman and around the region in 1986 to encourage the sides to agree on basic ground rules for a conference so that any later conference might be rendered less harmful.* Shultz let these talks proceed essentially because we had no other productive subject matter at that time with which to fuel Mideast diplomacy.

Unfortunately, we paid a price for not telling the truth as to what we really thought. In April 1987, at a secret meeting in London, after months of negotiation, Israeli foreign minister Shimon Peres and Jordan's King Hussein reached agreement on a set of ground rules for a conference.[46] Imagine their chagrin when they discovered from Shultz's unenthusiastic reaction that the United States really did not want a conference at all.[47]

The Soviets were not particularly helpful in this period in any case. There had been a burst of hope in 1984–85, when Shimon Peres had been prime minister (under the system of "rotation" after Israel's dead-locked 1984 election). The PLO was still weakened by the Israeli assault on it in Lebanon in 1981–82. Hussein and Arafat reached an important accord in Amman on February 11, 1985, that, in effect, refurbished Hussein's credentials to negotiate for the Palestinians.[48] The willingness of the PLO to take a background role and let Hussein come forward was a breakthrough for the U.S. strategy. The U.S. government had always been convinced that the moderate, pro-Western King Hussein had a far better chance of obtaining concessions from Israel than the radical, pro-Soviet PLO. Unfortunately, the Soviets did their best to sabotage the Amman accord. Their propaganda denounced it as a betrayal of the PLO's sanctified role as "sole legitimate representative of the Palestinian people"—doing all they could, together with the Syrians, to undercut Arafat after this undesirable display of moderation on his part. For this reason, among others, Arafat backed out of the Amman accord in April 1986. While Hussein continued to negotiate with the United States and Israel over the ground rules for an international conference, the shine had gone off Hussein's credentials to negotiate, and the Soviets had once again proved their unsuitability as a partner in the diplomacy.

Gorbachev's Middle East policy thus displayed certain contradictions, to put it politely. On the positive side was the conciliatory posture toward Israel: Soviet Jewish emigration opened up again; conspicuous diplomatic contacts multiplied (though I, ever the skeptic, tended to see these as an easy substitute for the full diplomatic relations that Israel wanted rather than necessarily a precursor).

---

*These ground rules included, for example, that the conference would not impose any settlement but only facilitate direct talks; that the conference could not reconvene without all parties' consent; that new participants—read: the PLO—could not be invited without all parties' consent.

Gorbachev also expanded contacts with the Arab moderates. The So-viets returned an ambassador to Cairo in 1985 after years of trying to ostracize Egypt after Camp David; they agreed to reschedule Egypt's military debts, believed to total around $3 billion, to be repaid now over a lengthy twenty-five-year period.[49] Moscow improved its relations also with Jordan and with traditional Western clients on the Gulf (Oman, the United Arab Emirates, Bahrain, Kuwait). Even Saudi Arabia was wooed. This was a harder case. I had been in meetings between Kissinger and King Faisal a decade earlier in which the monarch had explained the Saudi view of the Jewish-Communist conspiracy: This sinister cabal of Zionists and Bolsheviks had inflicted Israel on the Middle East and was now advancing Jews into high positions in the U.S. government.[50] I have rarely seen Henry Kissinger at a loss for words, but this was one such occasion.

Gorbachev was also willing to spend some political capital with Syria. In April 1987, in a Moscow banquet speech honoring Asad, Gorbachev spoke pointedly of the need to deal with Israel. The absence of Soviet relations with Israel, Gorbachev announced, "cannot be considered nor-mal," and he advised the Syrian that "the dependence on military power in settling the conflict has come to be completely discredited."[51] Thus did he make clear his noncooperation with Asad's long-standing goal of achieving "strategic parity" with Israel with Soviet weaponry. The Soviets continued to sell Syria advanced equipment, but it fell short of Syria's demands both quantitatively and qualitatively.

The Soviets also seemed, at least in private conversations, to show more understanding of American theories about the negotiation. Dennis Ross, an NSC staffer in the later years of the Reagan administration and then a central figure in the Bush and Clinton Middle East policy, often told me how struck he was by the younger generation of Soviet diplomats, who were far less dogmatic than their seniors. Dennis developed a strong friendship with Aleksandr Zotov, then a mid-level diplomat in Wash-ington and later Soviet ambassador to Syria. Zotov seemed to share not only Dennis's interest in Washington Bullets basketball but also an ap-preciation of why the United States favored the step-by-step procedure and the notion of a transitional phase of self-government for the Palestinians.

But the contrary trends in Soviet policy were inescapably evident. In 1985–86, as noted, the Soviets helped force the abrogation of the Amman accord between Hussein and Arafat. In April 1986, as we saw earlier, Gorbachev refused to distance himself from Libya when the United States clashed with Qaddafi. Active Soviet involvement in terrorism also seems to have continued long into the era of "new thinking."[52] Gorbachev's public rebuff of Asad's dream of "strategic parity" was striking, but it only made explicit what had long been implicit in Soviet policy. As I have argued earlier, the Soviets never relished the idea of a new outbreak of war, which they usually figured their clients would lose.

The real issue for us was how much the Soviets would exert themselves to promote a realistic peace negotiation, and here, too, Gorbachev's record was not impressive. In April 1987, when the PLO broke off relations with Egypt, the Soviets defended the PLO. In early 1988, the Soviets promoted a reconciliation between the PLO and Syria, which could only come at the expense of Jordan or at the cost of a hardening of the Arab negotiating position. Even the titillating dialogue in Paris between Yulii Vorontsov and the Israeli ambassador in July 1985 was interesting to me less for the contact than for the content: Vorontsov reportedly expressed a keen desire for better relations, but he kept stressing that Moscow had important commitments to Damascus and that any negotiating process would have to have something in it for Syria.[53] The Syrians seemed to have more influence over Soviet policy than the other way around. The growing weakness of Soviet power in the world only compounded the problem. On a later visit to Moscow, Asad was quoted as lamenting "the attempts by certain circles in the West to use the fact that the Soviet Union is occupied with its own internal affairs to strengthen pressure on progressive forces and on the Arab world."[54] There is no indication that Gorbachev disagreed.

In December 1988, the PLO for the first time accepted UN Security Council Resolutions 242 and 338 and the existence of Israel and renounced terrorism. This laid the basis for the first official political talks between the United States and the PLO.[55] Washington hoped the dialogue would help move the PLO to support the negotiating procedures we thought the most productive. By the end of 1989, however, the Bush administration found to its frustration that the Soviets were encouraging the PLO to stiffen its position—to insist on an immediate PLO role in the Palestinian-Israeli dialogue as well as on a Soviet role in the process. Secretary of State Baker had labored for months to secure Israeli agreement to meet with a Palestinian delegation whose composition would have been shaped only indirectly by the PLO through Egyptian mediation. He and Ross thought they had Soviet support for the approach. After all this, Shevardnadze suddenly sent Baker a letter insisting that the Soviet Union be made a "co-convenor" of the Israeli-Palestinian talks, and a week later he reportedly sent a message to Arafat warning him against Israeli insincerity and any efforts to exclude the PLO from direct participation. The Americans were not amused. [56]

The PLO's acceptance of Resolutions 242 and 338 had thus presented the Soviets with their classic dilemma. They had been telling us for years that they wanted Arafat to take this crucial step and accept the basic premises of the peace process. Probably they had been telling us the truth; it was, after all, in their interest for their Palestinian clients to advance their status in the diplomacy by meeting that essential precondition. Yet, once it happened, the first result was to satisfy Washington's long-standing conditions for a U.S.-PLO dialogue—raising the specter that Arafat, too, would be seduced into a U.S.-dominated peace process, just like Sadat and Asad.

The only diplomacy with any serious potential continued to be ours— this, despite all our frustrating years of failure after the success of Camp David. No one else had any better chance of delivering the Israelis to the negotiating table. The Soviets' wooing of Israel was too timid; they still held back from full diplomatic relations for fear of alienating Arab clients. The Soviet position was rendered impotent by its many contradictions. Soon enough, the PLO "solved" the Soviets' problem, in a way: Renewed terrorist attacks on Israelis in 1989, which the PLO could not bring itself to disavow, scuttled the U.S.-PLO dialogue, leaving the PLO outside the process once again for four more years.

There the PLO remained when the Gulf crisis began, an episode that demonstrated as clearly as any other the schizophrenia and paralysis of Soviet policy in the Middle East.

THE SOVIETS AND THE GULF CRISIS

Before there was any Arab-Israeli peace process, both the Soviet Union and the United States had been more preoccupied with the Persian Gulf.

For imperial Russia, expansion southward is what impelled it into the competition with the British—known as the "Great Game"—over Southwest Asia and the routes to India. When the Ottoman Empire disintegrated after World War I, the British moved quickly to expand their sphere of influence into the Arab world, elbowing out the French and keeping the Russians—now the Soviet Russians—at bay. [57]

In November 1940, in discussions between Molotov and Ribbentrop after the Nazi-Soviet pact, the Germans proposed to recognize a Soviet sphere of influence in the regions "south of the territory of the Soviet Union in the direction of the Indian Ocean." By this proposal they were hoping to deflect Soviet attentions away from the Balkans. Stalin and Molotov, wary of Hitler's intent, came back a few weeks later with an amendment—a stipulation of "the focal point of the aspirations of the Soviet Union south of Batum and Baku in the general direction of the Persian Gulf." The talks went nowhere, given the mutual suspicions, but the temptation to carve up the spoils of a defeated British Empire was there on both sides.[58] Stalin took a run at it in 1946 with his brief occupation of northern Iran, until driven to withdraw by intense U.S. and British diplomatic pressure.

The postwar Middle East preoccupation of the United States was to establish its own presence in the Gulf region—at the expense of the British. The Soviets looked on with a kind of detached amusement: "Although she succeeded in recovering her colonies after the war," observed Andrei Zhdanov in September 1947, "Britain found herself faced there with the enhanced influence of American imperialism, which during the war had invaded all the regions that before the war had been regarded as exclusive spheres of influence of British capital (the Arab East, Southeast Asia)."[59] Much of the Anglo-American competition in the 1950s focused on the oil-rich Arabian Peninsula and Iran. The Americans won the competition.[60]

When the British withdrew from their last protectorate relationships in the Gulf in 1971, it fell to the United States to design a new concept for Gulf security. In 1970, at the NSC, I worked on a policy study that came to the conclusion that in the era of Vietnam a new American military commitment in the Gulf was politically impossible. Therefore, Nixon decided on a policy of promoting a regional condominium of our allies Iran and Saudi Arabia.

Despite the presumed historical and geopolitical importance of the Gulf to the Soviet Union, the Soviet position in this part of the Mideast, too, remained surprisingly weak through the entire postwar period. The oil-rich regimes—the shah's in Iran and the Gulf monarchies—were as ideologically conservative as could be ("feudal" would be a more accurate label in many cases), and they eagerly sought American protection against precisely the kind of danger that the Soviet Union and its radical allies represented. That is why it took four decades for Moscow to achieve any significant political access in the Arab Gulf (except Iraq) and why the shah remained a steadfast ally of the West despite the wary economic dealings that, as an immediate neighbor, he could not escape having with the Soviets.

The Iranian Revolution in 1978–79 therefore seemed at first glance a geopolitical windfall for the Soviets. The U.S. strategy for Gulf security was a wreck; a more anti-American regime in Tehran could not have been imagined. Unfortunately for Moscow, the theocracy of the ayatollahs was rabidly anti-Communist as well. It represented an atavistic rebellion against all forms of European, secular, and modernizing tendencies of contemporary life—in which it included atheistic Marxism. This ideological paranoia was coupled with a traditional nationalistic suspicion of the powerful neighbor to the north. The Soviets would soon come to fear the contagion of Islamic radicalism in their own Muslim republics of Central Asia. Thus, Brezhnev's tortured analysis in his February 23, 1981, report to the Twenty-sixth Party Congress:

> The revolution in Iran, which was a major event on the international scene in recent years, is of a specific nature. However complex and contradictory, it is essentially an anti-imperialist revolution, though reaction at home and abroad is seeking to change this feature. . . . The banner of Islam may lead into struggle for liberation. This is borne out by history, including very recent history. But it also shows that reaction, too, manipulates with Islamic slogans to incite counterrevolutionary mutinies. Consequently, the whole thing hinges on the actual content of any movement.[61]

In 1983, Iran expelled eighteen Soviet diplomats on charges of espionage and shut down the Tudeh (Communist) party, arresting hundreds of its members. Tudeh leaders were paraded on television confessing their crimes and the crimes of their Soviet masters.[62]

Yet the ayatollahs, like the shah, had their wary economic and diplomatic dealings with the Soviets. In January 1985, Iran agreed to resuscitate a Soviet-Iranian joint economic commission, and trade featured prominently in a deputy foreign minister's talks in Moscow in April. These developments helped trigger the Reagan administration's overeager overtures to Iran. Graham Fuller, then CIA national intelligence officer for the Near East and South Asia, wrote a memorandum to his boss, William Casey, on May 17, 1985, entitled "Toward a Policy on Iran." Fuller warned of "Soviet progress toward developing significant leverage in Tehran" and recommended that the United States try to restore some contacts with Iran (and, *inter alia*, consider allowing allies to sell Iran some weapons).[63]

Casey circulated Fuller's memo around the government, including to Shultz, while I was Shultz's director of policy planning. (Fuller had already sent me a copy.) Shultz asked my opinion. I responded with a critique of Fuller's analysis. In the Iran-Iraq war, which had been raging already for five and a half years, Iran seemed on the verge of winning. As I have discussed, I strongly supported the avowed U.S. policy of tilting *against* Iran and blocking its access to arms. To abandon this policy seemed to me a strategic blunder at that time, and I did not see the Iranian flirtation with the Soviets as amounting to anything deep or lasting. By February 1986, the intelligence community as a whole had adopted a less worried view of the Soviet-Iranian connection.[64]

Fuller was one of the CIA's most brilliant analysts, and he did not deserve the congressional pillorying he later suffered after the White House's secret Iran caper surfaced. He bore no responsibility for the misdeeds of the policymakers. Fuller was, in fact, one of those rare intelligence analysts who combined (a) a searching mind, (b) the courage to state his conclusions even when they were not popular in the rest of the government, and (c) an uncanny knack for being right much of the time. I had lunched with him regularly during Shultz's Lebanon diplomacy of 1983, and he regularly annoyed me with his calm predictions that the Syrians would never go along with it. He was, of course, right. Later in the 1980s he was one of the first in the government to focus on the Kurdish question and its ramifications for Turkey, Syria, Iraq, and the entire region. On Iran in 1985 I disagreed with him, and occasionally on other issues, but I always considered him a wise observer as well as a friend.

Fuller's early alarms about the Soviets in Iran were not borne out because the Iran-Iraq war was only exposing yet again the contradictions in Soviet policy. The Soviets were trying to ride two horses. Iraq was a major arms customer and signatory of a 1972 Friendship Treaty with Moscow; it was, moreover, backed fervently by all the Arabs in its war with the hated Persians. Thus, to antagonize Iraq would involve a heavy political price. At the same time, Iran seemed the much greater strategic prize because of its size, wealth, population, and potential dominance of the Gulf. The Soviets tried to remain in the good graces of both.

Toward the end of the Iran-Iraq war, in 1987, Kuwait turned to both the Soviet Union and the United States for help in protecting its shipping from Iranian attacks. (Kuwait was then Iraq's main lifeline to the outside world.) The Soviets moved first to offer such protection, which prompted the United States to preempt with its own offer to reflag Kuwaiti ships as U.S. vessels and convoy them in the Gulf. The Kuwaitis later showed their appreciation to the Soviets by extending Moscow a $300 million credit.[65] Nevertheless, for many months in 1988, as Iran defied UN cease-fire resolutions, the Soviets stalled any UN sanctions against Iran, even while assuring everyone of their desire for an end to the war. They lost significant goodwill among the Arabs for this duplicity while winning little with Iran.

The Americans this time had the easier task, having no serious hope of an intimate relationship with either Iran or Iraq (though, Lord knows, there were many illusions in both directions in our government). Henry Kissinger, then a pundit out of office, joked in news interviews that our aim should be to arrange it that both sides lost the war.

The second Gulf war—the U.S.-led coalition's war to liberate Kuwait from Iraqi occupation in 1991—was a supreme test of Mikhail Gorbachev's commitment to "new thinking" and to a new relationship with the West. Gorbachev passed the test, though not with the highest honors.

The Bush administration's diplomacy was built on the foundation of twenty-two UN Security Council resolutions that sought to undo Iraq's invasion of Kuwait and provided the indispensable political basis for the unity of the coalition. Congressional support at home might not have been forthcoming without the impressive international support that Bush and Baker had rallied. These UN resolutions would literally not have been possible without Soviet agreement or acceptance, given the Soviet veto power in the Security Council. Soviet acquiescence in the ensuing war meant Soviet acquiescence in a dramatic display of American military prowess and political ascendancy in the Middle East. At the same time, a mischievous undercurrent in Soviet diplomacy came close to derailing the U.S. strategy at important stages of the crisis.

When the crisis began, it was at the peak of the era of "new thinking" in Soviet foreign policy. In 1989, the Eastern European empire had dissolved without Soviet resistance. The first half of 1990 was consumed by the delicate negotiation whereby Moscow was induced to accept the unification of Germany within the Atlantic Alliance and the NATO military structure. Saddam Hussein's August 2 invasion of Kuwait found James Baker at one of his regular friendly meetings with Eduard Shevardnadze, this time in the Siberian city of Irkutsk on Lake Baikal, where the two men had gone fishing. Before the day was out they had approved a UN Security Council resolution (Resolution 660), which condemned Iraq's invasion and demanded its immediate and unconditional withdrawal. A day later, in Moscow, they issued a forthright joint statement not only condemning the invasion but calling for an international embargo on the transfer of arms to Iraq. Coming from Iraq's longtime patron and major arms supplier, this was a noteworthy event. By August 6, this U.S.-Soviet commitment was codified in UN Security Council Resolution 661, embargoing *all* exports and imports to and from Iraq or occupied Kuwait.

It soon became evident, however, that these cooperative steps were coming at the cost of excruciating pain inside the Soviet leadership.[66] The initial U.S.-Soviet statement of August 3 survived only after a harrowing all-night battle between Shevardnadze and a group of hard-line colleagues on Gorbachev's Presidential Council—especially Defense Minister Dmitrii Yazov, Prime Minister Valentin Pavlov, and KGB Director Vladimir Kryuchkov. They argued that the Soviet Union would risk its position in the Middle East if it backed an American campaign against Iraq. Iraq was a key client, signatory of a Friendship Treaty, and (not to be sneezed at) the purchaser of $17.5 billion in Soviet arms since 1986.[67]

As Graham Fuller observed later, the Gulf War "compelled the Soviet Union to wrestle more publicly than ever before with questions of genuine Soviet national interests in the Third World. The blunt fact is that, ever since the collapse of its ideology, the Soviet Union has been in a state of confusion about what constitutes its national interests."[68]

The proponents of cooperation with the United States were the more reformist elements in the leadership, personified and led by Shevardnadze. They included his younger associates in the Foreign Ministry, iconoclasts in the media, academia, and the Parliament, and all those in the Soviet system who felt the country's future lay with the West and with the repudiation of the regime's past associations with radicals and rogues in the Third World and elsewhere. They were the "Westernizers," the democrats, the economic and political reformers. Shevardnadze, in his address to the UN General Assembly on September 25, 1990—in which he denounced Saddam's invasion as "an act of terrorism . . . against the emerging new world order"—quoted Immanuel Kant on the rule of law and invoked universal principles of human rights and democracy.[69] Kant, a quintessential bourgeois liberal once denounced by Communists as hopelessly inferior to Hegel, was now in vogue in Moscow. A commentator on Moscow Radio expressed shame at the Soviet Union's earlier backing of Saddam:

[T]his situation now has revealed the absurdity and unnaturalness of our frequent, so-called aid, especially military aid to Third World countries. This paternalism of ours, this feeding by us of frequently odious dictatorial regimes, which call themselves anti-imperialist and progressive, and on this basis alone we send weapons, money, food, anything there. . . . More than once I have seen how this is done in deeds, how weapons are thrown about, in whose hands they end up—it is a terrible picture from every point of view. It is not just a matter of huge profits, because Angola, Ethiopia, Mozambique, Cuba, Cambodia, Vietnam and many other countries will never return even a small part of the expenditures on weaponry which we had supplied them with.[70]

Against these reformers were arrayed powerful traditional forces of the Soviet system. The military and the KGB, as noted, argued for holding on to Moscow's traditional client relationships with the radical Arabs, not sacrificing these valuable geopolitical assets for the illusory benefits of American goodwill or international law. They were joined, if not egged on by, the so-called "Arabists" in the Foreign Ministry and academic institutes. As Fuller has written, "For many it was not so much a matter of ideology, but of a deeply ingrained foreign policy orientation toward the Third World, now dramatically abandoned for uncertain benefits."[71]

The Soviet military were reluctant to abandon or withdraw the thousand or more Soviet military advisers working with the Iraqi army. They also feared that the rapid buildup of U.S. troops foreshadowed a permanent U.S. military presence of enormous scale in a region not far from Soviet borders. The analysis of Gen. Vladimir Lobov, the Warsaw Pact commander, was that the United States might be using the crisis to extend the reach of NATO along the Soviet Union's southern flank, establishing a bridgehead from which to control Middle East oil flows and put pressure on Moscow.[72]

Clearly something deeper was going on than just a debate over Middle East policy. At home, Gorbachev was poised on a knife edge. The heady self-confidence of *perestroika* had given way to a bitter and enervating political struggle.[73] The forces of nationalism and pluralism, once unleashed, could not be reined in. The Baltic states were openly rebellious. Pressures mounted on Gorbachev to crack down; the party elite was panicking at the erosion of central authority. The political openness that had been his historic innovation now benefited his opponents. Hard-line critic Viktor Alksnis contemptuously compared him with "a person who has missed the train and is dashing around the empty platform."[74] The unintended consequences of Gorbachev's reforms were coming home to roost—the chaos in the economy, the collapse of Soviet positions abroad.

The humiliation, most of all, in Eastern Europe was giving rise to a delayed backlash—not in Eastern Europe, where any attempt to reclaim the Soviet position was clearly futile, but on the lesser issue of the Gulf on which Shevardnadze's personal responsibility for the new stance left him particularly vulnerable. (Similarly, in the United States in the 1970s, the humiliation in Indochina led to a backlash that vented its force on other issues like U.S.-Soviet relations.) Playing the pliant partner to the United States in the Gulf was said to make a mockery of the Soviet Union's status as a superpower.

As war loomed in the Gulf, moreover, there was increasing uneasiness in the Soviet Union that the country's Muslim population, already feared to be susceptible to Islamic influence, would explode if the Soviet Union colluded with the West against a Muslim country. It was not a frivolous concern: Emerging nationalist and religious leaders in the previously supine Muslim republics were agitating against U.S. policy.[75] Thus, the eagerness to avoid a war in the Gulf reflected a perceptible Russian national interest and was not the exclusive concern of Communist diehards.

As a final irony, there were pressures on the government from the new Parliament to make no decisions on war and peace without consulting with the legislators. In October, there was a brief panic in the country that the Kremlin might even send troops to the Middle East to fight alongside the Americans. Yen Kim, a member of the Supreme Soviet International Affairs Committee, protested: "On what ground does Eduard Shevardnadze tell the [UN] Security Council . . . that if the UN decides to dispatch troops to the Persian Gulf region the Soviet Union will also take part in that action? Sending troops abroad is the right of the Supreme Soviet, but no one has consulted us."[76] The promises of more democratic decision making that had been one of the noblest post-Afghanistan reforms were now coming back to haunt those who had made the promises. A majority of the Soviet people were reported to be opposed to military involvement, and opponents of the government shamelessly invoked the "Afghanistan syndrome."[77]

If Shevardnadze was the embodiment of the line of cooperation with the West, the embodiment of the line that drove Washington to distraction was the wily Yevgenii Primakov. The former academic, director of the Institute of Middle East Studies, had risen to become first a key informal adviser and then a member of Gorbachev's Politburo and Presidential Council. He was widely believed to have ambitions to replace Shevardnadze as foreign minister. I had known him since our discussion of the regional issues at Reykjavik in 1986. He had many admirers in the West, from his days as an interlocutor in informal exchanges like the Dartmouth Conference, and had managed smoothly (like Arbatov) to make the transition from defender of the Brezhnev line to apostle of "new thinking."

Yet his thinking on Middle East issues—his specialty—proved, in the end, not all that new. *

Primakov had known Saddam Hussein since 1969, when he had covered the Middle East as a *Pravda* correspondent. He remembered Saddam as a young tough who kept a submachine gun in his office, influential in the Ba'ath wing that had recently taken power.[78] In 1990 Primakov was convinced that it was essential to head off a war by some kind of compromise; he was also convinced that only he had the possibility of convincing Saddam of this.

Primakov's theory consisted of two basic points: first, that Saddam could be induced to withdraw peacefully from Kuwait if some concessions were made to help him save face, and second, that the crisis could be defused by committing the superpowers to make rapid progress on the Arab-Israeli dispute, perhaps by an international conference. This would give Saddam and all the agitated, frustrated Arabs something to show for the climb-down that we were asking of him.

Primakov's arguments began to show up in Soviet policy. James Baker two years earlier had expressed to aides the hope that if the United States ignored the Soviet idea of an international conference, "sooner or later it'll go away."[79] His friend Shevardnadze startled him on September 4 with a speech in Vladivostok that called for "step[ping] up pressure" for an international conference on the Middle East on the grounds that the Kuwait crisis was only one of "several highly complex, interlocking problems" in the region, including the Palestinian problem and Lebanon.[80] It was the worst possible idea from the American point of view. An international conference was by itself undesirable, as I have argued above, and its defects were only multiplied if it were to be convened as a reward for Saddam, vindicating his aggression in Kuwait and making him a hero of the Palestinians.

But Gorbachev was feeling increasing heat from the hard-liners. The unification of Germany came formally into effect on October 3. Shevardnadze was pushing for rapid progress on two controversial arms reduction agreements, one on conventional forces in Europe and the other on strategic weapons, both involving significant Soviet concessions. And the Soviet Union's Gulf policy was under growing attack. All this made inevitable a retrenchment in foreign policy. In the Gulf it led Gorbachev to lean toward Primakov's line.

---

*Russian president Boris Yeltsin later appointed Primakov head of the Russian Foreign Intelligence Service, successor of the KGB, where the "newness" of his thinking was even less evident (as in the matter of espionage operations against the United States).

Gorbachev therefore decided in early September to step up the pressure on the United States for some sort of linkage to the Palestinian problem— thus, the Shevardnadze speech of September 4 and the strong pitch that Gorbachev made to Bush for this at their September 9 summit in Helsinki. The Soviets also staked out a firm position against the use of force. On October 29—while the United States was trying to escalate the pressure on Saddam—Gorbachev unhelpfully declared that the use of force by the international coalition would be "unacceptable."[81] At the United Nations the Soviets were grudgingly going along with resolutions that tightened the noose of economic sanctions on Iraq. There are reports that Gorbachev also ordered the Soviet military to brief Secretary of Defense Dick Cheney and his staff in October on "everything the Iraqi military has."[82] But Gorbachev also gave in to Primakov's importunings to let him go to Baghdad to try out his peace plan personally on Saddam Hussein.

Primakov made three trips to Baghdad. He floated various compromises that had the common feature that Saddam would withdraw, or at least commit to withdraw, in exchange for various face-saving formulas—such as negotiations with Kuwait over oil rights and border changes, a promise that all U.S. troops would leave the Gulf, or linkage to an international conference on the Palestinian issue. These formulas involved no admission of error on Saddam's part and would have violated several of the Security Council resolutions. Saddam nevertheless stubbornly resisted all compromise, not believing that he faced any serious threat of punishment—an impression that Primakov was indirectly reinforcing.

The American strategy was to deny Saddam any reward or face saving lest he claim it as a victory and emerge stronger in the region for having faced down the imperialists. Primakov's enterprise ran directly counter to that. It was also a way of positioning the Soviets cleverly somewhere between the Americans and the Iraqis, as a subtle signal to the Arabs that the Soviet Union could still be counted upon to shield them from American depredations. Perhaps most important, it was a way to flaunt that the Soviet Union was still a factor in the world and not a puppet of the Americans. On October 31, Primakov declared on Soviet television: "The Soviet flag has been shown, and it is being perceived very positively. We are a superpower and we have our own line, our own policies; we are demonstrating this point."[83]

Even after the bombing of Iraq began on January 17, 1991, Primakov kept up his energetic diplomacy, with Gorbachev's support—this time to head off a ground war. If only this or that concession could be offered, we were told, Saddam would show flexibility. Saddam's purported concessions, as relayed by Primakov, were always marginal or cosmetic, but Primakov regularly informed the media that there was "hope" or some "possibility" not excluded for a solution—all of which added to political pressures on the coalition partners to hold off a military escalation.

Gorbachev's endorsement of Primakov's diplomacy made it harder for Bush to reject it outright. Being far more of a gentleman than I would have been, Bush chose rather to deflect it gently, while proceeding with the military campaign that appeared to him both inevitable and necessary.

Bush's strategy toward the Soviets during this period was one of remarkable forbearance. In fact, it went beyond forbearance. The Soviet Union, whose position in the Middle East had been regarded—correctly—as a menace for thirty-five years, was now actively courted as a Middle East partner. A dying superpower was propped up by its former enemy to play a supporting role. The United States even went to the extraordinary length of inviting the Soviets to send a land or naval force to the Gulf (which they fortunately declined for the domestic reasons we have seen).[84] Despite Primakov's mischief, the administration made significant concessions to Moscow to purchase its continued acquiescence in the Security Council resolutions that counted. On November 29, the Security Council—as always, with Soviet concurrence—passed the crucial Resolution 678 authorizing the use of "all necessary means" should Saddam fail to comply fully with all preceding UN resolutions by the deadline of January 15.

The American quid pro quos began at the Helsinki summit on September 9, where Bush reversed fourteen years of U.S. policy and accepted the idea of an international conference on the Arab-Israeli conflict. He chose to keep this concession from the public for the time being but agreed publicly to the principle of a Soviet role in the Middle East. He was prepared to pay this symbolic price, according to sources, in order to reinvigorate his own relationship with Gorbachev, strengthen the Soviet leader against his hard-line critics at home, and thereby reinforce the trend of Soviet cooperation in the Gulf.[85] The Helsinki communiqué of September 9, 1990, therefore declared: "It is essential to work actively to resolve all remaining conflicts in the Middle East and Persian Gulf. Both sides will continue to consult each other and initiate measures to pursue these broader objectives at the proper time." This was a vague but unmistakable commitment to take up the Palestinian issue as soon as the Gulf crisis was over. Sequential linkage, if you will.

At the joint news conference in Finlandia Hall at the close of the summit, Gorbachev declared with evident satisfaction: "In our talks, the President said, 'You know, there was a long time when our view was that the Soviet Union had nothing to do in the Middle East . . . had no business being there.' This was something that we had to talk through during this meeting here in Helsinki, and what was said here is that it's very important for us to cooperate in the Middle East, just as it is on other issues of world politics."[86]

Washington's other significant concession lay in its very acquiescence in the Primakov diplomacy. Primakov was received at the White House by President Bush after some of his trips to Baghdad. Bush told aides he had "zero enthusiasm" for the first meeting with Primakov, on October 19, and no desire to "legitimize" what Primakov was doing. But he felt he *had* to see him, since he was, after all, Gorbachev's emissary. Not wanting to seem totally dismissive, Bush indicated to Primakov that he would not object to his returning to Baghdad to continue his efforts, provided he conveyed the U.S. position accurately.[87]

The price that the administration paid for this politeness to Primakov it would not learn until December. Every time Bush told Primakov or Gorbachev that he was "appreciative" of Primakov's efforts,[88] every time Bush told Primakov that "he thought he had learned many interesting things from him" or that "there was something new in a number of ideas that had been presented,"[89] he encouraged not only Primakov's endeavors but also Gorbachev's decision to keep Primakov in this role at the expense of Shevardnadze. Shevardnadze came very close to resigning as foreign minister on two occasions because of his humiliation at Gorbachev's undercutting him in this way—undercutting him not only procedurally but substantively because of the irritant it introduced into relations with the United States.

Shevardnadze was coming under mounting attack in the parliament for "losing" Eastern Europe, for being a tool of the Americans in the Middle East, and for the other foreign policy setbacks. He was being made the scapegoat—and Gorbachev was not backing him. On the contrary, Gorbachev continued to bypass him throughout the course of one of the major foreign policy crises of the period. On December 20, 1990, Shevardnadze rose before the Congress of People's Deputies and defended his record. He warned of the "onset of dictatorship"—a veiled reference to the ascendancy of the hard-liners, toward whom Gorbachev was drifting—and announced his resignation.[90] His audience, including his old comrade Gorbachev, sat in stunned silence.

Obviously Shevardnadze's departure had many fundamental causes. But the Bush team contributed to it. In not slapping down Primakov, they undermined Shevardnadze, the real architect of the foreign policy revolution of the previous five years. Out of solicitude for Gorbachev, they contributed to his tilt toward the right which squandered his moral credibility and began the unraveling of his position. (The last-minute Soviet efforts to head off the Gulf War in January coincided with a brutal military crackdown in Vilnius that left fifteen Lithuanians dead and several hundred wounded.) The coddling of Primakov was a serious miscalculation.

Baker went a step further in a meeting with Shevardnadze's successor, Aleksandr Bessmertnykh, in Washington on January 29, 1991. Unbeknownst to the White House, Baker and Ross negotiated a joint statement with the Soviets that gave reassurance of the limits of U.S. war aims:

> Secretary of State Baker emphasized that the United States and its coalition partners are seeking the liberation of Kuwait, not the destruction of Iraq. He stressed that the United States has no quarrel with the people of Iraq, and poses no threat to Iraq's territorial integrity. Secretary Baker reiterated that the United States is doing its utmost to avoid casualties among the civilian population, and is not interested in expanding the conflict. . . .

> The ministers continue to believe that a cessation of hostilities would be possible if Iraq would make an unequivocal commitment to withdraw from Kuwait. They also believe that such a commitment must be backed by immediate, concrete steps leading to full compliance with the Security Council resolutions.

This statement had the effect of winning credit for the Soviets in the Arab world for restraining the impetuous Americans. It is not self-evident that what the world needed at that point in time was reassurance about *American* behavior, since we were not responsible for the crisis. In any event, if we were going to give any such assurances, we should have done so to friends like Egypt or Saudi Arabia so they could get the credit in the Arab world. The statement also seemed to endorse the Soviet idea that a ground war could be avoided if only Iraq made a *promise* to withdraw, whereas Bush's position had been that Iraq had to withdraw completely.

In addition, the Baker-Bessmertnykh communiqué reiterated the importance of "mutual U.S.-Soviet efforts" to achieve a "comprehensive settlement" of the Arab-Israeli conflict in the "aftermath" of the Gulf crisis. Linkage was now explicit. The statement included some good language about "a just peace, security, and real reconciliation" as the goals of Arab-Israeli diplomacy. This was a small victory for Ross, who had long sought Soviet endorsement of this phraseology. But the victory was overshadowed by the uproar caused by the seeming softening of the U.S. position toward Saddam. The White House was infuriated, not least by the fact that the uproar took some of the limelight from Bush's State of the Union address.[91] On the substance, however, the main lines of the Baker-Bessmertnykh document were the main lines of the Bush policy—deliberately keeping the Soviets engaged as a partner in the Gulf as well as the Arab-Israeli diplomacy.

Historians will have to sift through the evidence and decide whether the Bush/Baker approach of pumping up the Soviet role in the Middle East was a strategy indispensable to keeping the Soviets on board or a gamble whose risks we were spared only because the regime collapsed before our very eyes a few months later. By the time the international conference on the Middle East was convened in Madrid on October 30, 1991, the August putsch attempt in Moscow had intervened, and Gorbachev was the political equivalent of the walking dead. He embarrassed everyone at the conference by a speech that dwelt on his own country's internal problems and pleaded for "practical support" (from, presumably, the rich Arabs in the hall), hoping the world would not remain "indifferent to our great cause."[92]

The Madrid conference itself was a historic success, because, on the model of Geneva in December 1973, its results were precooked, as I had long hoped.[93] The PLO, discredited because of its support for Saddam, was unable to block Palestinian residents of the occupied territories from coming forward to negotiate without direct PLO participation, which was the procedure we insisted upon at that stage. In an even more significant breakthrough, the Palestinians had accepted the procedure of negotiating first on a turnover of powers to an interim self-governing authority, deferring the issues of final status to a later negotiation. With the defeat of Saddam, the moderates in the Arab world—principally our best Arab allies, Egypt and Saudi Arabia—were strengthened. Syria was weakened by the collapse of Soviet power and eager to get back into the financial good graces of the Gulf Arabs; Asad therefore thought better of trying to block progress.

It was a breathtaking reversal, a tribute to how far the global balance of power and the regional balance of power had boh shifted in our favor. The Gulf War had reshuffled the deck, but so had the transformed superpower context. Just as the weakening of the Soviet position in 1972–73 had spurred the first series of breakthroughs toward peace, the further weakening of the Soviets and their traditional radical clients spurred an even more historic advance. At that stage it did not do great harm to "bring the Soviets into the Middle East."

THE FUTURE: THE NEW "GREAT GAME"

History, however, has a way of mocking the complacent. Ever since Gamal Abdel Nasser linked up with Nikita Khrushchev, the West faced the challenge of an Arab radicalism led by military strongmen under the banner of a leftist ideology and with the backing of the Communist superpower. But Saddam Hussein and Hafez al-Asad—the heirs of Nasser—may have been the last of a dying breed. With the Gulf War and the end of the Cold War, both were shrunken in power and influence. The tragic irony of the Middle East is that just as the traditional leftist source of radicalism was on the wane, the region was swept up by a new wave of radicalism from the opposite direction—revolutionary Islam. Around the time of the Iranian Revolution (1978–79), scholars debated whether a philosophy spawned among Shi'ite Persians would have resonance among the Sunni of the vast Arab world. By the beginning of the 1990s, there was no doubt of it. The second wave of Islamic fundamentalism—its spread among the Sunni Arabs—was in large part a function of the ideological vacuum left by the demise of "Arab socialism," and is therefore another byproduct of the end of the Cold War.

Thus, a new and very different kind of Great Game was in store, one in which the regional actors were no longer the pawns in a big-power contest but potentially the principal players. The reversal of fortune in the early 1990s was such that scholar Barry Rubin could begin an article in *Foreign Affairs* with the wry observation: "[I]n the 1980s it seemed plausible that the Soviet Union might invade a disintegrating Iran; in the 1990s it seems conceivable that Iran might take over defecting portions of a crumbling U.S.S.R."[94]

Even as Saddam Hussein clung to power in Baghdad, keeping the world nervous about his clandestine potential as a nuclear and chemical-weapons menace, Iran launched itself on a dramatic military buildup in all categories.[95] CIA director Robert Gates reported to Congress in June 1992 that Iran was making an "across-the-board effort," including programs for weapons of mass destruction. A $1.9 billion arms deal with Gorbachev's Soviet Union in July 1989 had included forty-eight MiG-29 fighters and 100 T-72 tanks. Iran's five-year plans, approved in 1990, included $10 billion more for foreign weapons purchases plus another $2 billion for its Defense Industrial Organization. In July 1991, a second arms accord with the Soviet Union, estimated at $6 billion, involved hundreds of new aircraft. An arms accord with China involved fighter planes, patrol boats, antiship and antiaircraft missiles, and artillery. North Korea assisted Iran with the development and production of intermediate-range ballistic missiles—the SCUD-C (five-hundred-kilometer range) and the North Korean No-Dong 1 (one-thousand-kilometer range). Iran announced with fanfare in February 1991 that its long-range missiles were now in "mass production."

The second Gulf War had unbalanced the region by deflating Iraq in the power equation. However, as long as Saddam was in power pursuing his nuclear program, Iraq was no fit partner for the Arab moderates or the West. The United States had no choice but to fill the security vacuum itself, expanding its military ties—arms sales, training, joint facilities, and exercises—with the Arab Gulf states.

Like Soviet Russia at an earlier period, Iran combined a geopolitical thrust with an ideological one. Its oil wealth gave it resources; its religious fervor and theocratic institutions impelled it to send funds far and wide to finance mosques, religious teaching, political organizing—and terrorism. Iran's influence in the radical factions of the Afghan resistance has already been described. From Algeria to Egypt to the Sudan to the West Bank and Gaza to southern Lebanon to Saudi Arabia to Pakistan (and even to Indonesia), radical Islam spread—as a political movement, not simply a spiritual reawakening. The Muslim republics of the former Soviet Union seemed vulnerable, though, at least initially, the Soviet-trained elites in those new states remained resistant to religious agitation. The full scope of Iran's challenge to the world is yet to be determined.

For post-Communist Russia, its southern flank was now a priority foreign policy problem, if not obsession. The Central Asian republics, while no longer part of the USSR, remained part of the Russian-led Commonwealth of Independent States (CIS), and their stability and orientation constituted a "maximum interest" of Russian policy, according to aides of Russian president Boris Yeltsin.[96] As turmoil festered in the Caucasus and burst forth in Tajikistan, Yeltsin asked the world community's blessing for Russia's "special responsibility" to keep order in the former Soviet sphere: "Stopping all armed conflicts on the territory of the former USSR is Russia's vital interest. The world community sees more and more clearly Russia's special responsibility in this difficult undertaking. I believe the time has come for distinguished international organizations, including the United Nations, to grant Russia special powers as guarantor of peace and stability in regions of the former USSR."[97] It was the 1990s equivalent of Prince Gorchakov's diplomatic note of 1864 justifying Russian expansion in Central Asia.[98]

The same interest was bound to impel Russia to nurture a complex relationship with Iran. As analyst Stephen Blank has observed, Russia has many objectives—to be a regional player, to sell arms and receive aid, to shield itself and the CIS from the Islamic menace: "Such objectives at home and abroad inevitably lead policymakers to cooperate with Iran. Whatever issue one examines—Gulf security, Afghanistan, the new Transcaucasian and Central Asian states, or arms sales—bilateral cooperation with Iran is increasingly evident."[99] Russia has therefore, among other things, lent diplomatic support to Tehran's view that the Gulf's security cannot be assured unless all its littoral states, including Iran, are involved. Moscow has questioned American attempts to build a Gulf security structure exclusively with the Gulf Arabs, arrangements clearly aimed at excluding and counterbalancing Iran.[100]

Yet Russian policy continues to confront its familiar modern dilemmas. Reconciling good relations with Iran and with the moderate Arabs is no easier for Moscow now than a few years ago. A visit by Russian foreign minister Andrei Kozyrev to the Arab Gulf states in May 1992 produced an offer by Kozyrev to guarantee the sovereignty and territorial integrity of the United Arab Emirates (UAE). Russia's relations with Saudi Arabia, Kuwait, and the UAE developed rapidly after Madrid (with the same financial as well as geopolitical motives on Moscow's part). Likewise, Turkey, with which Russia has historically always had a wary relationship, is another moderate country with which it now seeks better relations.

However torn Moscow is by conflicting interests, its diplomatic activism in the region bespeaks an ambition to remain a factor in the Middle East. It is now attempting to do so not by the policies of anti-Western agitation of the past but by more conventional diplomatic engagement. Kozyrev declared during his Gulf tour: "Russia will remain a great power, with global and regional interests, and we have satisfied ourselves that this is what the states of the region want."[101] Moscow's basic interest is in maintaining a regional balance of power on its southern flank not dominated by a hostile regional power and not left to the exclusive influence of the United States.

Russia shares many of its concrete interests with us. Fearing the spread of weapons of mass destruction and of revolutionary Islam, Russia today has a basic interest in regional stability, not subversion or any form of radicalism. The strategy of Lenin, Khrushchev, and Brezhnev has been laid to rest. George Bush's summit in Washington with Boris Yeltsin in June 1992 even produced a remarkable agreement to collaborate on anti-ballistic-missile defenses. After all the controversies over Reagan's SDI—and his much-derided dream of sharing the effort with the Soviets—the two countries now contemplated the miasma of the contemporary Middle East, which is, after all, in much closer missile range of Russia than of the United States.

At the same time, Russian interests will not be, and cannot be, identical to ours. Nationalist suspicions of the West and protectiveness toward Russian security interests will inevitably reappear in Russian policy. Russia is bound to be wary of too assertive Western involvement in the Middle East (as in the Balkans); it has already begun to assert its own role in both places. The vestiges of the USSR's former client relationships with some of the less enlightened forces in the Middle East also remain, including arms sales. These links will be especially important to the Russian military, not to mention the country's foreign-exchange earnings.[102] Closer to home, the newly independent Muslim republics may not be eager for Russian tutelage, but the shadow of Russian power looms over them again, at this writing.

The assertion of a Russian national interest is not only a feature of ex-Communist diehards and the hide-bound military. Andrei Kozyrev made the point (quoted earlier). The most enlightened of Russians, like Sergei Stankevich, argue for a foreign policy that is true to Russia's uniqueness— its "Eurasian" vocation as a crossroads and link among Europe, Asia, and the Middle East; its historical and cultural amalgam tugging it toward the East as well as the West; its Dostoyevskian vision of a singular spiritual mission. The modern world and objective interests pull it toward friendly association with the West, Stankevich acknowledges, but Russia's nature is nevertheless distinct. This is the case he makes for "balance" in Russia's foreign policy.[103] In a passage echoing Charles de Gaulle, he has argued that only a country that means something to itself can be of value as a partner to others:

> Many people are calling for Russia to take steps toward the speediest integration into the Western community. . . . The reply to that is as follows. Only something that is already established, with a definite qualitative nature, can integrate into something else without disastrous consequences. Then it is possible to act as a partner. . . . First we must put down our own roots, become a power, create a national market, and only then raise the question of integration. . . . The main emphasis should be on identifying and formulating our own national interests and priorities.

"Russia is entirely capable of getting back on its feet again rapidly," Stankevich encouraged his compatriots in 1993, but first it must reconstitute itself as a system of authority, a set of values, and a strategy.[104]

Bismarck is reputed to have observed that "Russia is never as strong or as weak as it appears." That is perhaps the wisest advice of all. Russia *is* getting back on its feet, sooner than many anticipated. It will always be a major power. If there is any area outside of Europe where this will be evident, it is the Middle East.

AMERICA AND THE POST–COLD WAR WORLD

IMPACT ON THE THIRD WORLD

The human cost of the Cold War struggle in the Third World was devastating. In Afghanistan, by the end of the Soviet occupation, nearly 1 million had died, over half a million were disabled veterans, a third of all villages were destroyed. In Indochina, at least seventy thousand perished in the post-1978 phase of the Cambodian conflict. In Central America, the death toll in El Salvador and Nicaragua was around 100,000. In southern Africa (Angola and Namibia), an estimated 1.5 million died between 1980 and 1988.[1] And this covers only the conflicts since the late 1970s, not the earlier wars in Korea, the Congo, Vietnam, and elsewhere.

A debate could rage endlessly over which side was most responsible for the conflicts and the carnage, but there could be no debate over the magnitude of the economic and social disaster that befell these countries, perhaps irretrievably. Much responsibility lay with local leaders and political movements—hence, the virulence of many of these conflicts (especially Angola) even after the superpowers disengaged—but no one could deny that the overlay of the Cold War competition had added to the destructive firepower available to the local contenders.

Nevertheless, the end of the U.S.-Soviet contest in the Third World at the end of the 1980s was not an unadulterated blessing for all those who may have considered themselves its victims. For decades, the developing countries had polished their considerable skills at their own Great Game of playing the two sides against each other. They knew quite well, for example, how to scare the West into boosting economic and military assistance. Recall Khrushchev's wry comment to Indian foreign minister Morarji Desai: "They [the Americans] will give you more aid as soon as we give you aid."[2] From the platform afforded by the East-West competition, the nonaligned movement put forward its redistributionist economic programs, such as Mexican president Luis Echeverria's

"New International Economic Order," which called for the fixing of commodity prices and expanded transfers of aid to developing countries. At gatherings of the nonaligned movement and in the UN General Assembly, the Third World claimed a pivotal role on international political questions ranging from nuclear disarmament to East-West conflicts—a role that the larger powers were afraid to deny. In the 1960s, as we have seen, both superpowers even succumbed for a while to the fear that the global balance of power would be decided in the Third World.

When the Cold War ended, Third World countries found they had lost much of their leverage over the West. Nonalignment lost its meaning when there were no two sides to "align" with or against. To add injury to insult, much of the West's resources and attention was now drawn to the plight of the newly liberated countries of Central and Eastern Europe and the former Soviet Union.

In Latin America, for example, the United States had been galvanized for at least half a century by fears of an extrahemispheric threat exploiting the region's discontents. Franklin Roosevelt's cultivation of the Latins, while reflecting his humane impulses, was spurred in the early 1940s by worries of Nazi influence in some of the authoritarian regimes of South America; so was John Kennedy's Alliance for Progress stimulated in large part by fear of the Red menace. With the Soviet threat gone in the 1990s, the Latins faced, for the first time in memory, the possibility of North American strategic indifference.

Similarly elsewhere. Poorer countries, especially in Africa, worried that the end of the East-West split would only confirm and expand the gap between North and South, between the richest and poorest hemispheres of the planet. Third World countries had been rendered "politically and strategically irrelevant," lamented a Nigerian scholar, who feared that the end of the Cold War would simultaneously break down the cohesion that had provided the collective political strength of the nonaligned movement.[3]

Owen Harries, editor of the journal the *National Interest*, summed up the political blow the nonaligned suffered: "The tactic of playing one side against the other is not available in the absence of such a competition. Third World countries no longer have a ready-made, automatic way of linking themselves to the central issues of world politics—as counters in a game, as trophies to be won, or as reluctant neutrals to be seduced."[4] As Harries pointed out, even the much-heralded revitalization of the United Nations was no victory for the Third World. What was revitalized by the end of the East-West rivalry was the Security Council—the instrument of the great powers—at the expense of the General Assembly, which had been the stomping ground of the nonaligned through the decades.[5]

In the Introduction, I quoted a common lament in the developing world about the superpowers in the Cold War: "When the elephants fight, the grass suffers." In many cultures there is also a variant: "When the elephants make love, the grass suffers."

There is a school of thought that the Cold War also imposed a degree of discipline and restraint on a violent world and that these qualities are now missed. Superpower caution, especially after the Cuban Missile Crisis, ensured that the proxy competition in the Third World never reached the point of drawing the two sides into a nuclear or even a wider conventional conflagration. Saddam Hussein's invasion of Kuwait has even been cited as an example of an aggression that might have been restrained if Moscow had been at the peak of its influence.[6] This view had adherents in the Bush administration, which explains some of its hesitations in embracing the new world that the total collapse of Soviet power entailed. Deputy Secretary of State Lawrence Eagleburger mused in September 1989: "Nor is the multipolar world into which we are moving necessarily going to be a safer place than the Cold War era from which we are emerging, given the existence and indeed the proliferation of weapons of mass destruction. For all its risks and uncertainties, the Cold War was characterized by a remarkably stable and predictable set of relations among the great powers."[7]

There is truth in this analysis, but it should not be overstated. As we saw in the last chapter, the United States often put pressure on the Soviets in a Mideast crisis on the theory that they could be induced to exert some restraining influence. But it did not happen automatically. Brezhnev-era Soviet policy was never especially eager (or even able) to stand in the way of radical clients in 1967 or 1970 or 1973. Even into the Gorbachev era, the Soviets fueled conflict by arms transfers and obstructed diplomacy as often as they dampened conflict and contributed to ending it. One should restrain one's nostalgia for the Soviet Union and its foreign policy.

For better or worse, the collapse of the Soviets left most of the Third World alone with the West and with the necessity of redefining its relationship with the technically advanced societies that it simultaneously emulated and envied. The Bolsheviks had had a good run at exploiting the developing countries' historical resentments; now they (the Bolsheviks) were gone. The two main players left were essentially the same as at the beginning of the drama—the former colonial domains and the industrialized West—with all the complexes about each other that had survived the tumultuous century. The civilizations of the developing world would have to come to terms on their own, one way or another, with the West's economic and technological preeminence and its political and cultural influence. The process promised to be an emotional and turbulent one, even without the disruptive distraction of Marxism-Leninism.

The end of the Cold War had many other economic and political consequences.

ECONOMIC PROSPECTS

When the Cold War ended, official development assistance from the wealthier countries to the poorer had already been declining for some time, for a variety of reasons. The West was wrestling with its own economic difficulties ever since the 1970s. (The poignant irony here is that these economic difficulties were in part produced by OPEC's oil price gouge of the 1970s, which the Third World had cheered on as a matter of ideological solidarity.) In any case, by the 1980s and the era of Reagan, the industrial countries were imposing stricter conditions for their official aid, demanding major structural reforms of recipient-country economies to dismantle the state sector and expand the scope for free enterprise. This was painful medicine for governments reared on the once-fashionable theories of socialism. By the 1990s, however, there was no recourse: Not only Western governments but also the international financial institutions (the International Monetary Fund, the World Bank, and regional development banks), all dominated by the major capitalist powers, were imposing the same conditions for their aid.

The acceptance of such conditions may have been a political come-down, but from the neutral point of view of economic analysis, structural reforms of this kind had much to be said for them. The new seriousness about economic policy may turn out to be the Third World's biggest gain from the end of the Cold War. In 1991, the World Bank's *World Development Report* celebrated the policy revolution that was under way— the rapid spread of free-market structural reforms and the growing understanding of how to unleash the productive forces in developing societies. The World Bank projected that real per-capita incomes in the developing world would grow at a vigorous 3 percent a year through the 1990s, a figure that might be raised or lowered 0.5 to 1.0 percentage points by external conditions (terms of trade, etc.) but could be raised further by 1.5–2 percentage points if even more vigorous and comprehensive structural reforms were undertaken. "[T]he opportunity for rapid development is greater today," said the World Bank, "than at any time in history."[8] The pervasiveness of market-oriented reforms, the *Economist* noted, was the main factor that allayed the fears of the famous Third World debt crisis that had so haunted the international financial system in the 1980s.[9]

In other words, whatever the decline of "strategically minded" attention from the great powers, the transformation had the potential to be enormously positive for developing nations. The bad news—or the good news, depending on how one looked at it—was that responsibility was thrown back on their own shoulders. Richard Bissell observed: "The move toward democracy and open markets in Eastern Europe is not a threat to the countries of the erstwhile Third World. The most important mobilization occurring in both regions is internal, not external. The power to mobilize resources is far greater within any country than outside it."[10] To put it positively, their future was in their own hands.

An additional economic benefit, particularly for Latin America, was expected to come through trade. Reagan had often spoken of his dream of a North American free-trade arrangement—even a Western Hemisphere free-trade zone stretching from the Arctic Circle to Tierra del Fuego,[11]—which ran counter to the conventional wisdom that the Latins were ideologically allergic to such an intimate relationship with the "Colossus of the North." But after a U.S.-Canada Free Trade Agreement came into effect on January 1, 1989, negotiations immediately began on a broadened agreement, including Mexico, which was signed in 1992 by Presidents George Bush and Carlos Salinas de Gortari and approved by the U.S. Congress in 1993 under President Clinton. Bush's 1990 "Enterprise for the Americas" Initiative opened the door for other Latin American states to negotiate with the United States for free-trade arrangements of their own.

As described earlier, this evolution represented the overcoming of complexes that had stood for years in the way of such a natural trade grouping. The collapse of ideology and of the socialist alternative models gave way to a new maturity, freeing the Latins to act in their rational economic self-interest. There was no sensible alternative to becoming part of a hemispheric market of which the United States was the engine. Illusions that the Communist bloc was a viable economic partner had long since been exploded. For a brief time this was supplanted by a hope that the European Community might fulfill that role; this hope, too, was dashed at the beginning of the 1990s as the Latins saw the West Europeans' attentions and resources consumed by the problems of Central and Eastern Europe.

The combination of sound economic policies at home and open markets abroad thus offered a chance for real economic development. The success of Salinas's Mexico and post-Indira India pointed the way. The industrial nations needed, however, to rediscover and redefine their own stake in this process. The developing nations were not the only ones prompted to do some rethinking.

Strategic panic would no longer suffice as a motivation for the West's concern. Altruism was important, but foreign-aid programs had long since run up against budgetary constraints. The economic importance to the industrial countries of their trade with the growing markets in the Third World was an increasing incentive. (In 1990, developing countries supplied 40 percent of U.S. imports and bought 34 percent of U.S. exports.)[12] So was the fear of political instability, which was raising a new specter—mass migrations of people fleeing poverty and hopelessness to the Promised Land of North America and Western Europe. The ex-Communist countries were one source of new tides of migrants; also North Africa, South Asia, and East Asia. Western European countries, not accustomed to seeing themselves as anything but racially homoge-neous, were suffering unprecedented social strains. If the positive incen-tives of trade and political stability were not sufficient to convince the advanced countries of their stake in the economic progress of their poorer cousins, then the negative incentives—the fear of upheaval and immi-gration pressures—might prove to be.

Here was a creative task of leadership for the United States. Integrating the developing countries into a harmonious international system had been Woodrow Wilson's vision; now, as then, Americans had the idealism to reach out to these new nations and ensure their inclusion in international arrangements. As the great twentieth-century drama of decolonization came to its conclusion, just as at its beginning, a constructive task of statesmanship presented itself, which had never been only a function of the U.S.-Soviet rivalry.

POLITICAL TRENDS

The Cold War's end also accelerated a trend toward democracy in the developing world, though here the overall picture is more mixed. The collapse of socialism as an economic model was paralleled by the dis-crediting of the leftist radicalism that had relied—for legitimacy as well as for arms—on the Communist political model. Not wrongly did the Soviets often proclaim that the health of the international socialist move-ment depended on the health of the socialist motherland.

Gorbachev contributed to this process by delegitimizing his own system and its policies. In the television age, news spreads fast. Even Afghanistan had its reverberations in Eastern Europe as anti-Communists were emboldened by the failure of Soviet power, as some had predicted.[13] The Chinese dissidents who were suppressed at Tiananmen Square in June 1989 had hailed Gorbachev, the reformer, as representing the antithesis of the tyranny they suffered in China; Eastern Europeans then watched events in China and sensed that communism was weakening everywhere, if people could only muster enough courage. When the satellite Communist dictatorships were blown away in Central and Eastern Europe, the effects, in turn, reverberated back into the Third World: The equation of Hafez al-Asad with Nicolae Ceaucsescu and Erich Honecker became a staple of Middle East discourse.[14]

Samuel Huntington called attention in 1991 to what he saw as a "third wave" of democratization in modern history. The first wave had been the spread of democracy in Latin America and Europe in the nineteenth century; the second wave followed the Second World War. The latest wave of democratization (which he dated from 1974) began with Portugal and Spain and accelerated in the 1980s.

Authoritarian and totalitarian regimes around the world, according to Huntington, had suffered an acute crisis of legitimacy in that period as the idea of human rights spread. In some cases, these regimes were discredited by economic or military failures (as in Latin America). Meanwhile, global rises in living standards and education in much of the world since the 1960s had produced an expanded middle class, more politically conscious and insistent on its political voice. Another important factor was the doctrine of the Catholic church, which had shifted in the 1960s to an opponent instead of a defender of authoritarianism. Roughly three-quarters of the newly democratic countries between 1974 and 1989 were predominantly Catholic. The early successes of democracy in Portugal and Spain also had a demonstration effect, especially in Latin American nations influenced by Iberian culture.[15]

Beginning with the Helsinki process in the early 1970s, Huntington wrote, U.S. and Western European foreign policy had become more assertive in championing human rights. Then the Soviet Union under Gorbachev began its ideological retreat that ultimately ended its role as chief sponsor of totalitarianism and radicalism.

Outside of Europe, as the 1990s began, democratic practices indeed seemed to be a trend or a hope on every continent. The idea of democracy spread even to sub-Saharan Africa, where poverty and underdevelopment had long been thought to render it impossible. Zambia's longtime ruler Kenneth Kaunda was replaced in a free election in November 1991;

contested elections have been held in more than two dozen countries across the continent. Pressures mounted on Zaire's dictator Mobutu and on Kenya's authoritarian president Daniel arap Moi, not to mention South Africa's white-ruled regime, which went through its own extraordinary Gorbachev-like surrender of power under F. W. de Klerk.

With the collapse of the leftist ideology and Soviet backing that had constituted the principal source of radicalism for four decades, it is not surprising that many developing countries now had more of a chance for a normal political life. In the absence of a virulent radicalism, local politics was less a matter of life and death. Procedures of moderate politics, like the alternation of parties in office, became conceivable.

As at earlier periods of history, the ex-colonial countries were also attracted by the appeal of a winner. There had been a brief wave of interest in Western-style constitutionalism in the Arab world in the 1920s after Woodrow Wilson's inspirational appearance on the scene as the victor of World War I. The Western model had seemed vindicated then, too. Unfortunately, as Elie Kedourie has pointed out with respect to the Mideast, those experiments proved not to be durable.[16] Fascism had its Third World imitators in the 1930s and 1940s (in Latin America as well as the Arab world), and then Nasser championed the new style of dictatorship in the 1950s when leftism took its star turn as the "wave of the future." The post–Cold War tide of democratization confronts enormous obstacles—economic frustration, the continuing dislocations of modernization, ethnic and racial animosities, demographic upheavals, even a degrading ecology that promises to aggravate economic and social ills.[17] Its ultimate success is hardly guaranteed.

The part of the Third World where the prospects for democracy are the most problematic is the Muslim world, whose future is clouded by history's cruel joke that just as leftist radicalism wanes, an Islamic form of radicalism has risen to take its place. This promises a turbulent politics in that region for the foreseeable future.

The phenomenon that provokes such concern is not religious fervor—by that standard, America's allies Saudi Arabia and Pakistan are fundamentalist countries—but the distinctive *political* movement, driven by a powerful anti-Western ideology, that appeared on the scene with the Iranian Revolution of 1978–79. Such political agitation and radicalism are not even deeply rooted in Islam, marking, in fact, an innovation for a clergy that has traditionally eschewed worldly political activity.[18] This ideology is, as we have seen, anti-Communist as much as anti-Western, viewing communism as just a deviant form of Western secularism. Yet its main animus, even before the collapse of communism, was directed against the West. Scholar Ghassan Salamé has written: "Islamists would like to be viewed as the true anti-imperialist force, pushing the struggle a step further by resisting not only the West's political hegemony but also its intrusive ideas like liberalism, socialism, and secularism."[19]

A religious revival is evident in many societies—including the United States—and is one form of a widespread rebellion against the corrupting effects of modern culture on traditional values; it feeds on the social dislocations and psychological stresses that come inevitably with modernization, urbanization, and other transformations.[20] In the Islamic world, however, it also feeds on a potent brew of other historical resentments—the humiliations of a thousand years of European military and technological superiority, the bitterness at the West's perceived condescension. It is, as Bernard Lewis has called it, the politics of rage.[21] Barely two years after his optimistic prognosis on the "third wave" of democracy, Samuel Huntington came out with a new analysis foreshadowing a profound schism in world politics along cultural lines—a "clash of civilizations," born of anti-Western resentment in the Islamic world and among other non-Western cultures.[22]

Like the earlier leftist form of Third World radicalism, Islamic rage is directed not only at the West but against the Westernized, modernizing elites in its own societies. Militant Islam is thus another form of the civil war *within* developing societies between those who aspire to be part of the Western world and those who resent and despise the Western world, between those who share the Wilsonian dream of their country's integration in the world community and those who view the world community, dominated by the West, as the source of all ills. From Frantz Fanon to the Ayatollah Khomeini is not that great a philosophical leap.

There are thoughtful observers who worry that the West is rushing too fast to enshrine Islam as its new enemy to take the place of Soviet communism. They fear that the West always seems to need an external enemy to unite it and give it purpose. They caution against prejudging Islamic fundamentalism in this way, perhaps making it a self-fulfilling prophecy.[23]

This is thoughtful and well-meant advice, but it also misstates the problem, which is less a psychological condition of the West than it is the empirical reality of a new revolutionary movement on the world scene. Islamic radicalism's avowed attitude toward the international system is what diplomatic historians would call revisionist: Its openly proclaimed goal is a transformation of the region, if not of the world, to diminish our influence and undermine our friends. Political Islam is a proselytizing ideology with a spreading appeal in Muslim countries. The resemblance to earlier revolutionary movements—including Soviet communism—is analytic, not psychosomatic.

It is no accident, therefore, that radical Islam is stimulating a debate in the West that bears an uncanny resemblance to the intellectual rift that bedeviled Western thinking for decades about how to deal with leftist radicalism and the Soviet Union. The arguments on *both* sides bear an extraordinary similarity to those of the earlier debate.

The starting point of the contrarian analysis, for example, is that the spread of militant Islam in far-flung regions of the world, from Morocco to Indonesia, is the product mainly of indigenous forces. It is not, the argument runs, masterminded from Tehran by some kind of conspiratorial "Khomeintern." The unrest, rather, derives from deep-seated, local political, social, and economic causes, too long neglected by us and by the governments we have supported. In Algeria, the Islamic Salvation Front was on the verge of winning local elections all over the country in 1992 before it was blocked by a military crackdown; its electoral appeal derived, as journalist Robin Wright has pointed out, from "mass grievances over chronic housing shortages, unemployment, substandard education and social services" and an estimated 14 million of the country's 25 million people living below the poverty line.[24] Therefore, columnist Leslie Gelb concluded, "if the Saudis, Egyptians and others fear fundamentalism, the best place to counter that problem is not in Tehran, but in their own countries—with better care for their own people."[25]

We have seen similar arguments often over the years, from China to Cuba to Indochina to Central America, as our bourgeois society wrestled with the phenomenon of revolution against governments friendly to us. A radical movement, whose ideology is anti-Western on its face, is explained as a powerful popular phenomenon—an expression of the very democracy that we purport to be encouraging around the world. Is it a threat or not? The critics argue against reflexive opposition and put the blame for the unrest on the governments we are supporting. Just as Harvard professor Stanley Hoffmann used to insist that the United States had to come to terms with leftist revolution, so others today suggest that radical Islam is a historical tide that must be understood, not frontally fought.[26] If anything, the West is seen as in large part responsible for the rage against it. America's support for flawed governments, its backing of Israel, its acquiescence in the Algerian crackdown against the Islamists, its eagerness to go to war to defeat Iraq in 1991 in contrast to its reluctance to aid Muslims in Bosnia in 1992–94—all these have been cited by Western writers as explanations of Islamic resentments.[27]

The prescriptions for U.S. policy also embrace familiar themes. If the ideological threat is overstated, it follows that the West should not prejudge the foreign policy orientation of either Iran or other Islamic movements but should work with them in order to encourage moderation. This view is strongly held among some of our West European allies, who argue that a continuing "critical dialogue" with Iran will help moderate it. [28]

Some Arab governments (especially Jordan) have adopted a strategy of co-opting their Islamic parties, so far with some success. Critics take this analysis a step further and apply it to U.S.-Iranian relations as well. In this perception, U.S.-Iranian tensions reproduce several of the more unfortunate syndromes of the Cold War—mutual miscalculation (as in the Cuban Missile Crisis); the vicious cycle of action and reaction (like the U.S.-Soviet arms race); even an Iranian fear of encirclement (reminiscent of Soviet claims during the Stalin period). All these themes appear in an analysis by Shireen Hunter, a scholar at the Center for Strategic and International Studies:

> [B]ecause of the weakness of the post-Soviet Asian republics, Iran has increasingly come to be seen as an active threat to U.S. interests and to those of its allies such as Turkey. . . . This very well may be a legitimate concern to the United States. Nevertheless, it has generated in Iran a feeling that U.S. policy in the region is basically aimed at isolating and encircling Iran. . . . This portrayal of Iran as the new enemy has, in turn, fed certain fears and insecurities within Iran, leading to a military buildup. . . .
>
> Because of recent changes, including the introduction of the U.S. military presence in the Persian Gulf, Iran feels threatened [as well by] the efforts of certain regional countries to exclude Iran from all regional security plans for the Persian Gulf. This approach, in turn, has forced Iran to improve its defensive capability by exacerbating its security fears. [29]

Iran, for its part, denies its involvement in fueling terrorism or violent upheaval in other countries and professes its eagerness for better economic and political relations with the West.

There is a more skeptical school of thought, to which I subscribe. Iran's geopolitical thrust—its nuclear and conventional military buildup, its bullying of the smaller Gulf Arab states over territorial disputes, its hostility to the Arab-Israeli peace process—is not a figment of a hyperactive imagination. Secretary of State Warren Christopher, not known as a rabid hawk, has called Iran the "most worrisome" of a group of "dangerous states" that are contributing to regional tensions. [30] The U.S.

Central Command today considers that Iran, because of its military buildup, is "the single greatest threat to peace and stability in the Central Region."[31] Iran's deeply felt convictions lead it to lend not only moral but also financial and logistical support to fraternal radical movements— quite definitely including terrorists: It has been caught in the act in southern Lebanon (Hezbollah), the Sudan, and elsewhere—even Northern Ireland. The deep-seated indigenous social and economic causes of discontent cannot be disputed, but their *exploitation* by a revolutionary state ideologically hostile to us poses a strategic challenge that indeed bears comparison to the one we faced for the seventy years after 1917.

The Sandinistas used to refer to their "internationalist duty" and their "revolution beyond our borders."[32] The identical enthusiasm appears in Iranian rhetoric, as in this 1989 interview by Javad Larijani (often described in the West as a moderate):

> [W]e accept the world's geographic boundaries in order to avoid trouble. [But] our Islamic responsibility does not go away. This responsibility passes across borders. . . . No country other than Iran can lead the Islamic world, and this is a historical position.[33]

The Soviet Union did not create the conditions for revolution in Central America but stood nonetheless to profit from it strategically. In the same terms, one can imagine the strategic bonanza for Iran if one or more pro-Western Arab governments were to succumb to an Islamic upheaval, whatever its indigenous origins. An Islamic takeover in Algeria would inevitably have a shock effect in Egypt.

Experts can point to the diversity of the Islamic phenomenon and the tenuousness of the link between Tehran and its distant cousins. Yet it is hard to deny that even where Iranian funding does not reach, the prestige of the Iranian Revolution gives strength to the ideology. One need only reflect on how thoroughly the radical Left in Europe, Latin America, and Africa has been deflated and demoralized by the discrediting of communism in the Soviet motherland. There is at the very least a psychological connection between Iran and its distant imitators.

The United States needs always to be willing to settle differences and coexist peacefully if that should be Iran's course. But the very concept of coexisting peacefully, alas, is more the West's concept than Iran's. At the present juncture it is essential first to interpose countervailing power— just as the West did to the Soviet Union—to contain Iran's ambitions pending some ultimate erosion of its revolutionary élan. That means bolstering our regional allies, punishing terrorism, blocking Iran's access to militarily useful advanced technology, and maintaining a strong U.S. deterrent presence in the Gulf and in the Middle East.

Egypt, Jordan, Lebanon, Saudi Arabia, Morocco, Tunisia, the Gulf states—these are friends of the West and reasonably benign governments by Middle Eastern standards. They should be encouraged to reach out to all moderate elements in their societies, including Islamists, but should not be pushed into political experiments they consider dangerous. The West is under no obligation to commit strategic suicide out of guilt at social conditions whose improvement, after all, is more likely to come about from the Third World's integration into the world community than from terrorism and upheaval. There are millions of moderate, modern men and women in Muslim countries struggling against this obscurantism, and we do them a grave disservice if we assume the inevitable triumph—or, even worse, the democratic necessity—of the revolutionary tide.

For while Islamic leaders may be willing to seek power through parliamentary means, their program is an all-embracing social, political, and cultural mobilization that—as exemplified by Iran—is the negation of the constitutionalism that is the essence of democracy as we know it. Limitation of the power of government; respect for individual civil and political (including women's) rights; the alternation of parties in office—such features tend to be absent from revolutionary Islamic doctrine and practice.[34] The key question is not how a movement comes into power but what it can be expected to do with that power once it has attained it. The West need not be so relativist about the meaning of democracy as to concede away its fundamental elements. In the end, the issue for the West may be less the question of how it should conduct foreign policy than of whether it believes in itself.

The debate over policy toward the Soviet Union has thus been transplanted—consciously—to the new venue. For Robin Wright, a conciliatory policy toward Iran and Islam is mandated by what she sees as the lesson of the Cold War: "Generally the West is not applying the most important lesson of the Cold War: co-option is far more effective than confrontation in undermining a rival, in this case one perceived rather than real."[35] But for Anthony Lake, now President Clinton's national security adviser, the containment analogy is more apt. He has quoted from George Kennan's 1947 "X" article and argued for the same strategy of patience and firmness, on the theory that we encourage Iranian moderation best by frustrating its radical thrust.[36]

The euphoria about our strategic success in this region of the developing world may thus be short-lived in view of its volatility and passions. But it would be most tragic if the West's response to this new challenge were hampered by the same intellectual confusion that so tormented our policies during the Cold War.

AMERICA'S CHOICES

That intellectual confusion is one of the main themes of this book. Of all the battlefronts on which the Cold War was fought, the competition in the Third World seems to have posed the most anguishing moral dilemmas for Americans. Whatever debates there may have been in the United States over the strategic arms race and European security, they paled beside the bitter controversies over Vietnam and Central America, over covert action and presidential power, over jungle wars and the dilemmas of defending flawed allies. In this sphere, American idealism and American strategic necessities seemed too often in conflict. We were a superpower that wrestled with its conscience all the while that it battled with an unscrupulous adversary that—just as Walter Lippmann had predicted in 1947—often deliberately chose to challenge us on the messiest moral terrain.[37]

The American philosophy of foreign policy includes many strands. As we saw in the opening chapters, there is an anticolonial heritage and sympathy for the downtrodden—the vestige of our own revolutionary tradition—and it is not confined to a guilt-ridden intelligentsia; it is a feature of the American popular tradition. There is a Wilsonian expectation on all sides that the grubby way international politics has commonly been conducted can be reformed by an America that sets a higher standard.

Often the liberals have been the conscience of the nation, as in their revulsion at rightist dictatorships and their support for diplomatic solutions. At other times, their allergy to considerations of power has led to monumental misjudgments, with both strategic and moral consequences, as in the U.S. abdication in Cambodia and Angola in 1975. Conservatives have had fewer illusions about the nature of our Cold War adversary, but they, too, occasionally shied away from the Third World geopolitical contest and even more often from the inescapable task of shaping a positive political and diplomatic strategy. Left and Right have had in common a moral impulse that was classically American—the liberals in their inhibitions about the use of power and the conservatives in their aversion to legitimizing evil by a diplomatic dialogue with it.

Americans, in short, refuse to accept the grimness they see around them; evil is not something to adjust to but something to undo. After a century as grim and ridden with evil as the twentieth century, this refusal is evidence of an extraordinary faith. It is in large part *because* of an America that possessed such faith that the world has managed to survive that century and overcome its horrors. But the other side of the coin of this moral optimism is a moral discomfort with the means of engagement in an imperfect world.

Arkady Shevchenko writes of a conversation he once had with his boss, Andrei Gromyko, in the 1970s: "One day, while we were lunching at his dacha at Vnukovo, I asked Gromyko what he saw as the greatest weakness of U.S. foreign policy toward the Soviet Union. 'They don't comprehend our final goals,' he responded promptly. 'And they mistake tactics for strategy. Besides, they have too many doctrines and concepts proclaimed at different times, but the absence of a solid, coherent, and consistent policy is their big flaw.' "[38] In the short run, Gromyko was right: The United States often floundered in its response to the Soviet challenge. But in the long run, of course, he was wrong. From the contemporary vantage point the record of U.S. policy since 1945 shows, if not steadfast consistency, then at least an extraordinary resilience.

Containment was the watchword for the first postwar decades and commanded a bipartisan consensus. Vietnam then tore that consensus apart for a time, as we saw, and the strategic consequences of our abdication were severe. It was of that period that Shevchenko wrote. Nixon and Kissinger navigated this treacherous passage, compensating for the domestic weakness by strategic coups with China and Egypt. Then, at the end of the 1970s, the American people reacted to a string of humiliating events (especially the Iran hostage crisis and the invasion of Afghanistan) by endorsing a more assertive foreign policy that banished the guilt and self-torment that Vietnam had spawned. This was what Ronald Reagan embodied.

Nixon and Kissinger had tried in vain to educate the public about what they saw as the excesses of Wilsonian moralism. In the name of restraint and realism, they had mistrusted ideology on all sides, not only Soviet but American; at the same time, they strived mightily to keep America engaged in the geopolitical contest. It was an experiment that aborted, for a variety of reasons.[39] Reagan, in contrast, championed a shamelessly ideological policy that not only trumpeted the superiority of Western democracy but challenged the internal legitimacy of our Communist opponents. At the same time, it was Reagan who managed to reengage the United States on the geopolitical battlefield in the Third World—the field whose abandonment Kissinger had so deplored in 1975.

That success was not an accident. In the gloomy 1970s, Kissinger himself had often argued that the global balance of power was being undermined not by a failure of American resources or physical capacity but by a collapse of will: "America has the material assets to do the job. Our military might is unmatched. Our economic and technological strength dwarfs any other. Our democratic heritage is envied by hundreds of millions around the world.

"Our problems, therefore, are of our own making—self-doubt, division, irresolution."[40] He was right—but what restored the country's will turned out to be Reagan's ideological energy, which Nixon and Kissinger (and many others) had disparaged. Reagan's unabashed trumpeting of Western democracy and resistance to totalitarianism, as in his 1982 Westminster speech, was of a piece with his political mission of restoring the country's faith in itself—and this had strategic consequences.

America's reengagement restored the balance of the international system after a period of Soviet overreaching. The Soviets had to learn their limits, just as Americans had to learn that retreat was not an option for them. That restoration of balance is what made possible the successful East-West diplomacy of the 1980s in most of the crisis spots of the developing world that we have discussed in this book.

Where American policy succeeded, it was because it had bipartisan support, reflecting the deeper motivations of the country. The strength of the democratic idea around the world is no small vindication of the Wilsonian ideal. Many Third World countries have been beneficiaries of aid to institutions (parties, newspapers, labor unions, human rights monitors) provided by the National Endowment for Democracy—the congressionally funded agency created, with bipartisan support, after Reagan's speech at Westminster. Promotion of democracy was a principal feature of Bill Clinton's 1992 presidential campaign—his speeches even written by some of the same moderate Democrats who had backed the ideological theme of democracy in Reagan's Central America policy. George Bush suffered by his seeming preference for Nixonian realpolitik—his "embrace of stability at the expense of freedom," his "eagerness to befriend potentates and dictators," as Clinton put it.[41]

The lesson of the 1980s was the success of a foreign policy that reconciled America's moral impulses and its strategic necessities. In Central America, the United States supported the democratic center against both military thugs and Communist fanatics; by such a policy—and only by such a policy—could Reagan hold together, for much of his term, any kind of bipartisan majority in Congress—a majority that would probably have been more solid had it not been for the blunder of Iran-Contra.

Not only in Central America but globally, the United States refused to accept the pretensions of Communist permanence and rallied itself for a defense buildup and activist policy in the Third World. Reagan tapped the Wilsonian tradition as a motivation for the accomplishment of a Nixonian strategic purpose.

For all its clumsy bureaucratic infighting, the Reagan administration taught another lesson. Not only is it important to harness American idealism in the service of our strategic interests; it is also essential to harness American power in the service of political objectives. George Shultz's two-track approach—negotiations plus leverage—was essentially vindicated, despite its occasional stumbles amid the pressures from both the Right and Left. The military instrument (especially if it could be applied quietly) worked, and taught a basic truth about conflict resolution: Diplomacy certainly requires mediating skills, fairness, patience, and perseverance, but the diplomats have no chance to succeed unless the fundamental political forces at work are brought into balance by the application of leverage, wielding the power of the United States. Shaping the political forces in this way—not the display of lawyerlike negotiating skill—is the true job of foreign policy.

Critics who disdained the military instrument understood, at least, that strength is barren without a political purpose; our power was most effective when applied to a negotiating objective. As the Cold War regional rivalry wound down, liberals and conservatives alike were—one could hope—coming to understand that power and diplomacy must go hand in hand.*

No sooner does one phase of our history end with its lessons seemingly absorbed, however, than another era dawns and reopens some of the same questions. The challenge of reconciling our ideals and our power has already reappeared in new guises in the post–Cold War era.

One manifestation is the concept of multilateralism. As George Bush demonstrated deftly in the Gulf crisis, the United States can maximize its effectiveness through working with other nations. Superpower cooperation played an important role in the Gulf War and the Arab-Israeli peace process. Even Bush, chided by both liberals and neoconservatives as too much the power politician, described his vision in largely Wilsonian terms. He condemned Saddam Hussein's aggression in Kuwait not merely

---

*It was amusing to see liberals rediscover this lesson in the case of Serbian aggression in the former Yugoslavia. The idea that diplomacy depends on the wielding of power gained an eloquent advocate, for example, in Anthony Lewis, who had regularly dismissed such analysis throughout the Cold War.[42]

as a strategic challenge but as a defiance of the world's hopes for a better future after the Cold War; he painted a picture of a world governed by international cooperation, by collective security against aggression—"a world where the rule of law, not the law of the jungle, governs the conduct of nations."[43]

But multilateralism can take a multitude of forms. There is what I have called a "mushy" multilateralism—a policy that makes deference to an international consensus a cardinal principle for the United States, a policy of shying away from unilateral American action, particularly if it involves an assertion of American power.[44] This kind of multilateralism can become an excuse for inaction. Walter Lippmann once referred to it as "the internationalism of the isolationist."[45] We see signs of it in Bill Clinton's policy in Bosnia.

Contrasted to this is a more "muscular" multilateralism, which sees international cooperation not as an end in itself but as a means to an end. This approach—which more precisely characterizes Bush's performance in the Gulf crisis—first of all sees that the factor of power, in its classical forms, is still relevant in the new era despite the contemporary cliché about the obsolescence of traditional concepts of security. Saddam Hussein and Slobodan Milosevic have had a marvelous pedagogical impact in this respect.

The more muscular form of multilateralism sees, moreover, that American leadership is needed to *shape* the international consensus. The coalition that fought Iraq in 1991 would not have existed had America not taken the lead. The world community has been ineffectual in Bosnia in part because the United States gave no sustained, forceful lead; similarly, in the case of the world's failure so far to block North Korea's acquisition of a nuclear weapon. Sometimes the prospect of *unilateral* American action has had a galvanizing effect on international cooperation: Economic and diplomatic cooperation against Libya improved enormously after the U.S. military confrontation with Tripoli in 1986. The hopes for international norms of conduct and international collaboration in enforcing them depend crucially on an America that maintains its strength, is vigorous and confident, and is comfortable with its power and with the lonely responsibility that goes with it.

A second recent manifestation of the traditional American dilemma is a new theory on the subject of military intervention. The United States has found itself, since the Gulf War, drawn into a series of military actions on humanitarian grounds—first, the troop deployment in northern Iraq to protect the Kurds following the Gulf War; then the engagement in Somalia in 1992–94 in response to civil war, anarchy, and mass starvation;

then the halting involvement against Serb aggression and atrocities in Bosnia in 1992–94; and an aborted intervention in Haiti in 1993. Most of these interventions or proposed interventions had a compelling moral and legal case—the combating of evil, the rescue of suffering human beings, the upholding of international norms of conduct. The arguments for military action were made strongly in humanitarian terms, less so in terms of U.S. strategic interest.

The good news was the apparent end of liberal diffidence about the use of American military power. The bad news was that—yet again—it was still divorced from rigorous analysis of strategic or military realities. In some circles, strategic arguments were actively disparaged: Anthony Lewis, in a public debate, criticized Bush as a "gutless wimp" for not intervening to save Bosnia. When reminded that Bush had taken half a million Americans to war over Kuwait, Lewis replied mockingly: "Yes, he did because of oil, *O-I-L*, the famous three-letter word."[46] The final irony is that the end of the Cold War, while breaking some of the remaining Vietnam-era taboos against the use of our power, has produced an intellectual vacuum on the question of where the American national interest lies.

A whole new academic field has developed under the rubric of "humanitarian intervention."[47] Its modern origins can be traced to a passage in Harvard philosopher Michael Walzer's 1977 book *Just and Unjust Wars*, explaining how a moral duty to intervene can sometimes arise.[48] The doctrine was elaborated by the French socialist and activist Bernard Kouchner and was much discussed at the United Nations throughout 1991 in the context of Saddam's continuing persecution of the Kurdish minority in Iraq. By 1992, a study commission sponsored by the Carnegie Endowment for International Peace was hailing what it saw as a "new principle of international relations"—namely, that respect for a nation's sovereignty was no longer justified if it was violating human rights on a large scale, or if it otherwise presented what the report called a "humanitarian crisis." The United States and the world's nations had not only a right to intervene, by force if necessary, but a duty.[49] It was a remarkable reversal for a segment of our intellectual community that had criticized U.S. interventionism throughout the Cold War on the basis of the sacred principle of noninterference in the internal affairs of other states.

The motive of humanitarian intervention is noble, but the risks are great. It is difficult to imagine the American public's *sustaining* a military involvement—especially if it is large-scale, protracted, and costly in casualties—without a clear perception that a concrete national interest is involved, beyond the humanitarian impulse. The popular and congressional agitation that drove Clinton out of Somalia is a case in point. There is an undercurrent of isolationism in the country—not a tide but a mood—given the disappearance of our major strategic threat. The humanitarian interventionists risk discrediting the very internationalism that they are now rediscovering after two decades of ambivalence.

A third reappearance of America's intellectual dilemmas is its difficulty in the mid-1990s in coming to terms with the evolution in Russian foreign policy. With the end of communism there had been a profound Wilsonian confidence—first, that democracy would take firm root in Russia, and second, that a democratic Russia would conduct a wholly beneficent foreign policy. Both expectations have met with disappointments.

The demise of the Communist Soviet Union has been an enormous boon to the world. This book has traced some of its effects. Even a reassertive Russian policy lacks the Leninist thrust that commanded a strategy of undermining Western strategic positions globally, especially in the developing world. Even a nationalist Russia has little interest today in destabilizing Latin America, Africa, South or Southeast Asia; and in the Middle East, the region of the developing world in which Russia is most likely to remain engaged, its core interest is in stability, out of fear of the forces of radical Islam. Nor has Russia yet recommenced a strategic arms race or made moves to restore the previous status quo in Central or Eastern Europe.

Even so, Russia has surprised the world by the speed with which it has begun to restore its geopolitical position even while it remains a basket case economically. This is shown most vividly in what Russians call the "near abroad"—those republics of the former USSR in which Moscow has acted in classical fashion to restore its dominance in the name of restoring order. Russia has also sought to block the incorporation of its former Warsaw Pact allies into NATO. There will be no more "unilateral concessions" in foreign and defense policy, President Boris Yeltsin announced to the Parliament in February 1994—in the same week that he sent Russian troops to Bosnia.[50]

Today's Russia is neither an enemy nor an ally. It is a phenomenon well known to history—a great power, impelled by a conception of its national interest and destiny, acting according to morally neutral laws of geopolitics. History, geography, and the facts of power reassert themselves. For Americans who had bet their hopes on a moral conversion, this is a great disillusionment, a return to a balance-of-power world uncongenial to the Wilsonian tradition.[51]

THE FUTURE

For Americans, the post–Cold War world thus presents a conundrum: With a major threat ended, how do we define the mission of our foreign policy? The new era's challenges are multiple and varied; in the developing world, only a few of them reach the level of a strategic danger for us. But some do—especially the renegade regimes (North Korea, Iran, Iraq) actively seeking nuclear, chemical, and biological weapons capabilities and the ballistic missiles with which to deliver them. As Charles Krauthammer has written, these "radical Weapon states" may be the "single biggest threat to international security for the rest of our lives."[52]

The outlines of a new international system may not yet be sharply clear, but quite a lot is already evident. There is, first of all, no shortage of challenges and dangers to international *security*. The cliché that traditional security problems are obsolete is, as noted, false. Second, the world community at the present stage of its evolution is still dependent on American leadership. Without our willingness to take the initiative and the lead, there will simply be no effective response to the security challenges—or the humanitarian challenges. Whatever the issue—disarray in Europe, the reemergence of Russia, the new power of Germany and Japan, Third World renegades with weapons of mass destruction, a precarious international trading system, dangers to the global environment—there is no possible solution without us. The cliché about its being a shrinking planet on which America's fate is increasingly tied to that of others is true. Isolation is not an option.

America's self-confidence and steadfastness turn out to be, yet again, a decisive factor in the new international order. We do not dominate, but our influence is pivotal. We cannot wield this influence effectively without coherence in our policy and energy in carrying it out—qualities that are not easy for a democracy to attain. We need to prove Gromyko wrong all over again. The ability of Congress and the president to work together, our people's comfort with morally complex issues of power and diplomacy, our seriousness about maintaining our military and intelligence capabilities, our presidents' ability to assure bureaucratic discipline and boldness in the executive branch—these elements, or their absence, will have repercussions beyond our shores.

They are all a function of political will. "Imperial overstretch" is certainly not our problem. Our limits in the 1970s were to a great extent self-imposed, especially after Vietnam. And never has a more cost-effective policy been devised than our modest support for those challenging the Soviets in the 1980s—forcing the Soviets to confront *their* imperial overstretch. Our own difficulties, economic and political, have had more to do with philosophical confusion and deadlocks in our governmental system than with any exhaustion of our nation's energy or underlying strength. Our triumphs came when we were unified—and clearheaded—about our necessities. They came when we found in our morality a source of faith in ourselves, not of guilt or paralysis.

We are in the extraordinary position of the world's only superpower— yet a nation uniquely trusted by others. This is a tribute to us as a superpower with a conscience. The world is more afraid of our abdication than of our dominance. We are called upon to harness once again our moral convictions and our strategic insight, to respond to a new era of challenges as successfully as we did in the long struggle known as the Cold War.

NOTES

In order to keep the number of endnotes from proliferating even more than they have done, I have chosen not to provide a citation for the many quotations from senior American statesmen and officials when they are readily accessible in standard reference sources. For Woodrow Wilson, for example, the authoritative source is the multivolume Princeton compilation: Arthur S. Link et al., ed., *The Papers of Woodrow Wilson* (Princeton: Princeton University Press, 1982). Franklin D. Roosevelt's speeches and statements can be found in Samuel I. Rosenman, ed., *The Public Papers and Addresses of Franklin D. Roosevelt* (New York: Harper & Brothers, 1938–1950). For other presidents beginning with Herbert Hoover, official statements and documents are compiled in the annual volumes of the *Public Papers of the Presidents*, published in Washington by the U.S. Government Printing Office as well as (in recent decades) the *Weekly Compilation of Presidential Documents*. Statements by senior officials of the Department of State—secretaries of state and also deputy secretaries, under secretaries, and assistant secretaries—may be found in the *U.S. Department of State Bulletin* or, since September 1990, the weekly *U.S. Department of State Dispatch*. Unless otherwise indicated, all such quotations herein are taken from these sources.

FRONTISPIECE

1. Melba Porter Hay, ed., *The Papers of Henry Clay* (Lexington, KY: University of Kentucky Press, 1991), Vol. 10, pp. 945–46.

INTRODUCTION

1. Bill Keller, "Afghanistan: Last Man Out," *New York Times*, February 16, 1989, p. A8; interview with Gromov in *Sovietskaya Rossiya*, November 15, 1989, translated by the U.S. Department of Commerce, *Foreign Broadcast Information Service* (FBIS), in FBIS-SOV-89-223, 21 November 1989 (captioned as "Gromov Recalls Afghanistan, Life, Career"), pp. 107–8.

2. Woodrow Wilson, "A Talk to the Gridiron Club," Washington, D.C., February 26, 1916.

3. Jefferson letter to the Marquis de Lafayette, October 28, 1822, in Paul Leicester Ford, ed., *The Writings of Thomas Jefferson* (New York: G. P. Putnam's Sons, 1892–1899), Vol. X, p. 227.

4. Dean Acheson, "Morality, Moralism, and Diplomacy," address delivered at the University of Florida, Gainesville, February 20, 1958, in Dean Acheson, *Grapes from Thorns* (New York: W. W. Norton, 1972), p. 126.

5. Daniel P. Moynihan, "The Politics of Human Rights," *Commentary*, August 1977, pp. 23, 26.

CHAPTER 1

1. Arthur S. Link, *Woodrow Wilson and the Progressive Era, 1910–1917* (New York: Harper Torchbooks/Harper & Row, 1963), p. 275.

2. Arthur S. Link et al., eds., *The Papers of Woodrow Wilson* (Princeton, N.J.: Princeton University Press, 1982), Vol. 40, p. 409.

3. Link, *Woodrow Wilson and the Progressive Era*, pp. 224–30, 239–41.

4. Eric F. Goldman, *Rendezvous with Destiny: A History of Modern American Reform*, 25th anniversary ed. (New York: Vintage Books/Random House, 1977), p. 190.

5. Cobb's interview with Wilson can be found in Ray Stannard Baker, *Woodrow Wilson: Life and Letters* (Garden City, N.Y.: Doubleday, 1927–39), Vol. VI, pp. 506–7, and is quoted in Goldman, *op. cit.*, p. 191, and in Link, *Woodrow Wilson and the Progressive Era*, p. 277. Link dates the interview to March 19, 1917. See Arthur Link, "That Cobb Interview," *Journal of American History*, Vol. 72 (June 1985), pp. 7–17.

6. Gilbert Ziebura, *World Economy and World Politics, 1924–1931: From Reconstruction to Collapse*, translated by Bruce Little (Oxford, Eng.: Berg, 1990), Tables 1 and 2, p. 40.

7. Arthur S. Link, *Woodrow Wilson: Revolution, War, and Peace* (Arlington Heights, Ill.: Harlan Davidson, 1979), p. 3.

8. Wilson's preface to the fifteenth printing of his *Congressional Government* (1900), quoted in ibid., pp. 3–4.

9. Arno Mayer, *Wilson vs. Lenin: Political Origins of the New Diplomacy, 1917–1918* (Cleveland and New York: Meridian Books/World Publishing Company, 1964), pp. 346–48; Inga Floto, "Woodrow Wilson: War Aims, Peace Strategy, and the European Left," in Arthur S. Link, ed., *Woodrow Wilson and a Revolutionary World, 1913–1921* (Chapel Hill: University of North Carolina Press, 1982), pp. 129–32.

10. Goldman, *op. cit.*, p. 193.

11. Link, *Woodrow Wilson: Revolution, War, and Peace*, p. 81.

12. Quoted in Branko Lazitch and Milorad M. Drachkovitch, *Lenin and the Comintern* (Stanford, Calif.: Hoover Institution Press, 1972), Vol. I, p. 31.

13. Arthur Walworth, *Wilson and His Peacemakers: American Diplomacy at the Paris Peace Conference, 1919* (New York: W. W. Norton, 1986), p. 488 n. 22; Link, *Woodrow Wilson: Revolution, War, and Peace*, p. 81; Mayer, *op. cit.*, Chapter 9.

14. David Fromkin, *A Peace to End All Peace: The Fall of the Ottoman Empire and the Creation of the Modern Middle East* (New York: Avon Books, 1990), Part XII.

15. Jane Degras, ed., *Soviet Documents on Foreign Policy*, Vol. I, 1917–24 (London: Oxford University Press, 1951), pp. 15–17, quoted in Mayer, *op. cit.*, p. 295.

16. N. Gordon Levin, *Woodrow Wilson and World Politics: America's Response to War and Revolution* (London: Oxford University Press, 1968), *passim*; William Appleman

Williams, *The Tragedy of American Diplomacy*, 2d ed. rev. & enl. (New York: Dell Publishing Co./A Delta Book, 1972), Chapter 1.

17. Link, *Woodrow Wilson: Revolution, War, and Peace*, pp. 7–8.

18. Letter from Sir Cecil Arthur Spring Rice to Sir Edward Grey, February 7, 1914, in Link, *The Papers of Woodrow Wilson*, Vol. 29, pp. 228–31.

19. Levin, *op. cit.*, p. 24.

20. Link, *Woodrow Wilson: Revolution, War, and Peace*, pp. 9–11.

21. Walworth, *op. cit.*, p. 73.

22. Ibid, Chapter 4.

23. Lansing, Confidential Memoranda and Notes, December 30, 1918, Lansing MSS, Library of Congress, quoted in Levin, *op. cit.*, pp. 247–48.

24. Karl Marx, "The Future Results of British Rule in India," *New York Daily Tribune*, August 8, 1853; in Shlomo Avineri, ed., *Karl Marx on Colonialism and Modernization* (Garden City, N.Y.: Doubleday, 1968), p. 125.

25. Avineri, *op. cit.*, introduction, p. 12.

26. Marx, *loc. cit.*

27. Dana Torr, ed., *Marx and China: 1853–1860: Articles from the New York Daily Tribune* (London: Lawrence & Wishart, 1951), p. 45; Margot Light, *The Soviet Theory of International Relations* (New York: St. Martin's Press, 1988), pp. 75–78.

28. V. I. Lenin, "Report on the Work of the All-Russian Central Executive Committee and the Council of People's Commissars," delivered at the First Session of the All-Russia Central Executive Committee, Seventh Convocation, February 2, 1920, in V. I. Lenin, *Collected Works* (Moscow: Progress Publishers, 1965), Vol. 30 (September 1919–April 1920), p. 325.

29. V. I. Lenin, *Imperialism: The Highest Stage of Capitalism*, 1916, in V. I. Lenin, *Collected Works* (New York: International Publishers, 1942), Vol. XIX, pp. 91–196.

30. Mayer, *op. cit.*, p. 298.

31. V. I. Lenin, *The Discussion on Self-Determination Summed Up*, 1916, in *Collected Works* (New York), Vol. XIX, p. 287.

32. Quoted in Jane Degras, ed., *The Communist International 1919–1943: Documents* (London: Frank Cass, 1971), Vol. I, p. 138.

33. Lazitch & Drachkovitch, *op. cit.*, pp. 389–90.

34. V. I. Lenin, "Report on the International Situation and the Fundamental Tasks of the Communist International," July 19, 1920, in Lenin, *Collected Works* (Moscow), Vol. 31, p. 232.

35. V. I. Lenin, *Preliminary Draft Theses on the National and the Colonial Questions*, Points 2, 3, 5 in Lenin, *Collected Works* (Moscow), Vol. 31, pp. 145ff.

36. Ibid., Point 11.

37. M. N. Roy, *Memoirs* (Bombay: Allied Publishers Private Ltd., 1964), Chapter 46.

38. Ibid., p. 379.

39. Ibid.

40. Lazitch & Drachkovitch, *op. cit.*, p. 389.

41. Ibid.

42. Ibid., p. 402.

43. Ibid, p. 403.

44. Roy, *op. cit.*, p. 393.

45. Henry L. Roberts, "Russia and America," in Ivo J. Lederer, ed., *Russian Foreign Policy: Essays in Historical Perspective* (New Haven and London: Yale University Press, 1962), p. 588.

46. Ibid., p. 589.

47. George F. Kennan, *Soviet-American Relations, 1917–1920: Russia Leaves the War* (Princeton, N.J.: Princeton University Press, 1956), p. 28.

48. John Lewis Gaddis, *The Long Peace: Inquiries into the History of the Cold War* (New York: Oxford University Press, 1987), pp. 10–12, 18, 35.

49. Roberts, *loc. cit.*, pp. 590–91.

50. Harold Nicolson, *Peacemaking 1919* (London: Constable, 1943).

51. Hermann Kesser, *Neue Zuercher Zeitung*, October 27, 1918; quoted in *Cambridge Magazine* (November 16, 1918), p. 143, and in Mayer, *op. cit.*, p. 393.

CHAPTER 2

1. Margot Light, *The Soviet Theory of International Relations* (New York: St. Martin's Press, 1988), pp. 90–92.

2. David Fromkin, *A Peace to End All Peace: The Fall of the Ottoman Empire and the Creation of the Modern Middle East* (New York: Avon Books, 1989), pp. 394–401.

3. Ibid., pp. 385–87; 494–96.

4. Bruce D. Porter, *The USSR in Third World Conflicts: Soviet Arms and Diplomacy in Local Wars, 1945–1980* (Cambridge, Eng.: Cambridge University Press, 1984), p. 9.

5. Fromkin, *op. cit.*, pp. 421–23.

6. Henry S. Bradsher, *Afghanistan and the Soviet Union* (Durham, N.C.: Duke University Press, 1983), p. 15; Adam Ulam, *Expansion and Coexistence: The History of Soviet Foreign Policy, 1917–67* (New York: Frederick A. Praeger, 1968), p. 123.

7. Fromkin, *op. cit.*, p. 456.

8. Ibid., pp. 455–62.

9. Ulam, *op. cit.*, p. 145.

10. Franz Borkenau, *World Communism: A History of the Communist International* (Ann Arbor: University of Michigan Press, 1962), pp. 293–94; Branko Lazitch and Milorad M. Drachkovitch, *Lenin and the Comintern* (Stanford, Calif.: Hoover Institution Press, 1972), Vol. I, pp. 412–13.

11. Bradsher, *op. cit.*, pp. 14–15.

12. Quoted in Light, *op. cit.*, p. 94.

13. Porter, *op. cit.*, p. 10.

14. Borkenau, *op. cit.*, pp. 292–93.

15. Porter, *op. cit.*, pp. 11–12.

16. Ibid., p. 12.

17. Michael Novak, *The Spirit of Democratic Capitalism* (Lanham, Md.: Madison Books, 1991), especially Chapter XVIII.

18. *Addresses Delivered During the Visit of Herbert Hoover, President-elect of the United States, to Central and South America November–December 1928* (Washington, D.C.: Pan American Union Press, 1929), p. 16; quoted in Alexander DeConde, *Herbert Hoover's Latin-American Policy* (Stanford, Calif.: Stanford University Press, 1951), p. 59.

19. Reported remark of Wilson to Sir William Tyrrell, secretary to British foreign secretary Sir Edward Grey, November 13, 1913, in Burton J. Hendrick, ed., *The Life and Letters of Walter H. Page*, Vol. I (Garden City, N.Y.: Doubleday, 1922), pp. 204–5; quoted in Harley Notter, *The Origins of the Foreign Policy of Woodrow Wilson* (Baltimore, Md.: Johns Hopkins University Press, 1937), p. 274.

20. Franklin D. Roosevelt, note dictated to Vice President Henry Wallace on the origin of the Good Neighbor Policy, May 13, 1942, in Edgar B. Nixon, ed., *Franklin D. Roosevelt and Foreign Affairs*, Vol. I (Cambridge, Mass.: Belknap Press of Harvard University Press, 1969), pp. 20–21.

21. Franklin D. Roosevelt, "Our Foreign Policy: A Democratic View," *Foreign Affairs*, Vol. 6, No. 4 (July 1928), pp. 584.

22. Ibid., p. 586.

23. Willard Range, *Franklin D. Roosevelt's World Order* (Athens: University of Georgia Press, 1959), pp. 104–5.

24. Wm. Roger Louis, *Imperialism at Bay: The United States and the Decolonization of the British Empire, 1941–1945* (New York: Oxford University Press, 1978), pp. 123–25.

25. Ibid., p. 30.

26. Walter Lippmann, "The Post Singapore War in the East," *Washington Post*, February 21, 1942; quoted in ibid., pp. 134–35.

27. Cordell Hull, *Memoirs*, Vol. II (New York: Macmillan, 1948), pp. 1482–85.

28. Winston S. Churchill, *The Second World War: The Hinge of Fate* (Boston: Houghton Mifflin, 1950), pp. 212–14.

29. Ibid., p. 214.

30. Elliott Roosevelt, *As He Saw It* (New York: Duell, Sloan and Pearce, 1946), p. 74.

31. Churchill, radio address, November 10, 1942, in *The Times* (London), November 11, 1942; in Louis, *op. cit.*, p. 200.

32. Churchill, *The Hinge of Fate*, pp. 219–20.

33. Louis, *op. cit.*, pp. 150, 571.

34. Elliott Roosevelt, *op. cit.*, p. 24.

35. Ibid., p. 74; see also p. 115.

36. Memorandum by Taussig, March 15, 1944, cited in Louis, *op. cit.*, p. 486; see also the president's conversation with Stanley Hornbeck, ibid., p. 425, and the comments in the same vein by Sumner Welles, ibid., pp. 498–99.

37. Elliott Roosevelt, *op. cit.*, pp. 115–16.

38. Ibid., pp. 164, 203–4.

39. Ibid., pp. 206–7.

40. Louis, *op. cit.*, p. 198.

41. Ibid., p. 199.

42. Elliott Roosevelt, *op. cit.*, p. 75.

43. Roosevelt to Churchill, March 17, 1943, in Elliott Roosevelt, ed., *F.D.R.: His Personal Letters, 1928–1945*, Vol. II (New York: Duell, Sloan and Pearce, 1950), p. 1413.

44. Roosevelt's address at Monterrey, Mexico, April 20, 1943.

45. Range, *op. cit.*, p. 105; Louis *op. cit.*, p. 28.

46. Hull, *op. cit.*, p. 1597; see also the president's remarks to the Pacific War Council, July 21, 1943, in Louis, *op. cit.*, p. 277.

47. U.S. Department of State, *Foreign Relations of the United States: The Conference at Cairo and Tehran, 1943* (Washington, D.C.: U.S. Government Printing Office, 1961), pp. 485, 509.

48. Louis, *op. cit.*, pp. 90–95, 458.

49. U.S. Congress, Senate, Committee on Armed Services, *United States–Vietnam Relations, 1945–1967: Study Prepared by the Department of Defense* (Washington, D.C.: U.S. Government Printing Office, 1971), Book I, pp. A3–8, 28–50.

50. Central Intelligence Agency, "The Break-up of the Colonial Empires and Its Implications for US Security," ORE 25–48, 3 September 1948, p. 2, declassified in Michael Warner, ed., *CIA Cold War Records: The CIA Under Harry Truman* (Washington, D.C.: Central Intelligence Agency, Center for the Study of Intelligence, History Staff, 1994), p. 223.

51. John Lewis Gaddis, *The United States and the Origins of the Cold War, 1941–1947* (New York and London: Columbia University Press, 1972), pp. 299–301. For the

text of Stalin's address of February 9, 1946, see U.S. Congress, House of Representatives, Committee on Foreign Affairs, *The Strategy and Tactics of World Communism*, Report of Subcommittee No. 5, with Supplements I and II, House Document No. 619, 80th Congress, 2nd Session (Washington, D.C.: U.S. Government Printing Office, 1948), Supplement I ("One Hundred Years of Communism, 1848–1948"), pp. 168–78.

52. For an inside account of the crucial months of 1947, see Joseph Marion Jones, *The Fifteen Weeks* (New York: Harcourt, Brace & World, 1964).

53. Walter Lippmann, *The Cold War: A Study in U.S. Foreign Policy* (New York: Harper & Brothers, 1947), pp. 14, 21, 21–23.

54. E.g., Harry S. Truman, speech to the Swedish Pioneer Centennial Association, Chicago, June 4, 1948; see also Under Secretary of State Dean Acheson's testimony to the Senate Foreign Relations Committee, March 24, 1947, quoted in Jones, *op. cit.*, p. 190.

55. Milovan Djilas, *Conversations with Stalin* (New York: Harcourt, Brace & World, 1962), p. 182.

56. Ulam, *op. cit.*, pp. 425–28; Gaddis, *op. cit.*, pp. 309–12.

57. Andrei Zhdanov, "The International Situation," address to the founding conference of the Cominform, September 1947, in U.S. House of Representatives, *Strategy and Tactics of World Communism*, pp. 215–17.

58. Ye Zhukov, "Problems of the National-Colonial Struggle Since the Second World War," *Voprosy Economiki*, No. 9, 1949, in *Current Digest of the Soviet Press*, Vol. I, No. 49 (January 3, 1950), pp. 4–5.

59. The story is told in Arnold Krammer, *The Forgotten Friendship: Israel and the Soviet Bloc, 1947–53* (Urbana: University of Illinois Press, 1974).

60. See John Lewis Gaddis, *The Long Peace: Inquiries into the History of the Cold War* (New York: Oxford University Press, 1987), Chapter 4.

61. Ronald Steel, *Walter Lippmann and the American Century* (New York: Random House/Vintage Books, 1981), pp. 469–76.

62. Kathryn Weathersby, "Soviet Aims in Korea and the Origins of the Korean War, 1945–1950: New Evidence from Russian Archives," Working Paper No. 8, Cold War International History Project (Washington, D.C.: Woodrow Wilson International Center for Scholars, November 1993); see also "Secrets of the Korean War," *U.S. News & World Report*, August 9, 1993, pp. 45–47.

63. Nikita S. Khrushchev, *Khrushchev Remembers: The Glasnost Tapes*, translated and edited by Jerrold L. Schecter with Vyacheslav V. Luchkov (Boston: Little, Brown, 1990), pp. 144–46; Weathersby, *loc. cit.*, pp. 23–25; see also Nikita Khrushchev, *Khrushchev Remembers*, with an introduction, commentary, and notes by Edward Crankshaw (Boston: Little, Brown, 1970), pp. 368–69, where he refers to Stalin's initial doubts.

64. Khrushchev, *Khrushchev Remembers*, p. 221.

65. NSC 68 ("A Report to the President Pursuant to the President's Directive of January

31, 1950") in U.S. Department of State, *Foreign Relations of the United States, 1950*, Vol. I, *National Security Policy* (Washington, D.C.: U.S. Government Printing Office, 1977), pp. 287–88.

66. NSC 73/4 ("Report by the National Security Council, "The Position and Actions of the United States with Respect to Possible Further Soviet Moves in the Light of the Korean Situation"), August 25, 1950, in ibid., pp. 379–89.

67. Porter, *op. cit.*, p. 16.

CHAPTER 3

1. Remarks by Acheson in a news conference, February 14, 1951, in *New York Times*, February 15, 1951; Adam Ulam, *Expansion and Coexistence: The History of Soviet Foreign Policy, 1917–67* (New York: Frederick A. Praeger, 1968), Chapter X.

2. Margot Light, *The Soviet Theory of International Relations* (New York: St. Martin's Press, 1988), pp. 100–6.

3. Nikita Khrushchev, *Khrushchev Remembers: The Last Testament*, translated and edited by Strobe Talbott (Boston: Little, Brown, 1974), p. 296.

4. On the bureaucratic and policy background of the Eisenhower speech of April 16, 1953, to the American Society of Newspaper Editors, see W. W. Rostow, *Europe After Stalin: Eisenhower's Three Decisions of March 11, 1953* (Austin: University of Texas Press, 1982).

5. Address by G. M. Malenkov, chairman of the Council of Ministers, to the Supreme Soviet of the USSR, August 8, 1953, in *Pravda* and *Izvestia*, August 9, 1953, in *Current Digest of the Soviet Press*, Vol. V, No. 30 (September 5, 1953), pp. 9–10.

6. Joseph S. Berliner, *Soviet Economic Aid: The New Aid and Trade Policy in Under-developed Countries* (New York: Frederick A. Praeger, for the Council on Foreign Relations, 1958), pp. 15–16.

7. Keith Kyle, *Suez* (New York: St. Martin's Press, 1991), pp. 66, 577 note 14.

8. S. Nihal Singh, *The Yogi and the Bear: Story of Indo-Soviet Relations* (Riverdale, Md.: Riverdale Company, 1986), p. 14.

9. Ulam, *op. cit.*, pp. 561–62.

10. Khrushchev, *op. cit.*, pp. 295–343.

11. Oles Smolansky, *The Soviet Union and the Arab East Under Khrushchev* (Lewisburg, Pa.: Bucknell University Press, 1974), pp. 30–31; Jon D. Glassman, *Arms for the Arabs: The Soviet Union and War in the Middle East* (Baltimore and London: Johns Hopkins University Press, 1975), p. 10.

12. Report by Comrade N. S. Khrushchev, first secretary of the Central Committee of the CPSU, to the 20th Party Congress, February 14, 1956, in *Pravda*, February 15, 1956, and *Current Digest of the Soviet Press*, Vol. VIII, No. 4 (March 7, 1956), p. 7.

13. Light, *op. cit.*, pp. 113–42; Rajan Menon, *Soviet Power and the Third World* (New Haven: Yale University Press, 1986), pp. 19–21.

14. Francis Fukuyama, "Soviet Strategy in the Third World," in Andrzej Korbonski and Francis Fukuyama, eds., *The Soviet Union in the Third World: The Last Three Decades* (Ithaca, N.Y.: Cornell University Press, 1987), pp. 27–28.

15. Berliner, *op. cit.*, subtracting the 1957 figures (Table 7, p. 60) from the 1945–57 figures (Table 6, p. 57) to estimate the totals through 1956.

16. A. M. Rosenthal, "Dulles Meets Nehru in Hope for Accord," *New York Times*, March 10, 1956, pp. 1–2.

17. See, e.g., Henry A. Kissinger, *Nuclear Weapons and Foreign Policy* (New York: Harper and Brothers, for the Council on Foreign Relations, 1957), pp. 316–61.

18. NSC 153/1 ("Restatement of Basic National Security Policy"), June 10, 1953, in U.S. Department of State, *Foreign Relations of the United States, 1952–1954*, Vol. II (Washington, D.C.: U.S. Government Printing Office, 1984), p. 578.

19. NSC 162/2 ("Basic National Security Policy"), October 20, 1953, in ibid., pp. 588–590.

20. Henry A. Wallace, *Toward World Peace* (New York: Reynal and Hitchcock, 1948), pp. 36–37.

21. Ibid., pp. 45–46.

22. Central Intelligence Agency, "The Break-up of the Colonial Empires and Its Implications for US Security," ORE 25–48, 3 September 1948, p. 3, declassified in Michael Warner, ed., *CIA Cold War Records: The CIA Under Harry Truman* (Washington, D.C.: Central Intelligence Agency, Center for the Study of Intelligence, History Staff, 1994), p. 224.

23. Max F. Millikan and Walt W. Rostow, *A Proposal: Key to an Effective Foreign Policy* (New York: Harper and Brothers, 1957). For a history of the development of these ideas, see W. W. Rostow, *Eisenhower, Kennedy, and Foreign Aid* (Austin: University of Texas Press, 1985).

24. Millikan and Rostow, *op. cit.*, pp. 14–15.

25. Ibid., pp. 10, 11, 19, 25.

26. Rostow, *Eisenhower, Kennedy, and Foreign Aid*, Chapters 4, 10.

27. Rostow summarizes the debate with Bauer in ibid., especially pp. 36–56.

28. Robert A. Goldwin, ed., *Why Foreign Aid? Two Messages by President Kennedy and Essays* (Chicago: Rand McNally, 1963).

29. Hans J. Morgenthau, "Preface to a Political Theory of Foreign Aid," in ibid., p. 82; see also Edward C. Banfield, *American Foreign Aid Doctrines* (Washington, D.C.: American Enterprise Institute, 1963), pp. 14–15.

30. Morgenthau, *loc. cit.*, p. 84.

31. Henry A. Kissinger, *The Necessity for Choice: Prospects of American Foreign Policy* (New York: Harper and Brothers, 1961), pp. 290–91.

32. See especially the works of Lawrence E. Harrison, *Underdevelopment Is a State of Mind—The Latin American Case* (Lanham, Md.: Harvard Center for International

Affairs and University Press of America, 1985), and *Who Prospers? How Cultural Values Shape Economic and Political Success* (New York: Basic Books, 1992), and a forthcoming work by Francis Fukuyama.

33. Nicholas Eberstadt, *Foreign Aid and American Purpose* (Washington, D.C.: American Enterprise Institute, 1988), pp. 6, 79–80.

34. Ibid., p. 10.

35. Rostow, *Eisenhower, Kennedy, and Foreign Aid*, pp. 32–33.

36. Sarvepalli Gopal, *Jawaharlal Nehru: A Biography*, Vol. II (Delhi, India: Oxford University Press, 1979), p. 63; quoted in Singh, *op. cit.*, p. 20.

37. John Foster Dulles, "Challenge and Response in United States Policy," *Foreign Affairs*, Vol. 36, No. 1 (October 1957), pp. 38–39.

38. Letter from C. D. Jackson to Henry Luce, April 16, 1956, reporting on his conversation with Secretary Dulles, April 14, 1956, in Rostow, *Eisenhower, Kennedy, and Foreign Aid*, Appendix G, pp. 259–60. (Some of Dulles's concerns found their way into a speech he delivered before the annual luncheon of the Associated Press in New York, April 23, 1956.)

39. Ibid., p. 261.

40. Sen. John F. Kennedy, remarks at Fourth Annual Rockhurst Day Banquet of Rockhurst College, Kansas City, Missouri, June 2, 1956, in *Congressional Record* (84th Congress, 2nd Session), Vol. 102, Senate, June 6, 1956, p. 9615 (inserted in the *Record* by Sen. Stuart Symington). For Kennedy's Algeria speech of July 1957, see John F. Kennedy, *The Strategy of Peace*, edited by Allan Nevins (New York: Harper & Row, 1960), pp. 65–81.

41. Stephen E. Ambrose, *Eisenhower: The President* (New York: Simon and Schuster, 1984), p. 539.

42. William Bragg Ewald, Jr., *Eisenhower the President: Crucial Days, 1951–1960* (Englewood Cliffs, N.J.: Prentice-Hall, 1981), pp. 119–20.

43. William J. Lederer and Eugene Burdick, *The Ugly American* (New York: W. W. Norton, 1958). The film was produced by U-I/George Englund.

44. Raymond Cartier, *Paris-Match*, March 24, 1956, abridged and translated as "Why Does the World Hate America?" *National Review*, May 2, 1956, p. 13.

45. Morarji Desai, *Story of My Life*, Vol. II (New Delhi: S. Chand, 1974), p. 156; quoted in Singh, *op. cit.*, p. 18.

46. Marshall I. Goldman, *Soviet Foreign Aid* (New York: Frederick A. Praeger, 1967), pp. 191–92.

47. Barbara Ward, "For a New Foreign Aid Concept," *New York Times Magazine*, March 11, 1956, p. 42.

48. Ibid., p. 44.

49. See, e.g., the testimony of Deputy Secretary of State Clifton Wharton before the

Subcommittee on International Economic Policy, Trade, Oceans and Environment of the Senate Foreign Relations Committee, July 14, 1993.

50. Miles Copeland, *The Game of Nations: The Amorality of Power Politics* (New York: Simon and Schuster, 1969); Laurie Mylroie, *The Future of Iraq*, Policy Paper No. 24 (Washington, D.C.: Washington Institute for Near East Policy, 1991), pp. 55–56.

51. Kyle, *op. cit.*, pp. 56–57, 71–72; Shimon Shamir, "The Collapse of Project Alpha," in Wm. Roger Louis and Roger Owen, *Suez 1956: The Crisis and Its Consequences* (Oxford, Eng.: Clarendon Press, 1989).

52. Kyle, *op. cit.*, p. 75.

53. Ibid., p. 84.

54. Ibid., p. 99.

55. U.S. Department of State, *Foreign Relations of the United States 1955–1957*, Vol. XV, *Arab-Israeli Dispute: January 1–July 26, 1956* (Washington, D.C.: U.S. Government Printing Office, 1989), p. 419.

56. U.S. Congress, Senate, Committee on Foreign Relations, *Executive Sessions of the Senate Foreign Relations Committee (Historical Series)*, Vol. VIII, 84th Congress, 2nd Session, 1956 (made public December 1978), pp. 514–16.

57. Kyle, *op. cit.*, p. 130.

58. Ibid., p. 129.

59. Ibid., pp. 132–34.

60. Sir Anthony Eden, *Memoirs: Full Circle* (London: Cassell, 1960), pp. 427–28.

61. Ibid., p. 498.

62. Kyle, *op. cit.*, pp. 181, 267–68.

63. U.S. Department of State, *Foreign Relations of the United States 1955–1957*, Vol. XVI, *Suez Crisis, July 26–December 31, 1956*, (Washington, D.C.: U.S. Government Printing Office, 1990), pp. 132–33, 149–50, 156–60.

64. Ibid., p. 334.

65. Ibid., p. 357.

66. *New York Times*, October 3, 1956, p. 8. The official Department of State version differs from the *Times* text in a few nuances that tend to tone it down. See U.S. Department of State, *Department of State Bulletin*, Vol. XXXV, No. 903 (October 15, 1956), p. 577.

67. Nixon quoted in Herman Finer, *Dulles over Suez: The Theory and Practice of His Diplomacy* (Chicago: Quadrangle Books, 1964), p. 397.

68. Kyle, *op. cit.*, pp. 376–77.

69. Sanford J. Ungar, *Africa: The People and Politics of an Emerging Continent* (New York: Simon and Schuster, 1985), p. 64–65.

70. Dulles, *Foreign Affairs*, p. 27.

71. Kyle, *op. cit.*, p. 550; Smolansky, *op. cit.*, p. 51.

72. Sources collected in Bruce D. Porter, *The USSR in Third World Conflicts: Soviet Arms and Diplomacy in Local Wars, 1945–1980* (Cambridge, Eng.: Cambridge University Press, 1984), pp. 18–19.

73. Chester L. Cooper, *The Lion's Last Roar: Suez, 1956* (New York: Harper & Row, 1978), p. 181.

74. Selwyn Lloyd, *Suez 1956: A Personal Account* (New York: Mayflower Books, 1978), p. 219. Dulles acknowledged to Lloyd that there had been a difference "over method." To Robert Bowie, a defender of the administration's policy, the episode in the hospital is "puzzling and ambiguous" and not evidence of genuine regret. (See Robert R. Bowie, "Eisenhower, Dulles, and the Suez Crisis," in Louis and Owen, *op. cit.*, p. 214.) The evidence is cumulative, however, and seems incontrovertible.

75. Christian Pineau, *1956 Suez* (Paris: Laffont, 1976), p. 195; quoted in Lloyd, *op. cit.*, p. 258.

76. Lloyd, *op. cit.*, pp. 257–58.

77. Author's conversation on May 28, 1992, with Ambassador Ephraim Evron, who was Ambassador Harman's deputy chief of mission in the embassy of Israel in Washington at the time. Harman visited Eisenhower in 1967 to ask if the former president would publicly confirm the assurances that he had given to Israel in 1957 as part of the Suez settlement. (He would.) Harman recounted the conversation to Evron upon his return from Gettysburg.

78. Richard Nixon, "My Debt to Macmillan," *The Times* (London), January 28, 1987, p. 16; letter from Nixon to the author, February 25, 1992.

79. Richard Nixon, *1999: Victory Without War* (New York: Simon and Schuster, 1988), p. 205.

CHAPTER 4

1. Henry A. Kissinger, *White House Years* (Boston: Little, Brown, 1979), p. 1059.

2. Barbara W. Tuchman, *Stilwell and the American Experience in China, 1911–45* (New York: Macmillan, 1971).

3. Letter of transmittal from Secretary Acheson to the president, July 30, 1949, U.S. Department of State, *United States Relations with China* (Washington, D.C.: U.S. Government Printing Office, 1949), pp. XV–XVI.

4. See the *Resolution on Certain Questions in the History of our Party Since the Founding of the People's Republic of China*, adopted by the Sixth Plenary Session of the Eleventh Central Committee, June 27, 1981, *Beijing Review*, Vol. 24, No. 27 (July 6, 1981). Deng's view, however, was that Mao was 30 percent wrong and 70 percent correct. Ross Terrill, *Mao: A Biography* (New York: Touchstone/Simon & Schuster, 1993), p. 15. On the death toll under Mao, see Daniel Southerland, "Repression's Higher Toll," *Washington Post*, July 17, 1994, p. A1.

5. Harrison E. Salisbury, *The New Emperors: China in the Era of Mao and Deng* (Boston: Little, Brown, 1992), Chapters 2, 10.

6. John Lewis Gaddis, *The Long Peace: Inquiries into the History of the Cold War* (New York: Oxford University Press, 1987), Chapter 6.

7. NSC 34/2, "U.S. Policy Toward China," February 28, 1949, in U.S. Department of State, *Foreign Relations of the United States, 1949*, Vol. IX (Washington, D.C.: U.S. Government Printing Office, 1974), pp. 494–95.

8. John Foster Dulles, letter to Dean Acheson, November 30, 1950, quoted in Gaddis, *op. cit.*, p. 174.

9. See the recently published communications between Mao and Stalin, in Thomas J. Christensen, "Threats, Assurances, and the Last Chance for Peace: The Lessons of Mao's Korean War Telegrams," *International Security*, Vol. 17, No. 1 (Summer 1992).

10. T. N. Kaul, *Diplomacy in Peace and War: Recollections and Reflections* (New Delhi: Vikas, 1979), p. 12; quoted in S. Nihal Singh, *The Yogi and the Bear: Story of Indo-Soviet Relations* (Riverdale, Md.: Riverdale Company, 1986), p. 13.

11. Adam Ulam, *The Communists: The Story of Power and Lost Illusions: 1948–1991* (New York: Charles Scribner's Sons, 1992), p. 176.

12. Mao quoted in ibid., p. 178.

13. "Talk with Anna Louise Strong," August 1946, in *Selected Readings from the Works of Mao Tsetung* (Peking: Foreign Languages Press, 1971), p. 349.

14. Nikita Khrushchev, *Khrushchev Remembers: The Last Testament*, translated and edited by Strobe Talbott (Boston: Little, Brown, 1974), p. 255.

15. "Statement of Conference of World Communist Parties," continuation, *Pravda*, December 6, 1960; in *Current Digest of the Soviet Press*, Vol. XII, No. 49 (January 4, 1961), pp. 3, 6.

16. Daniel S. Papp, *Soviet Policies Toward the Developing World During the 1980s: The Dilemmas of Power and Presence* (Maxwell Air Force Base, Ala.: Air University Press, 1986), pp. 8–12; Alvin Z. Rubinstein, ed., *Soviet and Chinese Influence in the Third World* (Boston: Frederick A. Praeger, 1975).

17. Walter Lippmann, *The Communist World and Ours* (Boston: Little, Brown/Atlantic Monthly Press, 1959), p. 41.

18. Ibid., p. 13.

19. The quotes following are from N. S. Khrushchev, "Report at a Joint Meeting of the Party Organizations of the Higher Party School, the Academy of Social Sciences, and the Party Central Committee's Institute of Marxism-Leninism," January 6, 1961, in *Current Digest of the Soviet Press*, Vol. XIII, Nos. 3 and 4 (February 15 and 22, 1961).

20. Michael R. Beschloss, *The Crisis Years: Kennedy and Khrushchev, 1960–1963* (New York: HarperCollins, 1991), p. 61.

21. Ibid.

22. Ibid., p. 60.

23. Walter Lippmann, *The Coming Tests with Russia* (Boston: Little, Brown/Atlantic Monthly Press, 1961), p. 18.

24. See, e.g., Alvin Z. Rubinstein, *Moscow's Third World Strategy* (Princeton, N.J.: Princeton University Press, 1988), pp. 78–95; Beschloss, *op. cit.*, pp. 60–61, 63–64.

25. Rubinstein, *op. cit.*, pp. 92–95.

26. Roger Hilsman, *To Move a Nation: The Politics of Foreign Policy in the Administration of John F. Kennedy* (Garden City, N.Y.: Doubleday, 1967), pp. 413–14.

27. Lt. Col. T. N. Greene, ed., *The Guerrilla—and How to Fight Him*, (New York: Frederick A. Praeger, 1962).

28. William P. Yarborough, "Counterinsurgency: the U.S. Role—Past, Present, and Future," in Richard H. Shultz, Jr., et al., eds., *Guerrilla Warfare and Counterinsurgency: U.S.-Soviet Policy in the Third World* (Lexington, Mass.: Lexington Books/D.C. Heath, 1989), pp. 103–4.

29. See, e.g., William Odom, *On Internal War: American and Soviet Approaches to Third World Clients and Insurgents* (Durham, N.C.: Duke University Press, 1992), Chapter II.

30. W. W. Rostow, *Eisenhower, Kennedy, and Foreign Aid* (Austin: University of Texas Press, 1985), pp. 170–73.

31. Tad Szulc and Karl E. Meyer, *The Cuban Invasion* (New York: Ballantine Books, 1962), p. 57.

32. See Tad Szulc, *Fidel: A Critical Portrait* (New York: William Morrow, 1986), Part IV, Chapter 1.

33. Szulc and Meyer, *op. cit.*, especially pp. 85–89.

34. This and subsequent quotations are from U.S. Department of State, *Cuba* (Department of State Publication 7171, Inter-American Series 66), April 1961.

35. Szulc and Meyer, *op. cit.*, pp. 92–93, 106–7.

36. Beschloss, *op. cit.*, p. 120.

37. Philip Benjamin, "Robert Frost Returns with Word of Khrushchev," *New York Times*, September 10, 1962, p. 8. Frost disputed the press's interpretation of Khrushchev's remark, but his refutation leaves room for doubt whether his own interpretation was the same as Khrushchev's meaning. See F. D. Reeve, "Robert Frost Confronts Khrushchev," *Atlantic*, September 1963, pp. 33–39.

38. "Program of the CPSU," *Pravda*, November 3, 1961, in *Current Digest of the Soviet Press*, Vol. XIII, No. 45 (December 6, 1961), p. 12.

39. Stephen E. Ambrose, *Eisenhower: The President* (New York: Simon and Schuster, 1984), pp. 614–15.

40. Joseph Kraft, "John F. Kennedy: Portrait of a President," *Harper's*, January 1964, p. 98.

41. David Halberstam, *The Best and the Brightest* (New York: Random House, 1972), p. 76.

42. Sanford J. Ungar, *Africa: The People and Politics of an Emerging Continent* (New York: Simon and Schuster, 1985), p. 60.

43. Nyerere quoted in an address by Thomas L. Hughes, deputy director of intelligence and research, Department of State, "Soviet Foreign Policy—Its Implications for the West," before the conference on "the Sino-Soviet Bloc," Bernadotte Institute on World Affairs, Gustavus Adolphus College, St. Peter, Minnesota, May 4, 1962.

44. Nixon and Kennedy quoted in Ungar, *op. cit.*, p. 60.

45. Ibid., pp. 60–61.

46. Ibid., p. 62.

47. Ibid.

48. Madeleine G. Kalb, *The Congo Cables: The Cold War in Africa—From Eisenhower to Kennedy* (New York: Macmillan, 1982), is the best account of the Congo crisis.

49. Ibid., Chapters 6–8.

50. Arkady N. Shevchenko, *Breaking with Moscow* (New York: Alfred A. Knopf, 1985), pp. 102–3.

51. See the letter to the *Guardian* (London) by George Ivan Smith and Conor Cruise O'Brien, September 11, 1992, reported in the AP dispatch "Ex–U.N. Officials Question Hammarskjöld Crash," *New York Times*, September 13, 1992, p. 21.

52. Beschloss, *op. cit.*, pp. 329–32.

53. Ibid., pp. 331–32.

54. See, e.g., Beschloss, *op. cit.*, pp. 382–90; Nikita Khrushchev, *Khrushchev Remembers*, with an introduction, commentary, and notes by Edward Crankshaw (Boston: Little, Brown, 1970), pp. 492–95.

55. Khrushchev, *Khrushchev Remembers*, p. 494; see also Fedor Burlatsky, *Khrushchev and the First Russian Spring: The Era of Khrushchev Through the Eyes of His Adviser* (New York: Charles Scribner's Sons, 1991), pp. 171–74.

56. Max Frankel, "Khrushchev Trip to U.S. Expected Within 2 Months," *New York Times*, October 18, 1962, p. 1; Khrushchev interview with Raymond Scheyven, September 18, 1962, quoted in "Soviet May Put Berlin Up to U.N.," *New York Times*, October 22, 1962, p. 8; Max Frankel, "U.S. Sees Moscow Caught Off Guard," *New York Times*, October 24, 1962, p. 1. See also Burlatsky, *op. cit.*, pp. 173–74.

57. Juan de Onis, "Cuba Compromise Urged in Brazil," *New York Times*, October 28, 1962, p. 39; *Business Week*, November 3, 1962, p. 27; Henry M. Pachter, *Collision Course: The Cuban Missile Crisis and Coexistence* (New York: Frederick A. Praeger, 1963), pp. 80–81.

58. Harlan Cleveland, "Crisis Diplomacy," *Foreign Affairs*, Vol. VI, No. 4 (July 1963), p. 639 (emphasis in original); see Peter W. Rodman, "The Missiles of October: Twenty Years Later," *Commentary*, October 1982.

59. "Is Russia Slowing Down in Arms Race?" interview with McNamara in *U.S. News & World Report*, April 12, 1965, p. 52.

60. McNamara quoted in U.S. Congress, Senate, Committee on Armed Services, *Military Procurement Authorization for FY 1964, Hearings*, 88th Congress, 1st Session (Washington, D.C.: U.S. Government Printing Office, 1963), p. 507; see sources collected in Rodman, *loc. cit.*

61. N. S. Khrushchev, "The Present International Situation and the Foreign Policy of the Soviet Union," Report to Session of USSR Supreme Soviet, December 12, 1962, in *Current Digest of the Soviet Press*, Vol. XIV, No. 52 (January 23, 1963), p. 3.

62. Khrushchev, *Khrushchev Remembers: The Last Testament*, p. 512.

63. Kissinger quoted in Richard K. Betts, *Nuclear Blackmail and Nuclear Balance* (Washington, D.C.: Brookings Institution, 1987), p. 125; see also Henry A. Kissinger, statement on the Strategic Arms Limitation Treaty (SALT II) before the Senate Foreign Relations Committee, July 31, 1979, in U.S. Congress, Senate, Committee on Foreign Relations, *The SALT II Treaty, Hearings*, 96th Congress, 1st Session (Washington, D.C.: U.S. Government Printing Office, 1979), Part 3, pp. 164–65, 177–178, 224.

CHAPTER 5

1. Ho Chi Minh, "The Path Which Led Me to Leninism," *L'Echo du Vietnam* (July 1960), in Jean Lacouture, *Ho Chi Minh*, translated by Peter Wiles (London: Allen Lane/The Penguin Press, 1968), p. 22.

2. The "Pentagon Papers" provide a collection of biographical materials on Ho Chi Minh. See U.S. Congress, House of Representatives, Committee on Armed Services, *United States–Vietnam Relations, 1945–1967*, Study Prepared by the Department of Defense (Washington, D.C.: U.S. Government Printing Office, 1971), Book 1, Section IC; see also Robert F. Turner, *Vietnamese Communism: Its Origins and Development* (Stanford, Calif.: Hoover Institution Press, 1975), Chapter 1, and Douglas Pike, *Vietnam and the Soviet Union: Anatomy of an Alliance* (Boulder, Colo.: Westview Press, 1987), Chapter 1.

3. "Pentagon Papers," Book 1, pp. C41–42, 103.

4. Ibid., pp. C1–30.

5. Vo Nguyen Giap, *Immediate Military Tasks for Switching Over to the General Counter-Offensive* (Ha Dong: Resistance and Administrative Committee of Ha Dong Province, 1950), p. 14; quoted by Gareth Porter, "Vietnamese Policy and the Indochina Crisis," in David W. P. Elliott, ed., *The Third Indochina Conflict* (Boulder, Colo.: Westview Press, 1981), p. 88.

6. For this analysis, see Henry A. Kissinger, *Diplomacy* (New York: Simon and Schuster, 1994), Chapter 26.

7. Taylor quoted in Richard Reeves, *President Kennedy: Profile of Power* (New York: Simon and Schuster, 1993), p. 509.

8. For a good account, see ibid., pp. 541–652.

9. See "Memorandum for the Record of a Meeting, Executive Office Building, Washington, November 24, 1963, 3 P.M.," in U.S. Department of State, *Foreign Relations of the United States, 1961–1963*, Volume IV, *Vietnam: August–December 1963* (Washington, D.C.: U.S. Government Printing Office, 1991), pp. 636–37.

10. William E. Odom, *On Internal War: American and Soviet Approaches to Third World Clients and Insurgents* (Durham, N.C.: Duke University Press, 1992), p. 63.

11. Henry A. Kissinger, *White House Years* (Boston: Little, Brown, 1979), pp. 287–95, 1031–35; Kissinger, *Years of Upheaval* (Boston: Little, Brown, 1982), pp. 310–14.

12. "Pentagon Papers," Book 1, Section II, pp. B12–13.

13. Bruce D. Porter, *The USSR in Third World Conflicts: Soviet Arms and Diplomacy in Local Wars, 1945–1980* (Cambridge, Eng.: Cambridge University Press, 1984), pp. 19–20.

14. Pike, *op. cit.*, pp. 45–49.

15. *The Russians Are Coming! The Russians Are Coming!* by UA-Mirisch, 1966, produced and directed by Norman Jewison.

16. Lin Piao, "Long Live the Victory of People's War!" *Peking Review*, Vol. VIII, No. 36 (September 3, 1965), pp. 9–30.

17. Liu Shaoqi, Speech at Trade Union Conference of Asian and Australasian Countries, November 16, 1949, cited in Chalmers Johnson, *Autopsy on People's War* (Berkeley: Quantum Books/University of California Press, 1973), p. 16.

18. Johnson, *op. cit.*, pp. 16–23.

19. Lin Piao, *op. cit.*, p. 27.

20. D. P. Mozingo and T. W. Robinson, *Lin Piao on "People's War": China Takes a Second Look at Vietnam*, Memorandum RM-4814-PR (Santa Monica, Calif.: RAND Corporation, November 1965).

21. Edgar Snow, "Interview with Mao," *New Republic*, February 27, 1965, p. 17.

22. McGeorge Bundy, "A Trial Balance in Foreign Affairs," address to the annual meeting of the Harvard Club of Boston, *Harvard Alumni Bulletin*, Vol. 65, No. 13 (April 20, 1963), p. 551.

23. Thomas C. Schelling, *The Strategy of Conflict* (Cambridge, Mass.: Harvard University Press, 1960), pp. 5, 9 (emphases in original).

24. Testimony of Secretary of Defense Robert S. McNamara, February 20, 1963, in U.S. Congress, Senate, Committee on Armed Services, *Military Procurement Authorization: Fiscal Year 1964, Hearings*, 88th Congress, 1st Session (1963), p. 85.

25. Harlan Cleveland, "Crisis Diplomacy," *Foreign Affairs*, Vol. 41, No. 4 (July 1963), p. 639.

26. Arthur M. Schlesinger, Jr., *A Thousand Days: John F. Kennedy in the White House* (Boston: Houghton Mifflin, 1965), p. 841.

27. David Halberstam, *The Best and the Brightest* (New York: Random House, 1972), p. 515.

28. "Bill Moyers Talks About LBJ, Power, Poverty, War, and the Young," *Atlantic*, July 1968, pp. 29–30.

29. "Pentagon Papers," Book 4, Part C (2) (c), p. 36.

30. Ibid., Part C (3), pp. 31, 36.

31. Ibid., p. 40.

32. Ibid., p. 43.

33. Lyndon Baines Johnson, *Vantage Point: Perspectives of the Presidency, 1963–1969* (New York: Holt, Rinehart and Winston, 1971), p. 129.

34. Adm. U. S. G. Sharp, USN, "Report on Air and Naval Campaigns Against North Vietnam and Pacific Command-wide Support of the War, June 1964–July 1968," in U.S. Department of Defense, *Report on the War in Vietnam (as of 30 June 1968)*, (Washington, D.C.: Department of Defense, 1968), Section I, p. 18.

35. Harrison Salisbury, *Behind the Lines—Hanoi* (New York: Harper & Row, 1967), pp. 194–97.

36. See, e.g., President Johnson's remarks to the American Alumni Council on July 12, 1966: Indonesia's success in having "pulled back from the brink of Communism" was one of the positive developments that had occurred while South Vietnam and her allies "have been busy holding aggression at bay."

37. Sharp, *op. cit.*, pp. 18, 22.

38. Kissinger, *White House Years*, pp. 167–68.

39. Richard Nixon, *RN: The Memoirs of Richard Nixon* (New York: Grosset & Dunlap, 1978), p. 298. Nixon's campaign position on Vietnam was laid out in his remarks to the Republican National Convention, Committee on Resolutions, August 1, 1968, in *Nixon Speaks Out: Major Speeches and Statements by Richard M. Nixon in the Presidential Campaign of 1968* (New York: Nixon-Agnew Campaign Committee, October, 25, 1968), pp. 234–37.

40. Kissinger, *White House Years*, pp. 129–30. For a critical view of "linkage," see Raymond L. Garthoff, *Détente and Confrontation: American-Soviet Relations from Nixon to Reagan* (Washington, D.C.: Brookings Institution, 1985), *passim*, and Kiron K. Skinner, "Linkage," in Albert Carnesale and Richard N. Haass, eds., *Superpower Arms Control: Setting the Record Straight* (Cambridge, Mass.: Ballinger, 1987), Chapter 10.

41. Kissinger, *White House Years*, pp. 135–36.

42. Ibid., pp. 137–38.

43. Ibid., pp. 265–69.

44. The importance to the Soviets of the German treaties is stressed by Georgii Arbatov, *The System: An Insider's Life in Soviet Politics* (New York: Times Books/Random House, 1992), pp. 184–85.

45. Pike, *op. cit.*, p. 96.

46. The story is told in Kissinger, *White House Years*, Chapters XXVI and XXVII; see, especially, pp. 1200–01.

47. Pike, *op. cit.*, pp. 125–26.

48. Elmo R. Zumwalt, Jr., *On Watch: A Memoir* (New York: Quadrangle/New York Times Book Co., 1976), p. 319. Kissinger disputes much of Zumwalt's account.

49. Kissinger, *White House Years*, p. 228.

50. See the Eisenhower news conference of April 7, 1954; see also *NSC 124/2* ("United States Objectives and Courses of Action with Respect to Southeast Asia"), June 25, 1952, in U.S. Department of State, *Foreign Relations of the United States, 1952–1954*, Vol. XII, *East Asia and the Pacific*, Part 1 (Washington, D.C.: U.S. Government Printing Office, 1984), p. 127.

51. Arthur M. Schlesinger, Jr., "Make War Not It: Vietnam, the Revised Standard Version," *Harper's*, March 1982, p. 72.

52. See Bernard Gwertzman, "Gloom on World Situation Grips Kissinger and Aides," *New York Times*, March 20, 1975, p. 3.

53. David Kimche, *The Last Option: After Nasser, Arafat and Saddam Hussein: The Quest for Peace in the Middle East* (New York: Charles Scribner's Sons, 1991), p. 52.

54. Peres interview with Israel's Army Radio as reported by Reuters, in Robert Gary, "Indochina events justify decision against concessions, Israel says," *Boston Globe*, April 13, 1975, p. 17.

55. Gwertzman, *loc. cit.*

56. Earl C. Ravenal, "Consequences of the End Game in Vietnam," *Foreign Affairs*, Vol. 53, No. 4 (July 1975), p. 658.

57. *U.S. Department of State Bulletin*, Vol. LXXII, No. 1877 (June 2, 1975), pp. 737–38; see also Prime Minister Lee's address to the New Zealand National Press Club, April 7, 1975, reported in the *Washington Post*, April 13, 1975, and discussed by Ravenal, *loc. cit.*, p. 661.

58. Anthony Lake, "Introduction," in Anthony Lake, ed., *The Vietnam Legacy: The War, American Society and the Future of American Foreign Policy* (New York: New York University Press for the Council on Foreign Relations, 1976), p. xxii.

59. Alastair Buchan, "The Indochina War and the Changing Pattern of World Politics," in Lake, *op. cit.*, pp. 10–16.

60. Edward Shils, "American Society and the War in Indochina," in Lake, *op. cit.*, pp. 53, 61–62.

61. Ibid., pp. 64–65.

62. For a fuller discussion, see Peter W. Rodman, "The Imperial Congress," *National Interest*, Vol. I, No. 1 (Fall 1985), and Richard Haass, *Congressional Power: Implications for American Security Policy*, Adelphi Paper No. 153 (London: International Institute for Strategic Studies, Summer 1979); see also President Ronald Reagan's

address to the Center for Strategic and International Studies, Washington, April 6, 1984.

63. Letter from President Johnson to Eugene Rostow, as described by Professor Rostow to the author.

64. These data come from U.S. Department of Defense, *White Paper on the Department of Defense and the Congress*, Report to the President by the Secretary of Defense, January 1990; Ken Adelman, "Coming to Grips? Vulnerable Adversary," *Washington Times*, March 6, 1992.

65. French National Assembly Debates, May 6, 1976 (author's translation).

66. Address of Saddam Hussein to the Arab Cooperation Council Summit in Amman, February 24, 1990, in FBIS-NES-90-039, 27 February 1990, p. 5.

67. Saddam interview on CBS News, August 29, 1990, quoted in Reuters dispatch "Saddam Denies Secret Talks, and Warns United States in T.V. Interview," August 30, 1990.

68. Lawrence Freedman and Efraim Karsh, *The Gulf Conflict, 1990–1991: Diplomacy and War in the New World Order* (Princeton, N.J.: Princeton University Press, 1993), pp. 276–85; Barry Rubin, "The United States and Iraq: From Appeasement to War," in Amatzia Baram and Barry Rubin, eds., *Iraq's Road to War* (New York: St. Martin's Press, 1993), p. 264.

69. H. D. S. Greenway, "How the War Was Won, Mostly," *New York Times Book Review*, January 24, 1993, p. 2.

70. See the Iraqi record of the conversation between American ambassador April Glaspie and Iraqi president Saddam Hussein, July 25, 1990, as released by the Iraqi foreign ministry in September 1990, in *New York Times*, September 23, 1990, p. 19. The transcript is suspect in many respects, but in this respect probably not.

CHAPTER 6

1. Georgii Arbatov, *The System: An Insider's Life in Soviet Politics* (New York: Times Books/Random House, 1992), p. 246.

2. The "Ballerina" reference comes from Sergei N. Khrushchev, *Khrushchev on Khrushchev: An Inside Account of the Man and His Era*, edited and translated by William Taubman (Boston: Little, Brown, 1990), p. 32; see also Fedor Burlatsky, *Khrushchev and the First Russian Spring: The Era of Khrushchev Through the Eyes of His Advisor* (New York: Charles Scribner's Sons, 1992), Chapter 11.

3. Arbatov, *op. cit.*, p. 246.

4. Burlatsky, *op. cit.*, pp. 213–14.

5. Elizabeth Kridl Valkenier, "The Soviet Union and the Third World: From Khrushchev's 'Zone of Peace' to Brezhnev's 'Peace Program,' " in Roger E. Kanet and Donna Bahry, eds., *Soviet Economic and Political Relations with the Developing World*. First International Slavic Conference, Banff, Alberta, 1974 (New York: Frederick A. Praeger, 1975), p. 5.

6. Fritz Ermarth, "The Soviet Union in the Third World: Purpose in Search of Power," *Annals of the American Academy of Political and Social Science*, Vol. 386 (November 1969), pp. 39–40.

7. Leo Tansky, "Soviet Foreign Aid: Scope, Direction, and Trends," in U.S. Congress, Joint Economic Committee, *Soviet Economic Prospects for the Seventies*, 93rd Congress, 1st Session (Washington, D.C.: U.S. Government Printing Office, 1973), p. 766.

8. I. Shatalov, "The Leninist Foreign Policy and the National Liberation Movement," *International Affairs* (Moscow), No. 1 (January 1969), p. 72.

9. A. A. Gromyko, "Report to the 24th Congress of the CPSU," April 3, 1971, quoted in Raymond L. Garthoff, *Détente and Confrontation: American-Soviet Relations from Nixon to Reagan* (Washington, D.C.: Brookings Institution, 1985), p. 61.

10. This and subsequent Brezhnev quotes come from L. L. Brezhnev, "Report of the CPSU Central Committee and the Immediate Tasks of the Party in Home and Foreign Policy," February 24, 1976 (Moscow: Novosti Press Agency Publishing House, 1974), pp. 10–12, 20–22.

11. Constitution (Basic Law) of the Union of Soviet Socialist Republics, *Pravda* and *Izvestia*, October 8, 1977, in *Current Digest of the Soviet Press*, Vol. XXIX, No. 41 (November 9, 1977), p. 4.

12. See, e.g., G. Shakhnazarov, "On the Problem of the Correlation of Forces," *Kommunist*, February 1974; Col. S. Tyushkevich, "The Correlation of Forces in the World and Factors of War Prevention," *Kommunist of the Armed Forces*, May 1974; S. P. Sanakoyev, "The World Today: Problems of the Correlation of Forces," *International Affairs* (Moscow), No. 11 (November 1974); A. Sergiyev, "Leninism on the Correlation of Forces as a Factor of International Relations," *International Affairs* (Moscow), No. 5 (May 1975); G. Shakhnazarov, "The Victory—the World Balance of Strength—Peaceful Coexistence," *New Times*, No. 19, May 1975. For Western commentaries on the "correlation of forces," see Rajan Menon, *Soviet Power and the Third World* (New Haven: Yale University Press, 1986), pp. 22–23; John Lenczowski, *Soviet Perception of U.S. Foreign Policy: A Study of Ideology, Power, and Consensus* (Ithaca, N.Y.: Cornell University Press, 1982), pp. 51–59; Michael J. Deane, "The Soviet Assessment of the 'Correlation of World Forces': The Implications for American Foreign Policy," *Orbis*, Vol. 20, No. 3 (Fall 1976); and Margot Light, *The Soviet Theory of International Relations* (New York: St. Martin's Press, 1988), Chapter 9.

13. V. I. Lenin, " 'Left-Wing' Childishness and the Petty-Bourgeois Mentality," May 1918, in V. I. Lenin, *Collected Works*, Vol. 27 (Moscow: Progress Publishers, 1965), p. 328.

14. Light, *op. cit.*, pp. 254–60.

15. See Shakhnazarov, in *Kommunist*, February 1974, *loc. cit.*, p. 86; cited in Deane, *loc. cit.*, pp. 627–29.

16. Menon, *op. cit.*, pp. 22–33.

17. Lenczowski, *op. cit.*, Chapter 5, especially p. 231.

18. G. Trofimenko, "From Confrontation to Coexistence," *International Affairs* (Moscow), No. 10 (October 1975), p. 38.

19. V. V. Zagladin, "The Revolutionary Process and International CPSU Policy," *Kommunist*, September 1972, p. 22; quoted in Deane, *loc. cit.*, p. 632.

20. Sergiyev, *loc. cit.*, pp. 105–6.

21. "X" (George F. Kennan), "The Sources of Soviet Conduct," *Foreign Affairs*, Vol. 25, No. 4 (July 1947).

22. See Henry A. Kissinger, *White House Years* (Boston: Little, Brown, 1979), pp. 119–20; Henry A. Kissinger, *Diplomacy* (New York: Simon and Schuster, 1994), pp. 711–14.

23. Walter Lippmann, *The Communist World and Ours* (Boston: Little, Brown, 1959), p. 13; see Chapter 4 above.

24. Brezhnev, *loc. cit.*, p. 56.

25. Quoted in Garthoff, *op. cit.*, p. 41 (emphasis added by Garthoff).

26. G. A. Arbatov, "An Event of World Significance," *SShA*, No. 8 (August 1972), p. 9; quoted in Garthoff, *op. cit.*, p. 62 (emphasis added by Garthoff).

27. Garthoff, *op. cit.*, p. 49.

28. Henry Trofimenko, "The Third World and the U.S.-Soviet Competition: A Soviet View," *Foreign Affairs*, Vol. 59, No. 5 (Summer 1981), p. 1027.

29. Ibid., pp. 1026–27.

30. Most of the military data in this and following paragraphs, except where otherwise indicated, come from sources collected in Bruce D. Porter, *The USSR in Third World Conflicts: Soviet Arms and Diplomacy in Local Wars, 1945–1980* (Cambridge, Eng.: Cambridge University Press, 1984), Chapter 3, and Henry D. Bradsher, *Afghanistan and the Soviet Union* (Durham, N.C.: Duke University Press, 1983), p. 133.

31. Central Intelligence Agency, National Foreign Assessment Center, *Communist Aid Activities in Non-Communist Less Developed Countries, 1979 and 1954–79*, Research Paper ER 80-10318U, October 1980, Table 2, p. 6.

32. Ibid., Table 1, p. 5 (military agreements) and Table 4, p. 7 (economic aid agreements).

33. Daniel Patrick Moynihan with Suzanne Weaver, *A Dangerous Place* (Boston: Atlantic Monthly Press/Little, Brown, 1978), p. 248.

34. See Kissinger, *White House Years*, Chapter VII.

35. Porter, *op. cit.*, pp. 200–5.

36. See Brzezinski's address to the Foreign Policy Association, Washington, December 20, 1978, quoted in Bernard Gwertzman, "Brzezinski Says Soviet Arms Pact Will Not Weaken U.S.," *New York Times*, December 21, 1978, p. A3.

37. This analysis draws on Francis Fukuyama, "Soviet Strategy in the Third World," in Andrzej Korbonski and Francis Fukuyama, eds., *The Soviet Union and the Third*

World: The Last Three Decades (Ithaca, N.Y.: Cornell University Press, 1987), Chapter 2. See also Porter, *op. cit.*, pp. 29–30.

38. Porter, *op. cit.*, p. 239.

39. Ibid., p. 244.

40. See, e.g., Keith A. Dunn, "Soviet Involvement in the Third World: Implications of US Policy Assumptions," in Robert H. Donaldson, ed., *The Soviet Union in the Third World: Successes and Failures* (Boulder, Colo.: Westview Press, 1981), Chapter 20; Robert Legvold, "The Super Rivals: Conflict in the Third World," *Foreign Affairs*, Vol. 57, No. 4 (Spring 1979).

41. Kissinger, *White House Years*, pp. 1250, 1253–57.

42. See Kissinger's more recent discussion of these issues in *Diplomacy*, especially Chapter 29.

43. Zbigniew Brzezinski, *Power and Principle: Memoirs of the National Security Adviser, 1977–1981* (New York: Farrar Straus Giroux, 1983), p. 189.

CHAPTER 7

1. James Duffy, *Portugal in Africa* (Cambridge, Mass.: Harvard University Press, 1962), pp. 38–43. On the early history of Angola, see also John Marcum, *The Angolan Revolution: The Anatomy of an Explosion (1950–1962)*, Vol. 1, (Cambridge, Mass.: MIT Press, 1969).

2. Robert S. Jaster, *The 1988 Peace Accords and the Future of South-West Africa*, Adelphi Paper No. 253 (London: Brassey's/International Institute for Strategic Studies, Autumn 1990), p. 8.

3. Sanford J. Ungar, *Africa: The People and Politics of an Emerging Continent* (New York: Simon and Schuster, 1985), p. 71.

4. Mohamed A. El-Khawas and Barry Cohen, eds. and introduction, *The Kissinger Study of Southern Africa: National Security Study Memorandum 39 (Secret)* (Westport, Conn.: L. Hill, 1976); Anthony Lake, *The "Tar Baby" Option: American Policy Toward Southern Rhodesia* (New York: Columbia University Press, 1976).

5. Ungar, *op. cit.*, p. 71.

6. See the address of President F. W. de Klerk to a special joint session of the South African Parliament, March 24, 1993, in FBIS-AFR-93-056, 25 March 1993, p. 5; Darryl Howlett and John Simpson, "Nuclearisation and Denuclearisation in South Africa," *Survival*, Vol. 35, No. 3 (Autumn 1993), pp. 155–57.

7. William G. Hyland, *Mortal Rivals: Superpower Relations from Nixon to Reagan* (New York: Random House, 1987), pp. 131–35.

8. Chester A. Crocker, "Report on Angola," CSIS Report (Washington, D.C.: Center for Strategic and International Studies, February 20, 1976), pp. 3–4.

9. Ibid., p. 4; Kenneth L. Adelman, "Report from Angola," *Foreign Affairs*, Vol. 53, No. 3 (April 1975), p. 567.

10. Fred Bridgland, *Jonas Savimbi: A Key to Africa* (New York: Paragon House Publishers, 1987), Chapter 4.

11. Crocker, *op. cit.*, p. 5.

12. Chas. W. Freeman, Jr., "The Angola/Namibia Accords," *Foreign Affairs*, Vol. 68, No. 3 (Summer 1989), p. 127; Colin Legum, "A Study of Foreign Intervention in Angola," in Colin Legum and Tony Hodges, *After Angola: The War Over Southern Africa* (London: Rex Collings, 1976), pp. 28–29.

13. Compare especially Raymond L. Garthoff, *Détente and Confrontation: American-Soviet Relations from Nixon to Reagan* (Washington, D.C.: Brookings Institution, 1985), pp. 505–15, with Hyland, *op. cit.*, pp. 136–40. The sequence of events as described here is taken mainly from these two sources, plus Secretary of State Kissinger's Senate testimony of January 29, 1976, in U.S. Congress, Senate, Committee on Foreign Relations, Subcommittee on African Affairs, *Angola, Hearings*, 94th Congress, 2nd Session (Washington, D.C.: U.S. Government Printing Office, 1976).

14. Rosa Coutinho interviewed in Georgie Anne Geyer, "How Angola Was Given Away," *Washington Times*, July 15, 1988, p. F4.

15. Garthoff, a critic of the Ford-Kissinger policy, acknowledges that the Soviet decision to ship arms was probably made in January, before Ford's decision on the $300,000, *op. cit.*, p. 507. Freeman, *loc. cit.*, p. 128, dates to March the decision to send the Cubans.

16. See especially Seymour M. Hersh, "Early Angola Aid by U.S. Reported," *New York Times*, December 19, 1975, p. A1.

17. Davis's account can be found in Nathaniel Davis, "The Angola Decision of 1975: A Personal Memoir," *Foreign Affairs*, Vol. 57, No. 1 (Fall 1978).

18. Hyland, *op. cit.*, pp. 137–40.

19. Kissinger testimony, January 29, 1976, *loc. cit.*, p. 17.

20. Gabriel García Marquez, "Cuba in Africa: Seed Che Planted," *Washington Post*, January 12, 1977, p. A12.

21. Bruce D. Porter, *The USSR in Third World Conflicts: Soviet Arms and Diplomacy in Local Wars, 1945–1980* (Cambridge, Eng.: Cambridge University Press, 1984), pp. 172–73.

22. Garthoff, *op. cit.*, pp. 527–30; see also Colin Legum, "Angola and the Horn of Africa," in Stephen S. Kaplan, ed., *Diplomacy of Power: Soviet Armed Forces as a Political Instrument* (Washington, D.C.: Brookings Institution, 1981), p. 592.

23. Porter, *op. cit.*, pp. 175–78.

24. Ibid., pp. 164–70; Arkady N. Shevchenko, *Breaking with Moscow* (New York: Alfred A. Knopf, 1985) p. 272; Robert E. Quirk, *Fidel Castro* (New York: W. W. Norton, 1993), Chapter 28.

25. Hyland, *op. cit.*, p. 143.

26. Porter, *op. cit.*, p. 165.

27. Georgii Arbatov, *The System: An Insider's Life in Soviet Politics* (New York: Times Books, 1992), pp. 193–95.

28. Hyland, *op. cit.*, p. 145.

29. Kissinger testimony, January 29, 1976, *loc. cit.*, p. 18.

30. Seymour M. Hersh, "Angola—Aid Issue Opening Rifts in State Department," *New York Times*, December 14, 1975, p. A1.

31. "What to Do About Angola: Debate and Discussion," *Baltimore Sun*, December 27, 1975.

32. "Congress Divided Over Angola Aid," *Washington Post*, December 27, 1975.

33. Hersh, "Early Angola Aid by U.S. Reported," December 19, 1975, *op. cit.*

34. John H. Averill, "Virtually All Democratic Candidates Oppose U.S. Angola Role," *Washington Post*, January 6, 1976, p. A2.

35. Ibid.

36. Marilyn Berger, "U.S. Angola Cost: $80 Million," *Washington Post*, December 12, 1975.

37. "The Angola Issue," *Washington Post*, December 18, 1975.

38. David B. Ottaway, "Rep. Diggs Hits Ford on Angola," *Washington Post*, January 12, 1976, p. A1.

39. Colin Legum, "A Letter on Angola to American Liberals," *New Republic*, January 31, 1976, p. 16.

40. Kissinger testimony, January 29, 1976, pp. 21–23.

41. Ibid., pp. 23–25.

42. Daniel Patrick Moynihan with Suzanne Weaver, *A Dangerous Place* (Boston: Atlantic Monthly Press/Little, Brown, 1978), pp. 247–53.

43. Shevchenko, *op. cit.*, pp. 271–72.

44. Gerald R. Ford, *A Time to Heal* (New York: Harper & Row/Reader's Digest Association, 1979), p. 354.

45. Ibid.

46. Neto interview on Vienna Radio, January 29, 1976, cited in Legum, "A Study of Foreign Intervention in Angola," p. 19.

47. Garthoff, *op. cit.*, p. 521 (emphasis in original).

48. Kissinger testimony, January 29, 1976, pp. 19, 21.

49. Ibid., p. 16.

50. Arbatov, *op. cit.*, pp. 195–96.

51. "What to Do About Angola: Debate and Discussion," *Baltimore Sun*, December 27, 1975.

52. Ford, *op. cit.*, p. 346.

53. Author's conversation with John Carbaugh, former aide to Senator Helms, June 3, 1993.

54. Kissinger testimony, January 29, 1976, p. 19.

CHAPTER 8

1. Henry A. Kissinger, *White House Years* (Boston: Little, Brown, 1979), p. 1383 and pp. 1495–96 (note 3 to Chapter XXXII).

2. Ibid.

3. Testimony of Dennis J. Doolin, deputy assistant secretary of defense for international security affairs, June 6, 1973, in U.S. Congress, House of Representatives, Committee on Foreign Affairs, Subcommittee on Asian and Pacific Affairs, *U.S. Policy and Programs in Cambodia, Hearings*, 93rd Congress, 1st Session (Washington, D.C.: U.S. Government Printing Office, 1973), p. 85; also Prince Norodom Sihanouk, *War and Hope: The Case for Cambodia* (New York: Pantheon Books, 1980), pp. 14–15, 20, 24–27, 71–72.

4. Democratic Kampuchea, *The Black Book: Facts and Proofs of Vietnam's Acts of Aggression and Annexation Against Kampuchea* (Phnom Penh, September 1978), Chapter V, Section 2(c).

5. For a compilation of the legislative restrictions, see Henry A. Kissinger, *Years of Upheaval* (Boston: Little, Brown, 1982), pp. 337–39.

6. Sihanouk, *op. cit.*, pp. 21–23, 64–65; see also Democratic Kampuchea, *The Black Book*, Chapter V, Section 2(b).

7. François Ponchaud, *Cambodia: Year Zero* (New York: Penguin Books, 1978), p. 37; Kenneth M. Quinn, "Political Change in Wartime: The Khmer Krahom Revolution in Southern Cambodia, 1970–1974," *Naval War College Review*, Spring 1976, especially pp. 3, 8–9.

8. Anthony Lake, "At Stake in Cambodia: Extending Aid Will Only Prolong the Killing," *Washington Post*, March 9, 1975.

9. Sydney H. Schanberg, "The Enigmatic Cambodian Insurgents: Reds Appear to Dominate Diverse Bloc," *New York Times*, March 13, 1975, p. 1.

10. Anthony Lewis, "Avoiding a Bloodbath," *New York Times*, March 17, 1975, p. 29.

11. Editorial, "Cambodian Aid: Administration's Choice," *Washington Post*, March 17, 1975.

12. Editorial, "Out of the Past," *Los Angeles Times*, April 11, 1975.

13. Sydney H. Schanberg, "Indochina Without Americans: For Most, a Better Life," *New York Times*, April 13, 1975, Section IV, p. 1.

14. Testimony of Charles H. Twining, Department of State, July 26, 1977, in U.S. Congress, House of Representatives, Committee on International Relations, Sub-

committee on International Organizations, *Human Rights in Cambodia, Hearings*, 95th Congress, 1st Session (Washington, D.C.: U.S. Government Printing Office, 1977), p. 13.

15. Ponchaud, *op. cit.*, p. 107. On Khieu Samphan's economic and social ideas, see also Karl D. Jackson, "The Ideology of Total Revolution," in Karl D. Jackson, ed., *Cambodia 1975–1978: Rendezvous with Death* (Princeton, N.J.: Princeton University Press, 1989), pp. 42–43, and Jackson's concluding essay, "Intellectual Origins of the Khmer Rouge," in the same volume, especially pp. 245–48.

16. The best systematic account of the period of Khmer Rouge rule is the volume by Jackson, *op. cit.*; see also Ponchaud, *op. cit.*; John Barron and Anthony Paul, *Murder of a Gentle Land* (New York: Reader's Digest Books, 1977); Jean Lacouture, "The Revolution That Destroyed Itself," *Encounter*, May 1979, pp. 53–57, and "Ho Chi Minh, Pol Pot, and the Consequences," *Encounter*, November 1979, p. 92; U.S. Department of State, Submission on the "Human Rights Situation in Cambodia" to the United Nations Human Rights Commission, July 6, 1978.

17. Charles McGregor, *The Sino-Vietnamese Relationship and the Soviet Union*, Adelphi Paper No. 232 (London: International Institute for Strategic Studies, August 1988), pp. 28–30.

18. Elizabeth Becker, *When the War Was Over: The Voices of Cambodia's Revolution and Its People* (New York: Touchstone/Simon and Schuster, 1987), Chapter 8.

19. Douglas Pike, *Vietnam and the Soviet Union: Anatomy of an Alliance* (Boulder, Colo.: Westview Press, 1987), p. 202.

20. Kissinger, *Years of Upheaval*, p. 28.

21. Ibid., pp. 58–60.

22. McGregor, *op. cit.*, pp. 14–27.

23. Ibid., p. 32.

24. Becker, *op. cit.*, pp. 317–36.

25. Quoted in Singapore Ministry of Foreign Affairs, *From Phnom Penh to Kabul*, (Singapore: September 1980), p. 4.

26. Stephen J. Solarz, "Cambodia and the International Community," *Foreign Affairs*, Vol. LXIX, No. 2 (Spring 1990), p. 102n.

27. U.S. Congress, *Country Reports on Human Rights Practices for 1979*, Report to the House of Representatives, Committee on Foreign Affairs, and the Senate, Committee on Foreign Relations, in Accordance with Sections 116(d) and 502B(b) of the Foreign Assistance Act of 1961, as Amended, 96th Congress, 2nd Session, February 4, 1980 (Washington, D.C.: U.S. Government Printing Office, 1980), pp. 464–66; statement by Deputy Secretary of State Warren Christopher to the Conference on Kampuchean Relief, Geneva, May 26, 1980; William Shawcross, "Food Aid: Tale of Deceit, Obstruction," *Washington Post*, March 18, 1980, p. 1.

28. Editorial, "Vietnam: Genocide," *Washington Post*, October 12, 1979, p. A14.

29. Vietnamese vice foreign minister Nguyen Co Thach, news conference, Colombo, June 9, 1979, AFP report, in FBIS-APA-79-113, 11 June 1979, p. K15.

30. Kissinger, *Years of Upheaval*, pp. 233, 294–295, 1173.

31. Cyrus Vance, *Hard Choices: Critical Years in America's Foreign Policy* (New York: Simon and Schuster, 1983), Appendix I, p. 450.

32. Frederick Z. Brown, *Second Chance: The United States and Indochina in the 1990s* (New York: Council on Foreign Relations Press, 1989), pp. 21–31.

33. Raymond L. Garthoff, *Détente and Confrontation: American-Soviet Relations from Nixon to Reagan* (Washington, D.C.: Brookings Institution, 1985), p. 704; Zbigniew Brzezinski, *Power and Principle: Memoirs of the National Security Adviser, 1977–1981* (New York: Farrar Straus Giroux, 1983), pp. 207, 211–12, Annex I.

34. Brzezinski, *op. cit.*, p. 196.

35. Becker, *op. cit.*, p. 440.

36. Vance, *op. cit.*, pp. 126–27.

37. Nayan Chanda, *Brother Enemy: The War After the War* (New York: Harcourt Brace Jovanovich, 1986), pp. 363–69.

38. Ibid., p. 379.

39. E.g., Arthur M. Schlesinger, Jr., "Make War Not It: Vietnam, the Revised Standard Version," *Harper's*, March 1982, p. 72.

40. Elaine Sciolino, "Tainted Cambodia Aid: New Details," *New York Times*, November 1, 1988, p. A3.

41. Brown, *op. cit.*, pp. 40–41.

42. Ibid., pp. 45, 80.

43. E.g., Al Santoli, "Endless Insurgency: Cambodia," *Washington Quarterly*, Vol. VIII, No. 2 (Spring 1985), pp. 61–72.

44. Statement by Richard Holbrooke, assistant secretary of state for East Asian and Pacific affairs, before the Senate Foreign Relations Committee, Subcommittee on Asian and Pacific Affairs, March 24, 1980.

45. Chanda, *op. cit.*, p. 397.

46. Holbrooke, *loc. cit.*; see also Pike, *op. cit.*, pp. 193–95.

47. Chanda, *op. cit.*, pp. 404–6.

CHAPTER 9

1. This was said, for example, by a young Soviet military officer to my White House colleague James Pinkerton on the latter's visit to the USSR in June 1990. See Pinkerton's unpublished paper "Reflections on the Revolution in Russia," July 3, 1990, Part 4. The same thought was expressed by Soviet journalist Artyom Borovik on September 26, 1990, in Washington at the 1990 Sea Power Forum of the Center for Naval Analyses; see Eric Miller (rapporteur), *Beyond Afghanistan: Changing Soviet Perspectives on Regional Conflicts* (Alexandria, Va.: Center for Naval Analyses, undated), p. 12.

2. Henry S. Bradsher, *Afghanistan and the Soviet Union* (Durham, N.C.: Duke University Press, 1983), p. 9.

3. From George Vernadsky, ed., *A Source Book for Russian History: From Early Times to 1917*, Vol. III (New Haven: Yale University Press, 1972), p. 610; see the discussion in Firuz Kazemzadeh, "Russia and the Middle East," in Ivo J. Lederer, ed., *Russian Foreign Policy: Essays in Historical Perspective* (New Haven: Yale University Press, 1962), pp. 494–95.

4. J. Bruce Amstutz, *Afghanistan: The First Five Years of Soviet Occupation* (Washington, D.C.: National Defense University, 1986), p. 5, and sources in endnotes, p. 419.

5. Mir Sultan Mahomed Khan Munshi, ed., *The Life of Abdur Rahman: Amir of Afghanistan*, Vol. 2 (London: John Murray, 1900), p. 150; quoted in Mahnaz Z. Ispahani, *Roads and Rivals: The Political Uses of Access in the Borderlands of Asia* (Ithaca, N.Y.: Cornell University Press, 1989), p. 98.

6. Amstutz, *op. cit.*, pp. 10–15.

7. See the documents from the Joint Chiefs of Staff, National Security Council, and State Department quoted in Bradsher, *op. cit.*, p. 20.

8. A fascinating study is Ispahani, *op. cit.* The quote is from Vartan Gregorian, *The Emergence of Modern Afghanistan: Politics of Reform and Modernization, 1880–1946* (Stanford, Calif.: Stanford University Press, 1969), p. 161, cited by Ispahani, p. 99.

9. Ispahani, *op. cit.*, especially pp. 124–37.

10. Declassified Department of State memorandum of conversation, "Meeting of the President and Prince Naim," Washington, September 27, 1962, quoted by Amstutz, *op. cit.*, p. 28.

11. E.g., Fred Halliday, "Revolution in Afghanistan," *New Left Review* (No. 112), 1978, pp. 30, 43; Selig S. Harrison, "The Shah, Not Kremlin, Touched Off Afghan Coup," *Washington Post*, May 13, 1979, pp. C1, C5; Selig S. Harrison, "Dateline Afghanistan: Exit Through Finland?" *Foreign Policy*, No. 41 (Winter 1980–81), pp. 163–87.

12. Bradsher, *op. cit.*, pp. 60–67; Raymond L. Garthoff, *Détente and Confrontation: American-Soviet Relations from Nixon to Reagan* (Washington, D.C.: Brookings Institution, 1985), pp. 893–94.

13. There are conflicting versions of who did what in the April coup and why, but Garthoff, *op. cit.*, p. 895, considers this the most likely account.

14. Ibid. p. 897; see also the account of Aleksandr Morozov, deputy KGB station chief in Kabul at the time, reported in Michael Dobbs, "Secret Memos Trace Kremlin's March to War," *Washington Post*, November 15, 1992, p. A32.

15. "Coups and Killings in Kabul: A KGB Defector Tells How Afghanistan Becomes Brezhnev's Vietnam" (interview with former KGB officer Vladimir Kuzichkin), *Time*, November 22, 1982, p. 33; see also Bradsher, *op. cit.*, pp. 82–84, and Kuzichkin's

memoir, *Inside the KGB: My Life in Soviet Espionage*, translated by Thomas B. Beattie (New York: Pantheon Books, 1990), p. 311.

16. Cyrus Vance, *Hard Choices: Critical Years in America's Foreign Policy* (New York: Simon and Schuster, 1983), pp. 384, 386.

17. Anthony Lake, "Wrestling with Third World Radical Regimes: Theory and Practice," in John W. Sewell, Richard E. Feinberg, and Valeriana Kallab, eds., *U.S. Foreign Policy and the Third World: Agenda 1985–86*, U.S.–Third World Policy Perspectives, No. 3 (New Brunswick, N.J.: Transaction Books/Overseas Development Council, 1985), p. 125.

18. Ibid., p. 121.

19. Brzezinski quoted in Thomas T. Hammond, *Red Flag over Afghanistan: The Communist Coup, The Soviet Invasion, and the Consequences* (Boulder, Colo.: Westview Press, 1984), p. 13.

20. Zbigniew Brzezinski, *Power and Principle: Memoirs of the National Security Adviser, 1977–1981* (New York: Farrar Straus Giroux, 1983).

21. Hammond, *op. cit.*, p. 63.

22. Lake, *loc. cit.*, p. 145, note 6.

23. Editorial, "Communist Coup in Afghanistan," *New York Times*, May 5, 1978, p. A28.

24. David D. Newsom, Under Secretary of State for Political Affairs, "South Asia: Superpowers and Regional Alliances," address before the Council on Foreign Relations, New York, October 18, 1978.

25. Simon Winchester, "Afghan Leaders Seem Determined to Stay Independent," *Washington Post*, May 8, 1978, p. A16.

26. Brzezinski, *op. cit.*, p. 426.

27. Taraki interview with *Die Zeit*, in FBIS-MEA-78-112, 9 June 1978, p. S3.

28. Bradsher, *op. cit.*, p. 96.

29. Garthoff, *op. cit.*, p. 899, citing estimates by the U.S. embassy in Kabul.

30. Messages from U.S. embassy in Kabul to the State Department, later published by the Iranian government after the "liberation" of copies found in the U.S. embassy in Tehran after its seizure in November 1979, cited in Kimberly Marten Zisk, *Soviet Civil-Military Relations and the Decision to Use Force Abroad*, Discussion Paper No. 114 (Santa Monica, Calif.: California Seminar on International Security and Foreign Policy, April 1990), p. 14.

31. Louis Dupree, *Red Flag over the Hindu Kush, Part III: Rhetoric and Reforms, or Promises! Promises!*, American Universities Field Staff Report 23 (Hanover, N.H.: American Universities Field Staff, 1980), p. 4.

32. Bradsher, *op. cit.*, pp. 100–1; Garthoff, *op. cit.*, p. 900.

33. Brzezinski, *op. cit.*, p. 427.

34. Garthoff, *op. cit.*, p. 923.

35. Michael Getler, "U.S. Reportedly Is Supplying Weapons to Afghan Insurgents," *Washington Post*, February 15, 1980, p. A28; Garthoff, *op. cit.*, p. 923. Garthoff put the question to a senior Carter administration official, who would neither confirm nor deny U.S. aid to the rebels before the Soviet invasion. U.S. aid *after* the Soviet invasion is, of course, widely known.

36. Brzezinski, *op. cit.*, p. 427.

37. E.g., Amstutz, *op. cit.*, p. 40.

38. See an *Izvestia* article in April 1980, cited in ibid., p. 42.

39. "Replies of L. I. Brezhnev to Questions of a Correspondent of *Pravda*," *Pravda*, January 13, 1980, in FBIS-SOV-80-009, 14 January 1980, p. A2.

40. Nikita Khrushchev, *Khrushchev Remembers*, with an introduction, commentary, and notes by Edward Crankshaw (Boston: Little, Brown, 1970), p. 508; see also Nikita Khrushchev, *Khrushchev Remembers: The Last Testament*, translated and edited by Strobe Talbott (Boston: Little, Brown, 1974), pp. 298–300.

41. See notes 7 and 10 above.

42. "How We Went into Afghanistan," *Literaturnaya Gazeta*, September 20, 1989, p. 14; quoted in Jeanette Voas, *Preventing Future Afghanistans: Reform in Soviet Policymaking on Military Intervention Abroad*, Occasional Paper (Alexandria, Va.: Center for Naval Analyses, August 1990), pp. 8–9.

43. "Dzasokhov on 1979 Afghanistan Decision" (Report on the decision to send troops into Afghanistan, presented by Aleksandr Dzasokhov at the 24 December session of the Second Congress of USSR People's Deputies in the Kremlin), Moscow Television, 24 December 1979, in FBIS-SOV-89-248, 28 December 1989, p. 72; see also Artyom Borovik, *The Hidden War: A Russian Journalist's Account of the Soviet War in Afghanistan* (New York: Atlantic Monthly Press, 1990), pp 10–11.

44. Garthoff, *op. cit.*, p. 923.

45. Boris Ponomarëv, *Pravda*, April 21, 1979, cited in Zisk, *op. cit.*, p. 18; see also the article by Igor Belyaev in *Literaturnaya Gazeta*, March 12, 1980, quoted in Garthoff, *op. cit.*, p. 922.

46. Garthoff, *op. cit.*, pp. 921–22.

47. Bradsher, *op. cit.*, pp. 156–57. On the Islamic factor in the resistance, see Olivier Roy, *Islam and Resistance in Afghanistan*, 2nd ed., Cambridge Middle East Library No. 8 (Cambridge, Eng.: Cambridge University Press, 1990).

48. Amstutz *op. cit.*, p. 42. Author Amstutz was the U.S. chargé in Kabul who spoke with the East German.

49. Remarks of Sergei Tarasenko at the conference "Retrospective on the Cold War," Session V: "Afghanistan and the Limits of Empire," sponsored by the John Foster Dulles Program for the Study of Leadership and International Affairs, the Woodrow Wilson School of Public and International Affairs, Princeton University, February

27, 1993 [hereinafter cited as Princeton Conference], stenographic transcript, pp. 19–20.

50. Andrei Kolosov [reportedly a *nom de plume* for an aide to Deputy Foreign Minister Vladimir Petrovsky], "Reappraisal of USSR Third World Policy," *International Affairs* (Moscow), No. 5 (May 1990), p. 36. FBIS-SOV-90-099-A, 22 May 1990, p. 2.

51. Amstutz, *op. cit.*, p. 45.

52. Garthoff, *op. cit.*, p. 931.

53. Reporting messages in June and July 1979 from U.S. embassy in Kabul to the State Department, later published by the Iranian government, cited ibid., pp. 917–18.

54. Philip Johnston, "Interpreting Soviet Involvement in Afghanistan: April 1978–December 1979," unpublished paper for the author's seminar on U.S. and Soviet diplomacy in Third World conflicts, the Paul H. Nitze School of Advanced International Studies, the Johns Hopkins University, June 3, 1992; see Brzezinski, *op. cit.*, p. 427, and Garthoff, *op. cit.*, p. 943.

55. Brzezinski, *op. cit.*, p. 432; Vance, *op. cit.*, p. 386.

56. Amstutz, *op. cit.*, pp. 33, 44; Kuzichkin interview in *Time*, p. 33.

57. KGB documents cited in Dobbs, *loc. cit.*, p. A32.

58. Kuzichkin, *op. cit.*, p. 315; see also Amstutz, *op. cit.*, pp. 43–44; remarks by Artyom Borovik to CNA Sea Power Forum, September 26, 1990, in Miller, *op. cit.*, p. 3.

59. Kuzichkin interview in *Time*, p. 34.

60. Kuzichkin, *op. cit.*, p. 318.

61. Nikolai Berlev, interview in *Komsomolskaya Pravda*, quoted in Dobbs, *loc. cit.*, p. A32.

62. Dzasokhov report, *loc. cit.*, p. 73.

63. Dobbs, *loc. cit.*, pp. A1, A32.

64. Don Oberdorfer, *The Turn: From the Cold War to a New Era: The United States and the Soviet Union, 1983–1990* (New York: Poseidon Press, 1991), pp. 236–37.

65. Lt. Col. A. Oliynik, "The Sending of Troops to Afghanistan: Participants in the Events Tell and Documents Attest to How the Decision Was Made," *Krasnaya Zvezda*, November 18, 1989, pp. 3–4, in JPRS-UMA-90-004, Afghanistan, February 8, 1990 (captioned as "Defense Archival Material on Decision to Invade,"), p. 76.

66. "KGB's Kalugin Interviewed on Career," *Moscow News*, No. 25 (1–8 July 1990), p. 13, in FBIS-SOV-90-126, 29 June 1990, p. 58. Kuzichkin also defends the KGB's analytic soundness, *loc. cit.*, p. 33; see also Georgii Arbatov, *The System: An Insider's Life in Soviet Politics* (New York: Times Books, 1992), pp. 199–200.

67. "Lubyanka: Characters and Patrons," *Sobesednik*, No. 36 (September 1990), translated in "KGB Colonel Condemns Andropov, Corruption," FBIS-SOV-90-170, 14 September 1990, p. 39.

68. Arbatov, *op. cit.*, pp. 201–2.

69. "General Varennikov Interviewed on Afghanistan," *Ogonëk*, No. 12 (18–25 March 1989), in FBIS-SOV-89-062, 3 April 1989 (Annex), p. 1.

70. Arbatov, *op. cit.*, p. 199; remarks by Aleksandr Bessmertnykh at the Princeton Conference, p. 11.

71. Raju G. C. Thomas, "The Afghanistan Crisis and South Asian Security," *Journal of Strategic Studies*, Vol. IV, No. 4 (December 1981), p. 424.

72. Remarks by Aleksandr Bessmertnykh at the Princeton Conference, p. 12.

73. George F. Kennan, "Was This Really Mature Statesmanship?" *New York Times*, February 1, 1980, p. A27.

74. Garthoff, *op. cit.*, pp. 949–65.

75. Ibid.

76. See, e.g., Theodore L. Eliot, Jr., and Robert L. Pfaltzgraff, Jr., eds., *The Red Army on Pakistan's Borders: Policy Implications for the United States*, Special Report (Washington, D.C.: Pergamon-Brassey's, for the Center for Asian Pacific Affairs, The Asia Foundation, and Institute for Foreign Policy Analysis, 1986).

77. Telegram from the chargé in the Soviet Union (Kennan) to the secretary of state, February 22, 1946, in U.S. Department of State, *Foreign Relations of the United States: 1946*, Vol. VI, *The Soviet Union* (Washington, D.C.: U.S. Government Printing Office, 1969), pp. 699–700.

78. Steve Coll, "Anatomy of a Victory: CIA's Covert Afghan War," *Washington Post*, July 19, 1992, p. A24.

79. Carl Bernstein, "Arms for Afghanistan," *New Republic*, July 18, 1981, p. 8; see also Getler, *loc. cit.*

80. Coll, *loc. cit.*

81. The text may be found in "Transcript of President's Interview on Soviet Reply," *New York Times*, January 1, 1980, p. 4, or in the ABC News transcript reprinted in U.S. Department of State, *American Foreign Policy: Basic Documents, 1977–1980* (Washington, D.C.: Department of State, 1983), pp. 811–12.

82. Resolution ES-6/2, adopted by the UN General Assembly, January 14, 1980.

83. E.g., Bernard Nossiter, "U.N., Easing Tone, Again Urges Soviet to Get Out of Afghanistan," *New York Times*, November 21, 1980, p. A1.

84. Stephen J. Blank, *Operational and Strategic Lessons of the War in Afghanistan, 1979–90* (Carlisle Barracks, Pa.: U.S. Army War College, Strategic Studies Institute, September 1991), pp. 29–30.

85. Bruce D. Porter, *The USSR in Third World Conflicts: Soviet Arms and Diplomacy in Local Wars, 1945–1980* (Cambridge, Eng.: Cambridge University Press, 1984), p. 57.

86. Francis Fukuyama, *Soviet Civil-Military Relations and the Power Projection Mission*, R-3504-AF (Santa Monica, Calif.: RAND Corporation, April 1987), pp. 22–24; see

also Garthoff, *op. cit.*, pp. 683–87, though he cautions against exaggerating the point.

87. Blank, *op. cit.*, p. xi and Chapters 2 and 4.

88. Varennikov, *loc. cit.*, p. 4.

89. Observation of Dr. Ivan Antonovich in a discussion, "Perestroika, the 19th Party Conference and Foreign Policy," in *International Affairs* (Moscow), No. 7 (July 1988), p. 15.

90. Remarks of Artyom Borovik and Aleksandr Prokhanov to CNA Sea Power Forum, September 26, 1990, in Miller, *op. cit.*, pp. 6–7.

91. On the resistance, see Abdul Rashid, "The Afghan Resistance," in Rosanne Klass, ed., *Afghanistan: The Great Game Revisited* (New York: Freedom House, 1987), and Roy, *op. cit.*

92. Bill McCollum, "The CIA Has Bungled It," *Washington Post*, September 10, 1989, p. C1; Zalmay Khalilzad, "Ending the Afghan War," *Washington Post*, January 7, 1990, p. B4; Coll, *loc. cit.*

93. For a summary of the early negotiating efforts, see Amstutz, *op. cit.*, pp. 323–69. For a fuller account by the Pakistani negotiator, see Riaz M. Khan, *Untying the Afghan Knot: Negotiating Soviet Withdrawal* (Durham, N.C.: Duke University Press, 1991). Cordovez's perspective is reflected in Selig S. Harrison, "Inside the Afghan Talks," *Foreign Policy*, No. 72 (Fall 1988).

CHAPTER 10

1. E.g., André Gunder Frank, *Capitalism and Underdevelopment in Latin America* (New York: Monthly Review Press, 1967); Fernando Henrique Cardoso and Enzo Faletto, *Dependency and Development in Latin America* (Berkeley and Los Angeles: University of California Press, 1979); see Robert Packenham, *The Dependency Movement* (Cambridge, Mass.: Harvard University Press, 1992).

2. Michael Novak, *The Spirit of Domestic Capitalism* (Lanham, Md.: Madison Books, 1991), especially Chapter 18; Lawrence E. Harrison, *Underdevelopment Is a State of Mind: The Latin American Case* (Lanham, Md.: Harvard Center for International Affairs/University Press of America, 1985), Chapter 8.

3. Hernando de Soto, *The Other Path: The Invisible Revolution in the Third World* (New York: Harper & Row, 1989).

4. Carlos Rangel, *The Latin Americans: Their Love-Hate Relationship with the United States* (New York: Harcourt Brace Jovanovich, 1977); Novak, *op. cit.*, especially Chapter 14; Harrison, *op. cit.*, and also Lawrence E. Harrison, *Who Prospers? How Cultural Values Shape Economic and Political Success* (New York: Basic Books, 1992).

5. Rangel, *op. cit.*, p. 182.

6. Pope Paul VI, *Octogesima Adveniens* (1971), paragraph 35, in Joseph Gremillion, ed., *The Gospel of Peace and Justice* (Maryknoll, N.Y.: Orbis Books, 1976), p. 501; quoted in Novak, *op. cit.*, pp. 245–46.

7. Jefferson letter to Adams, May 17, 1818, in Paul Leicester Ford, ed., *The Writings of Thomas Jefferson* (New York: G. P. Putnam's Sons, 1892–1899, 10 vols.), Vol. X, p. 107; quoted in Robert W. Tucker and David C. Hendrickson, *Empire of Liberty: The Statecraft of Thomas Jefferson* (New York: Oxford University Press, 1990), p. 253.

8. The quote is from Moynihan's 1985 Godkin Lectures at Harvard, to be found in Daniel Patrick Moynihan, *Family and Nation* (San Diego: A Harvest/HBJ Book/ Harcourt Brace Jovanovich, 1987), p. 190; see Harrison, *Who Prospers?*, p. 1.

9. Mark Falcoff, "Somoza, Sandino, and the United States," *This World*, No. 6 (Fall, 1983).

10. Walter Lippmann, *Men of Destiny*, (New York: Macmillan, 1928), pp. 221–22.

11. Roland A. Ebel, "The Development and Decline of the Central American City-State," in Howard J. Wiarda, ed., *Rift and Revolution: The Central American Imbroglio* (Washington, D.C.: American Enterprise Institute, 1984), Table 4-1, p. 94.

12. Henry A. Kissinger, *White House Years* (Boston: Little, Brown, 1979), pp. 653–667.

13. An excellent account of the Carter policy is Anthony Lake, *Somoza Falling* (Boston: Houghton Mifflin, 1989).

14. Resolution Adopted by the Seventeenth Meeting of Consultation of Ministers of Foreign Affairs of the American Republics, Washington, June 23, 1979, from Organization of American States, Inter-American Commission on Human Rights, *Report on the Situation of Human Rights in the Republic of Nicaragua* (OAS document OEA/Ser. L/V/11.53, doc. 25, June 30, 1981), pp. 2–3.

15. Letter from the Junta of the Government of National Reconstruction to OAS Secretary-General Alejandro Orfila, July 12, 1979, ibid., pp. 4–5.

16. Anthony Lake, "Wrestling with Third World Radical Regimes: Theory and Practice," in John W. Sewell, Richard E. Feinberg, and Valeriana Kallab, eds., *U.S. Foreign Policy and the Third World: Agenda 1985–86* (New Brunswick, N.J.: Transaction Books/Overseas Development Council, 1985), p. 124.

17. Deputy Secretary of State Warren Christopher, statement before the Subcommittee on Foreign Operations of the House Appropriations Committee, September 11, 1979.

18. O'Donnell remarks in Hans Binnendijk, ed., *Authoritarian Regimes in Transition* (Washington, D.C.: U.S. Department of State, Foreign Service Institute, Center for the Study of Foreign Affairs, 1987), pp. 147–48.

19. U.S. Department of State, *"The 72-Hour Document": The Sandinista Blueprint for Constructing Communism in Nicaragua: A Translation* (Washington, D.C.: U.S. Department of State/Coordinator of Public Diplomacy for Latin America and the Caribbean, February 1986), pp. 3, 5, 11–12, 16.

20. Ibid., pp. 4, 13–14.

21. Shirley Christian, *Nicaragua: Revolution in the Family* (New York: Random House,

1985), pp. 148–57; Jiri and Virginia Valenta, "Sandinistas in Power," *Problems of Communism*, September-October 1985, pp. 16–17.

22. Christian, *op. cit.*, pp. 139–40.

23. Boris Ponomarëv, "The Inevitability of the Liberation Movement," *Kommunist* (Moscow), No. 1 (January 1980), p. 11–27; quoted in Valenta, *loc. cit.*, p. 21.

24. The National Bipartisan Commission on Central America (the "Kissinger Commission"), *Report* (Washington, January 1984), pp. 91–92.

25. Lippmann quoted in Ronald Steel, *Walter Lippmann and the American Century* (New York: Vintage Books/Random House, 1981), pp. 566–67.

26. E.g., James Chace, *Solvency: The Price of Survival: An Essay on American Foreign Policy* (New York: Random House, 1981); see the author's review of Chace in *Commentary*, June 1981, pp. 72–75.

27. U.S. Department of State, *"Revolution Beyond Our Borders": Sandinista Intervention in Central America*, Special Report No. 132 (Washington, D.C.: September 1985), pp. 5–13, 37–38.

28. Constantine C. Menges, *Inside the National Security Council: The True Story of the Making and Unmaking of Reagan's Foreign Policy* (New York: Simon and Schuster, 1988), p. 103.

29. Jeane J. Kirkpatrick, "Dictatorships and Double Standards," *Commentary*, November 1979, and "U.S. Security and Latin America," *Commentary*, January 1981, especially pp. 35–39.

30. Lake, *op. cit.*, pp. 260–64; Arturo Cruz, "What Went Wrong," in Binnendijk, *op. cit.*, pp. 132–33.

31. Robert Pastor interview in Christian, *op. cit.*, p. 69.

32. Cruz, *loc. cit.*, p. 133.

33. Lou Cannon, *President Reagan: The Role of a Lifetime* (New York: Simon and Schuster, 1991), pp. 22–26.

34. See the Economic Declaration issued by the G-7 Economic Summit participants in Bonn, May 4, 1985.

35. For much of the analysis in this chapter I am indebted to a forthcoming book by Robert W. Kagan, to be published by The Free Press, as yet untitled, which looks to be the definitive history of U.S. policy toward the Nicaraguan Revolution.

36. See, e.g., Roy Gutman, *Banana Diplomacy: The Making of American Policy in Nicaragua 1981–1987* (New York: Simon and Schuster, 1988); James Chace, *Endless War: How We Got Involved in Central America—and What Can Be Done* (New York: Vintage Books, 1984).

37. Ronald Reagan, *An American Life* (New York: Simon and Schuster/Pocket Books, 1990), pp. 238–39; see also Cannon, *op. cit.*, pp. 336–37.

38. Republican party platform, July 15, 1980, in *Congressional Quarterly Almanac, 1980* (Washington, D.C.: Congressional Quarterly, 1981), p. 82B.

39. Christopher Dickey, *With the Contras: A Reporter in the Wilds of Nicaragua* (New York: Simon and Schuster, 1985), p. 75.

40. U.S. Department of State, *Communist Interference in El Salvador*, Special Report No. 80, February 23, 1981; Mark Falcoff, "The El Salvador White Paper and Its Critics," in *AEI Foreign Policy and Defense Review*, Vol. 4, No. 2 (1982).

41. Cynthia J. Arnson, *Crossroads: Congress, the Reagan Administration, and Central America* (New York: Pantheon Books, 1989), p. 101.

42. George Gallup, "2 of 3 in U.S. See El Salvador Becoming 'Another Vietnam'," *Washington Post*, March 26, 1981, p. A2.

43. Alexander M. Haig, Jr., *Caveat: Realism, Reagan, and Foreign Policy* (New York: MacMillan, 1984), p. 125.

44. Ibid., p. 122.

45. See Caspar W. Weinberger, *Fighting for Peace: Seven Critical Years in the Pentagon* (New York: Warner Books, 1990), pp. 29–32; Michael K. Deaver with Mickey Herskowitz, *Behind the Scenes* (New York: William Morrow, 1987), pp. 39, 111, 168; Haig, *op. cit.*, pp. 127–30; Don Oberdorfer, "Applying Pressure in Central America," *Washington Post*, November 23, 1983, p. A10.

46. Arturo Cruz, Jr., *Memoirs of a Counterrevolutionary* (New York: Doubleday, 1989), pp. 116, 119–20, 125.

47. Interview with Cerna, December 31, 1981, on Radio Sandino, Managua, in FBIS-LAM-82-001, 4 January 1982 (captioned as "Security Chief on U.S. Plans, Insurgent Activity"), p. P12.

48. Christian, *op. cit.*, p. 191. She lists the date as June 23, though other commentators have it as August 25, 1981.

49. Gregory A. Fossedal, *The Democratic Imperative: Exporting the American Revolution* (New York: Basic Books/A New Republic Book, 1989), pp. 160–63; Malcolm Wallop, "U.S. Covert Action: Policy Tool or Policy Hedge?" *Strategic Review* (Summer 1984), reprinted in Walter F. Hahn, ed., *Central America and the Reagan Doctrine* (Washington, D.C.: Center for International Relations at Boston University/United States Strategic Institute, 1987), pp. 272–73.

50. Dickey, *op. cit.*, p. 291n.

51. Kagan interview with Enders, August 28, 1990, in Kagan, *op. cit.*, 1981 chapter; Bob Woodward, *Veil* (New York: Simon and Schuster, 1987), p. 173.

52. Don Oberdorfer and Patrick E. Tyler, "U.S.-Backed Nicaraguan Rebel Army Swells to 7,000 Men," *Washington Post*, May 8, 1983, p. A1.

53. Kagan interview with Enders, August 28, 1990, in Kagan, *op. cit.*, 1981 chapter; Patrick E. Tyler and Bob Woodward, "U.S. Approves Covert Plan in Nicaragua," *Washington Post*, March 10, 1982, p. A1; Patrick E. Tyler, "Nicaragua: Hill Concern on U.S. Objectives Persists," *Washington Post*, January 1, 1983, p. A1.

54. Haig, *op. cit.*, pp. 132–36.

55. Raymond W. Copson and Richard P. Cronin, "*Reagan Doctrine*": Assisting Anti-

Marxist Guerrillas, Issue Brief IB86113 (updated) (Washington, D.C.: Library of Congress/Congressional Research Service, May 1, 1987), p. 17; see also by the same authors, "The 'Reagan Doctrine' and Its Prospects," *Survival*, Vol. XXIX, No. 1 (January/February 1987), p. 44. For a censored text of the finding, see Arnson, *op. cit.*, p. 77n; see also Tyler and Woodward, "U.S. Approves Covert Plan in Nicaragua," *Washington Post*, March 10, 1982, p. A1.

56. Al Haig, "Where the Contra Policy Went Wrong," *Christian Science Monitor*, February 16, 1988, p. 16.

57. Tyler, "Nicaragua: Hill Concern on U.S. Objectives Persists," *Washington Post*, January 1, 1983, pp. A1, A10; Don Oberdorfer, "U.S. Support Bolsters Rebels' Confidence Inside Nicaragua: Washington's Role Troubles Congress," *Washington Post*, April 3, 1983, p. A1; Oberdorfer and Tyler, "U.S.-Backed Nicaraguan Rebel Army Swells to 7,000 Men," *Washington Post*, May 8, 1983, p. A1.

58. Kagan interview with Craig Johnstone, Enders's deputy, in Kagan, *op. cit.*, 1981 chapter; Gutman, *op. cit.*, p. 86; Frank McNeil, *War and Peace in Central America* (New York: Charles Scribner's Sons, 1988), p. 153.

59. McNeil, *op. cit.*, pp. 152–53.

60. Arnson, *op. cit.*, pp. 103–7. The Boland Amendment became law as Section 793 of the Department of Defense Appropriations Act, 1983, incorporated in the Continuing Appropriations Resolution for Fiscal Year 1983 (Public Law 97-377).

61. Interview with CIA Director William Casey, *U.S. News & World Report*, April 23, 1984, pp. 27–28.

62. See, e.g., Jim Wright, *Worth It All: My War for Peace* (Washington, D.C.: Brassey's [US], 1993), p. 60.

63. Cannon, *op. cit.*, pp. 357–60.

64. Nixon quoted in Lou Cannon, "Hang the Polls, Conviction Is What Counts on Latin Policy," *Washington Post*, May 14, 1984, p. A2.

65. E.g., Benjamin Weiser, "Company Man," *Washington Post Magazine*, May 17, 1992, p. 25, and the discussion in Arnson, *op. cit.*, pp. 155–62; but see also Jane Perlez, "For Moynihan, a Search for Middle Ground," *New York Times*, April 12, 1984, p. A10, and Michael A. Ledeen, *Perilous Statecraft: An Insider's Account of the Iran-Contra Affair* (New York: Charles Scribner's Sons, 1988), pp. 60–63.

66. Bernard Gwertzman, "Moynihan to Quit Senate Panel in Dispute on C.I.A.," *New York Times*, April 16, 1984, p. A8.

67. Ledeen, *op. cit.*, pp. 62–63; Woodward, *op. cit.*, pp. 319ff; Perlez, *loc. cit.*; and other accounts I have heard indirectly from participants.

68. See Mark Falcoff, "The Apple of Discord: Central America in U.S. Domestic Politics," in Wiarda, *op. cit.*

69. Karen J. Winkler, "Organizers of El Salvador 'Teach-In' Hope It Will Be Catalyst for Protesters," *Chronicle of Higher Education*, April 13, 1981; quoted in ibid., p. 366.

70. McNeil, *op. cit.*, p. 23.

71. Quoted in Arnson, *op. cit.*, p. 63.

72. Sen. Christopher J. Dodd, "Democratic Response to President Reagan's Address to Joint Session of Congress," April 27, 1983, News Release, p. 7.

73. *Congressional Record*, March 19–20, 1986, p. H1400. This and the subsequent quotations from the *Congressional Record* are drawn from "Running from Reality," a June 1986 compilation by Rep. Newt Gingrich.

74. E.g., Richard Fagen, "Dateline Nicaragua: The End of the Affair," *Foreign Policy*, No. 36 (Fall 1979), especially pp. 180–81. Compare Mark Falcoff, "Somoza, Sandino, and the United States," *loc. cit.*

75. *Congressional Record*, March 19–20, 1986, p. H1345.

76. Ibid., p. H1380.

77. Ibid., p. H1456.

78. Ibid., p. H1340.

79. Ibid., p. H1351.

80. Wright, *op. cit.*, p. 45.

81. The pope's remarks at Puebla, January 1979, are quoted by Christian, *op. cit.*, p. 211.

82. Speaker Tip O'Neill with William Novak, *Man of the House* (New York: Random House, 1987), p. 370.

83. Geraldine O'Leary de Macias, in *National Catholic Register*, October 16, 1983, reprinted in Mark Falcoff and Robert Royal, eds., *Crisis and Opportunity: U.S. Policy in Central America and the Caribbean* (Washington, D.C.: Ethics and Public Policy Center, 1984), pp. 425–32.

84. Daniel Wattenberg, "The Lady Macbeth of Little Rock," *American Spectator*, Vol. 25, No. 8 (August 1992), p. 32.

85. See Arnson, *op. cit.*, pp. 184–85.

86. See, e.g., "Neither Pure Nor Simple: The AFL-CIO and Latin America," in *NACLA Report on the Americas*, Vol. XXII, No. 3 (May/June 1988), 13–40 (a special issue on the subject); see also the critical but less splenetic Paul G. Buchanan, "The Impact of U.S. Labor," in Abraham F. Lowenthal, ed., *Exporting Democracy: The United States and Latin America: Themes and Issues* (Baltimore, Md.: Johns Hopkins University Press, 1991).

87. E.g., Charles Krauthammer, "Nicaraguan Nettle," *New Republic*, May 9, 1983, pp. 15–16; Ronald Radosh, "Darkening Nicaragua," *New Republic*, October 24, 1983, pp. 7–12.

88. On the connection with Middle Eastern and other terrorist groups, see U.S. Department of State, *The Sandinistas and Middle Eastern Radicals* (Washington, D.C.: Department of State, August 1985), and Douglas Farah, "Managua Blasts Rip Lid Off Secrets," *Washington Post*, July 14, 1993, p. A16.

89. U.S. Department of State, *Report of the Secretary of State's Panel on El Salvador* (Washington, D.C.: Department of State, July 15, 1993).

90. Remarks by Vice President George Bush at a dinner hosted by Salvadoran president Alvaro Magaña, San Salvador, December 11, 1983, Press Release by the Office of the Press Secretary to the Vice President, in U.S. Department of State, *American Foreign Policy: Current Documents, 1983* (Washington, D.C.: Department of State, 1985), p. 1389.

91. McNeil, *op. cit.*, pp. 175–76.

92. George P. Shultz, *Turmoil and Triumph: My Years as Secretary of State* (New York: Charles Scribner's Sons, 1993), p. 291.

93. Gutman, *op. cit.*, p. 66.

94. Ortega address to the UN General Assembly, October 7, 1981, in FBIS-LAM-81-195, 8 October 1981, pp. P3–12.

95. Speech by Tomás Borge at ceremonies marking the second anniversary of the Nicaraguan Revolution, July 19, 1981, in FBIS-LAM-81-139, 21 July 1981, p. P10.

96. U.S. Department of State, *Comandante Bayardo Arce's Secret Speech Before the Nicaraguan Socialist Party (PSN)*, Department of State Publication 9422 (Washington, D.C.: March 1985), p. 4.

97. Gutman, *op. cit.*, *passim.*

98. Shultz, *op. cit.*, p. 322.

99. The story of Shultz's encounters with the conservatives is told, from the latter's point of view, in Menges, *op. cit.*, Chapter 3. For Shultz's perspective, see Shultz, *op. cit.*, Chapter 19.

100. Fred C. Iklé, under secretary of defense for policy, "U.S. Policy for Central America—Can We Succeed?" remarks to the Baltimore Council on Foreign Relations, Baltimore, September 12, 1983, News Release (Washington: Office of the Assistant Secretary of Defense for Public Affairs, September 12, 1983), pp. 3–4.

101. Shultz, *op. cit.*, p. 305.

102. Ibid., pp. 297, 299.

103. Cannon, *op. cit.*, p. 381.

104. Ibid., p. 337.

105. Shultz, *op. cit.*, pp. 310–16; Don Oberdorfer, *The Turn: From the Cold War to a New Era: The United States and the Soviet Union 1983–1990* (New York: Poseidon Press, 1991), pp. 41–42.

106. Cruz, Jr., *op. cit.*, p. 141.

107. The degenerate quality of the Grenada regime is revealed in the documentary archive later retrieved; see U.S. Department of State and U.S. Department of Defense, *Grenada Documents: An Overview and Selection*, with an introduction by Michael Ledeen and Herbert Romerstein (Washington, D.C.: September 1984).

108. Editorial, "Goliath in Grenada," *New York Times*, October 30, 1983, Section IV, p. 18.

109. U.S. government photograph of Moscow television broadcast, October 1983, copy in author's possession.

110. Gutman, *op. cit.*, pp. 172–75; McNeil, *op. cit.*, pp. 175–76.

111. Shultz, *op. cit.*, p. 402; Menges, *op. cit.*, pp. 124–29. For a later version of the proposal, see Gutman, *op. cit.*, Appendix I, pp. 378–81.

112. Excerpts from the June 25, 1984, NSPG meeting are from an NSC transcript released in the Oliver North trial, quoted in Kagan, *op. cit.*, 1984 chapter.

113. The second Boland Amendment was enacted as Section 8066(a) of the Department of Defense Appropriations Act, 1985, as part of the Further Continuing Appropriations Resolution for Fiscal Year 1985 (Public Law 98-473).

114. Kagan, *op. cit.*, 1981 chapter.

115. Kagan interview with Ambassador Harry Shlaudeman, April 9, 1991, ibid.

116. Menges, *op. cit.*, pp. 105, 113.

117. Gutman, *op. cit.*, especially Chapter 5.

CHAPTER 11

1. McFarlane conversation with the author, January 17, 1991; Lou Cannon, *President Reagan: The Role of a Lifetime* (New York: Simon and Schuster, 1991), p. 372.

2. Charles Krauthammer, "The Reagan Doctrine," *Time*, April 1, 1985, pp. 54–55; see also Cannon, *op. cit.*, p. 369.

3. Henry A. Kissinger, *White House Years* (Boston: Little, Brown, 1979), pp. 222–25.

4. See the comment by NSC official Donald Fortier disavowing a "doctrine" for these reasons, in Patrick E. Tyler and David B. Ottaway, "Casey Enforces 'Reagan Doctrine' with Reinvigorated Covert Action," *Washington Post*, March 9, 1986, p. A10.

5. Author's conversation with John Carbaugh, June 3, 1993. The Madison Group included Carbaugh and James Lucier (aides to Sen. Jesse Helms), James Gidwitz, William Schneider, Richard Perle, Frank Gaffney, Christopher Lehman, David Sullivan, Michael Pillsbury, Carl Ford, Margot Carlisle, Charles Kupperman, and others.

6. Republican Advisory Council on National Security and International Affairs, "The Carter Administration: On the Wrong Side in Africa," (Washington, D.C.: Republican National Committee, April 1978).

7. Republican party platform, July 15, 1980, in *Congressional Quarterly Almanac, 1980,* (Washington, D.C.: Congressional Quarterly, 1981), pp. 80B, 82B.

8. Constantine C. Menges, *The Twilight Struggle: The Soviet Union v. the United States Today* (Washington, D.C.: The AEI Press, 1990), pp. 5–6.

9. See Peter Schweizer, *Victory: The Reagan Administration's Secret Strategy That*

Hastened the Collapse of the Soviet Union (New York: Atlantic Monthly Press, 1994), pp. 130–32.

10. Stephen Sestanovich, "Do the Soviets Feel Pinched by Third World Adventures?" *Washington Post*, May 20, 1984, p. B1; see also Margot Light, *The Soviet Theory of International Relations* (New York: St. Martin's Press, 1988), Chapters 5, 10.

11. State Department memorandum (drafted by Abrams) dated October 27, 1981, from Deputy Secretary William P. Clark and Under Secretary for Management Richard T. Kennedy to Secretary of State Alexander Haig, and approved by Haig, excerpted in *New York Times*, November 5, 1981, p. A10.

12. See George P. Shultz, *Turmoil and Triumph: My Years as Secretary of State* (New York: Charles Scribner's Sons, 1993), pp. 969–75.

13. Cannon, *op. cit.*, p. 337.

14. Stephen J. Solarz, "It's Time for the Democrats to Be Tough-Minded," *New York Times*, June 30, 1985, p. A27; see also Christopher Layne, "The Solarz Report: Hawks, Doves, and Democrats," *New Republic*, May 19, 1986, p. 11.

15. Stephen S. Rosenfeld, "The Guns of July," *Foreign Affairs*, Vol. 64, No. 4 (Spring 1986), p. 706.

16. See Stephen J. Solarz, "When to Intervene," *Foreign Policy*, No. 63 (Summer 1986), pp. 20–39.

17. Raymond W. Copson and Richard P. Cronin, "The 'Reagan Doctrine' and Its Prospects," *Survival*, Vol. XXIX, No. 1 (January/February 1987), pp. 44, 45.

18. Ibid., pp. 41, 44.

19. Ibid., p. 44.

20. William J. Casey, "Collapse of the Marxist Model: America's New Calling," speech to the Union League Club, New York, January 9, 1985, in Herbert E. Meyer, ed., *Scouting the Future: The Public Speeches of William J. Casey* (Washington, D.C.: Regnery Gateway, 1989), p. 171; quoted in Menges, *op. cit.*, pp. 3–4; see also Roy Gutman, *Banana Diplomacy: The Making of American Policy in Nicaragua 1981–1987* (New York: Simon and Schuster, 1988), pp. 266–71.

21. See Shultz, *op. cit.*, pp. 646–51, 677–78. On the bureaucratic struggle over Lebanon, see ibid., pp. 226–31.

22. E.g., George P. Shultz, "Terrorism: The Challenge to the Democracies," address to the Jonathan Institute, Second Conference on International Terrorism, Washington, June 24, 1984; address to Park Avenue Synagogue, New York, October 25, 1984; "The Ethics of Power," address at Yeshiva University, New York, December 9, 1984; "Low Intensity Warfare: The Challenge of Ambiguity," address before the Low Intensity Warfare Conference, National Defense University, January 15, 1986.

23. Constantine C. Menges, *Inside the National Security Council: The True Story of the Making and Unmaking of Reagan's Foreign Policy* (New York: Simon and Schuster, 1988), pp. 243–48.

24. E.g., Zbigniew Brzezinski, "Afghanistan and Nicaragua," *National Interest*, No. 1 (Fall 1985).

25. Don Oberdorfer, *The Turn: From the Cold War to a New Era: The United States and the Soviet Union, 1983–1990* (New York: Poseidon Press, 1991), pp. 59, 115.

26. Ronald Reagan, *An American Life* (New York: Pocket Books/Simon and Schuster, 1990), p. 606.

27. Rosenfeld, *loc. cit.*, especially pp. 709, 713–14.

28. Selig S. Harrison, "Afghanistan: Soviet Intervention, Afghan Resistance, and the American Role," in Michael T. Klare and Peter Kornbluh, eds., *Low-Intensity Warfare: Counterinsurgency, Proinsurgency, and Antiterrorism in the Eighties* (New York: Pantheon Books, 1988), pp. 183–206.

29. Daniel Patrick Moynihan, "Reagan's Doctrine and the Iran Issue," *New York Times*, December 21, 1986, p. E19; see also the essays by Stanley Hoffmann and Louis Henkin in Louis Henkin et al., *Right v. Might: International Law and the Use of Force* (New York: Council on Foreign Relations, 1989) and second edition published in 1991.

30. Charles Krauthammer, "Morality and the Reagan Doctrine," *New Republic*, September 8, 1986, pp. 17–24.

31. See Daniel Patrick Moynihan with Suzanne Weaver, *A Dangerous Place* (Boston: Atlantic Monthly Press/Little, Brown, 1978), pp. 247–53.

32. E.g., Stanley Hoffmann, "Foreign Policy: What's to Be Done?" *New York Review of Books*, April 30, 1981, pp. 33–37.

33. Robert W. Tucker, *Intervention and the Reagan Doctrine* (New York: Council on Religion and International Affairs, 1985), p. 13.

34. Ibid., pp. 8–9, 13.

35. Charles Krauthammer, "The Poverty of Realism," *New Republic*, February 17, 1986, p. 21.

36. Casey address of January 9, 1985, quoted in Gutman, *op. cit.*, p. 269.

37. Alexei Izyumov and Andrei Kortunov, "The Soviet Union in the Changing World," *International Affairs* (Moscow), No. 8 (August 1988), p. 52.

38. See Gregory A. Fossedal, *The Democratic Imperative: Exporting the American Revolution* (New York: Basic Books/A New Republic Book, 1989), Figure 7.1, p. 154.

39. Tucker quoted in Stephens Broening, "Many Feel Reagan Moves Helped Spark Soviet Shift," *Baltimore Sun*, January 8, 1989, p. 12.

40. E.g., Roger D. Hansen, "The Reagan Doctrine and Global Containment: Revival or Recessional," *SAIS Review*, Vol. 7, No. 1 (Winter-Spring 1987), pp. 54–55.

41. Earl C. Ravenal, "The Reagan Doctrine in Its Strategic and Moral Context," *Small Wars and Insurgencies*, Vol. 1, No. 1 (April 1990).

42. For a useful compilation of the arguments that follow, see Copson and Cronin, *loc. cit.*

43. Robert H. Johnson, " 'Rollback' Revisited—A Reagan Doctrine for Insurgent Wars,"

Policy Focus (Washington, D.C.: Overseas Development Council, January 1986), p.8.

44. See Andrew J. Pierre, ed., *Third World Instability: Central America as a European-American Issue* (New York: Council on Foreign Relations, 1985).

45. Michael A. Ledeen, *Perilous Statecraft: An Insider's Account of the Iran-Contra Affair* (New York: Charles Scribner's Sons, 1988), pp. 55–56.

46. Jeane J. Kirkpatrick, "The Reagan Doctrine and U.S. Foreign Policy" (Washington, D.C.: Heritage Foundation/ Fund for an American Renaissance, 1985), p. 11.

47. Angelo Codevilla, "The Reagan Doctrine—(As Yet) A Declaratory Policy," *Strategic Review*, Summer 1986, reprinted in Walter T. Hahn, ed., *Central America and the Reagan Doctrine* (Washington, D.C.: Center for International Relations at Boston University/United States Strategic Institute, 1987), Chapter 15.

48. Michael T. Klare, "The New U.S. Strategic Doctrine," *Nation*, December 28, 1985/ January 4, 1986.

49. Fred Halliday, *From Kabul to Managua: Soviet-American Relations in the 1980s* (New York: Pantheon Books, 1989), pp. 17, 109, 134; see also Mammo Muchie and Hans van Zon, "Soviet Foreign Policy Under Gorbachev and Revolution in the Third World: An Ideological Retreat or Refinement?" in Mary Kaldor, Gerard Holden, and Richard Falk, eds., *The New Détente: Rethinking East-West Relations* (London/ Tokyo: Verso/United Nations University, 1989), pp. 195–97.

50. Halliday, *op. cit.*, pp. 109, 134.

51. Ibid., p. 134.

52. Ibid., pp. 134–35.

CHAPTER 12

1. Don Oberdorfer, *The Turn: From the Cold War to a New Era: The United States and the Soviet Union, 1983–1990* (New York: Poseidon Press, 1991), p. 151; Lou Cannon, *President Reagan: The Role of a Lifetime* (New York: Simon and Schuster, 1991), pp. 749–50.

2. Kozyrev on ABC News, *This Week with David Brinkley*, August 25, 1991. From ABC News, Brinkley transcript #513, p. 7.

3. Gorbachev remarks at Soviet embassy reception in Washington, June 1990, in FBIS-SOV-90-107, 4 June 1990, p. 15.

4. Soviet spokesman Gennadii Gerasimov, press briefing in Helsinki, October 25, 1989, quoted in Bill Keller, "Gorbachev, in Finland, Disavows Any Right of Regional Intervention," *New York Times*, October 26, 1989, p. A1.

5. See Peter W. Rodman, "The Last General Secretary," *National Review*, January 20, 1992, pp. 11–14, from which some of this is taken.

6. Mikhail Gorbachev, "The Ideology of Renewal for Revolutionary Restructuring," address to the Plenary Meeting of the CPSU Central Committee, February 18, 1988 (Moscow: Novosti Press Agency Publishing House, 1988), pp. 35–36.

7. L. I. Brezhnev, "Report of the Central Committee of the CPSU to the XXVI Party Congress of the CPSU and the Immediate Tasks of the Party in Home and Foreign Policy," February 23, 1981 (Moscow: Novosti Press Agency Publishing House, 1981), pp. 6, 20–27.

8. Elizabeth Kridl Valkenier, "New Soviet Thinking About the Third World," *World Policy Journal*, Vol. IV, No. 4 (Fall 1987), pp. 669–70.

9. K. Brutents, "The Liberated Countries and the Anti-Imperialist Struggle," *Pravda*, January 10, 1986, pp. 3–4; quoted in ibid., p. 669.

10. Valkenier, *loc. cit.*, pp. 670–71.

11. G. Mirskii, "On the Question of the Developing Countries' Choice of Path and Orientation," *MEMO*, No. 11, 1987, p. 76; quoted in Mammo Muchie and Hans van Zon, "Soviet Foreign Policy Under Gorbachev and Revolution in the Third World: An Ideological Retreat or Refinement?" in Mary Kaldor, Gerard Holden, and Richard Falk, eds., *The New Détente: Rethinking East-West Relations* (London/ Tokyo: Verso/ United Nations University, 1989), p. 191.

12. Georgii Arbatov, *The System: An Insider's Life in Soviet Politics* (New York: Times Books/Random House, 1992), p. 258.

13. See Fedor Burlatsky, *Khrushchev and the First Russian Spring: The Era of Khrushchev Through the Eyes of His Advisor* (New York: Charles Scribner's Sons, 1991).

14. Arbatov, *op. cit.*, especially Chapter 4; Frederick Kagan, "The Secret History of Perestroika," *National Interest*, No. 23 (Spring 1991), pp. 33–42.

15. Andropov speech at CPSU Central Committee Plenum, June 15, 1983, in FBIS-SOV-83-117, 16 June 1983, pp. R9, 11.

16. Ibid., p. R12.

17. Stephen Sestanovich, "Do the Soviets Feel Pinched by Third World Adventures?" *Washington Post*, May 20, 1984, p. B1.

18. Charles Wolf, Jr., "Costs of the Soviet Empire," *Wall Street Journal*, January 30, 1984, p. 32; see also Charles Wolf, Jr., et al., *The Costs of the Soviet Empire*, Research Report R-3073/1-NA (Santa Monica, Calif.: RAND Corporation, 1984); U.S. Congress, House of Representatives, *The Soviet Union in the Third World, 1980–85: An Imperial Burden or Political Asset?* Report prepared for the Committee on Foreign Affairs by the Congressional Research Service, Library of Congress, Committee Print, 99th Congress, 1st Session (Washington, D.C.: September 23, 1985).

19. U.S. House, *The Soviet Union in the Third World*, pp. 203–4, citing unclassified data from Central Intelligence Agency, National Foreign Assessment Center, *Communist Aid Activities in Non-Communist Less Developed Countries, 1979 and 1954– 79*, Research Paper ER80-10318U, October 1980, pp. 18, 39.

20. Michael R. Beschloss and Strobe Talbott, *At the Highest Levels: The Inside Story of the End of the Cold War* (Boston: Little, Brown, 1993), p. 6.

21. Oberdorfer, *op. cit.*, p. 109.

22. Dusko Doder, " 'A Nice Smile, But Iron Teeth'," *Washington Post*, March 17, 1985, p. A1.

23. For a critical political biography of Gorbachev, see Dmitry Mikheyev, *The Rise and Fall of Gorbachev* (Indianapolis: Hudson Institute, 1992).

24. Richard Schifter, assistant secretary of state for human rights and humanitarian affairs, "*Glasnost:* The Dawn of Freedom?" address at the annual meeting of the American Academy of Political and Social Science, Philadelphia, April 28, 1989, published by U.S. Department of State, Bureau of Public Affairs, Public Information Series, June 1989.

25. Gorbachev speech to plenary meeting of CPSU Central Committee, March 11, 1985, in *Pravda* and *Izvestia*, March 12, 1985, translated in *Current Digest of the Soviet Press*, Vol. XXXVII, No. 9 (March 27, 1985), p. 8.

26. U.S. House, *The Soviet Union in the Third World*, p. 434.

27. TASS report, "Conversation Between M. S. Gorbachev and D. Ortega," March 14, 1985, in FBIS-SOV-85-050, 14 March 1985, p. K1.

28. TASS statement, April 12, 1985, in FBIS-SOV-85-072, 15 April 1985, p. K2.

29. U.S. House, *The Soviet Union in the Third World*, pp. 435–46; Dusko Doder, "Gorbachev Warns on Afghan Aid," *Washington Post*, March 16, 1985, p. A1, A28.

30. Ronald Reagan, *An American Life* (New York: Simon and Schuster, 1990), p. 617.

31. Mikhail Gorbachev, press conference at Soviet Press Centre, Geneva, November 21, 1985, in *Geneva: The Soviet-U.S. Summit, November 1985: Documents and Materials* (Moscow: Novosti Press Agency Publishing House, 1985), pp. 22–24.

32. Reagan, *op. cit.*, p. 644.

33. Ibid., p. 648.

34. Francis Fukuyama, *Gorbachev and the New Soviet Agenda in the Third World*, Research Report R-3634-A (Santa Monica, Calif.: RAND Corporation, June 1989), p. 14.

35. N. Simonya, "The Charter of Freedom and Independence (25 Years of the Declaration on the Granting of Independence to Colonial Countries and Peoples)," *International Affairs* (Moscow), No. 1 (January 1986), pp. 56–57.

36. Anatolii Gromyko and Vladimir Lomeiko, "New Way of Thinking and 'New Globalism,'" *International Affairs* (Moscow), No. 5 (May 1986), p. 20.

37. Richard Ovinnikov, "Doctrine of Neoglobalism and Washington's Imperial Policy," *International Affairs* (Moscow), No. 10 (October 1986), p. 119; see also V. Kazakov, "Regional Conflicts and International Security," *International Affairs* (Moscow), No. 2 (February 1986), pp. 45–50, 56.

38. Vladimir Bolshakov, "A Doctrine of International Brigandage," *International Affairs* (Moscow), No. 11 (November 1986), p. 100.

39. Mikhail Gorbachev, speech at dinner in honor of Algerian president Chadli Benjedid, March 26, 1986, in FBIS-SOV-86-059, 27 March 1986, p. H5.

40. Ibid., p. H4.

41. Communiqué of the Conference of the Warsaw Pact Political Consultative Committee, *Pravda*, June 12, 1986, in FBIS-SOV-86-114, 13 June 1986, p. BB3.

42. "An Interview with Gorbachev," *Time*, September 9, 1985, p. 29.

43. Yevgenii Primakov, "New Philosophy of Foreign Policy," *Pravda*, July 9, 1987, in FBIS-SOV-87-134, 14 July 1987 (captioned as "Primakov on 'New Philosophy' in Foreign Policy"), p. CC6.

44. Ibid., p. CC5.

45. Stephen Sestanovich, "Gorbachev's Foreign Policy: A Diplomacy of Decline," *Problems of Communism*, Vol. XXXVII, No. 1 (January/February 1988), p. 5.

46. TASS report of Gorbachev meeting with Ali Salim al-Beidh, February 10, 1987, in FBIS-SOV-87-029, 12 February 1987, p. H2. I am indebted to my friend, Egyptian diplomat Ramzy Ezzeldin Ramzy, for calling this to my attention.

47. Mikhail Gorbachev, *Perestroika: New Thinking for Our Country and the World* (New York: Harper & Row, 1987), p. 147.

48. For good analyses of Gorbachev's "new thinking," see Valkenier, *loc. cit.*; Margot Light, *The Soviet Theory of International Relations* (New York: St. Martin's Press, 1986), Chapter 10; Vernon V. Aspaturian, "Gorbachev's 'New Political Thinking' and Foreign Policy," in Jiri Valenta and Frank Cibulka, eds., *Gorbachev's New Thinking and Third World Conflicts* (New Brunswick, N.J.: Transaction Publishers, 1990), Chapter 1; Allen Lynch, *Gorbachev's International Outlook: Intellectual Origins and Political Consequences*, Occasional Paper Series No. 9 (New York: Institute for East-West Security Studies, 1989). On the changes in defense doctrine, see Raymond L. Garthoff, *Deterrence and the Revolution in Soviet Military Doctrine* (Washington, D.C.: Brookings Institution, 1990).

49. Dobrynin's lengthy presentation of the new philosophy, in his speech of May 27, 1986, was reprinted as "For a Nuclear-Free World, Approaching the 21st Century," *Kommunist*, June 1986.

50. Peter W. Rodman, "The Changing Soviet Challenge in the Third World: How Significant the Changes?," paper delivered to a conference on "The Changing Soviet Challenge in the Third World," December 11, 1987, at the Center for Strategic and International Studies, Washington, D.C. An updated version was later published as "The Case for Skepticism," *National Interest*, No. 12 (Summer 1988), pp. 83–90.

51. Yegor Ligachev, speech in Gorkii, August 5, 1988, in FBIS-SOV-88-152, 8 August 1988, p. 39.

52. TASS report, "Glorious Date in Mankind's History," *Pravda*, July 12, 1989, in FBIS-SOV-89-133, 13 July 1989 (captioned as "Yakovlev Addresses Meeting on French Revolution"), pp. 33–34.

53. Eduard Shevardnadze, "An Unconditional Requirement—Turn to Face the Economy," July 4, 1987, quoted in Sestanovich, "Gorbachev's Foreign Policy," *loc. cit.*, p. 3.

54. Mikhail Gorbachev, address at seventieth anniversary celebration of the Great Oc-

tober Socialist Revolution, November 2, 1987, in FBIS-SOV-87-212, 3 November 1987, p. 54.

55. Vyacheslav Dashichev, "East-West: Quest for New Relations: On the Priorities of the Soviet State's Foreign Policy," *Literaturnaya Gazeta*, May 18, 1988, in FBIS-SOV-88-098, 20 May 1988 (captioned as "Historian Questions Past Foreign Policies"), pp. 7–8.

56. V. I. Dashichev, "Topical Interview," *Komsomolskaya Pravda*, June 19, 1988, in FBIS-SOV-88-118, 20 June 1988 (captioned as "Past Foreign Policy 'Blunders' Criticized"), p. 57.

57. Eduard Shevardnadze, "The 19th All-Union CPSU Conference: Foreign Policy and Diplomacy," July 25, 1988, in *International Affairs* (Moscow), No. 10 (October 1988), pp. 8–12, 19–21.

58. Francis Fukuyama, "Patterns of Soviet Third World Policy," *Problems of Communism*, Vol. XXXVI, No. 5 (September-October 1987), p. 7.

59. Program of the CPSU, in *Current Digest of the Soviet Press*, Special Supplement, December 1986, quoted and discussed in Fukuyama, *loc. cit.*, p. 7.

60. Fukuyama, *loc. cit.*, pp. 7–8.

61. Elizabeth Kridl Valkenier, "*Glasnost* and *Perestroika* in Soviet–Third World Economic Relations," *Harriman Institute Forum*, Vol. 5, No. 2 (October 1991), p. 3.

62. Unclassified figures provided by CIA to the author in August 1988 for use in a speech, "Framework for U.S.-Soviet Relations—A Balancing of Interests?," delivered at the Fourth General Chautauqua Conference on U.S.-Soviet Relations, Tbilisi, Georgia, USSR, September 20, 1988.

63. *Izvestia*, March 2, 1990, in FBIS-SOV-90-043, 5 March 1990, pp. 8–84.

64. Yelena Arafyeva, "Charity or Ideology?" *Izvestia*, July 25, 1990, in FBIS-SOV-90-146, 30 July 1990 (captioned as "Charity to Replace Ideology in Aid Policy"), p. 7.

65. E.g., Yuriy Kornilov, "How Much Do Weapons Cost?" *Literaturnaya Gazeta*, January 31, 1990, in FBIS-SOV-90-024, 5 February 1990 (captioned as "Arms Shipments to Third World Questioned"), pp. 2–3.

66. Speech by N. P. Shmelëv at June 8, 1989, session of Congress of USSR People's Deputies, in FBIS-SOV-89-110S, 9 June 1989 (captioned as "Shmelev Urges Draconian Measures"), p. 28.

67. Andrei Kozyrev, "Confidence and the Balance of Interests," *International Affairs* (Moscow), No. 11 (November 1988), pp. 7–8.

68. Andrei Kolosov, "Reappraisal of USSR Third World Policy," *International Affairs* (Moscow), No. 5 (May 1990), pp. 35–36.

69. The editors of *Time*, *Mikhail Gorbachev: An Intimate Biography* (New York: New American Library, 1988), p. 126.

70. Reagan, *op. cit.*, p. 639.

71. Gorbachev, Political Report to the 27th Party Congress, February 25, 1986, in

Current Digest of the Soviet Press, Vol. XXXVIII, No. 8 (March 26, 1986), p. 29.

72. The official Afghanistan casualty figures were announced on May 25, 1988, in a news conference by Gen. A. D. Lizichev, director of the Soviet army and navy's chief political administration, reported in *Izvestia*, May 26, 1988, p. 8, in *Current Digest of the Soviet Press*, Vol. XL, No. 21 (June 22, 1988), p. 25. But the figures are suspect, according to Soviet sources. See the remarks by Sergei Tarasenko at the conference "Retrospective on the Cold War," Session V: "Afghanistan and the Limits of Empire," sponsored by the John Foster Dulles Program for the Study of Leadership and International Affairs, the Woodrow Wilson School of Public and International Affairs, Princeton University, February 27, 1993, stenographic transcript, pp. 50–51. The 60-billion-ruble figure was cited by Shevardnadze in a Foreign Ministry speech in April 1990, in FBIS-SOV-90-081, 26 April 1990, p. 9. On the squandering of gold and diamond reserves, see the Communist party documents published in June 1992 as reported in Michael Dobbs, "Yeltsin Aides Seek to Link Gorbachev to Terrorism," *Washington Post*, June 6, 1992, p. A19, and the reports in FBIS-SOV-92-110, 8 June 1992, pp. 25–27, and FBIS-SOV-92-112, 10 June 1992, p. 39.

73. Artyom Borovik, *The Hidden War: A Russian Journalist's Account of the Soviet War in Afghanistan* (New York: Atlantic Monthly Press, 1990), pp. 13–14.

74. Marion Recktenwald, *Soviet Third World Policy in a Changing Society: Afghanistan to the Gulf War*, Occasional Paper 4 (College Park, Md.: University of Maryland Center for International Security Studies, 1991), pp. 3–4; Molly Moore, "A Post-Afghan Syndrome?" *Washington Post*, October 1, 1989, p. D1; see also the letter to *Komsomolskaya Pravda* from an Afghan veteran, January 8, 1986, in *Current Digest of the Soviet Press*, Vol. XXXVIII, No. 1 (February 5, 1986), pp. 1–3, 16.

75. Interview with Marshal Akhromeyev, "A Soldier Talks Peace," *Time*, November 13, 1989, p. 59.

76. Recktenwald, *op. cit.*, pp. 13–24.

77. Andrei Sakharov, *Memoirs* (New York: Alfred A. Knopf, 1990), p. 509.

78. Yevgenii Primakov, "USSR Policy on Regional Conflicts," *International Affairs* (Moscow), No. 6 (June 1988), pp. 4–5.

79. George P. Shultz, *Turmoil and Triumph: My Years as Secretary of State* (New York: Charles Scribner's Sons, 1993), p. 589.

80. Cannon, *op. cit.*, p. 753.

81. Reagan, *op. cit.*, p. 675.

82. George F. Kennan, interview on *The MacNeil/Lehrer Newshour*, December 21, 1988, in George F. Kennan, *After the Cold War* (Washington, D.C.: American Committee on U.S.-Soviet Relations, February 1989), p. 16; see also George F. Kennan, "The G.O.P. Won the Cold War? Ridiculous," *New York Times*, October 28, 1992, p. A21.

83. "X" (George F. Kennan), "The Sources of Soviet Conduct," *Foreign Affairs*, Vol. 25, No. 4 (July 1947), pp. 581–82.

84. Strobe Talbott, "Rethinking the Red Menace," *Time*, January 1, 1990, p. 69.

85. Ibid., p. 70.

86. Alexei Izyumov and Andrei Kortunov, "The Soviet Union in the Changing World," *International Affairs* (Moscow), No. 8 (August 1988), pp. 48, 49, 51, 55; see Chapter 11, above.

87. Mikhail Gorbachev, Report to the Plenary Meeting of the CPSU Central Committee, October 15, 1985, quoted in *On the New Edition of the CPSU Programme* (Moscow: Novosti Press Agency Publishing House, 1986), pp. 13–15; also in FBIS-SOV-85-200, 16 October 1985, pp. R3, 6.

CHAPTER 13

1. Selig S. Harrison, "Inside the Afghan Talks," *Foreign Policy*, No. 72 (Fall 1988), pp. 39–47.

2. Politburo meeting records quoted in Michael Dobbs, "Dramatic Politburo Meeting Led to End of War," *Washington Post*, November 16, 1992, p. A16.

3. Cordovez quoted May 12, 1983, in *The Muslim* (Islamabad). For this and other points I am indebted to a detailed chronology prepared by Don Oberdorfer; see also Harrison, *loc. cit.*, p. 43.

4. William K. Stevens, "Pakistani Aide Doubts Afghan Solution Is in Sight," *New York Times*, June 16, 1983, p. A6.

5. Harrison, *loc. cit.*, pp. 44–46.

6. Yossef Bodansky, "Soviet Military Involvement in Afghanistan," in Rosanne Klass, ed, *Afghanistan: The Great Game Revisited* (New York: Freedom House, 1987), pp. 255–56; Olivier Roy, *The Lessons of the Soviet/Afghan War*, Adelphi Paper No. 259 (London: Brassey's/International Institute for Strategic Studies, Summer 1991), pp. 18–21; Stephen J. Blank, *Operational and Strategic Lessons of the War in Afghanistan, 1979–90* (Carlisle Barracks, Pa.: Strategic Studies Institute, U.S. Army War College, September 1991), Chapter 5.

7. Riaz M. Khan, *Untying the Afghan Knot: Negotiating Soviet Withdrawal* (Durham, N.C.: Duke University Press, 1991), p. 174.

8. Peter Schweizer, *Victory: The Reagan Administration's Secret Strategy That Hastened the Collapse of the Soviet Union* (New York: Atlantic Monthly Press, 1994), p. 208.

9. Roy, *op. cit.*, pp. 19–20.

10. Harrison, *loc. cit.*, pp. 32–51.

11. Dobbs, *loc. cit.*

12. Oberdorfer interview with Primakov in Geneva (on background), November 19, 1985, in Oberdorfer chronology.

13. Mikhail Gorbachev, Report at the Fourth Session of the USSR Supreme Soviet of the Eleventh Convocation, in *Geneva: The Soviet-US Summit, November 1985: Documents and Materials* (Moscow: Novosti Press Agency Publishing House, 1985), p. 71.

14. Don Oberdorfer, *The Turn: From the Cold War to a New Era: The United States and the Soviet Union 1983–1990* (New York: Poseidon Press, 1991), pp. 237–39; Steve Coll, "Anatomy of a Victory: CIA's Covert Afghan War," *Washington Post*, July 19, 1992, p. A24.

15. Dobbs, *loc. cit.*

16. Remarks of Gorbachev adviser Anatolii Chernyayev at the conference "Retrospective on the Cold War," Session V: "Afghanistan and the Limits of Empire," sponsored by the John Foster Dulles Program for the Study of Leadership and International Affairs, the Woodrow Wilson School of Public and International Affairs, Princeton, University, February 27, 1993, stenographic transcript, pp. 40–41.

17. Mikhail Gorbachev, Political Report to the Twenty-seventh Party Congress, February 25, 1986, in *Current Digest of the Soviet Press*, Vol. XXXVIII, No. 8 (March 26, 1986), p. 29.

18. Henry A. Kissinger, *White House Years* (Boston: Little, Brown, 1979), pp. 269–77, 282–95.

19. Mikhail Gorbachev, speech in Vladivostok, July 28, 1986 (Moscow: Novosti Press Agency Publishing House, 1986), pp. 37–38.

20. Craig Karp, "Afghanistan: Seven Years of Soviet Occupation," in U.S. *Department of State Bulletin*, Vol. 87, No. 2119 (February 1987), pp. 112–13.

21. Richard Mackenzie, "Afghan Front Rests on Capitol Hill," *Insight*, June 11, 1990, pp. 22ff.

22. Raymond Copson and Richard P. Cronin, *"Reagan Doctrine": Assisting Anti-Marxist Guerrillas*, Issue Brief IB86113 (updated) (Washington, D.C.: Library of Congress/ Congressional Research Service, May 1, 1987), pp. 3, 12–13.

23. Selig S. Harrison, "Are We Fighting to the Last Afghan?" *Washington Post*, December 29, 1983, p. A17; Selig S. Harrison, "Nearing a Pullout from Afghanistan," *New York Times*, June 7, 1983, p. A23.

24. Selig S. Harrison, "The Soviets Are Winning in Afghanistan," *Washington Post*, May 13, 1984, p. C1.

25. Richard J. Barnet and Eqbal Ahmad, "Bloody Games," *New Yorker*, April 11, 1988.

26. Mackenzie, *loc. cit.*

27. Stephen J. Solarz, "When to Intervene," *Foreign Policy*, No. 63 (Summer 1986), pp. 26–27.

28. Harrison, "Inside the Afghan Talks," pp. 33, 51–52.

29. E.g., Leon B. Poullada, "The Road to Crisis, 1919–1980," in Klass, *op. cit.*, p. 63.

30. Constantine C. Menges, *The Twilight Struggle: The Soviet Union v. the United States Today* (Washington, D.C.: American Enterprise Institute, 1990), p. 69.

31. Author's conversation with Bud McFarlane, December 16, 1993. McFarlane was present at earlier meetings between Shultz and the president at which Shultz foreshadowed the issue, but McFarlane had left office by the time the decision was

finally made. It is known that the NSC staff cleared off on the December 1985 decision, however; see David K. Shipler, "Reagan Didn't Know of Afghan Deal," *New York Times*, February 11, 1988, p. A3.

32. Harrison, "Inside the Afghan Talks," pp. 43, 49.

33. Ibid., p. 49.

34. For a more conventional view of the Geneva negotiations by a Pakistani diplomat, see Khan, *op. cit.*

35. Jeffrey Goldberg, "4 Injured as Antitank Shell Rips into Gas Pump," *Washington Post*, August 20, 1986, pp. C1, 5; "Sentence Delayed in Shooting Case," *Washington Post*, April 4, 1987, p. B5.

36. Chris Schroeder, "Arming the Afghan Resistance: Factors Affecting U.S. Policy," paper for the author's seminar on U.S. and Soviet diplomacy in Third World conflicts, the Paul H. Nitze School of Advanced International Studies, Johns Hopkins University, December 6, 1991, pp. 10–12.

37. Ibid., p. 12; John Gunston, "Su-24s, Tu-16s, Support Soviet Ground Forces," *Aviation Week & Space Technology*, October 29, 1984; David C. Isby, "Stinger in Afghanistan: The Soviets Try to Adapt," *Rotor & Wing International*, February 1990, p. 56.

38. For accounts of the Stinger decision and the bureaucratic battle, see John Walcott and Tim Carrington, "Role Reversal: CIA Resisted Proposal to Give Afghan Rebels U.S. Stinger Missiles," *Wall Street Journal*, February 16, 1988, p. 1; David B. Ottaway, "What Is 'Afghan Lesson' for Superpowers?" *Washington Post*, February 12, 1989, p. A1.

39. Schweizer, *op. cit.*, pp. 213–14; coll, *loc. cit.*, p. A24.

40. Ottaway, *loc. cit.*

41. Walcott and Carrington, *loc. cit.*

42. Fred Bridgland, *Jonas Savimbi: A Key to Africa* (New York: Paragon House Publishers, 1987), pp. 467–68.

43. Walcott and Carrington, *loc. cit.*

44. Reported by Rep. Charles Wilson, quoted in Tony Capaccio, "It's Official: Stinger Tipped Afghan War," *Defense Week*, June 12, 1989.

45. On the U.S. Army study, see David B. Ottaway, "Stingers Were Key Weapon in Afghan War, Army Finds," *Washington Post*, July 5, 1989, p. A2; Capaccio, *loc. cit.*

46. Col. V. G. Safronov, "How It Was," *Voyenno-Istoricheskiy Zhurnal*, No. 5, 1990, in FBIS-SOV-90-138-A, 18 July 1990, Annex (captioned as "Soviet Involvement in Afghanistan Viewed"), p. 16.

47. Coll, *loc. cit.*, p. A24.

48. Roy, *op. cit.*, p. 23.

49. Schweizer, *op. cit.*, pp. 252, 271–72.

50. Oberdorfer, *op. cit.*, p. 239.

51. Don Oberdorfer, "A Diplomatic Solution to a Stalemate," *Washington Post*, April 17, 1988, p. A31.

52. Minutes of the Politburo meeting of November 13, 1986, quoted in Dobbs, *loc. cit.*

53. Oberdorfer, *op. cit.*, pp. 239–40.

54. "Answers by M. S. Gorbachev to Questions from the Indonesian Newspaper *Merdeka,*" *Pravda*, July 23, 1987, in FBIS-SOV-87-141, 23 July 1987, p. CC7.

55. George P. Shultz, *Turmoil and Triumph: My Years as Secretary of State* (New York: Charles Scribner's Sons, 1993), pp. 571–74, 576–77, 702, 744; Oberdorfer, *op. cit.*, pp. 121–23, 313.

56. Shultz, *op. cit.*, p. 987; Oberdorfer, *op. cit.*, pp. 234–35.

57. Kissinger, *op. cit.*, pp. 1341–45.

58. Shultz, *op. cit.*, pp. 1089–90.

59. Harrison, "Inside the Afghan Talks," p. 56, quoting Robert Legvold, who took part in the meeting with Gorbachev.

60. See statement by General Secretary Gorbachev, February 8, 1988, in FBIS-SOV-88-025, 8 February 1988, pp. 34ff.

61. Shultz, *op. cit.*, pp. 1087–88; Oberdorfer, *op. cit.*, p. 274, and other accounts I have heard from CIA friends.

62. E.g., Aleksandr Prokhanov, "A Writer's Opinion: Afghan Questions," *Literaturnaya Gazeta*, February 17, 1988, in *Current Digest of the Soviet Press*, Vol. XL, No. 8 (March 23, 1988), pp. 13–14; Aleksandr Prokhanov, "Afghanistan," *International Affairs* (Moscow), No. 8 (August 1988). Prokhanov had been a leading supporter of the Afghan involvement.

63. For Shultz's account of the run-up to the Geneva accords, see Shultz, *op. cit.*, pp. 1090–93.

64. Asad interview with *Time* editors, Radio Damascus, March 27, 1989, in FBIS-NES-89-058, 28 March 1989, p. 40.

65. Rosanne Klass, "U.S. Must Reassess Afghan Policy," *Wall Street Journal*, October 18, 1989, p. A25, quoting General Gromov.

66. Patrick E. Tyler, "Soviets Said to Be 'Pouring' Arms, Equipment into Afghanistan," *Washington Post*, February 9, 1990, p. A21.

67. Roy, *op. cit.*, p. 37.

68. David B. Ottaway, "U.S. Misread Gorbachev, Official Says," *Washington Post*, September 10, 1989, p. A1; Lally Weymouth, "Afghanistan: Where the Credit Belongs," *Washington Post*, April 23, 1992, p. A23.

69. Roy, *op. cit.*, p. 24.

70. Charles G. Cogan, "Shawl of Lead: From Holy War to Civil War in Afghanistan," *Conflict*, Vol. 10 (1990), p. 196.

71. Roy, *op. cit.*, p. 36.

72. See Lally Weymouth, "An Afghan Rebel Chief Tells America 'No Deal,' " *Washington Post*, September 17, 1989, p. C1.

73. Selig Harrison, *Le Monde Diplomatique*, February 1989, p. 1; quoted in Cogan, *loc. cit.*

74. Anthony C. Beilenson, "End Aid to the Afghan Rebels," *New York Times*, May 22, 1989, p. A17.

75. Bill Bradley, "It's Time to Work for Peace in Afghanistan," *Washington Post*, June 8, 1989, p. A23.

76. David B. Ottaway, "Sen. Pell Urges Political Settlement in Afghan War," *Washington Post*, October 2, 1989, p. A22; see also Lee H. Hamilton, "Negotiate an End to Afghanistan's War," *Christian Science Monitor*, March 14, 1990, p. 18.

77. Al Kamen, "Afghan Aid Questioned in Congress," *Washington Post*, March 12, 1990, p. 1.

78. David Rogers, "Bush Seeking $280 Million to Maintain CIA's Covert Aid for Afghan Insurgents," *Wall Street Journal*, November 9, 1989, p. A18.

79. McCollum, *loc. cit.*

80. Elaine Sciolino, "Legislators Send Letter to Baker on Kabul Shift," *New York Times*, February 9, 1990, p. A9.

81. Andrei Kolosov, "Reexamining Policy in the Third World," *International Affairs* (Moscow), No. 5 (May 1990), p. 39. The Russian version of the article appeared in April.

82. Elaine Sciolino, "U.S., Deeming Policy Outmoded, May Cut Off Aid to Afghan Rebels," *New York Times*, May 12, 1991, p. A1.

83. Roy, *op. cit.*, p. 44.

84. Kozyrev interview, *Komsomolskaya Pravda*, August 28, 1991, p. 3, in FBIS-SOV-91-168, 29 August 1991 (captioned as "Kozyrev on Foreign Ministry's Record, Future"), p. 98.

85. Pavel Felgengauer, "The Soviet Government's Afghan War Is Over," *Nezavisimaya Gazeta*, September 14, 1991, p. 2.

86. Selig S. Harrison, "Afghanistan," in Anthony Lake et. al., *After the Wars: Reconstruction in Afghanistan, Indochina, Central America, Southern Africa, and the Horn of Africa*, U.S.-Third World Policy Perspectives, No. 16 (New Brunswick, N.J.: Transaction Publishers for the Overseas Development Council, 1990), pp. 45–46.

87. Roy, *op. cit.*, pp. 30–31, 63–64.

CHAPTER 14

1. Chester A. Crocker, "Southern Africa Eight Years Later," *Foreign Affairs*, Vol. 68, No. 4 (Fall 1989), pp. 147–48.

2. Chas. W. Freeman, "The Angola/Namibia Accords," *Foreign Affairs*, Vol. 68, No. 3 (Summer 1989), p. 127.

3. Chester A. Crocker, *High Noon in Southern Africa: Making Peace in a Rough Neighborhood* (New York: W. W. Norton, 1993), Chapter 3. Paul Wolfowitz, director of Haig's policy planning staff, seems to have originated the linkage idea, however.

4. Ibid., especially Chapters 11–13.

5. Robert S. Jaster, *The 1988 Peace Accords and the Future of Southwestern Africa*, Adelphi Paper No. 253 (London: Brassey's/International Institute for Strategic Studies, Autumn 1990), p. 15.

6. Interview in *Afrique-Asie*, cited in ibid., p. 16.

7. Communiqué of Gorbachev meeting with dos Santos, March 14, 1985, from *Krasnaya Zvezda*, March 15, 1985, in FBIS-SOV-85-051, 15 March 1985 (captioned as "Gorbachev, Gromyko Receive Angola's dos Santos"), p. J1.

8. See Bayard Rustin and Carl Gershman, "Africa, Soviet Imperialism and the Retreat of American Power," *Commentary*, October 1977.

9. See Arch Puddington, "Jesse Jackson, the Blacks & American Foreign Policy," *Commentary*, April 1984, pp. 19–27.

10. Peter Wise, "Disagreement About Strategy Surfaces Among Angolan Rebels," *Washington Post*, February 22, 1985, p. A22.

11. Bernard Gwertzman, "Angola, Angry over Rebel Aid Issue, Ends U.S. Talks," *New York Times*, July 14, 1985, p. 3.

12. Quoted in Crocker, *op. cit.*, p. 294.

13. Quoted in Constantine C. Menges, *Inside the National Security Council: The True Story of the Making and Unmaking of Reagan's Foreign Policy* (New York: Simon and Schuster, 1988), p. 241.

14. Shultz interview on NBC News, *Meet the Press*, November 24, 1985.

15. Reagan remarks reported in "Reagan Says U.S. Favors Covert Aid to Angola Rebels," *New York Times*, November 23, 1985, pp. 1, 6.

16. Crocker, *op. cit.*, pp. 203–4, 457.

17. James T. Hackett, ed., *The State Department vs. Ronald Reagan: Four Ambassadors Speak Out*, The Heritage Lectures, No. 44 (Washington, D.C.: Heritage Foundation, 1985).

18. See George P. Shultz, *Turmoil and Triumph: My Years as Secretary of State* (New York: Charles Scribner's Sons, 1993), Chapter 15.

19. Stephen J. Solarz, "When to Intervene," *Foreign Policy*, No. 63 (Summer 1986), pp. 32–33.

20. E.g., testimony of Richard E. Bissell, October 31, 1985, in U.S. Congress, House of Representatives, Committee on Foreign Affairs, Subcommittee on Africa, *Angola: Intervention or Negotiation, Hearings*, 99th Congress, 1st Session (Washington, D.C.: U.S. Government Printing Office, 1985), pp. 21, 27.

21. Fred Bridgland, *Jonas Savimbi: A Key to Africa* (New York: Paragon House Publishers, 1987), p. 464; see also George Lardner, Jr., "How Lobbyists Briefed a Rebel Leader," *Washington Post*, October 8, 1990, p. A21.

22. David B. Ottaway, "House, Senate Panels Vote to Bar Saudi Arms Sale," *Washington Post*, April 24, 1986, p. A16; Raymond W. Copson and Richard P. Cronin, *"Reagan Doctrine": Assisting Anti-Marxist Guerrillas*, Issue Brief IB86113 (updated) (Washington, D.C.: Library of Congress/Congressional Research Service, May 1, 1987), p. 13.

23. E.g., *The Federalist*, Number 64.

24. Abraham D. Sofaer, *War, Foreign Affairs and Constitutional Power: The Origins* (Cambridge, Mass.: Ballinger, 1976).

25. Ibid., pp. 203–4.

26. Prepared testimony of Morton H. Halperin, director, ACLU Washington Office, April 8, 1987, in U.S. Congress, House of Representatives, Permanent Select Committee on Intelligence, Subcommittee on Legislation, *H.R. 1013, H.R. 1371, and Other Proposals Which Address the Issue of Affording Prior Notice of Covert Actions to the Congress, Hearings*, 100th Congress, 1st Session (Washington, D.C.: U.S. Government Printing Office, 1987), p. 96.

27. Allan E. Goodman, "Reforming U.S. Intelligence," *Foreign Policy*, Number 67 (Summer 1987), p. 131.

28. See the letter from Prof. Eugene V. Rostow to William G. Miller, staff director, and Frederick A. O. Schwartz, Jr., chief counsel, of the Senate Select Committee to Study Government Operations with Respect to Intelligence Activities (the Church Committee), September 23, 1975, reprinted in *Yale Law Report*, Spring 1976, pp. 12ff; see also footnotes 23 and 24 above.

29. Miles Copeland, *The Game of Nations: The Amorality of Power Politics* (New York: Simon and Schuster, 1969), Chapters 1 and 2; Miles Copeland, *Without Cloak or Dagger: The Truth about the New Espionage* (New York: Simon and Schuster, 1974), especially Chapters 6, 7, and 9. On covert action, see also W. Michael Reisman and James E. Baker, *Regulating Covert Action: Practices, Contexts, and Policies of Covert Coercion Abroad in International and American Law* (New Haven: Yale University Press, 1992); and Richard H. Shultz, Jr., and B. Hugh Tovar, "Covert Action," in Roy Godson, ed., *Intelligence Requirements for the 1990s: Collection, Analysis, Counterintelligence, and Covert Action* (Lexington, Mass.: Lexington Books, 1989).

30. Theodore Shackley, *The Third Option: An American View of Counterinsurgency Operations* (New York: Reader's Digest Press, 1991).

31. Prepared statement of Henry A. Kissinger, secretary of state, January 29, 1976, in U.S. Senate, Committee on Foreign Relations, Subcommittee on African Affairs, *U.S. Involvement in Civil War in Angola, Hearings*, 94th Congress, 2d Session, (Washington, D.C.: U.S. Government Printing Office, 1976), p. 20.

32. Donald R. Fortier, "U.S. Foreign Policy and Regional Security: Trends and Tools," Remarks to the Dean Witter Reynolds Annual Metals and Mining Forum, New York, February 25, 1985, pp. 16–17 (emphasis in original).

33. Kissinger testimony, January 29, 1976, *loc. cit.*, pp. 20, 51.

34. Ibid., p. 40.

35. Lee Hamilton, "Angola: Open Talk, Covert Aid," *Washington Post*, June 12, 1986, p. A25.

36. Remarks of Senator Byrd, *Congressional Record*, June 2, 1989, p. S6090; see also the letter from Senator Claiborne Pell, chairman of the Senate Foreign Relations Committee, to Sen. David Boren, chairman of the Senate Select Committee on Intelligence, quoted in Lionel Barber, "Where the covert and the overt collide," *Financial Times*, (London), July 6, 1989.

37. Gregory A. Fossedal, *The Democratic Imperative: Exporting the American Revolution* (New York: Basic Books/A New Republic Book, 1989), p. 151.

38. Malcolm Wallop, "U.S. Covert Action: Policy Tool or Policy Hedge?" *Strategic Review* (October 1984), reprinted in Walter F. Hahn, ed., *Central America and the Reagan Doctrine* (Washington, D.C.: Center for International Relations at Boston University/United States Strategic Institute, 1987), pp. 266–67, 278–79.

39. *The Need to Know*, Report of the Twentieth Century Fund Task Force on Covert Action and American Democracy (New York: Twentieth Century Fund Press, 1992), Chapter 8.

40. Reisman and Baker, *op. cit.*, p. 141.

41. Ibid., pp. 136–38.

42. U.S. Congress, House of Representatives, *Intelligence Authorization Act, Fiscal Year 1991, Conference Report to Accompany H.R. 1455*, Report 102–106, 102nd Congress, 1st Session, July 25, 1991.

43. Crocker, *op. cit.*, p. 355.

44. For much of this military account I have relied on Jaster, *op. cit.*, pp. 17ff.

45. Ibid., p. 17.

46. Ibid., pp. 17–18.

47. Fidel Castro Moncada Barracks Anniversary Speech, July 26, 1988, in FBIS-LAT-88-145, 28 July 1988, p. 16.

48. See the address by Defense Minister Raúl Castro at a ceremony marking the return of Cuban troops, May 27, 1991, in FBIS-LAT-91-105, 31 May 1991 (captioned as "Raul Castro Welcomes Internationalists"), p. 1.

49. *Cape Times*, 4–7 January 1988, cited in Jaster, *op. cit.*, p. 18.

50. James Brooke, "Cubans on Patrol in South Angola," *New York Times*, December 16, 1987, p. A11.

51. Jaster, *op. cit.*, p. 19.

52. Fidel Castro Moncada Barracks Anniversary Speech, July 26, 1988, *loc. cit.*

53. Jaster, *op. cit.*, p. 21.

54. P. W. Botha interview with Arnaud de Borchgrave, *Washington Times*, March 14, 1988; quoted in ibid., p. 20.

55. Crocker, *op. cit.*, p. 415.

56. Ibid., p. 409.

57. Questions about the U.S. mediating role are examined in G. R. Berridge, "Diplomacy and the Angola/Namibia Accords," *International Affairs* (London), Vol. 65, No. 3 (Summer 1989), pp. 467–70.

58. Freeman, *loc. cit.*, pp. 131–32.

59. See, e.g., Savimbi's remarks in William Claiborne, "Angola's Twilight Zone," *Washington Post*, October 4, 1987, pp. C1, 4.

60. Crocker, *op. cit.*, p. 291.

61. Ibid.

62. Michael Parks, "Angola: Civil War Has No End in Sight," *Los Angeles Times*, January 4, 1988.

63. The Savimbi quote is from his news conference in Jamba, September 3, 1988, in FBIS-AFR-88-172, 6 September 1988, p. 9.

64. Copy of letter in author's files; see also Constantine C. Menges, *The Twilight Struggle: The Soviet Union v. the United States Today* (Washington, D.C.: AEI Press, 1990), pp. 131–32.

65. Rowland Evans and Robert Novak, "Liberals Reassess Savimbi," *Washington Post*, July 2, 1988, p. A23.

66. Copy of letters from Michel and the senators in author's files.

67. "Hill Support for Guerrillas in Angola . . . Helps Kill Funds for U.N. Peacekeepers," *Congressional Quarterly*, October 29, 1988, pp. 3142–43.

68. See David Brock, "Mr. Symms Goes to Jamba," *Policy Review*, Winter 1992. Compare Peter W. Rodman, "The Imperial Congress," *National Interest*, Vol. 1, No. 1 (Fall 1985).

69. Freeman, *loc. cit.*, p. 126.

70. George Lardner, Jr., "Covert Aid to Angola Rebels Facing House Floor Debate," *Washington Post*, October 3, 1990, p. A29.

71. "Angola: The Stake in Savimbi," *Economist*, October 21, 1989, p. 43.

72. Statement by Warren Clark, Jr., acting assistant secretary of state for African affairs, before the Subcommittee on Africa of the House Foreign Affairs Committee, September 27, 1989 (emphasis added).

73. Shawn McCormick, "Angola: The Road to Peace," *CSIS Africa Notes*, No. 125 (Washington, D.C.: Center for Strategic and International Studies, June 6, 1991), p. 2.

74. Michael R. Beschloss and Strobe Talbott, *At the Highest Levels* (Boston: Little, Brown, 1993), especially pp. 108–12; Don Oberdorfer, *The Turn: From the Cold*

War to a New Era: The United States and the Soviet Union, 1983–1990 (New York: Poseidon Press, 1991), especially pp. 369–74.

75. Lally Weymouth, "Is the Reagan Doctrine Dead in Angola?" *Washington Post*, October 23, 1989, p. A15.

76. Lally Weymouth, "Endgame in Angola," *Washington Post*, March 25, 1990, p. C1.

77. "Jesse Jackson Calls for U.S. Recognition of Angola," *Reuters*, June 16, 1989.

78. "Why Is the U.S. Prolonging War in Angola?" advertisement sponsored by the United Church of Christ, Commission for Racial Justice, *Washington Post*, October 5, 1989, p. A29, and *New York Times*, October 5, 1989, p. A22.

79. Howard Wolpe, "More U.S. Aid for Savimbi? It Will Heat Up the Civil War," *New York Times*, June 10, 1989, p. A27.

80. Radek Sikorski, "The Mystique of Savimbi," *National Review*, August 18, 1989, p. 36.

81. John Kifner, "Mandela Assails U.S. Aid to Savimbi," *New York Times*, June 25, 1990, p. B8.

82. For a good summary of the 1989–1991 negotiation, see McCormick, *op. cit.*

83. Ibid., pp. 3–4.

84. David B. Ottaway, "Angolan War in Showdown as Superpowers Plan Settlement," *Washington Post*, March 19, 1990, p. A18.

85. Statement by Department of State spokeswoman Margaret Tutwiler, January 8, 1990, quoted in Norman Kempster, "U.S. Charges Soviet Role in Angola Battle," *Los Angeles Times*, January 9, 1990.

86. Quoted in McCormick, *op. cit.*, p. 5.

87. Ottaway, *loc. cit.*

88. Michael Wines, "House Openly Debates C.I.A. Aid in Angola," *New York Times*, October 18, 1990, p. A11.

89. McCormick, *op. cit.*, p. 9.

90. Christopher S. Wren, "Ex-Rebel Leader Returns to Luanda," *New York Times*, September 30, 1991, p. A3.

91. Copy of letter and Hill and Knowlton press release in author's files.

92. E.g., Leon Dash, "Blood and Fire: Savimbi's War Against His UNITA Rivals," *Washington Post*, September 30, 1990, p. D1.

93. E.g., Fred Bridgland, "Angola's Secret Bloodbath," *Washington Post*, March 29, 1992, p. C1.

94. Clifford Krauss, "Angolan Rebel Lays Killings to a C.I.A. Plot," *New York Times*, May 5, 1992, p. A7.

95. UNAVEM II, "Summary of Findings of the Provincial Investigative Committees on the Conduct of the Electoral Process," October 16, 1992, p. 3.

96. "Democracy in Angola: Executed Under a White Flag?" Transition Brief No. 92-T 143 (Washington, D.C.: Center for Security Policy, November 18, 1992).

97. Margaret Anstee, letter to the editor, *Economist*, March 6, 1993, p. 8. On the inadequacy of the UN effort, see also International Institute for Strategic Studies, *Strategic Survey, 1992–1993* (London: Brassey's/International Institute for Strategic Studies, 1993), pp. 35–36, and Chester A. Crocker, "Angola: 'Can This Outrageous Spectacle Be Stopped?' " *Washington Post*, October 13, 1993, p. A20.

CHAPTER 15

1. Interview with Humberto Ortega, April 11, 1991, in the manuscript of the forth-coming book by Robert W. Kagan, to be published by The Free Press.

2. Ibid.

3. U.S. Department of State, *Comandante Bayardo Arce's Secret Speech Before the Nicaraguan Socialist Party (PSN)*, Publication No. 9422, Inter-American Series 118 (Washington, D.C.: March 1985), p. 4.

4. Ibid., pp. 4–7.

5. The Coordinadora's election program of December 1983 is reprinted in Robert S. Leiken and Barry Rubin, *The Central American Crisis Reader* (New York: Summit Books, 1987), pp. 284–85.

6. See the comments by Representative Solarz on the House floor, *Congressional Record*, April 24, 1984.

7. The "Dear Commandante" letter of March 20, 1984, is reproduced in Jim Wright, *Worth It All: My War for Peace* (Washington, D.C.: Brassey's [US], 1993), Appendix 2, pp. 266–67. The controversy over the letter is discussed by Wright on pp. 66–68.

8. Kagan, *op. cit.*, 1984 chapter.

9. U.S. Department of State, *Comandante Bayardo Arce's Secret Speech*, p. 8.

10. Roy Gutman, *Banana Diplomacy: The Making of American Policy in Nicaragua 1981–1987* (New York: Simon and Schuster, 1988), p. 243; Robert Leiken, "Nicaragua's Untold Stories," *New Republic*, October 8, 1984, pp. 20–21.

11. Gutman, *op. cit.*, p. 243.

12. Leiken, *loc. cit.*, pp. 21–22.

13. Arturo J. Cruz, *Nicaragua's Continuing Struggle* (New York: Freedom House, 1988), p. 16–17.

14. *Congressional Record*, September 25, 1984, p. S6658; see Leiken article in note 10 above.

15. Cynthia J. Arnson, *Crossroads: Congress, the Reagan Administration, and Central America* (New York: Pantheon Books, 1989), p. 172.

16. Ibid., p. 175.

17. Joanne Omang, "Sandinista Foe Backs 'Contra' Aid," *Washington Post*, January 4, 1985, p. A18.

18. McCurdy interview in Arnson, *op. cit.*, p. 176.

19. Alejandro Bendaña, *Una Tragedia Campesina: Testimonios de la Resistencia* ("A Peasant Tragedy: Testimonies of the Resistance"), Managua, 1991, quoted in Stephen Schwartz, "Pro & Contra," *Commentary*, April 1992, p. 62.

20. Hedrick Smith, "A Larger Force of Latin Rebels Sought by U.S.," *New York Times*, April 17, 1985, p. 1.

21. George P. Shultz, "America and the Struggle for Freedom," address before the Commonwealth Club of San Francisco, February 22, 1985.

22. Margaret Shapiro and Joanne Omang, "Speaker Says House May Aid 'Contras,'" *Washington Post*, May 7, 1985, p. A1.

23. Interview in Arnson, *op. cit.*, p. 187.

24. *Congressional Record*, June 12, 1985, p. H4148, quoted in ibid. See also Wright, *op. cit.*, p. 79.

25. Durenberger interview, "Inquiry," *USA Today*, February 26, 1985.

26. The full text is in *Congressional Record*, June 11, 1985, pp. H4093–94.

27. Interview in Arnson, *op. cit.*, p. 189.

28. U.S. Department of State, *Democracy in Latin America and the Caribbean: The Promise and the Challenge*, Special Report No. 158 (Washington, D.C.: March 1987), p. 1.

29. State Department memorandum (drafted by Abrams) dated October 27, 1981, from Deputy Secretary of State William P. Clark and Under Secretary for Management Richard T. Kennedy, to Secretary of State Haig, and approved by Haig, excerpted in *New York Times*, November 5, 1981, p. A10.

30. Author's conversation with Robert McFarlane, January 17, 1991.

31. Sandinista minister of social security, Reynaldo Antonio Tefel, quoted in Stephen Kinzer, "Sandinistas Press Attacks on Rebels," *New York Times*, June 4, 1985, p. A10; U.S. Department of State, *Nicaragua Biographies: A Resource Book*, Special Report No. 174 (Washington, D.C.: January 1988), pp. 5–6.

32. Paul Berman, "Neckties and Mass Graves," *The Village Voice*, March 5, 1991, p. 35; Ambrose Evans-Pritchard, "Nicaragua's Killing Fields," *National Review*, April 29, 1991, pp. 38–40.

33. U.S. Department of State, *The Sandinista Constitution*, Publication No. 9523 (Washington, D.C.: August 1987), pp. 7–15.

34. U.S. Department of State, *Human Rights in Nicaragua under the Sandinistas: From Revolution to Repression*, Publication No. 9467 (Washington, D.C.: December 1986), pp. 3, 7, 9.

35. U.S. Department of State, *The Sandinista Military Build-up*, Publication No. 9432, Inter-American Series 119 (Washington, D.C., May 1985).

36. Patrick J. Buchanan, "The Contras Need Our Help," *Washington Post*, March 5, 1986, p. A19.

37. Arnson, *op. cit.*, pp. 192–93.

38. *Congressional Record*, March 19, 1986, p. H1337.

39. Ibid., p. H1365.

40. Ibid., p. H1369.

41. Ibid., p. H1368.

42. Ibid., p. H1400.

43. Quoted in *Congressional Quarterly Almanac, 1986*, Vol. XLII (Washington, D.C.: Congressional Quarterly, 1987), p. 402.

44. Gutman, *op. cit.*, p. 330; Constantine C. Menges, *Inside the National Security Council: The True Story of the Making and Unmaking of Reagan's Foreign Policy* (New York: Simon and Schuster, 1988), pp. 295–302.

45. Arnson, *op. cit.*, pp. 195–96.

46. U.S. Department of Defense, *Prospects for Containment of Nicaragua's Communist Government* (Washington, D.C.: May 1986).

47. Menges, *op. cit.*, p. 303.

48. Joanne Omang, "Reagan Rallied for Aid Til the Hill Surrendered," *Washington Post*, January 2, 1987, p. A29.

49. Ibid.

50. Editorial, "The Sandinista Road to Stalinism," *New York Times*, July 10, 1986, p. A22.

51. U.S. Department of State, *Crackdown on Freedom in Nicaragua and Profiles of Internal Opposition Leaders* (Washington, D.C., August 1986), p. 1.

52. Testimony of Robert C. McFarlane in U.S. Congress, House of Representatives Select Committee to Investigate Covert Arms Transactions with Iran and Senate Select Committee on Secret Military Assistance to Iran and the Nicaraguan Opposition, *Testimony of Robert C. McFarlane, Gaston J. Sigur, Jr., and Robert W. Owen*, Joint Hearings, May 11, 12, 13, 14, and 19, 1987, 100th Congress, 1st Session (Washington, D.C.: U.S. Government Printing Office, November 1987), pp. 5, 10 (hereinafter cited as Joint Committee Hearings).

53. Ibid.

54. Michael K. Deaver with Mickey Herskowitz, *Behind the Scenes* (New York: William Morrow, 1987), p. 259.

55. The President's Special Review Board, *Report* (Washington, D.C.: U.S. Government Printing Office, February 26, 1987), p. B-100.

56. Presidential finding, January 17, 1986, reprinted in *Congressional Quarterly Almanac, 1986*, p. 418.

57. U.S. Congress, Senate Select Committee on Secret Military Assistance to Iran and the Nicaraguan Opposition and House of Representatives Select Committee to Investigate Covert Arms Transactions with Iran, *Report of the Congressional Committees Investigating the Iran-Contra Affair, with Supplemental, Minority, and Additional Views*, S. Rept. No. 100-216, H. Rept. No. 100-433, 100th Congress, 1st Session (Washington, D.C.: U.S. Government Printing Office, November 1987) Section I (hereinafter cited as Joint Committee Report).

58. See Lawrence E. Walsh, *Iran-Contra: The Final Report* (New York: Times Books/ Random House, 1994).

59. Theodore Draper, *A Very Thin Line: The Iran-Contra Affairs* (New York: Hill & Wang, 1991); Paul Berman, "The Vanities of Patriotism," *New Republic*, July 1, 1991, pp. 29–35.

60. See The White House, Office of the Press Secretary, Press Briefing by Marlin Fitzwater, May 14, 1987 (#2072-05/14), pp. 13, 17.

61. Joint Committee Report, *op. cit.*, Section II.

62. *United States v. North*, 910 F.2d 843, *modified*, 920 F.2d 940 (D.C. Cir. 1990).

63. See Jeffrey Toobin, *Opening Arguments: A Young Lawyer's First Case: United States v. Oliver North* (New York: Viking, 1991). For Abrams's account, see Elliott Abrams, *Undue Process: A Story of How Political Differences Are Turned into Crimes* (New York: Free Press, 1992); see also Michael Ledeen, "Lawrence Walsh, Grand Inquisitor," *American Spectator*, March 1993, and Marjorie Williams, "Burden of Proof," *Washington Post Magazine*, April 11, 1993.

64. See Peter W. Morgan, "The Undefined Crime of Lying to Congress: Ethics Reform and the Rule of Law," *Northwestern University Law Review*, Vol. 86, No. 2 (Winter 1992), pp. 177–258; Peter W. Morgan, "The Dangerously Undefined Crime of Lying to Congress," *Wall Street Journal*, September 30, 1992, p. A15.

65. *United States v. Nixon*, 418 U.S. 683 (1974).

66. David Boren, "Can America Have One Voice Again?" *Washington Post*, February 19, 1987, p. 27.

67. The President's Special Review Board, *op. cit.*, pp. V-4–5.

68. See the president's message to Congress, March 31, 1987, enclosing the full declassified text of NSDD 266.

69. Robert M. Gates, "CIA and the Making of American Foreign Policy," address at the Woodrow Wilson School of Public and International Affairs, Princeton University, September 29, 1987, p. 15.

70. Steven A. Holmes, "Administration Is Fighting Itself on Haiti Policy," *New York Times*, October 23, 1993, p. 1.

71. Gates, *loc. cit.*, pp. 16–17.

72. Robert M. Gates, "The CIA and American Foreign Policy," *Foreign Affairs*, Vol. 66, No. 2 (Winter 1987/88), p. 225.

73. Sources collected in Arnson, *op. cit.*, p. 202.

74. On the details of the Arias peace plan, see Gutman, *op. cit.*, pp. 343ff.

75. Ibid., p. 343.

76. Ibid. See also Arias's speech to the UN General Assembly in September 1986, quoted in George P. Shultz, *Turmoil and Triumph: My Years as Secretary of State* (New York: Charles Scribner's Sons, 1993), p. 956.

77. See, e.g., Mark Falcoff, "A Tropical Yalta," *Second Thoughts*, Vol. I, No. 2 (Fall 1989), p. 9. Falcoff was told this by the American to whom Aria spoke.

78. Wright, *op. cit.*, pp. 116, 120–22; Arnson, *op. cit.*, p. 204.

79. John M. Barry, *The Ambition and the Power* (New York: Viking, 1989) pp. 321, 494, 500–10. For Speaker Wright's version of some of these events, see Wright, *op. cit.*, Chapter 7.

80. Barry, *op. cit.*, pp. 321–23.

81. Ibid., p. 586.

82. Shultz, *op. cit.*, pp. 963–68; Wright, *op. cit.*, pp. 153–54.

83. The text of the Wright-Reagan Plan of August 5, 1987, can be found in U.S. Department of State, *Negotiations in Central America, 1981–1987 (Revised)*, Publication No. 9551 (Washington, D.C.: October 1987), pp. 14–15. Wright's account is in Wright, *op. cit.*, Chapter 6.

84. Robert Kagan, "On Conservative Conspiracy Theories" (letter to the editor), *Policy Review*, Spring 1989, p. 81; see also Shultz, *op. cit.*, pp. 958–59.

85. Menges, *op. cit.*, p. 327.

86. Shultz, *op. cit.*, p. 957.

87. The Guatemala City ("Esquipulas II") accords of August 6–7, 1987, can be found in U.S. Department of State, *Negotiations in Central America, 1981–1987 (Revised)*, *op. cit.*, pp. 16–20.

88. Barry, *op. cit.*, p. 586.

89. Ramirez remarks at León, September 21, 1987, broadcast over Radio Sandino, September 22, 1987, in FBIS-LAT-87-185, 24 September 1987 (captioned as "Ramirez Rejects Amnesty for Ex-Somozists"), p. 29.

90. H. Res. 290, introduced by Reps. Robin Tallon (D-S.C.) and Rod Chandler (R-Wash.), October 22, 1987, and passed December 8, 1987, as the Byron-Chandler amendment to the FY1988-1989 International Security and Development Assistance Authorization bill; see *Congressional Record*, December 8, 1987, pp. H11036–40.

91. Arturo Cruz, Jr., and Mark Falcoff, "Who Won Nicaragua?" *Commentary*, May 1990, p. 36.

92. Borge remarks at party meeting in León, Reuters report, July 17, 1988, in FBIS-LAT-88-138, 19 July 1988 (captioned as "Borge Warns of 'Institutional Violence' "), p. 16; Stephen Kinzer, "Sandinistas' Rationale," *New York Times*, July 18, 1988, p. A8.

93. Deaver interview with Lou Cannon, in Lou Cannon, *President Reagan: The Role of a Lifetime* (New York: Simon and Schuster, 1991), p. 382.

94. Baker comment to Lou Cannon, ibid.

95. The text of the Bipartisan Accord may be found in *U.S. Department of State Bulletin*, Vol. 89, No. 2147 (June 1989), p. 57.

96. Ibid.

97. The White House, Office of the Press Secretary, "Remarks of President Arias of Costa Rica During Question and Answer Session with the Press," April 4, 1989, p. 1.

98. Helen Dewar, "Arias Said to Favor Contra Aid Till February," *Washington Post*, August 30, 1989, p. A37.

99. *Immigration and Naturalization Service v. Chadha*, 462 U.S. 919 (1983).

100. Robert Pear, "Unease Is Voiced on Contra Accord," *New York Times*, March 26, 1989, p. 1. Gray was rebuked by the White House for committing the sin of telling the truth. Bernard Weinraub, "White House Rebukes Counsel on Pact," *New York Times*, March 28, 1989, p. A6.

101. Humberto Belli, "Election Nearing," *New Republic*, November 27, 1989, pp. 16–19.

102. The Center for Democracy, "Violence at Masatepe: An Eyewitness Report by a Center for Democracy Observer Delegation to the Nicaraguan Election," typescript (Washington, D.C., December 14, 1989); Mary Speck, "One Killed in Nicaraguan Election Riot," *Washington Post*, December 11, 1989, p. A1; William Branigin, "U.S. Team Says Violence Imperils Managua Vote," *Washington Post*, December 12, 1989, p. A40.

103. "Sandinista Fix?" *New Republic*, February 19, 1990, p. 9.

104. Statement of spokeswoman Margaret Tutwiler at Department of State daily press briefing, January 22, 1990 (DPC #14), p. 1.

105. Robert S. Leiken, "Vote Wasn't Bought, Sandinistas Blew It," *Los Angeles Times*, March 4, 1990; Robert S. Greenberger, "Nicaraguan Opposition Slowed by Delay in Election Aid Funds Pledged by U.S.," *Wall Street Journal*, December 11, 1989, p. A11.

106. Quoted in John M. McClintock, "Confident of Win, Ortega Invites Bush," *Baltimore Sun*, February 25, 1990.

107. Larry Bensky, "Campaigning with the Sandinistas," *Nation*, March 5, 1990, p. 302.

108. Quoted in Jim Drinkard (Associated Press), "Opening to Managua Possible," *Fort Worth Star-Telegram*, February 2, 1990.

109. Quoted in Doyle McManus, "U.S. Gets Ready for Likely Sandinista Election Victory," *Los Angeles Times*, February 24, 1990; see also Robert S. Greenberger, "U.S. Obsession with Central America, A Reagan Legacy, Wanes Under Bush," *Wall Street Journal*, February 12, 1990, p. 11.

110. Quoted in James M. Dorsey, "U.S. officials view fair vote as chance to close old issue," *Washington Times*, February 26, 1990.

111. Robert S. Leiken, "Oops," *New Republic*, March 19, 1990, p. 16.

112. Costa Rican government sources as recounted to me by Elliott Abrams; see also Cruz and Falcoff, *loc. cit.*, p. 32.

113. See "A No Vote for Ortega," *Newsweek*, March 12, 1990, pp. 34–35.

114. Solarz on *MacNeil/Lehrer Newshour*, quoted in Leiken, "Oops," *loc. cit.*

115. Howard Schuman, ". . . 3 Different Pens Help Tell the Story," *New York Times*, March 7, 1990, p. A25; see also Norman Ornstein, "Why Polls Flopped in Nicaragua . . . ," ibid.

116. Alexander Cockburn, "U.S. Backed Terrorism Won in Nicaragua, Not Democracy," *Wall Street Journal*, March 1, 1990, p. 17; see other examples quoted in Cruz and Falcoff, *loc. cit.*, p. 38.

117. Robert Pear, "Washington Set to End Embargo and Aid Chamorro Government," *New York Times*, February 27, 1990, p. A13; see also note 113 above.

118. Ann Devroy and Al Kamen, "Bush Opens Way to Lifting Sanctions," *Washington Post*, February 27, 1990, p. A16.

119. Editorial, "The Morning After in Nicaragua," *New York Times*, February 27, 1990, p. A22.

120. Andres Oppenheimer, *Castro's Final Hour: The Secret Story Behind the Coming Downfall of Communist Cuba* (New York: Simon and Schuster, 1992), pp. 202–4.

121. Arias address and remarks to the American Society of Newspaper Editors, Washington, April 14, 1988, quoted in Danna Walker, UPI dispatch, April 14, 1988.

122. Michael R. Beschloss and Strobe Talbott, *At the Highest Levels* (Boston: Little, Brown, 1993), p. 57.

123. Ibid.

124. Ibid., pp. 57–58.

125. Ibid., p. 59.

126. Michael Kramer, "Anger, Bluff—and Cooperation," *Time*, June 4, 1990, p. 38.

127. Ibid., p. 45.

128. William Branigin and Julia Preston, "President Indicates Sandinistas May Try to Keep Control of Army," *Washington Post*, February 28, 1990, p. 1; Elliott Abrams, "So Far from God," *National Review*, September 20, 1993, pp. 34–41.

129. Octavio Paz, "Marxism Is Out; Gringo-Bashing, Too," *Los Angeles Times*, March 1, 1990.

130. Ibid.

131. Mark Falcoff, "Notebook: Orphans of Utopia," *New Criterion*, Vol. 9, No. 10 (June 1991), pp. 76–77.

CHAPTER 16

1. Press conference of Maj. Gen. Nguyen Van Thai, deputy head of Political Department, Ministry of Defense, Ho Chi Minh City (Saigon), September 20, 1989, in FBIS-EAS-89-181, 20 September 1989, p. 68. The figures he announced were 55,300 killed, 110,000 seriously wounded. The official U.S. death toll in our Indochina war has crept up to around 58,000.

2. Charles McGregor, *The Sino-Vietnamese Relationship and the Soviet Union*, Adelphi Paper No. 232 (London: International Institute for Strategic Studies, Autumn 1988), pp. 43–44.

3. Ibid., pp. 44–45.

4. Paul Lewis, "Soviets Said to Double Cambodia Aid," *New York Times*, October 6, 1989, p. A3.

5. Steven Erlanger, "Aid to Cambodia Non-Communists Is Detailed," *New York Times*, November 16, 1989, p. A16.

6. Frederick Z. Brown, *Second Chance: The United States and Indochina in the 1990s* (New York: Council on Foreign Relations Press, 1989), pp. 72, 79, citing the testimony of Rear Adm. Timothy W. Wright, acting deputy assistant secretary of defense for international security affairs (East Asia and Pacific) before the Subcommittee on Asian and Pacific Affairs, House Committee on Foreign Affairs, March 1, 1989.

7. Frederick Z. Brown, *Cambodia and the Dilemmas of U.S. Policy*, Critical Issues 1991: 2/3 (New York: Council on Foreign Relations Press, 1991), p. 11. On the Chinese policy of "bleeding" Vietnam, see Nayan Chanda, *Brother Enemy: The War after the War* (New York: Harcourt Brace Jovanovich, 1986), p. 379, and Chapter 8, above.

8. Elizabeth Becker, *When the War Was Over: The Voices of Cambodia's Revolution and Its People* (New York: Touchstone/Simon and Schuster, 1987), p. 440.

9. Mikhail Gorbachev, address at Vladivostok, July 28, 1986 (Moscow: Novosti Press Agency Publishing House, 1986), p. 35.

10. "Answers by M. S. Gorbachev to Questions from the Indonesian Newspaper *Merdeka, Pravda*," July 23, 1987, in FBIS-SOV-87-141, 23 July 1987, pp. CC1ff.

11. Sino-Soviet joint statement on Cambodia, February 6, 1989, in FBIS-SOV-89-023, 6 February 1989, p. 29; Brown, *Second Chance*, pp. 49–50.

12. Brown, *Second Chance*, p. 51.

13. Joint Declaration of the Governments of the People's Republic of Kampuchea, the Lao People's Democratic Republic and the Socialist Republic of Vietnam, April 5, 1989, in FBIS-EAS-89-064, 5 April 1989, pp. 35–36.

14. Stephen J. Morris, "Thailand's Separate Peace in Indochina," *Wall Street Journal*,

September 6, 1989, p. A19; Lally Weymouth, "The Cambodian Cockpit," *Washington Post*, April 30, 1989, p. C4.

15. Weymouth, "The Cambodian Cockpit."

16. For this discussion of the Cambodia diplomacy I am indebted to Brown, *Second Chance*, pp. 54–60; see also Nayan Chanda, "Civil War in Cambodia?" *Foreign Policy*, No. 76 (Fall 1989).

17. Chanda, "Civil War in Cambodia?" pp. 34–38.

18. Atkins quoted in Mary McGrory, "More Bad Ideas for Cambodia," *Washington Post*, May 14, 1989, p. C1.

19. Hon. Edmund S. Muskie, testimony to the Senate Foreign Relations Committee Subcommittee on East Asian and Pacific Affairs, February 28, 1990, reprinted in *Congressional Record*, April 26, 1990, pp. S5145–47.

20. Elizabeth Becker, "Vietnam's Gift to Cambodia," *New York Times*, April 11, 1989, p. I31.

21. Mary McGrory, "New Policy, Old Hang-Up," *Washington Post*, July 24, 1990, p. A2.

22. Elizabeth Becker, "Take Vietnam Off the Enemy List," *Washington Post*, April 11, 1989, p. A19.

23. Comment of Dr. Erwin Parson, ABC News/*Time* Forum, "Beyond Vietnam," April 26, 1990, ABC News transcript #ABC-14, p. 23.

24. E.g., Jeremy J. Stone and William E. Colby, "Block the Khmer Rouge," *Washington Post*, April 28, 1989, p. A25.

25. ABC News, *Peter Jennings Reporting*, April 26, 1990, ABC News transcript #ABC-13; see also U.S. Senate, Democratic Policy Committee, "Cambodia: Military Cooperation Between the Khmer Rouge and the Non-Communist Resistance," DPC Special Report SR-7-Foreign Policy (Washington, March 11, 1991). For Solarz's rebuttal, see ABC News/*Time* Forum, p. 10; Solarz letter to the editor, *New York Times*, June 12, 1990, p. A20; and his article, "Cambodia and the International Community," *Foreign Affairs*, Vol. LXIX, No. 2 (Spring 1990), p. 111n. While minimal amounts of weaponry might have changed hands via the black market, if there was any significant transfer of equipment it was in the other direction, since the Khmer Rouge were more than amply supplied by the Chinese.

26. Some of this discussion of Bush administration policy appeared in Peter W. Rodman, "Cambodia: Supping with Devils," *National Interest*, Number 25 (Fall 1991), pp. 44–50.

27. Solarz, "Cambodia and the International Community," p. 99.

28. Brown, *Second Chance*, p. 43.

29. Ibid., p. 80.

30. The senatorial quotations, unless otherwise indicated, are from the floor debate on the Robb Amendment, *Congressional Record*, July 20, 1989, pp. S8413–8424.

31. Stephen S. Rosenfeld, "Khmer Rouge in the Wings," *Washington Post*, July 27, 1990, p. A27.

32. Office of the Vice President, Text of Remarks by the Vice President, "U.S. Policy in Asia: The Challenges for 1990," Heritage Foundation, Asian Studies Center Conference, Washington, D.C., June 22, 1989, pp. 8–13 (emphasis in original).

33. On the Paris conference generally, see Brown, *Second Chance*, Chapter 10; William S. Turley, "The *Khmer* War: Cambodia after Paris," *Survival*, Vol. XXXII, No. 5 (September/October 1990), pp. 440–42.

34. Anonymous U.S. briefer (in fact, Solomon) quoted in Steven Greenhouse, "Cambodia Talks Said to Collapse," *New York Times*, August 30, 1989, p. A1, and in Elizabeth Becker, "U.S. Blames Phnom Penh Regime for Cambodia Talks' Stalemate," *Washington Post*, August 30, 1989, p. A38.

35. Editorial, "Bleeding Cambodia," *New York Times*, September 1, 1989, p. A26.

36. Brown, *Second Chance*, p. 69; Turley, *loc. cit.*, p. 447; Solarz, "Cambodia and the International Community," p. 99n.

37. Brown, *Cambodia and the Dilemmas of U.S. Policy*, pp. 16ff.

38. Steven Greenhouse, "Greater U.N. Role Is Urged to Settle Cambodia Conflict," *New York Times*, January 17, 1990, p. A1; see text of the joint statement on p. A6.

39. Turley, *loc. cit.*, p. 447.

40. Brown, *Cambodia and the Dilemmas of U.S. Policy*, p. 19.

41. David Rogers, "Senate Panel Votes to End Covert Aid to Non-Communist Forces in Cambodia," *Wall Street Journal*, June 29, 1990, p. 14; Dan Morgan, "House Approves Aid to Cambodian Resistance," *Washington Post*, June 28, 1990, p. 10; Brown, *Cambodia and the Dilemmas of U.S. Policy*, pp. 34–36.

42. Chatichai quoted in FBIS-EAS-90-045, 7 March 1990, pp. 61–63.

43. Nate Thayer (AP), "Cambodian guerrillas make major advances," *Washington Times*, July 18, 1990, p. 11.

44. U.S. Department of State, Office of the Assistant Secretary/Spokesman, "Remarks of Secretary of State James A. Baker III and Soviet Foreign Minister Shevardnadze at the Conclusion of Bilateral Meeting," Paris, July 18, 1990 (press release), p. 2; see also Al Kamen, "Domestic Politics a Factor in U.S. Shift," *Washington Post*, July 19, 1990.

45. Steven Erlanger, "Allies in Southeast Asia Criticize Washington's Shift on Cambodia." *New York Times*, July 24, 1990, p. A2.

46. "Non-Communists Oppose Policy," AP dispatch, *New York Times*, July 19, 1990, p. A10.

47. Kerry remarks in *Congressional Record*, July 26, 1990, p. S10687.

48. Atkins quoted in Kamen, *loc. cit.*

49. Copy of senators' letter in author's files.

50. Brown, *Cambodia and the Dilemmas of U.S. Policy*, p. 34.

51. David Brock, "Mr. Symms Goes to Jamba," *Policy Review*, No. 59 (Winter 1992), p. 35.

52. Frederick Z. Brown, "Cambodia in 1991: An Uncertain Peace," *Asian Survey*, Vol. XXXII, No. 1 (January 1992), p. 90.

53. Clifford Kraus, "U.S. Is Encouraged by Hanoi Cabinet," *New York Times*, August 18, 1991, p. 9.

54. "Cambodia: The red solution," *The Economist*, August 17, 1991, pp. 30–31.

55. Brown, "Cambodia in 1991," p. 90.

56. Mitterrand quoted in Alan Riding, "3 Cambodian Factions Sign a U.N.-Enforced Peace Pact; Khmer Rouge Shares Rule," *New York Times*, October 24, 1991, pp. A1, A16.

57. Brown, "Cambodia in 1991," pp. 91–92.

58. Mary McGrory, "Who Invited the Khmer Rouge?" *Washington Post*, December 3, 1991, p. A2.

59. Atkins quoted in ibid.

60. Elizabeth Becker, "Showdown with the Khmer Rouge," *Washington Post*, November 8, 1992, p. C7.

61. Chanda, "Civil War in Cambodia?" p. 36.

62. Philip Shenon, "Sihanouk Backs Trials in Khmer Rouge Terror," *New York Times*, November 17, 1991, p. 18.

63. Brown, "Cambodia in 1991," p. 95.

64. Ibid.

65. Brown, *Cambodia and the Dilemmas of U.S. Policy*, pp. 22–24.

66. Frederick Z. Brown, *Cambodia in Crisis: The 1993 Elections and the United Nations*, Asian Update (New York: The Asia Society, May 1993), p. 5.

67. Remarks of John MacKinlay, senior research associate at the Thomas J. Watson, Jr., Center for International Studies, Brown University, at a panel discussion at the Johns Hopkins Foreign Policy Institute, Washington, February 11, 1993.

68. William Shawcross, "The Nightmare Is Over," *New York Times*, October 12, 1993, p. A23; see also Sichan Siv, "Help Can Work in Renascent Cambodia," *International Herald Tribune*, April 8, 1994, p. 6.

69. Sichan Siv and Richard H. Solomon, "The United Nations Is on the Verge of Retreating in the Face of a Success," *Los Angeles Times*, August 22, 1993, pp. M2, M6.

CHAPTER 17

1. Dulles memorandum of conversation with the president at the White House, September 17, 1956, in U.S. Department of State, *Foreign Relations of the United*

States, 1955–1957, Vol. XVI, Suez Crisis: July 26–December 31, 1956 (Washington, D.C.: U.S. Government Printing Office, 1990), p. 506.

2. George Dragnich, "The Soviet Union's Quest for Access to Naval Facilities in Egypt Prior to the June War of 1967," in Michael McGwire, Kenneth Booth, and John McDonnell, eds., Soviet Naval Policy: Objectives and Constraints (New York: Frederick A. Praeger, 1975).

3. William B. Quandt, "U.S.-Soviet Rivalry in the Middle East," in Marshall D. Shulman, ed., East-West Tensions in the Third World (New York: W. W. Norton, 1986), p. 32.

4. Eduard Shevardnadze, dinner remarks in Damascus, February 18, 1989, in FBIS-SOV-89-033, 21 February 1989, p. 20.

5. Daniel S. Papp, Soviet Policies Toward the Developing World During the 1980s: The Dilemmas of Power and Presence (Maxwell Air Force Base, Ala.: Air University Press, 1986), p. 229.

6. Attassi speech excerpted in International Documents on Palestine, 1967 (Beirut: Institute for Palestine Studies, 1970), pp. 501–2, quoted in Paul Jabber and Roman Kolkowicz, "The Arab-Israeli Wars of 1967 and 1973," in Stephen S. Kaplan, Diplomacy of Power: Soviet Armed Forces as a Political Instrument (Washington, D.C.: Brookings Institution, 1981), p. 420.

7. Jabber and Kolkowicz, loc. cit., pp. 424–25.

8. CIA report, "Soviet Official's Comments on Soviet Policy on the Middle Eastern War," TDCS-314/08242-67 (1967) (LBJ Library, approved for release, February 28, 1984; sanitized, May 3, 1984). I am grateful to Prof. Eugene V. Rostow for bringing this document to my attention.

9. Alfred L. Atherton, Jr., "The Soviet Role in the Middle East: An American View," Middle East Journal, Vol. 39,. No. 4 (Autumn 1985), pp. 690–91. Atherton's is the best summary of the U.S.-Soviet relationship in the 1960s and 1970s.

10. See Arthur J. Goldberg, "Negotiating History of Resolution 242," in Georgetown University, Edmund A. Walsh School of Foreign Service, Institute for the Study of Diplomacy, U.N. Security Council Resolution 242: A Case Study in Diplomatic Ambiguity, introduction by Joseph J. Sisco (Washington, D.C.: Institute for the Study of Diplomacy, 1981); see also the essays by Eugene V. Rostow, Vernon Turner, and Meir Rosenne in Washington Institute for Near East Policy, UN Security Council Resolution 242: The Building Block of Peacemaking, Washington Institute Monograph (Washington, D.C.: Washington Institute for Near East Policy, 1993).

11. Henry A. Kissinger, White House Years (Boston: Little, Brown, 1979), Chapters 10 and 14; see also Richard Nixon, RN: The Memoirs of Richard Nixon (New York: Grosset & Dunlap, 1978), pp. 478–79.

12. Nixon, op. cit., p. 477.

13. Richard Nixon, "U.S. Foreign Policy for the 1970's: A New Strategy for Peace," A Report to the Congress, February 18, 1970 (Washington, D.C.: U.S. Government Printing Office, 1970), p. 77.

14. Ibid., p. 80.

15. See William B. Quandt, *Peace Process: American Diplomacy and the Arab-Israeli Conflict since 1967* (Washington, D.C.: Brookings Institution and University of California Press, 1993), p. 95; Kissinger, *White House Years*, pp. 585–86.

16. Kissinger, *White House Years*, pp. 586–89.

17. Ibid., pp. 630–31; see also Quandt, *Peace Process*, p. 533, note 19.

18. Atherton, *loc. cit.*, p. 698; Quandt, *Peace Process*, pp. 112–13.

19. Atherton, *loc. cit.*

20. Kissinger, *White House Years*, pp. 579–80.

21. See the CPSU documents declassified in 1992 in connection with the trial of the CPSU before the Russian Constitutional Court, described in FBIS-SOV-92-110, 8 June 1992, pp. 25–27. See also Claire Sterling, *The Terror Network* (New York: Holt, Rinehart & Winston, 1981), and Ray S. Cline and Yonah Alexander, *Terrorism: The Soviet Connection* (New York: Crane Russak, 1984).

22. Henry A. Kissinger, *Years of Upheaval* (Boston: Little, Brown, 1982), pp. 201–2. On Nixon's sharing of this preoccupation with the Soviets, see Kissinger, *White House Years*, p. 563.

23. Kissinger, *White House Years*, pp. 1246–94; see also ibid., notes 3 and 4 to Chapter 28, pp. 1493–94, for the texts of the communiqué language and of the "general working principles."

24. Ibid., p. 1248.

25. Anwar el-Sadat, *In Search of Identity: An Autobiography* (New York: Harper & Row, 1978), p. 229.

26. "Arab Aide's Talk with Nixon Called Factor in Sadat Decision," *New York Times*, July 24, 1972, p. 2; Mohamed Heikal, *The Road to Ramadan* (New York: Quadrangle Books, 1975), pp. 183–84.

27. Sadat, *op. cit.*, Appendix, 1, p. 319.

28. Kissinger, *White House Years*, p. 1293.

29. Sadat, *op. cit.*, p. 230. Some see the expulsion as a hoax in which the Soviets connived to mask the war plans, but I find this hard to reconcile with Sadat's subsequent behavior. Cf. David Kimche, *The Last Option: After Nasser, Arafat & Saddam Hussein: The Quest for Peace in the Middle East* (New York: Charles Scribner's Sons, 1991), Chapter 1.

30. Sadat, *op. cit.*, p. 238.

31. Ibid., p. 269.

32. Kissinger, *Years of Upheaval*, pp. 637–40.

33. The text of the Egyptian-Israeli agreement can be found in ibid., in notes 5 and 6 to Chapter 18, pp. 1250–51.

34. Robert D. Kaplan, "Syria: Identity Crisis," *Atlantic*, February 1993, pp. 22–27.

35. The story of the 1974 Syrian shuttle is told in Kissinger, *Years of Upheaval*, Chapter 22, and the text of the Syrian-Israeli agreement can be found in ibid., note 3, pp. 1253–54.

36. Ibid., p. 1094.

37. Ibid., pp. 1104–5

38. Ibid., Chapter 20.

39. *Cf.* Quandt, *Peace Process*, pp. 266–68; see also Martin Indyk, *"To the Ends of the Earth": Sadat's Jerusalem Initiative*, Harvard Middle East Papers (Modern Series), No. 1 (Cambridge, Mass.: Harvard Center for Middle Eastern Studies, 1984).

40. Galia Golan, "The Soviet Union in the Middle East after Thirty Years," in Andrzej Korbonski and Francis Fukuyama, eds., *The Soviet Union and the Third World: The Last Three Decades* (Ithaca, N.Y.: Cornell University Press and the RAND/ UCLA Center for the Study of Soviet International Behavior, 1987), p. 182.

41. Transcript of Gromyko meeting with Arafat in the Kremlin, November 13, 1979, from copies of PLO documents captured by the Israel Defense Forces in Lebanon in June 1982, in author's possession; see also Cline and Alexander, *op. cit.*, Appendix, Document I, pp. 97–99.

42. For the Soviet Middle East proposal of July 30, 1984, see FBIS-SOV-84-147, 30 July 1984, p. H1.

43. The meeting between the Soviet and Israeli ambassadors in Paris is described in the *Jerusalem Post*, July 21, 1985, cited in Golan, *loc. cit.*, pp. 205–6.

44. E.g., *Toward Peace in the Middle East: Report of a Study Group* (Washington, D.C.: Brookings Institution, 1975), p. 17–18; Quandt, *Peace Process*, p. 237.

45. See the author's critique of the concept in Peter W. Rodman, "Middle East Diplomacy after the Gulf War," *Foreign Affairs*, Vol. 70, No. 2 (Spring 1991), pp. 10–14.

46. A purported text of the London accord, April 7, 1987, was published in *Ma'ariv*, January 1, 1988. See FBIS-NES-88-001, 4 January 1988, pp. 30–31, and the discussion in Quandt, *Peace Process*, pp. 360–63.

47. For Shultz's more coy version of events, see George P. Shultz, *Turmoil and Triumph: My Years as Secretary of State* (New York: Charles Scribner's Sons, 1993), pp. 936–40.

48. For the text of the February 11, 1985, Amman accord, see William B. Quandt, ed., *The Middle East: Ten Years after Camp David* (Washington, D.C.: Brookings Institution, 1988), Appendix F, pp. 473–74.

49. Galia Golan, "Gorbachev's Middle East Strategy, *Foreign Affairs*, Vol. 66, No. 1 (Fall 1987), p. 49.

50. Kissinger, *Years of Upheaval*, p. 661.

51. Gorbachev dinner toast for Asad, April 26, 1987, in FBIS-SOV-87-081, 28 April 1987, p. H7.

52. See the CPSU documents cited in note 21 above and also Michael Dobbs, "Yeltsin Aides Seek to Link Gorbachev to Terrorism," *Washington Post*, June 6, 1992, p. A19.

53. Peter W. Rodman, "The Case for Skepticism," *National Interest*, No. 12 (Summer 1988), p. 86.

54. Statement on Asad-Gorbachev meeting, Moscow, April 28, 1990, in FBIS-SOV-90-083, 30 April 1990, p. 22.

55. See Shultz, *op. cit.*, pp. 1034–45.

56. John P. Wallach, "U.S. Says Soviets Are 'Not Being Helpful' in Mideast Peace Talks," Hearst News Service Dispatch, December 4, 1989.

57. See David Fromkin, *A Peace to End All Peace: The Fall of the Ottoman Empire and the Creation of the Modern Middle East* (New York: Avon Books, 1990).

58. See Raymond L. Garthoff, *Détente and Confrontation: American-Soviet Relations from Nixon to Reagan* (Washington, D.C.: Brookings Institution, 1985), pp. 941–42n. Garthoff argues that it was more a German than a Soviet idea, but the Soviets bit nonetheless—and added the reference to the Gulf.

59. Andrei Zhdanov, "The International Situation," address to the founding conference of the Cominform, September 1947, in U.S. Congress, House of Representatives, Committee on Foreign Affairs, *The Strategy and Tactics of World Communism: Report of Subcommittee No. 5, with Supplements I and II*, House Document 619, 80th Congress, 2d Session (Washington, D.C.: U.S. Government Printing Office, 1948), Supplement I ("One Hundred Years of Communism, 1848–1948"), pp. 213–14.

60. See Daniel Yergin, *The Prize: The Epic Quest for Oil, Money and Power* (New York: Simon and Schuster, 1991), especially Chapters 20–23.

61. L. I. Brezhnev, "Report of the Central Committee of the CPSU to the XXVI Congress of the Communist Party of the Soviet Union and the Immediate Tasks of the Party in Home and Foreign Policy," February 23, 1981 (Moscow: Novosti Press Agency Publishing House, 1981), p. 23.

62. Robin Wright, *In the Name of God: The Khomeini Decade* (New York: Touchstone/Simon and Schuster, 1990), p. 124.

63. Graham Fuller, "Toward a Policy on Iran," NIC 02545-85, May 17, 1985, reproduced in U.S. Senate, Select Committee on Secret Military Assistance to Iran and the Nicaraguan Opposition and U.S. House of Representatives, Select Committee to Investigate Covert Arms Transactions with Iran, *Report of the Congressional Committees Investigating the Iran-Contra Affair* (hereinafter cited as Joint Committee Report), S. Rept. No. 100-216, H. Rept. No. 100-433, 100th Congress, 1st Session (Washington, D.C.: U.S. Government Printing Office, 1987), Appendix A, Vol. 1, Source Documents, pp. 968–72.

64. "Iran: Prospects for Near-Term Instability," Special National Intelligence Estimate, February 1986, cited in Joint Committee Report, Section II, p. 523.

65. Thomas McNaugher, "Walking Tightropes in the Gulf," in Efraim Karsh, ed., *The*

Iran-Iraq War: Impact and Implications (New York: St. Martin's Press, 1989), pp. 171–200.

66. On the internal strains in Moscow during the Gulf crisis, see especially Suzanne Crow, "Primakov and the Soviet Peace Initiative," *RFE/RL Research Institute Report on the USSR*, March 1, 1991, pp. 14–17; Marion Recktenwald, *Soviet Third World Policy in a Changing Society: Afghanistan to the Gulf War*, Occasional Paper 4 (College Park: University of Maryland Center for International Security Studies, 1991), pp. 13–29; Galia Golan, *Moscow and the Middle East: New Thinking on Regional Conflict* (New York: Council on Foreign Relations Press for the Royal Institute of International Affairs, 1992), Chapter 5.

67. Michael R. Beschloss and Strobe Talbott, *At the Highest Levels: The Inside Story of the End of the Cold War* (Boston: Little, Brown, 1993), p. 247.

68. Graham E. Fuller, "Moscow and the Gulf War," *Foreign Affairs*, Vol. 70, No. 3 (Summer 1991), p. 56.

69. Shevardnadze address to 45th UN General Assembly, September 25, 1990, in FBIS-SOV-90-187, 26 September 1990, pp. 2, 7.

70. Igor Fesunenko, Moscow Radio domestic service, August 25, 1990, in FBIS-SOV-166, 27 August 1990, p. 35.

71. Fuller, "Moscow and the Gulf War," p. 58.

72. Lobov quoted in Bill Keller, "Soviets Issue Their First Criticism of American Presence in the Gulf," *New York Times*, August 31, 1990, p. A13.

73. Dmitry Mikheyev, *The Rise and Fall of Gorbachev* (Indianapolis: Hudson Institute, 1992), pp. 110–14.

74. Alksnis in *Sovietskaya Rossiya*, November 21, 1990, quoted in ibid., p. 113.

75. Fuller, "Moscow and the Gulf War," p. 68.

76. Yen Kim interview in *Sovietskaya Rossiya*, October 4, 1990, quoted in Recktenwald, *op. cit.*, pp. 18–19.

77. Recktenwald, *op. cit.*, p. 21, and note 82 on pp. 38–39.

78. Yevgeni Primakov, "The Inside Story of Moscow's Quest for a Deal," *Time*, March 4, 1991, p. 41.

79. Beschloss and Talbott, *op. cit.*, p. 63.

80. Shevardnadze address at Vladivostok, September 4, 1991, in FBIS-SOV-90-172, 5 September 1990, p. 5.

81. Alan Riding, "Gorbachev, in France, Says His Envoy Found Signs of Shift by Iraq," *New York Times*, October 30, 1990, p. A13.

82. Beschloss and Talbott, *op. cit.*, p. 274; see also Marshal Sergei Akhromeyev, "Soviet Briefings Aided Allied Assault," letter to the editor, *Wall Street Journal*, April 11, 1991, p. A15, and AP report, "Soviets Provide U.S. Intelligence on Iraq Military," *Los Angeles Times*, January 17, 1991.

83. Interview with Primakov on Central Television, October 31, 1990, in FBIS-SOV-90-212, 1 November 1990, p. 9.

84. Beschloss and Talbott, *op. cit.*, p. 251.

85. Ibid., pp. 257–65.

86. Gorbachev at Helsinki, September 9, 1990, in *New York Times*, September 10, 1990, p. A9; see Andrew Rosenthal, "Bush, Reversing U.S. Policy, Won't Oppose a Soviet Role in Middle East Peace Talks," *New York Times*, September 11, 1990, p. A1.

87. Beschloss and Talbott, *op. cit.*, pp. 276–77.

88. Ibid., p. 276; Jim Hoagland, "The Shevardnadze Surprise," *Washington Post*, August 1, 1991, p. A15; Yevgeni Primakov, "My Final Visit with Saddam Hussein," *Time*, March 11, 1991, p. 45.

89. Primakov, "My Final Visit with Saddam Hussein," p. 47.

90. Shevardnadze address to the Fourth Congress of People's Deputies, December 20, 1990, in FBIS-SOV-90-245, 20 December 1990, pp. 11–12.

91. Beschloss and Talbott, *op. cit.*, pp. 324–33.

92. Gorbachev address to the Middle East Peace Conference, Madrid, October 30, 1991, in FBIS-NES-91-210, 30 October 1991, p. 14.

93. See Peter W. Rodman, "A Mideast Peace Conference—But Precook It Carefully," *Washington Post*, April 16, 1991, p. A19.

94. Barry Rubin, "Reshaping the Middle East," *Foreign Affairs*, Vol. 69, No. 3 (Summer 1990), p. 131.

95. The data on this paragraph are from Patrick Clawson, *Iran's Challenge to the West: How, When, and Why*, Washington Institute Policy Papers, No. 33 (Washington, D.C., Washington Institute for Near East Policy, 1993), Chapter 2.

96. Quoted in Stephen Blank, "Russia and Iran in the Middle East," *Mediterranean Quarterly*, Vol. 3, No. 4 (Fall 1992), p. 109.

97. Yeltsin speech to Civic Union forum, Moscow, February 28, 1993, in FBIS-SOV-93-038, 1 March 1993, p. 21.

98. Prince Gorchakov's diplomatic note, November 1864, in George Vernadsky, ed., *A Source Book for Russian History: From Early Times to 1917*, Vol. III (New Haven: Yale University Press, 1972), p. 610. See Chapter 9 above.

99. Blank, *loc. cit.*, p. 110.

100. Ibid., p. 114.

101. Kozyrev quoted in ibid., p. 111.

102. Andrei Volpin, *Russian Arms Sales Policy Toward the Middle East*, Policy Focus, Research Memorandum No. 23 (Washington, D.C.: Washington Institute for Near East Policy, October 1993).

103. Sergei Stankevich, "A State in Search of Itself: Notes on Russian Foreign Policy,"

Nezavisimaya Gazeta, March 28, 1992, in FBIS-SOV-92-069, 9 April 1992 (captioned as "State Counselor Views Foreign Policy Goals"), pp. 20–22. A version of the essay appears as Sergei Stankevich, "Russia in Search of Itself." *National Interest*, No. 28 (Summer 1992), pp. 47–51.

104. Sergei Stankevich, "Russia Has Its Place in the World," *Rossiyskiye Vesti*, February 27, 1993, in FBIS-SOV-93-039, 2 March 1993 (captioned as "Stankevich Views Russia's Place in the World"), pp. 17–19.

CHAPTER 18

1. Anthony Lake, "Introduction," in Lake et. al., *After the Wars: Reconstruction in Afghanistan, Indochina, Central America, Southern Africa, and the Horn of Africa*, U.S.-Third World Policy Perspectives, No. 16 (New Brunswick, N.J.: Transaction Publishers for the Overseas Development Council, 1990), p. 4.

2. Morarji Desai, *Story of My Life*, Vol. II (New Delhi: S. Chand, 1974), p. 156; quoted in S. Nihal Singh, *The Yogi and the Bear: Story of Indo-Soviet Relations* (Riverdale, Md.: Riverdale Press, 1986), p. 18; see Chapter 3 above.

3. Nigerian scholar Claude Ake, in remarks at the conference on "Conflict Resolution in the Post-Cold War Third World," sponsored by the United States Institute of Peace, Washington, October 3, 1990; see United States Institute of Peace, *In Brief*, No. 25 (January 1991), p. 3.

4. Owen Harries, "The Third World: R.I.P.," *National Interest*, No. 26 (Winter 1991/92), p. 110.

5. Ibid., p. 111.

6. E.g., Graham E. Fuller, *The Democracy Trap: The Perils of the Post-Cold War World* (New York: Dutton, 1991), pp. 83–85.

7. Deputy Secretary of State Lawrence S. Eagleburger, "Uncharted Waters: U.S. Foreign Policy in a Time of Transition," Samuel D. Berger Memorial Lecture, Georgetown University, September 13, 1989.

8. The World Bank. *World Development Report 1991: The Challenge of Development* (New York: Oxford University Press for the World Bank, 1991), pp. 3–4, 10–11.

9. "The Debt Crisis R.I.P.," *Economist*, September 12, 1992, pp. 15–16, and "Third World debt: The disaster that didn't happen," ibid., pp. 21–23.

10. Richard E. Bissell, "Who Killed the Third World?" *Washington Quarterly*, Vol. 13, No. 4 (Autumn 1990), pp. 30–31.

11. E.g., Reagan's announcement of his presidential candidacy, November 13, 1979, which included a proposal for a North American free trade arrangement; see *New York Times*, November 14, 1979, p. A1, and Lou Cannon, *President Reagan: The Role of a Lifetime* (New York: Simon and Schuster 1991), pp. 461, 832–33.

12. U.S. Department of Commerce, *Foreign Trade Highlights, 1990*, cited in Rosemarie Philips, *U.S. Foreign Policy and Developing Countries: Discourse and Data 1991*, Conference Report (Washington, D.C.: Overseas Development Council, 1991), p. 29.

13. E.g., Fred Halliday, *From Kabul to Managua: Soviet-American Relations in the 1980s* (New York: Pantheon Books, 1989), pp. 134–35.

14. Itamar Rabinovich, "Stability and Change in Syria," in Robert B. Satloff, ed., *The Politics of Change in the Middle East* (Boulder, Colo.: Westview Press/Washington Institute for Near East Policy, 1993), p. 18; Alan Cowell, "Trouble in Damascus," *New York Times Magazine*, April 1, 1990, pp. 32–33.

15. Samuel P. Huntington, "Democracy's Third Wave," *Journal of Democracy*, Vol. 2, No. 2 (Spring 1991); Samuel P. Huntington, *The Third Wave: Democratization in the Late Twentieth Century* (Oklahoma City: University of Oklahoma Press, 1991).

16. Elie Kedourie, *Democracy and Arab Political Culture* (Washington, D.C.: Washington Institute for Near East Policy, 1992), especially Chapter 6.

17. See especially the sobering analysis of Robert D. Kaplan, "The Coming Anarchy," *Atlantic*, February 1994.

18. Martin E. Marty and R. Scott Appleby, "Conclusion: An Interim Report on a Hypothetical Family," in Martin E. Marty and R. Scott Appleby, eds., *Fundamentalisms Observed* (Chicago: University of Chicago Press, 1991), pp. 825–27.

19. Ghassan Salamé, "Islam and the West," *Foreign Policy*, No. 90 (Spring 1993), p. 22.

20. Marty and Appleby, *loc. cit.*

21. Bernard Lewis, "The Roots of Muslim Rage," *Atlantic*, September 1990.

22. Samuel P. Huntington, "The Clash of Civilizations?" *Foreign Affairs*, Vol. 72, No. 3 (Summer 1993).

23. E.g., David Ignatius, "Islam in the West's Sights: The Wrong Crusade?" *Washington Post*, March 8, 1992, pp. C1–2; John L. Esposito, *The Islamic Threat: Myth or Reality?* (New York: Oxford University Press, 1992); Leon T. Hadar, "What Green Peril?" *Foreign Affairs*, Vol. 72, No. 2 (Spring 1993); Robin Wright, "Islam, Democracy and the West," *Foreign Affairs*, Vol. 71, No. 3 (Summer 1992).

24. Wright, *loc. cit.*, p. 134.

25. Leslie H. Gelb, "Iraq Balancing Iran?" *New York Times*, January 17, 1993, p. E17.

26. Compare Stanley Hoffmann, "Foreign Policy: What's to Be Done?" *New York Review of Books*, April 30, 1981, pp. 33–34, with Graham E. Fuller, "Respecting Regional Realities," *Foreign Policy*, No. 83 (Summer 1991), pp. 39–46, and Timothy D. Sisk, *Islam and Democracy: Religion, Politics, and Power in the Middle East* (Washington, D.C.: United States Institute of Peace Press, 1992), especially Chapter 2.

27. E.g., Caryle Murphy, "West Has Helped Fuel New Islamic Militancy," *Washington Post*, May 1, 1993, p. A15.

28. E.g., joint press conference of Belgian Foreign Minister W. Claes and EC Commissioner H. Van den Broek, New York, September 28, 1993, from EC press release.

29. Shireen Hunter, "Dynamics of Recent U.S.-Iran Relations," in Hooshang Amirahmadi and James A. Bill, eds., *The Clinton Administration and the Future of U.S.-*

Iran Relations, Middle East Insight Policy Report No. 3 (Washington, D.C.: International Insight, 1993), p.17.

30. Secretary of State Warren Christopher, "America's Partnership with the European Community," statement at the conclusion of the EC Ministerial, Chateau du Kirchberg, Luxembourg, June 9, 1993.

31. U.S. Central Command, *Posture Statement*, presented to the 103d Congress by Gen. Joseph P. Hoar, commander in chief, U.S. Central Command (1994), p. 20.

32. E.g., speech by Tomás Borge at ceremonies marking the second anniversary of the Nicaraguan Revolution, July 19, 1981, in FBIS-LAM-81-139, 21 July 1981, p. P10; see Chapter 10 above.

33. Dr. Javad Larijani, interview in *Resalat* (Tehran), August 7, 1989, in FBIS-NES-89-164, 25 August 1989, p. 49.

34. Bernard Lewis, "Islam and Liberal Democracy," *Atlantic*, February 1993; Martin Kramer, "Islam vs. Democracy," *Commentary*, February 1993; Judith Miller, "The Challenge of Radical Islam," *Foreign Affairs*, Vol. 72, No. 2 (Spring 1993); Peter W. Rodman, "Islam and Democracy," *National Review*, May 11, 1992.

35. Wright, *loc. cit.*, p. 143.

36. Anthony Lake, "Confronting Backlash States," *Foreign Affairs*, Vol. 73, No. 2 (March/April 1994), p. 55.

37. Walter Lippmann, *The Cold War: A Study in U.S. Foreign Policy* (New York: Harper and Brothers, 1947), pp. 13–14, 17, 21–30; see Chapter 2 above.

38. Arkady N. Shevchenko, *Breaking with Moscow* (New York: Alfred A. Knopf, 1985), p. 279.

39. See Kissinger's own reassessment in Henry A. Kissinger, *Diplomacy* (New York: Simon and Schuster, 1994), Chapter 29.

40. Secretary of State Henry A. Kissinger, "The Permanent Challenge of Peace: U.S. Policy Toward the Soviet Union," address to the Commonwealth Club and the World Affairs Council of Northern California, San Francisco, February 3, 1976.

41. Gov. Bill Clinton, "Democracy in America," remarks in Milwaukee, October 1, 1992, reportedly drafted by Penn Kemble of Freedom House and Joshua Muravchik of the American Enterprise Institute, Democratic moderates who had both supported the Nicaraguan resistance.

42. See, e.g., Anthony Lewis, "Candor and Fortitude," *New York Times*, May 3, 1993, p. A15.

43. George Bush, address to the nation, January 16, 1991. See also his addresses to the UN General Assembly, October 1, 1990, and to the Czecho-Slovak Federal Assembly on November 17, 1990.

44. See the author's remarks at the conference on "Conflict Resolution in the Post-Cold War Third World," sponsored by the U.S. Institute of Peace, October 5, 1990, in Sheryl J. Brown and Kimber M. Schraub, eds., *Resolving Third World Conflict:*

Challenges for a New Era (Washington, D.C.: U.S. Institute of Peace Press, 1992), pp. 268–69.

45. Lippmann quoted in Charles Krauthammer, "Isolationism, Left and Right," *New Republic*, March 4, 1985, p. 20.

46. Charles Krauthammer, "How the Doves Became Hawks," *Time*, May 17, 1993, p. 74.

47. E.g., Laura W. Reed and Carl Kaysen, *Emerging Norms of Justified Intervention* (Cambridge, Mass.: American Academy of Arts and Sciences, 1993); David J. Scheffer, Richard N. Gardner, and Gerald B. Helman, "Three Views on the Issue of Humanitarian Intervention," Study Group on Post-Gulf War Challenges to the UN Collective Security System (Washington, D.C.: U.S. Institute of Peace, June 1992); Larry Minear, "Humanitarian Intervention in a New World Order," Policy Focus, No. 1 (Washington, D.C.: Overseas Development Council, 1992).

48. Michael Walzer, *Just and Unjust Wars* (New York: Basic Books, 1977), pp. 101–8,

49. Winston Lord et al., *Changing Our Ways: America and the New World*, report of the Carnegie Endowment National Commission on America and the New World (Washington, D.C.: Carnegie Endowment for International Peace, 1992), pp. 50–51.

50. Boris Yeltsin, address to the Federal Assembly, February 24, 1994, in FBIS-SOV-94-037, 24 February 1994, p. 20.

51. Kissinger, *Diplomacy*, Chapter 30.

52. Charles Krauthammer, "America and the Post Cold War World," Henry M. Jackson Memorial Lecture, Washington, September 18, 1990 (Seattle: Henry M. Jackson Foundation, 1991), pp. 12–13; Charles Krauthammer, "The Unipolar Moment," *Foreign Affairs*, Vol. 70, No. 1 (America and the World 1990/91), pp. 29–32.

INDEX